No. 3278
$34.95

MS-DOS UTILITY PROGRAMS

Add-On Software Resources

Ronny Richardson

Published by **Windcrest Books**
FIRST EDITION/FIRST PRINTING

© 1989 by **Windcrest Books**. Reproduction or publication of the content in any manner, without express permission of the publisher, is prohibited. The publisher takes no responsibility for the use of any of the materials or methods described in this book, or for the products thereof.

Library of Congress Cataloging-in-Publication Data

Richardson, Ronny.
    MS-DOS utility programs : add-on software resources / by Ronny
Richardson.
        p.   cm.
    Includes index.
    ISBN 0-8306-9278-9 : ISBN 0-8306-3278-6 (pbk.)
    1. MS-DOS (Computer operating system)   2. Utilities (Computer
programs)   I. Title.
QA76.76.063R543   1989
005.4′3—dc20   89-35335
                                                                      CIP

TAB BOOKS Inc. offers software for sale. For information and a catalog, please contact TAB Software Department, Blue Ridge Summit, PA 17294-0850.

Questions regarding the content of this book should be addressed to:

Windcrest Books
Division of TAB BOOKS Inc.
Blue Ridge Summit, PA 17294-0850

Ron Powers: Director of Acquisitions
David Harter: Technical Editor
Katherine Brown: Production

Contents

_______________________PART ONE_______________________
PROGRAMS FOR BEGINNERS

FILE AND DISK MAINTENANCE

PART FOUR

MEMORY RESIDENT AIDS

PART FIVE

EXPANDING DOS

APPENDICES

Acknowledgments

Personally, I want to thank my wife Cicinda, my son Tevin and my daughter Dawna for their support and patience. Because I have only a limited pool of time available, some of the time I spent writing this book had to come from the time I would have spent with my family. They were all very understanding and supportive.

Professionally, there are two groups I would like to thank. First, all the public relations specialists that helped me pull this book together. Although they are too numerous to name, this book would not have been possible without them. Many times I called someone to tell them I needed a copy of a software package on a moment's notice or needed some information and they always came through.

Second, I want to thank all the public domain and shareware authors and especially those who graciously allowed me to include their software on the optional diskette set. Public domain and shareware authors have made a major contribution to this book.

There are a couple of individuals and firms to whom I owe a special note of thanks. They are:

1) Hal Reinish and IBM. Hal made the arrangements for IBM to loan me an IBM Model 70 to use for writing this book. Without such a powerful computer, the book would have been much more difficult to write.

2) Valerie Ward and Datavue. Valerie arranged for Datavue to loan me a Snap 1 + 1 portable computer for writing this book. My primary purpose for borrowing the computer was to test file transfer programs and to have an isolated computer for virus testing. I ended up doing a lot of writing with the

Snap 1 + 1 in my lap as I ran the software I was reviewing on the Model 70. Being able to write about the software as I was using it made me much more productive.

3) Meg Filipi, Will Matlack and Plus Development Corporation. Meg and Will arranged for Plus Development to loan a Passport drive to me for the book. I used the Passport drive for testing disk optimization software because it was an isolated system I could leave unchanged. I also used it to test the format recovery programs, because I was not about to format my primary drive on purpose.

4) Charles Guzis, the president of Sydex. I partitioned the Passport drive into two logical drives. I spent a lot of time creating a very fragmented file structure on one of the partitions to test the disk optimizing program. My original plan was to leave that drive as the benchmark, and copy the structure to the other partition for testing. It turned out that none of my backup software or tape drives could do this. Charles wrote a sector copy program just for this test, Thanks Charles.

Introduction

This book is for anyone who uses a computer. Anyone using a computer occasionally has to deal with DOS. This book covers a lot of programs to make dealing with your computer easier.

HOW THIS BOOK IS STRUCTURED

Each chapter in this book covers programs that perform a specific task generally associated with DOS. The first section covers programs for beginners. The chapters are:

1) DOS Learning Aids. This chapter covers programs that pop up with information designed to make it easier to use DOS.

2) DOS Menus. This chapter covers the programs that run other programs from a menu.

3) DOS Shells. This chapter covers the programs that replace DOS with a menu-driven program.

The second section covers File/Disk Maintenance. These are the programs you generally think of when you talk about DOS Utilities. The chapters are:

4) File Maintenance. This chapter covers the software like the Norton Utilities designed to overcome the ERASE *.* type mistakes we all make.

5) Utility Sets. This will cover sets of utilities where the set contains significant file or disk maintenance utilities.

6) Disk Maintenance. This chapter covers the software, like *Disk Technician Advanced,* for recovering from hard disk errors.

7) Format Recovery. This chapter covers programs to unformat a hard disk.

8) Disk Optimization. This chapter covers programs to optimize a hard disk.

9) Console Speed-up Programs. This chapter covers programs that speed up some DOS operations.

10) Programs to Speed Up a Hard Disk. This chapter covers mainly caching programs.

11) Hard Disk Drive Installation Utilities. This chapter covers the software that makes it easy to install hard disks.

Section 3 covers Protecting Your Data. The chapters are:

12) Backups. This chapter covers the backup software that replaces the awful backup/restore software that comes with DOS. It will also cover hardware.

13) Document Indexing Programs. This chapter covers programs that make it easy to locate information in text files.

14) Data Translation. This protects your data from loss when you switch programs.

15) Restricting Access to Your Computer/Data. This chapter covers password programs/hardware intended to restrict the access to your computer.

16) Dealing with copy protection. Copy protection is about dead, and very few people miss it. However, it hangs on in a few programs. This chapter tells you how to deal with it.

17) Anti-Viral Programs. This chapter covers this new category of software designed to protect users from the anti-social individuals producing programs to destroy the data on computers. J.D. Abolins helped me write this chapter.

Section 4 covers Memory Resident Aids. The chapters are:

18) File Noting Software. This chapter covers the programs that let you add descriptions to file names as well as notes to applications.

19) Memory resident managers. This chapter covers programs that aid in managing TSR software.

20) Print Buffers. This chapter covers programs (and hardware) that accept output from the computer and send it to the printer at a slower pace.

Section 5 covers programs for Expanding DOS. The chapters are:

21) This chapter covers the numerous public domain, shareware and commercial programs designed to replace specific DOS commands.

22) Batch File Software. This chapter covers software designed to help you write batch files.

23) File Compression Software. This chapter covers software designed to reduce the disk space required by files.

24) Software to Emulate EMS Using Hard Disk/Extended Memory. This chapter covers programs that allow you to use your hard disk or extended as Lotus expanded memory.

25) This section covers alternatives to DOS. This chapter briefly discusses your alternatives if you are looking for more than DOS offers.

Section 6 covers *Other,* the things that did not fit nicely into one of the other sections.

26) Other. This chapter covers other programs of interest.

27) Sharing Data When the Disk Drive Sizes are Different. This section covers the software/hardware designed to help users deal with two problems: sharing data with another user who has a different size drive; and moving data between a portable and a desktop computer.

MEMORY

This book gives the memory requirements for most programs. Memory requirements are not clear when the program loads from the DOS prompt. Its exact memory requirement depends on how you have your system configured.

Each program loaded from DOS gets a full copy of your environment. Normally, the environment is 160-bytes long. So each program started from the DOS prompt gains 160-bytes by getting a full copy of the environment. Because the environment stores your PATH, COMSPEC, and SET variables, many users expand its size. Under certain versions of DOS, you can expand the environment to 32K. Regardless of the size of the environment, each DOS program gets a full copy. Therefore, the exact memory requirements for any program loaded from DOS depends on the size of the environment.

ABOUT DOS 4.X

DOS 4.01 has only been out a short time at this writing. Many of the discussed programs are not compatible with DOS 4.01. When they are not, I mention that fact. However, it is not a "big deal." Over the next few months, most programs will be upgraded to support DOS 4.01, so by the time you read this only a few programs will be incompatible. If DOS 4.x support is important to you, check before purchasing.

ABOUT THE BOOK

I tested all of the software on an IBM Model 70 running at 16 MHz. This machine has 6 Meg of RAM, a 130 Meg hard disk and VGA display. It was running under DOS 4.01 from IBM. The Model 70 had a 40 Meg Plus Development Passport removable cartridge hard drive attached to it. I used this primarily for testing disk optimization and format recovery programs. A few of the programs would not run under DOS 4.01. For these, I booted from a DOS 3.3 disk and used the Passport drive. Because I had it formatted with 20 Meg partitions, I could access it under DOS 3.3 even though it was formatted with 4.01.

J.D. Abolins did most of the virus testing, but the testing I did was on a Snap 1 + 1 without a hard disk. I was able to isolate any problems to floppy disks and turn the Snap 1 + 1 off between programs to eliminate any chance of transfer. I also used the Snap 1 + 1 to test file transfer programs.

When I needed to print a copy, I used an HP Laserjet +. The word processor I used was Microsoft Word 4.0. I checked the text using RightWriter style checking software. I captured most screen shots using Hotshot and printed them on the HP Laserjet + printer. Hotshot would not work with a few programs. When that happened, I used Hijaak.

NOTE TO SOFTWARE AUTHORS

As DOS and the products that support it evolve, this book will require updating. If you would like for me to consider your software for future editions, please contact me in care of TAB BOOKS.

## Part One

Programs for Beginners

1
DOS Learning Aids

DOS is not something that comes naturally to a new computer user. In fact, it is probably one of the most difficult things a new user has to learn about his computer. This is especially difficult because of the fairly brief DOS manuals.

What the DOS manuals lack, book publishers and software vendors rush to provide. There is a wealth of information available to help users pick up on both DOS fundamentals and advanced features. The books are best suited for detailed study. When all you need is the syntax for the BACKUP command, you do not want to take the time or suffer the aggravation of finding the right book. Even then, you have the problem of finding the information in the book. You want the information right now. Software offers that instant access. It also offers another major advantage over books. A book is easy to misplace, and someone usually has borrowed a book just when you need it. However, software is always sitting on your hard disk just waiting on you.

I have divided these learning aid programs into two different categories: DOS tutorials and DOS aids. A tutorial is a stand-alone teaching program that electronically teaches DOS. A DOS aid is a "manual on a disk" program. It gives you instant access to DOS syntax and a brief explanation of the commands. These programs might be memory resident. However, being memory resident might not be a big advantage. When you want help with DOS, you are usually at the DOS prompt. (You could also use these programs while editing a batch file, your AUTOEXEC.BAT or your CONFIG.SYS file.) When you are at the DOS prompt, a stand-alone program is as convenient as a memory resident program. In addition, it does not have the memory requirement and possible conflict problems of a memory resident program.

DOS TUTORIALS

I work in an office where it is occasionally necessary to teach a new employee to use computers. This usually involves teaching them a few hardware basics, how to use DOS, and how to use a few application programs. Our main application programs are Lotus 1-2-3 and Microsoft Word. Both have excellent tutorials (for Lotus we use the tutorial that came with version 1A). These DOS tutorials offer the same tutorial-based teaching for DOS that the other tutorials offer for their specific application program.

DS Tutor.COM

DS Tutor.COM is really four separate programs: a stand-alone tutor, a glossary, a testing program and memory resident help.

Installation The installation program is a batch file to install the programs on a hard disk—you control which subdirectory by entering it on the command line after the INSTALL command. The installation program insists on running from the A-drive but the ASSIGN A=B command corrects this.

Operation When you start DS Tutor.COM, it presents you with a list of several topics to explore. They are:

- Hardware information.
- Disk operating system.
- Software information.

  You also have the option to:

- Resume prior session. This lets you pick up exactly where you left off last time.
- Configure colors.
- Keyboard installation. This lets you tell the program if you have a PC/XT, AT or PS/2 keyboard.
- Test selections. This lets you run the testing program.

For each major topic, there is a long list of minor topics. The menu lets you read about a single topic and return to the menu to select another topic. It also lets you select to read all topics in sequence.

As you work through each topic, you read a screen of information and press Return to the next screen. The tutorial is not interactive. It never stops to ask you a question.

Figure 1-1 is a screen shot of the DS Tutor.COM lesson on printers. DS Tutor.COM does not use graphics to illustrate the lessons. It does, however, use IBM high-order ASCII characters to draw simple drawings like Fig. 1-1.

Many programs leave you confused if their lessons use a term you do not understand. Not DS Tutor.COM. You can press the F1 key and access a glossary. The glossary has a list of terms across the left side of the screen. You scroll through the list and select the term you want to learn more about. When you press Return, a full description of that term appears on the right side of

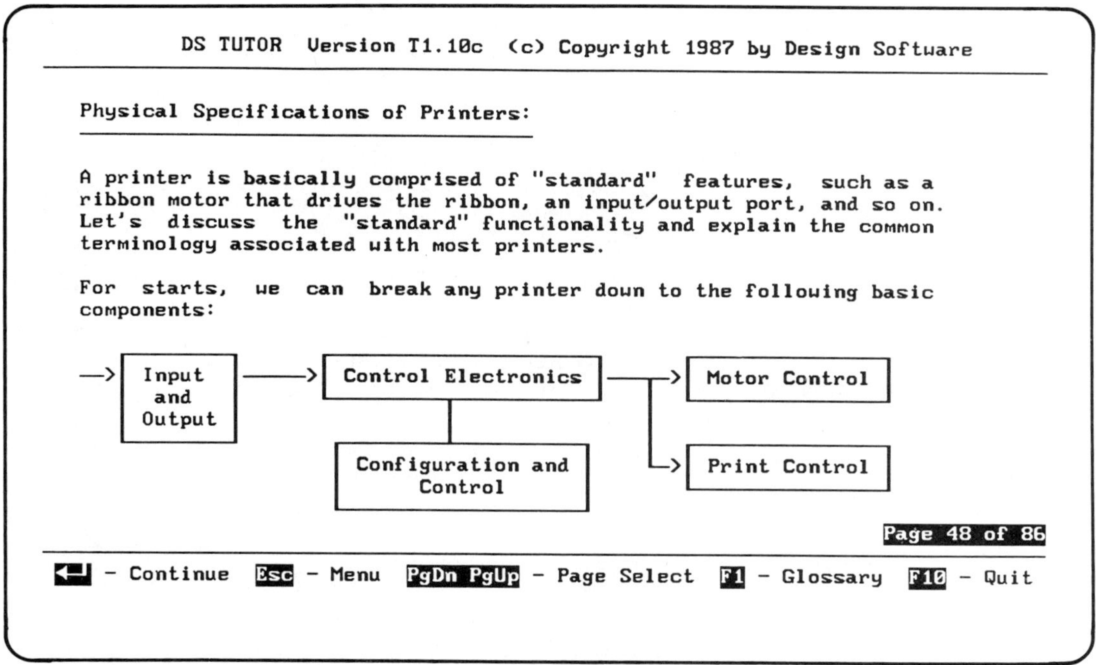

Fig. 1-1. DS Tutor.COM presents information on a broad range of computer topics.

the screen. Figure 1-2 shows this. After reading the description of a term, you can either move the cursor to another term or press Escape. Pressing Escape returns to your lesson.

Once you have finished your lessons, DS Tutor.COM has a built-in testing program. You can use this program to see how well you understood the lessons. The tests are all multiple choice. After you finish a test, DS Tutor.COM computes your score and tells you which questions you missed.

Once you have completed your lessons, DS Tutor.COM does not stop helping you. It includes a copy of the memory resident half of DS Help. I cover DS Help later in this chapter, but it is basically a memory resident help program.

Limitations   All of the text screens are right justified. The programmers padded the words with extra spaces between them to make the right margins equal. With only sixty to seventy characters per line that makes the text appear to have "rivers of white space" running through it. Sometimes there is so much padding the text is difficult to read. This is even worse in the glossary where the item descriptions are only about forty-five characters wide.

DS Tutor.COM will run on any computer, so it never uses graphics to illustrate a point. At best, it occasionally uses the IBM high-ordered graphic characters to "draw" something on the screen. The lack of illustrations makes DS Tutor.COM less effective than it could be.

The memory resident version of DS Help included with DS Tutor.COM refused to run under DOS 4.01. It would load into memory and take up place. The remove option would reclaim the memory, however DS Help would not

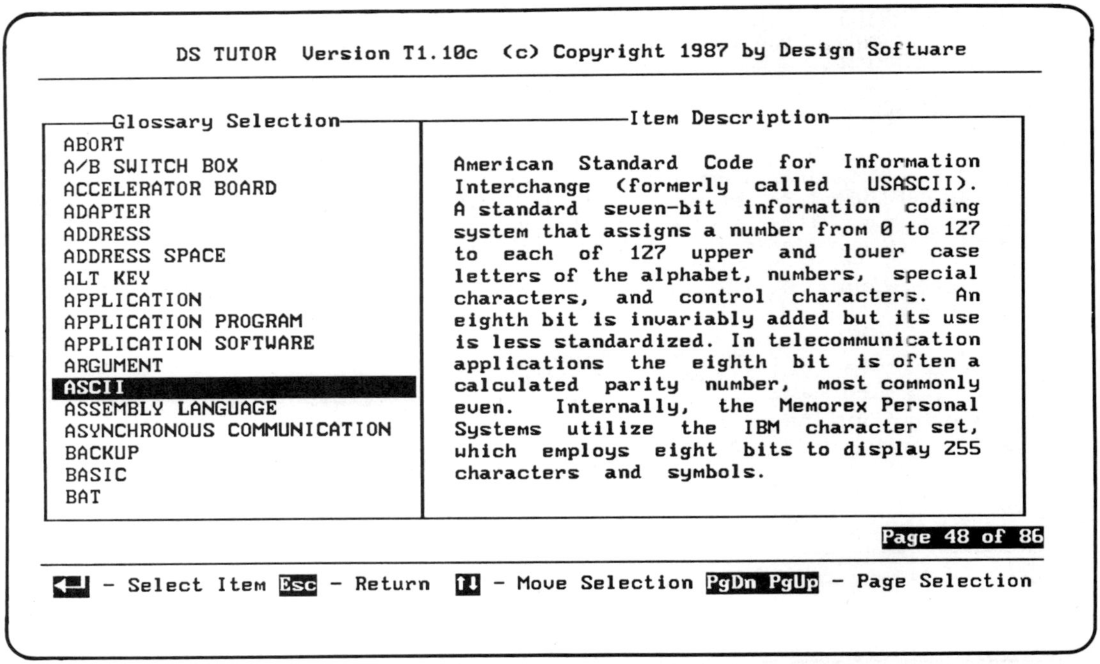

```
 DS TUTOR  Version T1.10c  (c) Copyright 1987 by Design Software

 ┌─Glossary Selection─────────┐   ┌─Item Description──────────┐
  ABORT                            American  Standard  Code  for  Information
  A/B SWITCH BOX                   Interchange  (formerly  called  USASCII).
  ACCELERATOR BOARD                A standard  seven-bit  information  coding
  ADAPTER                          system that assigns a number from 0 to 127
  ADDRESS                          to  each  of  127  upper  and  lower  case
  ADDRESS SPACE                    letters of the alphabet, numbers,  special
  ALT KEY                          characters,  and  control  characters.  An
  APPLICATION                      eighth bit is invariably added but its use
  APPLICATION PROGRAM              is less standardized. In telecommunication
  APPLICATION SOFTWARE             applications  the  eighth  bit  is often a
  ARGUMENT                         calculated  parity  number,  most commonly
  ASCII                            even.   Internally,  the  Memorex Personal
  ASSEMBLY LANGUAGE                Systems  utilize  the  IBM  character set,
  ASYNCHRONOUS COMMUNICATION       which  employs  eight  bits to display 255
  BACKUP                           characters  and  symbols.
  BASIC
  BAT

                                                        Page 48 of 86

  ◄┘ - Select Item  Esc - Return  ↑↓ - Move Selection  PgDn PgUp - Page Selection
```

Fig. 1-2. DS Tutor.COM has a full glossary that lets you look up terms in the lessons that you do not understand.

pop up. When I rebooted the machine off a DOS 3.3 disk, DS Help functioned properly. The version in the stand-alone DS Help package worked fine under DOS 4.01. The DS Help package includes both a memory resident and a stand-alone version of DS Help. DS Tutor.COM only contains the memory resident version.

Manual   Like most of the programs in this chapter, the DS Tutor.COM is very slim. About all it does is give brief instructions on installing and starting the program. That is acceptable. Once you get DS Tutor.COM going, you are not likely to need the manual.

Conclusion   DS Tutor.COM is a good tutoring program. The glossary and DS Help programs make this package an excellent buy.

```
Product:    DS Tutor
Price:      $39.95
Category:   Commercial
Publisher:  Design Software, Incorporated
Address:    19808 Nordhoff Place
            Chatsworth, California 91311
Phone:      (800) 231-3088
            (818) 885-9000
Memory:     256K for stand-alone programs
            46K for memory resident Help
```

Learning DOS

Learning DOS is both an interactive tutorial and a help program. Its main thrust is being a tutorial. As such, it does a good job introducing new users to DOS. Its help program is not memory resident. Rather, it is a stand-alone program that runs from the DOS prompt.

Installation   You can copy the files to a subdirectory or to a working floppy diskette. It comes with a floppy version and a hard disk version. However, you can use either version with either system. There is not a program to automatically install Learning DOS.

Operation   The tutorial begins by asking your name. If you enter your name, it will track the lessons you have taken in prior sessions. Learning DOS can track the names and places of several individuals. The first menu gives the following options:

1)   How to use this course
2)   What you can do with DOS (an overview)
3)   Using DOS (the main course)
4)   Practicing what you have learned (tests)
5)   Index (pick a specific subject to learn about)
6)   Quit

The using DOS option takes you into the core of the course. It begins with the basics such as "starting DOS" and "running an application." The course finishes up with fairly complex topics. These include "backing up to a floppy" and "fixed settings (AUTOEXEC.BAT and CONFIG.SYS files)." In between, you gain a fairly complete understanding of using DOS. After you complete each lesson, you have the option of taking a test or moving on.

Need to know how to tell DOS to treat a subdirectory as drive D (SUBST D: C:\directory)? Need to know how to configure your keyboard as a German keyboard (KEYBGR)? Cannot find your DOS manual? Then HELP is the program for you. Help is part of the Learning DOS package. You copy Help and its associated files to a subdirectory in your PATH. Anytime you enter Help from the DOS prompt, you get an index of DOS commands. Entering a specific command gives a one screen summary of that command with examples of specific usage. Experienced users will find that Help presents enough information on most DOS 3.x commands to allow you to avoid using your DOS manual.

Limitations   The tutorial presents each topic as a series of screens where you have to press the space bar to move between screens. Some screens begin with a graphics display. Learning DOS forms other screens by adding information to the current screen. The program redraws the screens at about the right speed on an AT-type machine. It seems slow on an IBM PC.

Manual   The manual is brief but adequate. Once you get Learning DOS up and running, it is unlikely you will need the manual. The program is so easy to use, the manual is almost optional.

Conclusion   The tutorial is an excellent way to introduce new users to DOS. It never gets frustrated and it never forgets to cover a topic. With the tutorial, you can select topics as needed, either from the menu or the index. That ability makes it an excellent tool for the intermediate user. Even if you have already learned to use DOS, you can use it to brush up on a topic in which you are weak. The Help program is a valuable replacement for the DOS manual for most questions. The tutorial makes excellent use of graphics to explain topics. The only drawback to the program is how slow it runs on a 8088 machine. Learning DOS is a bargain.

```
Product:      Learning DOS
Price:        $49.95
Category:     Commercial
Publisher:    Microsoft Corporation
Address:      16011 Northeast 36th Way
              Post Office Box 97017
              Redmond, Washington 98073
Phone:        (800) 426-9400
Memory:       256K
```

Tutor.COM

Tutor.COM is an interactive tutorial without a help program. Its tutorials often stop to ask you questions rather than simply presenting information on the screen.

Installation   To install Tutor.COM, you copy the files to a subdirectory or to a working floppy diskette. There is no installation program and the documentation does not explain the process.

Operation   Tutor.COM runs off of a single menu. The topics available from that menu are:

1) A brief explanation of Tutor.COM.
2) The keyboard and special keys.
3) A history of computers. While this information is not necessary to understand computers or operate a PC, I found it especially interesting.
4) Introduction to computers #1. This, along with the next section, covers the basic concepts of computing such as what a CPU and monitor are.
5) Introduction to computers #2.
6) Elementary DOS commands. This explains most of the simple commands, such as DIR and FORMAT.
7) Advanced DOS commands. This explains how to work with subdirectories.
8) Batch commands. This section explains how to write batch files.

For most screens, you move between screens using the plus key. You can go backwards with the minus key. Occasionally, Tutor.COM stops and asks you questions. You get three chances and then Tutor.COM gives you the correct answer. Tutor.COM is case insensitive but picky about the answers. For one

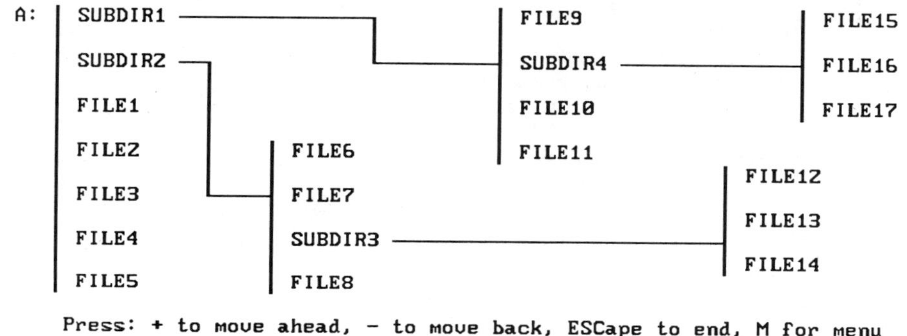

Fig. 1-3. Tutor.COM uses simple graphics to improve the appearances of some screens. These are constructed using built-in characters so they will look correct even on a monochrome system.

question, I entered "punch cards" which was incorrect. "Punched cards" was the correct answer.

Occasionally, Tutor.COM spices up the screens by using simple graphics. Figure 1-3 shows this. Tutor.COM produced all these using high-ordered ASCII characters (characters built into the computer). As a result, they do not slow down its operation and they will work on a monochrome system.

Limitations   Every time you start Tutor.COM, it asks you about color and sound. It should store your responses the first time through so it can skip these questions. I found moving between screens using the plus and minus keys to be awkward. The page up and page down keys would be a much better choice. The author has corrected these problems with a recent revision of the program.

Manual   There is very little documentation and it assumes you will be running Tutor.COM from a floppy drive. If that is the case, this lack of documentation is not a problem. You really do not need documentation to run the program. If you register the program, Computer Knowledge sends you a nice manual. That manual collects most of the screens from Tutor.COM into a bound manual. That manual makes a handy reference book by itself.

Conclusion   Tutor.COM is not as good a tutorial as is Learning DOS. However, its price is much lower and you can try it out before you buy it because it is shareware. It is good enough to warrant a close look.

Product:	TUTOR.COM	
Price:	$10	Registration only
	$15	Registration with latest disk
	$20	Registration with Latest disk and manual
	$40	Registration with manual and tutorial building tools
	$150	Single Organization site license
	$200	Single Organization site license for the tutorial building tools
Category:	Shareware	
Publisher:	Computer Knowledge	
Address:	Post Office Box 91176 Los Angeles, California 90009	
Phone:	Not Available	
Memory:	256K	

DOS AIDS

A *DOS aid* program's most important characteristic is intelligent writing. It does you little good to have on-line information instantly available if that information is as hard to understand as a DOS manual. It is also important for the interface to the program to be easy to master. No one wants to spend a long time to occasionally retrieve information on a second program. If learning the program takes a long time; that time could be better spent learning DOS.

Finally, the information needs to be up to date. That proved to be a special problem here because I was using IBM DOS 4.01 which none of the programs supported. I did not consider that to be a major drawback. At this writing Microsoft had not released a version of DOS 4.0 for non-IBM computers. There is typically a lag between the release of a new version of DOS and its acceptance and support. However, any program that does not support DOS 3.3 is seriously lacking.

Boston Documentation for DOS

Boston Documentation for DOS is a stand-alone or memory resident program that provides help on DOS topics. It is far more difficult and confusing to operate than similar programs.

Installation   Installing Boston Documentation for DOS is about the only thing easy about the program. To install it, simply copy all the files to a subdirectory of your hard disk. If you plan to use Boston Documentation for DOS in stand-alone mode, then that subdirectory will need to be in your PATH. There is no program to automate the process.

Operation   Boston Documentation for DOS comes with a tutorial. This tutorial is really an on-line manual presented using Boston Documentation for DOS.

To use Boston Documentation for DOS as a stand-alone program, you enter: WBREAD DOS-GO from the DOS prompt.

You can get to this same point using the memory resident version—it just takes more work. Boston Documentation for DOS does not actually run in memory resident mode. It actually runs under a limited-function version of Switch-It. The Switch-It program lets you load two programs into memory at once. To get to Boston Documentation for DOS under Switch-It, you first Alt-1. This does not get you to help, it just brings in a prompt. Next, you enter the name of the Boston Documentation database you want to use. Boston Documentation supplies databases for several popular programs. Enter "DOS" and you finally get to the main menu.

From this menu, you select the topic that interests you. You had better make the correct selection. The only way to get back to this screen is to exit and reenter the program. When you get to the help screen on the topic you want, you can read the information. You also have four additional choices. Those choices are "Next," "Prev," "XRef," and "Print." Next is not for the next screen, rather, it is for the next set of information on the opening menu. You would think that Prev(ious) would take you back to the previous screen, namely the menu. It does not. Rather, it takes you to the set of instructions list just before the current set in the menu. XRef, or cross-reference, highlights a number of words on the information screen. You can chain to information screens on any of the highlighted words. However, doing so requires that you first go through a screen to confirm your selection. Naturally, you print the current information using the Print command.

You might expect to go back to a menu using the Escape key. If you try that, you are asked if you really want to exit the program. If you are running Boston Documentation for DOS as a stand-alone program, Escape takes you back to the DOS prompt. However, if you are running Boston Documentation for DOS as a memory resident program, Escape takes you back to Switch-It. You have to again press Alt-1 to get back to your original application. This is especially confusing because most other memory resident programs do not work this way.

Limitations   As explained above, Boston Documentation for DOS is far more difficult to operate than the other programs. It has additional problems. This information is out of date. As I write this, I am using DOS 4.01. The other programs all support through at least DOS 3.3. Boston Documentation for DOS only supports through DOS 3.1.

Manual   The manual has only nine pages. That might be enough if Boston Documentation for DOS had an intuitive interface. It does not and the manual proves to be very inadequate. About the only way to learn to use Boston Documentation for DOS is to play around with it.

Conclusion   New users will find it easier to learn to use DOS than to learn to use Switch-It and Boston Documentation for DOS.

Product:	Boston Documentation for DOS
Price:	$34.95
Category:	Commercial
Publisher:	Boston Documentation Design Incorporated
Address:	125 Adams Street
	Suite 301
	Newton, Massachusetts 02158
Phone:	(617) 965-5300
Memory:	256K in Stand-Alone Mode
	100K in Memory-Resident Mode

DOS Help!

DOS Help! is a memory resident or stand-alone program that provides help on DOS topics. It uses a "hyper-text" like feature that lets you move easily from topic to topic and back.

Installation   Installing DOS Help! is as simple as copying a couple of files to a subdirectory in your PATH. The instructions do not explain how to install DOS Help!. There is no program to automate the process.

Operation   DOS Help! has two modes of operation, memory resident or stand-alone. When DOS Help! is memory resident, you can get to the menu any time by pressing Alt-H. You can remove DOS Help! from memory at the DOS prompt if it was the last program loaded by entering EXIT. In stand-alone mode, you can enter HELP TOPIC to get help on a specific topic. You can also simply enter HELP to select a topic from the main menu.

Once you get to the menu, the memory resident and stand-alone version work exactly the same. You select the topic of interest and press Return. After you work through the menus, you see the topic of interest. If you are using the program in stand-alone mode, you can avoid these menus by entering HELP Topic. That takes you directly to information on the specified topic.

Not only does DOS Help! display information on the topic of interest, but it also has a method to chain to related information rapidly and later return to your original point. For each topic, several related topics are highlighted. By moving the cursor to any of these and pressing Return, you can instantly go to that topic. That topic will have other topics highlighted to which you can move. When you have finished, each time you press Escape, the program takes you back one level.

Not only does DOS Help! give you the basic information, but it also points out useful information you do not expect to find in this type of product. For example, DOS Help! points out that you may have trouble reading the target diskette after you DISKCOPY from a 360K drive to a 1.2 Meg drive. It also points out that DISKCOPY also copies disk fragmentation between disks. Under the RECOVER command, it points out "Use RECOVER with care. If you fail to specify a filespec, you could effectively lose all data on your hard disk!" And under the JOIN command, it points out that the JOIN command is "not very useful."

If you do not know the exact name of a command, DOS Help! gives you enough hints as you work through the screens that you are likely to find just the command you need.

Limitations DOS Help! is a very useful program without significant limitations. The version I used did not yet support DOS 4.x, but that will likely change soon.

Manual DOS Help! does not exactly have a manual. DOS Help! comes with a single page (one-sided) of instructions. These instructions do little more than tell you how to start the program in stand-alone or memory resident mode. They tell you to make a backup. If you do not know how to make a backup, the instructions tell you to enter HELP DISKCOPY.

The instructions clearly need a little work. DOS Help! does not need a thick manual. Like the other help programs, you will rarely need a manual once you get the program running. However, better instructions on installing DOS Help! on a hard disk and how to make backups would make getting started easier.

Conclusion DOS Help! is an excellent program. It is a well designed program with several menus for users with different levels of experience. Its ability to move quickly between related topics and then jump back make DOS Help! an especially useful program.

Product:	DOS Help!
Price:	$49.95
Category:	Commercial
Publisher:	Flambeaux Software
Address:	1147 East Broadway
	Suite 56
	Glendale, California 91205
Phone:	(818) 500-0044
Notes:	Has both a memory resident and stand-alone mode.
Memory:	64K

DOS Helper

DOS Helper is a stand-alone or memory resident program that provides help on DOS topics. It is very easy to modify DOS Helper to include any information you need.

Installation Installing DOS Helper proved to be extremely frustrating. I placed the program disk in my B-drive and logged onto that drive to run the installation program. My first problem was DOS Helper expected to use the A-drive even though I had the computer logged onto the B-drive. I corrected that with an ASSIGN A=B statement. This ASSIGN A=B is a handy command to remember if you have a PS/2 computer with an external 5.25 inch drive.

After issuing the ASSIGN command, my problems were far from over. Going through the next time, I changed the default directory. DOS Helper expects you to install it in the HELPDOS directory, which I was already using for another program in this chapter. The first time through I changed this to the HELPDOS2. For some unexplained reason, DOS Helper does not work with subdirectories longer than seven characters. DOS allows up to eight with an additional three-character extension. When it tried to create this subdirectory, it shortened HELPDOS2 to HELPDOS and quit because it existed.

I ran the program again and selected the subdirectory HELPER. It modified the program files then tried to create a HELPDOS subdirectory anyway. Once again, it stopped because HELPDOS existed. At this point, I decided to run DOS Helper from the B-drive. When I logged onto the B-drive and tried to start DOS Helper, it responded that the subdirectory HELPER did not exist. Next, I tried to run the installation program to tell it to use the B-drive. When I told it I wanted to install DOS Helper for a single drive, it responded that running off a single disk required no installation. At this point there was no way to run it off the floppy drive.

I decided that DOS Helper had to be in my HELPDOS subdirectory so I moved all those files to a HELPDOS2 subdirectory. Then I deleted the HELP-DOS subdirectory so DOS Helper could create it. Once again, I ran the installation program. This time, I made the mistake of entering the subdirectory as \HELPDOS. The prompt warns you not to do that. When I tried to start DOS Helper, it responded that the directory C:\\HELPDO did not exist. (Since DOS Helper only allows seven characters, adding the "\" at the first caused it to drop the "S" at the end.) So I installed DOS Helper once again. This time I got everything right.

There are several other problems with the installation program, as hard as that is to believe. To change the hot-key for the memory resident program, you have to enter its ASCII code. The installation program only displays codes for a few combinations of the control, alternate, shift, and function keys. There is an additional problem when it prompts you for the new subdirectory. It does not prompt for something like "Enter the subdirectory for the data files." Rather, it asks you to "Modify F1 (DEFAULT = HELPDOS)." To make matters worse, the default in the prompt is wrong if you have already installed DOS Helper and changed the default. Accepting the default accepts what exists, even though you cannot find out what it is, rather than accepting HELPDOS.

Operation   DOS Helper does not exactly use a modern interface. Figure 1-4 shows the main menu. You do not use a moving lightbar or other such cursor to select a topic from a menu. All the menu does is display the files that are available. You have to enter the name of the help file you want. If a file name.hlp file exists, DOS Helper displays it. Otherwise, it gives you an error message. At least this approach makes it easy to add information, as explained in Appendix B. Figure 1-5 shows the information on the BACKUP command.

Limitations   Because each topic is a separate file, you end up with a lot of files. Just after installation, I had 112 files. On a floppy disk where the minimum size is 1K this does not represent a major problem. However, with certain types of hard disks and versions of DOS, the minimum file size is 8K. On those

```
F1=helpdos F2=unused! F3=unused! F4=unused! F5=unused! F6=unused! Use:C:\helpdos

     INTRODUCTION to DOS-Helper(R).  (c) Copyright Aristo Software 1985.

    |~~~~~~~~~~~~~~~~~~~~~~ MAIN FEATURES MENU ~~~~~~~~~~~~~~~~~~~~~~~|
    |                                                                 |
    |  PARAMETER     HELP                                             |
    |  ------------  ------------------------------------------------ |
    |  INTRO.........Introduction and general help (this file).       |
    |  CONTENT.......Logically ordered list of the help topics.       |
    |  INDEX.........Alphabetical list of the help topics.            |
    |  COMMANDS......List of the DOS commands + brief explanation.    |
    |  command_name..Help for the given DOS command.                  |
    |  topic_name....Help for the given topic.                        |
    |  SYNTAX........Definitions of DOS related syntax conventions.   |
    |  OWN...........How to create your own help files.               |
    |  ?.............Select one.                                      |
    ~~~~~~~~~~~~~~~~~~~~~~~~~~~~~~~~~~~~~~~~~~~~~~~~~~~~~~~~~~~~~~~~~~~

  The above menu summarizes the key features of the help system.  Additional
  help is provided below...
<↑><↓>=Line Scroll; <PgUp><PgDn><Space>=PageScroll; <HOME><END>=File Top,Bottom
CTRL/P=print; <Tab>=Previous Help;            Select help:[        ] <ESC>=exit
```

Fig. 1-4. The DOS Helper main menu. You select a topic by entering the name of the topic.

```
F1=helpdos F2=unused! F3=unused! F4=unused! F5=unused! F6=unused! Use:C:\helpdos

Command: BACKUP -- Back up disk files -- <E> <2.0>

Typical Usage: BACKUP C:\  A:/S

Syntax:
BACKUP d:[path][filespec]  d:[/S][/M][/A]

Function:
Back up files from a fixed (hard) disk to as many diskettes as needed.

This is the only way to backup a file (or group of files) that is too
large for an individual diskette.

(See other media backup for DOS 3.0 below.)

Detailed Description:

PARAMETERS:

   (FOR DOS 3.00 & up  [d:][path] can be specified before the command to
<↑><↓>=Line Scroll; <PgUp><PgDn><Space>=PageScroll; <HOME><END>=File Top,Bottom
CTRL/P=print; <Tab>=Previous Help;            Select help:[        ] <ESC>=exit
```

Fig. 1-5. The DOS Helper screen on the BACKUP command.

systems, these 112 files would require over 900K. (A few of the files are larger than 8K.) In addition, DOS Helper has a very poor installation program.

Manual   The manual is barely adequate. For some important information, like how to create your own databases, it refers you to a help topic.

Conclusion   DOS Helper is an adequate help program once you get it installed, and it is very easy to add additional information.

<table>
<tr><td>Product:</td><td>DOS Helper</td></tr>
<tr><td>Price:</td><td>$35</td></tr>
<tr><td>Category:</td><td>Commercial</td></tr>
<tr><td>Publisher:</td><td>Aristo Computers, Incorporated</td></tr>
<tr><td>Address:</td><td>6700 S.W. 105th Avenue
Suite 307
Beaverton, Oregon 97005</td></tr>
<tr><td>Phone:</td><td>(800) 537-7417</td></tr>
<tr><td>Notes:</td><td>Has both a memory resident
and stand-alone mode.</td></tr>
<tr><td>Memory:</td><td>72K in Memory Resident Mode
128K in Stand-Alone Mode</td></tr>
</table>

DS Help

DS Help is a stand-alone or memory resident program that provides help on DOS topics. The manual does not document the stand-alone version.

Installation   There is a batch file to install DS Help automatically. It insists on being run from the A-drive. However, the ASSIGN command easily fools it into running from the B-drive.

Operation   DS Help is simple to work with, once you have it installed and know the hot-key. After that, it is unlikely you will need the manual at all. DS Help operates as a memory resident program. You press Alt-H to bring up the main menu. Figure 1-6 shows this main menu. From there, you have five choices:

1) Analyze a command. This looks at the command you are now entering at the DOS prompt and displays the screen for that command. I found that DS Help had a lot of difficulty recognizing commands. It would give the help screen for the FORMAT command if I had entered: FORMAT but would fail to give me the same screen if I had entered: FORMAT A: Other commands had this same problem.

2) Subject reference. This would display general topics in English statements. Figure 1-7 shows what you see when you select a topic, like "Redirect Drive." DS Help gives you a list of commands from which to select—all related to your topic. Once you select a topic, you get the same set of screens you would get using option 3 below.

3) Command reference. Using this method, you select the command name from an alphabetical list. Once you get to the help screen, you use the cursor keys to read the several screens of information. After using either

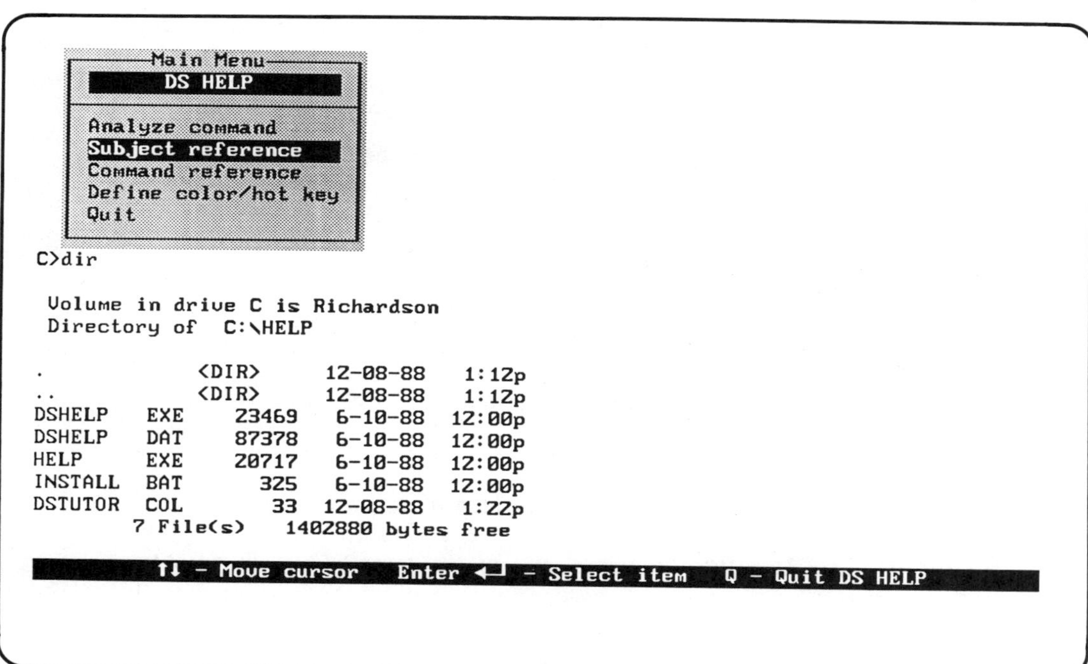

Fig. 1-6. The DS Help main menu lets you analyze a command, look up information by topic, or look up a specific command.

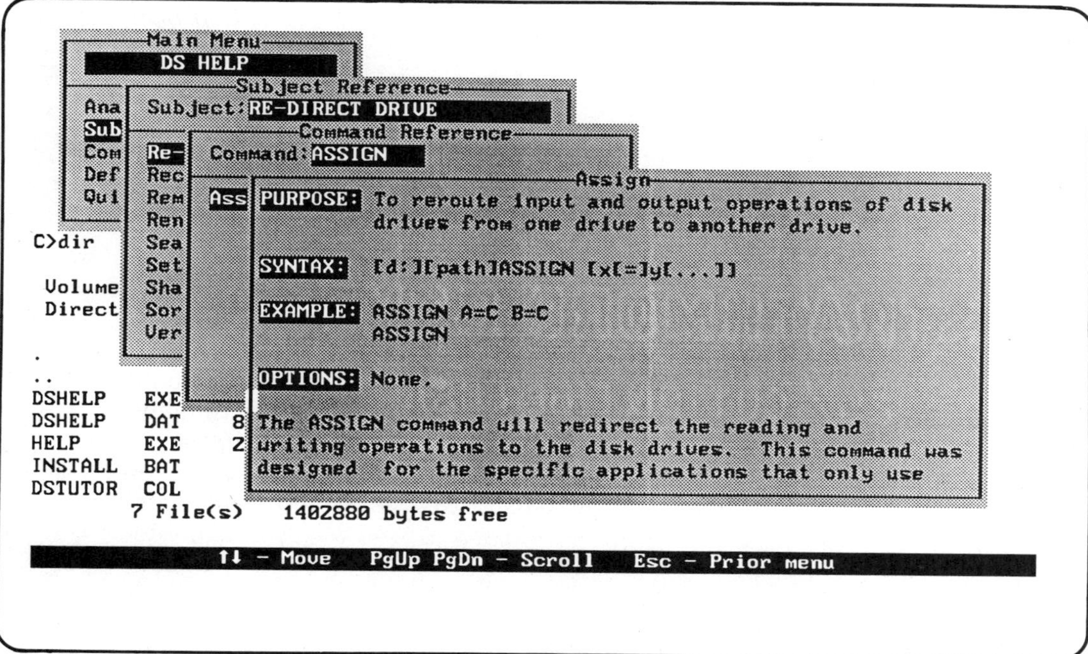

Fig. 1-7. As you work through the various levels of DS Help menus, all the prior menus are partially visible so you always know how you managed to reach a specific point.

method to reach the help screen, you exit. You can use Alt-H rather than Escape to exit. Using Alt-H causes DS Help to leave the help screen showing after you get back to DOS. Of course, you must position the contents carefully because you will not be able to scroll the screen from DOS.

4) Define color/hot key. This lets you control how DS Help appears and its hot key.

5) Quit. This lets you exit to DOS.

There is a separate stand-alone version of DS Help, called Help. Help does everything DS Help does except pop up while you are doing something else. To use it, you must be at a clear DOS prompt so you can enter the program name. This, of course, prevents you from using option 1 to analyze a command. Otherwise it functions the same as DS Help including being able to leave information on the screen. Getting help before entering a DOS command is not difficult—especially because you can leave that information on the screen. I preferred this version to the memory resident version.

Limitations   DS Help uses the industry standard of using the Escape key to back up one menu. However, this adherence to the standard stops when you reach the main menu. To exit the main menu and return to DOS, you must use the "Quit" command on the menu. Pressing Escape will not exit the program.

Manual   The manual is a brief nine pages. It adequately documents how to install and use DS Help. After all, you really do not need a manual to run DS Help. However, it fails to document the stand-alone Help program at all.

Conclusion   DS Help has a low price. That, and its ability to leave information on the screen when you exit, are significant advantages. *DS HELP* is worth careful consideration.

Product:	DS Help
Price:	$29.95
Category:	Commercial
Publisher:	Design Software, Incorporated
Address:	19808 Nordhoff Place
	Chatsworth, California 91311
Phone:	(800) 231-3088
	(818) 885-9000
Memory:	46K in Memory Resident Mode

Help!!

Help!! is a stand-alone or memory resident program that provides help on DOS topics. It has a low price and is easy to use.

Installation   Installing Help!! is a two-step process. First, you copy the files to a subdirectory in your PATH. Next, you run an installation program to tell Help!! where to find its data files. New users (the primary market for this product) could find the manual confusing because it only explains the second step. There is no program to automate the process.

Operation Help!! is simple to operate. In stand-alone mode you can enter the HELP Command to get help on a specific command. You can also enter HELP to select a command from the menu. In memory resident mode, you must work through the menus. You select a command, press Return and Help!! displays information in a second window. Figure 1-8 shows this. The information in Help!! is not as complete as DOS Help, but most users will find it adequate. Offsetting that is how easy it is to add data or modify existing data in the database. Appendix B explains this process.

Limitations Help!! includes several different databases of help information, including one on DOS 4.0. However, the program makes it very difficult to switch databases. Only one database is available for use at a time. To switch, you must:

1)   RENAME HELP.DAT to something else.
2)   RENAME the new database to HELP.DAT.
3)   Run an included program to index the new database.

I avoided this by placing several versions of Help!! in different subdirectories. These had slightly different names (HELP-DOS, HELP-40, and so on). Each version had a different HELP.DAT file. That is clumsy. The program should handle multiple databases easily if it is going to handle multiple databases.

Manual As explained above, the manual does a poor job of explaining how to install Help!!. The manual does an adequate job of explaining how to operate Help!! and how to modify the existing databases. It does not explain how to

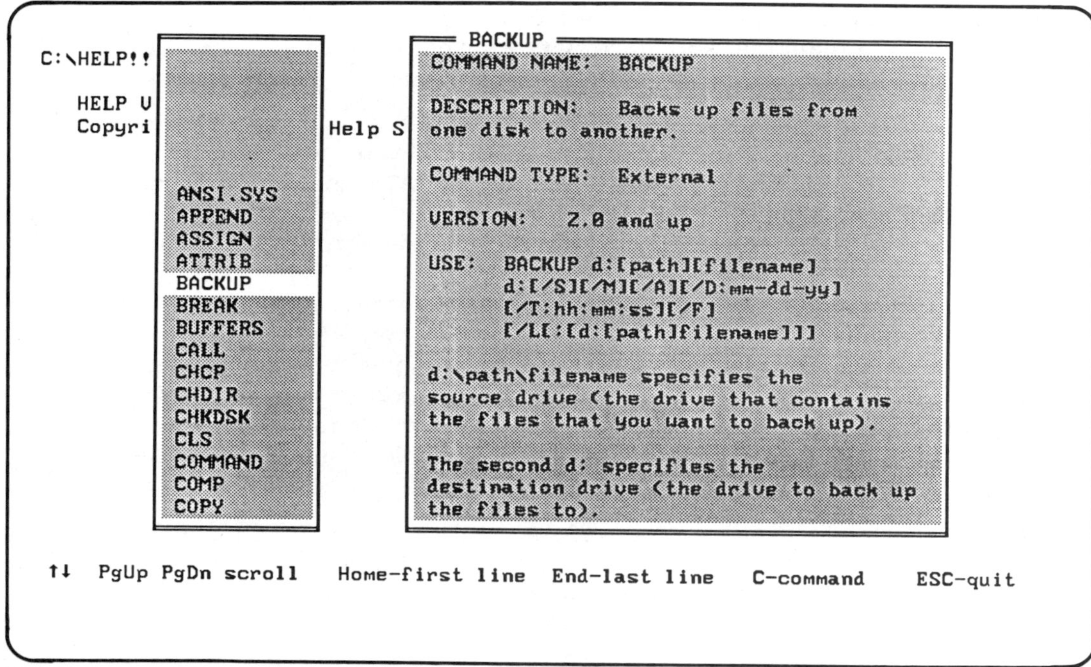

Fig. 1-8. Help/Pop-Help displaying information on the BACKUP command.

swap databases—I had to figure that one out myself. All in all, the missing information does not bode well for beginners.

Conclusion   Help!! is a good "engine" for someone looking to create their own database. Appendix B explores that aspect of the program. It is also an adequate program for DOS help. This is especially true if you can stick with the default database or can get some help with setting up the program.

Product:	Help!!
Price:	$25
Category:	Shareware
Publisher:	Help Software
Address:	16706 Bradley Court
	Belton, Missouri 64012
Phone:	(816) 331-5809
Memory:	256K Stand-Alone
	67K Memory Resident Mode

HelpDOS

HelpDOS is a stand-alone program that provides all the information in your DOS manual electronically. Because it is not memory resident, you can install HelpDOS on any machine without worrying about the memory requirements.

Installation   You must install HelpDOS in a subdirectory in your PATH statement. The best way to install HelpDOS is to create an individual subdirectory for HelpDOS and adding that subdirectory to your path statement. The electronic manual included on the HelpDOS disk adequately describes this process, but there is no program to automate it.

Operation   HelpDOS has two modes of operation. If you know exactly for which command you want help (for example the FORMAT command), you can go directly to that set of help screens with the command: HELP FORMAT

If you are not sure exactly which command you need help on, you can simply enter: HELP

That brings up the main menu. You then work your way through one or more layers of menus to hone in on the topic on which you need help.

HelpDOS does a very good job of explaining the topics, and has well laid out screens (see Fig. 1-9). You can scroll one line up or down with the cursor arrows. You can also use the page up and page down keys to move one screen at a time. If you want to print the explanation for a topic, a single key stroke does that for you.

Limitations   HelpDOS is an excellent product with no major limitations. Its only minor limitation is it does not follow the industry convention of using the Escape key to move back one menu at a time. The version I used did not yet support DOS 4.x, but that will likely change soon.

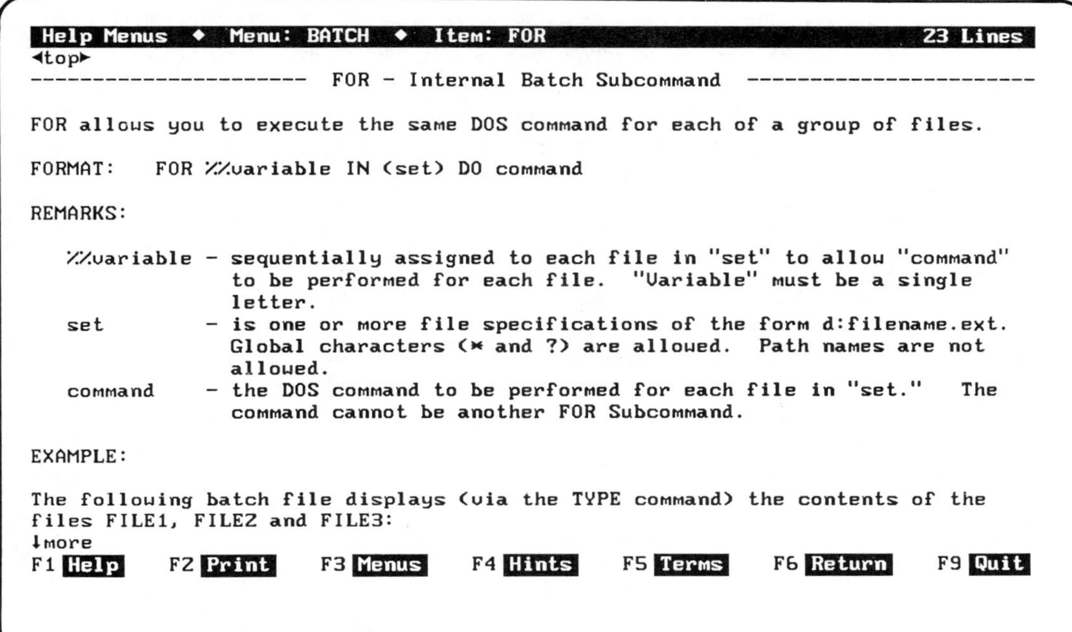

Fig. 1-9. The HelpDOS Help for the FOR command.

Manual   The electronic manual on the disk does an adequate job of explaining how to get HelpDOS up and running. After that, it is hard to imagine needing the manual for anything because HelpDOS is easy to use and self-explanatory.

Conclusion   HelpDOS is an excellent program for beginners who either do not know the syntax of a command or cannot remember it. It is also a good program for experienced users—those who always seem to misplace their DOS manual just when they need to look up the syntax on some infrequently used command. HelpDOS is available on the optional diskette set.

Product:	HelpDOS
Price:	$15
Category:	Shareware
Publisher:	Help Technologies
Address:	17955 Plaza Oriente
	Sonora, California 95370
Phone:	(209) 532-1062
Notes:	The optional diskette set includes a copy of this program.
Memory:	128K

RONNY'S PICKS

For DOS tutorials, the Learning DOS package from Microsoft is the better choice, unless you have a slow or monochrome display adapter machine. Its use of graphics makes it a much more interesting program to use. Of course the graphics also increases the requirements on the computer and slows the package down. Another advantage to Learning DOS is that it comes from Microsoft: the people who write DOS. While not received in time to include in this book, Microsoft has released a copy of Learning DOS to support DOS 4.x.

For DOS aids, my preference is for a program that runs from the command line. Because you generally want command line help, that mode of operation is adequate and saves memory. Even better is a program that gives you a choice of either running in memory resident mode or command line mode. A DOS aid does you little good if it does not have up to date information. Of all these programs, DOS Help! has the best information and works in either mode.

2
DOS Menus

Back in 1983, the organization I worked for got its first few computers. Over twenty users shared these computers. Most of them did not know much about using computers. After answering "how do I start Lotus" at least fifty times, I developed a menu system for the most frequently used computer. That menu system was very much like the one I describe in Appendix C. The MIS manager was not pleased with it, but several days later I saw him copying it onto the other computers: The menu had become so popular with the users that he had no choice.

I have slightly modified the menu system over the years. I have to do that every time I add or delete a program. Otherwise, it is very similar to the system I installed in 1983.

Menus have long had the reputation as something used by people too lazy to learn even a few DOS commands. The DOS shells covered in the next chapter share that reputation. That seems to be slowly changing. There seem to be two major reasons for the shift in opinions about these programs:

A new "generation" of computer users are coming along. The original PC users were those who shifted to the PC from other systems that were popular before the PC. These older systems lacked the support modern users take for granted so users were in the habit of doing things for themselves.

The second generation of computer users were what the marketing folks call "early adopters." Early adopters begin using a technology for the sake of the technology rather than what that technology can do for them.

Both of these generations of computer users are beginning to be outnumbered by the third generation. The technology interests this generation only for what that technology can do for them.

The menus and shells are getting better. Older programs were hard to set up and used a lot of memory in their operations. They were also fairly limited in what they could do. While this type of program has a place, the newer programs are far more powerful. Many of them offer features not even available directly from DOS. For example, with DOS the only way to move a handful of files from one subdirectory to another is to copy them one at a time. You then must delete them from the original subdirectory. This is time consuming—especially if the names do not lend themselves to using wildcards. Some of the newer shells will let you tag the files with a cursor and move them all with a single command. As these programs become more powerful, even hard-core command-line users are adopting them for their speed and ease of use.

WHY A MENU

The purpose of a menu system is to handle much of the overhead involved in running programs from a hard disk. For the most part, menus are more trouble than they are worth on a floppy diskette. Before developing a menu system, it is important to have a well structured hard disk. If you need more information on structuring your hard disk, you will find it in Appendix D.

WHAT THE MENU WILL DO FOR YOU

Basically, a menu will start a program for you with just a keystroke or two. It does this no matter how many DOS commands you would have to enter to start that program. Some menuing systems add simple DOS functions such as file copying and renaming.

My basis for evaluating the menu systems is:

1) Ease of setup. The majority of menu users are new to computing. They simply do not have the skills necessary to set up a complex program. Menu programs are unlike most other programs in that physically installing the software on your computer is the least of your problems. Once physically installed, you have to configure the menu program to operate with your software.

2) Ease of modification. It should not be difficult to add or delete a program from your menu.

3) Memory. The less memory a menu program takes up while you are running other applications the better. This is one advantage of the build-your-own menu system in Appendix C. It takes no memory while you are running other applications.

4) Ease of use. Menus should make using the computer easier for new or infrequent users. The easier they are to use, the better. In fact, a menu program should be so easy and straightforward to use that you find it boring.

This chapter discusses a wide array of menu programs with a wide array of features. It is important to select a menu program with the right combination of features and value for your own personal needs. The menu program you select directly influences how you use your computer. The chapter lists the programs alphabetically. The next chapter discusses DOS shells.

MENUS HAVE DRAWBACKS

In non-computer terms, the basic issue is how much should you know mechanically about a car in order to drive it. Clearly, you really only need to know how to add gas, check the oil, and change a flat. Anything beyond that will save you time and money, but is not necessary to operate a car.

The same is true of computers. There is little reason for a user to know how to change the environment or write batch files in order to simply use his computer. In that respect, a menu is like a good mechanic. It takes over the hard stuff so you can just productively use your computer.

The issue boils down to: more risk for greater ease of use. If you avoid menus, you are going to have to learn more about your computer to become productive. Therefore, you are going to be able to solve more of the problems you encounter. If you decide to go with a menu, you will become productive sooner. However, you are not going to have to learn the details that would help you in solving problems as they arise.

WHEN A SHELL IS A MENU

The next chapter covers DOS shells. These are programs that automate many of the processes of working with DOS. For example, to erase files you might perform the following steps:

1) Select the erase command from a menu.
2) Mark the files to erase by moving the cursor through a list of files and tagging them by pressing the space bar.
3) Carry out the erasure by pressing Return.

One thing you will notice is the last thing in this chapter: a listing of other programs you should look at. Many of them are DOS shells. My original outline for this book called for menus and shells to be in a single chapter called "Automating DOS." I had to divide them because there are so many of these programs.

It turns out that there are actually three types of programs. One type is the strictly menu program. Those are in this chapter. Another type is the strictly DOS shell. Those are in the next chapter. The third type is the program that does both. They are in the chapters where they fit best. You will find a listing of them at the end of this chapter. If you are new to computing, these combination programs represent an excellent value. You essentially get two programs for the price of one. The menu program lets you figure out the commands to start your programs once and then has the program remember and recall those commands. The shell program automates many of your everyday DOS functions.

Automenu

Automenu is a shareware menu program. It uses a script language that makes it more powerful than standard menu programs. The same script language makes it more difficult to configure Automenu.

Installation   Automenu does not come with an installation program. The manual-on-the-disk instructs you to:

1) Create a subdirectory especially for Automenu.
2) Add that subdirectory to your PATH.
3) Copy all the files from the distribution disk to this subdirectory.

Configuration   The default menu delivered with Automenu contains an option to edit the menu file. I started by creating a new menu file with only a few entries in it. I forgot to include any editing command or even an exit to DOS command. I then made that script the default menu file. I now had no way to edit the menu and no way to even exit. I ended up rebooting and renaming and copying over some files. The message is clear. When all menu functions flow through the user-defined menu, the menu builder must make sure and include all necessary options.

Automenu includes an editor for its menu scripting language. Figure 2-1 shows this. In this script language, the first character of each line is very important. The first character tells Automenu what the line does. For example, a "." marks a comment line that Automenu does not process. A "?" marks

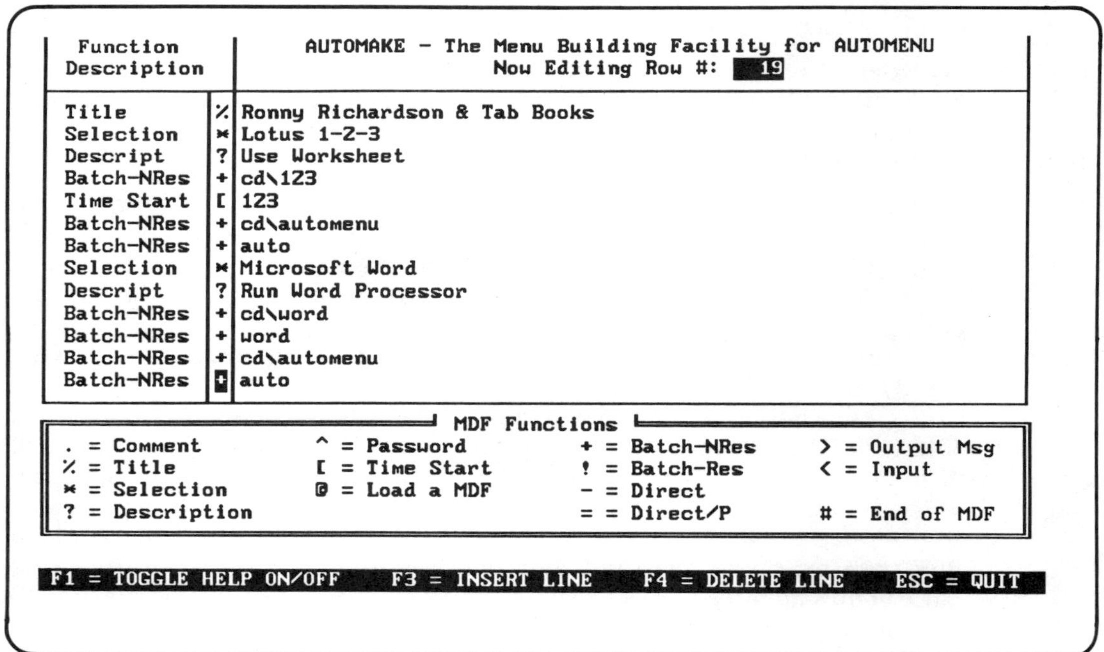

Fig. 2-1. Automenu uses a script file to define its menus. Automenu includes a program for editing this script file.

a line that more fully describes menu options. The editor takes this into account and marks off the first column as special. Once you enter the first character, the function description on the left side of the screen changes to describe the function of that line. It bases this description on the first character.

A "*" line is a menu option line. Everything until the next menu option line or new page line relates to this menu item. There should be a line "?" describing this menu option. Automenu automatically centers and displays this description at the bottom of the screen when this option is highlighted. You can enter as many DOS commands as you like. Automenu executes these commands when you select a menu item. If you start the line with a " + " then Automenu removes itself from memory before running these commands. They function just like a batch file with Automenu taking no memory. The last line must contain the command "AUTO" to run a batch file and restart Automenu. DOS command lines can also start with a "!" which functions just like a " + " except Automenu remains in memory. These two types of lines cannot be intermixed.

If there is only one line of DOS commands and Automenu is to remain in memory, you can start that line with a "-" for faster reloading. You can also use a " = " line. It is the same as a "-" line except Automenu pauses after executing the command. This lets you read the screen. You cannot mix these commands or use them with the " + " or "!" DOS commands.

Automenu has several other interesting types of lines. Starting a line with a "[" causes Automenu to automatically run that selection at a specific time. Automenu must be active at that time. Starting a line with a "∧" defines a valid password for that option. More than one valid password can be active for an option. A ">" line prints information on the screen for the user. A "<" prompts the user for information. Automenu places the first query in the DOS %1 variable, the second in %2 and so on through the DOS limit of nine. A "@" loads a new menu file. Using this option, Automenu can chain in and out of different menu files.

The editor stores the resulting menu file as a strait ASCII file. You can edit it with any word processor as well as the Automenu editor. Automenu is very picky about errors and will not load a menu file with any errors. As a result, using an external editor is somewhat difficult. It does give you the line number for the first error to aid you in tracking down errors. Each menu can have eight options. There is no limit to the number of menus you can create in a single file.

Operation   You select a menu option on the current menu using one of two methods. You either move the cursor to that option and press Return, or you enter the number associated with the menu option. Automenu automatically provides that number. You move to other menus using the page up and page down keys. You must move through the menus sequentially. From menu number seven, you can go directly to only menu six and eight. There are two exceptions to the sequentially accessed rule. Home takes you to the first menu from anywhere and end takes you to the last menu.

Limitations   Automenu has a screen saving feature that blanks the screen after a few moments of inactivity. However, the screen does not go completely blank when this feature kicks in. Rather, it places a box in the middle of the screen with a message telling you to press the space bar. Automenu shows the date and time below the box. Rather than staying still, the box begins to roll down the screen. When it reaches the bottom, it pops back up to the top. This constant movement keeps the box and message from burning into the screen. The constant motion ends up being very annoying if you are trying to sit and work at your desk.

Manual   Like most shareware products, the manual exists as a file on the disk. You must either use an ASCII listing program to read the manual from the screen, or print the manual yourself. You can print the manual using either the PRINT command or your word processor. The Automenu manual is very good. It has a fairly simple section for new users and a technical section for advanced users.

Conclusion   Automenu is more difficult to configure that some other programs. However, its menu scripting language gives you the power to create complex menus. Automenu would not be a good choice for someone looking for a menu to run a few programs. If you are looking for a departmental menu to manage a complex set of programs, Automenu would be an excellent choice. If you want a central computer center to configure and administer the menu, Automenu would be an excellent choice.

<table>
<tr><td>Product:</td><td>Automenu</td></tr>
<tr><td>Price:</td><td>$69.95</td></tr>
<tr><td>Category:</td><td>Shareware</td></tr>
<tr><td>Publisher:</td><td>Magee Enterprises,
Incorporated</td></tr>
<tr><td>Address:</td><td>Post Office Box 1587
Norcross, Georgia 30091</td></tr>
<tr><td>Phone:</td><td>(404) 446-0271</td></tr>
<tr><td>Notes:</td><td>Automenu releases memory
when running another
applications.

The optional diskette set
includes a copy of Automenu.</td></tr>
<tr><td>Memory:</td><td>32K</td></tr>
</table>

Direct Access

Direct Access is a menu program that allows two levels of menus with up to 400 programs. It has excellent usage tracking and good security.

Installation   Direct Access has a built-in installation program. This program works well and is very flexible. It allows you to select the hard disk and subdirectory for Direct Access and it asks before modifying your AUTOEXEC.BAT file. There is one minor drawback to the installation program: In addition to installing all the Direct Access files in the subdirectory, it places one file, MENU.BAT, in the root directory without informing you. Unlike many installation programs, this one will work fine from the B-drive without resorting the ASSIGN command. That is a plus to PS/2 users because Direct Access comes on a 5.25 inch disk. Overall, this is a very good installation program.

Configuration   You create and modify menus using the Menu Maintenance utility which you access by pressing F1. You can easily restrict a user from modifying the menus or seeing the passwords. To do that you simply erase the CONFIG.EXE program that performs the editing.

The main menu allows up to twenty entries. Figure 2-2 shows using the editor to modify the main menu. You have two choices for each line. First, you can enter the name of a single program to run. Second, you can enter the name of a submenu. Direct Access does not know the difference. How Direct Access treats it depends on what you do next.

When you are ready to work on a specific menu entry, you press F9 to modify a submenu. That command name is misleading. You have to do this even if the menu option is a single program rather than a submenu.

The submenu screen has twenty lines with room for all the information for a single program on each line. If you only enter one line, Direct Access treats the original menu entry as a program. It runs that program when you select that menu option. If you enter more than one line, Direct Access treats the original menu entry as the title of a submenu. When you select a submenu option, Direct Access displays the submenu. Direct Access uses the description you enter here as the options in the submenu.

Each line has room for a description, drive containing the files, subdirectory containing the files, and command to start the program. This command can be either a .EXE, .COM, or .BAT file. If it is a batch file, you must start the

```
            C R E A T E  ╱  M O D I F Y   M A I N   M E N U

                    The Main Menu Title Currently Is

            Menu for Ronny Richardson

      Sub-Menu Description      Password      Sub-Menu Description    Password
      ----------------------    -----         ----------------------  -----
   A) Lotus                     [123  ]  K)                              [      ]
   B) Microsoft Word            [Word ]  L)                              [      ]
   C) dBASE                     [dbase]  M)                              [      ]
   D) Norton                    [Norto]  N)                              [      ]
   E)                           [     ]  O)                              [      ]
   F) Miscellaneous             [     ]  P)                              [      ]
   G)                           [     ]  Q)                              [      ]
   H)                           [     ]  R)                              [      ]
   I)                           [     ]  S)                              [      ]
   J)                           [     ]  T)                              [      ]

    F1 Insert   F2 Delete   F3 Move   F7 Options   F9 Modify Sub-Menu   Esc Exit
```

Fig. 2-2. The main menu can contain up to 20 entries. The Menu Maintenance utility is used to modify the menu.

command with the word "batch." Once you enter a line, Direct Access checks to make sure the file you entered exists. If it does not, you have two options. You can change the name or have Direct Access search the entire hard disk for the file you specified. This is a nice feature. It saves you endless switching between menu construction and running applications to make sure you have entered everything properly. If you constantly set up menus for others, this feature alone makes Direct Access worth serious consideration. Figure 2-3 shows the submenu editor.

If you like, you can construct a batch-like command series from within Direct Access. You run these just like a menu option. Though most of a Custom Application are straight DOS commands, the first line can contain special Direct Access commands. These allow you to prompt for a password, diskette changing and/or additional parameters. Figure 2-4 shows the finished menu.

Operation Like most menus, you select Direct Access applications by selecting an application or submenu from a menu. It runs the application, and then returns you to the Direct Access menu. Direct Access can prompt you for a password before running an application. It gives you three tries at the password. If you fail all three times, all it does is return you to the main menu.

In addition to a password, Direct Access can prompt you for a user number and project number. It can compare these to a table of acceptable combinations. It will only allow you to proceed if the combination matches an entry in the table. Direct Access can store this information, along with the menu option selected and the time spent on that application, in a log file. This affords easy logging of the work performed on an application or project. Direct Access had one of the best project time tracking options of any menu program.

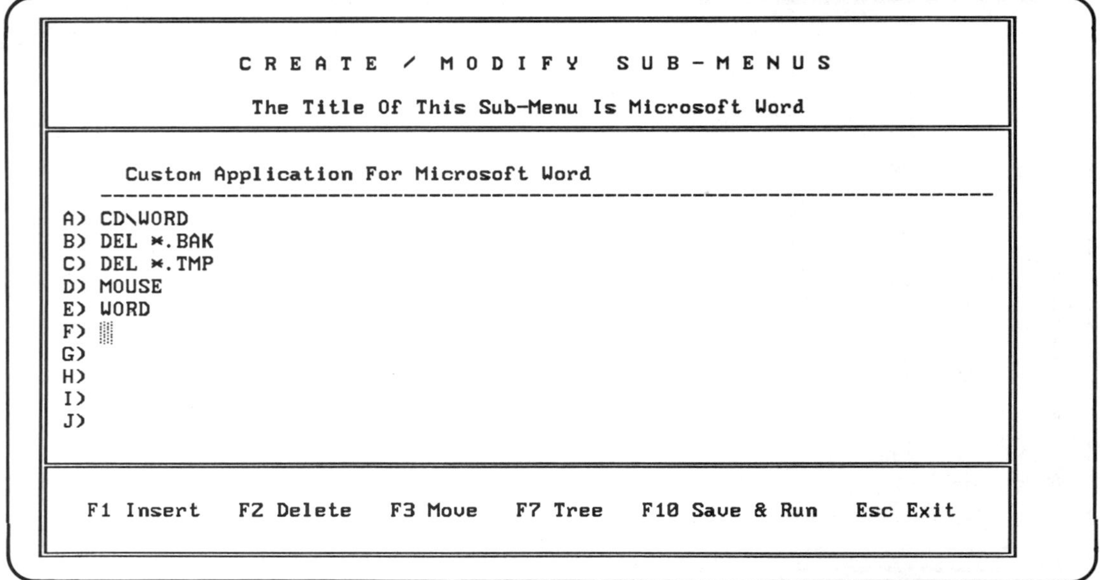

Fig. 2-3. Direct Access allows you to create Custom Applications that work almost exactly like batch files. Their only difference is that the first line can prompt for additional information, or for a specific diskette.

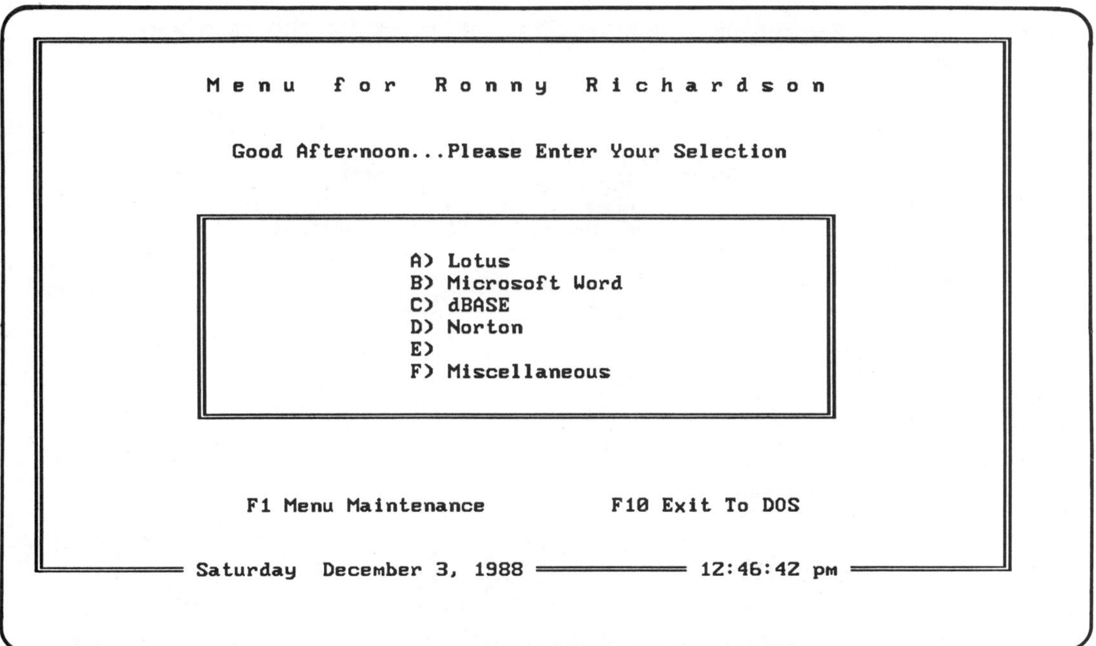

Fig. 2-4. This is the finished Direct Access menu.

Limitations   Direct Access allows you to password protect your programs. You can even password protect the exit to DOS command. Both are good ideas for some systems. With Direct Access, you will have to remember to protect the Maintenance Menu. If you do not, anyone can go to that menu and see the passwords. You protect the Maintenance Menu by erasing the file that performs the editing. Once you do that, you cannot add programs to the menu without first restoring this program. In fact, you cannot even change your password without restoring this program.

In addition, Direct Access breaks a cardinal rule of using passwords. When it asks for a password, the box that pops up is the same length as the password. So an unauthorized user knows right away the length of the password. Of course, Direct Access's is not perfect protection. An informed user can boot from a floppy diskette or hit Control-Break before Direct Access loads. This would allow him to gain access to the system without Direct Access getting in the way. This problem is not unique to Direct Access; most programs with security options face this problem. That does not excuse Direct Access for giving away the length of the password.

Manual   The manual is short but does an acceptable job of explaining how to install, configure and use Direct Access. There is no index, so it is hard to use the manual as a reference book. The program does not have help available while the program is running.

Conclusion   Direct Access is a very good menu program with excellent project time tracking. Its automatic verification that files exist makes it especially

easy to set up. This feature should not go unnoticed by anyone who often sets
up computers for others.

Product:	Direct Access
Price:	$89.95
Category:	Commercial
Publisher:	Delta Technology International
Address:	1621 Westgate Road
	Eau Claire, Wisconsin 54703
Phone:	(715) 832-7575
Note:	Direct Access requires only 64 bytes while other programs are running
Memory:	256K

DOSShell

DOSShell is the menu and DOS shell is the program included free with
DOS 4.x. It provides full mouse support.

Installation   You do not have to install DOSShell separately. Installing DOS
automatically installs DOSShell.

Configuration   You add a program to the DOSShell menu by pressing F10 to
bring up the program menu then selecting add. There are also commands
to . . .

- Modify an existing menu option.
- Delete a menu option.
- Copy a menu option to another name for editing.

Operation   To run a menu option, you move the cursor to that option and
press Return. DOSShell does not support pressing the first letter of the command. It does, however, support a mouse. You can run an option by moving the
mouse cursor to that option and clicking on it twice. DOSShell retains about
4K while it runs another program.

One of the menu options built into DOSShell is "File System." This is a full
DOS shell. DOSShell divides the default screen into five parts. At the very top
is the menu. Just below this are all the drives available, including SUBSTituted drives. You can log onto any two at once. Below that, it divides the major
part of the screen into half. On the left half is a graphical tree representation of
the hard disk structure. On the right is a list of files in the currently highlighted subdirectory. In addition to the file name and extension, it shows the
files size and creation date. It does not show the creation time. To the left of
each file is a graphical symbol representing the type of file it is. Programs have
one symbol, data files another, and so on. Below that is a single line listing the
function keys you can use with the system.

Once you have tagged files to operate on, the file menu has options to:

- Run a single program file.
- Print an ASCII file.
- Associate a file type to a program. This lets you associate all .DOS files, for
  example, with Microsoft Word. That way, any time you select "Open" while

on a .DOC file, DOSShell will automatically start Microsoft Word and supply it with the highlighted file name.

- Move files to another location. This move does not simply move the directory entry. Rather, it copies and then erases the file.
- Copy files.
- Delete files.
- Rename files.
- Change file attributes.
- View. This lets you view a file in either ASCII or hexadecimal mode.
- Create a subdirectory.
- Automatically select all files.
- Automatically deselect all files.

An options menu lets you control how DOSShell sorts files and which files it displays. There is also an arrangement menu. It lets you split the graphical tree and file list in half. That way you can look at two sections of the hard disk at once. The arrangement menu also lets you display all the file names on the hard disk without regard to the subdirectory they are in. You can tag files and operate in either of these displays just like in the first display.

Limitations You use the group command to reorder programs in the menu. However, using it is cumbersome: You first move the cursor to a menu option you want and select the group. You move the cursor to the new position for that option and press Return. You must repeat the entire process to move another menu option.

Manual The manual for DOSShell is extremely poor. The IBM DOS manual devotes a single page to explaining all the features of DOSShell. Luckily, DOSShell has very good context-sensitive help and is naturally very easy to use.

Conclusion DOSShell is a very good menu program and an excellent DOS shell. All it is missing is a "real" move command that relocates files by moving their directory entry without moving the actual file. It has the best mouse support of any of the programs. If I were using DOS 4.x I would not consider any other menu program or DOS shell—especially because DOS includes DOSShell for free.

Product:	DOSShell
Price:	free
Category:	Commercial
Publisher:	Microsoft
Address:	16011 North East 36th Way
	Redmond, Washington 98073
Phone:	(206) 882-8088
Notes:	DOSShell is included free as a part of DOS 4.x. Of course, you must pay $150 for DOS 4.x
	DOSShell releases all but 4K of memory when it runs another application
Memory:	128K

DS Manager

DS Manager is a full menu system and a full DOS shell combined into a single program.

Installation   DS Manager comes with an installation program to automatically install the program. It works from either the A- or B-drive. It prompts you before modifying your AUTOEXEC.BAT file and allows you to skip that step if you like. The installation program does not let you change the name of the subdirectory used to install DS Manager.

Configuration   DS Manager uses passwords and there is no way to avoid that. Your password tells DS Manager what level of access you have. Only the user with the PC Coordinator password can configure the system. Figure 2-5 shows the menu configuration screen.

Operation   Because it depends on batch files, DS Manager does not use any significant memory while another application is running. To select an application, you move the cursor to that menu item and press Return. You can also press the first capitalized key in the title.

In addition to a menu, DS Manager adds a full file manager. Figure 2-6 shows the file manager screen. The screen shows a graphical tree on the left side and the files in the highlighted subdirectory on the right side. The figure shows the file menu at the bottom of the screen. This menu lets you:

- Change disk drives.
- Change the file specification that lists the current subdirectory.

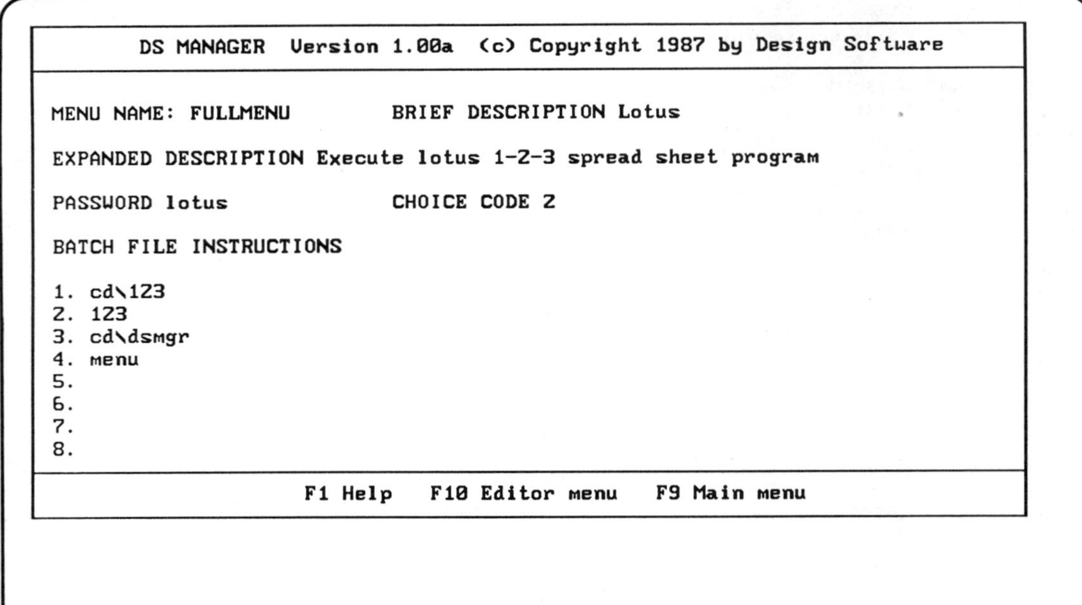

Fig. 2-5. This screen must be completed for each menu option in DS Manager.

```
 DS MANAGER    Version 1.00a   (c) Copyright 1987 by Design Software

——HIJAAK         AUTOEXEC.BAT      794   12-20-88  10:26a              Arc
——HOTDOS         CHAPTER1.DEL    42496    9-07-88  05:55p              Arc
——HOTSHOT        CHAPTER2.DEL    66560    8-16-88  06:20p              Arc
——HUNTER         CHAPTER3.DEL     7680    9-07-88  06:21p              Arc
——ICONSHEL       CHT-TEMP.DEL     1024    7-08-88  10:28a              Arc
   └——DOC         FIGURES.DEL     75776    7-29-88  06:47p              Arc
——JOBS           HEATPUMP.DEL     6144    6-19-88  08:31a              Arc
——JUNK           INTRO.DEL        9216    8-16-88  06:13p              Arc
——LIST           MORECAPT.DEL     5120    8-19-88  08:20a              Arc
——LOCKUP         OLDLABEL.DEL    43520    9-08-88  09:05p              Arc
——LOTUSFIG       OUTLINE.DEL      5120    9-07-88  06:32p              Arc
——LPTZDISK       RELEASEL.DEL     2560    9-16-88  09:18a              Arc
——MACE           REQUESTE.DEL     3584    7-15-88  02:17a              Arc
——MAGIC          STRATMAP.DEL     7168    9-08-88  09:02p              Arc

 Path: C:\JUNK

 DOS version:   4.0     # files:   17                  bytes free:  39954432
 # dirs     :   100     # bytes:   434458

Drive  Global  Locate  Make dir  Rem dir  Floppy  Stats  Bytes  Clock  Quit
Change current disk(ette) drive letter
```

Fig. 2-6. The DS Manager file manager has all the features of a stand-alone file manager.

- Locate files matching a given file specification.
- Add a new subdirectory.
- Remove an empty subdirectory.
- DISKCOPY a floppy disk.
- COMPARE two floppy disks.
- FORMAT a floppy disk.
- Display memory and disk usage statistics.
- Display the amount of free space on the current disk.
- Reset system date and time.
- Erase files. Once you select the delete function, you can then tag files for deletion by moving the cursor to the files to flag and pressing the space bar. Pressing Return carries out the command.
- Copy files, tagging them just as with the delete command.
- Move files, tagging them just as with the delete command.
- Rename files. Files can only be renamed one at a time.
- View ASCII files. You can only select one file to view.
- Edit an ASCII file using the DS Manager editor. You can only select one file for editing.
- Print an ASCII file. You can only select one file for printing.
- Changing file attributes, tagging them just as with the delete command. You cannot change the system attribute.

Limitations   The file manager does only a little better job of displaying subdirectories in the graphical tree than does WindowDOS. DS Manager can display a maximum of one hundred subdirectories no matter how many you have. The graphical tree is the only way DS Manager has for selecting subdirectories. As a result, you cannot manage the remaining subdirectories using DS Manager.

DS Manager makes very poor use of the screen. The menu is crammed into the bottom two lines. A two-line logo and single-line menu title have 15 or so lines in the middle of the screen.

I found the constant use of passwords to be cumbersome. Unfortunately, with DS Manager there is no way to turn off the use of passwords.

Manual   The manual is brief but does an adequate job of explaining how to use DS Manager.

Conclusion   DS Manager is a good menu manager and a good file manager. The menu manager does not make as good use of the screen as do other programs. DS Manager's inability to access more than one hundred subdirectories for any of its operations is a serious limitation for users with large hard disks.

Product:	DS Manager
Price:	$49.95
Category:	Commercial
Publisher:	Design Software, Incorporated
Address:	19808 Nordhoff Place
	Chatsworth, California 91311
Phone:	(800) 231-3088
	(818) 885-9000
Notes:	DS Manager does not use any memory while it is running another application.
Memory:	256K

HDM III

HDM III is a shareware hard disk menu system. Some of the menus work similarly to Lotus—moving lightbar menus.

Installation   Installing HDM III involves copying files and modifying your AUTOEXEC.BAT file. There is a program that automates the copying, but you must modify your AUTOEXEC.BAT file yourself.

Configuration   When you first start HDM III, you see a screen like the one in Fig. 2-7, but without the top box. HDM III divides the menu into two parts. The right section is the page index side. From here, you select the major menu you will be using with the appropriate function key. The left section holds the menu items for the currently active menu page. You select these using the numbers, or by moving the cursor and pressing Return.

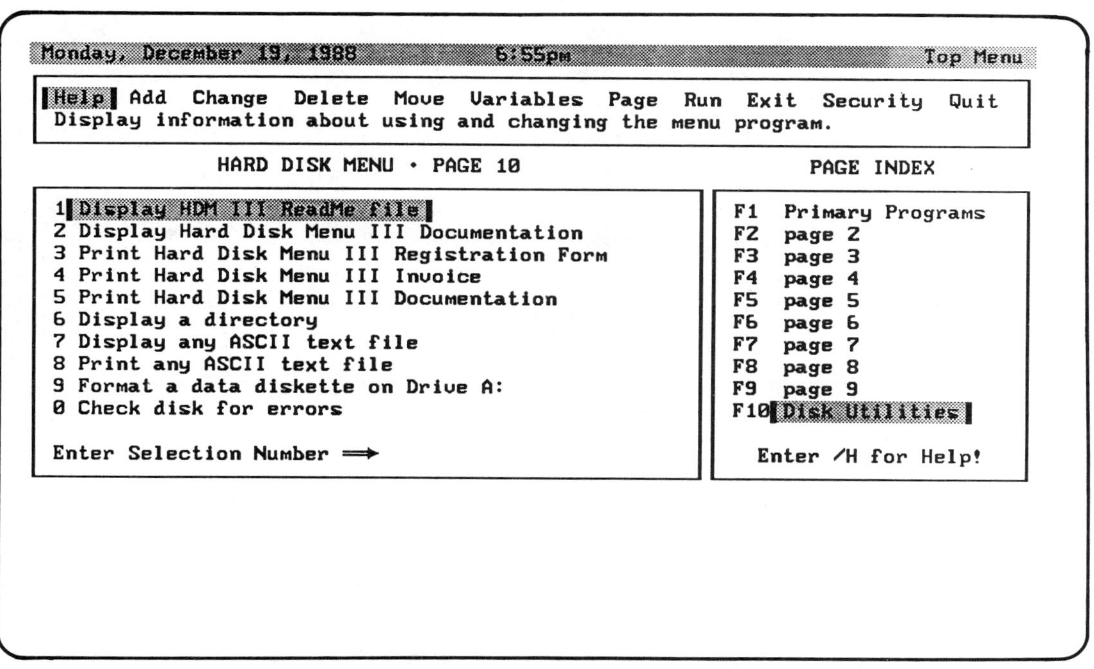

Fig. 2-7. The menu modification allows you to configure any of the menus.

Modifying or creating a menu requires the modification menu. Figure 2-7 shows this.

Operation　　Using the HDM III menus to run programs is simple. You press function keys to switch between menu pages. You use either the cursor keys or numbers to select a program to run from the currently active menu page.

Limitations　　The biggest limitation is the manual, as described below. In addition, there is no way to exit HDM III completely without rebooting. You can get to DOS, but HDM III is in memory waiting to kick in again when you enter EXIT. A memory resident manager like PopDrop could cure this problem.

Manual　　The manual is a disk-based ASCII file. It is fairly technical and an inexperienced user would find it very difficult to understand.

Conclusion　　HDM III is harder to set up than some of the other programs. Entering the DOS commands to start a menu application in a Lotus macro-like structure would be especially difficult for someone not familiar with Lotus macros. Once configured, HDM III is easy to use. There is a copy of HDM III on the optional diskette set.

```
Product:      HDM III
Price:        $25/$35
Category:     Shareware
Publisher:    Microfox
Address:      Post Office Box 447
              Richfield, Ohio 44286
Phone:        Not Available
Notes:        $25 to register
              $35 to register and receive latest version
              A copy of HDM III is included on the
              optional diskette set
              Only 60 bytes are used by HDM III when
              it runs another program
Memory:       128K
```

Hot

Hot, from the same company that produces *Xtree*, is a menu program with a full DOS shell. Hot comes in two parts: the menu builder and a runtime module. A menu designer uses the menu builder to construct a menu system and then installs it using a runtime module. That way the end-user cannot modify the menu.

Installation   Hot comes with an installation program that automatically installs Hot. It works from either the A- or B-drive without problems.

Configuration   You begin by selecting to edit a menu option, and providing the name of a menu file to edit. This takes you to the menu editor. Figure 2-8 shows this menu, which forms the nucleus of the menu editing functions. You move to a second screen when you enter the DOS commands required to run an application. The menu on the right side of the screen shows the Hot commands you can enter to customize an application. You can also, of course, enter DOS commands.

You can also begin your menu construction by running a program called Hotbuild. This program scans your hard disk and constructs a menu item for each program—sort of like Menu Works discussed below. I say "sort of" because Hotbuild does not do nearly as good a job as Menu Works. In fact, you are probably better off skipping Hotbuild and building all your menus from scratch.

Operation   Hot works like most menu programs. You highlight the menu choice you want to run and press Return. You can also press the first capitalized letter in each menu. When Hot runs a menu it retains 209K of RAM. This is far more than other menu programs and enough to interfere with programs that are relatively RAM insensitive.

Hot requires so much RAM because it has pop-up utilities that are available from within other applications. You access them by pressing the left Shift key twice. The pop-up utilities are:

- Notepad.
- File finding utility.

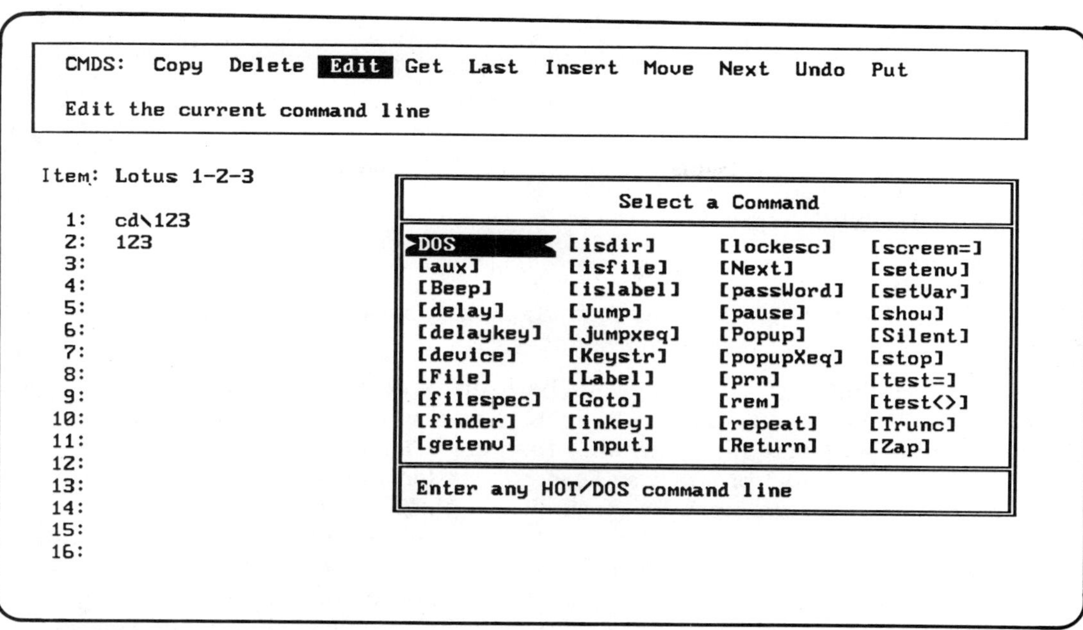

Fig. 2-8. When entering the DOS commands to start an application, Hot gives you a menu from which to select the available commands. You can, of course, also enter the commands manually.

- Calculator.
- Calendar.
- Blank the screen when the computer is not being used until the user presses a key.
- Appointment book.
- Miscellaneous utility that shows the ASCII tables, the ASCII characters used for box trading, change the keystroke rate and other such utilities.

You can, of course, reduce the memory required by Hot by removing some or all of these utilities.

In addition to a menu program, Hot includes a set of menus that perform most of the functions of a stand-alone DOS shell. There are commands to:

- Change directories. You can enter the directory manually or switch to a graphical tree display to select the subdirectory.
- List all the files in the currently active subdirectory.
- Create a new subdirectory.
- Remove an empty subdirectory.
- Run the SUBST command to treat a subdirectory as a disk drive when issuing DOS commands.
- Change file attributes.
- Copy files.
- Erase files.
- Use the built-in Hot editor to edit ASCII files.
- Change a file name.

- Print an ASCII file.
- Run the DOS BACKUP and RESTORE programs.
- View a file in either ASCII or hexadecimal mode.
- Run the CHKDSK program.
- Run the DISKCOPY program.
- Format a floppy diskette.
- Run the COMPARE program.
- Set up the serial port.
- Set up a printer.

There are even on-line help programs that pop-up help screens on topical DOS questions.

Limitations   Hotbuild tries to scan your hard disk and automatically construct a menu. However, this menu will likely require extensive modification. On my system, there were more mistakes than correct guesses. It misstated the Take Charge Diskmap program as Diagram Master and the Psearch program as Print Shop for example. Every single .BAT, .COM and .EXE file that Hotbuild finds that does not match anything in its database gets dumped into a menu of miscellaneous programs. This miscellaneous menu just lists the program name (e.g. 1.BAT) with no indication of what it does. On my system this miscellaneous program went on for fourteen full screens. This is not a very useful way to build a menu.

Manual   The manual does a good job of explaining how to set up Hot. There is not a second manual to be included with the runtime versions of your menu program. So the menu builder must write extensive documentation himself on using the Hot menus.

Conclusion   I found Hot to be more difficult to configure than some of the other menu programs. The included Hotbuild program is supposed to overcome this by building menus automatically. However, it makes so many mistakes it will end up costing you far more time than it saves you. You must configure Hot to skip all the memory resident software. Otherwise, you will end up with a menu system requiring so much memory it cannot run major applications.

Product:	Hot
Price:	$179.00
Category:	Commercial
Publisher:	XTree Company
Address:	4330 Santa Fe Road
	San Luisobispo, California 93401
Phone:	(805) 541-0604
	(800) 634-5545
	(800) 551-5353 in California
Notes:	Hot retains 209K of RAM memory when running another program
	Hot includes two runtime modules, additional runtime modules cost $49.95 each
Memory:	512K

Icon Shell

The *Icon Shell* is a quasi-graphical interface menu program. Its main purpose is as a glue to tie together various applications into a coherent system. It also functions as a DOS menu, though not a very good one.

Installation   The Icon Shell has a built-in installation program. It is as happy running from the A- or B-drive. It lets you select the hard disk on which you want the program installed. It does not let you change the name of the subdirectory—you must use \IS.

Configuration   Configuring the Icon Shell involves writing a script file, called IS.SCF. You must write this script file for each subdirectory where you plan to use the Icon Shell. The Icon = # statement reads a file called ISICONS.TXT. This text file contains all of the icons. Each icon consists of four lines of 13 characters. The characters are generally high-ordered ASCII characters so the drawings look crude. Using this method ensures that the Icon Shell can run on any system.

To develop a menu, you first begin by selecting or drawing an icon for each application.

Operation   The Icon Shell is fairly simple in operation. You move the cursor around to highlight an entire icon. You run a program by highlighting the icon representing the application you want to run and pressing Return. If there are more icons that will fit on one screen, you can scroll them. Because the Icon Shell does little else, its operation is smooth and simple.

Limitations   The Icon Shell is a program that cannot seem to make up its mind. Part of the manual and examples talk about setting the Icon Shell up as a DOS shell. Other parts talk about using it as a shell for running application programs you write yourself. There is even a Turbo Pascal example for programmers.

Manual   The manual begins by suggesting you start the program and learn it by osmosis. I think you could actually do that with some of the programs in this section. However, the Icon Shell is not one of them. The manual is written for someone technically inclined. That reader will have no difficulty. A new user simply looking for a menu program to automate using his computer will find the manual extremely difficult.

Conclusion   I like the idea of using icons in the menu. However, as a menu program, the Icon Shell is far outclassed by some of the other programs in this chapter.

Product:	Icon Shell
Price:	$49
Category:	Commercial
Publisher:	Saratoga Group
Address:	Post Office Box 91287
	San Diego, California 92109
Phone:	Not Available
Memory:	54K

Lazy Susan

Lazy Susan is a menu program with a user interface not well suited for many menu options. It has macro capabilities so common commands can be relegated to a single keystroke. The menu creation and menu running programs are separate so the menu builder can easily keep the menus from being modified.

Installation   The installation program will only run from the A-drive. ASSIGN B = A corrects the problem. The installation program does not let you pick the directory name, it always uses \SUSAN. It also does not let you pick the hard disk, it always assumes the C-drive. Fortunately, the manual gives directions on how to install Lazy Susan manually.

Configuration   Lazy Susan comes with two separate programs. You use one program to configure the menus. You use the second to run the menus. Lazy Susan comes configured with eight menus. You will end up deleting or modifying these.

When you select "add an item," Lazy Susan prompts to see if it will be a menu or a program. For programs, Lazy Susan prompts you for the menu under which the program will come. You select by moving the cursor to the appropriate menu and pressing Return. You then get a panel to file in, containing the information required to run the program. Figure 2-9 shows this.

In addition to menus, Lazy Susan does macros. A macro is a series of Lazy Susan keystrokes that it stores in a file. These can be replayed on command. These commands must all be Lazy Susan commands, the macros do not work

```
 Change Program Information:
 ─────────────────────────────────────────────────────────────────────
 Program Description: (As it will Appear on Lazy Susan Menu)
 Microsoft Word
 Program Name: (MS-DOS Filename of Program, Extension Optional)
 WORD
 Program Help:
 Run word processing program
 Program Location: (Drive and Directory)
 C:\WORD
 Location of Other Files Required by Program: (Drive and Directory)

 Initial Console Input to Program: (MS-DOS Command Line)

 Get Console Input Before Running Program? (Y or N)    Y

 Console Input Prompt: (If Y to Above)
 Enter the name of a file to edit to return to start a new file
 Hide Command Line? (Y or N)    Y

 Pause on Exit? (Y or N)    N



    ↑ and ↓ - Select Item to Change, F1 - Accept Screen,  F2 or Esc - Exit
```

Fig. 2-9. You configure Lazy Susan to run programs by completing the information in this panel.

outside of Lazy Susan. If you store the macro in a file with a single letter name, you can select the macro from a menu. You can also invoke it with Alt-<letter name>.

Operation   The second half of Lazy Susan is the menu running program. Figure 2-10 shows this. This half of Lazy Susan cannot create or modify any of the menus. It can, however, create and modify any of the macros. Lazy Susan has no macro editing facilities.

As you can see in Fig. 2-10, Lazy Susan shows all the menus and all the menu options on a single screen. The only benefit to placing options in different menus is for a meaningful division on the screen. It does not affect how Lazy Susan works.

Limitations   For the most part, I like the idea of separating the menu creation and menu execution programs. That way, when the menu builder and user are different individuals, the menu builder can easily keep his menus from being modified. However, the way Lazy Susan implements this arrangement makes it difficult on inexperienced users. The menu building program has no way to test menu entries to see if they work. To test, you have to switch programs. If you are having a difficult problem, you can end up switching back and forth a lot. An option to test menu entries would help a lot. Because it would be solely for testing, Lazy Susan would not have to release all of its memory to the application.

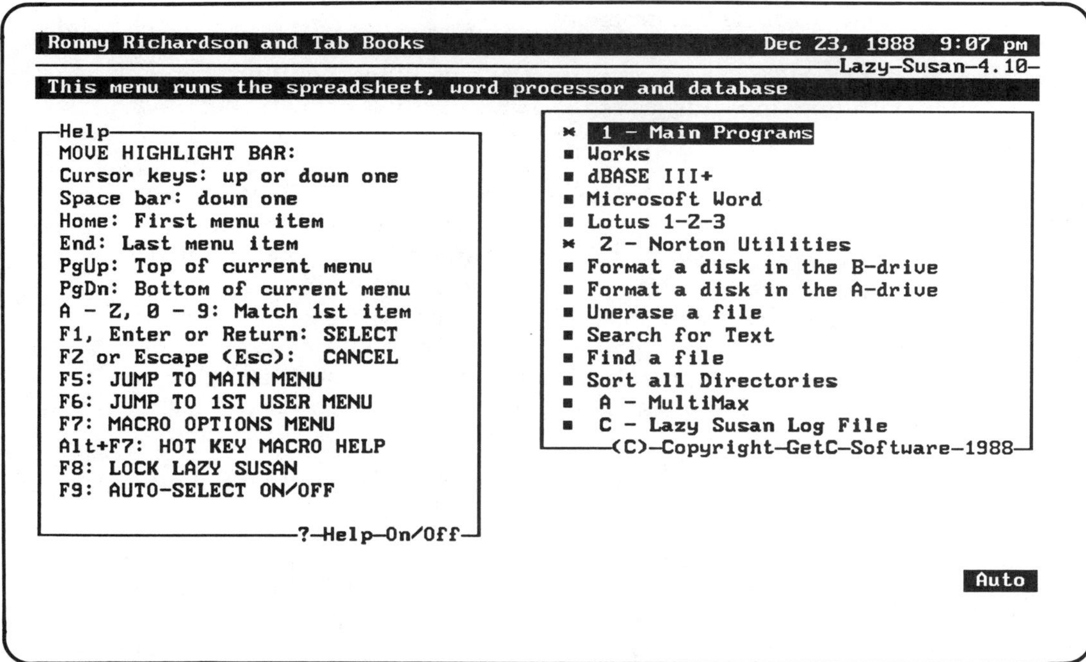

Fig. 2-10. Lazy Susan divides the menu creation and menu running program into two separate programs. This menu running program cannot edit or modify the menus. It can, however, create or modify macros.

You can select menu items by moving the cursor to them and pressing Return. You can also run them immediately by entering the first character of the menu. The manual suggests, quite appropriately, that using the first letter is the only way you should select commands in macros. You cannot depend on moving the cursor and pressing Return because you cannot be sure of the cursor location.

That does present a problem for complex menus. There are only 26 letters and 10 numerals with which you can start command titles. It also requires that you pay special attention to how you construct your menus. Pressing the first letter always runs the first match. If your menu contains both Microsoft Word and Microsoft Works in that order, you cannot run Works using the first letter approach. You end up with menu items like 1=Microsoft Word and 7=Microsoft Works. This is not visually very appealing and it still does not remove the 36 beginning character limitation.

The basic problem with Lazy Susan is that all of the menu options for every menu are all on the screen at once. That alone is not the problem. That arrangement actually works fairly well if you only want to have a few menu options. You can, of course, simulate this with other menu programs by placing all the options in a single menu.

As the number of menu options expands, Lazy Susan's method of selecting menu options becomes more cumbersome. You soon reach the point where all the keystrokes spent paging up and down exceeds the number of keystrokes needed to select submenus. The macros and first letter activation helps, but they in no way cure the problem.

An additional problem for programs that require a lot of memory is that Lazy Susan does not release as much memory as do other menu programs. The typical menu program needs less than 10K to get itself up and running again after you exit an application. A few do it with only a few bytes. In either case that is so little memory that you are not likely to miss it. Lazy Susan, on the other hand, needs 31K to get itself up and running again. That will not present a problem for many programs but a few may not be able to run.

When configuring Lazy Susan to run a program, it limits you to a single DOS command. Lazy Susan uses other information you enter to switch to the proper subdirectory, so most programs will run using a single command. If any of your applications require multiple command line entries to run, you will have to write a batch file to run them using Lazy Susan. Your alternative is to place each DOS command under a separate menu option and use a macro to run them sequentially.

Manual   The manual is adequate. An inexperienced user could read it and set up Lazy Susan without much difficulty.

Conclusion   I like the approach of separating the menu creation and menu operation into two separate programs. Placing all the menu options on the screen at once is acceptable also—as long as you will only be using short menus. With more menu options, the Lazy Susan user interface becomes just too clunky.

```
Product:      Lazy Susan
Price:        $79.95
Category:     Commercial
Publisher:    GetC Software Incorporated
Address:      Post Office Box 8110-182
              264 H Street
              Blaine, Washington 98230

              In Canada
              1280 Seymour Street
              2nd Floor
              Vancouver, British Columbia
              V6B 3N9
Phone:        (800) 663-8066
Notes:        When running another
              application, Lazy Susan retains
              between 25K and 31K of
              memory depending on
              configuration.
Memory:       256K
```

Magic Menus

Magic Menus is a shareware menu program with both a built-in DOS shell and a pop-up calculator.

Installation   Magic Menus comes with an installation program that automatically installs the program. Magic Menus is a shareware program and the documentation is a compressed file on the disk. The installation program neither copies the documentation to the hard disk or uncompresses it. In fact, Magic Menus does not have a program to decompress the documentation. The documentation is compressed using a common format and anyone commonly using shareware will have one or more decompression programs.

Configuration   Magic Menus selects the menu to use in an unusual fashion. The "other Menus" menu pops up a menu from which you select the applications menu you wish to either use or add a command to. To add the new menu item, you move to the "Applications" menu. This brings up the menu you just selected. The last two options let you add or edit an application. Figure 2-11 shows a sample user menu.

When you select add a command, you get a screen to fill in like the one in Fig. 2-12.

Once you complete this information, you have done everything needed to create a menu entry. That menu entry is immediately available. You do not have to reboot or exit Magic Menus and start it over again.

You can define up to ten menus, including the predefined main menu. Each menu can have up to 10 user defined entries. Each menu will automatically have the "Add application" and "Edit application" entries. Menu entries cannot lead to submenus, so Magic Menus can have up to 100 menu items.

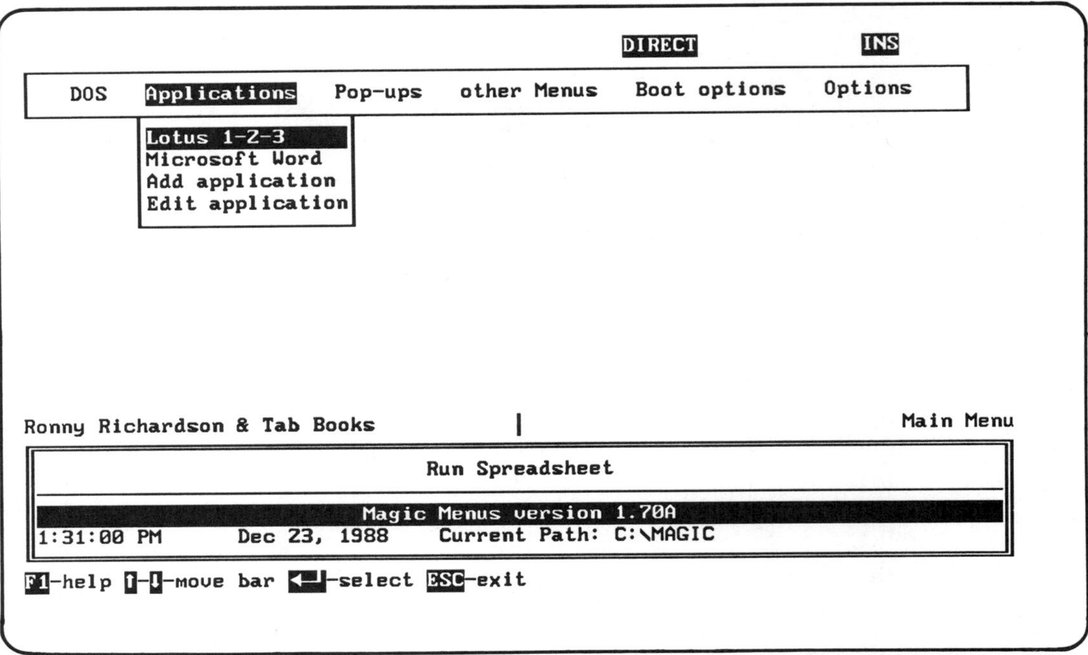

Fig. 2-11. You select programs to run from a menu and you add items to a menu using the "Applications" menu.

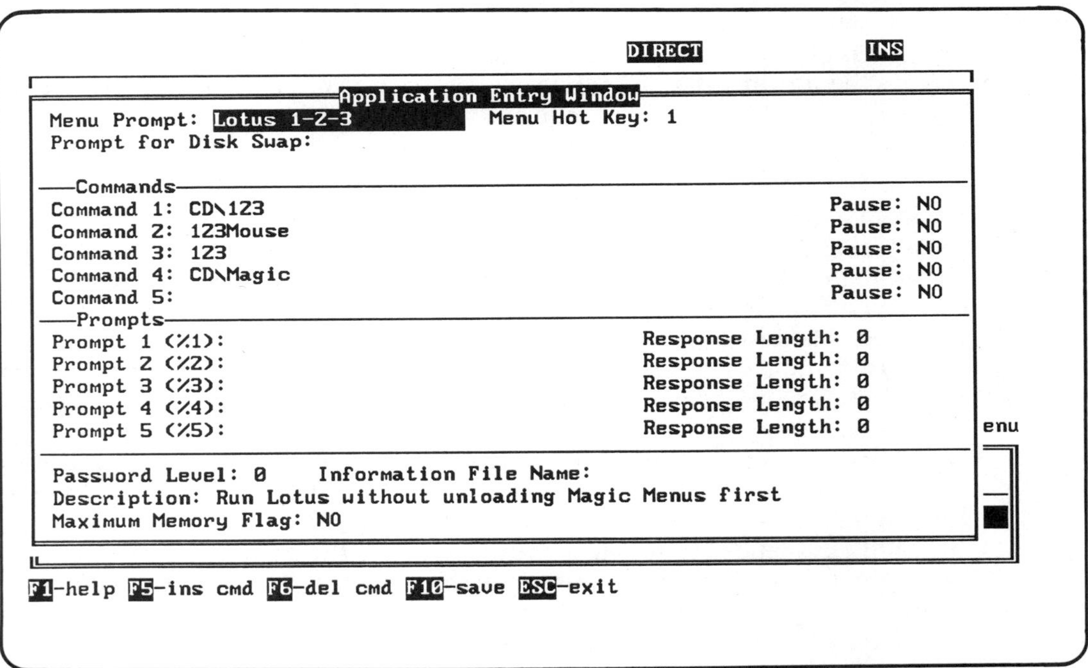

Fig. 2-12. When entering a new menu item into Magic Menus, or editing an existing one, you edit a single screen containing all the information about that application.

Magic Menus has several advanced features the menu builder can use. They are:

- Reusing information. If a menu item is to run several programs and you prompt the user for inputs, all the programs can use the responses.
- Easy file name selection. When prompting for a file, Magic Menus can optionally pop up a list of all those available.
- Response manipulating. Magic Menus lets the menu builder manipulate the response the user provides. For example, he can strip out all the directory information from a response and just retain the file name.
- Automatically pop up the printer control screen while processing another menu item. That way, you know Magic Menus has properly configured the printer for that application.
- Custom response menus. When prompting the user for information, the menu builder can create files that restrict the user to certain responses. Magic Menus displays this list as a menu when prompting the user for information.

All of these options taken together allow the creation of very intelligent menu systems.

Operation   If you have a mouse, Magic Menus has excellent mouse support. The left mouse button functions as a Return and the right button as the Escape key for backing out of menus. Moving the mouse will move you through menus just like the cursor keys.

In addition to a full menu system, Magic Menus offers several nice features along with a DOS shell. The features include:

- A directory selection window. After you configure this, it lets you select from a list of twenty directories. The list on the screen has 20-character English names. If the menu is being set up for someone else, you can completely isolate the user from subdirectories using this very nice feature.
- Printer control. This is another very nice feature that lets you select control strings to send to your printer. You select from an English list, just like the directory selection window. Of course, you have to spend an aggravating evening with your printer manual to set this feature up. After that, it works automatically.
- Window to DOS. This is a quick way to enter DOS commands. Magic Menus displays your last 10 commands. You can edit and reuse them. The minimum memory mode is not available here so you may not have enough memory to perform some tasks.
- Calculator. This is a nice pop-up four function calculator with simulated paper tape. You can send the tape to the printer.
- List of files. This gives you a pop-up listing of all the files in the current directory that match a file specification. Magic Menus prompts you for the file specification.

One of the menus in Magic Menus is a menu of DOS commands. It contains entries to:

- Get a DIRectory.
- Copy files.
- Rename files.
- DELete files.
- Change directories.
- Make a new directory.
- Remove an existing and empty directory.
- Set the date.
- Set the time.
- Run a DOS command. This option does have the minimum memory mode available so Magic Menus retains only 6K while the program is running. It does not retain prior commands for reuse.
- DOS shell. This option drops you out of Magic Menus to the DOS prompt, but keeps some or all of Magic Menus in memory. This option does have the minimum memory mode available so Magic Menus requires only 6K.

All of these features work, they just offer very little over DOS itself. The only advantage is that you select them from a menu. For example, when changing directories you cannot select the new subdirectory from a graphical tree. Most DOS shells offer this feature. When copying or deleting files, you cannot get a listing of files and move around that list tagging files to operate. Most DOS shells offer this feature.

Magic Menus has five password levels. Level five is the highest level and level one is the lowest. Someone who knows a level three password can also access level two and one options. You assign a single password to each level. You then assign levels to each menu item you generate in the same panel you use to generate that item. The password screen has prompts for assigning passwords to exiting Magic Menus and running the menu options that directly access DOS.

With passwords, you have to worry about how "sticky" they are. Assume someone sits down to work at the computer and has a level five password. When they leave the computer, a sticky password would let the next user continue accessing level five functions. To avoid this, the level five user must remember to cancel his password. That depends on human memory and can lead to problems. Magic Menus avoids this problem by requiring you to enter the password each time you run a menu selection.

Limitations   You use one menu to switch menus, and another to actually select menu items. As a result, moving around the menus in Magic Menus is more cumbersome than it should be. Using Magic Menus would be far easier if the actual menus would pop up on the left as you scrolled down the menu selections. Once you create menu entries, there is no way to reorder them or move them to another location. The DOS shell feature of Magic Menus would be far easier to use if it would show a graphical tree to move around, and lists of files for tagging before executing a command.

Magic Menus has a screen saving feature that blanks the screen after from one to 99 minutes. The delay is set by the user. That works fine. However, rather than completely blanking the screen, it displays a "> > > Screen Saver—Press any Key < < <" message in the center of the screen. This message then continually scrolls down the screen. Actually, scrolls is the wrong word. It appears on line one. Then disappears and reappears on line two. It continues to the bottom then reappears at the top. When I am at my desk and I am doing something away from the computer, I find this message flashing on and off often catches my eye. That causes me to look up from what I am doing. I find that extremely annoying. As a result, I set the screen saving delay to 99 minutes to avoid it as much as possible. There is also an option to turn this off completely. This is, of course, a personal opinion. It may not bother other users.

The "Add application" and "Edit application" prompts are always the last two prompts on the menus. You cannot remove them. If you are building menus for someone else to use, the only way you can prevent them from modifying the menus is to use password protection. Password protection interferes with using Magic Menus (this is true of passwords in general, not just Magic Menus) so you will probably want to avoid them. It would be very nice if Magic Menus had an option to hide the menu modification option.

Manual   The manual is very good. It is easy to read and follow. In addition, content sensitive help is always available while running Magic Menus by pressing the F1 key.

Conclusion   Magic Menus is an excellent choice for a menu program. It is easy to configure, easy to use, and low priced. A copy of Magic Menus is on the optional diskette set.

Product:	Magic Menus
Price:	$32.95
Category:	Shareware
Publisher:	Custom Technologies
Address:	Post Office Box 62118
	Colorado Springs, Colorado 80962
Phone:	(800) 541-6234 Sales
	(719) 282-0402 Technical Support
Notes:	A copy of Magic Menus is included on the optional diskette set
	Magic Menus can release all but about 6K of its memory when running another application.
Memory:	160K

Menu Works

Menu Works is an incredibly powerful menu program that installs itself. Not only does it install itself on your hard disk, it installs itself to run all your software!

Installation   Menu Works comes with an automatic installation program. Like many other programs, it expects to be in the A-drive. When I originally ran it from the B-drive, it locked up the computer and forced me to reboot. My old standby, ASSIGN A = B corrected that problem.

For most installation programs, once they copy the files on to your hard disk, they quit. A few will go on and configure a few things and perhaps ask you a few questions. Very few go beyond that. The Menu Works installation program goes well beyond that.

If you let it, the Menu Works installation program will look through your hard disk and set up menus. There are two ways to run this. The first checks every .COM and .EXE against its database and only installs the ones that match. The other creates a menu entry for every .COM and .EXE file it finds. Always use the first.

I was pretty cynical when I read about the automatic menu generation. I figured it would recognize a few major programs like Lotus and Wordstar and that would be it. Boy was I wrong!

I have a 130 Meg hard disk on my IBM Model 70 with over 90 Meg of software installed. At this writing, I have installed over half the software discussed in this book on my computer. In addition, I have installed the software I use in my writing and my everyday computer use. How could a program recognize all this?

Menu Works churned away at my hard disk. There were several counters going on the screen so I would know it was doing something. File names flew by the screen so fast I could not read them. In about five minutes, it finished.

Not only does Menu Works recognize software and auto-install it, it groups it into logical menus. It did a good job of this as well. For example:

- Under file utilities, it had menu entries for Fastback—a commercial and very popular program. It also had entrees for a number of shareware programs including Pattr, Psort, Ptouch and Pkarc.
- Under database programs, it had menu entries for the commercial programs Clipper and dBASE but missed the shareware Wampum.
- Under DOS utilities, it picked up the shareware programs EE2, Pcopy, Pdel and List. However, it missed all the Norton programs.
- Under general utilities, it picked up several competitive menu programs, 1Dir+ and Q-DOS II. It also picked up the Mace utilities but again missed the Norton Utilities.
- Under graphics, charting and drawing, it picked up Freelance but missed Lotus.
- It picked up all of my *PC Magazine* utilities and grouped them together.
- Under spreadsheets, it picked up MathCAD but failed to pick up Lotus. That is probably because I erased LOTUS.COM and always run Lotus using 123.EXE. That is the reason but not an excuse.
- Under word processing, it picked up sideways, Edlin and Anagram, a utility supplied with Microsoft Word. It failed to pick up Microsoft Word or Microsoft Works, although it picked Works under integrated software.

Altogether, I would say the auto-install program picked up 75% of the software I commonly use. That is, indeed, impressive. Figure 2-13 shows a menu generated solely by Menu Works.

Configuration   With Menu Works, you may not have to configure the menus at all. It is just possible that it will recognize all your software and do it for you. If it skips a program or two, adding them to the appropriate menu is easy.

You begin by pressing the Escape key at the main menu. This brings up the System Menu. From the System Menu, you select System Setup. The System Setup menu has an option for creating a new menu and modify an existing menu. Assuming you want to modify one of the menus Menu Works created for you, the next step is to supply the menu name. This is not the long name you see at the top of the menu. Rather, it is a short, eight character name. You will probably not know this, but pressing Return will give you a list to pick from.

This takes you to the actual menu construction area, called the Edit Menu. The Edit Menu lets you. . .

- Delete existing entries
- Modify existing entries
- Change a title
- Add a password
- Add a new entry to the end of the list
- Insert the new entry anywhere in the list

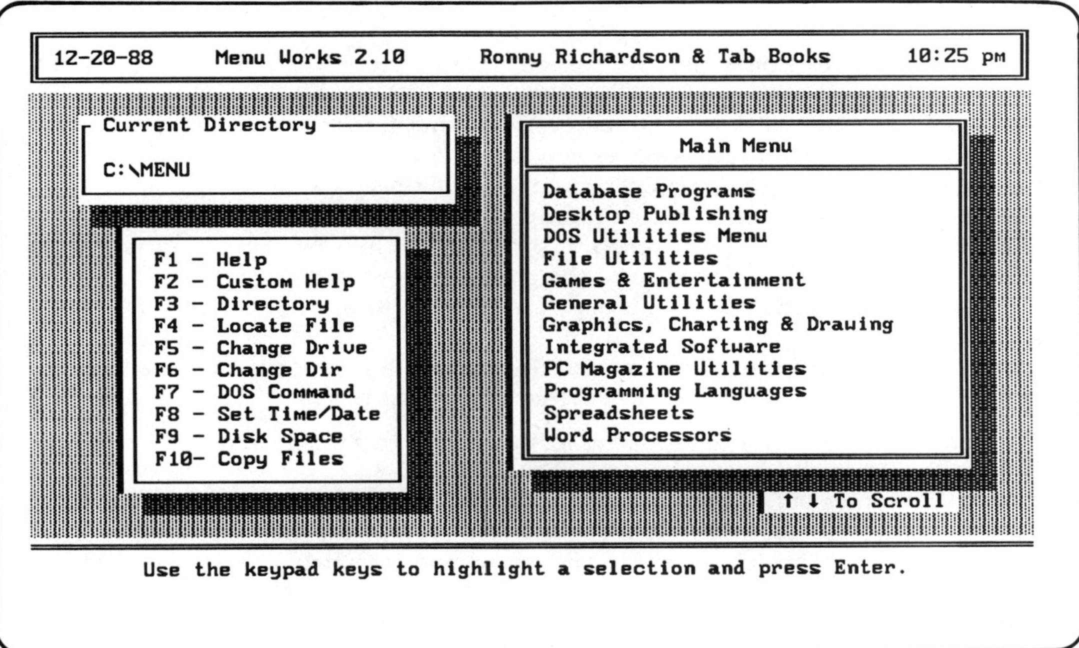

Fig. 2-13. Menu Works can automatically install itself for many popular programs without user assistance. This menu was generated solely by Menu Works.

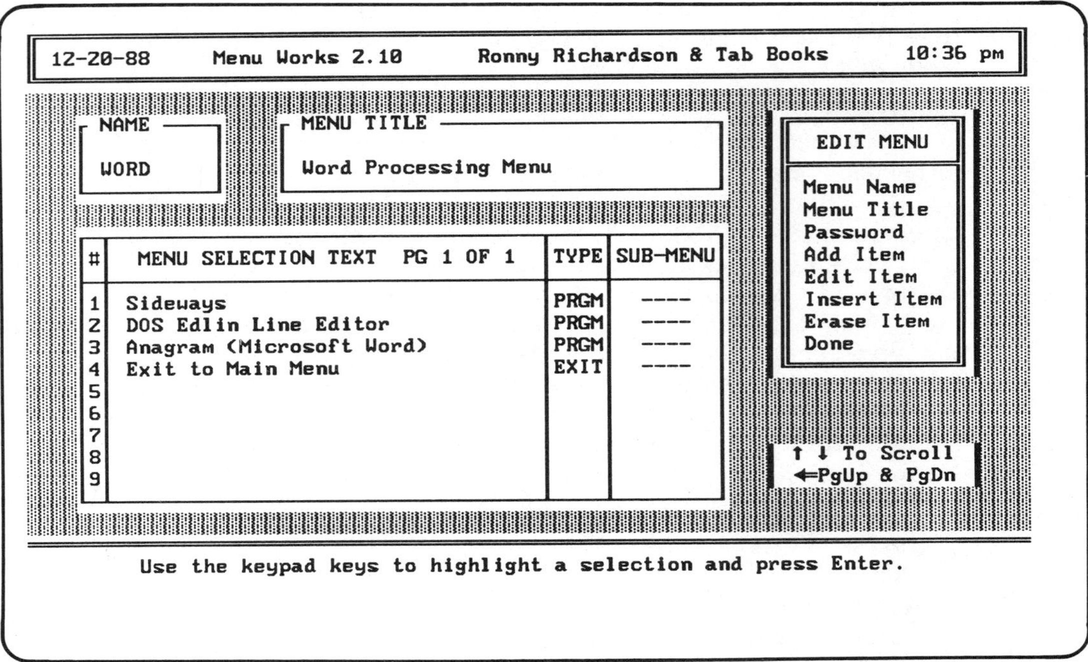

Fig. 2-14. With Menu Works, a painless series of menus leads you through creating a new menu or editing an existing one.

Figure 2-14 shows the Edit Menu.

When you select add an item, Menu Works prompts you for the text to be displayed on the menu itself. Next, you are asked if this item runs a program or leads to a submenu. Menu Works allows you to nest menus as deep as you like. If you are adding a program, the next prompt asks if it needs to multiply commands to start the program. The next prompt asks for the subdirectory to log onto before running the program. Next, it prompts for the DOS command to start the program. You are then asked if the program requires a lot of memory. If you answer yes, Menu Works removes all but about 8K of code before running the program.

While you may never need them, Menu Works has a nice set of advanced features an experienced user can incorporate into a menu:

- Custom help screens for an application. Of course, these help screens are only visible from within Menu Works.
- Up to fifteen lines of DOS commands to start an application.
- Prompting the user for information, such as disk drives and file names. You can even incorporate the user's response to one question into another prompt.
- Full password support for menus and programs within menus.

Operation   Operating Menu Works is easy. You use the up and down keys to select the menu you want to use. Pressing Return takes you to that menu.

Move the cursor to the program you want to run and press Return. Press Return again and Menu Works runs the program. When you exit your program, Menu Works automatically reloads.

Limitations   The database that Menu Works uses to auto-configure for various software packages is a minor limitation. There is simply no excuse for missing 123.EXE and WORD.COM.

Manual   The manual is excellent and easy for an inexperienced user to understand. While it does not talk down to the reader, it explains everything the reader needs to know clearly. The manual has large easy-to-read type.

Conclusion   If you are interested in using a menu system and not coding one, then purchase Menu Works. It automatically configures itself to much of your software, and does a good job at that. For those few packages it misses, manual configuration is easy. It is conceivable that you will have Menu Works up and running and fully configured within an hour of opening the box.

```
Product:     Menu Works
Price:       $24.95
Category:    Commercial
Publisher:   PC Dynamics, Incorporated
Address:     31332 Via Colinas
             Suite 102
             Westlake Village, California 91362
Phone:       (800) 888-1741
             (818) 889-1741
Notes:       Menu Works requires 132K when
             running but can reduce that to 8K when
             running a DOS command and 2K when
             running another program.
Memory:      132K/8K/2K
```

PC-Menu

PC-Menu is a powerful menu system that is easy to operate once installed and running. Setting up PC-Menu is difficult and beyond the ability of many beginners.

Installation   There is an automatic installation program that will run from any disk drive. It will let you specify any subdirectory name to use to install PC-Menu. The installation program needs to modify your AUTOEXEC.BAT file. It will prompt you for permission before doing this and skip this step if you want it to.

Configuration   Configuring PC-Menu is difficult. It involves writing complex batch file-like commands in a file called MENU.DEF. PC-Menu includes an example file that you can modify to suit your tastes. That makes the process somewhat easier. Still, a beginner would find it extremely difficult to configure PC-Menu without help.

Operation   Unlike the configuration process, operating PC-Menu is straightforward and fairly easy. Figure 2-15 shows the main PC-Menu menu. The

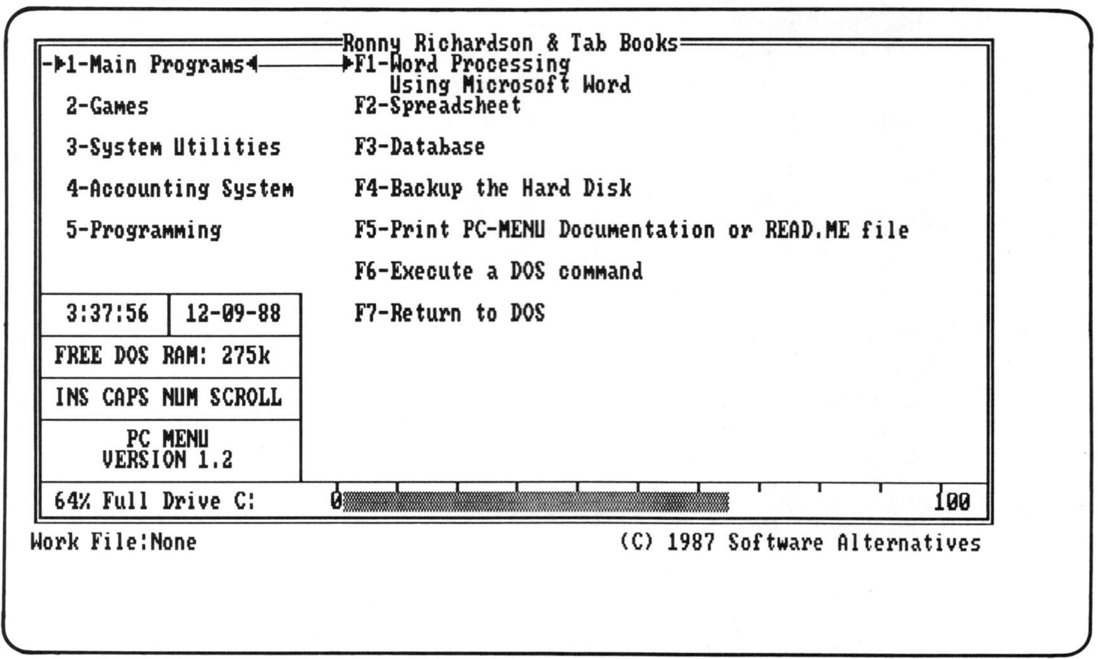

Fig. 2-15. The PC-Menu main menu is divided into up to six screens and each screen can have up to 10 options.

items down the left side are the menu pages. There can be up to six pages. Each page title can be up to 19 characters long. You select the page using either the number beside it or the page up and page down keys. The items down the right side are the actual menu options. There can be up to 10 of these on each page. Each option can be up to 49 characters long. You can add explanatory text below it. You select the menu item to run using the up and down arrows and pressing Return or using the function keys.

If you have a mouse, PC-Menu will be even easier to run. You can use your mouse to click on either the page or the menu item for rapid menu selections.

PC-Menu uses a script-like language to set the steps performed by each menu item. There is no practical limit on the number of steps performed by each menu item. Because PC-Menu uses this script-like language, the advanced user has almost unlimited power in designing menu options.

In addition to the menu pages, PC-Menu has one additional special menu. Here you can define up to 26 commands for PC-Menu to execute when you press an Alt-letter combination. Figure 2-16 shows this menu. You see the Alt menu anytime you press the Alt key.

Limitations   PC-Menu requires 54K and it releases none of that memory when you run a program from within PC-Menu. In addition, PC-Menu is very hard to configure.

Manual   The manual devotes only a few pages to operating PC-Menu. Of course, PC-Menu is so easy to use that a few pages are enough. The manual does a good job of explaining its operation.

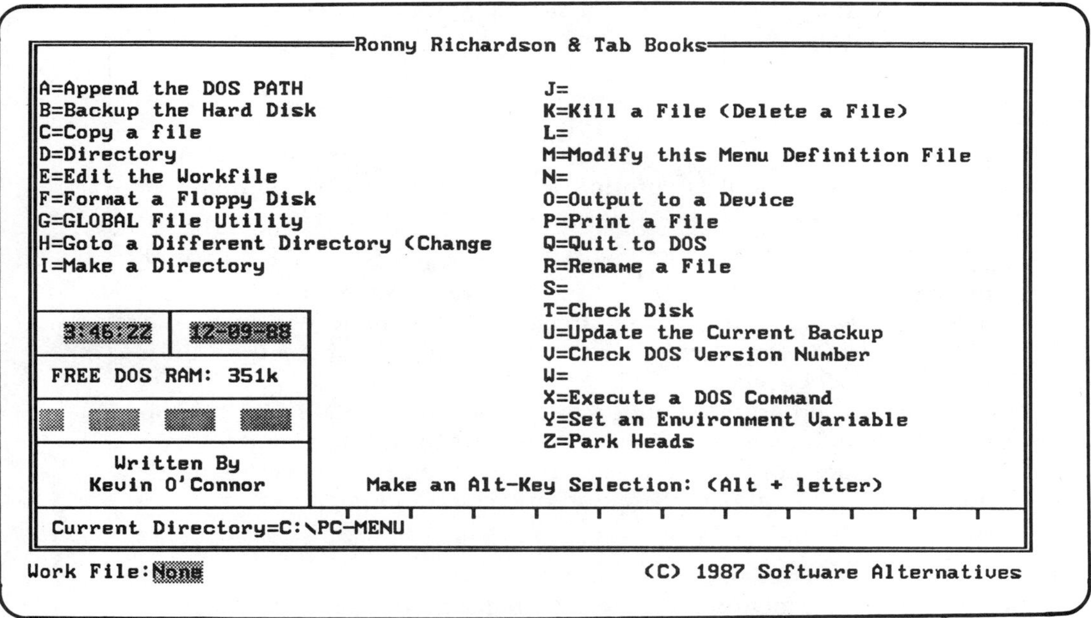

Fig. 2-16. With PC-Menu, you can specify up to 26 commands to be performed using an Alt-letter combination. These are shown in a special Alt menu.

The balance of the manual explains how to program using the PC-Menu script-like language. I found the manual a little hard to follow. In fact, I found that the best way to learn the language was to read the example MENU.DEF file and use that to figure out what was going on.

Conclusion   PC-Menu is an excellent choice for a company where there is a knowledgeable computer person to configure it. It is also an excellent choice for a computer store looking to configure customer computers. It is not a good

Product:	PC-Menu	
Price:	$15	Registration Only
	$20	Registration: Including next release on disk
	$35	Registration: Including next release on disk and typeset manual
Category:	Shareware	
Publisher:	Software Alternatives	
Address:	5170 East 65th Street Indianapolis, Indiana 46220	
Phone:	Not available	
Note:	A copy of PC-Menu is included on the optional diskette set PC-Menu does not release any of its menu when running another application	
Memory:	54K	

choice for a new user trying to make his own computer operations easier to manage.

PreCursor

PreCursor is an easy-to-configure menu program. It releases all of its memory to the application it is running. PreCursor includes a simple DOS shell menu.

Installation   The PreCursor manual tells you to begin by using the DISK-COPY command to make a backup. It then tells you to create a subdirectory for PreCursor and to log on to that subdirectory. At this point you enter A:IN-STALL to install PreCursor. The installation program will not run from the B-drive but an ASSIGN A=B corrects that.

The installation program demands to find a copy of ANSI.SYS on your hard disk even though PreCursor does not need ANSI.SYS to operate. If your AUTOEXEC.BAT does not contain everything required to run PreCursor, the installation program gives you the option of fixing it yourself or having the installation program do it for you.

Configuration   PreCursor requires a special maintenance program in order to create or modify the menus. The installation program gives you the option of installing this program or leaving it on the distribution floppy diskette. If you leave it on the diskette you need that diskette to change the menus.

To change the menus, you press the F4 key to go to the menu maintenance program. Figure 2-17 shows the main screen. Here you enter the menu

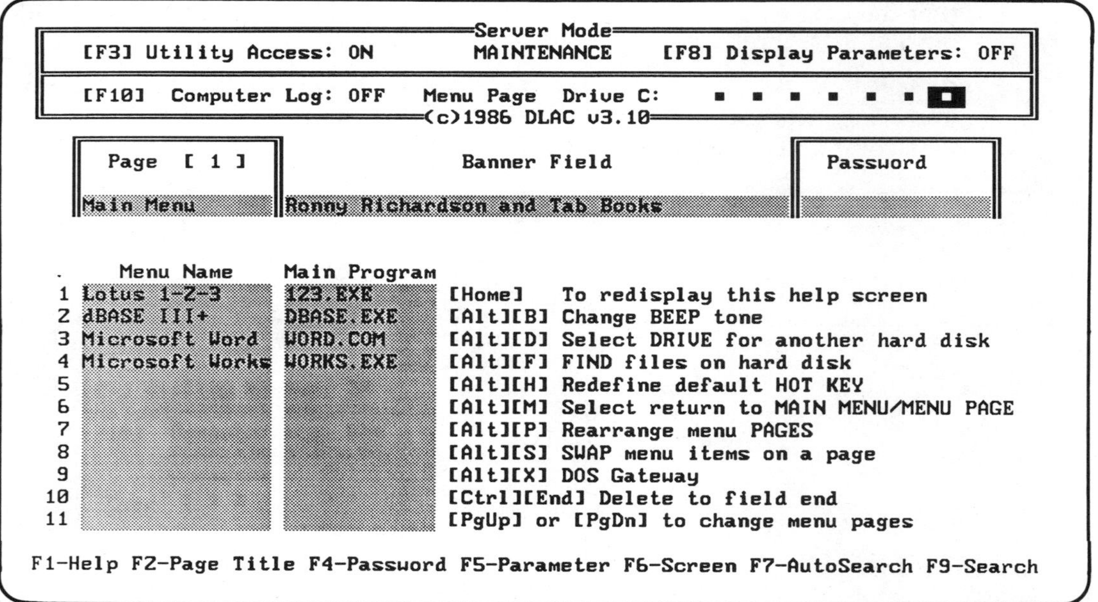

Fig. 2-17. With PreCursor, all that is required to create a menu item is the menu entry and the name of the program to run.

name and the program name. This is all PreCursor requires to define a menu item. When you exit this screen, PreCursor will search the hard disk for the programs specified so it will know the directory to switch to. If a program does not exist, it prompts you with an error message.

PreCursor has up to 14 menu pages and each page can have up to 12 options. One of the menu pages is automatically the main menu. You use it to switch between the other pages using the names you provide when you configured the menu. Another menu page is automatically a utility menu with file manipulation commands. A third page is the printer setup menu. That leaves up to 11 pages the user can define.

All PreCursor needs to define a menu is the name of the program. PreCursor searches the hard disk for the program name you enter. If you need more control, the program name you enter can be a batch file. PreCursor can also prompt the user for information, such as a file name to edit.

You can use PreCursor to track computer utilization by requiring the user to enter his name and a project ID. PreCursor stores that information along with the time spent on each menu item for future reference.

Operation When you start PreCursor, you see a menu like Fig. 2-18. You select the application to run by pressing the number associated with that menu entry or by moving the cursor to that entry and pressing Return. You can return to the main menu by pressing F2 and from there you can select menu pages. The main menu displays the title of each available menu.

When you run an application from within PreCursor, it releases all but a few bytes of memory to that application program. If you have used the DOS

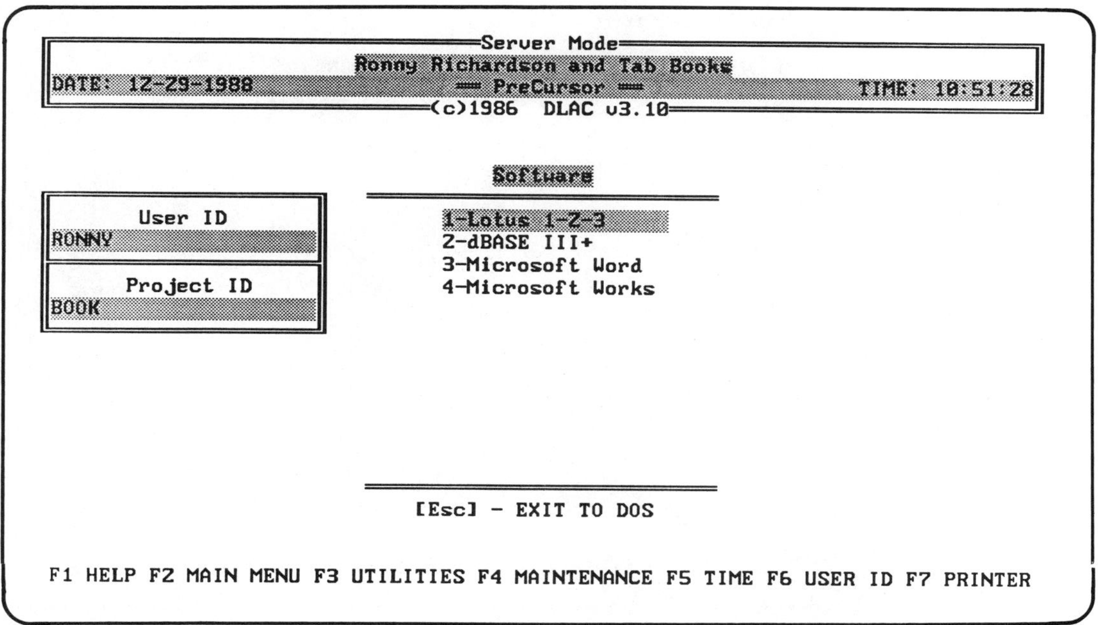

Fig. 2-18. To use PreCursor, all you do is select the program to run from the menu.

shell to tag files, PreCursor retains the name of the tagged files in a file. That way it does not have to keep that information in memory.

One of the menu pages, selected with the F3 key, is the utilities page. This menu functions as a limited DOS shell. There are menu items to:

- List all the files in a subdirectory or find files matching a file specification. Once you list the files, you can tag them for other operations by pressing F3.
- Run CHKDSK program
- Format a disk
- Run DISKCOPY program
- Copy files
- Erase files
- Rename files
- Move files
- List ASCII files to the screen
- List ASCII files to a printer
- Compare files for differences
- Run the DOS backup and restore programs
- Preview tagged files

Limitations   The DOS shell built into PreCursor lacks a graphical tree display. That makes it more difficult than other DOS shells to tag and untag files.

Manual   The manual does a very good job of explaining how to configure PreCursor and how to use it as a menu program. It only devotes a few pages to using the DOS shell menu. For additional information, the manual refers the reader to the on-line help information.

Conclusion   PreCursor is an easy-to-configure and easy-to-use menu system. Its DOS shell is very weak when compared to stand-alone DOS shell programs.

Product:	PreCursor
Price:	$96.00
Category:	Commercial
Publisher:	The Aldridge Company
Address:	2500 CityWest Boulevard
	Suite #575
	Houston, Texas 77042
Phone:	(713) 953-1940
Notes:	All but a few bytes of memory are released when PreCursor runs another program.
	The Aldridge Company has released a major to PreCursor since this review was prepared.
Memory:	256K

Program Director

The *Program Director* is an excellent menu program. It is easy to set up and requires very little memory while other programs are running.

Installation   The Program Director comes with an installation program. It automatically installs the program and configures your AUTOEXEC.BAT file so it will start when the computer boots. The installation program will not let you modify the name of the directory used to install the program.

The installation pamphlet that comes with the program gives you the wrong instructions. It tells you to first create a subdirectory and then run the installation program. This works, but the installation program does not use the subdirectory you create; rather, it installs the program in the \PROGDIR subdirectory. So you end up with an empty subdirectory. This may create confusion for new users. This is especially a problem because the directions for starting the program tell you to change to the (empty) subdirectory you just created. Luckily, the installation program adds the proper commands to the AUTOEXEC.BAT file so once you reboot, the program is available.

Configuration   Figure 2-19 shows the main menu. It has room for 16 options. Any of these can call up a submenu which would also have 16 options. You can only nest menus one deep so the submenu must have actual programs on it.

```
12-18-88                    THE PROGRAM DIRECTOR                 10:43:57 PM
                            ═══════════════════

        1   Lotus 1-2-3                  9  -

        2   Microsoft Word              10  -

        3   dBASE III+                  11  -

        4   DOS Commands (MENU)         12  -

        5   -                           13  -

        6   -                           14  -

        7   -                           15  -

        8   -                           16  -

                          Selection Number:


   F1 Help   F2 Instructions   F4 DOS Commands   F5 Modify Menu   F6 Setup   F7 Exit
```

Fig. 2-19. The main Program Director menu has room for 16 entries. Each of these can either run a program or lead to a submenu with room for 16 more programs.

The first thing you do is press F6 to set up the setup menu. Here you specify:

- Master password. You must have the master password to modify all other passwords. Entering the password in the setup is optional, but without a master password, none of the other passwords will operate. If you use the master password, you must have it to modify the menu and exit to DOS. All passwords are case-insensitive. They can contain up to eight characters with imbedded spaces. However, the spaces cannot be at the start or end of the password.
- Menu password. This password lets a user use all the menu options except modifying the menu, exiting to DOS or running DOS commands.
- Color. You can configure Program Director for monochrome or color. You cannot change the white-on-blue colors.
- Time and date format.

To modify or construct a menu option, you use the F5 "Modify Menu" option. The program prompts you for the number to modify. If you want to make that item a menu item, you will see a screen like Fig. 2-20. It contains four pieces of information:

1) Title. This is the title you see on the Program Director menu.
2) Password. This is the password needed to run this menu selection and is optional. Note that the master and menu passwords override this. If you

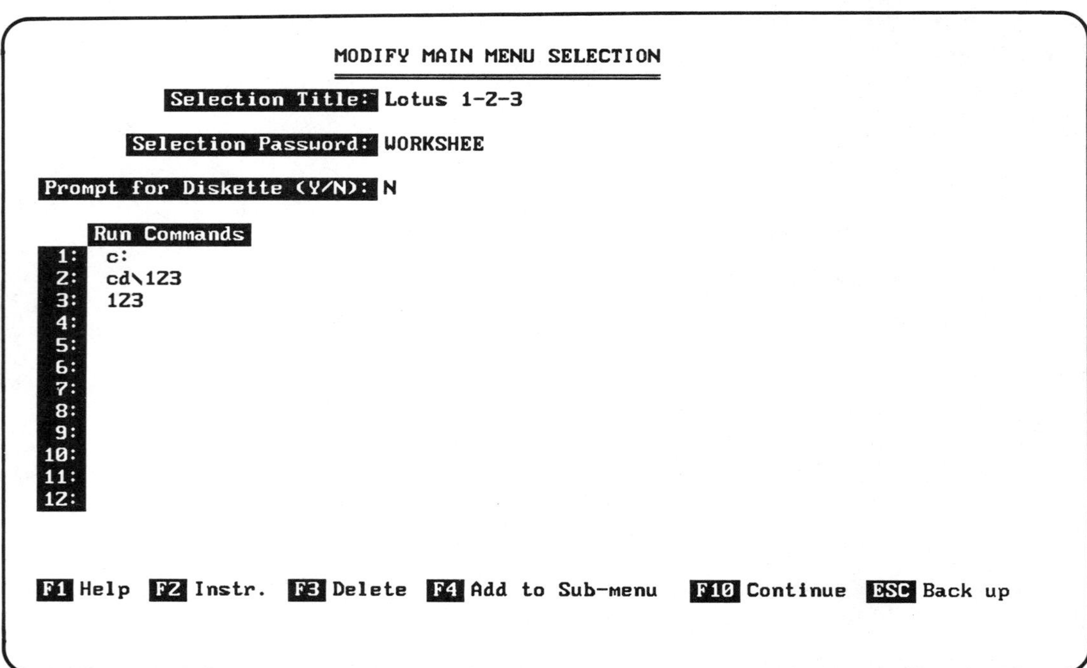

Fig. 2-20. To add an item to a menu, you supply Program Director with the DOS commands to run the program, a title and an optional password.

know the menu password, you can run a program without knowing this selection password.

3) Prompt for Diskette. If you answer yes, Program Director will stop and tell you to insert a disk. This is useful for copy protected programs that require a key disk.

4) Run Commands. These are the DOS commands required to start the application. Notice I have assumed nothing in configuring my menu in the screen shot. The first command makes sure I am using the C-drive and then the second changes to the proper subdirectory. There is room for at most 12. Of course, few programs require 12 commands to start. Also note there are no commands to restart Program Director once Lotus terminates. That is because Program Director takes care of that automatically.

Creating a submenu is also easy. If you press the F4 key while creating or modifying a main menu entry, Program Director will prompt you for a submenu name. The main menu will have the submenu name with the word menu in parentheses. The entry you are creating will become the first entry in the submenu. You edit the submenu entries just like the main menu entries except submenus cannot have additional submenus.

Operation   Operation is simple. If you are not using passwords, you press the number of the program you want to run and Program Director runs it. If you are using passwords and your password is valid for the program you select, Program Director will run it for you. (Remember, master and menu passwords are valid for all menu items.) If your password is not valid for a program, it prompts you for a password. You get as many shots at guessing the password as you like. While Program Director runs a program, it gives most of the memory it used over to the program. Program Director retains only 16 bytes in memory.

If you need to access DOS directly, you can press the F4 key. That brings up a screen where you can enter up to 12 DOS commands for Program Director to execute. Of course, any of these commands can run another program. Access to this menu and exiting to DOS requires the master password if Program Directory is using passwords.

Limitations   There is little not to like about Program Director. It does everything well.

Manual   The Program Director does not come with the typical manual one usually finds with a commercial software package. Rather, the manual is a hybrid shareware-like manual. The manual is a disk file. It is not a straight ASCII file as one finds with shareware. It has control codes imbedded. You read the manual using the F2 "Instructions" key. The control codes allow the reader to jump around the manual for a specific topic.

I miss the printed manual, but having the manual available electronically is actually a plus once you are used to it. No more worries about where you last left the manual, or trying to dig it up to answer a quick question. Just press the F2 key to get immediate access. Of course, it does take up a lot of disk space—25K to be exact. That should concern you only if you are running out of space.

The quality of the manual is very high. It is easy to read—even an inexperienced user will understand it.

Conclusion   Program Director is an excellent program. It is easy to configure. If you know the commands to start your application, then you know how to configure Program Director. When it runs a program, it gets out of the way leaving only a few bytes of code in menu; and at 16 bytes, it is unlikely to make the difference with any program.

Product:	Program Director
Price:	$59.95
Category:	Commercial
Publisher:	Power Up Software
	Corporation
Address:	2929 Campus Drive
	San Mateo, California 94403
Phone:	(800) 851-2917
	(800) 223-1479 in California
Notes:	Program Director releases all but a few bytes of memory when you run an application from its menu
Memory:	128K

Syorg

Syorg is a shareware menu program that has the ability to record who runs each application and for how long.

Installation   The documentation does not explain how to install the program and there is no installation program. Syorg should be in its own subdirectory and that subdirectory will need to be in the PATH.

Configuration   To configure Syorg, you write a menu script. Figure 2-21 shows a typical example. You write this file using an ASCII text editor. Syorg has no facilities to help you. The special characters are:

- Tells Syorg to center the text that follows.
+ Tells Syorg that the text that follows is a menu option. Syorg automatically generates the sequential numbers. You can create submenus by having a menu item call Syorg again with a new menu file.
* Tells Syorg that the following is a program or command to run when you select the menu item above this entry. You can have as many of these commands per menu option as you like.
% Prompts the user for their name.
? Prompts for a parameter and passes it to the application.
Causes Syorg to store a full statistical report when the user selects a program containing this. The report is appended to a file called MNUSTATS in the directory from which you started Syorg.

```
-Ronny Richardson and Tab Books    <-- Centered title
-================================   <-- Centered title
-                                   <-- Adds blank line
+Lotus 1-2-3                        <-- Menu option
*CD \123                           <-- Command that runs when menu selected
*123 %#                            <-- Command that runs when menu selected
*CD \                             <-- Command that runs when menu selected
+Microsoft Word                    <-- Menu option
*CD \word                         <-- Command that runs when menu selected
*word %#                          <-- Command that runs when menu selected
*CD \                             <-- Command that runs when menu selected
+dBASE                             <-- Menu option
*cd\dbase                         <-- Command that runs when menu selected
*dbase %#                         <-- Command that runs when menu selected
*cd\                             <-- Command that runs when menu selected
```

Fig. 2-21. Menu file for Syong.

You start Syorg with the command: SYORG FILE Switches

You can use two switches, EXIT and DOS. The EXIT switch allows the user to exit the program completely to DOS. Without that switch on the command line, the only way to exit Syorg is to reboot. The DOS switch allows the user to enter commands in place of menu items. These do not have to be DOS commands. The user can enter any program or batch file name. Syorg performs no checking, it just passes the command on to DOS.

Operation   Operation is very simple. No moving lightbars or first letter combination. To run a program, you enter its number and press Return. If you start Syorg with the DOS switch, you can also enter any DOS or program name to run while Syorg is waiting on a menu selection.

Syorg records data on each menu containing a ?#.

Limitations   Syorg will prompt the user for a name but has no function to make sure the user enters a valid name. Syorg does not release its memory when running another application. Syorg clears the screen between each command. If one of the commands leaves information on the screen you need to read (like DIR) Syorg erases it as soon as Syorg finishes executing that command. Adding a PAUSE line will not work because Syorg clears the screen between each line. Syorg does not do this for commands you enter if you start it with the DOS switch but always does it for menu scripts.

Manual   The documentation is very brief. I found it only a little difficult to set the program up because Syorg was one of the last menu programs I reviewed. However, I do think inexperienced users will have difficulty learning to use the program from the documentation.

Conclusion   Syorg has excellent computer utilization tracking as long as you can depend on your users to enter the correct name. Its scripting language is weak but acceptable. Its own screen appearance is poor.

Product:	Syorg
Price:	$29.95
Category:	Shareware
Publisher:	Jack Means
Address:	1612 East Oakland
	Bloomington, Illinois 61701
Phone:	Not Available
Memory:	46K

Take Charge

Take Charge is a commercial memory resident program. It has a wealth of features including a DOS shell, menu program and format recovery. I discuss most of these features elsewhere in this book. This chapter only covers the DOS shell.

Installation   Take Charge comes with an installation program. It lets you select the drive to install Take Charge on but requires you to use the \ TC! subdirectory. It runs from the A-drive and requires an ASSIGN A=B statement to run from the B-drive.

Configuration   To add an element, you move the cursor to the appropriate square and press F2. It prompts you to input if the entry is to be a program to run or a submenu. To build a program entry you complete a program definition window as shown in Fig. 2-22. If you configure it as a submenu, it prompts you for the menu name and then brings up a blank menu for you to configure.

Take Charge has several menu editing commands. The F4 key will move the currently highlighted entry to another location. The F5 key will delete the currently highlighted entry. If you forgot the name of a program or subdirectory, the F9 key will allow you to enter a DOS command. Figure 2-23 shows the final menu.

Operation   You can select a program to run by pressing the menu letter. That way, Take Charge will run the program automatically. If it is a menu, Take Charge will display the menu automatically. You can also move the cursor to the appropriate entry and press Return to run a program.

Limitations   Having Take Charge in memory disables DOS command editing. Normally, pressing F3 displays the past command and F2 will display the past command up to the key you press after F2. When you load Take Charge into memory, these no longer work.

I tried to log onto the PC-Link computer network with Take Charge loaded into memory but not active. PC-Link runs under a runtime version of the Deskmate program from Tandy. PC-Link was able to display all its graphic mode characters normally. PC-Link displayed all its text mode characters like static on a monitor display and were completely unreadable. Clearly, Take Charge interferes with either the runtime Deskmate or the PC-Link software.

While moving around many of the Take Charge menus and screens, pressing the 5-key in the middle of the number pad (which does nothing) will blank

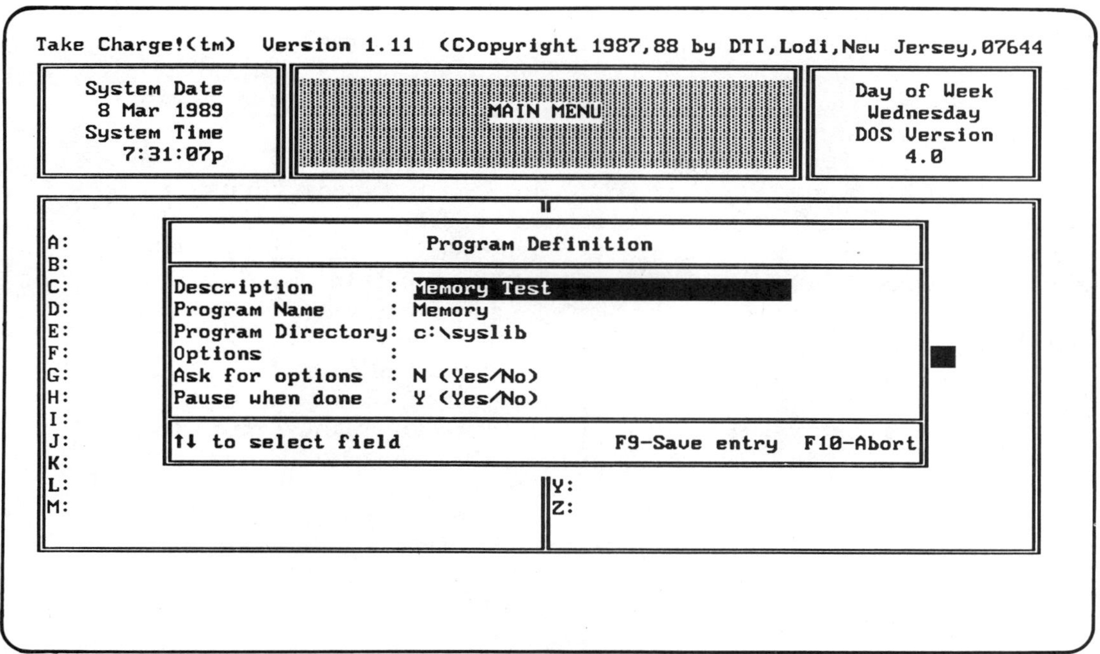

Fig. 2-22. To construct a Take Charge menu entry, you supply a description for the screen, the program name and subdirectory, and any options the program requires.

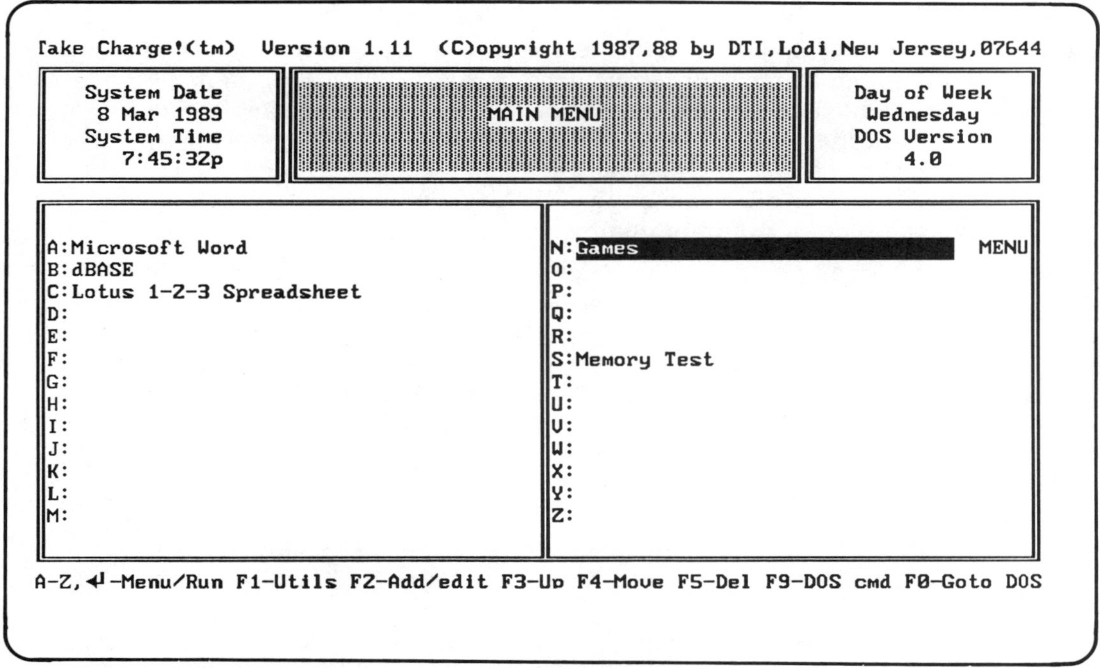

Fig. 2-23. The Take Charge menu after it has been configured to run programs.

the screen until you press another key. This ability to blank the screen would be an advantage if you activated it by some out of the way keystroke combination. However, the proximity of the 5-key to commonly used keys means you often accidentally blank the screen. New users may not be able to quickly identify the problem.

Because some Take Charge operations do not work under DOS 4.0, I copied the Take Charge programs to a DOS 3.3 disk. I then booted off that disk to run some tests. When I did that, the serial number Take Charge normally displays on the log-on screen changed to "bootlegged." This was especially annoying because I had a legal and registered copy. While the serial number changed, my name remained on the display. I guess that was to show where the "bootlegged" copy came from.

The Take Charge menu runs a program by creating a batch file called TC$$$.BAT on the fly to run the program. After you exit your application, this batch file hands control over to the menu program. The manual warns that you must include the .BAT in the program name if a menu option runs a batch file. That is so Take Charge can construct the batch file with a second copy of COMMAND.COM to regain control. This is necessary because most versions of DOS do not allow one batch file to call another. However, Take Charge does not check to see what kind of file it is running. If you enter a batch file name as a program name without the .BAT, Take Charge will run it normally. When you exit your application, Take Charge will not regain control.

When you enter information into the program definition screen, Take Charge appropriately checks to make sure you entered a valid subdirectory. However, it does not verify that the program name you enter is valid.

Manual   The Take Charge manual is very complete. It does a good job of explaining how to run all the features included in Take Charge. The manual is a paperback book and appears to be constructed of bound photocopied sheets. The paper used in the manual is low quality paper. Many of the pages were printed with the lines at a slight angle and some of them are printed with the ends of the lines chopped off. Not enough of the pages are misprinted to cause serious problems. The lack of print quality, however, is annoying.

Conclusion   Take Charge has a functional menu that is actually better than some of the programs in this chapter. However, it lacks advanced features like mouse support. It also lacks the ability to select programs from a graphical tree during menu construction and the ability to issue multiple commands to start an application. The real advantage of the Take Charge menu program is: it is only a small portion of the overall Take Charge package.

ALSO SEE. . .

The DOS shell *1Dir+*, covered in the next chapter, has the ability to create user defined menus and run programs. You can configure 1Dir+ to release all but a few bytes of memory while running these programs. 1Dir+ offers all the power of any of these menu programs. It is, however, significantly more difficult to use than the best of these. Of course, 1Dir+ includes a full DOS shell in addition to its ability to create menus.

The DOS shell *Direc-Tree Plus*, covered in the next chapter, has a menu program. It will store twenty programs on each of five pages of menus. Those menus are very easy to create and Direc-Tree Plus only requires 5K while other programs are running.

The DOS shell *Pathminder*, covered in the next chapter, has the ability to create user-defined menus and run programs. When you load Pathminder using its virtual version, it releases all but 4K of its memory when it runs another program. The menu feature of Pathminder is not as powerful as the best menu programs in this chapter. However, Pathminder includes a full DOS shell as well.

RONNY'S PICKS

I have a copy of DOS 4.01 from IBM. After using the DOS shell program that comes with DOS for several months, I believe it is every bit as good as the commercial menu programs. If you have DOS 4.x, then you have a good menu program and do not need to consider any other. If you are considering purchasing a menu program, then you should strongly consider spending that money on DOS 4.x. You would upgrade your DOS and get a free menu program in the bargain.

If DOS 4.x is not an option for you, then the best menu program you can buy is Menu Works. By their very nature, ease of setting them up is a major consideration for a menu program. When it comes to setup, the automatic configuration of Menu Works is miles ahead of any other program.

If you are in a computer department looking for a package you can configure for a number of individual users, then Automenu is an excellent choice. It uses script files for configuration. These are more difficult for beginners to master. However, experienced users can use their editor to reuse much of a script file over-and-over each time they set up a computer for new users.

3
DOS Shells

In the last chapter, I described the reasons that DOS menus are becoming more popular. These very same reasons are why DOS shells are far more popular today than ever before.

WHAT THE SHELL WILL DO FOR YOU

Basically, a shell takes the place of DOS. Instead of issuing cryptic commands, you use the shell to enter English-like commands or select commands from a menu. Some shells add simple menuing abilities. My basis for evaluating the shells was:

1) Ease of set up. The majority of shell users are new to computing. They simply do not have the skills necessary to set up a complex program.
2) Ease of use. It should not be difficult to use the software. If it is, you may as well learn and use DOS.
3) Power. Although shells are more commonly used by beginners, they must be powerful. Otherwise, the users will soon outgrow the program they spent time to learn.

This chapter discusses a wide array of shell programs with a wide array of features. It is important to select a menu program with the right combination of features and value for your own personal needs. Once you select a shell program, that program directly influences how you use your computer. The programs in this chapter are in alphabetical order.

1Dir +

1Dir + is a complete and powerful DOS shell as well as a full menu system for running other programs. It is significantly harder to learn to use than most of the other shell programs. 1Dir + rewards that difficulty with more power.

Installation   1Dir + comes with an installation program to automatically install it and get it running. There are also instructions in the manual on how to install it yourself. You use those if you do not wish to use the installation program. 1Dir + is very inflexible in its arrangement. It requires one file in the root directory and all other files in a subdirectory directly off the root directory called \ 1DIRPLUS. You can change this only if you point to the new subdirectory using an environmental variable.

Operation   When you first start 1Dir +, you see a colorful display with numerous boxes or windows. Figure 3-1 shows this. This display shows file names, extension and sizes. It also shows the menu, a quick reference section and a display containing some system information. 1Dir + called this a *face*. It also calls this *default face* the *Quick Reference face.*

There are seven other faces, all available using a Shift-function key combination. The other faces vary the information presented by 1Dir +.

- It calls the second face the Statistics face. It replaces the quick reference window with several windows displaying disk and memory usage.

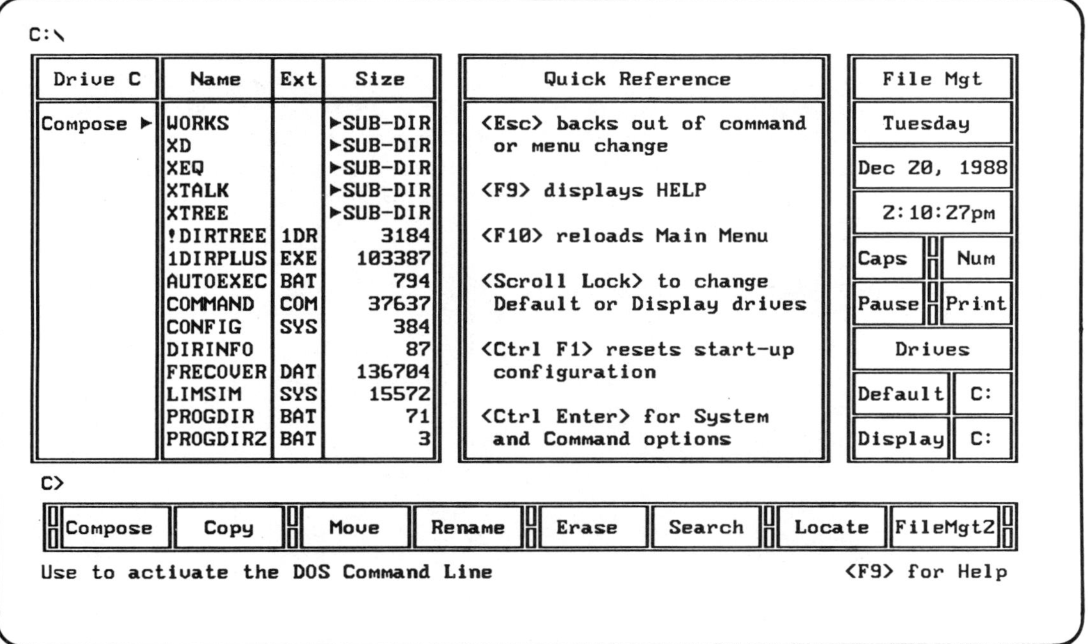

Fig. 3-1. 1Dir + is highly configurable. The main display can take on eight different looks. This is the default.

- It calls the third face the Extended Directory face. It replaces the quick reference window with additional information on the files. It contains the creation date and time along with the file attributes.
- It calls the fourth face the Wide Directory face. It replaces the quick reference window and the area containing the size with a new display showing four columns of file names and extensions.
- It calls the fifth face the Two Menu face. It is like the fourth except it shows fewer files. That leaves room for a second menu, the file management menu.
- It calls the sixth face the Global Directory face. This is like the Wide Directory face except files are shown in a continuous listing across subdirectories.
- It calls the seventh face the DOS face. This is actually straight DOS with the standard DOS prompt. However, 1Dir+ is in memory and just a keystroke away.
- It calls the eighth face the Menu Only face. This shows an expanded menu without showing any files.

As a file manager, 1Dir+ works like most of the others, only you go through a few more menus. For example, to erase several files from a subdirectory, you first move to that subdirectory. You can do that by moving the cursor to the first level subdirectory and pressing Return twice. You can repeat that to move another subdirectory level deep. You can also press Control-T to get a graphical tree. You then move the cursor directly to the subdirectory you wish to move to and press Return.

Once you can see the files you want to delete on the screen, you press F5 for the File Management menu. You then press F5 again to highlight erase. You move the cursor to each file you want to erase and press the space bar to tag it. When you finish tagging files, you press Return. 1Dir+ collects all the tagged files together. It then asks if you really want to erase them. When you respond yes, it drops to DOS. While at DOS, it erases the files and returns you to just where you left off. The other file management functions:

- Copying files
- Moving files to another location by moving the directory entry
- Renaming files
- Searching for a set of characters in files—usually ASCII files
- Looking for a specific file or files that match a file specification
- Removing subdirectories
- Formatting disks
- Copying a disk using DISKCOPY
- Comparing two disks using DISKCOMP

all work in a similar fashion.

In addition to functioning as a DOS shell, 1Dir+ can function as a full menu system. To begin, you construct what 1Dir+ calls commands. These are the individual menu items that you will later assemble into a menu. You select F8 "Wonder+" from the main menu. Then you select F3 "Menu Build" from that menu. This takes you to the Command and Menu Builder menu. Figure 3-2 shows the Command and Menu Builder menu.

You complete the Application Command Template to tell 1Dir+ how to run a program. Figure 3-3 shows this. The items on the template are:

- Name. This name will show up on the menu. 1Dir+ limits it to eight characters. The name does not have to be a file name.
- Description. This explanation will show up below the menu when this item is highlighted.
- Directory. This is the directory 1Dir+ logs onto before issuing the command.
- Command. This is the actual DOS command that 1Dir+ issues to start an application.
- Directory. This second directory is the one 1Dir+ changes to when the application terminates.
- Batch File. 1Dir+ needs to know if it is running a batch file rather than a program.

Once you complete the commands, you assemble them into menus. You do this using either the F4 "Create Menu" or F5 "Modify Menu" functions of the Command and Menu Builder. This brings up the Menu Builder Template. Figure 3-4 shows this.

The middle section of the Menu Builder Template contains every 1Dir+ command that is available. This includes all of the built-in commands and the

```
┌─────────────────────────────────────────────────────────────────┐
│                   Command & Menu Builder                          │
├──────────────────────────┬────────────────────────────────────────┤
│        Option            │           Description                  │
├──────────────────────────┼────────────────────────────────────────┤
│ F1 = Create Command      │ Use to program a new command           │
│ F2 = Modify Command      │ Use to change an existing command      │
│ F3 = Delete Command      │ Use to remove an existing command      │
├──────────────────────────┼────────────────────────────────────────┤
│ F4 = Create Menu         │ Use to make a new command menu         │
│ F5 = Modify Menu         │ Use to change an existing command menu  │
│ F6 = Delete Menu         │ Use to remove an existing command menu  │
├──────────────────────────┼────────────────────────────────────────┤
│ F7 = Print               │ Use to print commands and command menus │
│ F8 = Exit                │ Use to exit the Command and Menu Builder │
├──────────────────────────┴────────────────────────────────────────┤
│   Use the function keys <F1-F8> or the cursor keys <↑↓> to         │
│       select the desired command.   Then press <Enter>.           │
└───────────────────────────────────────────────────────────────────┘

Menu Builder - 2.13 - Copyright (c) Bourbaki, Inc. 1986, 1987
```

Fig. 3-2. The Command and Menu Builder in 1Dir+ is highly configurable. The main display can take on eight different looks. This is the default.

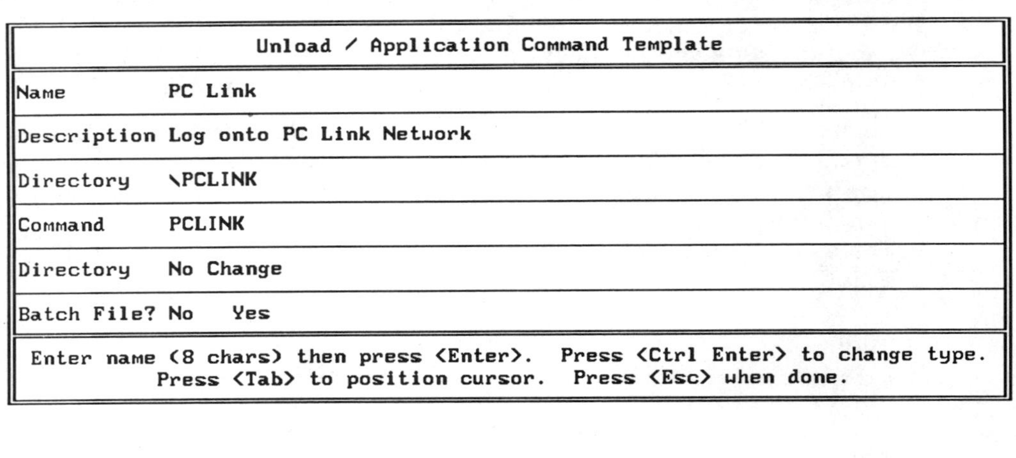

```
              Unload / Application Command Template

Name            PC Link

Description  Log onto PC Link Network

Directory       \PCLINK

Command         PCLINK

Directory       No Change

Batch File?  No    Yes

   Enter name <8 chars> then press <Enter>.  Press <Ctrl Enter> to change type.
          Press <Tab> to position cursor.   Press <Esc> when done.
```

Fig. 3-3. The Application Command Template is completed to tell 1Dir + how to run a menu command.

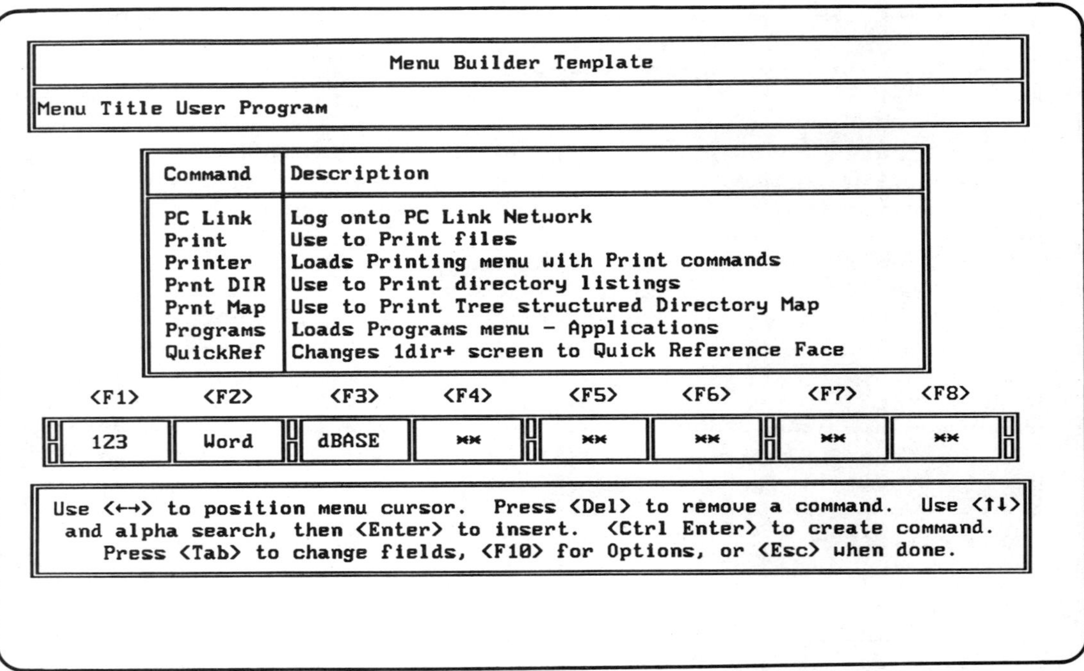

```
                      Menu Builder Template

Menu Title User Program

        Command    Description

        PC Link    Log onto PC Link Network
        Print      Use to Print files
        Printer    Loads Printing menu with Print commands
        Prnt DIR   Use to Print directory listings
        Prnt Map   Use to Print Tree structured Directory Map
        Programs   Loads Programs menu - Applications
        QuickRef   Changes 1dir+ screen to Quick Reference Face

    <F1>     <F2>      <F3>      <F4>      <F5>      <F6>      <F7>      <F8>

     123     Word     dBASE      ><        ><        ><        ><        ><

   Use <←→> to position menu cursor.  Press <Del> to remove a command.  Use <↑↓>
   and alpha search, then <Enter> to insert.  <Ctrl Enter> to create command.
       Press <Tab> to change fields, <F10> for Options, or <Esc> when done.
```

Fig. 3-4. The Menu Builder Template is used to assemble 1Dir + menus.

ones created by the user. You select up to eight of these to appear on a menu. You use the left and right arrows to position the cursor on the function key to receive the command. You use the up and down arrows to highlight the command. You then press Enter to insert the command into the menu. And now, when you bring up the menus, it shows the new commands.

You have several options when programs run. You can retain 1Dir+ fully in memory. This reduces the RAM available to your application by about 130K. This is probably best when running programs that do not require much memory. It allows 1Dir+ to start back very rapidly when you exit a program. For large programs, you can set 1Dir+ to only use 32K of RAM while the application is running. 1Dir+ can also be reduced to only a few bytes while an application is running, the best alternative for large programs.

While not reviewed for the book, Bourbaki sells a developers key for 1Dir+ called Muscle. Muscle adds:

- An expanded language for programming commands. The additional features include conditional operators, variable assignments, loops, prompts, parameter passing, character string passing, macros, and much more.
- Network and multi-user capabilities.
- A utility that prompts a user for his name and password and then configures 1Dir+ specifically for that user.
- File encryption.

Limitations   The biggest drawback to 1Dir+ is due primarily to its power: 1Dir+ is just plain hard to learn to use. It also eats keystrokes. Simple activities like erasing a file require far more keystrokes than with other shells.

Manual   The manual is dense. Everything you would ever want to know about 1Dir+ is in its manual. There is a complete table of contents and an index. The manual has all the right components, it is just hard to read and follow. Part of the problem is the complexity of 1Dir+. However, another large part of the manual is just not well written. Experienced users will just fuss about the manual. Inexperienced users will have a great deal of trouble understanding it.

Conclusion   1Dir+ is a very flexible program. "Power users" will find they can shape and mold it to fit their image of what a DOS shell should do. Power users are probably the best market for 1Dir+. The program is likely to overwhelm new users.

Product:	1Dir+
Price:	$95.00
Category:	Commercial
Publisher:	Bourbaki, Incorporated
Address:	615 West Hays
	Boise, Idaho 83702
Phone:	(208) 342-5849
Notes:	1Dir+ can be configured to require only a few bytes of memory while it runs other programs.
Memory:	256K

ClassiFILE

ClassiFILE is a powerful DOS shell program with a rudimentary menu program built in.

Installation   ClassiFILE is not copy protected but it brands itself when you first install the program. During the first installation, it asks your name and writes that to the disk and the program. About one out of 15 times, when you start the program it shows the registered name. There is a batch file that automates the installation program. The instructions tell you to start this batch file with the command: INSTALL A: C: \ directory

It will run as well from the B-drive if you replace the A: with a B:. However, the manual does not tell you this.

Operation   ClassiFILE starts rapidly because it only reads the information from the root directory. This display has room to enter a long description of each file and subdirectory. It stores this information in a special file so the descriptions are available each time you run ClassiFILE. If you need to see file attributes, you can swap the file descriptions for attributes. ClassiFILE can change any of these attributes except system.

If you need to edit an ASCII file, ClassiFILE has a built-in editor. This editor only works on ASCII files and has only simple editing commands.

ClassiFILE has the full complement of file management features. You can easily move or delete tagged files. There is even an option to copy specified files to another disk, useful for simple backups.

ClassiFILE supports a non-DOS feature called folders. Basically, you group files within a subdirectory into sets of folders. For example, all .DOC document files could go into one folder, all .CMP spell checker files could go into another. Until you specify otherwise, all you see on the ClassiFILE menu is the folder rather than the individual files. You can easily select all the files in the folder for file handling operations.

These folders only operate under ClassiFILE, they are completely transparent to DOS. The ClassiFILE manual recommends that you use folders rather than additional subdirectories. Traditional hard disk management recommends that you have a program subdirectory and then subdirectories under that for each major grouping of data files. ClassiFILE recommends that you just create the program subdirectory. You would then store all the data files in that subdirectory but view them as sets of folders. While files arranged under folders will work well while in ClassiFILE, it is not an arrangement I recommend. Individual data subdirectories make hard disk maintenance that ClassiFILE cannot perform, such as backups and unerasing, more difficult.

ClassiFILE has a configuration program. The configuration program lets you control how ClassiFILE operates. The main user-configurable feature is the program menu. This menu contains up to 20 programs that you can run from a ClassiFILE menu. ClassiFILE can run any other program from within ClassiFILE by moving the cursor to that program and pressing Return. When ClassiFILE runs a program, it swaps most of its code to either expanded memory or the hard disk. While running another program, ClassiFILE only uses 8K of memory.

The main screen for menu configuration shows the program name and control key. You can extensively configure the method ClassiFILE uses to run each of these programs.

ClassiFILE maintains a list of twenty relationships. You enter these into a list similar to the menu list. Once you form these relationships, ClassiFILE will run the related program when you click on a data file.

The idea of pairing data files to programs comes from Windows. It also works much better in Windows. Under Windows, every program is capable of receiving a data file name during start-up. Under DOS, many programs cannot start with a data file. For example, there is no way to pass a worksheet to load when you start Lotus. There is also no way to pass a database to load when you start dBASE. (You can, however, pass a program to run to dBASE.) This inability of many DOS programs to accept the data file from ClassiFILE limits the usefulness of this feature.

Another limitation is ClassiFILE's inability to specify certain information necessary for certain programs to run the way it does for the menu programs. For example, Lotus requires that you switch to the subdirectory containing its files before it will load. Of course, this represents much less of a problem if you use ClassiFILE's folders. That places the data files in the same subdirectory as the program files.

Limitations   I found the user interface cluttered and somewhat difficult to learn. With XTreePro, I sat down and began productively using the program before I read the manual. With ClassiFILE, I had to read the manual first. When I came back to ClassiFILE after not using it for several days, I had to glance through the manual to brush up before I could use the program. With XTreePro, I could just sit down and use it. ClassiFILE also requires you to press Return to confirm non-destructive operations such as running a program. I often found myself hitting confirm far more often than I would have liked.

Manual   The manual is complete and all the information is there; however, I found it difficult to read. It gave complex items, like folders, only a brief couple of pages of explanation, and often only a single example.

Conclusion   Although a little harder to use than XTreePro, ClassiFILE is still an excellent DOS shell. It makes up for its difficulty by offering an acceptable menu program built in and by reducing itself to 8K when running other programs.

Product:	ClassiFILE
Price:	$49.95
Category:	Commercial
Publisher:	SoftLogic Solutions, Incorporated
Address:	One Perimeter Road
	Manchester, New Hampshire 03101
Phone:	(800) 272-9900
Memory:	256K

Direc-Tree Plus

Direc-Tree Plus is a fairly straightforward and easy-to-use DOS manager with hints of a menu program built in.

Installation Direc-Tree Plus comes with an installation program that has s dual purpose. First, it brands the software, and second, it installs it on your hard disk. When branding, the installation program adds your name and company name to the software so it shows on the log-on screen. This discourages copying because the screen always shows the source of the copy.

The branding software worked properly but did not create the subdirectory or install the software. I next tried creating the subdirectory for it and rerunning the installation program. No luck. Finally, I copied the files manually. That worked.

Direc-Tree Plus has a customization program. Direc-Tree Plus will run without your running it. However, you can better configure Direc-Tree Plus to fit your needs using it. You probably should run Direc-Tree Plus long enough to understand how it works before running the configuration program.

The configuration program has two options, "See The addendum File" and "Customize Direc-Tree Plus." The first is merely a text reader for displaying the readme file. For some unknown reason, you have to supply the name of the file. Give it the name of a file that does not exist, and it will drop you right to DOS.

The customization option is important. It will let you:

- supply the default drive (usually C). That way, Direc-Tree Plus does not ask you for it each time.
- tell the program to alphabetize the graphical tree rather than using the order as it exists on the disk.
- decide if the menus are always visible.
- set the default file display mode. You can have 46 files if you want the size and date or 115 files if you only want the name.
- set the file sorting order.
- set the mode of operation for Direc-Tree Plus when it runs another program, normal or miser. Miser reduces the memory used by Direc-Tree Plus so you should always select that one.
- set the mode of operation, normal or miser, when running a word processor. You can configure Direc-Tree Plus to use your own word processor rather than its built-in editor when you select edit. Word processors are normally less memory intensive than other programs so normal should be acceptable. Normal causes Direc-Tree Plus to start up much faster when you return from running the word processor.
- set how text is displayed. You can configure it for color or black and white. You can also have Direc-Tree Plus correct for snow.
- set the printer port used by Direc-Tree Plus. You can only configure it for a parallel printer.
- specify if there is a complete menu for configuring your printer.
- specify the word processor to use for editing.

- specify the title to appear at the top of the user defined menus. You can only enter one title. Direc-Tree Plus uses it for all five pages of the menu.

Operation   When you first start the Direc-Tree Plus program, you see the main screen. Figure 3-5 shows the main screen. It has a graphical tree representation of your hard disk structure at the top, and the menu at the bottom. If you scroll down, the menu will automatically switch to the top. Direc-Tree Plus stores the menu in a disk file. That way the program does not have the 10- to 30-second delay normally associated with producing a complex tree.

One drawback to this tree is cursor movement. You can only move up and down the tree one line at a time, or go directly to either end of the tree using the Home and End keys. While not much of a problem on small trees, the single line movement can make moving around large trees slow.

You use the function keys to select the action you want to take. When you select an action, erasing files for example, Direc-Tree Plus expands to show all of the files in the currently highlighted subdirectory. It uses a two-column format that also shows the size and creation date. You tag files with the space bar and press Return to carry out the action.

Besides the default menu shown in Fig. 3-5, there are two additional menus. Pressing the Alt key brings up a brief menu. That menu will let you back up files, enter a password or look at a help screen. The backup command is not a backup in the normal sense. Rather, it is simply a copy that resets the archive bit after copying. It is good for backing up a few critical files at best. Direc-Tree Plus includes a security program that lets you password-protect

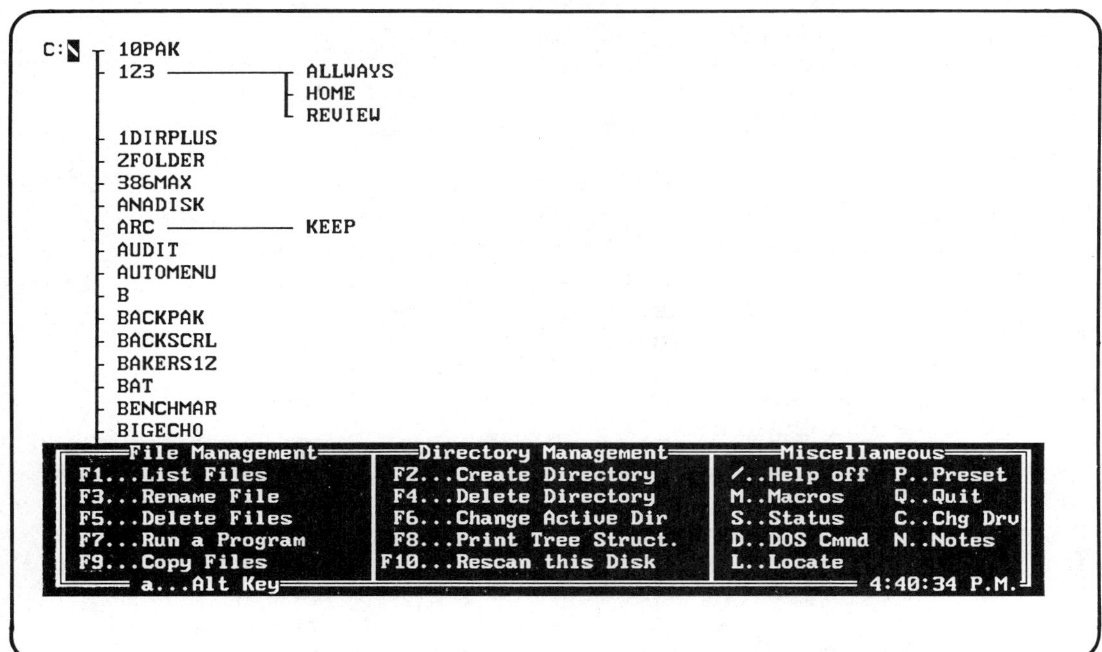

Fig. 3-5. The Direc-Tree Plus main screen shows a directory tree at the top of the screen and a menu at the bottom.

sections of your hard disk. You use the password command of the Alt menu to access these areas.

There is another brief menu that you access using the Control key. This menu lets you. . .

- type an ASCII file to the printer
- change file attributes
- edit a file using either the built in editor or a user defined editor
- move files
- rename directories
- change the default drive
- alphabetize the tree

I found changing the attributes to be especially difficult. You press a letter code and then tag files to toggle. The letter codes are A = archive, R = read only and H = hidden. Finally, you press Return when finished. All of this takes place without much in the way of visual clues of what is going to happen.

Direc-Tree Plus has three ways to run a program. The easiest way is using the D or "DOS Command" key. You can also move the cursor to the subdirectory containing the program and press F7. That will give you a list of all the files in that subdirectory. You can press Return over the program you wish to run. Direc-Tree Plus only displays the file list after you press the F7 command. Therefore, I do not understand why it shows all the files rather than just showing the files it can run. The third way to run a program is pressing P for the user-defined menu, discussed below.

When Direc-Tree Plus runs a program, two modes are possible. One way uses about 35K of code in memory while the second way uses less than 5K. You select between the two using the configuration program also discussed below. One interesting aspect of the way Direc-Tree Plus runs programs; it refuses to run FORMAT.COM. The manual says that FORMAT is too dangerous to run from the shell.

Direc-Tree Plus has a menu construction option. You press P to get to the user menu and Control-Z to modify it. You first select the entry to add or modify. Then you point to the file to run. You do this using the tree to select the subdirectory. After selecting the subdirectory, you then point to the file. The next prompt lets you add an include file. It also lets you select the memory miser mode to reduce the RAM Direc-Tree Plus use to 5K. Next you enter a menu title. After you finish, you end up with a menu similar to Fig. 3-6. This menu can hold 20 items and there are four more "pages." That gives you the ability to define up to one hundred programs.

Limitations   I found the approach Direc-Tree Plus takes to be quite natural. I would prefer the menu vertically so you could see more of the tree at a glance. (You can turn the menu off to see more of the tree. However, then you cannot see the menu. As a result, it only helps after you have used the program for a long time.) That could obscure the tree if you nest subdirectories more than about four deep. There, it would need an option to switch the menu back to horizontal for hard disks with complex structure.

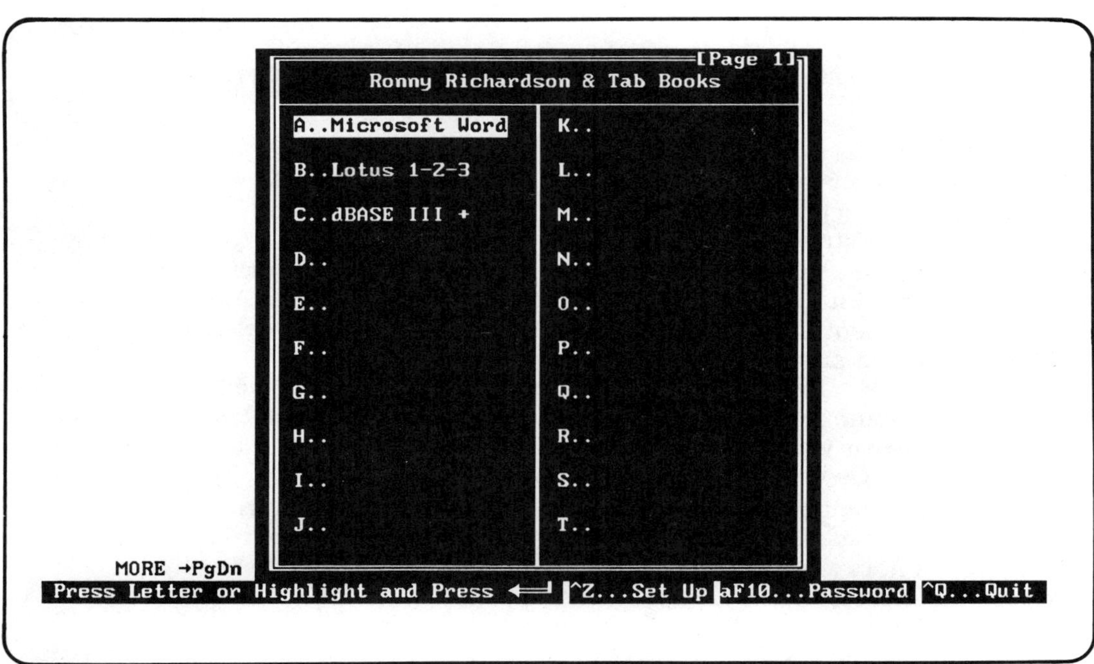

Fig. 3-6. Direc-Tree Plus lets you put together a menu of up to 20 programs. There are five pages to the menu so a total of 100 programs or macros can be defined.

I also found it awkward to move around the tree only one line at a time. Supporting the page-up and page-down keys, along with mouse support, would have added a lot.

Manual   The manual has a workman-like quality. It gets the job done and has no glaring flaws. However, I felt while reading it that it needed some work.

Conclusion   Overall, Direc-Tree Plus is an excellent DOS shell with only minor drawbacks. It does what a DOS shell needs to do without a lot of extras to hog memory and get in the way. While not my favorite, I really like this program.

Product:	Direc-Tree Plus
Price:	$59.95
Category:	Commercial
Publisher:	Micro-Z Company
Address:	4 Santa Bella Road
	Rolling Hills, California 90274
Phone:	(213) 377-1640
Memory:	42K

DOS Directory

DOS Directory is a copy-protected DOS shell. It cannot handle large hard disks.

Installation　Because DOS Directory is copy protected, you must install it using the supplied installation program. That proved to be impossible on my machine. DOS Directory is on a single 5.25 inch disk with no 3.5 inch exchange coupon. I tried to install it from the B-drive. It just began grinding my A-drive. I waited and waited for the DOS "Ignore, abort or retry" error message but I never got it. DOS Directory just kept grinding away at the A-drive. I did not want to reboot the machine. Finally, I stuck a blank disk in the A-drive and the installation program aborted.

Next, I tried the old ASSIGN A=B trick that has served me so well in the past. The exact same thing happened. I really didn't expect this trick to work. The copy protection has to bypass DOS. Otherwise it is too easy to break so DOS commands like ASSIGN do not effect the installation program.

At this point, memories of why I hate copy protected software were rapidly returning. It was clear I could not install the program on my Model 70. The disk would not fit in the A-drive and would not install in the B-drive. Finally, I tried running the program from the B-drive. Luckily, that worked. So I completed my review running DOS Directory off its floppy disk.

Operation　As I explain in the installation section, I ran DOS Directory from the B-drive. So the first thing I did when I started it was to use the log command to change over to the C-drive. I have about two hundred subdirectories and about three thousand files on my 130 Meg hard disk. When I changed over, DOS Directory responded with a "too many files, extras ignored" error message. DOS Directory has a limit of 180 subdirectories and 2,500 files. For many users, these limits may not present a problem.

The "missing" files and directories are still there, you just cannot work with them using DOS Directory. On my system, it read in all the subdirectories directly off the root directory properly. However, many of the subdirectories off these were missing. There is no command in the DOS Directory to swap the missing subdirectories into memory and swap out others. As a result, they are completely inaccessible.

Figure 3-7 shows the DOS Directory main screen. This display provides the following information:

1) Graphical tree. This is a display of the hard disk structure. You can change subdirectories by moving the cursor around this display.
2) Files. This is a partial listing of the files in the subdirectory highlighted by the cursor. You can switch this display to two other modes. One shows two columns of files along with the file size and file attributes. The other mode shows one column of files with the size, file attributes, creation date and creation time.
3) Menu. This shows some of the available commands. Additional commands are available by pressing the alternate key.

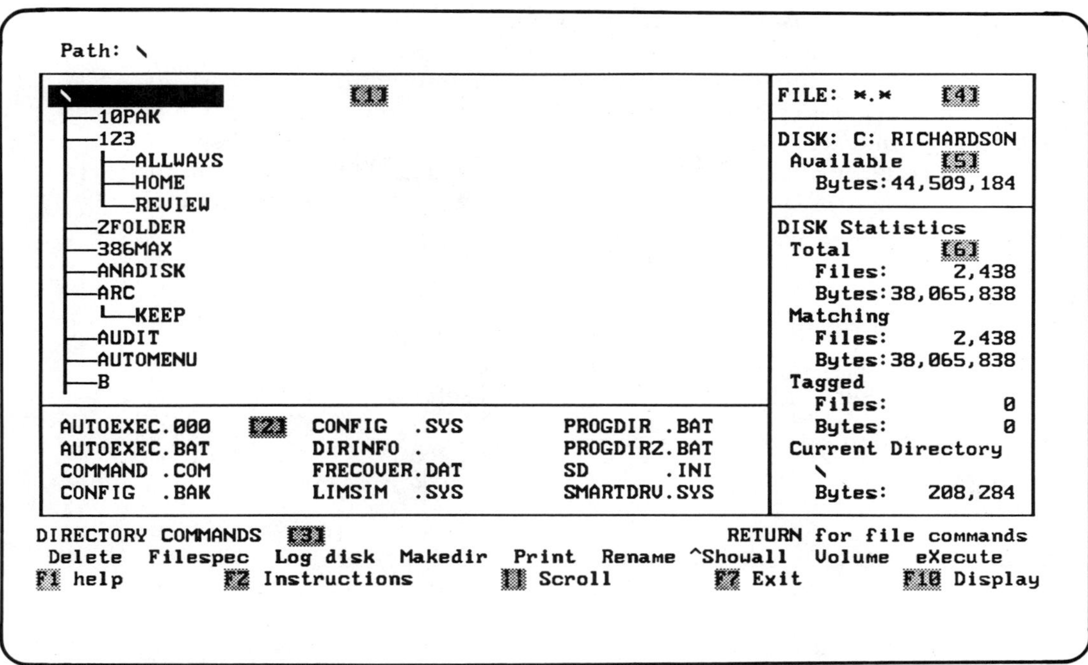

Fig. 3-7. The DOS Directory main screen shows a tree map of the hard disk, the files in the current subdirectory, summary statistics and the command menu.

4) File specification. This shows the currently active file specification.
5) Disk information. This shows the volume label, logged on drive, and free space.
6) Disk statistics. This shows information about the files on the hard disk. Notice that the total file size of all files matching the *.* file specification is slightly over 38 Meg. There are over 80 Meg of files on the hard disk. Therefore, DOS Directory missed over half the files when it ran out of room.

The commands in the main menu let you . . .

- delete an empty subdirectory
- change the file specification used to display files
- change logged on disk drive
- make a subdirectory
- print an ASCII file
- rename a subdirectory
- change the volume level
- execute DOS commands

Basically, they let you work on your disk at the subdirectory level. However, most of the time you will want to work at the file level.

To get to the file level, you press Return. This moves the cursor to the file box. It also changes the display in the file box. The new display is a single column display. It shows the file attributes, creation date and creation time. It also changes the menu at the bottom. The file menu has the usual commands. You can copy, erase, rename, and view files. These commands work in a slightly unusual fashion. Pressing "C" will copy the currently highlighted file. Pressing Control-C will copy all the tagged files. If you cannot see enough files using this display, you can press Return. The graphical tree menu goes away and the file menu expands to take its place. This is a toggle: pressing Return once more returns you to the original display.

Limitations   It is copy protected. Even if it were the best program in this chapter—which it is not—I cannot recommend copy protected software. To see why, just reread the installation section. If that is not enough, consider what you are going to do if you lose the use of your copy-protected software due to a hard disk crash. Remember, most copy-protected software will not work after a restoration.

In addition to being copy-protected, DOS Directory will not work with large hard disks. A significant number of directories were missing from the display for my 130 Meg hard disk.

Manual   The DOS Director does not come with the typical manual one usually finds with a commercial software package. Rather, the manual is a hybrid shareware-like manual. The manual is a disk file. It is not a straight ASCII file as one finds with shareware. It has control codes imbedded. You read the manual using the F2 "Instructions" key. The control codes allow the reader to jump around the manual for a specific topic.

I miss the printed manual, but having the manual available electronically is actually a plus once you are used to it. No more worries about where you last left the manual, or trying to dig it up to answer a quick question. Just press the F2 key to get immediate access. Of course, it does take up a lot of disk space, 25K to be exact. That should concern you only if you are running out of space.

The quality of the manual is very high. It is easy to read, even an inexperienced user will understand it.

Conclusion   Except being copy protected and having a limited capacity, DOS Directory is an adequate DOS shell. However, I cannot recommend it when there are non-copy protected DOS shells that are better and others that cost less.

Product:	DOS Directory
Price:	$49.95
Category:	Commercial
Publisher:	Power Up!
Address:	Post Office Box 7600
	San Mateo, California 94019
Phone:	(800) 851-2917
	(800) 851-2917 in California
Notes:	DOS Directory is copy protected
Memory:	128K

DS Optimize

DS Optimize is a commercial disk optimization program. In addition to unfragmenting disks, it has a serviceable DOS shell, unerasing routine and hard disk unformatting program.

Installation   DS Optimize comes with an automatic installation program. The program lets you enter any name for the subdirectory to install DS Optimize into. However, it expects to run from the A-drive. ASSIGN A = B corrects this.

Operation   In addition to performing optimization, DS Optimize has a built-in DOS shell. Figure 3-8 shows this. This shell provides the ability to:

- copy a file
- move files
- erase files
- rename files
- change file attributes
- create a new subdirectory
- delete an existing subdirectory
- find a file matching a file specification

The DOS shell does not allow you to move around tagging individual files to operate on. Rather, after you enter a command, DS Optimize will prompt you for the file specification to operate on. That is a far less useful method.

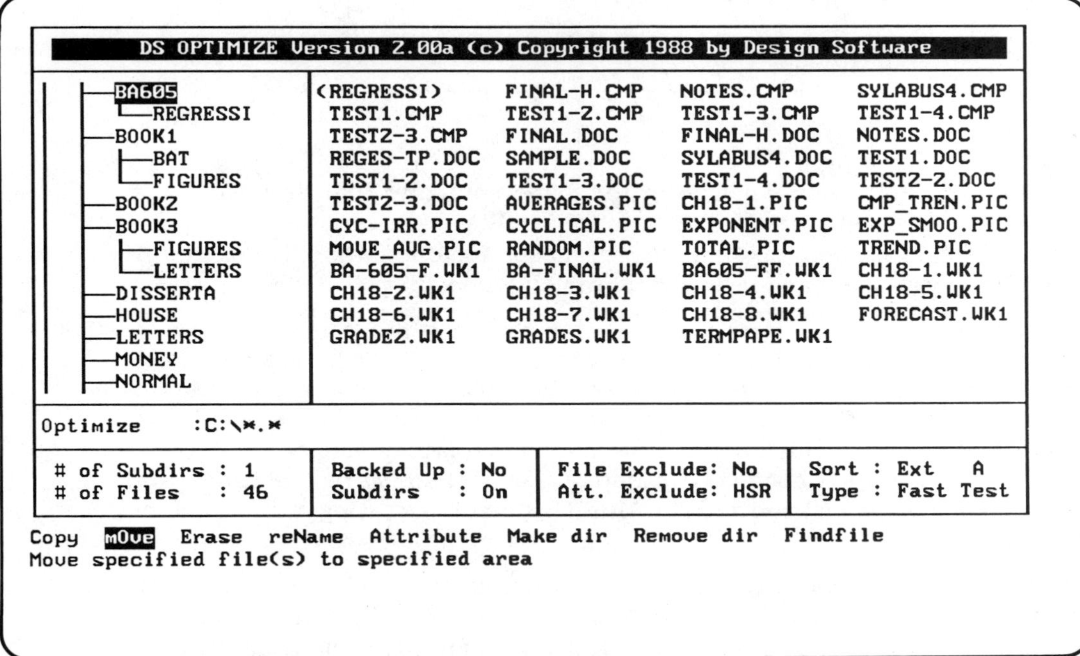

Fig. 3-8. DS Optimize includes a built-in DOS shell.

The utility menu has an option to recover unerased files. It works just like unerasing unprotected files in DS Recovery. DS Optimize also includes an unformatting routine that works just like the unformatting in DS Recovery.

Limitations   DS Optimize does not work with large hard disks. When I tried to run it on the 130 Meg hard disk on my IBM Model 70 DS Optimize would crash. DS Optimize is limited to a total of 5,000 files and subdirectories. It does not work under DOS 4.x either. Instead of reporting an invalid media or some other error message, after about five seconds it reports the disk has been successfully optimized.

Manual   The manual is small, only about five inches square. The type in the manual is so small that it is hard to read. Otherwise, the manual does a good job of explaining how to use DS Optimize.

Conclusion   The DOS shell in DS Optimize is not nearly as powerful as most of the other shells in this chapter. However, if you need both an optimizer and a shell, the shell in DS Optimize is good enough that you may not need to purchase a shell separately.

Product:	DS Optimize
Price:	$59.95
Category:	Commercial
Publisher:	Design Software, Incorporated
Address:	19808 Nordhoff Place
	Chatsworth, California 91311
Phone:	(800) 231-3088
	(818) 885-9000
Notes:	Not DOS 4.x Compatible
Memory:	256K

MultiMax

MultiMax is a DOS shell from the same company that produces Lazy Susan. You can configure MultiMax and Lazy Susan to work together. MultiMax suffers from a poor user interface and poor documentation. It comes with MaxEdit, a very good and user configurable ASCII editor.

Installation   MultiMax does not have an installation program. There are no instructions on how to install MultiMax in the manual. There is a "readme" file on the distribution diskette that briefly explains how to install the program. For a program intended to make using DOS easier for inexperienced users, the lack of any installation information is unacceptable.

No installation is needed on a floppy disk system. You should, however, make a copy of the diskette and run MultiMax using your copy rather than the original.

Operation   There are actually two different versions of MultiMax. One version is for small systems with a 40 Meg or smaller hard disk. The other is for systems larger than this. I performed all the work for this book using the large version.

MultiMax starts up with a warning "For your convenience, this program is not copy-inhibited; It [sic] is however serialized and traceable." That is not the sort of thing I expect to see when I load a program. However, once I got used to the idea it did not bother me. This is one of several alternatives software companies are exploring to reduce their loses due to software copying. Another approach is using the installation program to "brand" the software with your name. Any time you use the software it displays the name of the licensee. If they require such measures to avoid copy protection, then they are a much better alternative and I support them. The message does go away as soon as you press any key.

You may remember from the last chapter that the menu program Lazy Susan had menu entries for MultiMax and MaxEdit. You can configure Lazy Susan and MultiMax to work together. However, neither manual explains how. MaxEdit is the editor included as a part of MultiMax.

Figure 3-13 shows the main MultiMax screen. MultiMax divides its screen into four areas (noted in Fig. 3-9):

1) This is the menu area. It shows most of the commands available in Multi-Max. There are additional, less frequently used commands assigned to function keys and to Alt-letter combinations. Non-context sensitive help is available listing the keystrokes with commands assigned by pressing the "/" or the "?" keys.

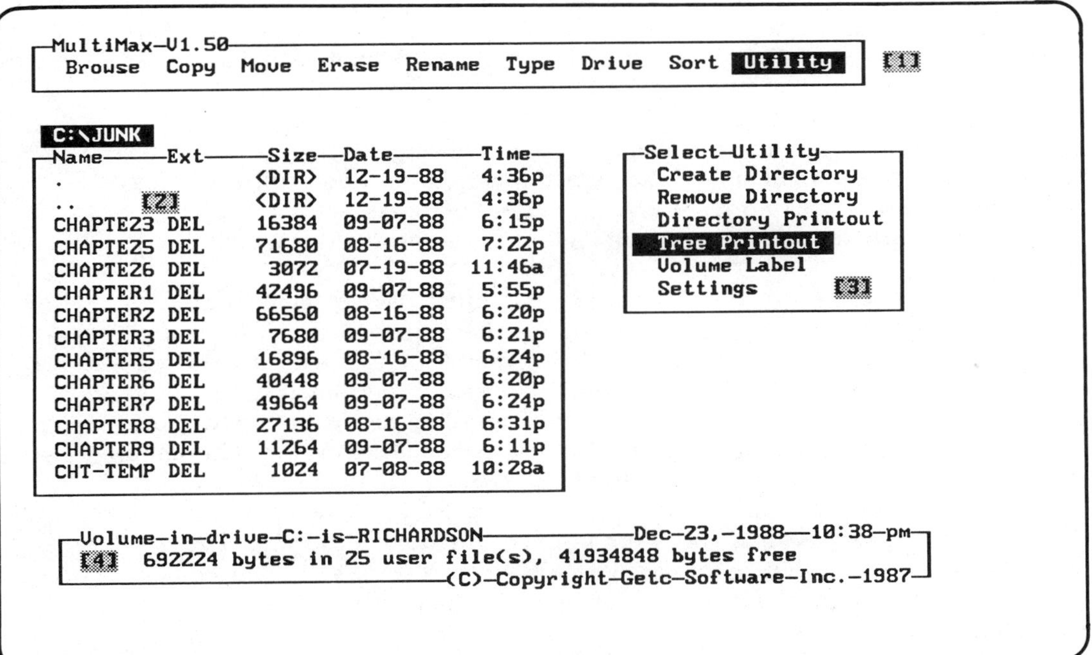

Fig. 3-9. The MultiMax screen is divided into four parts: the menu area, the submenu area, the file list area and the informational area. NameTab1: The NameTag display shows the DOS file name and extension, the 40-character comment added using NameTag, the file size and the file creation date.

2) This is the file area. It contains a listing of all the files in the currently
    logged subdirectory. If there are more files than will fit, the cursor will
    scroll the screen to show the remaining files. Notice that all the informa-
    tion about the files except their file attributes are visible. You can switch
    this area to a graphical tree for viewing a complex structure and for navi-
    gating around the hard disk.
3) This is the optional submenu. It is naturally visible only for those com-
    mands that have a submenu.
4) This is the summary area. It shows the disk volume label, the space used
    by the currently logged subdirectory, the total free space on the disk and
    several other pieces of information.

Moving around a complex hard disk structure is slightly more cumbersome than it should be. You move down one subdirectory level by moving the
cursor to the double-dot directory entry and pressing the F1 key. You can move
up a subdirectory from the current subdirectory by the same procedure. First
highlight the name of the subdirectory on the screen and press F1. To use the
graphical tree to move around, you press F6 to get the tree. Then you move the
cursor to the subdirectory to change to, press the F1 key, then press Escape.
The natural tendency is to highlight the subdirectory and press Return, but
that does not work. If you try that while in the graphical tree, you will get a
very worrisome "Confirm Erase" message.

The first time you use the F6 command to get a graphical tree each session, MultiMax takes a second or two to read in the tree structure. It retains
that in memory so you do not have to wait again. MultiMax does not store the
tree to disk, so it is reread each session.

To manipulate files, you first switch to their directory. You then tag the
files by moving the cursor to the files to tag and pressing the F1 key. A counter
at the top shows the total size of the tagged files but not the number of files.
You press Return to carry out the erasure. After you press Return, it prompts
you to confirm the erasure. A box pops up on the right to show which files it
erased.

With MultiMax, tagging a file for one operation, like erasing, only tags
them for that operation. If you decide to copy them instead, you will have to
retag them. This is not necessarily bad. It does force you to make sure the cursor is in the proper menu option before you begin tagging files. You can actually tag a few files for one operation, select another menu option without
carrying out the first operation, and tag a few more files. However, MultiMax
will only carry out the operation you have highlighted when you press Return.

In addition to functioning as a DOS shell, MultiMax can run programs.
There are two ways you can run a program from within MultiMax. The first
way is to press the F4 DOS command key. This lets you enter the command at
a simulated DOS prompt. Using this method, MultiMax requires 73K of memory. That reduces the memory available to the program you are running. The
second way to run a program is to highlight the program entry on the screen
and press F8. This method uses slightly less memory, 67K.

MultiMax comes with a simple editor called MaxEdit. This editor displays files when you select the Browse command. You can also use it to edit ASCII files by highlighting the file to edit and pressing the F7 key. MaxEdit is a good little editor for ASCII files. You can run it from the DOS prompt as well as from the shell, a nice touch. Another extremely nice touch that experienced users will appreciate is the MaxEdit command definition table. This is a file MaxEdit reads in each time you start it. This file controls most of the functions of Max-Edit, where the tabs are and what keystroke combination does what. If you do not like the way MaxEdit works, you can edit this file to make it work the way you want it to.

Limitations   MultiMax has an option to show hidden files. That option leads to two problems both very confusing but neither major. If you try to tag a hidden file for an operation, the program simply does nothing. DOS shells should not let you work on hidden files, at least without several precautions. Therefore, it was ok for MultiMax not to tag the files. The problem is MultiMax does not tell you why it is not tagging the files, it just sits there and does nothing.

The second problem is a result of the way DOS erases files. When you erase a file with DOS, DOS does not remove the file from the disk. Rather, in the directory entry, DOS replaces the first character of the file name by a special character. In addition, DOS releases the space the file occupied for other uses. Until another file uses that space, the file can be reclaimed by the unerasing programs covered elsewhere. Several times, when I logged onto a directory MultiMax would display the erased files in its file list with a blank first character. It did not do this consistently and I was unable to figure out what caused it.

MultiMax has an option on the utility menu to configure the program. This lets you turn on the color, set the video mode, select which editor you will use and so on. When you save this configuration, MultiMax actually modifies the program file. That is a very bad habit in these days of viruses. One of the things viruses do is modify program files. With MultiMax, it will be far more difficult to know if a modification to the program file was caused by MultiMax or by a virus.

Browsing a file requires that you have installed the included editor, Max-Edit, using the Utility menu. That is not a problem since MaxEdit comes with MultiMax. The manual even tells you how to install MaxEdit. The problem is: if you have not yet installed MaxEdit and you try to view a file, MultiMax will simply do nothing. It never displays an error message so you must figure out what is the problem.

Manual   There are two manuals, one for MultiMax and another for MaxEdit. The manual for MultiMax is inadequate. As discussed above, it begins by failing to tell you how to install the program. Beyond that, it explains many important features with only a few lines. The manual for MaxEdit is marginally better. It also fails to tell you how to install the program. Beyond that it does an adequate job of explaining how to use the program. It only briefly covers modifying the command definition file to change the keystrokes. However, the layout of the file is clear enough that anyone experienced enough to consider such a task should have little problem completing it.

Conclusion   MultiMax suffers from a poor user interface and poor documentation. There are enough better programs available. There is little reason to consider MultiMax.

Product:	MultiMax
Price:	$79.95
Category:	Commercial
Publisher:	GetC Software Incorporated
Address:	In United States:
	Box F110-182
	264 H Street
	Blaine, Washington 98230
	In Canada
	1269 Howe Street
	Vancouver, British Columbia
	V6Z 1R3
Phone:	(800) 663-8066
Notes:	When running another application, MultiMax retains between 67K and 73K of memory depending on the method used to run the program
Memory:	256K

Norton Commander

The *Norton Commander* is an easy-to-use DOS shell with excellent mouse support. It also allows you to build highly structured menus.

Installation   The Norton Utilities are for a more experienced user than the Norton Commander. It comes with an excellent installation program. You type in INSTALL and it does everything for you. It even has informational screens to let you know what it is doing. The Norton Commander is for a more inexperienced user than the Norton Utilities. It comes without any installation program at all. The manual does tell you how to install it—you just have to do everything yourself.

Operation   When you first start the Norton Commander, you see a screen like Fig. 3-10. It only takes up half the screen and you can see prior DOS commands on the other side. Notice the mouse cursor. The Norton Commander has full mouse support. However, the mouse support does not get in the way. All the commands work in an intuitive manner without the mouse.

If you like, you can add a second display to the left side. Figure 3-11 shows this. This figure also illustrates the two additional display modes available. On the left, files are shown in full format. This format shows the size, date and time. The right side shows the tree format. This is a sorted graphical representation of the structure of the hard disk. You can easily move around the hard disk by moving the cursor to the subdirectory you wish to move to. If you move the mouse cursor to the top (or bottom), the screen will scroll. You can do the same with the cursor control arrows so the lack of a mouse does not get in the way.

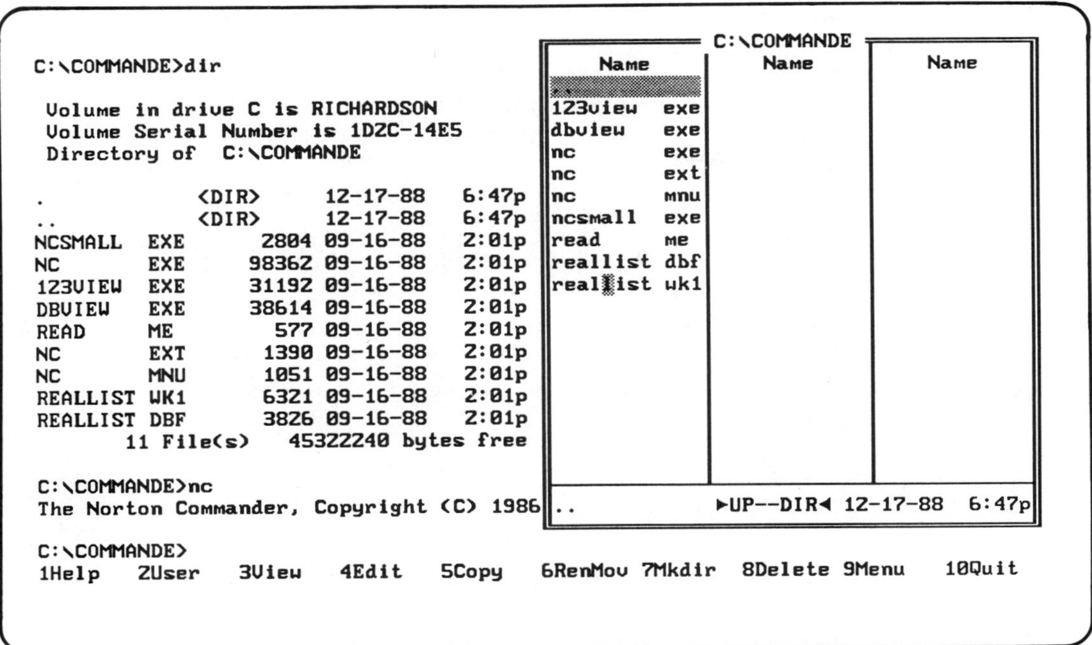

Fig. 3-10. The normal Norton Commander interface only takes up half the screen. Below that, you can see the DOS commands that were issued prior to using the Commander.

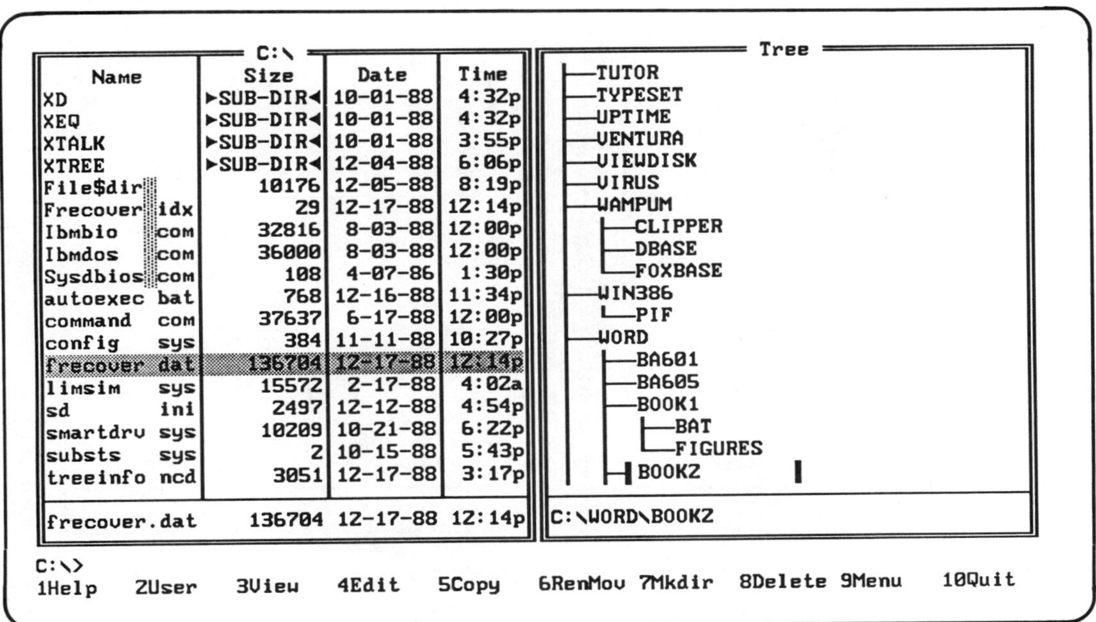

Fig. 3-11. In addition to the short listing in the first screen shot, files can be listed in two additional formats. The left side illustrates the long format where the size, date and time are shown. The right side shows the tree format. This is especially useful for moving around the hard disk.

The easiest way to enter commands is using the pull down menus. Press (or click on) F9 and then press the first letter of the menu you wish to use. Figure 3-12 shows this. You have probably noticed that all the figures have a DOS prompt in the bottom-left corner. At almost any time, you can enter a DOS command while the Norton Commander is operating. The one exception is when a pull-down menu is down; or looking at it another way, you can leave the Norton Commander active and use it only when it is helpful, and use DOS for everything else.

You perform actual file operations using the Files menu. This menu lets you:

- View and edit ASCII files.
- Copy files.
- Move files. This is like a copy followed by a delete command. However, the program only changes the directory information. It does not move the file to another location on the disk.
- Rename files.
- Delete files and whole directories.
- Create directories.

One additional option on the file menu lets you run a user defined menu. Figure 3-13 shows this menu. This menu lets you expand the Norton Commander to do most anything, but at a cost. The Norton Commander takes up 150K while running any program from this menu. That leaves enough mem-

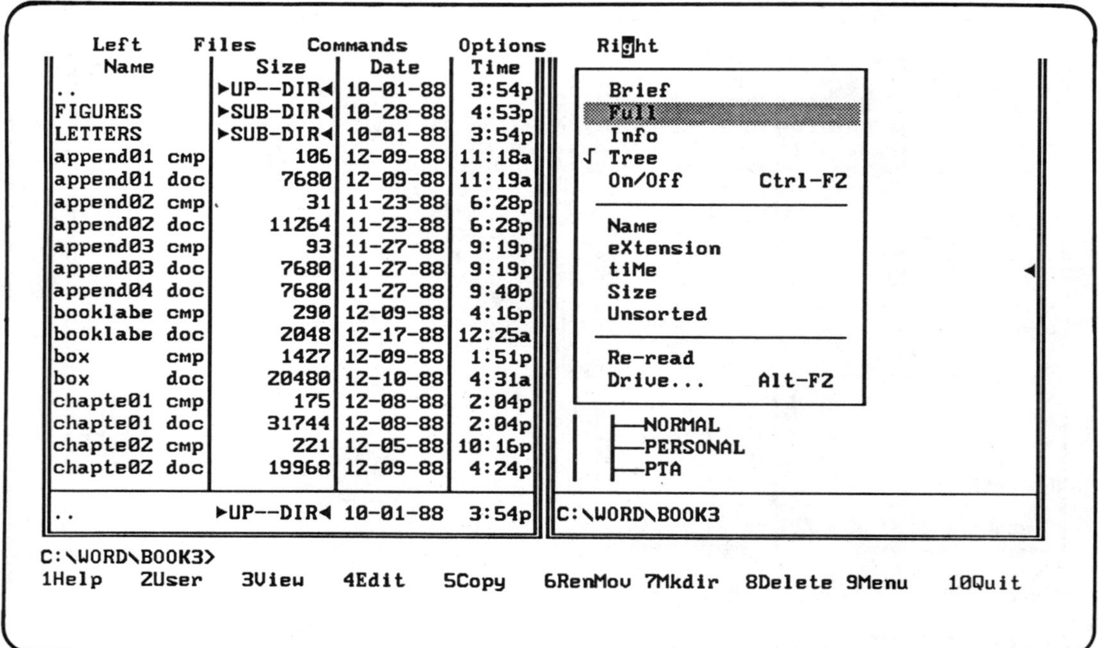

Fig. 3-12. All commands can be selected using pull-down menus, making it easy for an inexperienced user to find the command they are looking for.

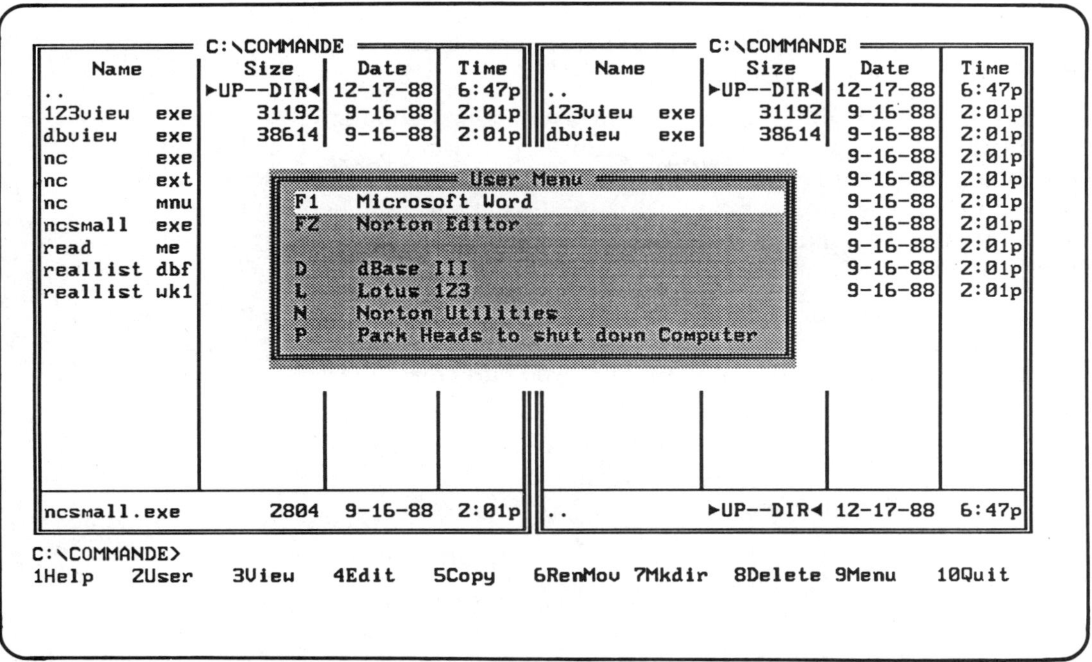

Fig. 3-13. One of the file options lets you run a user defined menu. This menu lets you expand the Norton Commander to run almost anything.

ory to run DOS programs like CHKDSK, but severely limits large programs like Lotus. There is a second version of Norton Commander that overcomes this problem by leaving only 18K in memory while running another program.

These menus are fairly easy to create. They bear a strong resemblance to a collection of batch files. In fact, if you can write batch files, you will find these menus to be a snap. Each menu can call another menu. As a result, the small memory version can function as a very good menu program. It gives you a combined file manager and menu program.

You can define links between data files and programs. For example, you can link .TXT files to WordStar. Every time you click on a .TXT file, the Norton Commander will automatically start WordStar. If the application program allows you to give it a file name on the command line, the Norton Commander will do that for you.

The Norton Commander dramatically expands your ability to view non-ASCII files with two programs. A dBASE viewer lets you view dBASE .DBF files. A Lotus viewer lets you view Lotus .WKS and .WK1 files. It also works on Symphony files. Neither the dBASE nor Lotus viewers let you modify the files.

If you have an EGA screen, the Norton Commander will run in 43-line mode. For a VGA screen, it will run in 50-line mode. The additional lines are optional. You can stick with the 25-line mode for extra readability. It runs in color, but you cannot adjust the colors—it only runs in white on blue.

Limitations   The Norton Commander shows hidden and system files. In fact, it lets you delete them easily. Those files are not visible for a reason. This is a minor flaw in an otherwise excellent product.

Manual   The Norton Commander comes with two manuals. The first is a typical reference manual. The second is a brief pictorial manual that highlights the major screens and functions. Both are well written and easy to read. The Norton Commander has on-line help—or at least sort of. The help is a single screen that summarizes the major commands. The program is easy enough to use that you are not likely to miss the help.

Conclusion   The Norton Commander is a near-perfect program. It offers all the power of the best file manager in an easy to use package with excellent mouse support. Using the small module, you can create excellent menus like the best menu packages.

Product:	Norton Commander
Price:	$89.00
Category:	Commercial
Publisher:	Peter Norton Computing, Incorporated
Address:	2210 Wilshire Boulevard
	Santa Monica, California 90403
Phone:	(213) 453-2361
Memory:	256K

Overdos.system

Overdos.system is a Windows-like DOS shell with very impressive graphics. Unfortunately, the graphical interface often gets in the way and makes Overdos.system one of the most difficult DOS shells to learn and operate.

Installation   Overdos.system has an automatic installation program. It willingly ran from the B-drive. I was easily able to change the name of the subdirectory for the files. The default subdirectory name is \SYSTEM. Many users are likely to already have DOS files in that subdirectory so Overdos.system's ability to easily modify the subdirectory name is welcome.

Operation   Figure 3-14 shows the main Overdos.system display. This computer has both an A and B floppy disk drive and a single hard disk: the C-drive. The remaining drives are subdirectories that DOS treats as a hard disk. You set these up using the SUBST command. SUBSTed subdirectories make working with a complex hard disk structure easier and make for a much shorter PATH statement. Notice the mouse-shaped pointer just below the B-drive icon. If you look close, you will see that both buttons are black. That means that both buttons will perform a function. In other situations, only one button will work so only that button will be visible.

If you move the mouse pointer to any drive and double-click the left button, you will see a display like Fig. 3-15. Each computer in the bottom half of the screen represents a subdirectory. Each block in the monitor represents a

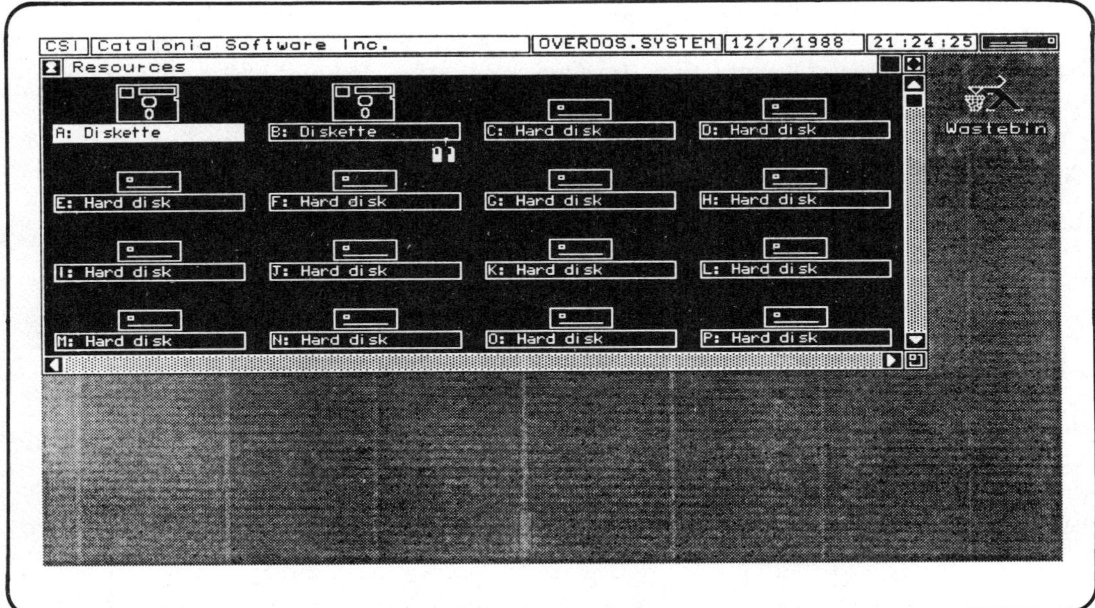

Fig. 3-14. The Overview main menu is a graphical representation of your hard disk structure.

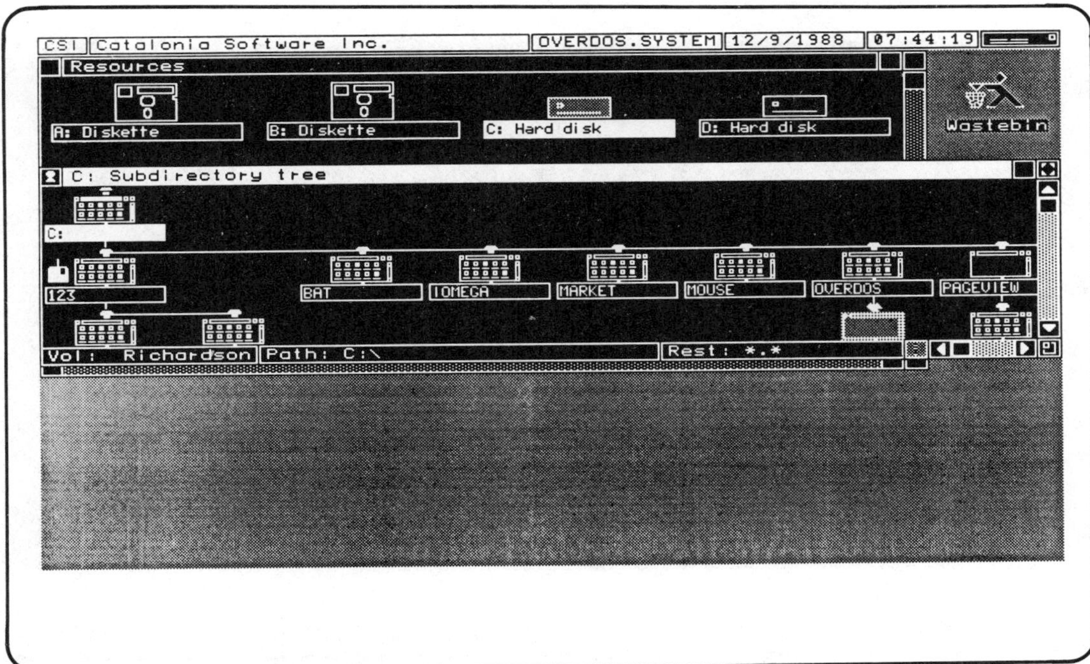

Fig. 3-15. Each computer in the bottom half of the screen represents a subdirectory. Each block in the monitor represents a file in that subdirectory.

file in that subdirectory. You can move the mouse cursor into the large box below the monitor representing the computer case, click the mouse button once, and hold it down. You can then drag the "computer" to another location and release the mouse button. That is how you create a subdirectory within Overdos.system. Once you do this, Overdos.system prompts you for the subdirectory name.

If you move the mouse pointer to any subdirectory icon and double click the left mouse button, you get the file display. The icons in the bottom third of the screen represent specific files. Overdos.system picks the type of icon based on the file extension.

At this point, you move the mouse icon to an empty space away from any icons and click the right mouse button. This gets you the Option Menu. Figure 3-16 shows the Option Menu. Once you get to this menu, you are ready to begin the actual file-level work. As you can see from the figure, this menu lets you perform all of the normal file maintenance like copying, deleting, and renaming. You can also delete files by dragging them to the wastebin icon, visible on some of the earlier figures. There is a procedure where you can mark any of these files so you can retain them and drag them to the wastebin later when it is once again visible.

Once you reach this level, you can run any executable program by clicking on it. Overdos.system gives you the chance to enter command line parameters before running the program, a nice touch. While you run the program, Over-

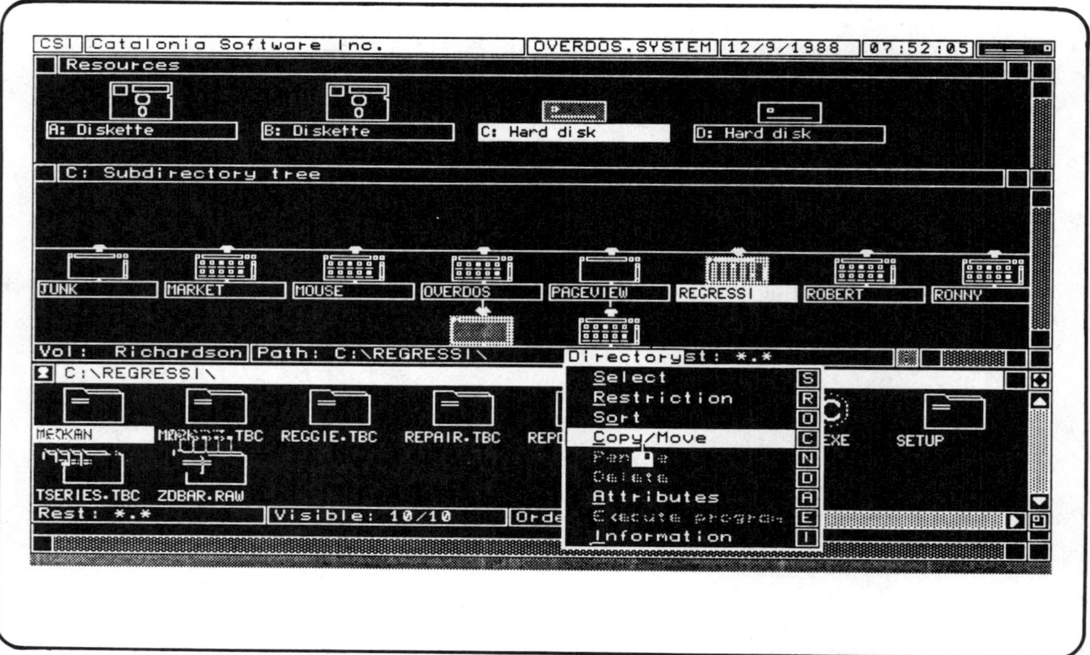

Fig. 3-16. When you have the file display, you click the right mouse cursor to get the Option Menu. This menu is where you perform the actual file-level work.

dos.system removes most of its code from memory. Therefore, you have most of the available memory to run your application. Only about 8K of Overdos.system remains in memory. When you exit the application, Overdos.system returns you to the main menu rather than to the point from which you left.

One disadvantage to working with files as icons is the missing information. You do not have the file size or creation date and time. Overdos.system can replace the icons with file names. Another interesting adjustment is Overdos.system's ability to switch from words on the menus to icons on the menus.

Limitations   The very first thing I do with these shell programs after installing them is try to run them. That is, before I have read anything other than the installation section of the manual. I do this to get a feel for how intuitive their interface is. If a program has a good interface, a user should be able to sit down and figure out how to use it. You cannot do that with Overdos.system. I have used Windows enough to know the basic point-and-shoot routine. Several times I ended up at places were the exit was not intuitive. In fact, I ended up rebooting several times. I was not able to sit down and do anything useful with Overdos.system without reading the manual.

Even after reading the manual several times and working through the tutorial several times, I was not comfortable with Overdos.system. Another advantage of an intuitive interface is that it is easy to pick up again after a long time away from it. After just a few days away from Overdos.system, I found myself having to work through the tutorial again.

Manual   More than any other manual, the Overdos.system manual is critical to its success. This manual is actually two oversized paperback books. One is strictly the tutorial while the other is the users manual. Both have numerous screen shots. There is rarely a page without several illustrations. While there are a number of illustrations, they look crude, as though they were printed on a dot matrix printer and then enlarged.

The tutorial works through all of the features of Overdos.system. It is actually very good. The users manual explains things well but it is poorly structured. It is often difficult to find the information you want. I often found myself thumbing through the manual looking for a picture relating to what I was doing.

Conclusion   Overdos.system has a lot of potential. In fact, it has far more potential than most of the other DOS shells. It seems to me that a good graphical interface has a lot to offer the new user. However, while Overdos.system has a lot of potential, it is unrealized potential. There is so much double-clicking on the right spot and following the right sequence of events with absolutely no indicators built into the display that Overdos.system is simply a pain to use.

Pull down menus or pull down help would help a lot. The best interface would be one where you used the icons and mouse clicking to move around the hard disk structure. Then you would use pull down menu to select what you wanted to do. I do not see why you have to double-click when a single-click will do. While Overdos.system has a lot of potential, I cannot recommend it in its present form.

```
Product:    Overdos.system
Price:      $99.95
Category:   Commercial
Publisher:  Catalonia Software, Incorporated
Address:    12930 Saratoga Avenue
            Suite B1
            Saratoga, California 95070
Phone:      (408) 446-2666
Notes:      Graphics card required
            Mouse recommended
            DOS 3.0 or later required
            Removes all but 8K of code when
            running another program from
            within Overdos.system
Memory:     512K
```

Pathminder

Pathminder is a good DOS shell with an acceptable menu program built in. Some of the ways it works are a little non-standard so it will take some getting use to.

Installation   You install Pathminder by placing the diskette in the A-drive and entering INSTALL. The installation program refuses to run from the B-drive even if the A-drive is not a 5.25 inch drive. An ASSIGN A = B statement corrects this problem. The documentation talks about a SET variable that must contain the name of the subdirectory storing Pathminder. However, the installation program forces you to install it in the \TOOLS directory.

The installation program renames any existing AUTOEXEC.BAT file to AUTOEXEC.OLD and copies its own AUTOEXEC.BAT file in its place. It does not do like most other installation programs and store a backup of the existing file and append its code to the end of the file. Rather it copies a whole new AUTOEXEC.BAT file into place containing nothing but the Pathminder start-up code.

This is an unacceptable practice. Some hardware requires you to run programs in the AUTOEXEC.BAT file in order to operate properly. Many other software packages require the same. In order to configure itself to run, Pathminder trashes every other program or hardware that depends on the AUTOEXEC.BAT file. Experienced users will be able to correct the problem. Inexperienced users are the ones most likely to purchase and use Pathminder. They will only be able to wonder what happened to their other programs and perhaps to some of their hardware.

This is simply not an acceptable way to install software. Luckily, there is a pause statement before copying the new AUTOEXEC.BAT file into place. That is also the last step in the installation program. When you see the message about copying the AUTOEXEC.BAT file, you should hit the control-break key combination to stop the program. The manual contains enough information to add the proper commands to your AUTOEXEC.BAT file manually.

Operation   When you first start Pathminder: The top section of the screen is a moving light-bar menu similar to a Lotus menu. The top line is a list of available commands. You can select a command by moving the lighted cursor to the command you want to run and pressing Return. You can also enter the first letter of the command. The second line gives a brief explanation of the highlighted command.

The left section of the screen shows the files and subdirectories in the subdirectory Pathminder is currently logged onto. You can move around these files, but not in the normal fashion. Normally, as you pressed the up and down arrows, the lighted cursor would move. When the cursor reached the top or bottom, it would quit moving and the files would begin scrolling up or down. With Pathminder, the lighted cursor always stays in the middle of the screen and the files scroll.

The default mode for the right section of the screen is a help screen. As the next few descriptions show, you can use it for other purposes:

- The graphical tree represents the hard disk structure. This tree does not work like a normal graphical tree. You cannot use it as a shortcut for moving around the hard disk as you can with other DOS shells. Other shells let you move around the graphical tree and press Return on the subdirectory you wish to select. In Pathminder, the graphical tree merely represents the location of the file highlighted on the left side. You cannot use it to maneuver around the hard disk.
- Using the Directory mode, the Pathminder screen converts to a single display. The additional room displays the date and time of file creation and the file attribute, if any.
- When in File=Find and you press the F8 key, Pathminder displays a new help screen on the right section of the screen. It also prompts you for the file specification to match. Once you enter the file specification, Pathminder goes out and finds the matches. You can scroll through the matching files on the left section of the screen. However, you cannot tag all the matches for further operation, like deleting all the .BAK files you find.

Selecting File from the main menu moves you the actual shell portion of Pathminder. Here there are more options than usual. They are:

- Find. This works just like the F8 key from the main menu. It will find all the files matching a file specification and allow you to examine them. However, you cannot tag all the matches for further operation, like deleting all the .BAK files you find.
- Copy. This lets you tag and copy files to another operation. Its operation is somewhat cumbersome. When you select copy, you get another menu where you select if you are copying to another subdirectory, another drive, or another drive and resetting the archive status. You then move the cursor and tag files by pressing the space bar. The space bar is a toggle so you can untag files already tagged by moving the cursor to that file and pressing the space bar. Once you have tagged all the files, you move the cursor to the destination subdirectory and press Return. You then must select yes to ver-

ify the copy or no to cancel it. The copy command will not let you copy the file to another file name either in the same directory or in another subdirectory.

- Type. This lets you list ASCII files on either the screen or the printer.
- Ren. This lets you rename a single highlighted file or subdirectory. Due to a limitation in DOS, renaming a subdirectory requires DOS 3.x or higher.
- Move. This quickly moves files to a different subdirectory on the same drive by only moving the subdirectory entry and leaving the physical file in the same location. File selection works the same as the copy command.
- Erase. This will erase a file or group of files. You tag the files with the space bar and press enter to carry out the erasure. Before erasing the files, it prompts you to verify you really want to erase the files.
- Kill. This is just like erasing a file, except that in addition to erasing the file the program Pathminder writes zeros over the space on the hard disk. As a result, no unerasing utility, like the Norton Utilities, can recover the data. It works just like the erasing command.
- Attrib. This lets you toggle the archive, read only, and hidden attributes on and off. When you select the attrib command, you get another menu where you select which of six options to carry out. These are archive on, archive off, read only on, read only off, hidden on or hidden off. You can only change one attribute at a time. You then use the space bar to toggle file selections on and off and press return to carry out the action. It then prompts you to verify that you really want to carry out the action. Pathminder cannot change the system attribute.
- Encrypt. This encrypts a file so no one else can use it. You first use the space bar to mark all the files you wish to encrypt using a single key. Next, you enter the encryption key. This is the password you must know to convert the file back to a useable format. Keys can be up to eighty characters long and can include spaces. Next, it prompts you on should it kill the original file after successful encryption. If you do not do this, the encrypted file gives you little protection since anyone can look at the original file. Next, it prompts you about do you really want to encrypt the files. At this point, Pathminder encrypts the file and creates a new file with the same name and the extension .OOO.
- Decrypt. This reverses the encryption process. First you select the files to decrypt using the space bar and the press return to activate. Next, you enter the decryption key. It then prompts you to see if you want the encrypted version erased after it decodes it. It then prompts you if you really want to continue. Pathminder will check the file and tell you if you entered the proper key. It will not continue unless you use the proper key. It restores the file to its original name. It prompts you before it overwrites an existing file with the same name.

In addition to the file command, the main Pathminder menu has several additional commands of interest. They are:

- Run. This runs a highlighted file if it is a .COM, .EXE, .BAT, or .BAS file. If you started Pathminder using the virtual version of Pathminder, it releases all but 4K of the Pathminder memory to run the application. If you used the other version, it releases none of its memory to the application. The only drawback to the virtual version is it takes slightly longer to start back when you exit an application. With only this minor drawback, everyone should use the virtual version.

- Directory. This leads to a submenu that lets you create, delete, open and close subdirectories. The creating and deleting correspond to the DOS MKDIR and RMDIR commands. Opening a directory adds the files in that directory to the main Pathminder display so you can scroll through them. Closing a directory removes its files from display.
- Edit. This brings up a simple file editor for editing ASCII files. It is a full screen editor that is much better than Edlin for editing batch files.
- Options. This brings up a submenu that lets you configure Pathminder. One of the options lets you turn off many of the confirmations Pathminder is always asking for. Another option, discussed below, lets you modify the Pathminder application menu.
- Compose. This lets you enter a DOS command directly. It also remembers the last command so you can edit it next time.
- Log. This lets you track computer usage in one personal and nine business accounts for client billing.

Because the virtual version of Pathminder only requires 4K while another program is running, you can use Pathminder as a menuing program. It is not as good as the better menuing programs, but it is quite acceptable for personal use. In addition, it is free with the shell. To create a menu, you first select an option from the main menu. You select menu from the option menu.

When you get to the application menu editor, it prompts you for the information it needs. That information includes . . .

- the name to appear on the menu.
- the explanation to appear when that name is highlighted.
- the program to run.
- several options features.

You select the program to run by pointing to in using the left section of the screen. In addition to entering items on one menu, you can have a menu item lead to a sub menu. As a result, you can construct quite complex menus.

Limitations   I covered the major limitations of Pathminder elsewhere, so I will just briefly mention them here. The installation program replaces any existing AUTOEXEC.BAT file with its own without retaining any of the commands from the original. It stores the original unchanged under a different name. The manual is difficult to read and shows signs of poor editing. Pathminder itself uses a slightly non-standard way of operation that often gets in the way, making it somewhat more difficult to use.

Manual   The manual shows numerous signs of poor or no editing. There are numerous occurrences of a word being hyphenated in the middle of a line, e.g., "mid-dle." Many word processors allow conditional hyphens. Those are hyphens that the word processor will use to split a word if that word is at the end of the line. Otherwise it does not print the hyphen. In the Pathminder manual, it is as though every conditional hyphen was printed. There are other editing problems, such as a title in all capital letters except one letter and punctuation without spacing after it.

Once you get past the (lack of) editing, the manual is complete and explains how to use Pathminder. However, I found the manual to be more difficult to read and understand than some of the other shell manuals.

Conclusion   Pathminder actually offers more than most of the other DOS shells. In addition to a full shell program with a wealth of features, it has a full menu program that takes up only 4K while other programs are running. As it stands, Pathminder is a good program. With more attention to the user interface and the manual, it could be a great one.

Product:	Pathminder
Price:	$59.95
Category:	Commercial
Publisher:	Westlake Data Corporation
Address:	Post Office Box 1711 Austin, Texas 78767
Phone:	(512) 328-1041
Notes:	All but 4K of the memory required by Pathminder is released when Pathminder runs another application.
Memory:	256K

PC Shell

PC Shell is just one of the many features of PC Tools Deluxe. For a discussion of the rest of the features of PC Tools Deluxe, see Chapter 5. PC Shell is an excellent DOS shell that can run as either a stand-alone program or a memory resident program.

Installation   PC Tools Deluxe comes with an installation program that will run from any drive and install PC Tools Deluxe in any subdirectory. The default name for the subdirectory is \PCTOOLS. If you already have an older version of PC Tools installed in that subdirectory, it is renamed to \PCTOOL4. In addition, the installation programs adds the PC Tools Deluxe subdirectory to the PATH statement in your AUTOEXEC.BAT file without asking permission. It saves the existing AUTOEXEC.BAT file as AUTOEXEC.SAV. It also renames any file named FORMAT.COM in your path to FORMAT!.COM. It creates a batch file called FORMAT.BAT that runs the PC Tools Deluxe formatting program.

In addition to these automatic changes, the PC Tools Deluxe installation program has several optional changes it can make. Basically, these changes are adding the necessary commands to the AUTOEXEC.BAT file to run several of the PC Tools Deluxe memory resident and special applications. The memory resident applications are a caching program and a shell program. The special program is a format recovery program that saves important information about the hard disk in a special file.

Operation   PC Shell can run as either a stand-alone program from the DOS prompt or as a memory resident program. When run as a memory resident program, PC Shell only uses 10K of memory while not in use. It uses 150K while active. PC Shell keeps it memory requirements low by leaving program and overlay files on disk and calling them as required. As a result, it runs a little slower and will not run from small capacity 360K or 720K floppy diskettes.

PC Shell uses pull down menus that you can access either through the keyboard with Alt-letter combinations or with a mouse. Figure 3-17 shows the PC Shell main menu with the "File" menu pulled down.

Clicking on the File menu brings up the following options:

- Copy. This lets you copy all the tagged files. Like all the menu options, if you have not tagged any files then the command only works on the currently highlighted file. You can also copy files by tagging them with the mouse and then dragging them to a new location with the mouse.
- Move. This lets you move the tagged files to another location on the same drive. It only changes the directory information so moves are very fast.
- Compare. This lets you compare the contents of tagged files against files you specify. The comparisons do not have to be against files with the same name in a different location.
- Find. This lets you enter ASCII or hexadecimal text and PC Tools Deluxe will find all files containing that text. When it finds that a match is found, it

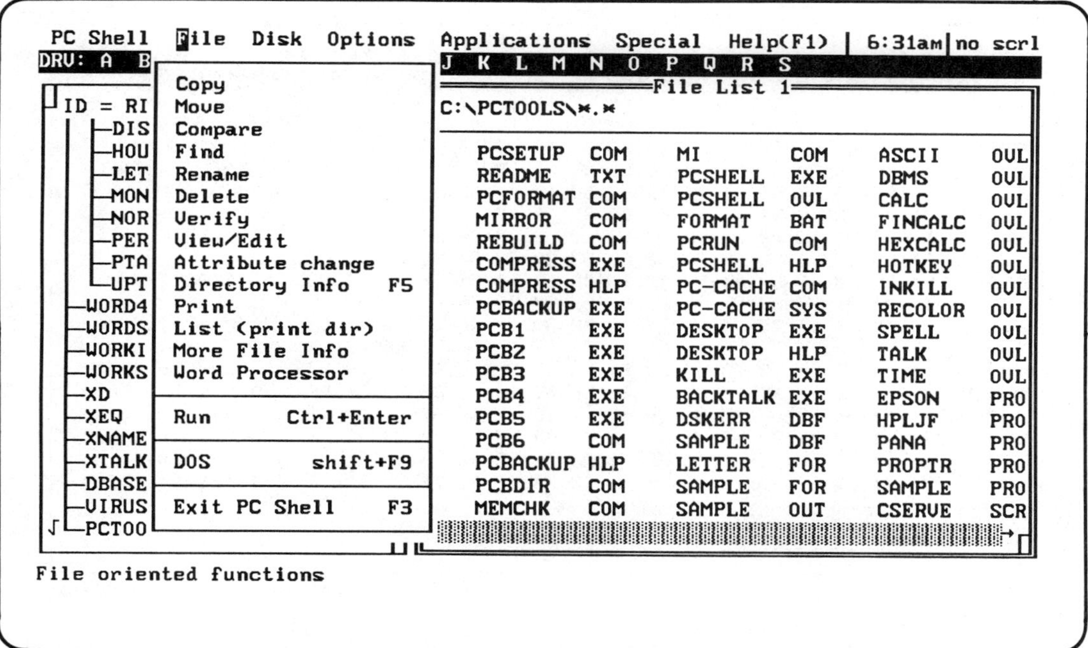

Fig. 3-17. PC Shell is part of the PC Tools Deluxe package. It makes extensive use of pull down menus and has excellent mouse support.

gives the file name, relative sector and offset. You have the option of stopping the search, continuing or editing the file that matched. It only searches tagged files.

- Rename. This lets you rename tagged files one at a time. For each tagged file, PC Shell pops up a screen for you to enter the new name and extension.
- Delete. This erases the tagged files. After selecting this command, a dialog box pops up that allows you to confirm each deletion. You can skip this by selecting "Delete All" from the dialog box.
- Verify. This verifies that all the tagged files are readable.
- View/Exit. This displays the files in ASCII mode on the screen. An option at the bottom of the screen lets you edit the file in ASCII or hexadecimal mode. Figure 3-18 shows this.
- Attribute change. This lists all the tagged files on the screen along with their current attributes, creation date and time and file size. You then move a cursor around double-clicking on files and attributes to change. It is a wonderfully easy way to change file attributes.
- Directory Information. This shows the total size of the files in the directory, the total size of the selected files and the available empty space on the disk.
- Print. This gives you the option of printing the tagged files as ASCII files, using the PC Shell print options or dumping each sector in ASCII and hexadecimal. Using the PC Shell print options lets you control such things as the page size, margins and headers/footers.
- List. This prints a file directory to your printer for the current directory.

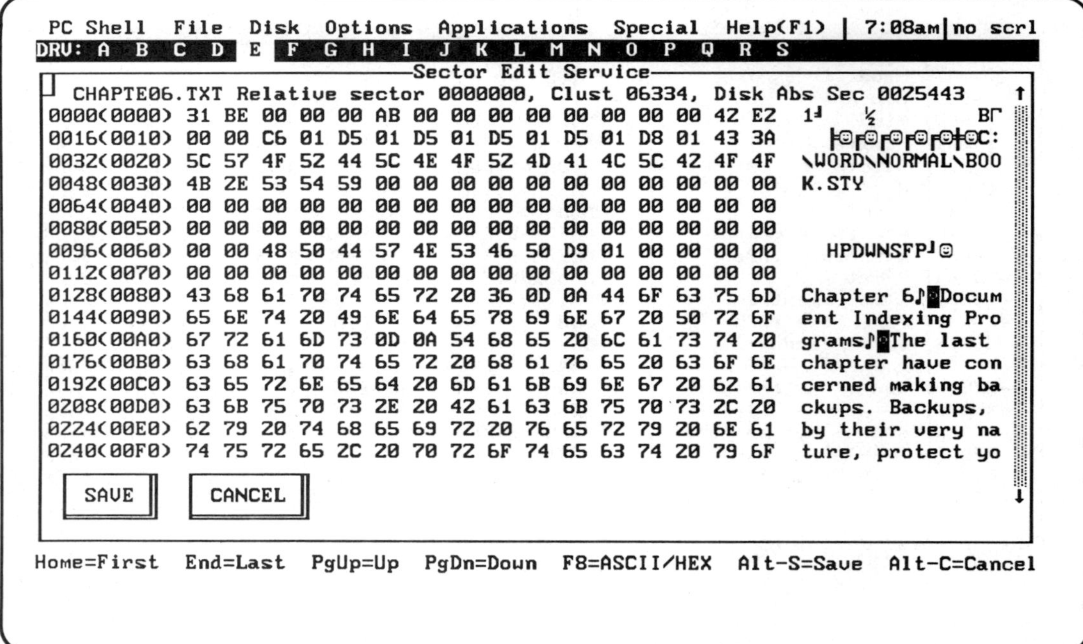

Fig. 3-18. The PC Shell View/Edit menu option lets you edit a file in either ASCII or hexadecimal mode.

- More File Information. For each tagged file, this shows a screen displaying technical information on the size.
- Word Processor. This runs the PC Shell built-in word processor on the tagged files. This word process offers a number of advanced features including search, search and replace, block deletes and block moves. Figure 3-19 shows this.
- Run. You use this to run the tagged program. You can also run a program by double clicking on it or by pressing Control-Enter while the program is highlighted.
- DOS. This lets you run DOS and return to PC Shell by entering EXIT.
- Exit PC Shell. This returns you to DOS if you started from the DOS prompt or to your application program if PC Shell is running in memory resident mode.

Clicking on the Disk menu brings up the following options:

- Copy Disk. This performs a DOS DISKCOPY-like operation to copy one diskette to another diskette. It copies the source diskette exactly and erases the target diskette.
- Compare Disk. This performs a DOS COMPARE-like operation to compare one diskette to another diskette. The two diskettes must be the same size. It performs a sector-to-sector comparison.
- Search Disk. This searches the entire disk for a character string you enter. Like the File menu Find option, this lets you enter ASCII or hexadecimal

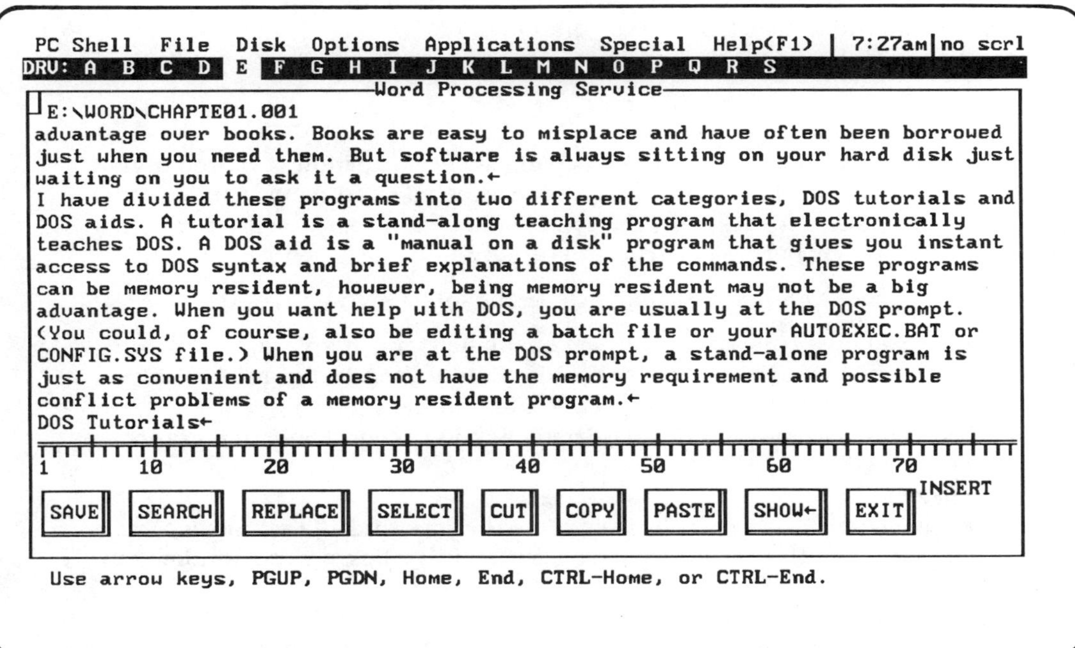

Fig. 3-19. PC Shell has a built-in ASCII word processor that offers such advanced features as search, search and replace, block deletes, block copies and block moves.

text. PC Shell then will find all files containing that text. When it finds a match, PC Shell gives the file name, relative sector and offset. You have the option of stopping the search, continuing or editing the file that matched. The only difference between Search Disk and Find is Find searches tagged files while Search Disk searches the entire disk.

- Rename Volume. This lets you change the volume label.
- Verify Disk. This verifies that it can read the entire hard disk.
- View/Edit Disk. This lets you edit anywhere on the disk. For editing, you can select:

Boot sector
First Fat sector
First Root DIR sector
First Data sector
Any cluster on the hard disk

- Locate File. This locates all the files matching the file specification you enter. If you like, you can then use PC Shell and all its functions on those files. For example, you could locate all your *.DOC files, tag them, and copy all them to a floppy disk for backup. This is a very handy way to work with certain types of files.
- Format Data Disk. This formats a floppy disk without the system files.
- Make System Disk. This formats a floppy disk with the system files.
- Disk Information. This displays technical information on the disk.
- Park Disk. This parks the heads on the current hard disk.
- Directory Maintenance. This gives you options to:

  - Add a subdirectory
  - Rename an existing subdirectory
  - Delete an empty subdirectory
  - Change the subdirectory DOS has flagged as the current subdirectory
  - Prune and graft. This lets you move the selected subdirectory and all its files to another location on the hard disk. This is an excellent way to rearrange your hard disk structure rapidly.

Clicking on the Options menu brings up the following menu options:

- Two List Display. This splits the screen in half and displays a separate graphical tree and file list in each half. This is handy for moving files around or copying files from one location to another.
- One List Display. This converts PC Shell back to showing only one graphical tree and file list.
- Reset Selected Files. This untags all files.
- Tree/Files Switch. This switches between the tree and file windows. You can also use the tab key. Mouse users can simply click on the window to use.
- Dir List Argument. Normally, PC Shell shows all files, e.g. *.*. This lets you change the display criteria so it shows only files matching your file specification.

- Active List Switch. When you are using the two window display, this switches between the two. You can also use the tab key. Mouse users can simply click on the window to use.
- Screen Colors. This changes the colors used by PC Shell.
- Size/Move Window. This changes how the windows appear on the screen.
- Date/Time. This lets you set or change the system time.
- File display Options. This lets you control what order PC Shell displays files in and what information it displays with the file. In addition to the file name, PC Shell can display the size, date, time, attributes and number of clusters. It can sort files by name, extension, size and creation date and time. Sorting can be in ascending or descending order. You cannot specify a tie-breaker for the sort.
- Modify Applications List. This lets you add your own programs to the applications list. That turns PC Shell into a quasi-menu program. However, you cannot layer menu options. That limits the number of items you can add to a menu. To add an application, you must complete a screen specifying the operating parameters for that application.
- Save Configuration. This saves the PC Shell setting to disk so it will start up next time just the way you want it.
- Quick Run. This turns the swapping of memory on and off. When quick run is on, PC Shell does not give its memory up to the application being run. That reduces the memory available to that application by 128K but allows PC Shell to load quicker when you exit the application.

The Applications menu runs the programs included with PC Tools Deluxe along with any applications you add using the Modify Applications List option on the Options menu. The applications included with PC Tools Deluxe are:

- Compress Disk
- PC Backup
- Mirror
- PC Format
- PC Secure

These are in other chapters.

Clicking on the Special menu brings up the following options:

- System Information. This shows technical information about the system.
- Undelete. This lets you undelete files and subdirectories. This can be automatic or you can search the disk and clusters to build the file manually.
- File Map. This highlights the clusters allocated to the highlighted file.
- Directory Sort. This lets you sort files by name, extension, size, creation date and time or by a number PC Shell assigns to each file. The sort can be ascending or descending. PC Shell allows you to see the results of the sort before writing it to disk. You can cancel the sort if you do not like the results.
- Memory Map. This shows how software is using the memory and can optionally show hooked vectors. Figure 3-20 shows this information.

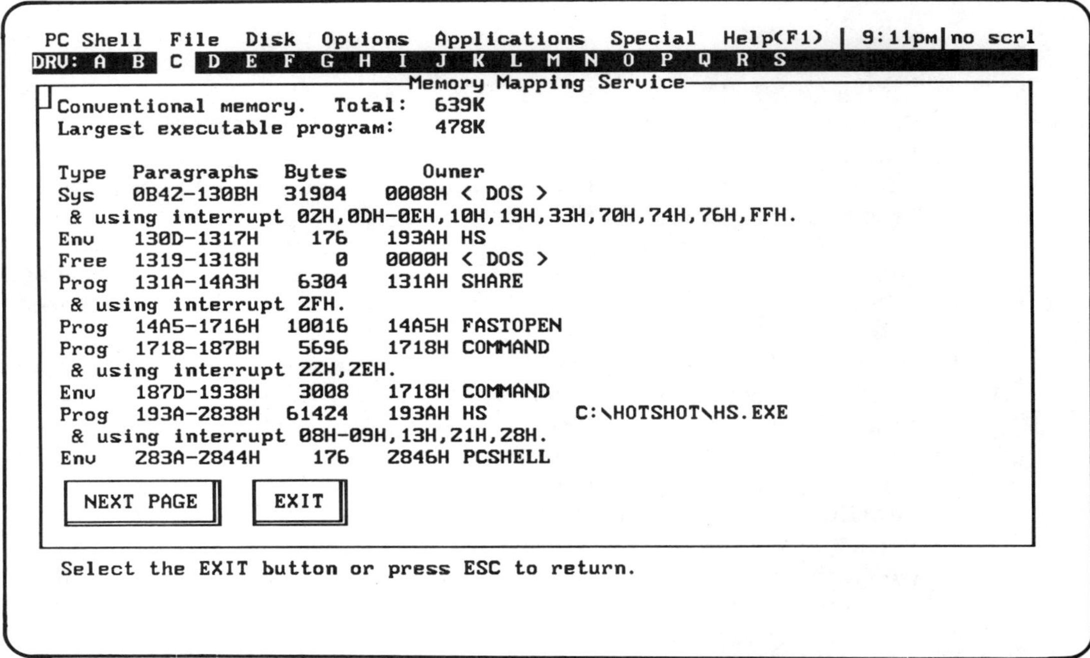

Fig. 3-20. PC Shell can display how memory is allocated along with vectors that have been hooked by the programs.

Limitations   PC Shell displays the letter for each available drive on the second line of the screen. These letters include the floppy disk drives, the hard disk drives and any logical drives created using the SUBST command.

The SUBST command is useful for working with programs that do not support subdirectories. It is also useful for making your PATH statement shorter since you can, for example, use an H: in place of C:\DBASE. This is important if you have a long PATH because DOS limits your PATH to 127 characters including the "PATH =" portion. Each time you try to log onto a drive created by the SUBST command, PC Shell locks the computer. With one graphical tree showing, you can recover with a warm boot. With two graphical trees showing, you must turn the computer off to restart. This is a major problem with PC Shell. With a mouse it is especially easy to click on a SUBSTed drive accidentally.

The PC Shell rename function is difficult to use. To rename all the *.TXT files to *.BAK files, you have to go through and enter the new name for every file. The park heads option on the disk menu is not able to park the heads on multiple hard disks.

PC Shell has only limited on-line help. You access it using either the F1 key or clicking on the help option of the menu. That displays a general window, the help is not context sensitive. You can select an index from this window that lists major topics. However, the topics are not in any specific order so you end up scrolling through the entire list to find the topic of interest.

Manual PC Tools Deluxe has a wonderful manual. Very few of the software packages in this book have manuals the caliber of this one. Each major program in the PC Tools Deluxe package has its own section. Each section explains how to use that program as though you have no experience with any of the other programs. With a few minor lapses, every menu option is explained in detail. The manual is lavishly illustrated with screen shots so you know exactly what to expect to see on the screen. It has an excellent table of contents and index. What makes all this especially surprising is PC Tools Deluxe is a fairly inexpensive utility.

Conclusion PC Shell is an excellent program. It is even a better bargain since it is only a small portion of the PC Tools Deluxe package. If you can live with the package hanging when you select SUBSTed drives or if you do not use SUBSTed drives, then this is one shell you should strongly consider.

<table>
<tr><td>Product:</td><td>PC Shell</td></tr>
<tr><td>Price:</td><td>$129.00</td></tr>
<tr><td>Category:</td><td>Commercial</td></tr>
<tr><td>Publisher:</td><td>Central Point Software, Incorporated</td></tr>
<tr><td>Address:</td><td>15220 NW Greenbrier Parkway
Suite 200
Beaverton, Oregon 97006</td></tr>
<tr><td>Phone:</td><td>(503) 690-8090</td></tr>
<tr><td>Notes:</td><td>PC Shell is only one small portion of the PC Tools Deluxe package.

In memory resident mode it requires 9K while not running and 170K while active.

In stand-alone mode it requires 256K.

256K is the minimum memory requirements; however, PC Shell will use all available memory.</td></tr>
<tr><td>Memory:</td><td>256K</td></tr>
</table>

Point & Shoot The Hard Disk Manager

Point & Shoot The Hard Disk Manager, or *Point & Shoot* for short, is a shareware DOS shell. It has a good menuing system and good mouse support. Other built-in features, like an editor and calculator, make it a good all-around hard disk management program.

Installation Point & Shoot comes with an installation program that automatically installs the program on your hard disk. It expects to run from the A-drive but an ASSIGN A = B statements corrects the problem.

Operation When you first start Point & Shoot, you see a screen like Fig. 3-21 only without the menu options. If you have an unregistered copy, there will be a flashing "Please Register" message just above the title. You can change the title to anything you like.

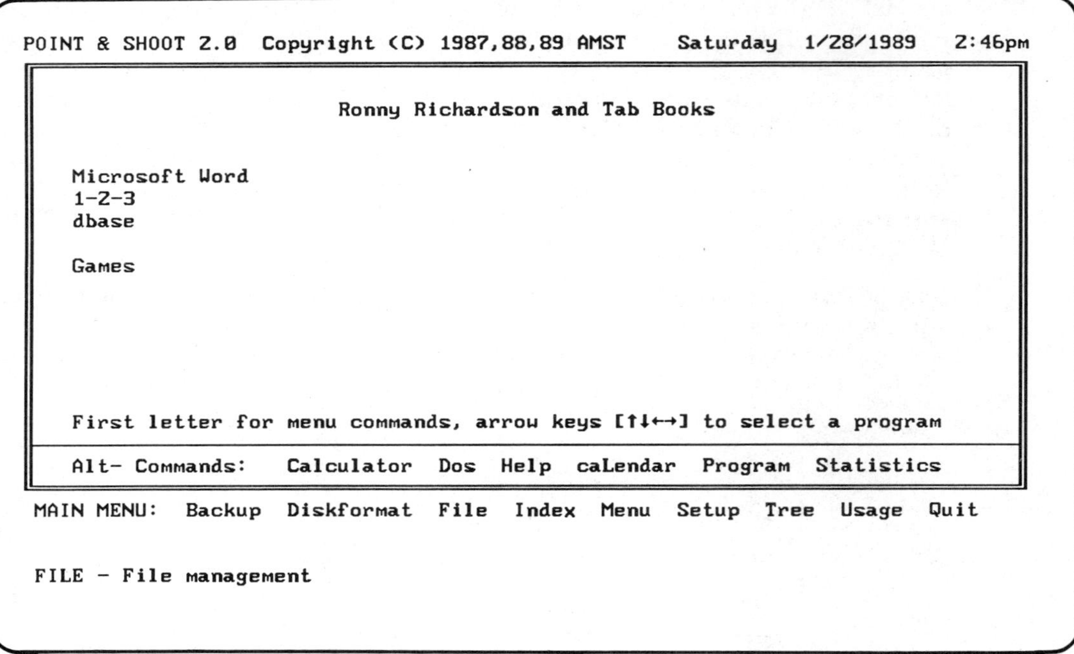

Fig. 3-21. The main Point & Shoot screen does not automatically show a graphical tree—you have to request one with the File command. That lets Point & Search switch easily between being a menu program and a shell program.

From this screen, several of Point & Shoot nicer features are available. Pressing Alt-C brings up a handy non-memory resident calculator. Pressing Alt-D lets you enter DOS commands directly. Point & Shoot lets you recall your last ten DOS commands for reuse or editing. Alt-H brings up non-context sensitive help. Alt-L brings up a calendar. Alt-P brings up shareware registration information and Alt-S brings up disk statistics and program defaults.

Adding menus to Point & Shoot is fairly easy. You select the Menu command. That brings up another menu that lets you . . .

- add a new menu entry.
- modify or delete an existing entry.
- change the location of menu entries.
- import menus from an older version of Point & Shoot.

There is room for thirty menu items on the Point & Shoot screen. You can place a menu entry in any of these thirty positions without regard for filling up all the ones before it.

Figure 3-22 shows a menu definition screen. The title you enter on the top row is on the Point & Shoot screen. If you leave the command line blank, Point & Shoot treats that entry as a submenu. It shows up to ten items on a pop up menu when that item is highlighted. As you see, you can enter multiple commands on a single line with them separated by vertical bars. You can also prompt the user for information. If this line is not enough, menu options can

```
POINT & SHOOT 2.0  Copyright (C) 1987,88,89 AMST     Saturday  1/28/1989   3:15pm

       MENU ENTRY TITLE     COMMAND TO EXECUTE    | = [Cr]  } = parm  ^ = stop
     *Games
SUB
  1  Aldo                   cd\games|aldo|cd\point&shot
  2  Breakout               cd\games|breakout 1 s-1|cd\word|cd\point&shoot
  3  Risk                   cd\games|EGARisk
  4
  5
  6
  7
  8
  9
 10

                      (blank path in submenu defaults to main entry path)
  APPLICATION PATH
  APPLICATION PASSWORD

F3=Set/Change Password        F5=Delete Line    F7=Select Path     Insert On
                              F6=Switch Lines   F8=Blank Field     F10=Accept

Use the commands shown to update the menu entries, [Esc] to abort
```

Fig. 3-22. Point & Shoot allows up to 30 menus on its screen. Each menu can be defined as a submenu containing up to 10 items.

run batch files. With a batch file, the last line of the batch file must be the command to start Point & Shoot. Point & Shoot releases all but a few bytes of memory when running a program from its menu.

Selecting the File commands moves you to the DOS shell area of Point & Shoot. Here you have a graphical tree on the right side of the screen and a file list on the left side. Figure 3-23 shows this. You move between the two top menus using the left and right cursor keys. You move between the menu options using the space bar. It is slightly cumbersome but Point & Shoot supports a mouse and that makes moving around easier. One especially nice feature is the ability to display multiple drives in a common display. This makes it easy to manage multiple drives.

Point & Shoot has all the usual DOS shell functions and they all work well. I especially liked the renaming function. It pops up the current name of the file in a window and for editing just like editing a name with a word processor. It uses an unusual method for copying and moving files. You move the cursor to the target subdirectory and select Target from the menu to flag that subdirectory. It moves and copies then automatically goes to the target subdirectory. That seems strange at first but after awhile I got to like that method.

Point & Shoot comes with an ASCII editor built in. It limits files to 64K but otherwise this is an excellent editor. If you need a better editor, you can attach most any other editor as the default editor.

Point & Shoot also comes with a flat-file database. It has a fixed format, meaning you cannot change the fields. There is room for an item name, cate-

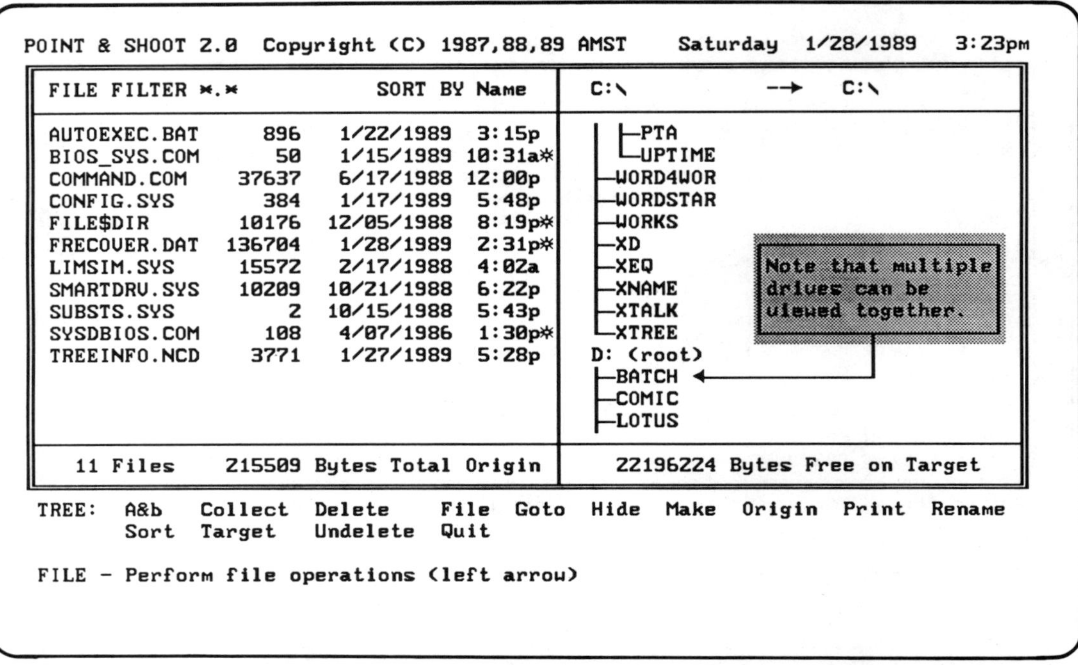

Fig. 3-23. The Point & Shoot file management area divides the screen into three parts. The left side shows a list of files, the right side shows a graphical tree and the bottom shows a menu.

gory, date, keywords and comments. You can use the database to store information on files. You can also use it to store any kind of information that fits its format.

Point & Shoot has a number of commands for working with the database. These commands let you . . .

- Add information
- Edit and delete existing information
- View the data in a tabular format
- Set up key fields
- Find information matching a user defined criteria
- Print a report

Limitations   Point & Shoot is an excellent program with no significant limitations other than the manual, discussed below.

Manual   Like most shareware programs, Point & Shoot comes with the manual in an ASCII file. When you register your copy, you get a printed manual. The manual explains how to use the program but often fails to give an adequate explanation of certain functions. For example, the section on the database devotes only one paragraph to explaining what a database is. After that, it launches into an explanation of index key files. New users are the primary target for DOS shells. They will be overwhelmed by such a short explanation.

Conclusion   Point & Shoot is an excellent choice if you are looking for an integrated menu program and DOS shell. Its low price and additional features, like the pop-up calculator, make it an excellent bargain.

<table>
<tr><td>Product:</td><td>Point & Shoot The Hard Disk Manager</td></tr>
<tr><td>Price:</td><td>$35</td></tr>
<tr><td>Category:</td><td>Shareware</td></tr>
<tr><td>Publisher:</td><td>Applied Micro Systems Technology</td></tr>
<tr><td>Address:</td><td>Post Office Box 1596
Welch Avenue Station
Ames, Iowa 50010</td></tr>
<tr><td>Phone:</td><td>(515) 292-0426
(800) 537-7417</td></tr>
<tr><td>Memory:</td><td>256K</td></tr>
</table>

Q-DOS II

Q-DOS II is an extremely fast DOS shell. It is easy enough to use that you will rarely need to refer to the manual.

Installation   Q-DOS II has an automatic installation program. It will let you install Q-DOS II from the B-drive and change the subdirectory to which it installs Q-DOS II; and all without any problems.

Operation   The main Q-DOS II screen contains five parts. Figure 3-24 shows this. These five parts are:

1) The menu. Here Q-DOS II shows what commands are available and gives a brief explanation of each.
2) The PATH. This box shows the current PATH Q-DOS II is using.
3) Statistics. This gives information about the current subdirectory including the number of files and the total size.
4) Function keys. This lists what commands the function keys perform.
5) Files. This area lists all the files and subdirectories in the current directory.

Figure 3-25 shows Q-DOS II makes it easy to move to a different subdirectory. When you press the D key, Q-DOS II gives you a map of the hard disk. In this map, it sorts the subdirectories in alphabetical order and is presented visually with each subdirectory connected by a line to its parent.

Q-DOS II has an editor included. The editor is good for editing batch files or other text files. In addition to editing standard ASCII files, this editor can view and edit files in hexadecimal. The editor limits files to 60K. If you do not find this editor to your liking, you can use the configuration program to replace it with another editor. Like the editor, the Q-DOS II view command can view files in either ASCII or hexadecimal. In addition, the view command can view WordStar files properly.

Limitations   Q-DOS II lets you search for all the files matching a specific file specification, *.BAK for example, and you can erase the files as you find them.

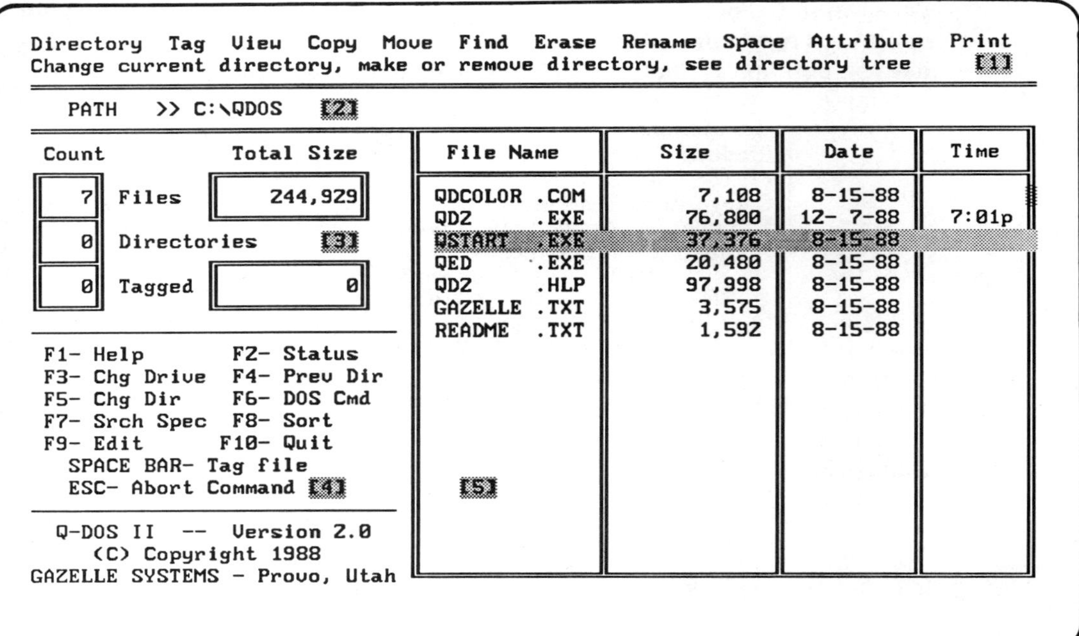

Fig. 3-24. The Q-DOS II main screen is divided into five sections. One has the menu, path, system information, function key assignment, and files in the current subdirectory.

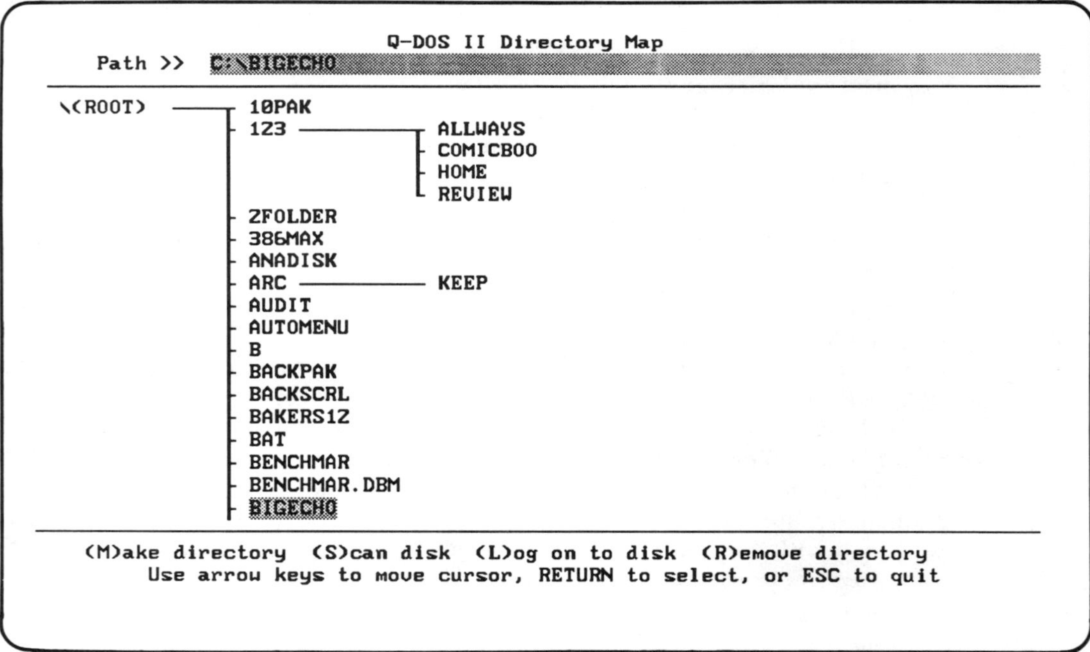

Fig. 3-25. Any time you press the D, Q-DOS II will give you a visual map of the hard disk. You can move to any subdirectory by moving the cursor to that directory on the map and pressing Return.

You cannot, however, tag them for a future operation as you find them. If you could, you could search for all *.WK1 Lotus files, tag them, and then copy them to a floppy disk for an easy backup. As it is, you have to tag them one directory at a time.

Q-DOS II cannot remove most of itself from memory and run memory and run another program the way XTreePro can. You can use a function key to run a program, but this method leaves 131K of code in memory.

Manual   The manual is well written. It has only a few screen illustrations. Q-DOS II has on-line context-sensitive help screens.

Conclusion   Q-DOS II uses moving light-bar menus like Lotus. That combined with its informative screen and context-sensitive help will make most users feel right at home. In addition, Q-DOS II is extremely fast. While Q-DOS II does not offer a lot of extra features, it is a good solid DOS shell. While not covered for this book, there is a version of Q-DOS II for networks. The vendor indicated it would work across all drives and respect all security restrictions.

Product:	Q-DOS II
Price:	$79.95
Category:	Commercial
Publisher:	Gazelle Systems
Address:	42 North University Avenue
	Suite 10
	Provo, Utah 84601
Phone:	(800) 233-0383
Memory:	256K

Qdisk

Qdisk is a memory resident shareware DOS shell. A copy is on the optional diskette set.

Installation   There is no installation program and the documentation does not mention how to install or start Qdisk. All that you have to do is copy QD334.COM to a subdirectory in your PATH and add the command to load it into memory in your AUTOEXEC.BAT file.

Operation   Qdisk pops up using the Alt-space bar combination. Figure 3-26 shows this. Qdisk does not display a graphical tree of your hard disk to move around. However, pressing return on any of the directories will move you to that directory.

Limitations   Qdisk does not tell you why it does not do something when you give it an invalid command. For example, if you tell it to remove a subdirectory with files in it or delete a read-only file, Qdisk will beep and not carry out the command. However, it will not tell you why it failed.

File sorting is always in ascending order. For example, you cannot sort by size from largest to smallest. The sort only effects the order inside Qdisk, when you exit to DOS the files will still be in their original order.

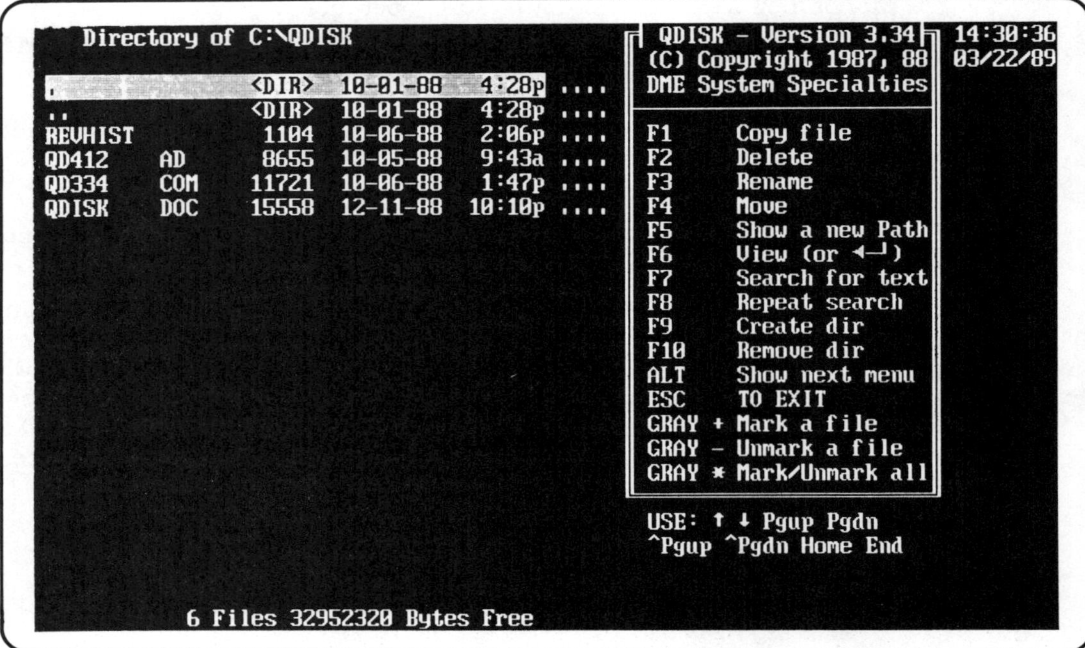

Fig. 3-26. Qdisk pops up and displays a list of files and directories on the left and a list of commands on the right.

Manual   The documentation for Qdisk does an adequate job of explaining how to use the program. However, the prompts for Qdisk are clear enough you are not likely to need the documentation.

Conclusion   Qdisk is a very good memory resident DOS shell. About all it is missing is a graphical tree display.

Product:	Qdisk
Price:	$39.95
Category:	Shareware
Publisher:	DME System Specialties
Address:	20432 Kinzie Street
	Suite 1
	Chatsworth, California 91311
Phone:	Not Available
Notes:	The optional diskette set includes a copy of this program.
Memory:	64K

Qfiler

Qfiler is a fairly simple to use DOS shell. It lacks many of the more powerful shell features, but all the basics are there and the price is fairly low.

Installation   Installing Qfiler involves copying the appropriate files to the sub-directory you want to contain the program. The best way is to create a special subdirectory for Qfiler. Regardless if you install Qfiler in a new or existing subdirectory that subdirectory should be in your PATH. The brief manual does not explain how to add the subdirectory to your PATH statement.

Operation   The files in the currently active subdirectory are in the left window. The right window currently contains the shareware notice. You can overlay that with a second subdirectory if you like. Figure 3-27 shows this. When you use the Pick command to select another subdirectory, Qfiler will use the right menu to show a map of the hard disk. You can easily move the cursor around the map to select the subdirectory you want to work with.

The moving lightbar menu along the bottom lets you:

- Quickly tag and untag all the files in the subdirectory.
- Copy either all the tagged files or the currently highlighted file to another location.
- Move either all the tagged files or the currently highlighted file to another location. A move is like a copy followed by a delete except. However, the files are not physically moved. The program only updates the directory information.
- Delete either all the tagged files or the currently highlighted file. If any of the files you select to delete are read-only, Qfiler will ask you if you want to delete them. If you say yes, it will delete them regardless of their read-only status.

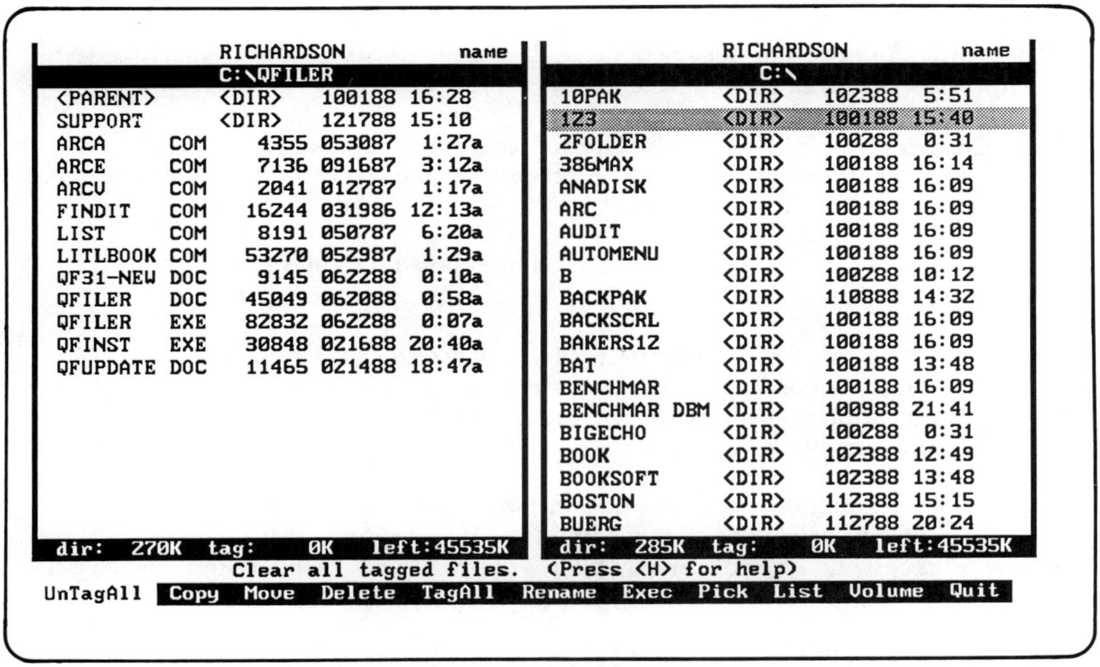

```
        RICHARDSON        name              RICHARDSON        name
           C:\QFILER                           C:\
<PARENT>      <DIR>    100188  16:28     10PAK       <DIR>    102388   5:51
SUPPORT       <DIR>    121788  15:10     1Z3         <DIR>    100188  15:40
ARCA     COM    4355   053087   1:27a    2FOLDER     <DIR>    100288   0:31
ARCE     COM    7136   091687   3:12a    386MAX      <DIR>    100188  16:14
ARCU     COM    2041   012787   1:17a    ANADISK     <DIR>    100188  16:09
FINDIT   COM   16244   031986  12:13a    ARC         <DIR>    100188  16:09
LIST     COM    8191   050787   6:20a    AUDIT       <DIR>    100188  16:09
LITLBOOK COM   53270   052987   1:29a    AUTOMENU    <DIR>    100188  16:09
QF31-NEW DOC    9145   062288   0:10a    B           <DIR>    100288  10:12
QFILER   DOC   45049   062088   0:58a    BACKPAK     <DIR>    110888  14:32
QFILER   EXE   82832   062288   0:07a    BACKSCRL    <DIR>    100188  16:09
QFINST   EXE   30848   021688  20:40a    BAKERS12    <DIR>    100188  16:09
QFUPDATE DOC   11465   021488  18:47a    BAT         <DIR>    100188  13:48
                                         BENCHMAR    <DIR>    100188  16:09
                                         BENCHMAR DBM <DIR>   100988  21:41
                                         BIGECHO     <DIR>    100288   0:31
                                         BOOK        <DIR>    102388  12:49
                                         BOOKSOFT    <DIR>    102388  13:48
                                         BOSTON      <DIR>    112388  15:15
                                         BUERG       <DIR>    112788  20:24
dir:   270K  tag:     0K   left:45535K   dir:   285K  tag:     0K   left:45535K
          Clear all tagged files.  (Press <H> for help)
UnTagAll   Copy   Move   Delete   TagAll   Rename   Exec   Pick   List   Volume   Quit
```

Fig. 3-27. The default Qfiler display can be modified to list two separate subdirectories—one on the left and one on the right.

- Rename either all the tagged files or the currently highlighted file.
- Run a program by selecting it from the file listing. Using this option, Qfiler can function like a simple menu program. The drawback is Qfiler does not release any of its memory first. As a result, it takes up 172K while the other program is running.
- Pick another subdirectory or disk drive to view.
- List an ASCII file. This requires that LIST.COM from Vernon D. Buerg be in your PATH.
- Change the volume label.

In addition to the menu, additional commands are available by using the function keys. They are:

- Create a subdirectory.
- Delete a subdirectory.
- Selecting subdirectories to show on the left and right windows.
- Sorting files by name, extension, size, or date.
- Tagging and untagging files.
- Setting and clearing the archive bit.
- Hiding and unhiding files.
- Turning the read-only bit on and off.
- Entering a file specification. That causes the program to only display certain files.

Even more commands and menus are available using control-keystroke combinations. They include:

- An archive menu. This uses separately licensed shareware programs to compress one or more files into a single compressed file. It also extracts files from a single compressed file.
- A backup command. This is not like the DOS backup. Rather, it copies newer copies of files in the source subdirectory to the target subdirectory.
- An alternate copy command where files are renamed while being copied.
- Shelling to DOS to run a program.
- Refresh the displays. This is useful if you have copied files and they do not appear on the screen.

Limitations   The two major limitations of Qfiler are the user interface, discussed above, and its poor manual, discussed below. An additional limitation is its reliance on additional shareware programs, which the user must license, to perform functions like listing ASCII files.

Manual   The manual is very brief. Experienced users, who least need any shell, will be able to use Qfiler after reading the manual. Inexperienced users will have a great deal of trouble using Qfiler if their only reference material is the manual.

Conclusion   The limitations of Qfiler are important limitations. They are also somewhat offset by its low price. A copy of Qfiler is on the optional diskette set.

```
Product:     Qfiler
Price:       $20
Category:    Shareware
Publisher:   Jamestown Software
Address:     2508 Valley Forge Drive
             Madison, Wisconsin 53719
Phone:       Not Available
Notes:       Site licenses and volume
             discounts are available
Memory:      192K
```

Scout

Scout is a shareware memory resident, pop-up DOS shell.

Installation   Installing Scout is a two-step process. First, you copy the Scout files to a subdirectory on your hard disk. The manual does not tell you how to do this. The next step is to run the configuration program. You have to do this to tell Scout where to find files it needs while running. The manual does explain how to run this program.

Operation   Scout is a memory resident program. When you start the program, it only reserves enough room in memory for 250 files per directory and 50 directories on a disk. To make room in memory for more files or directories, you add switches to the command line when you start Scout. Each additional file uses an additional 23-bytes. Each additional subdirectory uses an additional 39-bytes. In addition, Scout has command line switches to increase the buffers it uses. This speeds copying.

When you press the Scout hot-key (Alt-F10) it pops up. The main screen shows the files in the current subdirectory. The bottom left of the screen shows detailed information on the file currently highlighted. The remaining portion of the bottom shows disk information.

Scout makes extensive use of letters to execute commands. With no prompts visible, it is difficult to remember which letter performs which function. To overcome this, Scout will show a help screen when you press Control-H. Figure 3-28 shows this.

Limitations   The major limitation of Scout is its user interface. You probably noticed as you read through the list of commands in Fig. 3-28, many of the letters seemed to be arbitrarily assigned. To remember them, you will either have to keep referring to the manual or help screen. An intelligently designed menu using the bottom few lines of the screen would do wonders for Scout.

Scout does not show any subdirectories that you created by changing the subdirectory file attribute. Scout does not allow you to enter volume labels as both upper and lowercase. It only accepts uppercase. The menu program requires a lot of files spread across many subdirectories. In addition, it does not allow you to select commands from an English-like menu.

The Alt-D command shows the space available on all the available drives.

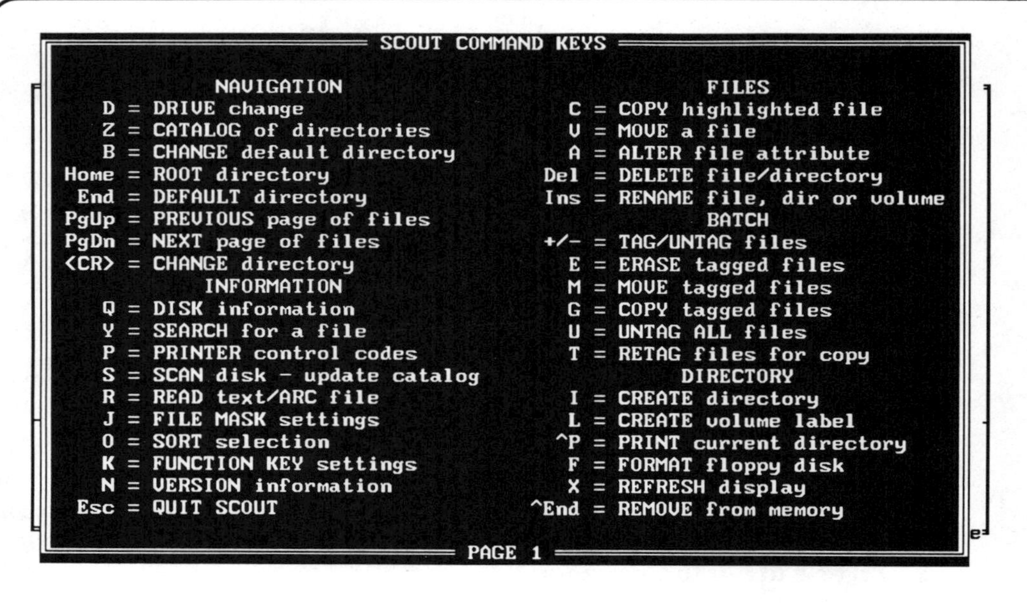

Fig. 3-28. Pressing the Control-H key while in Scout brings up this help screen. Pressing Page Down shows the functions performed by the Control-letter and Alt-letter combinations.

It also totals that space and displays that total as the space available for the system. If you use the SUBST command to treat a subdirectory as a drive, Scout becomes confused. For example, if you have a hard disk (C-drive) with 10 Meg free and you issue the command: SUBST C:\WORD D:

DOS will treat the \WORD subdirectory as the D-drive. Scout will show 10 Meg free on the C-drive, 10 Meg free on the D-drive and 20 Meg free on the system. Of course, C and D are on the same drive and only 10 Meg is free on the system.

Manual   Like most shareware, Scout has an electronic manual on its disk. This manual does a good job of explaining how to use Scout if you are an experienced DOS user. However, new users will find the explanations too brief.

Conclusion   I do not think a memory resident DOS shell has an advantage over a stand-alone shell. Generally, you will only be performing disk management when you are at a DOS prompt so the memory resident portion gives you no real advantage. With the letter commands, no prompts and only two screens of help information it is difficult to master Scout.

However, other than its poor user interface, Scout is a good, functional DOS shell. If you disagree with me and think a memory resident DOS shell would be useful, then Scout deserves a good look.

Product:	Scout
Price:	$30-$35
Category:	Shareware
Publisher:	New-Ware
Address:	6198 Agee Street
	Suite 71
	San Diego, California 92122
Phone:	(619) 455-6225
Notes:	$30 entitles you to use the program
	$35 entitles you to use the program, it also gets you a printed manual and one free upgrade
	$40 gets you the expanded memory version of Scout that only uses 6K of regular memory
	Exact memory requirements depend on your system configuration, the memory requirements listed below is the minimum Scout will use
	A version of Scout is available (for an extra fee) that loads all but 6K of the code into expanded memory
Memory:	64K

Still River Shell

Still River Shell is an adequate shareware DOS shell with an excellent site license policy. Still River Shell is highly configurable. That makes it a good choice for a central computer department, especially in light of the site license policy.

Installation   There is no installation program to install the Still River Shell. All the manual tells you to do is perform two steps. First, copy SR.EXE to a subdirectory in your PATH. Then, modify your CONFIG.SYS file to contain the proper number of buffers. This will get the Still River Shell up and running. However, it does not tell you what to do with the other files on the disk.

Operation   The Still River Shell screen is in sections. The left section lists the files in the current subdirectory. The right section lists technical information on the hard disk, and the bottom section contains the menu. The left section of the menu can also form a graphical representation of the hard disk. You can use this to select a new directory to work with.

Like other shells, you use menu options to tag and untag files. Once tagged, you can use the menu to operate on the files. When a menu option requires additional information, like where to copy files, you must enter that information manually. You cannot simply point using the graphical tree.

The Still River Shell lets you assign commands to function keys. For example, you could assign the commands to start your word processor to one of the function keys. You could then effectively use your word processor as an editor from within the shell. Unlike some other shells, you essentially write a DOS batch file to do this. Therefore, you need a high degree of familiarity with DOS to use this feature. In addition, Still River Shell has no kernel that stays in memory. Therefore, these function key assignments are only available from within the shell. In addition to the regular function keys, you can combine both the alternate and control keys with the function keys to yield even more key combinations. If you enter DOS commands from within the shell, using the Xdos command, the shell can recall your last twenty commands for reuse or editing.

There is a find command that will list all the files on the hard disk matching a certain file specification. It will find, for example, all the .BAK backup files. You can then easily mark any or even all the files it finds for deletion, copying or other file operations. If the list is too long to fit on one screen, you can even scroll back to see the files that were scrolled off the screen.

In addition to the Still River Shell, the disk contains three minor utilities. The first two work together. The first, PUSHD.EXE stores the current directory and changes to a specified directory. The second, POPD.EXE switches back to the directory stored by PUSHD.EXE. The third utility, XDOS.EXE, lets one batch file easily call another. Before DOS 3.3, when one batch file invoked another, control never returned to the original batch file. You could "trick" DOS into returning control to the original batch file by loading a second copy of COMMAND.COM, but the syntax is complex. XDOS.EXE makes it simple. In DOS 3.3, the CALL command automates this within DOS.

Limitations   As explained below, the biggest limitation of the Still River Shell is its documentation. The manual is completely inadequate for the new user. Like some of the other shells, the Still River Shell can run a program. You do this by pressing the Xdos command, which lets you run any DOS command. Pressing the insert key will place the name of the currently lighted program on the command line. When you execute a program using this method, Still River Shell releases none of the memory. As a result, the memory the program has is 102K lower.

Manual   The Still River Shell operates very intuitively. That is fortunately because the manual is inadequate for an inexperienced user. As I mentioned above, the details on installing the program are scarce. Very soon after the page on installation, the manual turns into a very technical manual. Even experienced DOS users will have to read the manual several times to understand what is going on. Inexperienced users may never understand.

Conclusion   The Still River Shell is a good solid program, especially if an experienced user is available to install and configure it. This combined with its relatively inexpensive site license makes this an excellent program for larger companies to consider. Inexperienced users without readily available help should consider another program.

```
Product:        Still River Shell
Price:          $25-$59
Category:       Shareware
Publisher:      Bill White
Address:        Post Office Box 57
                Still River, Massachusetts 01467
Phone:          (617) 456-3699
Notes:          $25 for registration only
                $39 for registration and manual
                $59 for registration, manual, and one upgrade
                $390 for one location site license
                Site license includes permission to duplicate the
                printed manual
                Phone number is for credit card orders only
Memory:         102K
```

Take Charge

Take Charge is a commercial package with a complete set of file and disk maintenance programs. The DOS shell is only a small portion of the Take Charge package.

Installation   Take Charge comes with an installation program. It lets you select the drive to install Take Charge on but requires you to use the \ TC! subdirectory. It runs from the A-drive and requires an ASSIGN A = B statement to run from the B-drive.

Operation   The File Services portion of Take Charge is a DOS shell. When you start the File Services, it displays the files in the current root directory of the current disk. Figure 3-29 shows this. You select commands along the top by moving the cursor to that command and pressing Return or by pressing the first letter of the command.

Limitations   Having Take Charge in memory disables DOS command editing. Normally, pressing F3 displays the past command and F2 will display the past command up to the key you press after F2. When you load Take Charge into memory, these no longer work.

I tried to log onto the PC-Link computer network with Take Charge loaded into memory but not active. PC-Link runs under a runtime version of the Deskmate program from Tandy. PC-Link was able to display all its graphic mode characters normally. PC-Link displayed all its text mode characters like static on a monitor display and were completely unreadable. Clearly Take Charge interferes with either the runtime Deskmate or the PC-Link software.

While moving around many of the Take Charge menus and screens, pressing the 5-key in the middle of the number pad (which does nothing) will blank the screen until you press another key. This ability to blank the screen would be an advantage if you activated it by some out of the way keystroke combination. However, the proximity of the 5-key to commonly used keys means you often accidentally blank the screen. New users may not be able to quickly identify the problem.

```
Attrib Copy Delete Edit Find Move Next Other Print Rename Space Tag Untag View
Change file attributes of current file or group of files.

 Path: A:\*.*
 No of files:     10  Filesize:       96881  Tagged files:      0 Filesize:        0

    Filename Ext       Filesize        Date       Time      Attribute(s)
    BOOK    .                 0   14 Mar 1989    05:17p   ..SUB DIRECTORY...
    HOTSHOT .                 0   14 Mar 1989    05:15p   ..SUB DIRECTORY...
    TC      .                 0   18 Mar 1989    06:10p   ..SUB DIRECTORY...
    AUTOEXEC.BAT             42   18 Mar 1989    07:59p   ...............Arc
    COMMAND .COM          25307   17 Mar 1987    12:00a   ...............Arc
    CONFIG  .SYS             42   14 Mar 1989    05:15p   ...............Arc
    IBMBIO  .COM          22100   18 Mar 1987    12:00a   R/O..Hid..Sys..Arc
    IBMDOS  .COM          30159   17 Mar 1987    12:00a   R/O..Hid..Sys..Arc
    IMAGECOP.EXE          10313   23 Feb 1989    11:43p   ...............Arc
    PLUSDRV .SYS           8918   30 Jun 1988    01:00a   ...............Arc

 ALT-A.Z-goto file F1-Chdir F2-Dir Cmds F3-Dir↑ F4-Dir↓ F5-Sort F6-Reread F0-Quit
```

Fig. 3-29. The Take Charge File Services program is a DOS Shell. Although not as powerful as a full DOS Shell, it can perform many useful functions.

Because some Take Charge operations do not work under DOS 4.0, I copied the Take Charge programs to a DOS 3.3 disk. I then booted off that disk to run some tests. When I did that, the serial number Take Charge normally displays on the log on screen changed to "bootlegged." This was especially annoying since I had a legal and registered copy. While the serial number changed, my name remained on the display. I guess that was to show where the "bootlegged" copy came from.

If you do not have a LASTDRIVE statement in your CONFIG.SYS file, the File Services will let you select from drives A-E for a copy command even though not all those drives exist. If you select a non-existent drive, it responds with the less than helpful "Cannot create destination file (Disk fill [sic] or R/O file exists??.)" error message. If you enter an improper file name or a file name with wildcards, it responds with the same error message. Some of the other options, like finding a file, have this same problem.

Manual   The Take Charge manual is very complete. It does a good job of explaining how to run all the features included in Take Charge. The manual is a paperback book and appears to have been constructed of bound photocopied sheets. The paper used in the manual is low quality paper. Many of the pages were printed with the lines at a slight angle and some of them are printed with the ends of the lines chopped off. Not enough of the pages are misprinted to cause serious problems, however, the lack of print quality is annoying.

Conclusion   The File Services portion of Take Charge is a functional DOS shell. Many of the programs in this chapter are better. However, File Services is only a small portion of the overall Take Charge package. Take Charge is covered in detail in Chapter 5. (See pg. 224 for ordering information.)

Tree86

Tree86 is a DOS shell with very good mouse support.

Installation   Tree86 does not come with an installation program. The manual explains how to create a subdirectory and how to install Tree86.

Operation   The default Tree86 display shows a graphical tree on the left side and displays summary on the right side.

You begin by selecting the subdirectory to work with from the graphical tree. When you click on a subdirectory or move the cursor to it and press return, you move to the file display in Fig. 3-30. The primary commands in this file menu are:

- List. You use this to move through the different subdirectories.
- Tag. This menu option provides a versatile set of tools for marking files.

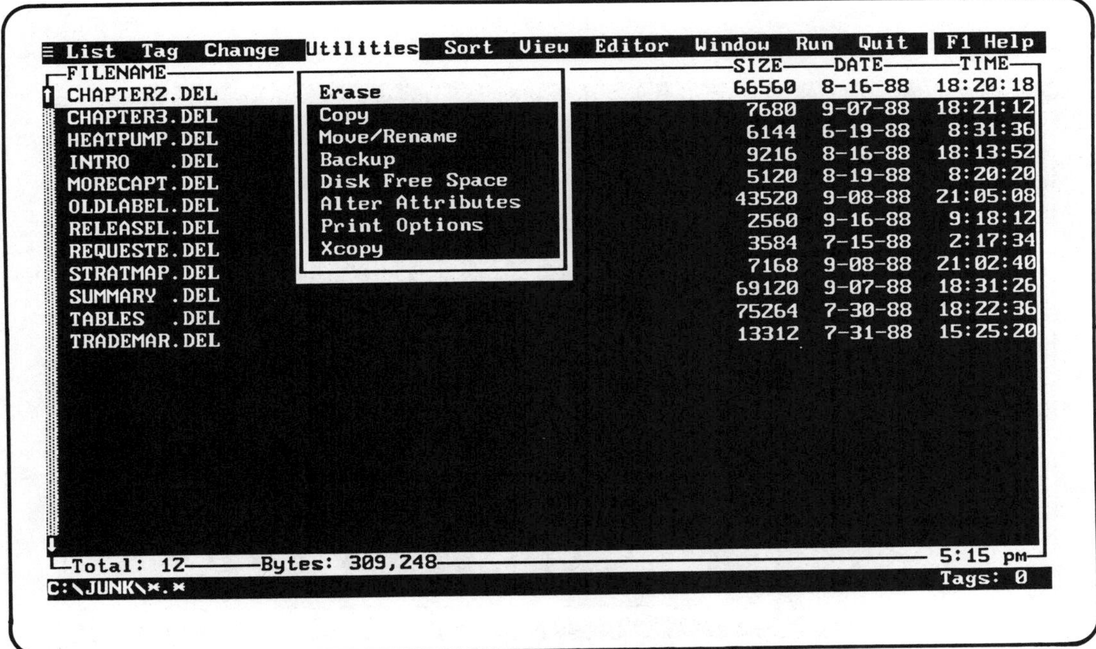

Fig. 3-30. Tree86 uses pull-down menus to perform the actual file management work.

- Utilities. This is the actual file management menu for working on tagged files.
- Sort. This lets you control how the program sorts the files in the window.
- View. This uses an external program to display ASCII files on the screen.
- Editor. This accesses your word processor. Tree86 does not include an editor, you must use the configuration program you specify your editor as the one to use.
- Window. This switches back to the graphical tree window.
- Run. This runs the program highlighted by the cursor.

The utility menu provides the following file manipulation function:

- erasing files
- copying files
- moving files
- renaming files
- displays the free disk space
- change attributes
- printing a copy of the graphical tree
- copying files using XCOPY

If you get stuck while using Tree86, it has full context sensitive help built in. Figure 3-31 shows a typical Tree86 help screen.

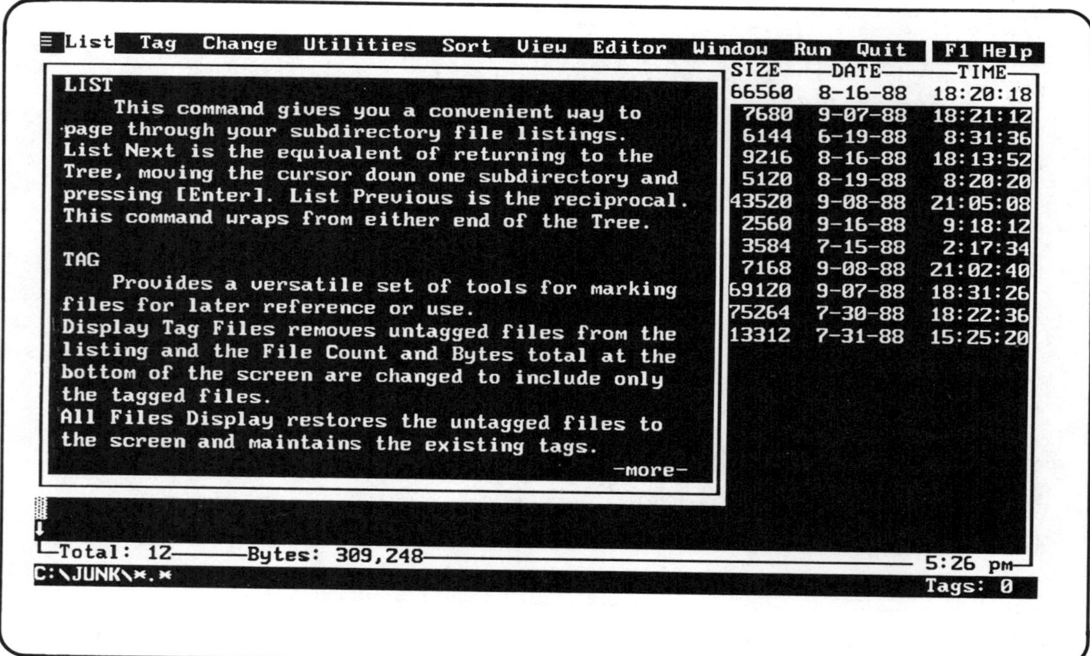

Fig. 3-31. While using Tree86, you are never far from help. Tree86 includes context-sensitive help when you press the F1 key.

Limitations   Some of the summary technical information displayed is incorrect. Under DOS 4.x, hard disks can be larger than 32 Meg. This causes Tree86 to display the incorrect total available space and the incorrect percentage of free space. Tree86 also displays the incorrect amount of extended memory.

Manual   The manual for Tree86 does a good job of explaining how to use Tree86.

Conclusion   Tree86 is a very good DOS shell with full mouse support and context sensitive help screens.

Product:	Tree86
Price:	$89.95
Category:	Commercial
Publisher:	The Aldridge Company
Address:	2500 CityWest Boulevard
	Suite #575
	Houston, Texas 77042
Phone:	(713) 953-1940
Memory:	256K

Treeview

Treeview is a shareware DOS shell.

Installation   Treeview does not come with an installation program. The disk-file manual instructs you to create a subdirectory for Treeview and copy all of the files to it. There is a list of what each file does so you can eliminate optional files if space is tight.

Operation   Figure 3-32 shows the default Treeview screen. Along the top row is the menu. You access these pull down menus by pressing the first letter of the command. Just below the menu is an area with disk information. It has . . .

- the total disk space
- the free space
- the number and size of the files matching the file specification
- the number and size of the tagged files

Treeview has a graphical tree display for moving around the hard disk. To see it, you select tree from the Dir menu. The tree completely replaces the files display. You can write a tree to disk so you do not have to wait for Treeview to read the disk and reconstruct the tree each time. Once you move to a directory of interest, you press return to see the files in that subdirectory.

To tag files, you press "T" to select the tag menu and then "C" for the currently highlighted file. You can also tag based on the date and time or name.

Once you have tagged the files, the normal file commands are available to operate on them. These include:

- changing the file attributes
- copying the files

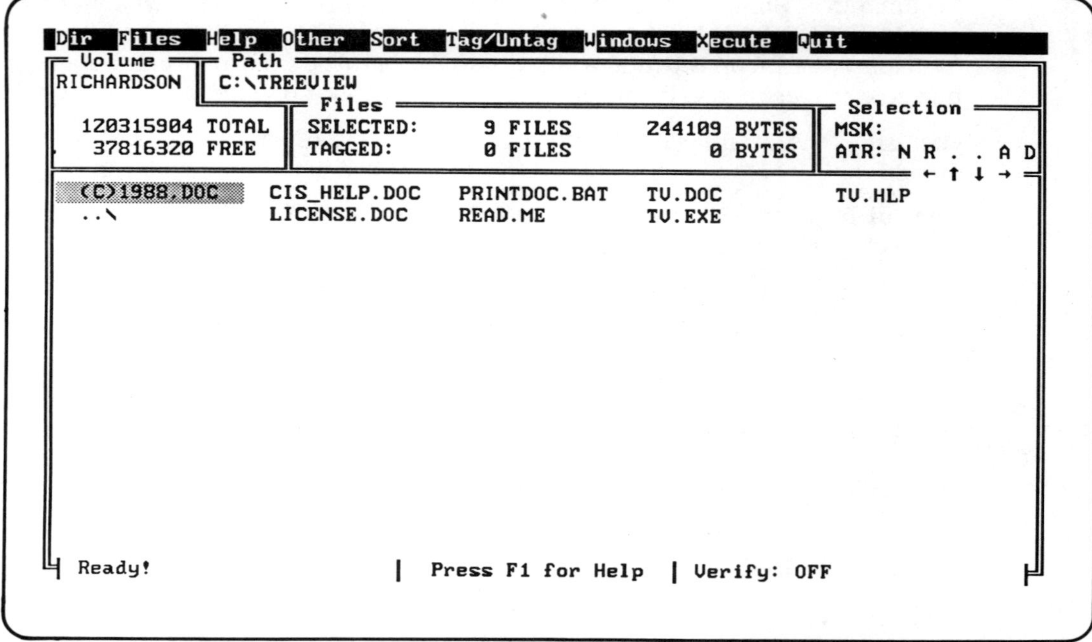

Fig. 3-32. The default Treeview screen has a menu along the top, summary disk information in the center, and a list of files in the bottom window.

- changing the creation date and time
- erasing the files
- renaming files
- moving files
- viewing the files
- running a file
- editing a file (To use this, you must have attached your editor to Treeview)

Treeview allows you to split the file window into several different windows. Each window can maintain a separate view on your hard disk. However, you cannot view a graphical tree in one window and files in another. Each time you select the tree command, it takes over the entire screen. Only after you press return does the normal display return.

Treeview is DESQview aware and can run in a small window under the Desqview multitasking program. Treeview can use expanded memory for storing some of its data, if expanded memory is available. Treeview can display information in 43-line mode on an EGA display and in 50-line mode on a VGA display.

Limitations   Treeview only shows the graphical tree when you are moving around. It does not display any files. As a result, it is more difficult to select the appropriate subdirectory. You must move to the subdirectory and press Return to see the files. If the files you want are not there, you must select the tree command to try again.

While moving around the tree, you cannot perform a speed search. If you knew you wanted to move to a subdirectory that started with an "S" a speed search would let you type in an "S" to move directly to first subdirectory starting with an "S." The page up and page down keys also do not work. You can move to the root directory with the home key and you can move to the last subdirectory with the end key. Between them, you can only move one subdirectory at a time using the up and down keys. That can make moving around a large hard disk very slow.

The menu has an execute command that lets you run either a DOS command or the highlighted program. This feature is not very useful since Treeview retains 162K of memory for itself.

Manual　　Like most shareware, the manual for Treeview is a file on the distribution diskette. You must view it with an ASCII file view or print it using your word processor. The manual for Treeview is quite good and explains how to use the program in a clear fashion.

Conclusion　　Treeview is a very good DOS shell. Its major limitations are the memory it requires while running another program and its inability to display a graphical tree and files at the same time. Depending on how you use a DOS shell, these could be very minor limitations.

Product:	Treeview
Price:	$50.00
Category:	Shareware
Publisher:	Magee Enterprises, Incorporated
Address:	Post Office Box 1587 Norcross, Georgia 30091
Phone:	(404) 446-0271
Memory:	128K

WindowDOS

WindowDOS is a DOS shell with the unique ability to run as a memory resident program. This gives you access to the DOS shell anytime. It can also run as a stand-alone program.

Installation　　There is no real installation program. The manual tells you to load WindowDOS and use it to copy the files you need.

Operation　　WindowDOS has two modes of operation, memory resident and stand-alone. When running as a memory resident program, it requires 53K. It can pop up over most programs and give you assess to all of its features while most any other program is running. I am not sure how advantageous it is to be able to erase a file or format a disk in the middle of typing a memo to my boss. However, if you want to do that, WindowDOS will let you. You can also load WindowDOS as a standard stand-alone DOS shell. I performed most of the testing for this book in stand-alone mode.

Figure 3-33 shows the WindowDOS screen. You use the cursor control keys to move around the files. Pressing the plus key tags a file. You press the

```
=C:\WINDOWDO=
.              December  26, 1988      12:24 am      phsuDa                 0

  .              @EXTKEYS HLP    @SCANKEY HLP    CAPTURE  EXE    WD2      EXE
  @ASCII   HLP   @LINES   HLP    @WD2     HLP    README   DOC    WD2-CFIG EXE
  @COLORS  HLP




  Copy  Dir  Erase  Format  Global  List  MkDir  Rename  Sort  Tree  View
```

Fig. 3-33. WindowDOS displays the files in the current subdirectory at the top of the screen and a list of commands at the bottom.

first letter of a command to activate that command. For example, to delete a file, you would move the cursor to that file, press the plus key to tag it and then the e-key to erase it.

WindowDOS gives you several ways to move around the subdirectories. You can press the tab key to move back one subdirectory at a time. You can press the t-key to get a graphical tree. You can then move the cursor to the subdirectory to move to and press Return. You can also move to the subdirectory directory entry and press Return.

In addition to the usual DOS shell features, WindowDOS has several interesting features:

- Viewing a file. WindowDOS can display a file in both ASCII and hexadecimal mode. The viewer automatically recognizes WordStar files and displays them properly.
- Viewing the environment. Figure 3-34 shows WindowDOS can display the DOS environment of the memory. This display shows the memory resident programs and the vectors they have hooked.
- Password locking. If you want to leave your computer without worrying about someone else using it, you can use WindowDOS to lock out the computer until you enter a password. Figure 3-35 shows this.
- Screen capture. WindowDOS includes a simple memory resident program to capture text screens. It can only store the screens in a format used by Basic or as a collection of ASCII characters. You can edit this ASCII file using most word processors.

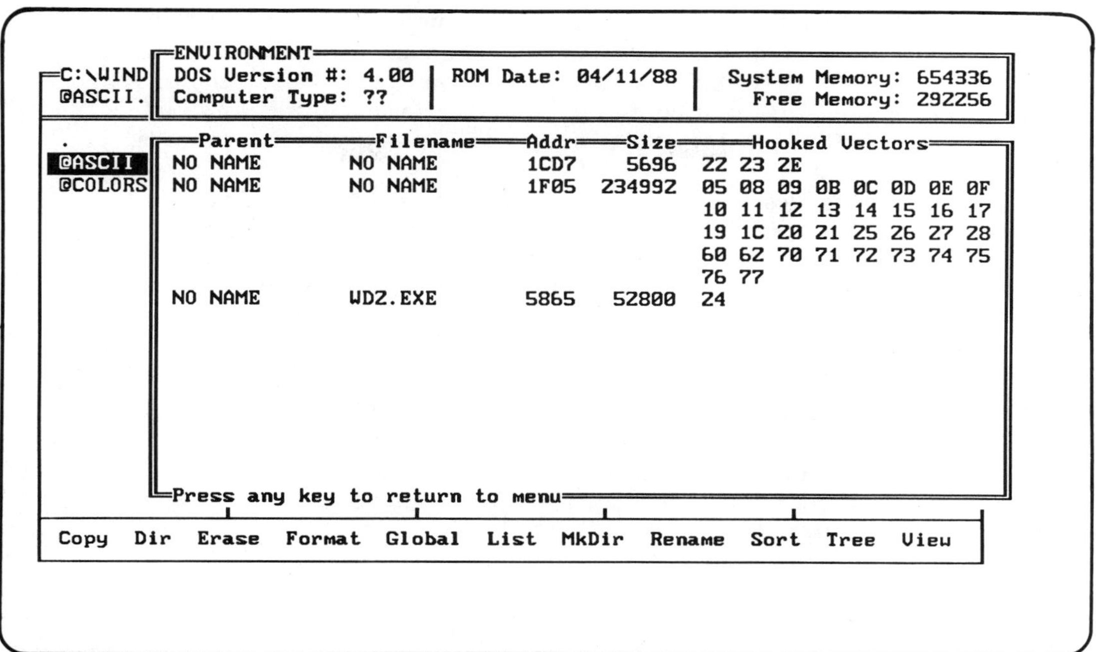

Fig. 3-34. WindowDOS can display information about the DOS environment, including the memory resident programs loaded and the vector they hook.

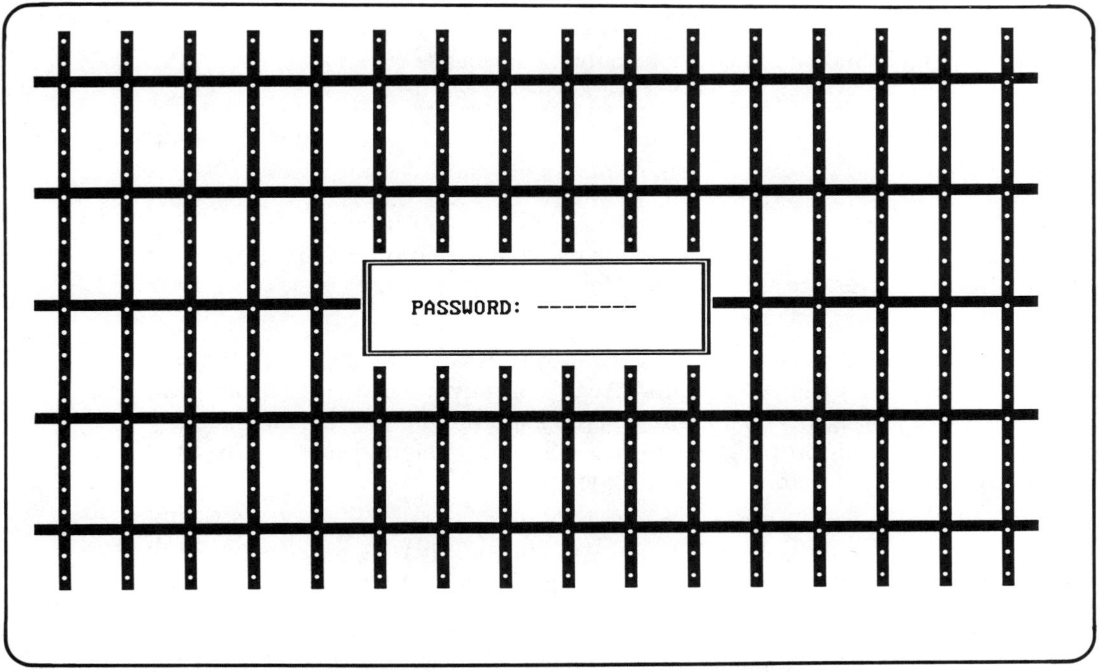

Fig. 3-35. WindowDOS can lock your computer until the password you designate is entered.

Limitations   WindowDOS has a tree command for displaying a tree diagram of the hard disk. It has, however, far less capacity than any other DOS shell. It was only able to list 82 of the subdirectories on my hard disk. Most programs did not hit their limit until well beyond 200 subdirectories. In memory resident mode, WindowDOS locks up when you try to display a tree that exceeds its capacity.

You can list all the files on a disk matching a file specification and you can even delete them all. However, you cannot tag them individually for deletion. If you only want to delete some of them, you will have to write down their location and delete them individually. I pressed control-break while WindowDOS was listing all the files. It immediately kicked me out to DOS.

Manual   The manual does a good job of explaining how to use WindowDOS.

Conclusion   WindowDOS is an acceptable stand-alone DOS shell. It offers a reasonable tradeoff between features, complexity and price. WindowDOS is the only memory resident DOS shell I covered. It functions identically as a memory resident program so you give up no features. You do, however, give up memory other programs could be using.

```
Product:      WindowDOS
Price:        $49.95
Category:     Commercial
Publisher:    WindowDOS Associates
Address:      Post Office Box 300488
              Arlington, Texas 76010
Phone:        (817) 467-4103
Memory:       53K in memory resident mode
              256K in stand-alone mode
```

XTreePro

XTreePro is a powerful yet easy to use DOS shell. While not as fully featured as some of the other shells, it performs all of the common functions with grace. The user interface is so straightforward that you may never need the manual.

Installation   XTreePro includes an automatic installation menu. It has one unusual quirk. If you want to install XTreePro in any subdirectory other than the default, you must exit the installation program and create the subdirectory yourself. The installation program for a DOS shell designed to simplify DOS cannot create a subdirectory for installation!

Operation   When you start XTreePro, it first reads the entire hard disk structure into memory. This is not a trivial task. On my 16 MHz Model 70 with a 130 Meg hard disk and four thousand plus files, this took almost 15 seconds.

XTreePro comes up with the main menu. Figure 3-36 shows this. The screen is in eight different parts:

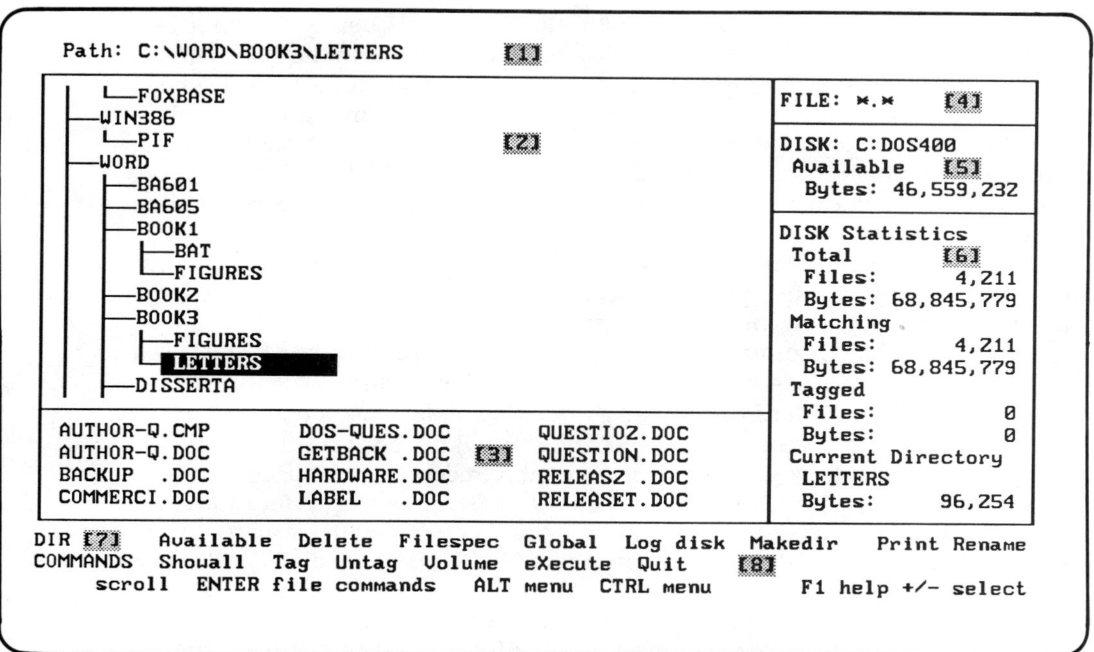

Fig. 3-36. The Xtree screen is divided into eight parts. Each part provides the user with specific information about the state of their hard disk.

1) PATH Line. This line indicates the PATH that XTreePro is currently working in.

2) Directory Window. This is a very nice representation of the structure of your hard disk. The root directory is at the top. It sorts the remaining directories and lists them below the root directory. It indents each sub-directory from and connected to its parent.

3) File Window. This lists all (or as many as will fit) the files that match the file specification.

4) File Specification Box. This is where you list the types of files you want shown in the File Window. The program allows wildcards.

5) Disk Specification Box. This shows the disk label and the available space.

6) Statistics Box. This shows a great deal of summary statistics. These include the total number of files and their size, the number of files that matched the file specification and their size, the number of files tagged and their size, and the size of the current directory.

7) Command Menu. This area is where XTreePro displays the available commands. These commands vary depending on which window the cursor is in.

8) Prompt Line. This line displays additional, and usually advanced, options.

You toggle between the Directory and File Windows using the enter key. Press enter while in the Directory Window and you move into the File Window for the subdirectory currently highlighted. This window displays twelve files. Press enter again and you get a larger version of the File Window that displays almost sixty files. Either window can be scrolled to show additional information. You can change the information in several of the smaller boxes using menu options. For example, XTreePro lets you update the file specification and volume label.

XTreePro has a global command that lets you display all the files on your system matching the file specification. You can, for example, display all the batch (.BAT) files on your hard disk. However, there is more. XTreePro can log onto more than one drive at a time. You could, therefore, display all the batch files on your hard disk, A-drive, and an external Bernoulli drive. You can tag files in either the standard display or global display for easy operation on all files. Using the global command, you could display, tag, and delete all the backup (.BAK) files on your hard disk to quickly recover extra space.

When working with a file subset, XTreePro lets you use up to four file specifications rather than a single one. You could display all the files you could run (.BAT, .EXE, and .COM) or all your graphics (.PCX, .IMG, and .PIC) files, for example.

XTreePro has a shell command that lets you enter and execute DOS commands from within XTreePro. However, the 208K required by XTreePro means you will only be able to run programs with small memory requirements. Using this method of entering commands, XTreePro allows you to recall and edit your last fifteen commands.

Learning to use XTreePro is easy. It always shows all the options in Command Menu. You either press the first letter of the command or press the control or alternate to bring up a secondary menu. No complex commands or keystrokes to learn here.

In addition to disk management, XTreePro includes a nice ASCII file editor. You access it using the edit command. It uses the WordStar command set so most users will feel comfortable with it. It proved to be great for editing batch files.

Limitations   The big limitation of XTreePro is its own power. It is possible to delete a bunch of files with an errant keystroke or two. However, DOS shares that problem. Many users can attest to the damage caused as the result of a DEL *.* command.

Manual   The manual is very good. It starts with a XTreePro tutorial and then has a reference section. The clear user interface of XTreePro and the on-line help mean that you will not be consulting the manual often.

Conclusion   This is one of the best shell programs, and the price reflects that. If cost is no object, the XTreePro is probably your best bet.

```
Product:    XTreePro
Price:      $129.95
Category:   Commercial
Publisher:  XTree Company
Address:    4330 Santa Fe Road
            San Luisobispo, California
            93401
Phone:      (800) 634-5545
            (800) 551-5353 in California
            (805) 541-0604
Notes:      Owner of XTree can upgrade to
            XTreePro for $45

            Owners of any competing
            commercially-available DOS
            shell can upgrade to XTeePro
            for $69

            A network version of XTreePro
            called XTreeNet is available for
            $395
Memory:     60K
```

XTree

XTree is a reduced version of XTreePro. The differences between them are:

- XTree does not use the DOS XCOPY command.
- XTree cannot print the contents of an ASCII file.
- XTree cannot change the volume label.
- XTree cannot change the date and time.
- XTreePro can log up to 26-drives while XTree can only log a single drive. XTreePro logs files up to seven times faster than XTree.
- XTree does not support ASCII and hexadecimal editing of files.
- XTreePro includes a multiple file specification capability. That makes it possible to display and work with up to four groups of files at one time while XTree does not.

Other than these differences, XTree and XTreePro are identical.

```
Product:    XTree
Price:      $69.95
Category:   Commercial
Publisher:  XTree Company
Address:    4330 Santa Fe Road
            San Luisobispo, California
            93401
Phone:      (800) 634-5545
            (800) 551-5353 in California
            (805) 541-0604
Memory:     60K
```

ALSO SEE. . .

DOSShell DOSShell is the menu and DOS shell program included free with DOS 4.x. I covered it in the last chapter. It is a good menu program and an excellent DOS shell. In fact, if you are purchasing DOS 4.x, there is no reason for you to consider any other menu or DOS shell program.

DS Manager The menu program *DS Manager,* covered in the last chapter has a DOS shell built in. It will perform most of the features of the DOS shells in this chapter. Its major limitation is an inability to manage more than one hundred subdirectories. If you have more than one hundred, DS Manager will not be able to access any beyond one hundred for any of its actions.

Magic Menus The menu program *Magic Menus,* covered in the last chapter, has a DOS shell built in. While not as good as some of the better shells in this chapter, it does include a full menu program and is modestly priced.

Point 'N Shoot Pop Up Menus *Point 'N Shoot Pop Up Menus* lets you perform many of the DOS commands using a mouse working with a custom menu. I covered it in the *Programs That Replace or Enhance DOS Commands and Functions chapter.*

PreCursor The *PreCursor* menu program includes a menu for performing most of the functions of a DOS shell. The PreCursor menu makes it somewhat more difficult to tag and untag files than do these DOS shells. Otherwise, the PreCursor is an acceptable DOS shell.

XD *XD* is a shareware program from ButtonWare. It has many of the features found in these DOS shells. It also gives you a choice. You can select the command to use by working through a menu or you can enter the command at the command line. I covered it in the *Programs That Replace or Enhance DOS Commands and Functions* chapter.

TakeTwo Plus *TakeTwo Plus* is a backup program. Its primary function is to store the data on your hard disk onto a set of floppies. That way, you can recover that data if anything happens to your hard disk. TakeTwo Plus also includes an acceptable DOS shell. I covered TakeTwo Plus in the Backup chapter.

RONNY'S PICKS

I have a copy of DOS 4.01 from IBM. After using the DOSShell program that comes with DOS for several months, I believe it is every bit as good as the commercial DOS shells. If you have DOS 4.x, then you have an excellent DOS shell and do not need to consider any other. If you are considering purchasing a DOS shell, then you should strongly consider spending that money on DOS 4.x. You would upgrade your DOS and get a free DOS shell in the bargain.

If, for some reason, you do not want to upgrade to DOS 4.x, then the Norton Commander is the best DOS shell available. It has full mouse support, the ability to display dBASE files and the ability to display Lotus files. Only the mouse support is available in a few other packages. If you do not use SUBSTed drives, then PC Shell is an excellent DOS shell made even better because it is only a small portion of PC Tools Deluxe. It offers a menu program, however it is weak.

If you are looking for a DOS shell and menu program in a single package, then Point & Shoot The Hard Disk Manager is an excellent choice. Its menus are as good as most menu programs and its DOS shell is excellent. Its low price is also attractive.

_________________Part Two_________________

File and Disk

Maintenance

____

4
File Maintenance

Your DOS disk comes with very few programs to actually maintain your computer files. However, a number of vendors have developed packages that greatly expand the file maintenance capabilities of DOS. The major features to look for are:

- File unerasing. When DOS erases a file, it does not remove the data from the disk. Rather, it just marks the space as free. The actual data stays on the disk until DOS uses that space to save another file. Anytime before that, you can recover the file (unerase it) by reconstructing the directory and file allocation table entries. While that sounds difficult, many programs will do it for you.
- Subdirectory unerasing. A subdirectory is nothing more than a special type of file. If the subdirectory has never had more than 62 files in it, then it is only a 2K file. On most systems that is one cluster so recover should be very easy.
- Unformatting. Many of these programs can do this, some better than others. Unformatting is covered in Chapter 7.
- Directory sorting. You can get a sorted directory in DOS by piping the output of the DIR command through SORT.EXE. However, DOS only shows this on the screen. The directory on the disk remains the same. Many programs can actually change the order DOS stores the directory entries on disk.
- Moving files. With DOS, your only alternative for moving files to a different location on the same disk is to copy the file to a new target. Once you have copied the file, you delete the original. This has three disadvantages. First,

it is error prone. You can end up deleting the original even if you copied it incorrectly. Second, until you delete the original it ties up twice the space of the file since two copies exist. For crowded drives and/or large files there may not even be enough room for two copies. Finally, it is slow especially for large files. Many programs add a move command that leaves the file alone and just changes the directory information. This is quick, safe, takes the same time for any size file and does not need any extra space.

These are just a few of the more popular features these packages offer. Most of them make it much easier to manage your files.

DS Recover

DS Recover is a commercial program that makes it easy to recover files erased accidentally. It also recovers from a formatted hard disk and a power failure.

Installation   The manual tells you to copy all the files to a subdirectory on your hard disk. There is no installation program to do this for you. The manual explains how to set up an environmental variable to point to the DS Recover files. However, the manual does not explain how to deal with an error message indicating the environment is full. The SET command is typeset in such a manner it appears as though you should include extra spaces in the command. If you enter these extra spaces, DS Recover will not understand its environment variable.

Operation   You invoke the DS Recover protection with the command:

SENTRY ON

This loads a 7K memory resident program. While the DS Recover Sentry program is active, you cannot "really" delete any files. Any time you delete a file with the DEL or ERASE commands Sentry converts it to a hidden file with a name like KR000023.SAV. As a hidden file, it does not show up on a directory.

To unerase files, you run the DS Recover Recovery program. The Recovery program lists all the files in the current subdirectory that you have deleted. Figure 4-1 shows this. The "Protected" files were files you deleted while Sentry was active. Notice it lists the entire file name. The "Unprotected" files were files you deleted while Sentry was inactive.

Recovering a protected file is as easy as highlighting it and pressing return. That is what you would expect. DOS never erased the protected files. All DS Recover had to do to recover them was change their name back and unhide them. There is also a Purge program to permanently erase files protected by Sentry. You recover unprotected files using the same method, except you must provide the first letter of the file name.

DS Recover includes a program to recover a hard disk after formatting. Chapter 7 on unformatting a hard disk provides more details.

DS Recover comes with a program called Snapshot. Snapshot is a memory resident program that saves the contents of your memory every thirty sec-

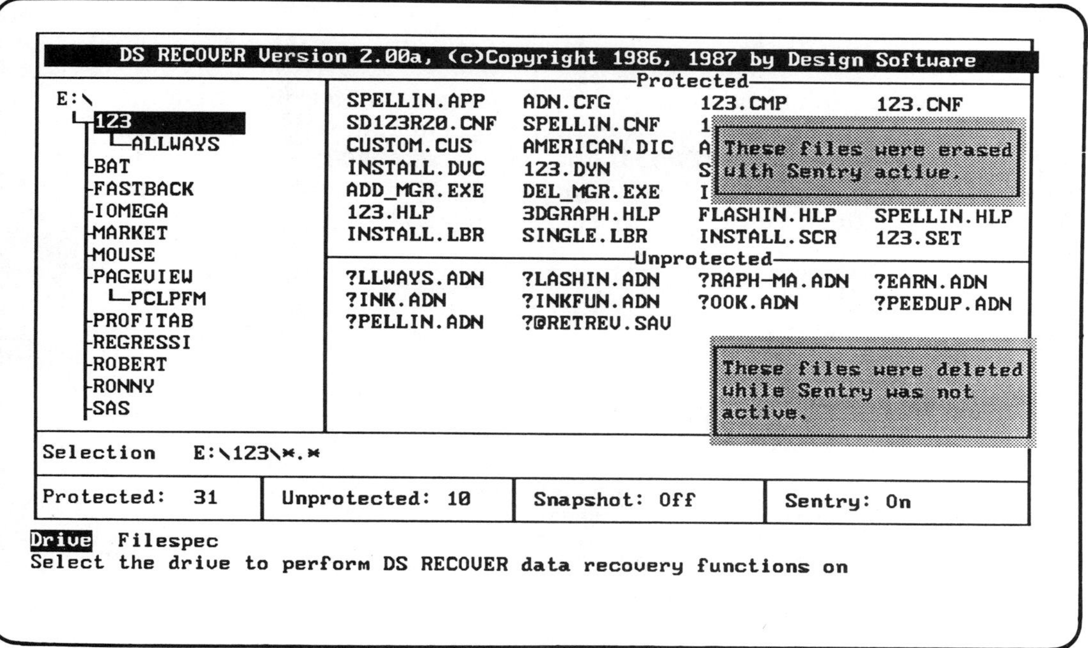

Fig. 4-1. The DS Recover recovery program lists all the files in the current subdirectory that have been deleted. The "Protected" files were deleted while Sentry was active. The "Unprotected" files were deleted while Sentry was inactive.

onds. If you accidentally reboot, lose power or the computer locks up, you can restore the system to the state it was in at the last Snapshot save.

Limitations   DS Recover has far fewer tools to unerase files that you erased while Sentry was inactive than other utilities in this chapter. It only runs in automatic mode. Sometimes it indicates that it restored files even when it restored them improperly. That can give users a false sense of security. Other times it refused to restore a file because the first cluster was in use. No program can restore all of a file with its first cluster in use by another file. However, programs like the Norton Utilities will let you look for some data to restore. That may be worthwhile with a text file.

When the Sentry program is running, it takes much longer than normal to delete files.

Manual   The manual is about five inches square and printed in small print. While it is small and hard to see, it does a good job of explaining how to use DS Recover.

Conclusion   The format recovery routine in DS Recover is as good as the ones with the other programs and is covered in detail in Chapter 7. The unerasing program will only work on unprotected files that have not had any of their clusters overwritten. If you are willing to get back only part of the file, you will need another program. The Snapshot program is a nice program if you have frequent power failures.

The key feature of DS Recover is its Sentry program. That memory resident program hides files anytime you try to erase them. You then have the option of recovering these files easily or purging them from your system. This approach is based on the assumption that most erasures are accidental and you will want to recover them. If you only occasionally try to recover an erased file, you will just find that this feature gets in the way.

```
Product:     DS Recover
Price:       $49.95
Category:    Commercial
Publisher:   Design Software, Incorporated
Address:     19808 Nordhoff Place
             Chatsworth, California 91311
Phone:       (800) 231-3088
             (818) 885-9000
Notes:       Not DOS 4.x Compatible
Memory:      7K     Sentry
             6K     Snapshot
             256K   DS Recover
```

Helpme

Helpme tests a number of systems attributes and reports on the results of those tests. Much of this information is very useful and not available from any other program.

Installation   The manual instructs you to copy all the files to the root directory or a subdirectory you create. There is no batch file provided to automate this. You should always install programs in a subdirectory and not in the root directory. The manual does not explain how to create a subdirectory.

Operation   Helpme is extremely easy to use. You enter HELPME at the DOS prompt to run the programs. Most of the time, the various screens simply require you to press a key. You press enter return after reading the report to continue, the end key to skip the remainder of that report or the "w" key to write suggested changes to your disk.

Figures 4-2 through 4-6 show some of the information provided by Helpme.

1) Figure 4-2 shows the Helpme CONFIG.SYS test. Note that Helpme reports that the new INSTALL and REM commands introduced in DOS 4.0 are invalid.
2) Figure 4-3 shows the Helpme map of disk usage. This map clearly shows the disk needs to be optimized. The map is not complete, again illustrating Helpme's incompatibility with DOS 4.01.
3) Figure 4-4 shows Helpme listing all the hidden and read only files.
4) Figure 4-5 shows Helpme listing duplicate file names across subdirectories.

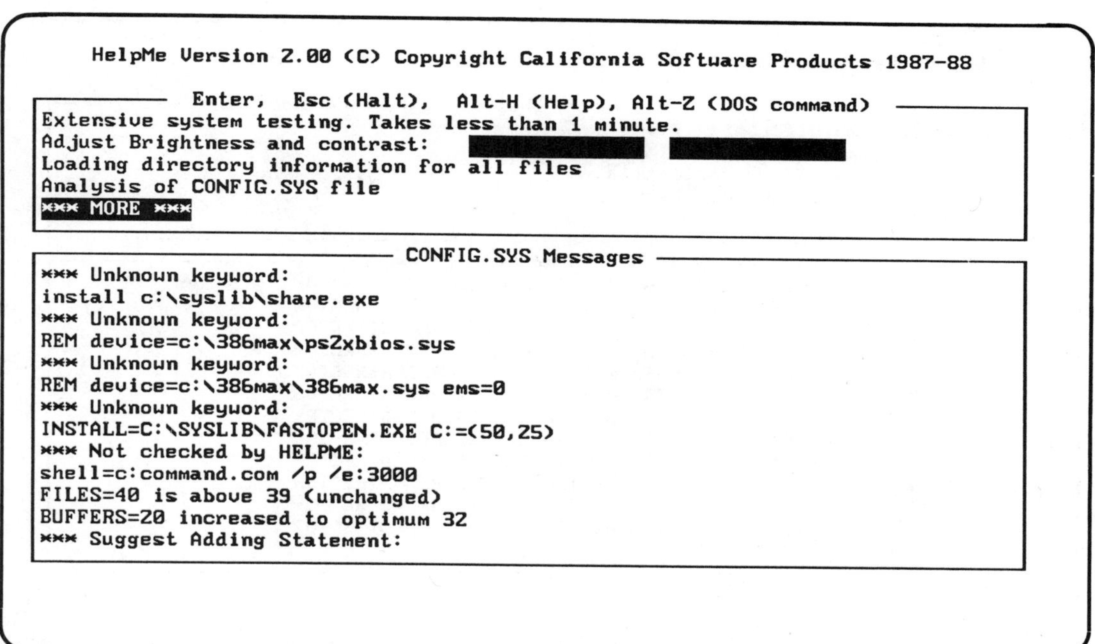

Fig. 4-2. The Helpme CONFIG.SYS test. Note that Helpme reports that the new INSTALL and REM commands introduced in DOS 4.0 are invalid.

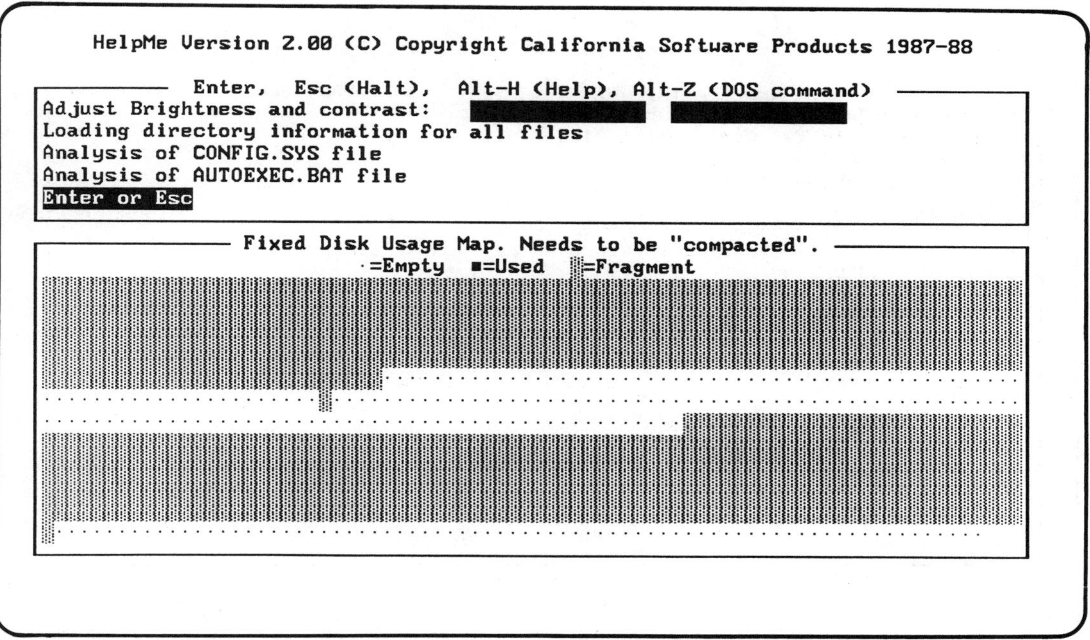

Fig. 4-3. The Helpme map of disk usage. This map clearly shows the disk needs to be optimized. The map is not complete, again illustrating Helpme's incompatibility with DOS 4.01.

```
HelpMe Version 2.00 (C) Copyright California Software Products 1987-88

 ───── Enter,  Esc (Halt),  Alt-H (Help),  Alt-Z (DOS command) ─────
Checking for Empty (0 byte) files
Checking for Invalid DATE & TIME fields
Checking for Invalid characters in name
Checking for Hidden or Read-Only files
xxx MORE xxx

 ───────────────── Hidden or Read-Only files ─────────────────
01        DIR       263     9-15-86    05:54p  C:\DISCARD\DIRECTOR
02        DIR       345     9-15-86    05:54p  C:\DISCARD\DIRECTOR
03        DIR      2509     9-15-86    05:55p  C:\DISCARD\DIRECTOR
04        DIR      4671     9-15-86    05:56p  C:\DISCARD\DIRECTOR
05        DIR      3903     9-15-86    05:57p  C:\DISCARD\DIRECTOR
06        DIR      3863     9-15-86    06:03p  C:\DISCARD\DIRECTOR
07        DIR       550     9-15-86    06:05p  C:\DISCARD\DIRECTOR
08        DIR      1698     9-15-86    06:06p  C:\DISCARD\DIRECTOR
09        DIR      3871     9-15-86    06:07p  C:\DISCARD\DIRECTOR
10        DIR       386     9-15-86    06:10p  C:\DISCARD\DIRECTOR
11        DIR      2518     9-17-86    04:48p  C:\DISCARD\DIRECTOR
12        DIR       591     9-17-86    04:48p  C:\DISCARD\DIRECTOR
123       EXE      7680     1-01-80    12:04a  C:\123
```

Fig. 4-4. Helpme listing all the hidden and read-only files.

```
HelpMe Version 2.00 (C) Copyright California Software Products 1987-88

 ───── Enter,  Esc (Halt),  Alt-H (Help),  Alt-Z (DOS command) ─────
Checking for Unusable PIF files
Checking for Selected Application files
Checking for DOS Version Information
Checking for Subdirectories with duplicate files
Enter or Esc

 ───────────────── Subdirectories with duplicate files ─────────────────
54   C:\WORD\BOOK2
28   C:\WORD\BOOK1
26   C:\WORD\BOOK3
21   C:\COMIC
17   C:\WORD\BOOK1\BAT
17   C:\COMIC\REAL
15   C:\COMPRESS
15   C:\HIJAAK
14   C:\SHOW
12   C:\WAMPUM\DBASE
12   C:\WAMPUM\CLIPPER
10   C:\WORDSTAR
10   C:\SYSLIB
```

Fig. 4-5. Helpme listing duplicate file names across subdirectories.

```
HelpMe Version 2.00 (C) Copyright California Software Products 1987-88

┌─────────── Enter,  Esc (Halt),  Alt-H (Help), Alt-Z (DOS command) ───────────┐
│ Checking for Subdirectories with duplicate files                             │
│ Duplicate names (hit End to skip)                                            │
│ IBM PS2 Adapter Information                                                   │
│ Non Standard conditions                                                      │
│ ▓▓▓ MORE ▓▓▓                                                                  │
└──────────────────────────────────────────────────────────────────────────────┘
┌───────────────────────────── Non Standard conditions ───────────────────────┐
│  1e.Multiple copies of command processor COMMAND COM                         │
│  2d.PS/2 Mouse                                                               │
│  4a.Enhanced Graphics Adapter(256 kb)+EnhDisplay                            │
│  7a.Extended diskette parameter support (INT13/AH=8)                        │
│      and table size (at INT1E) more than 11 bytes                           │
│  7b.Enhanced Keyboard Installed                                             │
│  7d.Model Code=F8,4  BIOS Level=2                                           │
│      BIOS uses DMA3,Cascaded IRQ2,Real Time Clock,Keyboard Hook            │
│ 12b.Media descriptor is not F8(fixed disk)                                  │
│ 12d.INT25 read(logical) does not call INT13(physical IO)                    │
│ 16a.Mouse driver installed.  Buttons=2                                      │
│ 19a.BREAK ON.  Any DOS call.  Unsafe for some programs.                     │
│ 21b.File Allocation Table (FAT) is not available  ◄──────  ┌───────────┐    │
│                                                            │ DOS 4.01  │    │
│                                                            │Incompatible│   │
│                                                            └───────────┘    │
└──────────────────────────────────────────────────────────────────────────────┘
```

Fig. 4-6. Helpme listing any conditions if found to be non-standard.

5) Figure 4-6 shows Helpme listing any conditions if found to be non-standard.

In addition to this main program, Helpme contains four other useful programs:

1) Browse. This program lists ASCII files to the screen. You can scroll forwards or backwards in the file.

2) Cfile. This program lists non-ASCII files to the screen. You can scroll forwards or backwards in the file. Figure 4-7 shows this.

3) Checka. This program tests floppy diskettes for read errors. This is a non-destructive test that only checks for read errors.

4) Checkhd. This program tests hard disks for read errors. This is a nondestructive test that only checks for read errors.

Limitations   As pointed out above, Helpme is not fully compatible with DOS 4.x. It runs, but some of the tests do not work properly. This is a minor limitation.

A more important limitation is Helpme's habit of occasionally "locking up" the computer. I performed most of the tests using an IBM Model 70 and Helpme worked flawlessly. I ran a few tests on an IBM Model 80 and a Compaq Deskpro 386. The Model 80 locked up once. The Compaq locked up every time I ran Helpme.

The manual discusses system crashes and quite correctly points out that many crashes are not the fault of Helpme. The programs make extensive use

```
File: C:helpme.exe  Sector = 30

0100: 8B 46 FE 89 46 FC 8B 46-FC 40 40 1E 50 E8 1C FF   |.F..F..F.@@.P...|
0110: 8B 76 FC 8B 04 89 46 FE-EB E0 8B E5 5D CB 55 8B   |.v....F.....].U.|
0120: EC 81 EC 04 00 A1 CA BB-89 46 FC 83 7E FC 01 72   |.........F..~..r|
0130: 52 C7 46 FE 01 00 B8 0C-00 F7 66 FE 97 83 C7 FC   |R.F.......f.....|
0140: C4 1E C2 BB 03 DF 8B D7-8B FB BE BB CA B9 03 00   |................|
0150: FC F3 A6 74 0D C4 1E C2-BB 8B F2 26 8B 00 3C 7E   |...t.......&..<~|
0160: 75 14 B8 0C 00 F7 66 FE-05 F4 FF C4 1E C2 BB 03   |u.....f.........|
0170: D8 06 53 E8 B6 FE 8B 46-FE 40 89 46 FE 48 3B 46   |..S....F.@.F.H;F|
0180: FC 75 B3 8B E5 5D CB 55-8B EC 81 EC 02 00 8B 46   |.u...].U.......F|
0190: 06 48 48 8B 76 04 8B D0-8B 44 E6 32 E4 F7 E2 3B   |.HH.v....D.2...;|
01A0: 76 04 8B 74 0A 03 44 0B-8B 76 04 03 44 F5 89 46   |v..t..D..v..D..F|
01B0: FE 8B 46 FE 8B E5 5D C2-04 00 55 8B EC 81 EC 02   |..F...]...U.....|
01C0: 00 8B 46 06 89 46 FE 8B-76 FE 8B 7E 04 8B 4D F8   |..F..F..v..~..M.|
01D0: 8B 46 08 33 D2 F7 F1 89-04 8B 46 08 33 D2 F7 F1   |.F.3.....F.3...|
01E0: 8B 7E 04 92 8B 4D F1 33-D2 F7 F1 89 44 02 8B 46   |.~...M.3....D..F|
01F0: 08 33 D2 F7 F1 42 89 54-04 8B E5 5D C2 06 00 55   |.3...B.T...]...U|


Esc-Exit    Home-First    End-Last    PgUp-Prev    PgDn-Next
```

Fig. 4-7. Using the Cfile program to look at the contents of a non-ASCII file.

of the hardware for testing and can find problems you would not normally encounter. I expect that the Compaq crashes were the result of a hardware problem since they always occurred during the same test.

Manual   The manual explains Helpme well. It contains a number of screen shots and illustrations. All that is missing is an index.

Conclusion   Helpme provides extensive tests simply not performed by any other program. Running Helpme once a week is an excellent way to spot problems early.

```
Product:      Helpme
Price:        $99
Category:     Commercial
Publisher:    California Software Products
Address:      525 North Cabrillo Park Drive
              Santa Ana, California 92701
Phone:        (714) 973-0440
Memory:       256K
```

Mace Utilities Gold

The *Mace Utilities Gold* are a collection of utilities very similar to the Norton Utilities Advanced Edition. Mace came on the scene later than Norton.

However, both Mace and Norton are currently locked in a battle for first place in the disk utility market. When Mace adds a nifty feature, Norton clones. When Norton adds something new, Mace clones it. The real winners are the users of both programs.

Installation   The Mace Utilities Gold comes with an installation program. It expects to run from the A-drive. The ASSIGN A = B command causes it to work properly. The installation program can modify your AUTOEXEC.BAT file to include the Mace directory in the PATH. It can also add the format recovery command.   The installation program prompts you before modifying the AUTOEXEC.BAT file so you can stop it if you like.

Operation   The Mace Utilities comes with the following utilities:

FindFile. FindFile should find files matching a specific file specification. For example, the command: FINDFILE C: *.BAK should find all the *.BAK files on the C-drive. This is identical to the Norton FileFind program. However, the Mace program would not work on my computer. In addition, the manual says to use the FINDFILE command as I show above. However, no such program exists. The real program name is FFIND.EXE.

Format-F. This is a safe formatting program for floppy diskettes. Unlike the menu-driven Norton formatting program, Format-F is command-line driven. Like Norton, it formats without deleting data. You can recover any data that is accidentally formatted over using the Mace Utilities Gold.

Format-H. This is a safe formatting program for hard disks. It only erases the file allocation table and root directory. If a hard disk is accidentally formatted using Format-H, you can restore it using the Mace Utilities Gold.

Fragchk. Fragchk checks the hard disk for file fragmentation. It first reports on technical information about the hard disk then it lists every single fragmented file. After the report finishes running, it lists some summary information.

Vaccine. This program helps protect your system against viruses. Chapter 17 covers this.

Mcache. Mcache is a caching program. Chapter 10 covers this.

Mkeyrate. Mkeyrate is a program that controls how fast keyboard characters repeat and how soon they begin repeating. It only works with AT and PS/2 computers.

Mace Utilities Sector Editor [MUSE]. MUSE is a sector editor for your disks. Think of it as a word processor for your disk. It lets you edit the sectors in either ASCII or Hexadecimal. First, you select a subdirectory containing the file you wish to edit. This brings up a list of files. You move to the file to edit and press Alt-I. That brings up a combination ASCII/hexadecimal listing of the file. Figure 4-8 shows this. Using the Alt-x and Alt-a commands, you can switch between editing in ASCII or hexadecimal.

While editing a file, MUSE offers four views of that file:

1) The file view. This is the combination ASCII/hexadecimal view shown above.

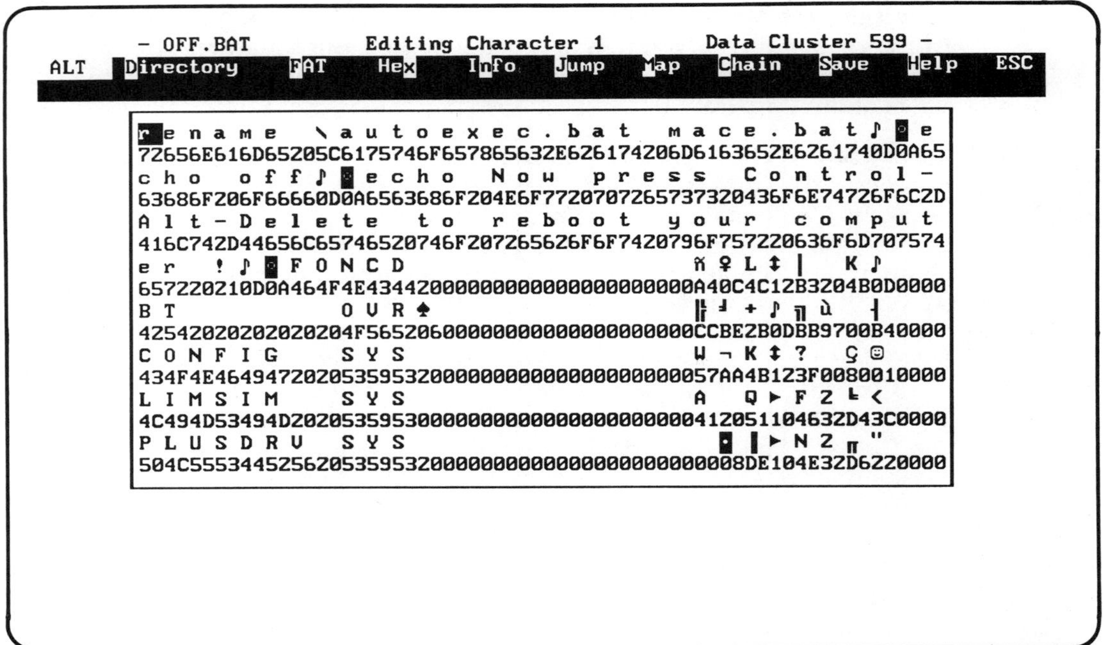

Fig. 4-8. Once you have selected a file, the Mace Utilities Sector Editor lets you edit that file in either ASCII or hexadecimal.

2) The directory view. This shows the directory entry for this file. Not only does it display the directory entry, but also it allows you to edit it. Figure 4-9 shows this.
3) The file allocation table [FAT] view. This shows the chain of FAT entries associated with the file and allows you to edit the chain. Figure 4-10 shows this.
4) The map view. This shows a map of the hard disk and points out the location of every file. This is the only view where you cannot edit the information.

MUSE can read drives that DOS refuses to read, e.g., the "Invalid drive specification" error message. It can also dump the information to another drive. As a result, you can use MUSE to recover information from drives DOS no longer recognizes.

Park. This moves the heads of your hard disk to a safe area. That way, if the computer gets bumped the heads will not crash into the spinning disk and destroy data. Issuing the PARK command once parks the heads on all the hard disks.

Remedy. Remedy will test the hard disk for errors. Depending on which mode Remedy is running in, it can also correct the errors it finds. Before it runs, Remedy always runs the DOS CHKDSK program first.

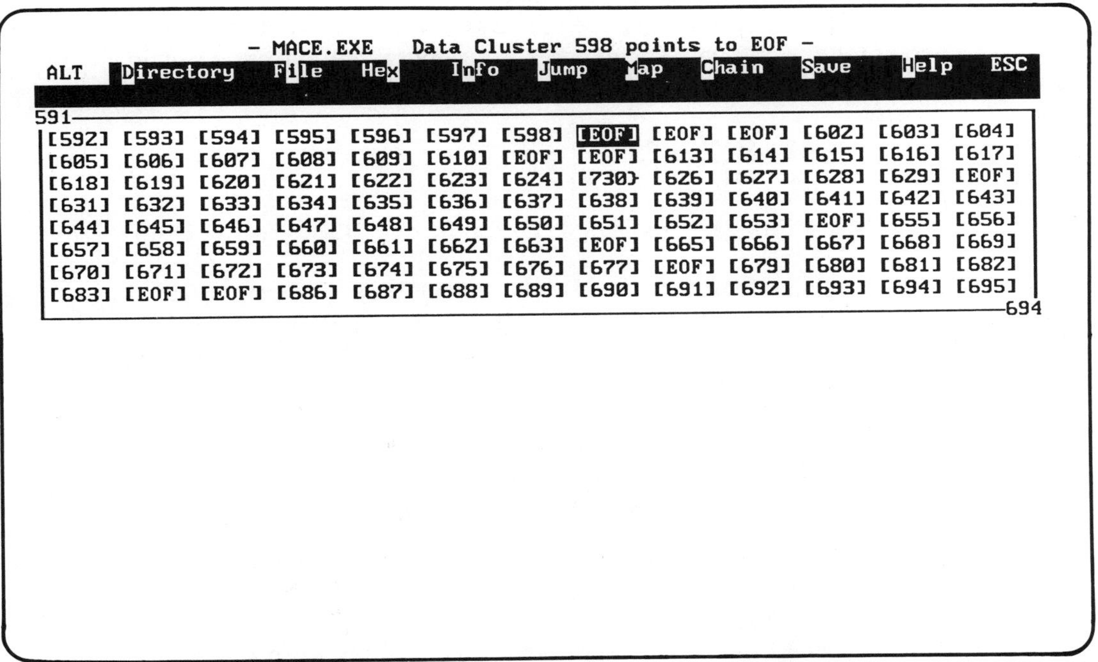

Fig. 4-9. The Mace Utilities Sector Editor directory view allows you to edit the directory entry for a file.

Fig. 4-10. The Mace Utilities Sector Editor file allocation table view shows the chain of FAT entries associated with the file and allows you to edit the chain.

As Remedy runs, it displays a map of the hard disk. As it tests different files, different areas of the hard disk map change colors. So in addition to testing your hard disk, Remedy puts on quite a show.

RxBak. This program copies the boot sector, file allocation table and root directory for Mace Utilities Gold to use when unformatting a hard disk. Chapter 7 covers this.

Sortd. This program sorts the directory entries into order. You have a choice of four orders:

1) Sorted by name order.
2) Sorted by extension order.
3) Sorted by date and time.
4) Sorted by size.

You can add a minus sign to any of these to reverse the sorting order. Unlike Norton's Dirsort program, Sortd remembers the last order you entered and uses it if you do not enter one after the program name.

Sqzd. This program squeezes directories by removing all entries for erased files. Because DOS searches all directory entries for certain commands, this can substantially speed up some operations. However, you will not be able to unerase files automatically after running Sqzd since no information on the erased files remains in the directory. As a result, you should wait and only run Sqzd after performing a backup.

Systat. This displays technical information about the computer.

Undelete. The Undelete program works exactly opposite to the DOS DEL command. With DEL, you must enter the file name to recover. With Undelete, you must also enter the file name to recover. It supports full paths and wild cards. If one is available, Undelete uses the BACKUP.M_U file created by RxBak to unformat a disk.

Unformat. Chapter 7 covers this.

UnFrag. Chapter 8 covers this.

The Gold   The *Mace Utilities Gold* adds the following utilities to the Mace Utilities:

dbFix. For some reason, dBASE *.DBF database files are extremely accident prone. Many times, for almost no reason, they seem to go south. One minute they will have 10,000 records and the next they will have 10. Or dBASE will not be able to read the records at all.

Part of the problem is the format of the .DBF file. It begins with a header that contains specific information about the file. Following that are the records in a fixed length format. Add one byte in the wrong place and all the records after that one byte are out of place and therefore improper to dBASE.

dbFix has two modes of operation. The first mode is Restore. You use that to correct problems with existing dBASE files. The second mode is Recover. You use that to recover erased dBASE database files. It ignores directory information and searches the hard disk for dBASE database headers.

To test dbFix, I loaded a large 1 Meg database file into my word processor. Then I added one byte (an ASCII value 027) near the top of the file. All of the records after the addition are offset. That causes the information to be incorrect so dBASE cannot use the database properly.

When you select the Restore command, dbFix prompts you for the disk drive. It then shows all the database files on the entire drive for you to select from. Figure 4-11 shows this. Once you have selected a database, dbFix gives you the options to:

- Examine the header information. dBASE has a fixed format for the header and it must be exactly correct.
- Check file integrity by record. dbFix will go through and check all the records for corruption. You can have it list all the files to the screen in several formats or only list the corrupted records. This failed to find any problems with the corrupted database in my test.
- Salvage a damaged file to another disk. This copies the file to another drive and gives you the option of correcting the header. This did correct the problem with the above file.
- Automatic salvaging. This works just like the salvage option above except that the program does not stop to show you problem records.

dbFix was also able to handle scrambled headers. It shows you the data and you have to point out the individual fields. It uses the information you provide along with what information remains in the header to reconstruct the header.

Backup/Verify/Restore. The Mace backup program proved to be completely inoperative on PS/2 computers. It uses a proprietary disk format. It would format and write to the disks properly until it reached track 72. At that

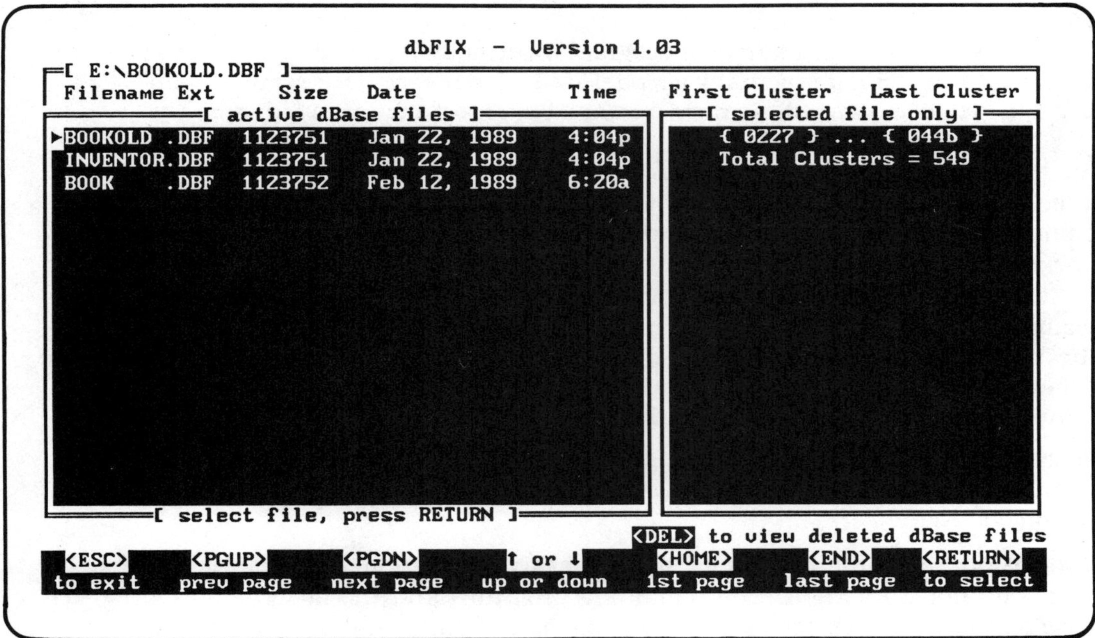

Fig. 4-11. dbFix lists all the dBASE database files on your hard disk for you to select from.

point it would begin flashing an error message to close the drive door. This in spite of the drive door being closed. Nothing would cause the program to proceed beyond track 72 of the first disk. I verified this problem on other PS/2 computers.

Power Out Protector [POP]. This is a nifty 10K memory resident program. It saves the contents of your RAM and video RAM and preset intervals between one and sixty minutes. If there is a power failure while you are working on something, you can recover. POP restores your computer to its state at the last POP save. If you were working on something, you can go ahead and save it once POP restores the memory.

TextFix. This is a file recovery program aimed specifically at word processing documents. It automatically recognizes the format for many word processors. Like dbFix, it has a number of features for reconstructing text documents. It can also search through the disk for text information not referenced under DOS.

Limitations   The FindFile program was not properly documented in the manual. It does not work anyway. The PARK command tries to park the heads on all the hard disks on your system including the pseudo-hard disks created with the DOS SUBST command. The Sortd directory sorting program runs much slower than the Norton Dirsort program.

On my 130 Meg hard disk with about 210 subdirectories, the Sqzd directory squeezing program would only squeeze the first 21 subdirectories. After that, it would stop as though it had processed all the directories. The manual gives the wrong command for the Sqzd program. It tells you to enter SORTD when you should enter SQZD.

The Systat System Statistical program incorrectly reported my computer as an IBM Model 80. It is actually a Model 70. It also reported the regular memory and lack of expanded memory but failed to report the extended memory.

The Undelete program is more difficult to use than the Norton Unerase program. With Norton, you can look at a list of all the unerased files to see which ones you want to recover. With Mace, you must list the files to recover using a file specification on the command line. That makes Norton easier to use, especially if you have trouble remembering the file name.

The dbFix program would not work on my 130 Meg hard disk. It began loading the disk information into memory and then locked up. When I copied the files to a 20 Meg Passport drive, dbFix worked properly. Sometimes when I edited with dbFix, my computer locked up with a "Memory allocation error Cannot load COMMAND, system halted" error message.

Manual   The manual does a good job of explaining how to use the Mace Utilities Gold. However, there are a number of typo's. Several places show the wrong command.

Conclusion   The manual shows signs of hasty production. Some of the programs do not work right. The remaining programs and the documentation have all the classic signs of a program rushed to market slightly ahead of its time. Mace has an excellent reputation and I feel comfortable stating that most of these problems will be corrected by the time this book is available. However that makes them no less annoying.

Most of you are probably trying to decide between Mace and Norton. On that count, I have to give a slight edge to Norton. Norton's programs have a better user interface. In addition, they have the polish the Mace's programs are currently lacking. However, from what I was able to see of the Mace backup program, once it is fixed it will be a big advantage for Mace.

Product:	Mace Utilities Gold
Price:	$149.00
Category:	Commercial
Publisher:	Paul Mace Software
Address:	400 Williamson Way
	Ashland, Oregon 97520
Phone:	(503) 488-0224
Memory:	256K

Norton Utilities

The *Norton Utilities* were one of the first disk utilities for the IBM-PC. When they first came out over five years ago, the utilities were "must buy" items for every computer owner. Like most good programs, the Norton Utilities were quickly imitated. Some added for features. Others had a lower price. Still others were free, placed in the public domain or published in various magazines.

Peter Norton has not stood still and depended on his name to sell his utilities. He has continued to improve his utilities until they have become one of the more powerful tools for a PC.

Beginning with Release 4.0, the Norton Utilities were split into two products, the Norton Utilities and the Norton Utilities Advanced Edition. The Advanced Edition contains all the tools of the regular edition plus some additional tools. This split continues with Release 4.5. Each utility is discussed below.

Installation   Prior versions of the Norton Utilities did not include an installation program. I guess the feeling was that anyone who knew how to use the utilities could figure out how to install them. That has changed. The current version has the finest installation program I have ever seen for a piece of software. Each step has pop-up screens to tell you what the program is doing and why. Several times, it stops to give you information and then asks if you want to continue, stop or just skip this step. One nice feature is at the start it searches all your disks looking for prior versions of the utilities. If it finds them, it will erase them for you, copy them to a backup directory, or simply leave them alone, all at your choice.

Operation   The Norton Utilities contain the following programs:

Ask. The last version of the utilities introduced a program called Ask. This program let a batch file prompt a user for information and set the DOS

ERRORLEVEL according to the response the user made. This new program removes ASK as a stand-alone program and incorporates it as a command in the Batch Enhancer program discussed below. Users who have incorporated the ASK command into existing batch files have two options. They can recode the batch file to use the new Batch Enhancer program or retain and continue to use the old Ask program. Either method is acceptable. The recoding required is minor. It involves adding three characters to each line using the Ask command. In addition, the old ASK program works fine under DOS 4.x and in conjunction with the new utilities.

Batch Enhancer. The Batch Enhancer, or BE for short, is a single program containing several commands to improve your batch files. You start it with the line "BE command."

The BE invokes and runs the Batch Enhancer while the Command gives BE a specific command. If you have a number of BE commands to process in a row, loading the program for each command can be very slow. In this case, you can replace Command with the name of a script file containing a set of BE commands. BE will execute each command in turn and after executing each command will return control to the batch file.

The commands added by BE are:

1) ASK. This new feature lets you get information from the user during a batch file. It returns information to the batch file by the ERRORLEVEL value, the only way DOS offers to communicate with a batch file. For more information on batch files, see my book MS-DOS Batch File Programming . . . Including OS/2. ASK has several options. They are:

   - A prompt to put on the screen.
   - A set of keys from which the user must select one. You use this for limiting choices.
   - A default key to assume if the user does not select a key in the specified time.
   - The time ASK will wait before assuming the default key.
   - Color control for the questions.
   - An offset. Experienced users can use the offset to pass the results of multiple questions back to a batch file using the single ERRORLEVEL slot available.

2) BEEP.   This sounds a beep on the computer speaker. This is useful to mark the end of a batch file or an error in a batch file. The syntax of the command allows you to control the sound frequency, duration and the wait between tones and the number of beeps. BEEP can read this information from a script file. The utilities even come with a sample script file to play "Mary Had A Little Lamb."

3) BOX.   This draws a box of specified color, location and size on the screen.

4) PRINTCHAR.   This prints a specified character a specified number of times. Useful for entering a lot of spaces without having to type each one in.

5) ROWCOL.   This positions the cursor at a specific location and prints text in a specified color.

6) WINDOW. This draws a window of specified color and size at any location on the screen. You can have the window zoom in as the program is drawn and have a shadow "behind" it.

Beep. Like Ask, Beep was incorporated into the Batch Enhancer. Like Ask, you must either retain the old Beep program or rewrite any batch files that use this program.

Directory Sort [**DS**]. This command allows you to sort a directory by name, extension, date, time, or size. You can use more than one sort key. A minus sign specifies reverse order. You can also move files within a directory around manually into any order.

Disk Information. Gives you a complete set of technical information about your disk drive. This information includes:

- The operating system used to format the disk. On my system, it is IBM DOS 4.0.
- The drive number. The "2" means it is the second drive. It also means the program failed to count my external IBM 5.25 inch drive. Do not worry, the rest of the utilities work fine on the B-drive.
- The bytes per sector. Unless you are using a non-standard formatting program, this will be 512.
- The sectors per cluster. This varies with the operating system.
- Number of file allocation table copies, or FATs. This will be 2 except for a RAM disk. It can be either 1 or 2.
- Root directory entries. This varies with the operating system and disk size. It is the maximum number of entries DOS can store in the root directory.
- Sectors per FAT. This varies depending on the operating system and disk size.
- Number of clusters. This varies depending on the operating system and disk size.
- Number of sectors. This is equal to the number of clusters you have times the number of sectors contained in each cluster.
- Offset to FAT. This is the sector number of the beginning of the FAT.
- Offset to directory. This is the sector number of the first part of the root directory.
- Offset to data. This is the sector number for the first data file.
- Sectors per track. This varies depending on the operating system and disk size.
- Sides. This number of logical sides of the disk.
- Hidden sectors. This indicates the first sector of the DOS partition.

Disk Test. Disk Test, or DT for short, tests a disk for damage. Command syntax allows you to test by files, sectors, or both. When it finds problems in unused sectors of the disk, it allows you to easily mark that sector as bad. When it finds a problem in an active sector of the disk, DT can automatically move the data to a safe location.

The function of disk test is entirely different from the function of the DOS program CHKDSK. CHKDSK checks the logical arrangement of the disk to make sure it agrees with the system area and that no two files share part of the same area. DT makes sure that all parts of the disk can be read. Files in areas of the disk that are risky can be automatically moved by the program. Running Disk Test once a week can prevent a number of disk problems.

File Attribute. File Attribute, or FA for short, allows you to control the attributes of any files. You can see the status of files and change files between any combination of normal, read only, archive, system, and hidden. There is also a clear command to remove all file attributes.

- Read only attribute. This attribute prevents files from being erased. This is useful for protecting important program files on shared computers. However, this can cause problems with some copy protection schemes and with any program file that the program writes to when default settings are changed.
- Archive attribute. This is a flag showing if the file has changed since the last backup.
- Hidden attribute. This flag prevents a file from showing up in a DIRectory. The file is still there and you can run it just as you always do, you just cannot see it or erase it. The manual makes one of its few mistakes on hidden files. It states "hidden programs cannot be executed" on page 76. This is incorrect, at least under DOS 3.3 and 4.01 the only versions I have access to. All executable files, including batch files, perform normally when hidden. Hiding a file is a simple way to keep curious users from seeing and wanting to run a program without affecting its operation.
- System attribute. You cannot see a file containing this attribute in a DIRectory. It is generally either a special DOS file or a copy protection file. You cannot erase them and you cannot run them.

File Date. This new program lets you change the date and time for a specified group of files or even remove the date and time altogether. You could always do this with the old utilities by editing a directory containing the files. This program just makes it much easier and safer than editing the directory.

File Find. File Find, or FF for short, searches all subdirectories for files matching the input criteria. This is useful for finding a worksheet on a complex hard disk if you know the name.

File Info. File Info is a non-memory resident way to attach a 65-character comment to file names. It stores the existing file name and the comment in a database file called FILEINFO.FI. Each time you enter the FI command, the program matches file names to display with comments. It has commands to add and modify comments and to remove comments for files that no longer exist. Since the program is not memory resident, it cannot update the file automatically when you delete, renamed or move a file.

Format Recovery. Chapter 7 covers this.

File Size. DOS allocates space to files in whole clusters. The size of a cluster varies depending on the size of the disk and the version of DOS in use. If the cluster size is 4K, then DOS will allocate a 1-byte file 4K of space. As a result, the file size you see when you do a DIRectory is only mildly related to the actual size of the file. File size reports the actual size of the files, the disk space used, the slack (Used-minus-Needed divided by Needed), and will tell you if the files will fit on the diskette you have in the specified drive.

List Directories. The List Directory command lists all the subdirectories on a hard disk (or even a floppy diskette) along with file names and sizes. It also displays the subdirectory trees in a graphical format.

Line Print. This is a simple replacement for the DOS PRINT program, offering more control over the printing. You can control line numbering, margins, page size, page numbering and headers. Also, it allows you to use wild cards. Just like PRINT, the program only works with ASCII files. The latest release adds page numbers, headers, 256 character lines, EBCDIC option, and Lotus-like setup strings.

Norton Change Directory. This is a nifty replacement for the DOS CD (change directory) command. Using it, you type NCD and enough of the subdirectory to be unique and it will change to that subdirectory. So without NCD, if you are in the WORDSTAR subdirectory you must enter: CD \ LOTUS \ PROJ-ECT1 \ COSTS \ VARIABLE to change to the VARIABLE subdirectory. If you have no other subdirectory named variable, using NCD you could enter: NCD VAR

You can also use NCD to "walk" to a subdirectory. You can move the cursor around the map till it is on the subdirectory you want to change to and press return to switch to that subdirectory. You can also use the speed search mode. You begin entering the name and as you enter each letter, NCD moves to the first directory matching that description. When it matches, press Return.

Norton Control Center. The Norton Control Center, or NCC for short, is a program to let you easily control a number of parameters about how your computer operates. It does this without resorting to complex MODE statements. Using NCC, you can:

- Change the cursor size. You can set the cursor to one of sixteen sizes.
- Set the DOS colors. You can set the foreground, background and border colors. These are not permanent, if you issue a CLS command, they are reset to white on black.
- Select the palette colors. EGA and VGA users can select sixteen colors from a set of sixty four.
- Select the video mode. You can select between 25x80 monochrome, 25x80 color, 40x80 color and 50x80 color depending on the type of display you have.
- Set the keyboard rate. This lets you select how fast DOS repeats characters and how long the delay is before it begins repeating.
- Set up the serial ports. You can set the port, baud rate, parity, databits, and stopbits.
- Set up to four timers to record events.
- Set the time and date.

You can set a few of these attributes from the command line. Most, however, must be set using a central program. When you enter NCC, you get a screen where the left side shows the options you can set. You move the cursor to the one to set, and tab over to the right side where you actually set the value.

Norton Disk Doctor. The Norton Disk Doctor, or NDD for short, is a program that corrects most physical or logical errors on a disk. NDD performs over 100 tests. The manual does not list all of them. Even if they were listed in the manual, they would be too numerous to list here. The major things NDD can do are:

- Testing each sector. If a sector is bad, it is marked as such. If it contains data, as much as possible is recovered and moved to a safe location.
- Making a disk bootable. Certain DOS files must be at a specific location to boot off a disk. If you format a disk as a data disk, those locations can have data written to them. Using this option, NDD will move that data to another location and install the system files properly.
- Revive a defective diskette. This formats a problem disk without erasing the data contained on the disk. The DOS formatting program always completely erases a floppy diskette.
- Recover from the DOS RECOVER command. This DOS command does not unerase files. In fact, it should only be used by a highly experienced user. If you do use the RECOVER command, you will find all your files in the root directory with strange names. NDD can help you recover from this.

Norton Integrator. Before version 4.0, the Norton Utilities were meant to run from the DOS prompt and nothing else. The Norton Integrator is a menu driven shell that lets you run any of the utilities from a central menu.

Norton Utilities Main Program. The Norton Utilities Main Program, or NU for short, is the capstone program, and the main reason for purchasing the entire set of utilities. This program offers two main features, unerasing files and exploring and changing a disk.

Let's face it, we all do it sometime. Entering: ERASE *.WK1 only to remember we needed one of the files; or entering: ERASE *.BAT when we meant to enter BAK not BAT. Erasing a file does not remove that file from the disk, it only removes the part of the associated directory entry. If you immediately try to unerase the file you can almost always get it (them) back. The longer you wait the less likely file recovery becomes. Once DOS stores another file in that now vacant area, you can never recover the erased file.

This program is completely menu driven and will lead you step-by-step through the process. If none of the space occupied by the erased file has been reused, then all you have to do is supply the first letter of the file name. The program will do everything else for you.

If part of the space used by the erased file is being used by another file, then you have a lot of work cut out for you. It is only worthwhile for text files and then only if you do not have an earlier backup of the file. If the program cannot determine where the remaining erased data is located, you have three alternatives:

1) The semi-automatic method where the program makes its best guess but then asks you to confirm that guess.
2) Searching for specific data, where you tell the program to search for "Dear John:". One problem with this method is that some word processors (WordStar for example) change the last letter of each word to a high

ordered bit. As a result, you would not find "Dear John:" even if it were still on the disk.

3) You tell the program which sector contains the data.

It has on-line help and a very clear tutorial in the manual.

The Exploring and Changing a Disk section of the program displays each section of the disk in both ASCII and hexadecimal format. It allows you to change what is on the disk in either format.

To a great extent, it is a disk processor instead of a word processor. It will also display directories and text. I had a case where the DOS BACKUP.COM program made an error writing a file name during backup. This made it impossible to restore from that disk when my hard disk "crashed." I was able to correct the file name using this option of the program. Since the directory is just another section of the disk, you can edit it like any other file. I have also used this option to edit COMMAND.COM to change the names of commands like DEL. One word of caution, a mistake can make a disk useless. This feature should be used with caution only by experienced users.

In addition to editing absolute sectors on a disk, this powerful program will let you edit:

- The root directory or any subdirectory.
- The file allocation table, or FAT.
- Partition table.

These are, of course, very powerful and dangerous tools. They let you edit the very items DOS uses to store information critical to its operation. If you do not know exactly what you are doing, it is possible to make a disk useless.

Quick Unerase. Quick Unerase will automatically erase only those files it can completely recover automatically. It has two modes. One, it will run unattended recovering every file it can. And two, it will ask you if you want to recover each file and then the first character of the file name. You can specify the files to recover on the command line.

Safe Format. Safe Format, or SF for short, is a menu driven formatting program designed to completely replace the DOS formatting program. In fact, the installation routine gives you the option of renaming your existing FORMAT.COM and replacing it with SF—although this can interfere with the DOS backup program.

SF does not erase data on a disk when it formats it, even if the disk is a floppy diskette. Rather, it leaves the data alone. If the data is erased, it remains erased but recoverable. SF has a number of options to control the formatting process. They include:

- Safe formatting. This uses a proprietary algorithm to format the disk without destroying data. It is also faster than a DOS format.
- Quick formatting. This formats a disk even faster by simply replacing the system area and ignoring the rest of the disk.
- DOS formatting. This uses exactly the same process and the DOS formatting program.
- Complete formatting. This is the same as safe formatting except it tests for and marks bad sectors so DOS will not use them.

Screen Attributes. This program was incorporated into the Batch Enhancer program. Like the other incorporated programs, if your batch files use this program you will either have to rewrite them or save the old program.

Speed Disk. Speed Disk, or SD for short, is a disk optimization program. Chapter 8 covers this.

System Information. This is the part of the utilities seen in computer reviews and ads. System information reports the following:

- What type of computer you are using, if it can find that information in the BIOS.
- The version of DOS being used.
- Total memory and available memory.
- Computing performance index. A 1.5 would mean that the computer was 50% faster than a standard PC. This measure does not consider disk speed.
- An optional test, selected with a switch, compares the hard disk to a standard PC hard disk.

Time Mark. This is a stop watch program. Time mark is useful for consultants who bill their time. It has four counters. The new version adds an optional comment.

Text Search. Text search, TS for short, will search the disk or specified files for a text string. TS is useful if your word processor stores files in ASCII format. Many other word processors (for example Microsoft Word) store text as ASCII while surrounding it with non-ASCII characters. You can use text search with these word processors as well. The new version is faster and shows more text.

A real limitation of text search is its inability to skip to the next file. If a file matches the search 30-times, you must tell it to continue searching 30-times. There is no "go to next file" command.

Unremove Directory. Unremove Directory will recover erased directories if the space they occupied is still free. This allows you to recover files even if you erase all the files then remove the directory. You can specify the name of the subdirectory to recover on the command line.

Volume Label. Volume Label allows you to add or change the disk volume label using a mixture of upper and lowercase letters. DOS only allows uppercase.

Wipe Disk. This program overwrites all the information on a disk with zeros. This prevents anyone from unerasing any files on the disk. It also "removes" the formatting on the disk so it must be reformatted. This, and the next program, are useful for protecting confidential data files you do not want recovered after being erased or after the disk is formatted.

Wipe File. Wipe file replaces the contents of a file with zeros and then erases the file. Even though you can recover the file by unerasing the file, the recovered file will be empty. Like the wipe disk program, this program helps protect confidential data.

Manual   There are actually three manuals. The first, *The Norton Utilities*, actually documents the program. The second, *The Norton Trouble Shooter*, is a paper "expert system." It lists a number of problems and no-nonsense solutions. Not all of these solutions involve the Norton Utilities. One even requires you to key in a short Basic program. The third, *The Norton Disk Companion*, explains how your disk operates and what those confusing terms, like FAT, really mean. Peter Norton has written numerous books and for most major computer magazines and it shows. All three books are excellent. This, combined with the on-line help, make these programs easy to use.

Differences Between the Regular and Advanced Edition   The advanced edition ($150 or $39 to upgrade from an earlier version) gives you everything you have read about. The regular edition ($100 or $25 to upgrade from an earlier version) leaves out the following:

- The Speed Disk optimizing program.
- The Unformatting program to recover your hard disk after formatting.
- The Norton Disk Doctor disk repair program.
- The Norton Trouble Shooter book.

In addition, the regular edition Norton Utility Main Program is missing several features:

- The partition editor.
- The file allocation table editor.
- The absolute sector editor.
- Maintenance mode.

Although these advanced features may seem like something you do not need now, you are going to want them later. Save yourself the trouble and go ahead and purchase the advanced edition. It is money well spent.

Conclusion   The Norton Utilities is an excellent product. Every computer user should own a copy. The Advanced Edition has useful features and includes all the basic features so that is the version you should purchase.

<table>
<tr><td>Product:</td><td>Norton Utilities</td></tr>
<tr><td>Price:</td><td>$100</td></tr>
<tr><td>Category:</td><td>Commercial</td></tr>
<tr><td>Publisher:</td><td>Peter Norton Computing, Incorporated</td></tr>
<tr><td>Address:</td><td>2210 Wilshire Boulevard
Santa Monica, California 90403</td></tr>
<tr><td>Phone:</td><td>(213) 453-2361</td></tr>
<tr><td>Notes:</td><td>The Norton Utilities consists of a number of separate utilities each with its own memory requirements. With 256K, you will be able to run any of the utilities</td></tr>
<tr><td>Memory:</td><td>256K</td></tr>
</table>

Professional Master Key

The *Professional Master Key* utilities are a set of useful shareware disk and file utilities. A copy of Professional Master Key is included on the optional diskette set.

Installation   There is no program to install the Professional Master Key on your hard disk or working floppy disk. The manual does not explain the process. There is a program labeled install but it only changes the defaults for the way the program operates.

Operation   You can run each of the major Professional Master Key utilities as a stand-alone program. There is also a master menu that automatically calls the major programs. The Professional Master Key has five sections:

1) The Professional Master Key. This is the major section of the program and is discussed below.
2) Fill Disk. This writes any message to all free sectors on a disk. It also zeros out all unused sectors so there is no trace of existing data. The program prompts you for the message to use. While Fill Disk writes the message you enter to the disk, it does not mark the sectors as used. As a result, the disk shows the same free space as before running Fill Disk. Generally that is what you want.
3) UnFormat protects hard disks from accidentally formatting and unformats the hard disk. Chapter 7 covers this.
4) Zero Disk. This permanently removes all traces of data on a disk by writing to each sector and removing all formatting information. It will not work on non-DOS formatted disks like an old Fastback backup disk.

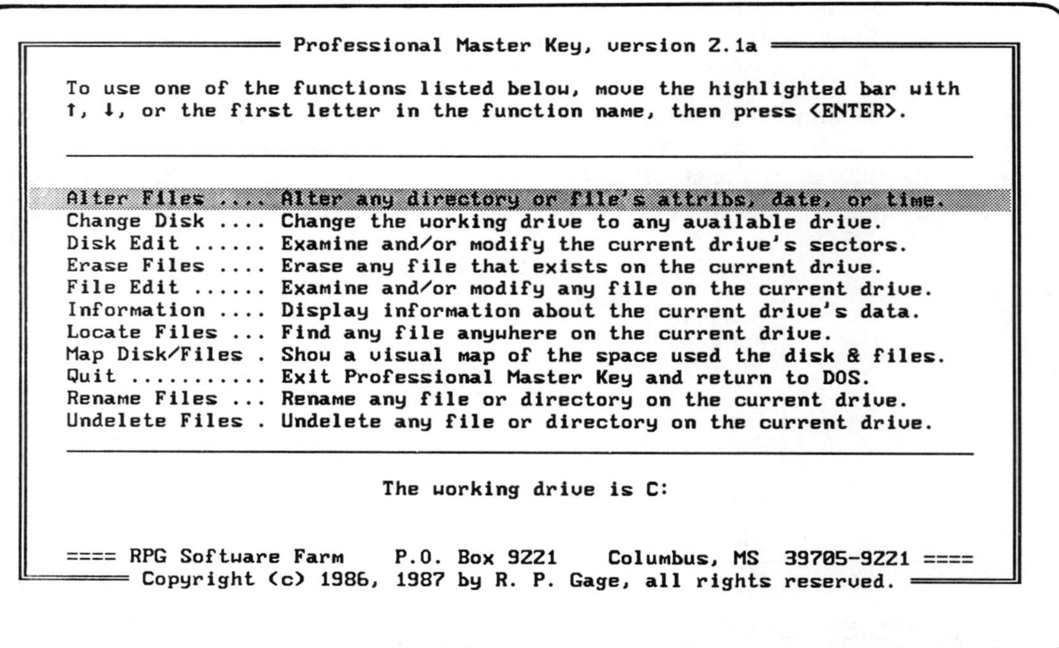

Fig. 4-12. The Professional Master Key menu option is the heart of the Professional Master Key utilities.

5) Zero File. This permanently removes any trace of a file by overwriting each sector in the file. You can configure Zero File so it will ask you to confirm each overwriting.

The utilities under the Professional Master Key menu option form the major portion of the Professional Master Key package. Professional Master Key is menu driven. Figure 4-12 shows its menu. The menu options are:

1) Alter Files. This programs lets you change file attributes and the date and time. When you press Return, it first asks you for the subdirectory to modify. You make your selection using a graphical tree. Once you select the subdirectory, Alter Files presents you with a list of files in that subdirectory. You move the cursor to the file to modify and press Return to modify it. Figure 4-13 shows this. Once you select a file, Alter Files gives you a screen with the old information on the left. You make your changes on the right so you can always see how things have changed. Figure 4-14 shows this.

2) Change Disk. This changes the disk drive that Professional Master Key is working on.

3) Disk Edit. You use Disk Edit to edit any sector on a disk in either ASCII or hexadecimal. Figure 4-15 shows this. The program has a help screen. It can go directly to any sector by number or the first or last sector in a file. It can also search for ASCII or hexadecimal data on the disk.

```
═══════════════════════════ File Altering ═══════════════════════════
Directory:    C:\TEMPORAR\

Name     Ext      Size     Date       Time       Attributes
README  .BAT        17   11/02/87   12:00pm    Archive
PMK-UTIL.INF      1280   11/02/87   12:01pm    Archive
FD      .EXE     20986   11/02/87   12:02pm    Archive
INSTALL .EXE     23386   11/02/87   12:03pm    Archive
PMK     .EXE     69434   11/02/87   12:04pm    Archive
PMK-MENU.EXE     25202   11/02/87   12:05pm    Archive
PMK-UTIL.DOC    129920   11/02/87   12:06pm    Archive
UF      .EXE     27296   11/02/87   12:07pm    Archive
ZERODISK.EXE     21218   11/02/87   12:08pm    Archive
ZEROFILE.EXE     20018   11/02/87   12:09pm    Archive
UNFORMAT.PMK      1024    4/02/89   11:50am    Archive




To select a file, move the highlighted bar with ↑, ↓, PgUp, PgDn, Home, or
End, then press <ENTER>.  Press <F10> to exit to the main menu.
```

Fig. 4-13. When Professional Master Key asks you to select a file, you make that selection by scrolling through a list of files.

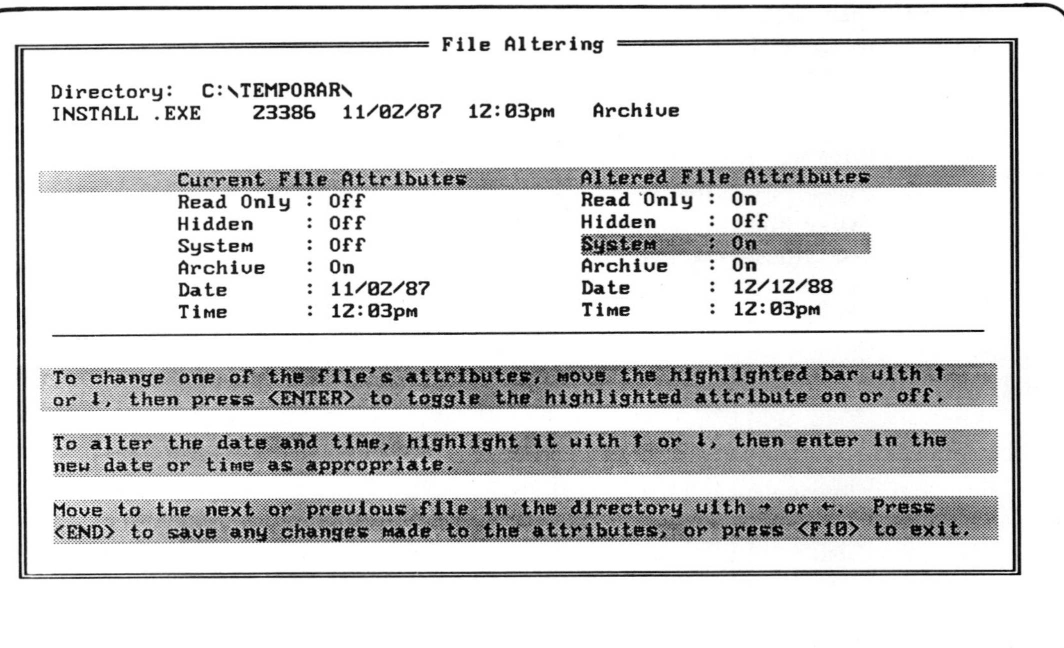

Fig. 4-14. With the Alter Files program in the Professional Master Key, you can see the old attributes as you make your changes.

4) Erase Files. This erases any file. You first select the subdirectory and file using the same method as in the Alter Files program. After selecting a file to delete, you must press "Y" to delete it. You can also press "S" to skip it if you made a mistake in selecting that file.

5) File Edit. You first select the subdirectory and file using the same method as in the Alter Files program. Once you select a file, you edit it in ASCII or hexadecimal just like in the Disk Edit program.

6) Information. This displays technical information on the disk.

7) Locate Files. This displays all the files on a disk matching the input criteria along with their subdirectory, size date and attributes.

8) Map Disk/Files. This shows a map of the hard disk and the area allocated to files, free space and bad sectors.

9) Quit. This exits the program.

10) Rename Files. You first select the subdirectory and file using the same method as in the Alter Files program. After selecting the file to rename, it gives you a template with the existing name and you type in the new name.

11) Undelete Files. You first select the subdirectory and file to undelete using the same method as in the Alter Files program. There is no manual undelete mode, Undelete Files performs all the work manually. After you undelete a file, Undelete Files displays the remaining erased files so you can undelete another file if you like.

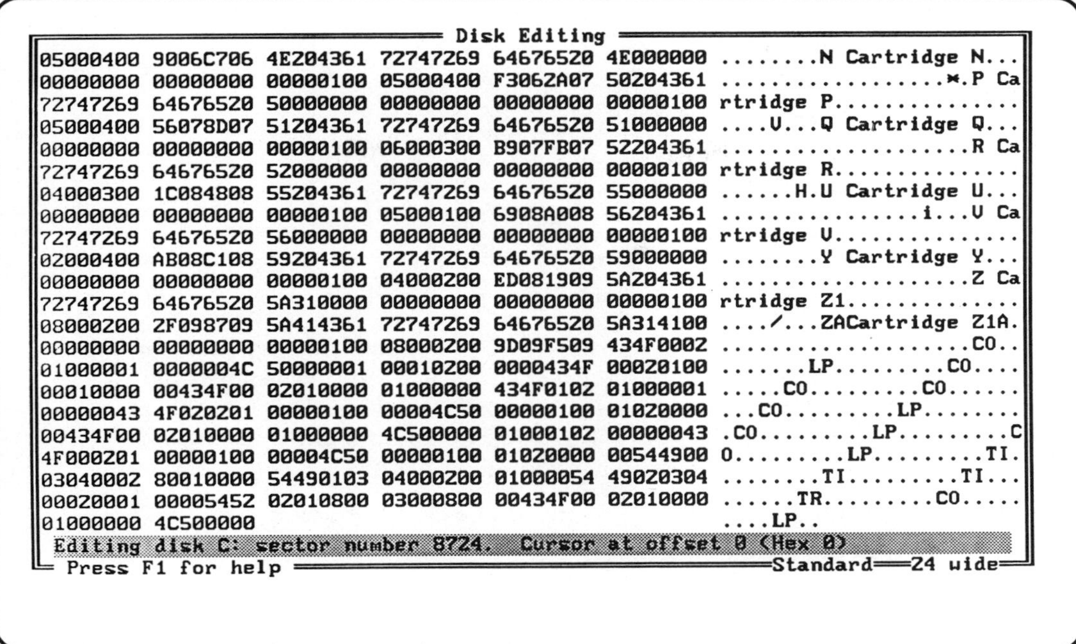

Fig. 4-15. The Disk Edit program in the Professional Master Key lets you edit any sector on the disk in ASCII or hexadecimal.

Limitations   The Professional Master Key will not run under DOS 4.x. In addition, it will not run on a PS/2 computer under DOS 3.x. It ran fine on a clone under IBM DOS 3.3.

The Alter Files program makes it very easy to alter file attributes, data and time on a single file. However, if you need to change a lot of files, then Alter Files is cumbersome. With Alter Files, there are only two ways to make changes. One is to work through the files one at a time. The other is to use the left and right keys to scroll through the files in the directory one at a time. The instructions on the screen tell you to press the End-key to save or the F10-key to exit. In fact, you must press the F10-key to exit. The End-key only saves your changes so far but does not let you exit.

The Erase Files program does not let you tag files to erase. You must work through all the menus for each file you select to erase. In the same fashion, the renaming program will only let you rename one file at a time.

Manual   Other than its lack of information on installing the Professional Master Key, the electronic manual does a good job of explaining how to use the program.

Conclusion   The Professional Master Key utilities are a very good shareware utility set, especially for light users. A copy of the Professional Master Key is included on the optional diskette set.

```
Product:      Professional Master Key Utilities
Price:        $25.00
Category:     Shareware
Publisher:    RPG Software Farm
Address:      Post Office Box 9221
              Columbus, Mississippi 39705
Phone:        Not Available
Notes:        The optional diskette set includes a
              copy of this program.
Memory:       128K
```

Rescue

Rescue includes four powerful functions. First, it will reconstruct corrupted Lotus *.WK1 files that give the dreaded "Not a valid worksheet file" error message. Second, it will unerase erased worksheet files. Third, it has an add-in to automatically save your worksheet after a specified time has elapsed. Finally, it will figure out the password associated with a file.

Installation   There is a batch file to install Rescue on a hard disk.

Operation   Rescue has four functions:

1) Reconstructing corrupted worksheet files.
2) Unerasing worksheet files.
3) Automatically saving worksheets.
4) Finding out the password associated with a file.

Each of these operations is discussed separately.

Reconstructing corrupted worksheet files. One of the most dreaded error messages Lotus gives is "Not a valid worksheet file". One way to get this error message is by trying to retrieve a non-worksheet file. Unfortunately that is not the only way. A Lotus file is a very special type of file where every byte relates to every other byte. In some cases, corrupting a single byte will keep a Lotus file from loading. When that happens, there is no way to use the file with Lotus.

In the five years I have been using Lotus, I have had this problem six times. It is a very frustrating problem because backups do not help and frequently saving your file does not help. A backup of a corrupted file is corrupted. The only time there is a problem is when the last version saved has the problem.

I learned about Rescue from the company that handles the computer maintenance for the computers at my office. The technician happened to be there the last time I had this problem so I asked him if he knew a cure. He pulled a Rescue disk from his case and had my file back in two minutes. If this were all Rescue could do, I would still recommend that every Lotus user own a copy, but it does much more.

I was not able to recreate this problem for testing while writing this book. I did the next best thing. I loaded a copy of ADDITION.WK1 into the Norton Utilities. Then I used the file editor to replace a couple of randomly selected bytes in the file to "00" using the file editing feature.

The file still loaded into Lotus, but most of it was missing. The first row of formulae was there as was half of the second row. Everything else was missing.

Next, I loaded the damaged file into Rescue. While running, it displays a bar chart showing its progress. I loaded the finished worksheet back into Lotus. Two formulae were missing, no doubt they contained the two bytes I modified. Everything else was there. This feature of Rescue is very impressive. Even more impressive because it requires nothing from the user other than the file name.

Unerasing worksheet files. New computer users often find it difficult to believe, but it is fairly easy to unerase files that you have just erased. The reason is simple. When you issue the command: ERASE WORKSHEET.WK1 DOS does not actually take the time to physically remove the data contained in WORK-SHEET.WK1 from your disk. Rather, it updates its map of your disk to reallo-cate the space that file used as empty. The data remains on the disk. Later, when you write another file to the disk and DOS decides to use the area that once contained WORKSHEET.WK1, then the new data will overwrite the exist-ing data. Until the data is overwritten, you can recover. Once overwritten, it is gone forever.

The easiest way to recover an erased file is with an unerasing utility like the Norton Utilities. The authors of Rescue claim that using a general utility for Lotus data can cause more problems than it cures. Therefore they claim the unerase feature of Rescue is the program of choice. I am not convinced. I have been unerasing worksheets with the Norton Utilities for over four years and they have worked on every recoverable file.

Unerasing a file is a multi-step process. The first step is to run ResQDisk. ResQDisk does not recover the data, it simply tells you where it is. The main menu has three options:

1) Search disk for Lotus data. This searches the entire disk for Lotus data. It prints out a list of all the areas on the disk containing any data created by Lotus along with address information required by other programs. All three direct their output to a printer. You cannot run these programs with-out a printer.
2) Find all Lotus file starts. You use this function to find all valid Lotus files on a disk and their starting address.
3) Find deleted Lotus file data. You supply the path and file name and it finds all the data belonging to that file. It prints the necessary file information for later use.

All three menu options simply create lists of disk addresses. You then use these in other programs. ResQView allows you to view these addresses. ResQView has a major advantage over the Norton Utilities. Both let you view the raw data on the disk. However, the Norton Utilities displays it as the binary information stored by Lotus while ResQView translates it into a readable form. This is the advantage of a specialized program over a general one. This feature does not work with password protected files.

You use ResQFile to actually unerase the files. You enter the addresses found by the ResQDisk and it reconstructs the files.

The more typical use of these programs is to unerase a file you accidentally erased. This three step process is far more difficult to use than the Norton Utilities. The Norton Utilities has, in my experience, worked well at unerasing worksheet files. So, I recommend you use Norton.

A less common use for these programs is trying to recover data from a formatted hard disk. Most format routines (Compaq and AT&T are the exceptions— they physically erase the hard disk during formatting) do not erase the hard disk during formatting. (All formatting routines erase floppy diskettes during formatting.) Rather, they erase the file allocation table [FAT]. The erased FAT prevents DOS from finding any files. It also prevents unerasing programs, like the Norton Utilities, from finding the data. These programs can find the data. If you do not have format protect (like that provided by the Norton Utilities Advanced Edition) then this is the only way to get your worksheets back.

Automatically saving worksheets. This add-in, called Guardian will automatically save your worksheet ever-so-often. It is a useful feature and it is compatible with SQZ.

Finding out the password associated with a file. Lotus uses the password you enter to encrypt the file as it is being saved. ResQPass can find out what the password was by using pattern matching on the file. It is not able to find the password to very small files because there are not enough cells to perform pattern matching.

To be honest, all this program did was convince me not to ever use Lotus passwords! After all, what good are they if a utility can figure them out?

Limitations All of the functions of ResQDisk direct their output to a printer. You cannot direct it elsewhere. As a result, you cannot run this program if you do not have an operational printer. The file unerase features are more difficult to use than they should be.

Manual The manual is for a "power-user." There is no table of contents or index. The explanations are brief and technical in nature. Do not let that keep you from buying Rescue. Its main ability is to recover corrupted Lotus files and you can do that without ever reading the manual. Simply type Rescue, and enter the source file name and a file name for the output. One thing about the manual that did impress me is a brief section on how to intentionally damage Lotus files so you could put Rescue through its paces.

Conclusion Every Lotus user should own a copy of Rescue, period. Its ability to uncorrupt a Lotus file is alone worth the purchase price. I was not impressed with its ability to unerase Lotus worksheets. It does work, but it requires much more work than the Norton Utilities and little in the way of advantages over the Norton Utilities. It is difficult enough to use that many new users will avoid it simply because it is too difficult. It will, however, unerase worksheet data from a formatted hard disk, something Norton will not do. Both Guardian and ResQPass worked without problem. Except the

Guardian add-in, Rescue works with all releases of Lotus and with any other program that creates Lotus-compatible *.WK? files.

Product:	Rescue
Price:	$84.95
Category:	Commercial
Publisher:	Spectrum Computer Services, Incorporated
Address:	133 Main Street
	Suite 209
	North Reading, Massachusetts 01864
Phone:	(617) 664-0337
Notes:	The add-in portion requires 20K. The stand-alone DOS utilities require 256K
Memory:	20K

Vopt

Vopt is primarily a commercial disk optimization program. However, it comes with several other handy utilities for maintaining your files.

Installation   There is no installation program. The manual merely instructs you to copy the files on the distribution disk to any convenient disk or sub-directory. Experienced users will have no trouble. Inexperienced users will find the installation instructions inadequate.

Operation   The primary program in the Vopt package is a disk optimizer. It proved to be inadequate. Chapter 8 covers it. The remaining programs are:

- CHKDSK. This has the same function as the DOS CHKDSK program and generally displays the same information. It runs with hard disks larger than 32 Meg, created using non-standard sector or cluster sizes. It does have a few additional switches. They are:

    /I   Causes CHKDSK to display the sector size, cluster size, volume size and FAT entry size.
    /V   Causes CHKDSK to verify each file.
    /G   Causes CHKDSK to check file contiguity for each file.

- VMap. This generates a map of the hard disk showing how it is used. Figure 4-16 shows this.
- VBench. This benchmarks your computer performance. It displays that information in a bar graph against either a 4.77 MHz PC or a 6 MHz AT depending on how fast your computer is. Figure 4-17 shows this for an IBM Model 70 running at 16 MHz.
- VColor. You use this to set screen colors. The first time you run it, it displays a matrix of color combinations. You scroll around and select the one you like. It then tells you the numeric code for that combination. For example, white on blue is 3F. After that, you enter VColor followed by the number to set the color directly.
- VLoc. You use this to locate files matching a given file specification on your hard disk.

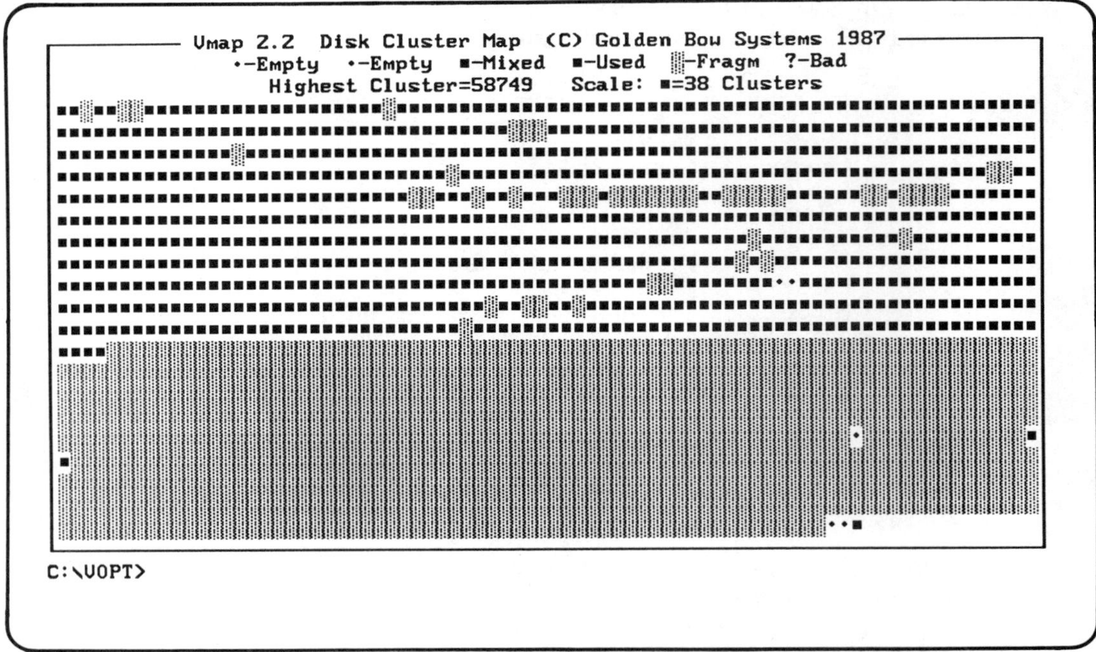

Fig. 4-16. Map displays a map of the hard disk and shows how files are stored on the hard disk.

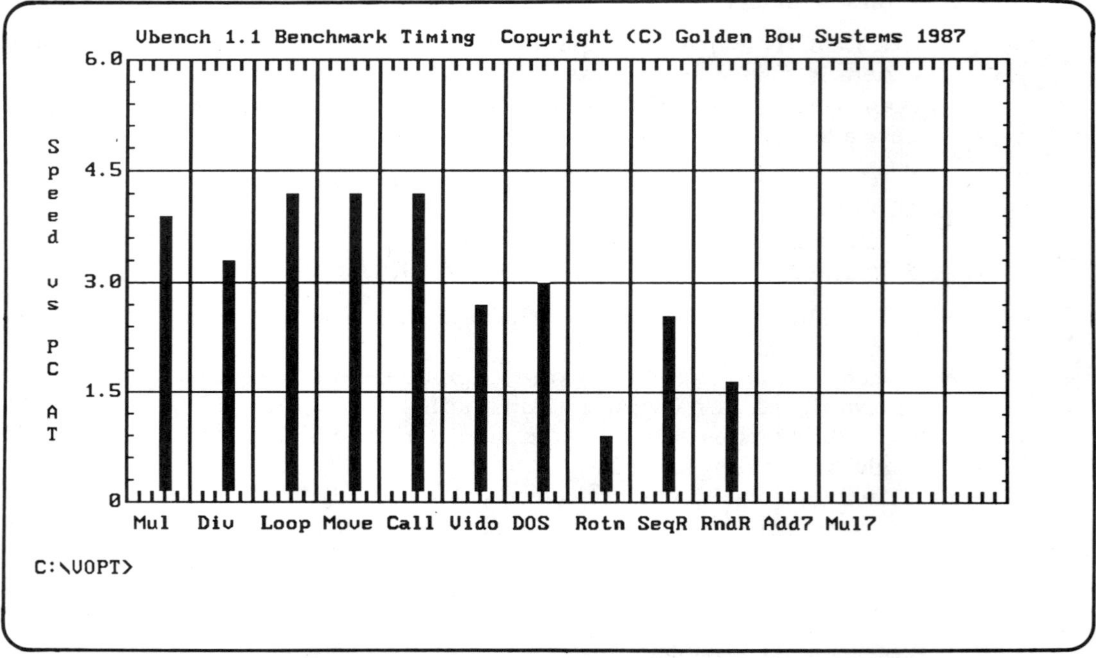

Fig. 4-17. VBench benchmarks your computer and graphically displays it compared to a 6 MHz AT.

- VMarkBad. This tests the entire hard disk and marks all the bad clusters it finds.
- VPrtSc. This is a 10K memory resident program that significantly speeds up print screens.
- Vrd. This program verifies a floppy diskette using a better test than the DOS FORMAT command. This program is especially useful for verifying that diskettes you plan to use for backup do not have problems. Figure 4-18 shows a copy of the Vrd display.
- VSeek. This program shows a graphical display of the seek time for every hard disk in the system.
- VSpeed. This tests the speed of a floppy disk drive and displays the results graphically.
- VTsr. This shows all the memory resident programs loaded into memory. It also shows their size and the interrupts they use.
- VoptDemo. This is a menu program you can use to run all the Vopt programs. Figure 4-19 shows the menu.

Limitations   I tried running Vopt on the 130 Meg hard disk on the IBM Model 70. Each time, it reported "Crosslinked Files" and did nothing. The DOS CHKDSK program and the Norton Disktest program found no problems. The Vopt CHKDSK program refused to run. It returned a "Disk error reading Sub-Directory" error message. The list of error messages in the manual does not

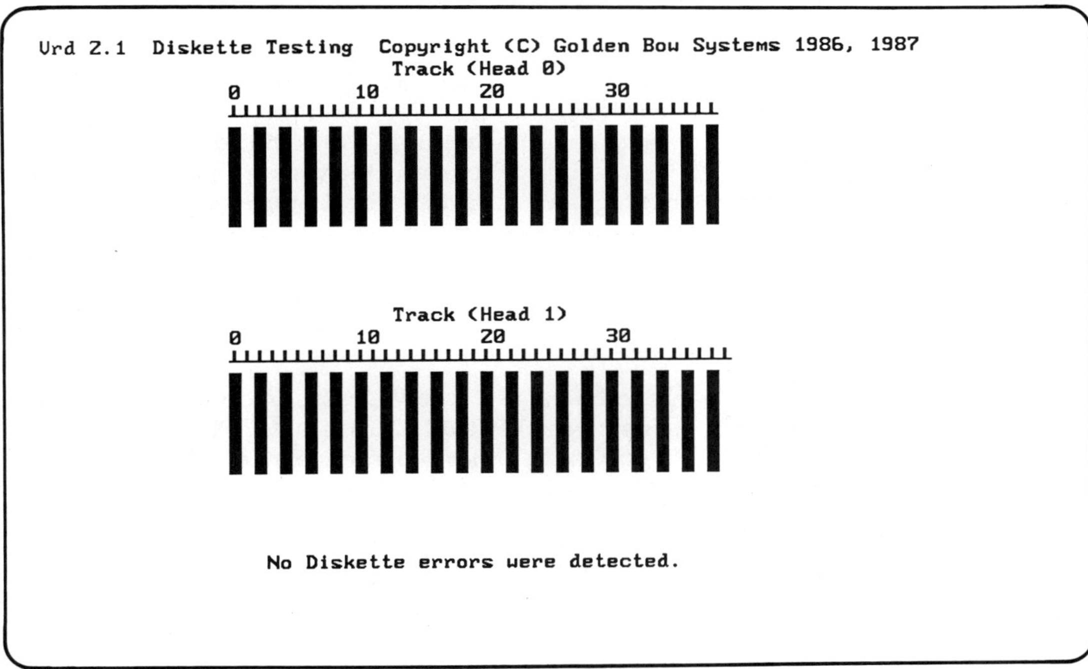

Fig. 4-18. Vrd tests floppy diskettes using a testing procedure that will find errors that the DOS FORMAT program will miss.

```
VoptDemo  Copyright (C) Golden Bow Systems 1987

    Select with F1 to F10.   Exit with Esc(ape)

        F1:     Vbench Timing

        F2:     Vcolor Screen Colors

        F3:     Vmap Disk

        F4:     Vmarkbad Clusters

        F5:     Vopt Optimize Disk

        F6:     Vrd Diskette Test

        F7:     Vseek (Fixed Disk)

        F8:     Vspeed Diskette Timing

        F9:     Vtsr Resident Programs

        F0:     Chkdsk
```

Fig. 4-19. VoptDemo is a menu program you can use to run all the Vopt programs.

contain this message. While CHKDSK would not run from the command line, it ran perfectly when running under VoptDemo, the Vopt menu program.

While VPrtSc did significantly speed up screen prints, it introduced a serious bug. On my IBM Model 70, performing a screen print with no printer causes no problem. The computer recognizes the printer is missing and skips the screen print without missing a beat. A clone I use at the office recovers in about ten seconds. Once you install VPrtSc, a screen print with no printer locks up the computer until you either reboot or connect a printer. The problem VPrtSc introduces is larger than the problem it corrects (slow screen prints) and I recommend you not use the program.

Manual   The manual devotes only seven pages to the Vopt disk optimizer. It includes an example of a batch file using the ERRORLEVEL and GOTO commands without any explanation. It covers the other programs just as briefly. Understanding the Vopt manual requires a good deal of experience.

Conclusion   Many of the Vopt utilities are very nice. However, the keystone disk optimization program does not work very well. That makes it very difficult to recommend the Vopt package unless you need one of these other utilities very badly.

```
Product:      Vopt
Price:        $59.95
Category:     Commercial
Publisher:    Golden Bow Systems
Address:      2870 Fifth Avenue
              Suite 201
              San Diego, California
              92103
Phone:        (619) 298-9349
Memory:       512K
```

ALSO SEE. . .

Some of the disk maintenance programs in Chapter 5 offer some type of file maintenance facilities. While usually not as extensive as the ones in this chapter, they may be adequate for you to avoid buying both types of programs.

RONNY'S PICKS

It is really no contest. The best disk utilities are the Norton Utilities.

5
Utility Sets

This chapter covers programs that are a set of utilities. These utility sets generally have a wealth of programs. Many of the features of these sets do things like file editing that is not a part of the book. However, I briefly covered these extra features to give the complete flavor of the package. For me to include a utility set in this chapter, it must have to have a significant number of options for performing file or disk maintenance. Utility sets that perform primarily file maintenance are in the prior chapter. Utility sets that perform primarily disk maintenance are in the next chapter.

Baker's Dozen

Baker's Dozen is a shareware collection of fourteen handy utilities. A copy of Baker's Dozen is included on the optional diskette set.

Installation   Baker's Dozen does not come with an installation program and the manual does not discuss how to install the program. Baker's Dozen should be in its own subdirectory and needs to be in the PATH to operate properly.

Operation   Baker's Dozen consists of fourteen individual programs. Each program operates individually. The programs are:

Button-Calc. Button-Calc is a stand-alone mini-spreadsheet. Figure 5-1 shows Button-Calc. This mini-spreadsheet only has this single page of cells. You cannot adjust the width of any of the columns. It allows you to save and recall information. Button-Calc has extensive on-line help, as shown in Fig. 5-2.

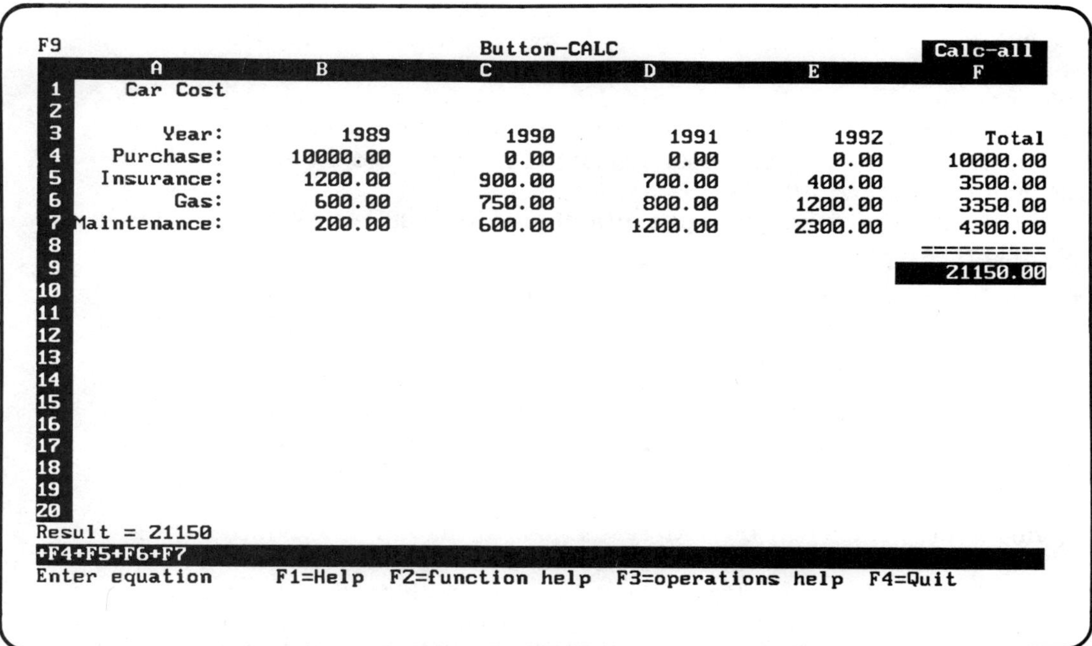

Fig. 5-1. Button-Calc is a stand-alone spreadsheet with a single "page" working space.

```
                    MISCELLANEOUS FUNCTIONS

x,y=(value)         n,r=(integer)

ABS(x)              ABS(14.5)      = 14.5      ABS(-14.5)      = 14.5
CEIL(x)             CEIL(2.1)      =  3.0      CEIL(-1.2)      = -1.0
COMB(n,r)           COMB(3,2)      =  3.0
EXP(x)              EXP(1)         =    e
FACT(n)             FACT(3)        =  6.0
FIX(x)              FIX(2.1)       =  2.0      FIX(-1.6)       = -1.0
FLOOR(x)            FLOOR(2.9)     =  2.0      FLOOR(-2.1)     = -3.0
LOG(x)              LOG(e)         =  1.0
LOG10(x)            LOG10(100)     =  2.0
MAX2(x,y)           MAX2(5,3)      =  5.0
MIN2(x,y)           MIN2(5,3)      =  3.0
MOD(x,n)            MOD(20.7,3)    =  2.7
PERM(n,r)           PERM(3,2)      =  6.0
REMAINDER(x)        REMAINDER(3.4) =  0.4      REMAINDER(-3.4) = -0.4
ROUND(x,n)          ROUND(27,-1)   = 30.0      ROUND(7.45,1)   =  7.5
SGN(x)              SGN(5)         =  1.0      SGN(-5)         = -1.0
SQRT(x)             SQRT(4)        =  2.0

                                              PgUp PgDn or Esc
```

Fig. 5-2. Button-Calc has extensive on-line help available.

Button-Calc looks very much like Lotus 1-2-3 but it does not act very much like Lotus 1-2-3. Most commands are control-letter combinations. For example, you load a file using Control-R(ead) and save a file using Control-W(rite.)

Calendar. The calendar can run as either a stand-alone or pop-up utility. It only displays information. To change dates, you must modify an ASCII data file. Figure 5-3 shows the calendar.

Diskutil. The disk utilities [Diskutil] are the heart of Baker's Dozen. It has the following features:

- Display technical summary of the disk. Like most of the Diskutil screens, it can route a copy to a file or the printer.
- Display a graphical tree illustrating the complete subdirectory of the selected disk.
- Display/edit the file allocation table [FAT]. Figure 5-4 shows this. This is the clearest representation of the FAT I have seen. Each cell on the screen represents a single cluster. Notice that clusters 00 and 01 are blank. (The cluster number is the sum of the number on the row and column. So the highlighted cluster in the FAT screen shot containing the number 39 is cluster 35. The 35 is the sum of the 30 row number and the 5 column number.) DOS reserves these for its own purposes. They store the version of DOS used to format the disk. An entry that starts with an F is the first cluster in the file. A number represents the next cluster in the file. A "- ->" means

```
 ┌──────────────────────────┐      ┌────────────────────────────────┐
 │   December    1989       │      │ Ronny Richardson & Tab Books   │
 ├──────────────────────────┤      └────────────────────────────────┘
 │ Su Mo Tu We Th Fr Sa     │
 ├──────────────────────────┤       15 Bill of Rights Day
 │                   1   2  │       17 Wright Brothers Day
 │                          │       21 Forefathers' Day
 │  3  4  5  6  7  8   9    │       22 Chanukah
 │                          │       25 Christmas
 │ 10 11 12 13 14 15  16    │       31 New Year's Eve
 │                          │
 │ 17 18 19 20 21 22  23    │
 │                          │
 │ 24 25 26 27 28 29  30    │
 │                          │
 │ 31                       │
 └──────────────────────────┘


 Press ←→ to change month
 Press ↓↑ to change years

 The Year of the Snake
 The Jewish Year: 5750


                        Copyright 1987 by WyndhamWare and ButtonWare
```

Fig. 5-3. The Baker's Dozen calendar displays holidays and other dates. To change these, you modify an ASCII file.

```
FAT: viewed in forward direction                         Press Esc to Exit
sectors: 00F7h-00FAh
 Dcml      0      1      2      3      4      5      6      7      8      9

    0                   F65     12     10     15     F9    -->     11     17
   10     13     14     28     16     19     24     18     43     20     21
   20     22     25    -->     26     29    End    -->     30     33     38
   30    -->     34    F36     41    -->     39    -->     42     53    -->
   40     44     49     55    102    -->    -->    -->    -->     50     59
   50    -->    -->     54     56     60     63    -->    -->     62     61
   60     64     68     67    End     72    130    F69     70     71     85
   70     76     73     81    -->    -->     77     79    -->     82    -->

   80     88     86    -->    -->    109     94    -->     90    -->     91
   90     93    -->     97     96    -->     98    103     99    105    -->
  100    -->    110    115    -->    106    111    -->    -->    112    119
  110    125    114    -->    117    116    134    123    -->    121    -->
  120    132    -->    128    -->    126    133    -->    End    139   F131
  130    195    135    137    136    150    138    142    140    End    145
  140    -->    151    -->    148   F146    147    154    149    160    153
  150    152    169    171    155    156    157    158    159    162    172

Last-Fat=10338                 G=Goto Request    ^G=Goto next/prev
                               L=ReLoad FAT      M=Modify value    R=Review Cluster
F1=Help F2=F/B F5=SymbDef      <-->↑↓ Home End ^Home ^End PgUp PgDn ^PgUp ^PgDn
```

Fig. 5-4. The Diskutil program of Baker's Dozen can display the file allocation table and how each cluster is allocated.

the file is continued in the very next cluster, e.g., no fragmentation. An "End" means that the cluster is the last cluster in the file.

Pressing Control-G takes you to the next cluster in that specific file. Pressing "R" lets you view and edit the contents of the highlighted cluster in both hexadecimal and ASCII. Pressing "M" lets you modify the entry for the highlighted cluster. You can:

1) Enter the next cluster in the file.
2) Mark the cluster as available.
3) Mark the cluster as the last cluster in a file.
4) Mark the cluster as reserved. If you do this, DOS will not use the cluster.
5) Mark the cluster as bad.

It does not write modifications to the FAT to disk immediately. You are given an opportunity to abort saving your changes to disk.

- Unerase a file. This is not as easy as the FAT editor. You select a file from a hexadecimal display of the directory. Diskutil them shows you a hexadecimal display of each cluster and asks you to verify if it belongs in the file. You can also manually add clusters to the file.
- Text search. Diskutil can search the disk for a text string. You can enter the string in ASCII or hexadecimal. You can limit the search to files or to specific clusters.

- Directory removal. Removing a subdirectory and all the associated files is easy. Just highlight it and press "E". That erases all the files in the subdirectory and all its child subdirectories then removes the subdirectory and child subdirectories.
- Change or add a volume label.
- Modify the directory information for a file. You can change the attributes, date, time, name and extension. You can also read and erase the file and display the FAT map for just that file.
- Create a special batch file. You can use Diskutil to tag specific files and then have it write a special batch file for those files. You enter a command (like COPY) to go in front of the file name and another (like A:) to go after the name. It creates one line for each tagged file.

FileComp. This program compares two ASCII files and points out the differences. It has a switch that causes the program to ignore blank lines.

Gkey. It displays information about the keys you press. It first asks you for the type of information you want. There are four options:

1) Hexadecimal ASCII value. This displays a table showing all the characters and their hexadecimal value.
2) Decimal ASCII value. This displays a table showing all the characters and their decimal value.
3) Keyboard values. This shows key values sent to the computer (interrupt 9) when you press a key. This brings up a chart showing the "Key Pressed" and "Key Released". It shows the value for each key you press until you press escape.
4) Scan code and character values. This shows the interrupt 16h scan code. It brings up a chart showing "Key Value Returned", "Character Value" and "Character". It shows the value for each key you press until you press Escape.

Locate. This will find every file on the disk matching the file specification you enter. It also shows the file date, time and size. You can also have it search for ASCII text within files matching the file specification.

P90. This program prints out ASCII files sideways on Epson-compatible dot matrix printers.

PC_Sort. PC_Sort is a replacement for the DOS SORT program with a couple of improvements. PC_Sort can handle files larger than 64K and it can sort on multiple keys.

PRN_File. This is a small memory resident program that directs all data sent to a printer into a disk file. It is useful for programs that do not have a write to disk option or that require a printer to run when you do not have one.

RDir. This is a nice little program that deletes all the files in a subdirectory and all its child subdirectories and then deletes the subdirectories. It first lists the subdirectories it is going to remove and asks if you are sure.

Snapshot. Snapshot is a 13K memory resident program that can capture an image to file of any text screen.

Swcom12. This small program switches COM:1 and COM:2. It is useful when using programs that do not support multiple COM ports.

Swlpt12. This small program switches LPT:1 and LPT:2. It is useful when using programs that do not support multiple printer ports.

Limitations   Button-Calc suffers from severe memory problems. The manual claims it will run in 256K. I was running it on a machine with 463K available to Button-Calc. After filling only thirty of the available 120 cells, Button-Calc began dropping to DOS due to lack of memory. The memory problems seemed especially severe when I tried to copy cells containing formulae. This must be some sort of memory allocation problem since I dropped temporarily to DOS (Control-E) and measured 264K of available memory.

The calendar requires a complex set of commands to load. A typical loading command looks like:

```
CALENDAR I = CAL.DAT R = Y M = ''RONNY RICHARDSON'' K = 6400
```

The I= statement defines the data file, there is no default. The R=Y tells the calendar to load as a memory resident program. The M= gives the calendar a title. You cannot store this title as part of the data file. The K=6400 defines the hot-key using scan code.

The complex data requirements to start the calendar are not its only problem. You cannot change any of the data while the calendar is active. To change data, you must modify an ASCII database. The program reads this database into the calendar only when it starts. As a result, to display changes you much remove the calendar from memory and then reload it.

As if that were not enough, I had a great deal of difficulty getting the calendar to pop up. It would not pop up while I was at the DOS prompt. It would pop up over some applications but not others.

The Diskutil program is not DOS 4.0 compatible. It would start and prompt you for a disk drive. After you entered that, it would try to read the disk then drop you to DOS with an out of memory error message. This happened even with a full 640K.

Manual   The manual is complete (except not explaining how to install the program) and explains how to use all the utilities. It has numerous illustrations and charts so you know what to expect while the program is running. However, when explaining the longer programs, like the spreadsheet, it jumps around and is sometimes hard to follow.

Conclusion   I actually found very little to like about Button-Calc. Since it is not memory resident, to use it I have to exit any other program and load Button-Calc. After going through all that, I see little advantage in loading Button-Calc over going ahead and loading Lotus 1-2-3. In addition to its memory problems, Button-Calc looks very similar but uses different commands. I was constantly trying to use Lotus commands in Button-Calc. I just found it confusing.

Like the spreadsheet, the calendar is just not up to par with its competition. Other memory resident calendars offer more features in a similar memory.

The Diskutil program offers some extremely powerful features that are not available elsewhere. Its FAT editor is the best there is. However, its user interface is terrible. Some things that are easy for beginners with a program like the Norton Utilities are difficult for experienced users with Diskutil. Some of the other programs, like Swcom12, are very useful in specialized situations.

All-in-all, Baker's Dozen is a mixed bag. Some of the utilities are very useful while others are so cumbersome they will not get much use. A copy of Baker's Dozen is included on the optional diskette set.

Product:	Baker's Dozen
Price:	$59.95
Category:	Shareware
Publisher:	Buttonware, Incorporated
Address:	Post Office Box 5786
	Bellevue, Washington 98006
Phone:	(206) 454-0479
Notes:	A copy of Baker's Dozen is included on the optional diskette set
Memory:	256K

PC Tools Deluxe

PC Tools Deluxe is a collection of a number of individual programs. Many of those (including a DOS shell, format recovery, disk optimization and caching) are covered in other chapters. The remaining PC Tools Deluxe tools are covered here. These tools are primarily a set of pop-up applications that replace items generally found on an office desk.

Installation   PC Tools Deluxe comes with an installation program that will run from any drive and install PC Tools Deluxe in any subdirectory. The default name for the subdirectory is \PCTOOLS. If you already have an older version of PC Tools installed in that subdirectory, it is renamed to \PCTOOL4. In addition, the installation program add the PC Tools Deluxe subdirectory to the PATH statement in your AUTOEXEC.BAT file without asking permission. It saves the existing AUTOEXEC.BAT file as AUTOEXEC.SAV. It also renames any file named FORMAT.COM in your path to FORMAT!.COM. It creates a batch file called FORMAT.BAT that runs the PC Tools Deluxe formatting program.

In addition to these automatic changes, the PC Tools Deluxe installation program has several optional changes it can make. Basically, these changes are adding the necessary commands to the AUTOEXEC.BAT file to run several of the PC Tools Deluxe memory resident and special applications. The memory resident applications are a caching program and a shell program. The special program is a format recovery program that saves important information about the hard disk in a special file.

Operation   PC Tools Deluxe is a collection of a number of excellent tools. The DOS shell is covered in Chapter 3 and I picked it as one of my favorites. The backup program is covered in Chapter 12. The format recovery program is covered in Chapter 7. It is not as good as some of the other programs on unprotected hard disks. However, it has additional features that make it an excellent choice for future protection. The disk optimizer is covered in Chapter 8. The data encryption program is covered in Chapter 15. The caching program is covered in Chapter 10.

PC Format. PC Format is a replacement for the formatting program that comes with DOS. Unlike the Norton formatting program, PC Format works with both floppy diskettes and hard disks. Its advantages over DOS are:

- When you format a floppy disk with data, PC Format will leave the data intact. It clears the File Allocation Table [FAT] and the first character of the file name in the directory. It stores that first character in one of the reserved bytes, 16-bytes after the beginning of the name in the directory. That allows Rebuild (the unformatting program covered in Chapter 7) to recover the data, including the full file name. If the disk is unformatted or the first two tracks are empty then PC Format will write overwrite every track with a hexadecimal F6 characters, just like DOS.
- When you use PC Format to format a hard disk, it also saves the first character of the file name. However, it only does this for the root directory since Rebuild can recover the full file names for subdirectory entries. PC Format only supports the 512-byte sectors.

This makes PC Format safer than the DOS formatting program. Since it works with hard disks as well as floppy disks, you can delete the FORMAT.COM that comes with DOS and rename PCFORMAT.COM to FORMAT.COM. That way, any program that needs to format a disk will use the safer PC Format program.

PC Format has a number of command line options to control how it operates. Many of these, like /S, duplicate DOS options. Additional options include:

/F This is a full format where it formats every track. However, PC Format still does not lose any data. It reads a track into memory, formats that track then writes the data back to the track. It clears the FAT and directory as usual so you must use Rebuild to recover any data.

/R This is just like the /F option except it does not clear the FAT and directory. You use it to clear up marginal disks but where you need to keep the data.

/Q This is a quick reformatting for diskettes that are already formatted. It clears the FAT and directory but does not scan the disk. It is a quick way to erase a disk.

PC Tools Desktop The PC Tools Desktop is a set of nine application programs bundled into a single program. You can run the Desktop as either a stand-alone program from the DOS prompt or as a memory resident program. Desktop requires only 40K as a memory resident program.

All of the applications run from a common menu, as shown in Fig. 5-5. The programs use pull down menus and have full mouse support. Each of the nine applications is discussed below:

Notepad. The Notepad can edit files up to 64K. It can create straight ASCII text or WordStar files. You can have up to fifteen windows open with the Desktop and if you like each can have a Notepad in it. The screen shot below shows the Notepad.

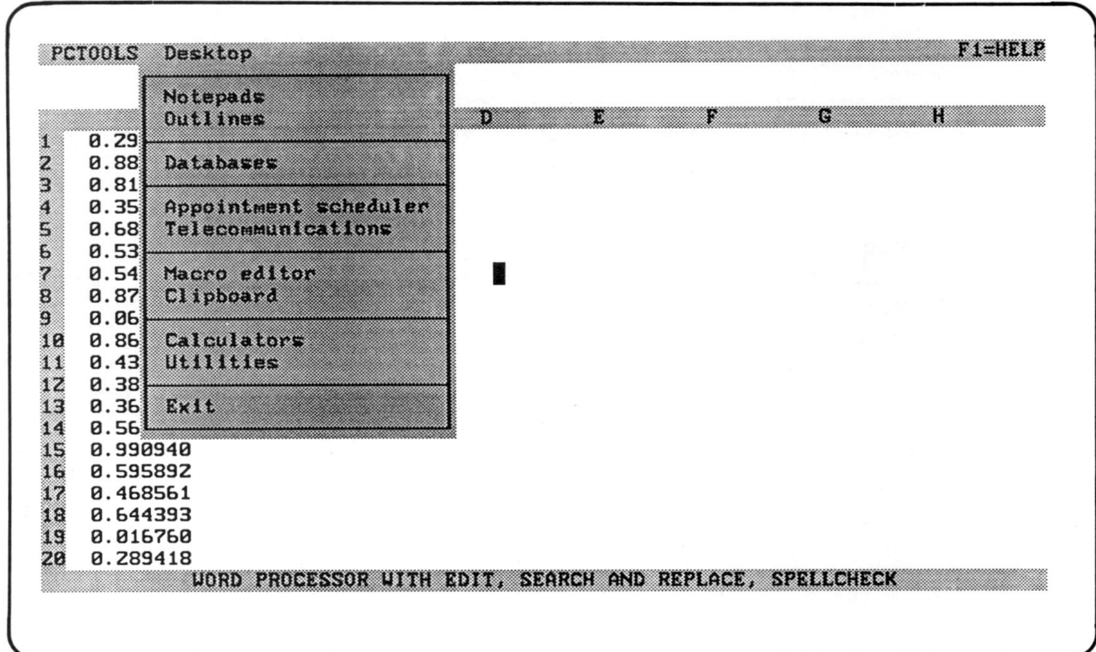

Fig. 5-5. The Desktop portion of PC Tools Deluxe is a pop-up program that gives you nine application programs for 40K of memory. You can also run Desktop as a stand-alone application.

The Notepad is very much a full-featured word processor. For many users, it is all the word processor they will ever need. A few of its major features are:

- Automatically saving the Notepad file at specified intervals without user intervention.
- Cutting and copying information to the Desktop Clipboard for use by other Desktop applications.
- Pasting information from the Desktop Clipboard.
- Checking the spelling of a word, screen or entire files.
- Searching for text and searching for text with replacement.
- Headers and footers.
- Automatic wordwrap and paragraph indenting.
- Block deletes. You can simulate block moves by cutting the block to the Clipboard and pasting it from the Clipboard at another location.

I found the Notepad to be a better notepad than most of the similar programs I have used.

Outlines. The Outline functions as a special Notepad application with additional commands to expand and contract the outline and to control the level of entries. The idea is to view higher levels of the outline as you are developing the paper. As you develop the paper, you view progressively deeper and deeper views of the outline. Normally, you would pop up the outline while working in your word processor or in the Notepad. Figure 5-6 shows the outline.

Databases. The Database uses dBASE III compatible *.DBF databases with the following limits:

- No index files.
- No memo fields.
- 4,000 characters per record.
- 128 fields per record.
- 3,500 records per database.

The Database supports four types of fields, character, numeric, logical and date. It allows you to create format files so the data will be displayed in the format you design inside the Notepad.

By combining the Database with the Notepad, you have an extremely easy to use mailmerge program. Just write your form in the Notepad. Everywhere you want data from the Database to appear, just include the field name in square brackets. Figure 5-7 shows two versions of the same Notepad document. The top version is attached to a comicbook database and shows its data. The bottom version is the same file in the Notepad without linking to the database. Notice how easy it is to add links between the document and database.

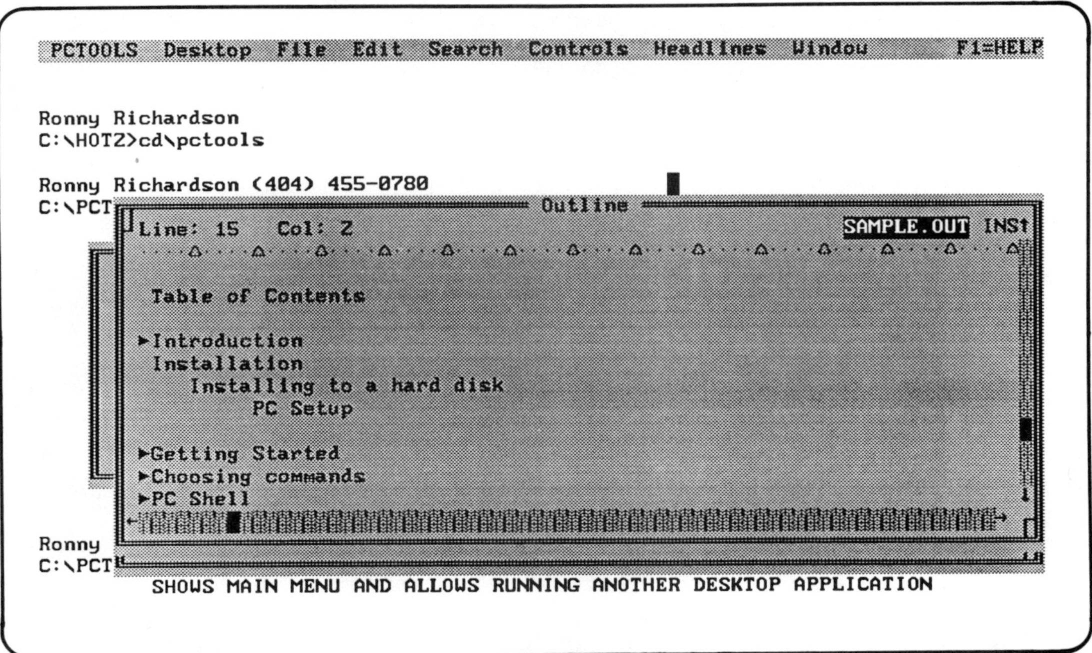

Fig. 5-6. The Outline is a special Notepad that can expand and collapse outline levels.

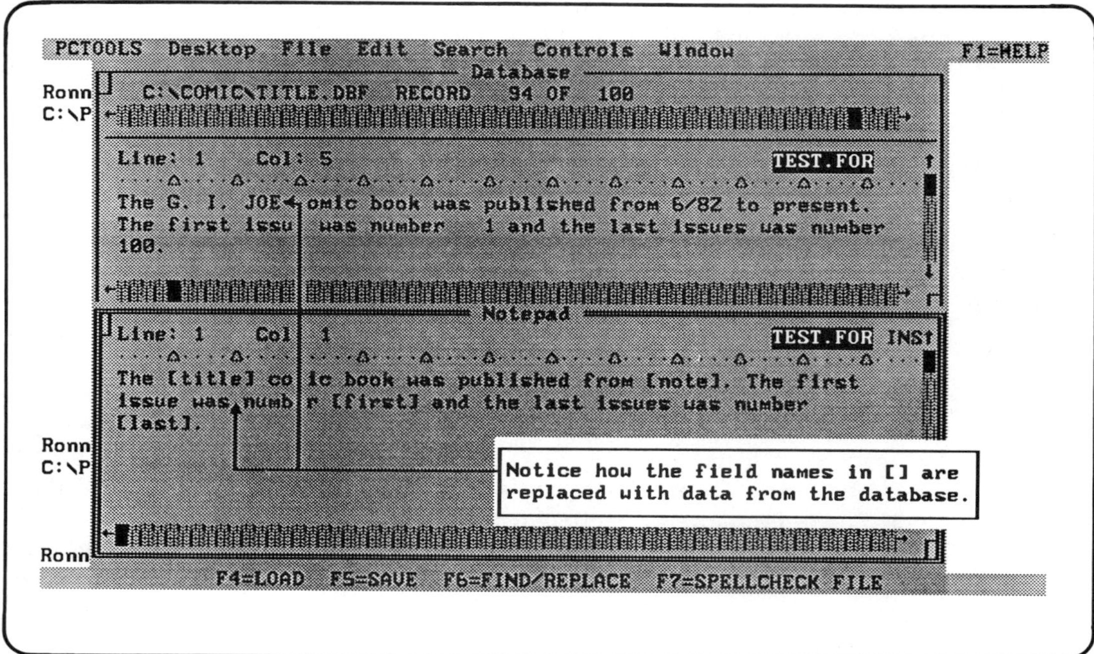

Fig. 5-7. By combining the Database and Notepad, the PC Tools Deluxe Desktop makes it very easy to create form letters that print out with data from a database. The database can be in PC Tools Deluxe or dBASE III format.

The Edit menu includes commands to:

- Add records.
- Delete records.
- Undelete records. The Database works like dBASE III. When you delete a record, it is only marked as deleted and can easily be undeleted.
- Pack the database. The Pack command physically removes the deleted records from the database. After that, you cannot recover deleted records.
- Hide the current record. This prevents the record from being viewed or printed. This allows you to scroll through the database and manually hide specific records before printing a form letter.
- Select all records. This displays all hidden records.
- Change the field names.
- Sort the database on any field.
- Input a selection criteria. This defines values for fields that are acceptable. It only displays and prints records matching these values.

In addition, the Search menu allows you to search for text in specific fields or in all fields. It also allows you to go to a specific record number.

Appointment Scheduler. The Appointment Scheduler screen consists of three parts. The top left shows a month-by-month calendar. The right of the screen shows your schedule in fifteen minute increments from 8 AM to 5 PM. The bottom left shows your to-do list.

To add an appointment, you click on the time. That brings up a second screen. Here you enter the start date and end date for the appointment. You can select a one-time appointment or every day, every workday, weekly, monthly on a fixed day and monthly on a fixed weekday. You also enter the duration, set an alarm and attach a note.

The Appointment Scheduler has a menu where you can select which holidays your firm celebrates and you can even add unique holidays. The Appointment Scheduler can also run a PC Tools Deluxe macro when an alarm goes off. For example, you could leave a disk in the computer and have a late alarm run the Compress program in batch mode to defragment your hard disk. The latter is especially nice since the Compress program is fairly slow.

The to-do list is a list of up to eighty items that you plan to do. The list is independent of the Appointment Scheduler so you only have to save it once. The Appointment Scheduler carries the to-do list forward every day. Items remain on the list until you delete them. You attach a priority from one to ten to each item in the to-do list. It lists all the priority one items first, then the priority two and so on. You cannot change the listing within a priority.

Telecommunications. The telecommunications program supports baud rates from 300 to 19200 and accepts most communications parameters. It will transmit in either ASCII or XMODEM. It can also operate in the background under macro control. You can have it log onto a network and download your mail and stock quotes while you write a memo to the manager.

Macro Editor. You write macros using a pop-up macro editor. Special keystrokes are stored inside angle brackets. You can define macros to be active only in Desktop, active everywhere except Desktop or active everywhere.

Clipboard. The Clipboard works very much like the Clipboard in Windows. It is a temporary storage area. While working in an application, you mark text and cut or copy it to the Clipboard. A cut deletes it from the current application and puts it in the Clipboard. A copy simply makes a duplicate version of the information in the Clipboard. Generally, you can only cut while within PC Tools Deluxe applications. With other applications you have to copy to the Clipboard.

Calculators. The Desktop has three calculators, algebraic, financial and programmers. The algebraic calculator works just like most of the stand-alone calculators being sold today. To add one to one, you enter one, plus, one, enter. The calculator displays two.

The financial calculator emulates the Hewlett-Packard HP-12C calculator, one of the more difficult to use calculators currently available. In fact, the manual warns "Central Point Software, Inc. does not guarantee that the keystroke sequences and the results are correct or suitable for your purposes. You are responsible for decisions you make when using the Financial Calculator." [page 426] To add one and one using this calculator, you enter one, enter, one, enter, plus. The calculator displays two. Figure 5-8 shows the financial calculator.

The programmers calculator lets you enter numbers or calculators in

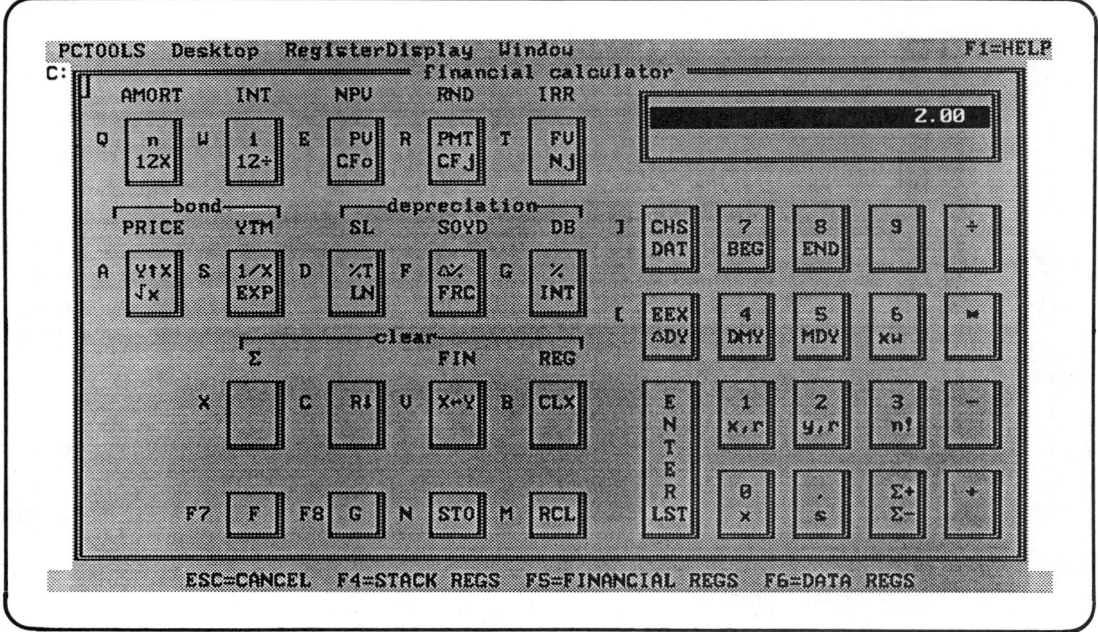

Fig. 5-8. The PC Tools Deluxe Desktop calculator can emulate the Hewlett-packard HP-12C financial calculator.

hexadecimal, octal, binary or decimal. The results are shown in all four categories.

Utilities. This menu lets you change the hot-keys the Desktop programs use, view an ASCII table, change the colors and unload the Desktop.

Limitations   Some of the PC Tools Deluxe programs discussed in other chapters have significant limitations. These are discussed in the appropriate chapters.

After creating a form letter in the Notepad for one of the databases in the Database, I was not able to unattach the form letter. Every time I tried to edit or view the database, the form letter appeared. I ended up having to erase the form letter in DOS to access the database normally. When using the Select option on the Edit menu to enter acceptable field values to select records to display, you can only use character fields. The manual does not mention this limitation.

While the macro editor is very useful, it falls short of dedicated macro programs like SuperKey. With SuperKey, you can define macros on the fly and record macros by working through the commands. With the PC Tools Deluxe macro program, you must pop up the editor and manually write your macros.

As you would expect, the Clipboard only works in text mode. However, it even has a few problems in text mode. In addition to 25-line mode an EGA screen can run in 43-line text mode and a VGA screen can run in either 43-line or 50-line mode. The Clipboard forces them into 25-line mode when it pops up to cut or paste. After exiting the Clipboard, the screens are completely unreadable. The information is there, you just cannot read it. In most programs you have to save and exit (without being able to read the screen). A few programs, like Microsoft Word, have commands to redraw the screen and will work properly from then on.

Manual   PC Tools Deluxe has a wonderful manual. Very few of the software packages in this book have manuals the caliber of this one. Each major program in the PC Tools Deluxe package has its own section. Each section explains how to use that program as though you have no experience with any of the other programs. With a few minor lapses, it explains every menu option in detail. The manual is lavishly illustrated with screen shots so you know exactly what to expect to see on the screen. It has an excellent table of contents and index. What makes all this especially surprising is PC Tools Deluxe is a fairly inexpensive utility.

Conclusion   PC Tools Deluxe reminds me a lot of a Swiss army knife. It has a number of features, many of them excellent. The shell is excellent. Other features, like its unerasing and macro program, are fairly weak. The decision to buy PC Tools Deluxe is still a fairly easy one. The PC Shell program is one of the best in its class and alone is worth the price of the PC Tools Deluxe package.

Product:	PC Shell
Price:	$129.00
Category:	Commercial
Publisher:	Central Point Software, Incorporated
Address:	15220 NW Greenbrier Parkway
	Suite 200
	Beaverton, Oregon 97006
Phone:	(503) 690-8090
Notes:	PC Shell is only one small portion of the PC Tools Deluxe package.
	In memory resident mode it requires 9K while not running and 170K while active.
	In stand-alone mode it requires 256K.
	256K is the minimum memory requirements; however, PC Shell will use all available memory.
Memory:	256K

Take Charge

Take Charge is a commercial memory resident program. It features a wealth of features including a DOS shell, menu program and format recovery. Many of these features are discussed elsewhere in this book. The remaining features are discussed here.

Installation   Take Charge comes with an installation program. It lets you select the drive to install Take Charge on but requires you to use the \ TC! subdirectory. It runs from the A-drive and requires an ASSIGN A = B statement to run from the B-drive.

Operation   Take Charge comes with a function menu program. The menu is covered in Chapter 2. It comes with a DOS shell program. The DOS shell is covered in Chapter 3. It comes with a format recovery program. The format recovery program is covered in Chapter 7.

Clipboard. Anytime you are running an application in text mode and Take Charge is active, you can use the Clipboard to transfer information. To capture the information, you press Alt-Space bar to activate Take Charge and then Alt-C to bring up the Clipboard. You move the cursor around the screen to capture just the information you want and then press Return to grab it. If you need to further refine the captured data, you can edit the data in the Clipboard using the built-in editor, discussed later. When you are ready to paste the information, you bring up Take Charge and press Alt-P.

Alarm Clock. When you press Alt-Space bar, it brings up the main Take Charge menu shown in Fig. 5-9. Pressing F1 brings up an alarm clock you can use to remind you of up to fifteen events. At the appropriate time, the Alarm Clock sounds a bell and it displays a single text line at the top of the screen to remind you. The bell sounds for three seconds and repeats until you press the Escape key.

Appointment Calendar. Pressing F2 brings up the Appointment Calendar. It shows a calendar on the left side of the screen. You move the highlighted

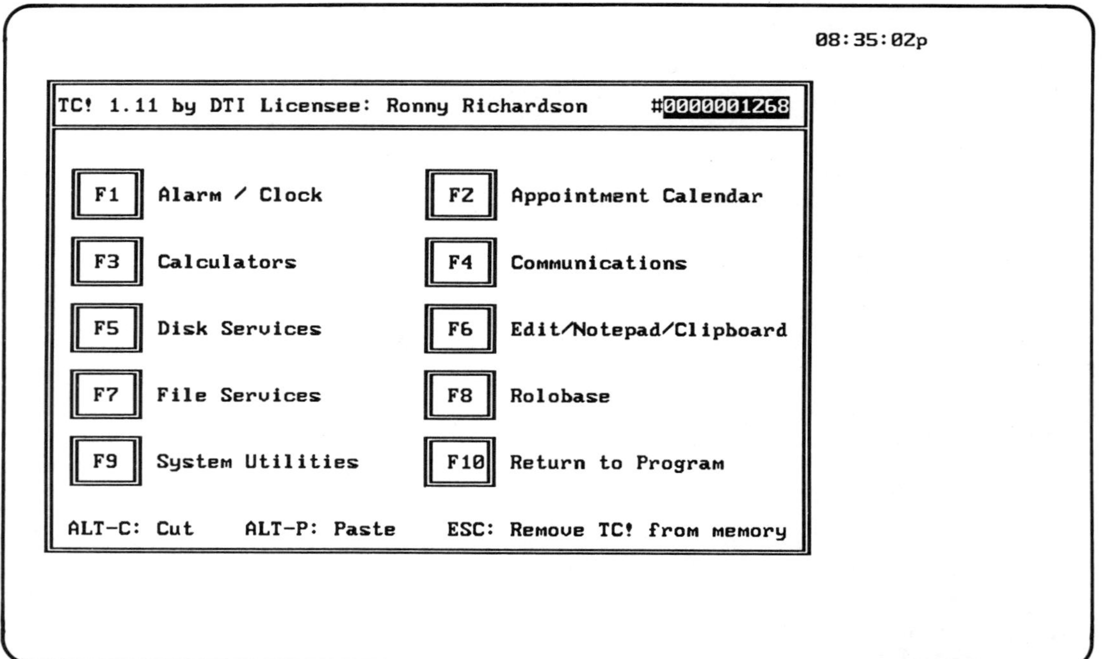

Fig. 5-9. Pressing the Take Charge hot-key brings up the main menu you use to run many applications.

cursor to the day you want to look at or edit and press Return. That brings up an appointment scheduler on the right side of the screen.

The appointment scheduler divides the day into 96 15-minute blocks. Unlike some other programs, it has room for the entire day from 12 AM to 12 PM. There are options to:

- Delete all the appointments for the current day.
- Delete all the appointments for a range of days.
- Print appoints for a day.
- Print appoints for a range of days.
- Add a single note to the top of the schedule for the day.

Calculators. Pressing F3 from the Take Charge lets you select from two different calculators. The first is a reverse Polish notation [NPR] calculator with a wealth of available features as shown in Fig. 5-10. Take Charge also has a standard adding machine type calculator complete with a tape.

Communications. The communications module is an easy to use program with the capacity to store up to 100 numbers for quick dialing. It has macro scripting ability. It supports ASCII, CRC Xmodem, Kermit and Xmodem protocols.

Disk Services. The Disk Services feature is the heart of the file maintenance features offered by Take Charge. Take Charge offers a menu to use the Disk Services programs by pressing the F5 key. Figure 5-11 shows this. However, you can also run these programs from the DOS command line, with or

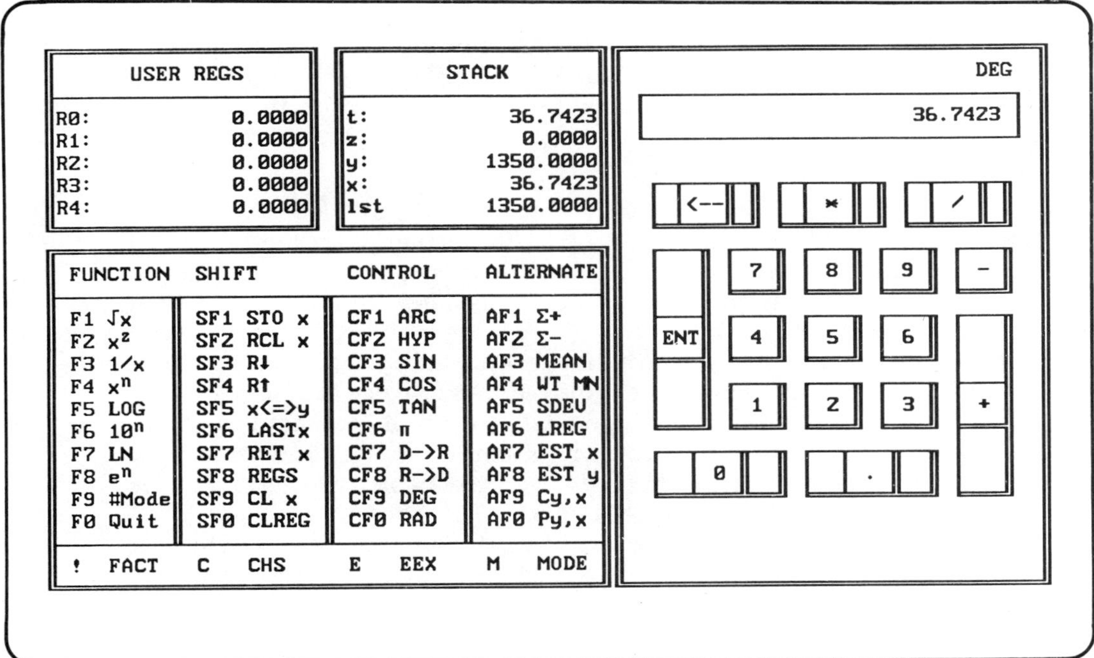

Fig. 5-10. The Take Charge reverse Polish notation calculator has a wealth of scientific and mathematical functions.

```
ABBR UTILITY FUNCTION              |              UTILITY DESCRIPTION

DD   Disk Directory       Overview:  DD is a graphic directory display command
DE   Directory Editor                showing the directories and files of an
DM   Disk Map                        entire disk.
DO   Disk Optimizer
DS   Directory Sort       Syntax  :  DD [d:path] [/bw]
DT   Disk Test
FI   FileInfo             [d:path]   the disk whose directories and files are
FL   File Locator                    to be displayed. A starting directory can
FR   Format Recovery                 be specified.
HE   Hex Editor
SW   Stop Watch           [/bw]      Shows all screen output in black & white.
TD   Tree Directory                  For monitors which cannot display colors
UD   UnDelete                        clearly.
VL   Volume Label
ZD   Zap Disk             Example:   View the disk directory structure of drive
ZF   Zap File                        C:, beginning at the current directory
                                     DD c:

TAB-Quick Mode                                          F1-Help   F10-Quit
```

Fig. 5-11. The Take Charge Disk Services menu can be used to run any of the file utilities. These can also be run from the DOS command link.

without Take Charge in memory. You do this by entering the two letter abbreviation along with any necessary switches. When you select the program from this menu, it prompts you for the switches while explaining them on the screen.

The features available are:

- Disk Directory. This shows a graphical tree of the hard disk on the top half of the screen. As you move around the tree, the display at the bottom shows the files in the currently highlighted subdirectory. It can display files in short format with only their name and extension or in long format with their size, date, time and attributes.

- Directory Editor. This lets you edit the attributes of each file in a subdirectory. It also allows you to change the file name, size (very dangerous), date, time and starting cluster (very dangerous). Because it can change the size and starting cluster, the Directory Editor can do major damage to your data. Unless you are very technically knowledgeable, you should erase DE.EXE from the Take Charge subdirectory.

- Disk Map. This shows a map of the hard disk similar to those shown by disk optimizers and shows a separate screen with technical information on the disk.

- Directory Sort. This sorts the files in name, extension, date, time or size order. The sorting can be ascending or descending. It can sort files across all subdirectories.

- Disk Test. This tests all or part of the disk to make sure it can read that portion of the disk being tested. It marks problem areas as bad.
- FileInfo. This appends a 60-character description onto the file. The program lets you create and edit these comments in a full-screen mode. The display can be toggled to display less of the comment and more information about the file. It stores the existing file name and the comment in a database file. Each time you enter the FI command, the program matches file names to display with comments. It has commands to add and modify comments and to remove comments for files that no longer exist. Since the program is not memory resident, it cannot update the file automatically when you delete, rename or move files.
- File Locater. This locates all the files matching a file specification it prompts you for.
- Hex Editor. This shows the file on a split screen with the hexadecimal values on one side and the ASCII values on the other. You can edit the file on either side.
- Stop Watch. Take Charge has ten separate timers built in. You can use these for timing your activities for billing purposes.
- Tree Directory. This reads in the current directory structure and displays a graphical tree on the screen. You can then move around this tree adding and deleting subdirectories.
- UnDelete. This unerases files. Take Charge reads the directory you select and displays a list of all the files it thinks it can recover. You begin undeleting by tagging the files to undelete. Then, if you press F1, Take Charge will undelete them automatically and pick its own character for the first letter of the name. Pressing F2 does the same automatic recovery except Take Charge prompts you for the first character of the file name. Pressing F3 lets you examine each cluster of the file and decide which ones to add to the recovered file. As part of the manual reconstruction you can search for text strings on the disk or go to absolute sectors. Take Charge will protect existing files by keeping you from manually adding a cluster from an existing file into a file you are recovering.
- Volume Label. This adds, deletes or changes the volume label on a disk.
- Zap Disk. This overwrites an entire disk or its erased space with an ASCII character so no file can be unerased.
- Zap File. This overwrites a file with an ASCII character so it cannot be successfully unerased.

Editor. Take Charge includes an excellent ASCII editor. Using it, you can edit up to 10 files at once. The size of each file is limited only by available disk space. In addition to editing files, the editor can edit the clipboard. The editor has block copies and moves along with search and replace.

Rolobase. The Take Charge Rolobase is a pop-up database with predefined fields. When you first start Rolobase, you see a screen that shows names and home and business phone numbers. Figure 5-12 shows this. By moving the cursor to a specific entry and pressing Return, you get detailed information on a specific entry. It uses a similar screen to enter and update information in the database. In addition to this, Rolobase can use a modem to dial

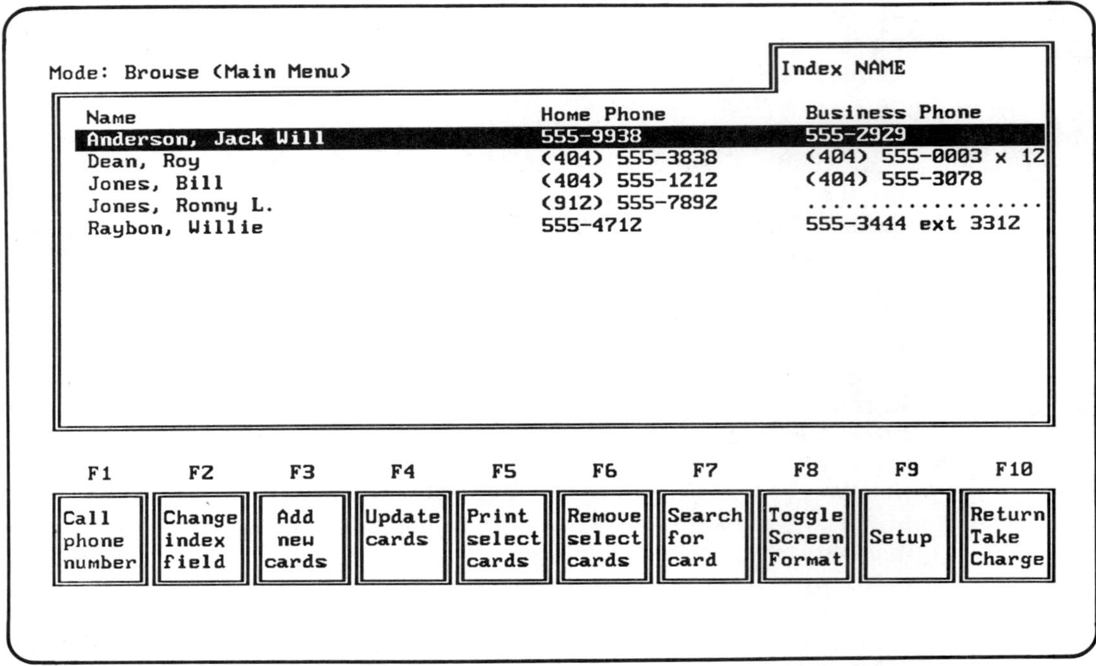

Fig. 5-12. When you first start the Take Charge Rolobase, it displays the names and phone numbers for the people in the database.

either the business or home numbers for any database entry. As you build larger databases, Rolobase has a search option for finding specific entries quickly.

System Utilities. The System Utilities menu controls the Take Charge environment. It has options to . . .

- Turn the alarm clock on and off.
- Turn the display of the clock on and off. When this is on, Take Charge displays the time in the upper right corner of the screen. The clock display is active even when Take Charge is not.
- Display a pop up ASCII table. This is improperly placed since it is not a configuration option. Rather, it is simply a display.
- Change the way Take Charge displays the date.
- Keyboard lock. Again this is not really a configuration. It prompts you for a password and then locks the keyboard until someone enters that password again.
- Printer redirect. This causes Take Charge to redirect printer output to a file with the name you specify.
- Screen Saver. This prompts you for the inactive time after which Take Charge should blank the screen. You can enter values between 0 and 99 minutes.
- Speed key toggle. If this is on and the computer supports it, Take Charge triples the repeat rate for the keys.

- System reset. This removes any programs from memory that you loaded into memory after Take Charge.

Limitations　　Having Take Charge in memory disables DOS command editing. Normally, pressing F3 displays the past command and F2 will display the past command up to the key you press after F2. When Take Charge is in memory, these no longer work.

I tried to log onto the PC-Link computer network while Take Charge was in memory but not active. PC-Link runs under a runtime version of the Deskmate program from Tandy. All of the PC-Link characters it displays in graphic mode appeared normally. All of the PC-Link characters that it displays in text mode looked like static on a monitor display and were completely unreadable. Clearly Take Charge interferes with either the runtime Deskmate or the PC-Link software.

While moving around many of the Take Charge menus and screens, pressing the 5-key in the middle of the number pad (which does nothing) will blank the screen until you press another key. This ability to blank the screen would be an advantage if you activated it by some out of the way keystroke combination. However, the proximity of the 5-key to commonly used keys means you often accidentally blank the screen. New users may not be able to quickly identify the problem.

Because some Take Charge operations do not work under DOS 4.0, I copied the Take Charge programs to a DOS 3.3 disk. I then booted off that disk to run some tests. When I did that, the serial number Take Charge normally displays on the log on screen changed to "bootlegged". This was especially annoying because I had a legal and registered copy. While the serial number changed, my name remained on the display. I guess that was to show where the "bootlegged" copy came from.

The Disk Directory in Disk Services can display only a limited number of subdirectories. When I tried to use in on a disk with about 200 subdirectories, it refused to display any of them other than the current subdirectory.

If you do not have a LASTDRIVE statement in your CONFIG.SYS file, the File Services will let you select from drives A-E for a copy command even though not all those drives exist. If you select a non-existent drive, it responds with the less than helpful "Cannot create destination file (Disk fill [sic] or R/O file exists??.)" error message. If you enter an improper file name or a file name with wildcards, it responds with the same error message. Some of the other options, like finding a file, have this same problem.

The manual claims that pressing F4 in the Systems Utilities menu will activate DOS command recall. This would have Take Charge store your DOS commands for reuse. F4 does not do this. Rather, it changes the way Take Charge displays dates. The command to activate DOS command recall is missing from Take Charge.

The Directory Editor and Directory Sort refused to run under DOS 4.0. It responded with a "no files" error message in most directories containing files. In a few large subdirectories, it responded there were too many files to load. Undelete refused to run as well. It displayed no error message.

Disk Map only works with hard disks that have 512-byte sectors. DOS 4.x increased the size of hard disk partitions by increasing the sector size to 2048-bytes on large hard disks. Disk Map will not work with these disks. The Disk Optimizer will not run under DOS 4.0 even on disks with 512-byte sectors. Disk Test ran on 512-sector disks under DOS 4.0 but would not run on disks with larger sectors.

The Hex Editor can only keep a small portion of the file in memory. When you try to scroll past what is in memory and you have made changes, the editor gives you the option of saving or discarding your changes. This is how the program should work. However, Hex Editor sometimes prompts you with this message even if you have changed nothing.

DOS allows spaces in the volume label. You can even enter them directly when formatting a disk with more recent versions of DOS. However, the Take Charge Volume Label program does not allow spaces. Since you enter the command on the command line, Volume Label must break the command line down into pieces. It treats all the text after the last space as a label. Therefore, it ignores any part of the label before the space.

Manual   The Take Charge manual is very complete. It does a good job of explaining how to run all the features included in Take Charge. The manual is a paperback book and appears to have been constructed of bound photocopied sheets. The paper used in the manual is low quality paper. Many of the pages were printed with the lines at a slight angle and some of them are printed with the ends of the lines chopped off. Not enough of the pages are misprinted to cause serious problems, however, the lack of print quality is annoying.

Conclusion   Take Charge has a wealth of features at a low price. It is especially attractive because it is able to do so much with so little memory. However, those features and functionality come with a long list of bugs. Take Charge has the appearance of a program that was rushed to market with inadequate testing. Only you can decide if the low price is worth dealing with the significant problems. (For ordering information, see page 224.)

ALSO SEE. . .

Many of the features of these programs replicate stand-alone programs that do a better job. However, collecting the individual stand-alone programs represents a significant investment. The primary decision you have to make is if the excellent price of either of these utilities is worth losing some functionality.

6
Disk Maintenance

Your hard disk is going to fail. While that is a depressing thought, there is no way you can avoid it. You can, however, prevent it from happening as soon as it otherwise would or causing as much damage as it otherwise would.

The single most important step to take is to make frequent backups. No program in this chapter in any way reduces your need to make frequent backups. Nothing is more comforting when your hard disk gives you an "Abort, Ignore, Retry or Fail" error message than a recent backup. In fact, most of the programs in this chapter warn you not to run them unless your backup is current.

Next to a backup, your next line of defense is running the DOS CHKDSK program often. CHKDSK does not spot physical problems with your hard (or floppy) disk. Rather, it spots logical problems. The two most common problems it spots are cross-linked clusters and non-allocated clusters.

A cross-linked cluster is a cluster that DOS thinks is part of two files. Because a cluster can only point to one following cluster, the files will be the same beyond the cross-linked cluster. (Actually, the file allocation table entry points to the next cluster, not the cluster itself. This is explained in detail in Appendix F.) This error means at least one of the files is damaged. A non-allocated cluster is a cluster that DOS has marked as in-use by the file allocation table but which is not part of any file. This is a lost chain. This can happen when you reboot or there is a power failure while the computer is writing a file. CHKDSK will correct both problems if you run it with the /F (or fix) option. However, the data recovered by CHKDSK may be incomplete or damaged. See Appendix F for more information on this.

The programs in this chapter can also help forestall hard-disk problems. They test your hard disk (some of them will also test floppy disks) and look for problems. When they find a problem, some of them will mark the area as bad so DOS will not try to use it. Still others will try to correct the problem first. This involves reading the data into memory and then performing a low-level format on just the bad spot on the disk. If this corrects the problem, then the program rewrites the data to its original location. Otherwise, it marks the spot as bad and writes the data to another location.

Some drives, especially hard disk cards, do not allow low-level formatting. This will reduce the effectiveness of these programs. If you are not sure about your drive, check with its manufacturer or with the maker of the maintenance program you select.

Anadisk

Anadisk is a shareware program that analyzes, inspects, edits, repairs and copies 5.25 and 3.5 inch diskettes. It does not work with hard disks. In addition to working with IBM format disks, it will work with Atari ST disks. Anadisk can also work with many non-DOS formats used to copy protect games. I did not test this.

Installation   Anadisk is shareware. Generally its files are compressed into a single archive file. Installing it requires that you unarchive these files. From that point, Anadisk has no installation program. However, it will run without additional installation.

Operation   When you start Anadisk, you first see an informational screen. After that, you reach the main menu. The options on this menu are:

- Scan. This reads every sector on the diskette and displays detailed technical information on the diskette. Figure 6-1 shows this. Scanning the disk will let you know the general readability of the disk. Scan can optionally search for a data pattern on the disk.
- Edit Sectors. This lets you edit the actual sector you specify without consideration for which file they are a part of. Figure 6-2 shows this. You can edit in either ASCII or hexadecimal.
- Edit Files. This functions just like edit sectors except you select files to edit rather than sectors. Once you select a file name, you can only edit sectors in that file.
- Repair. This scans the disk for readability and reconciles the state of each sector to the file allocation table [FAT]. Since this function depends on a DOS structured FAT, it only works with DOS disks.
- Copy. This is a sector-by-sector copy from one diskette to another regardless of the underlying diskette format. While not intended or promoted as such, this copying method will copy some copy protected disks. The copy program verifies its results by reading back the data after it writes it. When the copy program finds an error in the data, it copies the data with the error intact.

Fig. 6-1. Anadisk will scan a floppy disk and display detailed technical information on the disk.

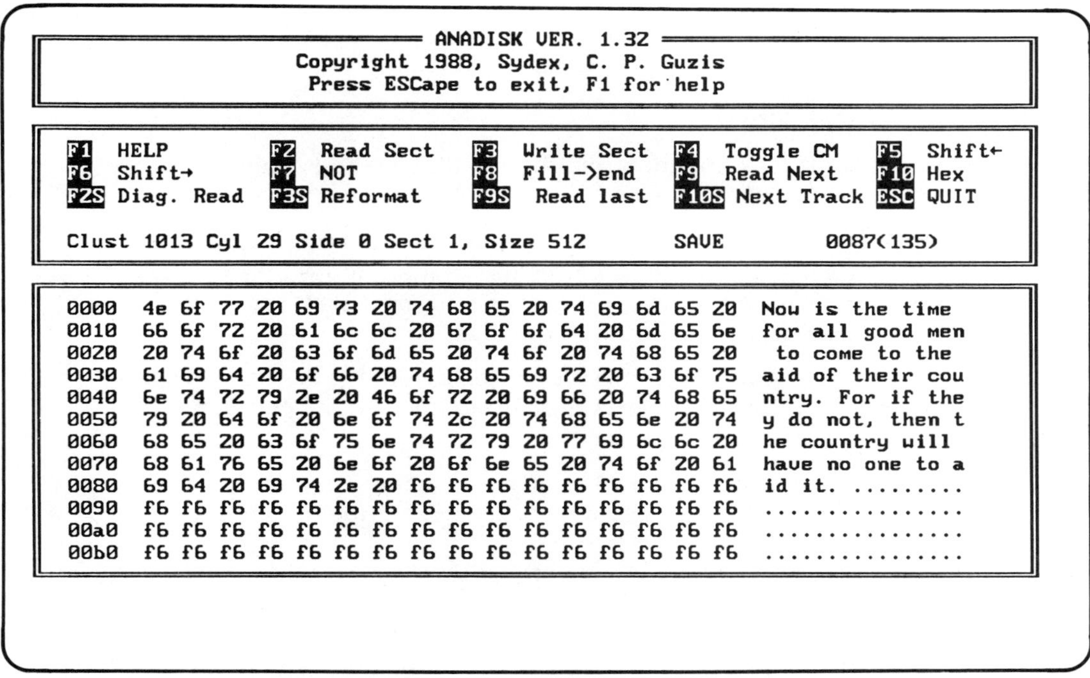

Fig. 6-2. Anadisk will allow you to edit a file in either ASCII or hexadecimal.

- Dump. This copies the data in a range of cylinders to a file for later processing. I found this useful when trying to recover data from a problem diskette. I was able to process the data from the dump without trying to work on the problem diskette itself.

Limitations   Anadisk is not extremely difficult to use. However, an experienced user would find it difficult to use Anadisk to recover damaged information off a floppy diskette. The main difficulty is in the manual. It tells how to use the program. However, it fails to provide enough background information for a new user trying to learn the program.

Manual   Like most shareware programs, Anadisk has its manual as an ASCII file on the disk. The manual does a good job of explaining how to use the features of Anadisk. As discussed above, the manual provides inadequate background for new users.

Conclusion   Anadisk is useful for recovering data from problem diskettes. A copy of Anadisk is on the optional diskette set.

```
Product:      Anadisk
Price:        $15     Non Commercial
Category:     Shareware
Publisher:    Sydex
Address:      153 North Murphy Avenue
              Sunnyvale, California 94086
Phone:        (408) 739-4866
Notes:        The optional diskette set includes a
              copy of Anadisk.
Memory:       128K
```

Disk Drive Analyzer

Disk Drive Analyzer is a commercial floppy disk testing program from Verbatim.

Installation   There is no installation. For technical reasons (not copy protection), Disk Drive Analyzer must run from its distribution floppy diskette. The manual does briefly tell how to transfer the system to the diskette to make it a bootable disk. This is not necessary to use the disk, however.

Operation   Disk Drive Analyzer is very easy to use. You put it in a floppy drive, log onto that drive and enter DDA. The program does the rest. It makes seven reports. They are:

1) Disk Speed. It tests the diskette revolution speed against the internal clock twenty times and issues a pass/fail report. It issues additional reports if the speed is more that .25% off.
2) Noise Tolerance. The enter-most track of the distribution disk is recorded at one half its normal width. The program tests the drive to see if it can read this track. This simulates a "worst-case" read test for the drive.
3) Write then Read. The program writes data to the disk and then reads to see if it is read without errors.

4) Track Alignment. The program tests for track alignment. If the drive fails, it reports if the failure was due to disk clamping eccentricity or erase crosstalk.

5) Positioner Backlash. A drive head positioner will normally have some backlash. This causes it to position the head differently depending on which direction it approaches a track from. The program reports if this is out of tolerance.

6) Clamping. A disk drive must physically position the disk in the center of the drive while you close the drive locking mechanism. If it does this improperly, the disk will be in different positions each time you insert it. If the program suspects a clamping error, it prompts you to repeat the test after removing and reinserting the diskette.

7) Erase Crosstalk. The heads in a disk drive contain elements that clear special zones between the tracks when the diskette is being written to. They do this so a drive can be slightly out of alignment without the heads receiving interference from adjacent tracks. Erase crosstalk errors result when these special elements begin to pick up signals. This signals defective heads. They cannot be repaired so you must replace them.

Limitations   Disk Drive Analyzer will only work on a 5.25 inch 360K drive. When Disk Drive Analyzer exits, it leaves the display in 40-column mode.

Manual   The manual is very brief. However, this program flags problems the average user is not going to be able to correct. Therefore, all the manual needs to do is tell you how to run the tests. It does that adequately. It also includes a two page quick reference card.

Conclusion   Disk Drive Analyzer does a good job of testing 360K floppy disk drives.

<table>
<tr><td>Product:</td><td>Disk Drive Analyzer</td></tr>
<tr><td>Price:</td><td>$39.95</td></tr>
<tr><td>Category:</td><td>Commercial</td></tr>
<tr><td>Publisher:</td><td>Verbatim Corporation</td></tr>
<tr><td>Address:</td><td>1200 W. T. Harris Boulevard
Charlotte, North Carolina 28213</td></tr>
<tr><td>Phone:</td><td>(800) 538-8589
(704) 547-6500</td></tr>
<tr><td>Memory:</td><td>128K</td></tr>
</table>

Disk Manager Diagnostics

Disk Manager Diagnostics is a commercial program for testing your hard disk and related systems. It will verify the hard disk, controller, cables and drive communications.

Installation   There is no installation program. The manual assumes you will be running the program from a floppy diskette. There are only two files and you can copy these to a subdirectory on your hard disk if you like.

Operation   When started, Disk Manager Diagnostics first reads the drive table. It asks you which drive to use if you have more than one. Once you have selected a drive, it displays the characteristics and asks if you want to use them. Normally, you would answer yes.

The main menu gives you the following options:

1) Run all tests. This runs most of the tests. However, it skips tests involving the customer engineer [CE] cylinder and the option to verify the media. (The customer engineer or CE cylinder is the last cylinder on the disk. This cylinder is reserved for the controller and is not normally used by DOS. Because it is not used by DOS, it was not formatted by DOS when the drive was initialized. Therefore it must be formatted before use.)

2) Run individual tests. This brings up another menu where you can select the following tests:

   - Controller tests. This tests the controller card and does not even need the hard disk connected to the controller. When it finds a fault, Disk Manager Diagnostics can display a detailed help screen to help you spot the problem. Figure 6-3 shows this.
   - Seek Tests. This performs a sequential, harmonic and random seek test on the hard disk.
   - Random read tests. This tests the overall disk by randomly reading selected areas of the disk.

```
THE HARD DISK BIOS RETURNED A STATUS WHICH INDICATES
THAT THE HARD DISK CONTROLLER HAS MALFUNCTIONED.

1-The hard disk controller card may be defective.
    Power off the computer, reseat the card, then retry
    diagnostics.  If this problem persists, replace the
    hard disk controller card.

2-Drive cables may be incorrectly installed or defective.
    Please refer to Appendix -B- of the diagnostic manual
    as a guide to installing cables and jumpers.




CONTROLLER RAM TESTS FAILED
Bad command received by controller.
                    Press any key to return.
```

Fig. 6-3. When Disk Manager Diagnostics finds a fault, it can display a detailed help screen to help you find the problem.

- Read/write tests. This test tries to write to and read from the CE cylinder.
- ECC read/write tests. This test forces errors onto the CE cylinder and then tests the controller's ability to correct those errors.
- Verify disk media. This is a nondestructive scan on the hard disk for read errors.

3) Repeat the tests. This lets you run the tests more than once. In fact, it lets you repeat them up to 9,999 times.

4) Allow CE cylinder writes. This is a toggle that lets the program write to the CE area.

5) Stop on error. This is another toggle that controls if Disk Manager Diagnostics continues once it finds an error.

6) Select drive. You use this option only if you have more than one hard disk installed. It lets you switch between available hard disks.

7) Format CE cylinder. You must do this before Disk Manager Diagnostics can write to the area.

8) Display all disk parameters. This shows technical information on the hard disk. Figure 6-4 shows this.

Limitations   When you start Disk Manager Diagnostics, it asks if you want to use drive one or two even if you only have one hard disk. If you select drive two and only have one drive, it responds with an error message. Because it knows you only have one drive, this is a senseless prompt. In addition, it is likely to cause confusion for new users. Disk Manager Diagnostics treats a hard disk as

```
        DISK MANAGER DIAGNOSTICS 1.04 SERIAL NO. 00002411
        COPYRIGHT (C) ONTRACK COMPUTER SYSTEMS INC. 1986

        PARAMETERS                      DRIVE ONE    DRIVE TWO

        SETUP TYPE                          0            0
        MEGABYTES                        297.7        781.1
        CYLINDERS                        21328        65460
        HEADS                              176          235
        REDUCED WRITE CURRENT            58891        45103
        WRITE PRE-COMP                   60192        58891
        ECC CORRECTION SPAN                  0          160
        CONTROL BYTE                       228          235
        STANDARD TIME OUT                   32            0
        FORMAT DRIVE TIME OUT              138          228
        CHECK DRIVE TIME OUT              224          160
        LANDING ZONE                     50186        63626
        SECTORS PER TRACK                  117           10


        Press F1 to modify DRIVE ONE       Press F2 to modify DRIVE TWO
        Press F10 to return to main menu.
```

Fig. 6-4. Before testing a drive, Disk Manager Diagnostics displays technical information on the drive.

one drive no matter how many partitions it has. For example, I often use an AT-clone with a 40 Meg hard disk running under DOS 3.3. The hard disk is partitioned into two logical 20 Meg hard disks. Most users with this setup are used to thinking about their C-drive and D-drive as two hard disks. However, under Disk Manager Diagnostics they are a single drive.

I tried to format the CE cylinder on the Plus Development Passport hard disk. Disk Manager Diagnostics responded with "Passport hard disks cannot be low-level formatted." This is the correct response. However, at this point the program locked up. All of the Disk Manager Diagnostics tests except the scan of the entire hard disk are completely DOS 4.0 incompatible.

Disk Manager Diagnostics can scan the disk and check for read errors. However, it cannot mark defective areas as bad so DOS will not use them. For that the manual tells you to reformat the disk.

Manual   The manual is very brief and requires a good deal of technical ability to understand. It includes a brief explanation on installing a hard disk.

Conclusion   Other products in this chapter offer disk testing programs that are easier to use and offer more complete testing. The major advantage of Disk Manager Diagnostics is its ability to test the controller card.

Product:	Disk Manager Diagnostics
Price:	$124.95
Category:	Commercial
Publisher:	Ontrack Computer Systems
Address:	6321 Bury Drive
	Eden Prairie, Minnesota 55346
Phone:	(800) 752-1333
	(612) 937-1107
Memory:	128K

Disk Technician Advanced

Disk Technician Advanced is a commercial disk testing program that uses a database and artificial intelligence to track and test your hard disk.

Installation   The manual suggests you copy the files to a diskette with the system on it. You use this disk to boot from to make sure the computer does not load any unnecessary software. Of course, if your system requires a device driver to access the hard disk you will need to add that to the boot disk.

Once you create this boot disk, you run the installation program off of this disk. That program gives you the option of installing Disk Technician Advanced on either the hard disk or floppy. The advantage of floppy diskette installation is it gives you a working copy of the program and database. You can use this for recovery if the hard disk fails completely. The installation program will automatically install a head parking program on your hard disk. It will also add the necessary command to your AUTOEXEC.BAT file to start it.

Operation   Disk Technician Advanced should be run every single day. The manual warns you to warm up the computer for at least two hours prior to running Disk Technician Advanced. You usually run the program from a floppy diskette. It stores information on this floppy diskette that it can use to help recover from major hard disk failures. Its ability to recover is limited if it stores that data on the hard disk. Its ability to recover is a function of the data; its ability to read the disk is a function of its recovery ability. However, for the bold the program will run from a hard disk and even gives you that option during installation.

If you do install Disk Technician Advanced on a hard disk, it makes provisions to boot using its own CONFIG.SYS and AUTOEXEC.BAT files. It restores your normal files after Disk Technician Advanced finishes testing.

Disk Technician Advanced uses information in its database to make decisions about how to treat the hard disk. It is critical that the database it uses is correct for the hard disk. To prevent mistakes, Disk Technician Advanced adds a number to the hard disk in an area it marks as bad. The program will only run when the database number matches this number. This is, however, not copy protection. You can easily reinstall Disk Technician Advanced from the distribution disk if you damage the working floppy disk or change computers.

The first time you run Disk Technician Advanced, it performs a "monthly" test. Before running the test, it shows an informational screen. This screen is blank and will be filled in after Disk Technician Advanced has run. Figure 6-5 shows this.

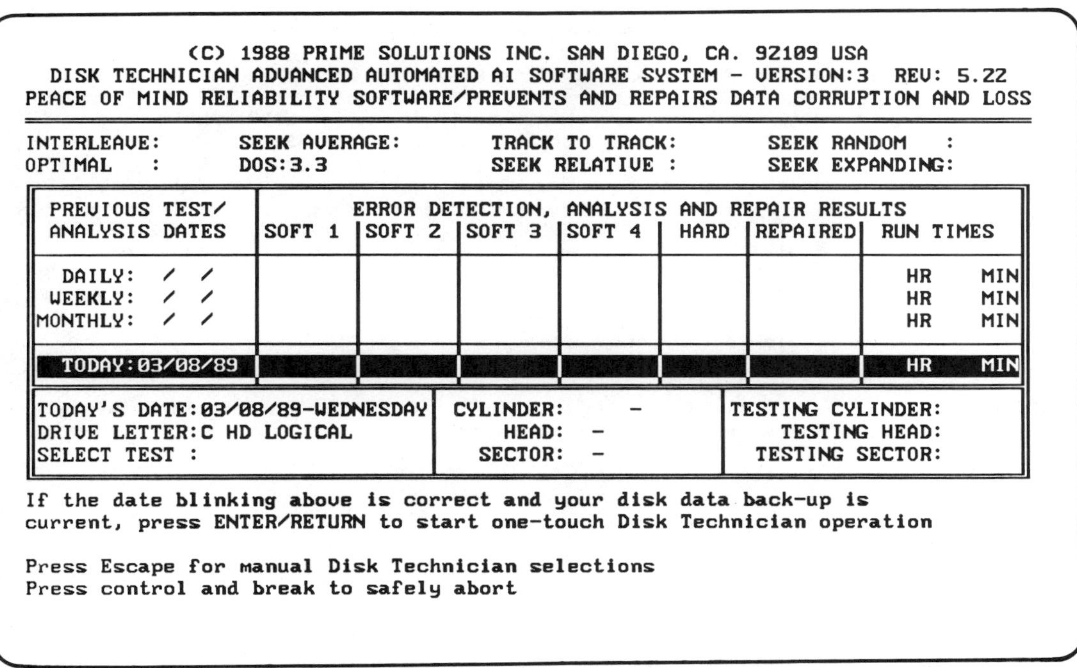

Fig. 6-5. The first time you run Disk Technician Advanced, the main screen has very little information about your computer.

The monthly test is a very long and very thorough test. I tested Disk Technician Advanced using a 12 MHz AT clone with a 40 Meg hard disk partitioned into two 20 Meg drives. The monthly test took one hour and thirty- seven minutes on one partition and a few minutes longer on the other. The test drive had several bad spots on it. These were flagged by the factory as bad. I recorded their location and changed their classification as good before running Disk Technician Advanced. It found every one of them. Rather than flagging them as bad, it successfully performed a low-level format and recovered them. It also flagged several other spots on its first test as marginal, an indication it is even more conservative than the factory testing program. Figure 6-6 shows the Disk Technician Advanced error report.

None of the factory-spotted bad spots had any data because they were flagged as bad until just before the test. However, several of the other spots flagged by Disk Technician Advanced did have data in them. The program recovered all the data without problem.

After the initial run, Disk Technician Advanced decides which test to run based on its database and the system date. In addition to a monthly test, it also has a daily and weekly test. The weekly test took about thirty-seven minutes per drive and the daily test took less than three minutes per drive. Disk Technician Advanced automatically tests all of your partitions. After running each type of test once, Disk Technician Advanced stores this information. It displays this information for later tests so you can estimate the time required. Figure 6-7 shows this.

```
Cumulative preventions/detections/repairs/recoveries from 03/08/89 TO 03/16/89
------------------------------------------------------------------------------
INTERLEAVE:2      SEEK AVERAGE:0      TRACK TO TRACK:         SEEK RANDOM   :
OPTIMAL   :2      DOS:3.3             SEEK RELATIVE :         SEEK EXPANDING:
FAULTS: |      2 |        17 |       0 |        0 |        0 |          19
BYTES:  |  1,024 |      8,704 |       0 |        0 |        0 |       9,728
------------------------------------------------------------------------------
  RELOCATED SECTORS |       SYSTEM SECTORS |                    TOTAL ERRORS
--------------------|----------------------|------------------------------
FAULTS: |      0 |                     0 |                             19
BYTES:  |      0 |                     0 |                          9,728
------------------------------------------------------------------------------
Total potential problem bytes continually
being specially monitored by each Disk Technician run: 17,408

Disk Technician has finished. Remove Disk Technician diskette and store safely
Press ENTER/RETURN then reboot system for normal use
```

Fig. 6-6. After Disk Technician Advanced runs, it gives you a report of what it found.

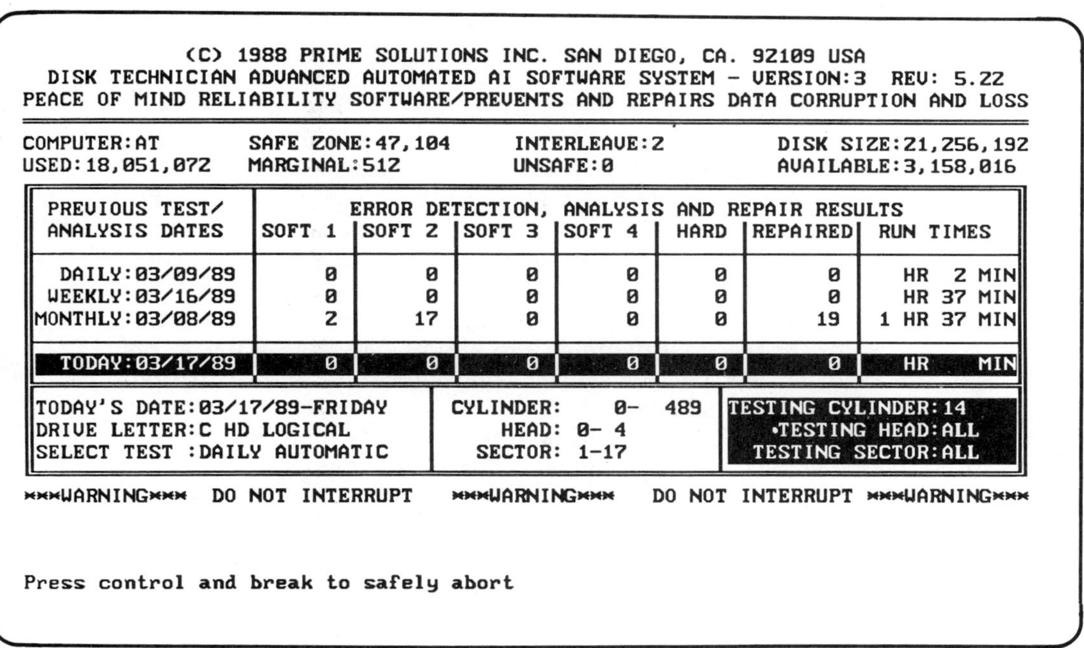

Fig. 6-7. After Disk Technician Advanced has run each test at least once, it remembers the results and displays them so you can estimate the time required for future tests.

As powerful as Disk Technician Advanced is, it is also easy to use. You boot from the working disk you make during installation and an AUTOEXEC.BAT file takes over. You answer a couple of prompts and it takes over and runs automatically. It is able to handle almost any problem without user intervention. This is an easy program to use, even for a beginner. Anything you can do with Disk Technician Advanced that will cause data loss had adequate warning to prevent accidental use.

Disk Technician Advanced is advertised as using artificial intelligence. In normal use, it uses complex algorithms to test your hard disk and monitor access times. As you use Disk Technician Advanced, it adjusts the algorithms to reflect the state of your hard disk. When it takes the program too long to read an area it tries to fix it. It reads the data into memory and then performs a low-level format on that area. After the formatting, it tests the area again. If the area tests good, the program writes the data back to its original space. If not, it flags the area as bad and moves the data to a new location.

I spoke with the technical support at Prime Solutions several times. Each time I came away very impressed with their knowledge of their product and hard disks in general. Support is unlimited and free but you pay for the call. Their technical support could end up as a great friend in need if you ever have a major disk crash.

One of the things I regretted was my inability to perform long term experiments to see how disk maintenance software performed over long periods on problem equipment. Fortunately, others have. *PC Magazine* performed extensive testing of Disk Technician Advanced on two ill-fated CMI drives from the problem batch used on the IBM AT. These drives had failed enough that *PC Magazine* had put them in their "equipment morgue." After 120-hours of steady use, *PC Magazine* pronounced the drives cured. They did point out that each drive required over 15-hours of work with Disk Technician. While that is an interesting test, 120-hours on just two computers is hardly a vigorous or statistically valid experiment. Luckily, a better experiment was available.

According to John Livingston, the United States Air Force Inspection and Safety Center performed an extensive experiment. For almost twenty-three months they tracked 210 new computers. During that time, 63% of the computers required some form of maintenance and almost a third (32.6%) of this maintenance was hard disk related. After this twenty-three month period, they installed Disk Technician Advanced on all the machines. They monitored the computers for four months (up till press time) and there had been no hard disk failures since installing Disk Technician Advanced.

This Air Force study is impressive. They installed Disk Technician Advanced on a large number of machines with a proven track record of hard disk problems. It stopped all the problems. It is likely that other disk testing programs would have been as successful, however, no other programs were included in the experiment.

Limitations　　Disk Technician Advanced is not compatible with DOS 4.0. If you are running off of DOS 4.0 and have a hard disk with disk partitions less than 32 Meg each, you may be able to boot from a DOS 3.3 disk and run Disk Technician Advanced. If you have partitions greater than 32 Meg under DOS 4.0, you will not be able to use the program at all.

The installation program tries to write the commands to load the head parking program to the AUTOEXEC.BAT file. The first time I ran the program, I had my AUTOEXEC.BAT file configured as a read only and hidden file. (It still works fine that way. I had it configured that way so I would know if any installation program tried to modify it.) The installation program responded with an error message that my hard disk was full. It was not and I quickly corrected the problem. However, the error message gave me no help in identifying the source of the problem.

The manual instructs you to boot off a fresh DOS diskette before running the installation program. I forgot to do that the first time. My AUTOEXEC.BAT file configures a number of Substituted hard disks. I use these to both shorten my PATH statement and to shorten the COPY commands I use. One of the things the installation program does is create a "safe landing zone" on each drive for the head parking program. This is an area where DOS is not allowed to store data. As the installation program ran, it began attempting to create a safe landing zone for each of these Substituted pseudo-drives. I aborted the installation and checked with technical support. They said the program is intelligent enough it does not actually create safe landing zones for each SUB-STituted drive. It is just not intelligent enough to bypass those messages.

Disk Technician Advanced will not work with Plus Development drives, including the Hardcard and the Passport drives. This is not the fault of the program. Plus Development performs extensive testing of their drives at the factory and then low-level formats the drives before shipping them. The drives are configured in a manner that prevents the user from being able to perform a low-level format. If your drive requires a low-level format, you must return it to Plus Development for formatting. Disk Technician Advanced must be able to low-level format to work properly.

Manual   The manual I received was not a glossy printed manual. Rather, it was a set of double-sided photocopied papers stapled together. It included a note saying the manual was being upgraded and all registered users would receive a new manual in the future. It did not arrive during the test period.

The front of the manual has a section called the "10 Second Instruction Manual." This will quickly get a new user up and running. In fact, for many users this and the brief installation section is the only thing you will have to read. Disk Technician Advanced itself is easy enough to use that you may never need the manual.

Some users may find they cannot access all their hard disk drive partitions if they run Disk Technician Advanced from a floppy disk drive. Certain configurations require that the CONFIG.SYS file load a device driver. For example, Compaqs with multiple partitions require a device driver. The Disk Technician Advanced working disk also requires a CONFIG.SYS file to load this type of device driver. That information is buried in the manual. However, it is not in the installation or 10 Second Instruction Manual sections.

Conclusion   Extensive testing convinced me that Disk Technician Advanced is the best disk testing program I reviewed. It is well worth its asking price. The program will go a long way towards preventing a hard disk disaster. Disk Technician Advanced is the second most important thing you can do for your hard disk, after frequent backups.

Product:	Disk Technician Advanced
Price:	$189.95
Category:	Commercial
Publisher:	Prime Solutions, Incorporated
Address:	1940 Garnet Avenue
	San Diego, California 92109
Phone:	(619) 274-5000
Memory:	256K

HDtest (by Jim Bracking)

HDtest is a very powerful shareware hard disk testing program. A copy of HDtest is on the optional diskette set.

Installation   Like most shareware, HDtest comes as an archived file. You must decompress this file to run HDtest. Once you have done this, there is no installation program. The HDtest manual does not discuss how to install the program.

Operation   HDtest is a program to test your hard disk and correct any problems it finds. It can also measure the performance of the hard disk. HDtest has two types of tests, nondestructive and destructive. The nondestructive tests read and write to the diagnostic cylinder of the hard disk. The destructive tests write to the data portion of the drive.

If your hard disk does not have self retracting heads HDtest has a "park heads" feature. It moves the heads to the landing zone. You would do this just before turning off your computer.

HDtest has a very nice screen. The background shows technical information on the currently selected drives. The foreground shows the pull down menus. Figure 6-8 shows this. The help menu is used to read about program options on-line. You use the options menu to configure some of the program options.

The tests performed by HDtest from the disk tests menu are:

- Read/write/verify. This writes a data pattern, reads it back and verifies the contents.
- Seek test. This executes a seek to track 0 of every cylinder. Then it seeks to the first and last cylinders. Finally, it executes 1000 random seeks.
- Head select test. This executes a verify command for each head on the disk.
- ECC or error correction code test. The ECC logic allows the controller to correct temporary read errors where one or more data bits were invalid. The controller writes an ECC with every 512 byte sector. When it reads the data the controller uses an algorithm to determine if the data is correct. It will attempt to correct it if the data is incorrect. The implementation of this feature varies depending on the controller you have. This test:

1) Writes a data pattern.
2) Reads the data and ECC.

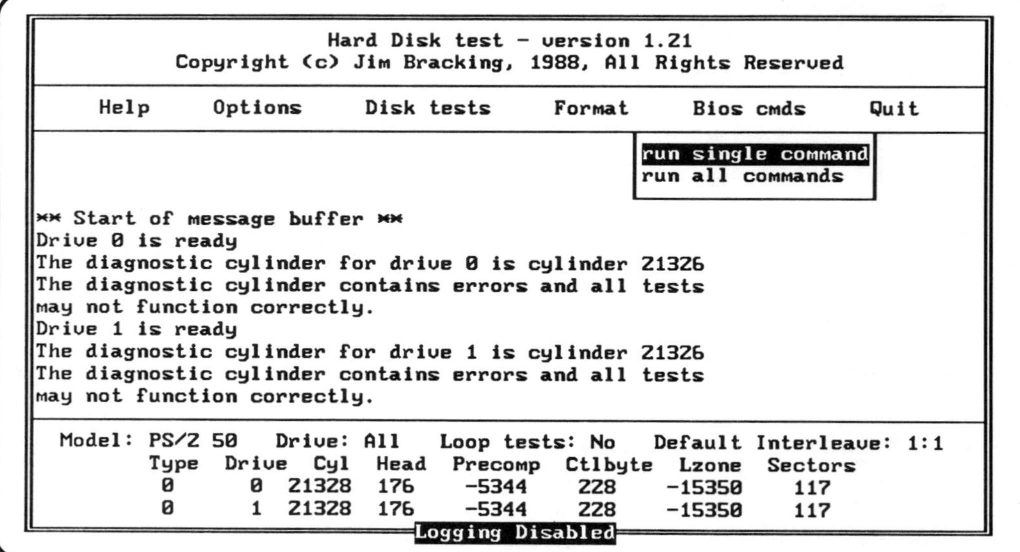

Fig. 6-8. The HDtest screen has pull-down menus in the foreground and technical information on the drive in the background.

3) Modifies one bit.
4) Writes the data and ECC.
5) Reads the data and verifies the data.

- Defect scan. This test verifies every sector on the hard disk and reports any errors it finds.
- Park the heads. This will move the heads to a safe landing zone.
- Interleave test. This test formats the diagnostic cylinder with interleave values from 1:1 to 7:1, executes 50 multi-sector reads and reports the average time the read took. You use this to select the best interleave.
- Performance test. This test executes a series of reads, track to track seeks and random seeks to determine the drive performance.

There is also a format menu. Most of the options on this menu destroy data. It has the following options:

- Format drive. This formats the entire hard disk. A secondary menu lets you either enter the defects or scan the disk for defects. The scan option only works on a previously formatted disk.
- Format track. This option lets you format up to one hundred individual tracks.
- Flag defective track. This option lets you enter up to one hundred tracks marked as defective.
- Format diagnostic cylinder. You must do this before using it. Since it does not store data, this does not cause you to lose any data.
- Surface analysis. This option writes a data pattern of xb66d to every sector on the hard disk then reads it back 3 times. If it finds any errors, the track is flagged as defective.
- Reformat drive. HDtest performs this formatting without losing data. It does this by first reading the data, formatting the track and then restoring the data. This is useful for refreshing the existing magnetic signal on the drive, correcting temporary errors and changing the interleave.

Finally, there is a BIOS menu that runs a number of tests to determine if the disk commands work properly. You can run all the tests at once or select a single command.

Limitations HDtest does not include support ESDI hard disks. HDtest was not compatible with the 130 Meg hard disk on my IBM Model 70 running under DOS 4.0. It would try to run the tests, but it would report nothing but errors.

Manual Like most shareware programs, HDtest comes with an electronic manual on a disk. The manual is for experienced users. However, to its credit it begins with an explanation of common concepts of hard disk operation. That makes it easier for an inexperienced user to get started.

Conclusion The testing performed by HDtest is less extensive than some of the programs like Disk Technician Advanced. However, HDtest will find many of the problems that plague hard disks and it is far less expensive that Disk Technician Advanced. A copy of HDtest is on the optional diskette set.

```
Product:     HDTest
Price:       $35.00
Category:    Shareware
Publisher:   Jim Bracking
Address:     967 Pinwood Drive
             San Jose, California 95129
Phone:       (408) 257-0945
Note:        For a registration fee of $50,
             the author sends out a disk
             with the latest versions
Memory:      180K
```

HDTest (by Peter Fletcher)

HDTest is a shareware hard/floppy disk testing program. It performs a comprehensive read/write test of most IBM compatible computers. HDTest can test the entire disk while preserving all the data on the disk.

Installation   The manual is very vague on the installation process. This should not be a major problem since someone planning on using this type of program is not likely to need hand-holding installation instructions.

Operation   HDTest can test almost any hard disk or floppy diskette. However, you do not have to worry about compatibility. HDTest includes a companion program, called HDChek, that checks the target device for compatibility. HDChek is a read-only test and can safely test all devices.

If the disk being tested contains data, HDTest can test it without losing any data. If HDTest finds a defective sector with date, it will attempt to recover as much data as possible. It will place that data in a safe location before marking the cluster as bad. Of course, data loss is always possible with bad clusters.

Most programs in this chapter test your disks by simply reading the existing data. They compare the cyclical redundancy check number for the data they read to the number stored on the disk. If they try to write to the disk at all, they only write once to blank areas. The Mace Utilities Gold and Norton Utilities Advanced Edition perform this test. HDTest, like Optune and Disk Technician, performs a much more exhaustive test.

HDTest has two modes of operation. In its slow mode, it writes 20 test patterns to each cluster. It then reads that pattern back and compares it to what it wrote. In order for HDTest to consider a cluster as good, it must pass every single one of these tests. If it fails even a single test, HDTest marks it as bad. Often, HDTest is able to spot a defective cluster before the errors get to DOS because many read/write errors are correctable by the hardware that controls the disk drive.

HDTest performs these tests on every cluster, even the ones containing data. When HDTest encounters a cluster with data, it reads that data into memory and stores it while testing the disk. If it finds no errors, it writes the data back to its original location. If it finds errors, it writes the data to a safe location and marks that cluster as bad.

One problem occurs when the cluster is so bad that HDTest has difficulty reading the data in the first place. While I was not able to perform extensive tests, HDTest does seem to try much harder than DOS to read your data. It got most of the data off a floppy diskette which I had stapled several times. (Of course I removed the staples before using the disk so it was actually the staple holes and not the staples that caused the problems.)

Another advantage to running HDTest is reinforcing the hard disk. The magnetic signals on your hard disk begin to fade the moment DOS writes something to your hard disk. This fading is hard to notice because it may take years for a signal to fade enough for DOS to have trouble reading it. In addition, the computer writes to many files over and over which strengthens the magnetic signal. Because HDTest reads all the data into memory and then writes it back to disk, it refreshes all the magnetic signals on the hard disk.

The manual discusses several things you should do before running HDTest. It recommends you begin by making a backup of the disk you are testing, especially the first time you run HDTest. This is a good suggestion. It should not present a problem because you run HDTest infrequently and you should be making frequent backups anyway.

After making a backup, the next step is to run the DOS CHKDSK program. CHKDSK primarily finds cross-linked files. Cross-linked files are two files that have a single cluster in common. In other words, the last individual cluster in file A points to cluster 1800, and the last individual cluster in file B also points to cluster 1800. Because cluster 1800 can only point to one following cluster, the files have common clusters after that. This is a logical error on the hard disk. It is generally caused by a power failure or rebooting while the disk is being written to.

Cross-linked files cause problems for HDTest if the cluster where the files join is defective and HDTest has to move it. You should, in general, run CHKDSK occasionally anyway to spot and correct cross-linked files. Correcting the problem requires you run CHKDSK/F.

After running CHKDSK, you are ready to run HDTest. The program wants a blank, formatted floppy disk in the A-drive when testing a hard disk. It uses this floppy to store a log of the session so you will know what HDTest did while you were sleeping. If the disk is not blank, HDTest will not overwrite data.

The only time HDTest requires input from the user while testing is when it finds a bad cluster in a file marked as a system, hidden or read-only file. When that happens, HDTest will ask for permission before moving the file. If HDTest finds bad clusters, it writes that data to a new cluster and back to the bad cluster. It stores the new location in memory but not written to the File Allocation Table [FAT]. At the end of the test, HDTest asks your permission to update the FAT. Usually, you would say yes.

HDTest needs to locate and use the ROM BIOS INT 13 entry point. It is able to do that automatically on all IBM computers, including PS/2. It sometimes fails to do this on less compatible systems. To get around this, HDTest is distributed on a disk with a modified boot sector. This modified boot sector allows identification of the INT 13 entry point on problem computers.

The modified boot sector copies properly with the DOS DISKCOPY command (no copy protection here) but not with the COPY or XCOPY command. Because HDTest is only distributed on 5.25 inch disks, HDTest includes a program called Bootload to create the modified boot sector on 3.5 inch disks.

To locate ROM BIOS INT 13, you place the special disk in the boot drive and reboot. Normally, when you boot from a floppy the boot sector on the code tries to locate and load DOS. The modification to the HDTest boot sector causes it not to load DOS. Rather, it reads and reports on the contents of the INT 13 vector. It then transfers the INT 13 vector to the unused INT 68 location. You then write down the vector location and remove the disk so DOS can continue booting from the hard disk. You then transfer this information to HDTest by starting HDTest with the appropriate command-line switch.

Limitations   HDTest is slow. It has an optional "fast" mode that only uses two test patterns. Even that is slow. It took twelve and a half minutes to test a 360K floppy in fast mode. A fast test on a 20 Meg Plus Development Passport drive took well over an hour. The slow test took all night. I did not have enough time to test the 130 Meg IBM Model 70 drive.

HDTest's lack of speed does not mean you should not use it. Much of the lack of speed is due to the exhaustive testing HDTest performs. You only need to run HDTest a few times per year and you can schedule those runs at night or over the weekend.

Although I was not able to test it, it seems that by reading and writing every cluster on the hard disk, HDTest has the potential to interfere with some copy protection schemes. This is especially true if the scheme modifies the information on the disk in a way not standard to DOS. You should check with the vendors of any copy protected software you have before running HDTest. Or better yet, upgrade to a non-protected version, even if you have to convert to another program.

Manual   Like most shareware, HDTest comes with an electronic manual on a disk. The manual assumes the reader is very familiar with the computer. This may not be a bad assumption, I expect that very few beginners try to perform a detailed analysis of their hard disk. However, a beginner could certainly use HDTest with clearer instructions especially if the computer was highly compatible.

Conclusion   HDTest performs an exhaustive test of the disk drive. It is probably overkill to test all your floppy disks, however, I would recommend testing the ones you use for backups. HDTest is an excellent test you use on your hard disk a few times each year, perhaps each time the seasons change. For highly compatible computers, it will test the hard disk will little user involvement. Just run the test overnight for small drives and over the weekend for larger ones.

Product:	HDTEST
Price:	$35
Category:	Shareware
Publisher:	Peter R. Fletcher
Address:	1515 West Montgomery Avenue
	Rosemont, Pennsylvania 19010
Phone:	Not Available
Memory:	320K

Optune

Optune is a disk optimization program with the ability to perform other hard disk "tune-ups" as well.

Installation   Optune has a program that automatically installs Optune. To run from the B-drive it requires an ASSIGN A=B statement. It includes a program called Opcolor you can use to change the colors it uses.

Operation   Most of the menus in Optune are three levels deep. You select the main area from the top menu. That brings up the second menu where you select the option you want to change. Figure 6-9 shows this.

Optune offers three types of optimizations. Chapter 8 discusses these. Optune can also recover from a formatted hard disk. Chapter 7 discusses this. This chapter discusses the other functions of Optune.

The Tune-Disk option performs two functions. First, it will read a sector into memory, then reformat that sector and then rewrite the data back onto that sector. This strengthens the magnetic signal on the disk. Second, if the disk has the wrong interleave factor, Optune can change it without destroying any data.

The Check-Disk option performs the same function as the DOS CHKDSK program. It verifies the File Allocation Table [FAT] and the subdirectory and

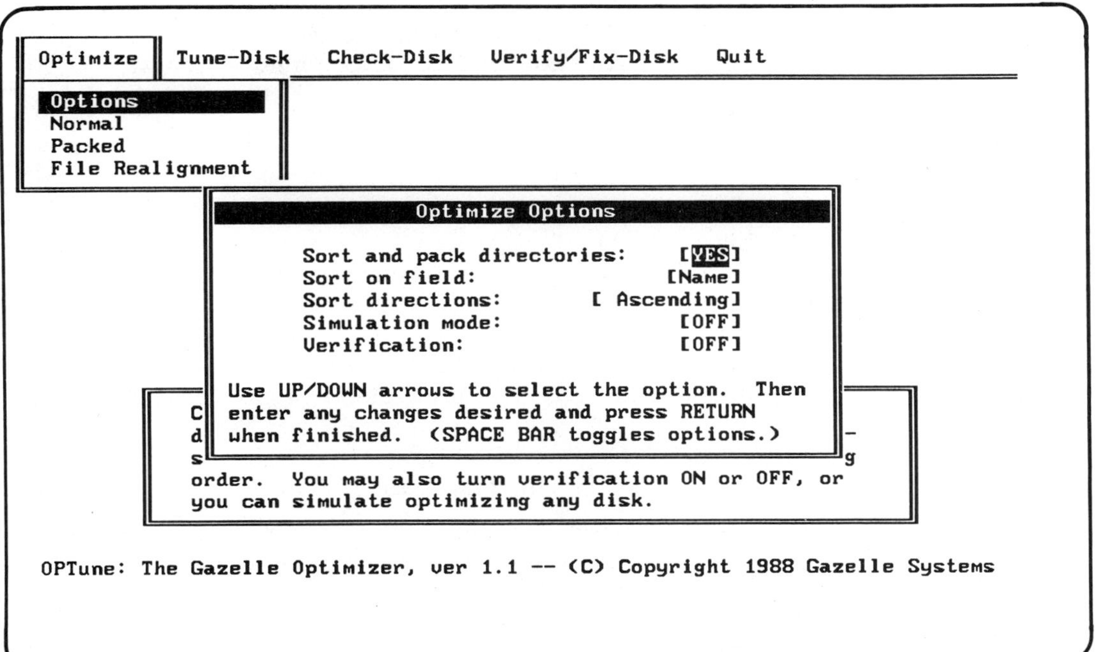

Fig. 6-9. Most of the menus in Optune are three levels deep. You select the main area from the top menu. That brings up the second menu where you select the option you want to change.

file entries. The Optune program is faster and will work with some non-standard drives.

The Verify/Fix option tests the physical integrity of the entire hard disk. It tries to read each sector. When it finds a bad or marginal one it locks them out so DOS will not use them. This can prevent future problems. DOS is not very picky about marginal spots. When it cannot read a sector the first time it tries three to five more times. If it succeeds on any of those tries, it assumes that area is perfect. Optune has four levels of tests:

1) Read-Only. Optune simply reads what is already on the disk, computes the cyclical redundancy check number and compares it to the disk. When they match, Optune assumes that area of the disk is good. This took 37 seconds on the 20 Meg Plus Development Passport drive.
2) Level 1. This reads any existing data into memory then writes a unique 512-byte bit pattern to the disk and then checks that pattern. After testing, it writes the original data back to the disk. This took 17 minutes and 12 seconds on the 20 Meg Plus Development Passport drive.
3) Level 2. First this performs a level 1 test. Then it writes and reads eight sets of 32-byte bit patterns. These patterns are hard disk manufacturer's standards. After that, it tries four more proprietary patterns. This took a little over two hours on the 20 Meg Plus Development Passport drive.
4) Level 3. First this performs a level 1 test. Then it writes and reads sixteen sets of 32-byte bit patterns. These patterns are hard disk manufacturer's standards. After that, it tries eight more proprietary patterns. This took five hours and twelve minutes on the 20 Meg Plus Development Passport drive.

Limitations　　The Optune manual is up-front about the technical limits of the program. They are:

- The DOS sector size is 16,384 or smaller. Most DOS versions have a 512-byte sector size so this is a fairly minor limitation. A few non-standard versions of DOS prior to version 4.0 used larger sector sizes. This was to increase the hard disk size above the 32 Meg limit earlier versions of DOS imposed.
- The DOS cluster size does not exceed 64K. This limit is also only a problem with versions of DOS that adjust the sector size to accommodate large hard disks.
- No single file is larger than 2,147 Meg.
- The total number of files and directories do not exceed 15,000.

The Tune-Disk option would not work on the Plus Development Passport drive I used successfully with Optune for the disk optimization test. It reported they were non-standard drives. It also failed to work with the 130 Meg hard disk IBM includes in their Model 70. IBM may be surprised to know these are also non-standard hard disks!

Manual　　The manual is very good. It is clearly written and easy to follow. There are enough screen shots so you know what to expect while running the program. There is a table of contents, index and list of error messages and what they mean.

Conclusion Optune is a serviceable disk optimizer. However, the Norton Utilities Advanced Edition gives you more optimization options. When it comes to testing your hard disk for errors, Optune is an extremely powerful program with few equals.

Product:	Optune
Price:	$99.95
Category:	Commercial
Publisher:	Gazelle Systems
Address:	42 North University Avenue
	Suite 10
	Provo, Utah 84601
Phone:	(800) 233-0383
Memory:	256K

RONNY'S PICK

The Disk Technician Advanced program impressed me, as did technical support. A good program with good support is a hard combination to beat. I was also impressed with the results of the large scale experiment showing Disk Technician Advanced actually worked as they claim.

7
Format Recovery

Using most versions of DOS, formatting a hard disk only destroys the root directory and file allocation table. All of your data is still on the hard disk, but DOS does not know how to access it. Recovering that data is more difficult than unerasing a file. When unerasing a file, the utility has access to hints. The directory still has the information on the file sans the first character of the name. All the utility has to do is reconstruct the FAT entries.

Typically, you use a format recovery program by periodically running a program that copies the information in the file allocation table, boot sector and root directory to an area of the disk not disturbed by formatting the disk. If the disk is later formatted then that information is blank. To recover existing data, the recovery program will copy that information from its file back on top of the blank information placed on the disk by the formatting program.

It sounds complex but it really is not. A couple of warnings are in order. First, this does not reduce your need to back up your hard disk. Second, it does not work with all versions and brands of DOS. Before you depend on it, check with your dealer to see if your version of DOS erases the hard disk during a format. Finally, you must run the program to update your format recovery information frequently.

Some programs will recover some of the data from an unprotected hard disk. They do this by scanning the hard disk looking for files that appear to be subdirectories. Once they have restored the subdirectories, restoring the files in that directory is much like unerasing them.

This mode has major drawbacks:

1) None of the programs work perfectly. This is due not to imperfect programs but to the nature of DOS. This is less of a problem with data files

where recovering some of the data is better than recovering none of the data. However, programs are likely not to run if even one byte of the recovered information is incorrect. Clearly, a format recovery program is no replacement for a recent backup.

2) Even after format recovery, all files in the root directory are lost. That is because the formatting clears the root directory so no information at all exists on files in the root directory. If you are skilled, you may be able to recover some or all of the files manually. If you have your hard disk set up properly, this will be a minor problem. Optimally, the root directory should contain only the COMMAND.COM, AUTOEXEC.BAT and CONFIG.SYS files. If there are any other files, they should be programs necessary to boot the computer, like device drivers. You can replace these easily from the distribution diskette.

3) The format recovery program cannot recover the names of your subdirectories in the root directory. As a result, it will name them something like DIR00000, DIR00001, and so on. If you are using DOS 3.0 or later, they can be renamed.

Table 7-1 summarizes their performance along with notes of interest. None of the programs took excessively long to recover a hard disk. In addition, hard disk recovery is a very infrequent activity. As a result, you should not base your choice on speed. Rather, pay close attention to the notes and to any other functions the program performs.

DS Optimize

DS Optimize is a commercial disk optimization program with a number of features in addition to format recovery. It works poorly as a format recovery program.

Installation   DS Optimize comes with an automatic installation program. The program lets you enter any name for the subdirectory to install DS Optimize into. However, it expects to run from the A-drive. ASSIGN A=B corrects this.

Operation   To recover an unprotected disk, you enter UNF and supply the drive to unformat. DS Optimize tries to do everything else automatically. Unfortunately, it recovered no useful data from the test disk. This is the same unprotected format recovery program that comes with DS Recovery. While DS Recovery also comes with a protected format recovery program, DS Optimize does not.

Limitations   None of the files recovered by DS Optimize from an unprotected hard disk were usable. In fact, I recovered no usable data from an unprotected hard disk.

Manual   The manual is about five inches square and printed in small print. While it is small and hard to see, it does a good job of explaining how to use DS Optimize.

Table 7-1. Results of Format Recovery Programs.

Program	Unprotected Time	Protected Time	Notes
DS Optimize	0:22	NA	1,2
DS Recovery	0:22	0:26	3
Mace Utilities Gold	2:48	1:43	4
Norton Utilities	1:20	0:12	5,6,7
Optune	N/A	:02	8
PC Tools Deluxe	2:03	0:24	9
Professional Master Key	N/A	:55	10
Take Charge	N/A	:43	11

Unprotected time is the time to unformat the hard disk when no information has been saved in advance. Protected time is the time to unformat the hard disk when information has been saved in advance.

Unless noted . . .

All times are on an IBM Model 70 running at 16 MHz.
All times are using a Plus Development Passport removable drive with a "standard" set of files.

---

1 No usable data was recovered.

2 DS Optimize includes the same UNFORMATTING program included with DS Recovery. This program recovers unprotected hard disks. The Save and Unformat programs from DS Recovery to protect and recover protected hard disks are not included with DS Optimize.

3 No usable data was recovered. The protected disk was recovered properly.

4 The Mace Utilities Gold would occasionally lock the computer up when trying to restore a formatted hard disk with the saved information file. This occurred several times but with no visible reason. This caused no real damage as Mace was able to restore the hard disk after rebooting.

5 When working without the saved information file, Norton created cross-linked subdirectories. Both subdirectories contained the same files. If you erased the file from one subdirectory, it disappeared from the other. The files were completely usable. However, it required a lot of file copying and erasing to correct the problem.

6 The recovery program caused two files to be cross-linked when working with a saved information file. Both were corrected by the Norton Disk Doctor.

7 The Norton programs to unerase subdirectories and unerase files will use the data stored by the unformatting program to aid in their operation.

8 Only works on protected hard disks.

9 PC Tools Deluxe was not able to completely recover data from an unprotected hard disk. Over 3.5 Meg of data was lost.

10 Professional Master Key was tested on a 10 Meg Bernoulli cartridge and a 12 MHz 80286 clone.

11 Only works on protected hard disks.

Conclusion   The format recovery program is completely unacceptable. It does not protect hard disks or recover data from protected hard disks. Its routine to recover unprotected hard disks not only does not work, it leaves the hard disk unrecoverable by other programs that can work with unprotected hard disks.

Product:	DS Optimize
Price:	$59.95
Category:	Commercial
Publisher:	Design Software, Incorporated
Address:	19808 Nordhoff Place
	Chatsworth, California 91311
Phone:	(800) 231-3088
	(818) 885-9000
Notes:	Not DOS 4.x Compatible
Memory:	256K

DS Recover

DS Recover is a commercial file maintenance program with a number of features in addition to format recovery. It works well as a format recovery program.

Installation   The manual tells you to copy all the files to a subdirectory on your hard disk. There is no installation program to do this for you. The manual explains how to set up an environmental variable to point to the DS Recover files. However, the manual does not explain how to deal with an error message indicating the environment is full. The SET command is typeset in such a manner it appears as though you should include extra spaces in the command. If you enter these extra spaces, DS Recover will not understand its environment variable.

Operation   To protect a hard disk, you run a program called Save or select Protect from the main DS Recover menu. Unlike most other programs, DS Recover does not write the information to the hard disk being protected. If you have only one hard disk, then you must write the information to a floppy disk. If you have multiple hard disks, you can store the file for one on another. The name of the file is PROTECTE.FMT and using the test 20 Meg Plus Development Passport drive, the file was 59K.

To recover an unprotected disk, you enter UNF and supply the drive to unformat. DS Recover tries to do everything else automatically. Unfortunately, I recovered no useful data from the test disk.

To recover a protected disk, you enter Unformat and supply the drive to unformat and the drive containing PROTECTE.FMT. After asking you twice if you really want to do this, it recovers everything automatically.

Limitations   The format recovery program is DOS 4.x compatible. However, the DS Recover program is not. To use the format recover under DOS 4.0, you must use the Save program.

None of the files recovered by DS Recover from an unprotected hard disk were usable. In fact, I recovered no usable data from an unprotected hard disk.

Manual   The manual is about five inches square and printed in small print. While it is small and hard to see, it does a good job of explaining how to use DS Recover.

Conclusion   The format recovery program for unprotected hard disks is completely unacceptable. It not only does not work, it leaves the hard disk bad off enough that other programs that can work with protected hard disks will no longer work. The protected format recovery program worked very well on protected hard disks.

```
Product:      DS Recover
Price:        $49.95
Category:     Commercial
Publisher:    Design Software, Incorporated
Address:      19808 Nordhoff Place
              Chatsworth, California 91311
Phone:        (800) 231-3088
              (818) 885-9000
Notes:        Not DOS 4.x Compatible
Memory:       7K     Sentry
              6K     Snapshot
              256K   DS Recover
```

Mace Utilities Gold

The *Mace Utilities Gold,* discussed in Chapter 4, includes a program called RxBak. This program copies the boot sector, file allocation table and root directory for Mace Utilities Gold to use when unformatting a hard disk. It creates a file in the root directory called BACKUP.M_U. When it creates this file, it renames the old file OLDBACK.M_U. On the test disk, this file was 39K.

To unformat a hard disk, you run a program called Unformat. You can also select this option from the menu. The program will ask you if the disk to unformat was protected or unprotected. If the hard disk was protected, the program will give you the option of using BACKUP.M_U OR OLDBACK.M_U. If your version of DOS uses a formatting program that erases a hard disk, Mace includes a hard disk formatting program that does not erase data.

Limitations   The unformatting program worked without problems. Other portions of the Mace Utilities Gold had significant problems. Chapter 4 discusses these.

Manual   The manual does a good job of explaining how to use the Mace Utilities Gold. However, there are a number of typo's. Several places show the wrong command.

Conclusion   The format recovery program works very well on unprotected hard disks. It works even better on protected hard disks.

```
Product:      Mace Utilities Gold
Price:        $149.00
Category:     Commercial
Publisher:    Paul Mace Software
Address:      400 Williamson Way
              Ashland, Oregon 97520
Phone:        (503) 488-0224
Memory:       256K
```

Norton Utilities

Earlier versions of Format Recovery, one of the *Norton Utilities* discussed in Chapter 4, only worked on protected hard disks. This version also works on hard disks the Format Recovery program was not protecting before the formatting. If you use a version of DOS that destructively formats the hard disk, Norton includes a safe floppy formatting program that will not format a hard disk. That will prevent an accidental hard disk format.

To protect a hard disk you run a program called FR, short for Format Recovery. This creates a 39K file in the root directory called FRECOVER.DAT. You have the option of saving the existing version as FRECOVER.BAK. You use the same FR program to recover a formatted hard disk. It has menu options for a protected and unprotected hard disk. After answering prompts to select the recovery method and drive, FR ran automatically.

Limitations   The unformatting program worked with only minor disk problems. The Norton Disk Doctor corrected these automatically. The unformatting program is only included in the Norton Utilities Advanced Edition.

Conclusion   The format recovery program works very well on protected hard disk. It has minor problems with unprotected hard disks but the Norton Disk Doctor corrects these.

<table>
<tr><td>Product:</td><td>Norton Utilities</td></tr>
<tr><td>Price:</td><td>$100</td></tr>
<tr><td>Category:</td><td>Commercial</td></tr>
<tr><td>Publisher:</td><td>Peter Norton Computing, Incorporated</td></tr>
<tr><td>Address:</td><td>2210 Wilshire Boulevard
Santa Monica, California 90403</td></tr>
<tr><td>Phone:</td><td>(213) 453-2361</td></tr>
<tr><td>Notes:</td><td>The Norton Utilities consists of a number of separate utilities each with its own memory requirements. With 256K, you will be able to run any of the utilities</td></tr>
<tr><td>Memory:</td><td>256K</td></tr>
</table>

Optune

Optune is a disk optimization program with the ability to perform other hard disk "tune-ups" as well. It can also recover from formatting a protected hard disk.

Installation   Optune has a program that automatically installs Optune. To run from the B-drive it requires an ASSIGN A=B statement. It includes a program called Opcolor you can use to change the colors it uses.

Operation   In addition to format recovery, Optune offers a wealth of features. Chapter 6 discusses disk testing and Chapter 8 discusses disk optimization.

To protect a hard disk, you run the program called Gz_save. This creates a file called GAZELLE_.SAV in the root directory. It is a read-only, hidden, system file. On the test 20 Meg Plus Development Passport drive, this file was 39K. To restore a protected formatted hard disk, you run a program called Gz_unfmt. It handles the restoration automatically but will prompt you to see if you want to continue.

Limitations The Optune manual is up-front about the technical limits of the program. They are:

- The DOS sector size is 16,384 or smaller. Most DOS versions have a 512-byte sector size so this is a fairly minor limitation. A few non-standard versions of DOS prior to version 4.0 used larger sector sizes to increase the hard disk size above the 32 Meg limit earlier versions of DOS imposed.
- The DOS cluster size does not exceed 64K. This limit is also only a problem with versions of DOS that adjust the sector size to accommodate large hard disks.
- No single file is larger than 2,147 Meg.
- The total number of files and directories do not exceed 15,000.

Optune only works on protected disks. If you accidentally format your hard disk and then purchase Optune, it cannot help you recover.

Manual The manual is very good. It is clear and easy to follow. There are enough screen shots so you know what to expect while running the program. There is a table of contents, index and list of error messages and what they mean.

Conclusion Optune is a serviceable disk optimizer. However, the Norton Utilities Advanced Edition gives you more optimization options. When it comes to testing your hard disk for errors, Optune is an extremely powerful program with few equals.

```
Product:     Optune
Price:       $99.95
Category:    Commercial
Publisher:   Gazelle Systems
Address:     42 North University Avenue
             Suite 10
             Provo, Utah 84601
Phone:       (800) 233-0383
Memory:      256K
```

PC Tools Deluxe

The format recovery program is only a small portion of the *PC Tools Deluxe* package discussed in Chapter 5. PC Tools Deluxe was able to recover all the data from a formatted protected hard disk. It had less success with a formatted unprotected hard disk.

Operation To protect the hard disk, you run a program called Mirror. It creates a protection file call MIRROR.FIL in the root directory. On the 20 Meg optimization test disk, this file was 39K. Mirror can also save the partition data to a floppy disk. It uses this information to recover from the "Invalid drive specification" error message. You only need to run this when you change the partitioning of the hard disk.

To recover a disk, you enter REBUILD at the DOS prompt. PC Tools Deluxe gives you several chances to abort the process and gives adequate warnings about the danger of the program. When you have not used the Mirror program to save disk information prior to the formatting, PC Tools Deluxe sometimes had problems recovering the disk. Its problems were directly proportional to the disk fragmentation. With no fragmentation, PC Tools Deluxe worked as well as the Norton Utilities or the Mace Utilities. As the fragmentation increased, its success rate dropped. On the highly fragmented disk optimizer test disk, PC Tools Deluxe was unable to recover over 3.5 Meg of data.

When run, Mirror has the option of storing the old MIRROR.FIL as MIRROR.BAK. That is the default setting and you should know that, especially if you have more than one disk. That way, you are protected if you realize you are reformatting a hard disk and reboot. Without that option, if your AUTOEXEC-.BAT file still existed, it could overwrite the existing (and good) MIRROR.FIL with one containing the structure for the partially formatted hard disk. When you run Rebuild on a protected hard disk, it lets you select which version of MIRROR.FIL to use. It runs fast and recovers everything.

In addition to protecting against formatting, Mirror can aid in unerasing files. When you run it with a /TD option, it loads a 500-byte memory resident program that records information about erased files inside MIRROR.FIL. The file unerasing program can use that to aid it in recovering erased files from a highly fragmented hard disk or a disk with a number of erased files.

Limitations PC Tools Deluxe was unable to recover as much data from unprotected fragmented disks as were the other programs. The Mirror program refused to work on the Plus Development Passport drive I was using to test these programs. It is a 40 Meg hard disk I had partitioned into two 20 Meg logical drives. Mirror responded that the drive had not been partitioned.

Manual The manual is excellent. It is well written with numerous illustrations of how the screen should look at any point.

Conclusion PC Tools Deluxe works as well as the other programs on protected hard disks and deserves serious consideration. However, if you are purchasing a program especially to recover a freshly formatted unprotected hard disk, PC Tools Deluxe is inadequate and other programs will work much better.

Product:	PC Tools Deluxe
Price:	$129.00
Category:	Commercial
Publisher:	Central Point Software, Incorporated
Address:	15220 NW Greenbrier Parkway
	Suite 200
	Beaverton, Oregon 97006
Phone:	(503) 690-8090
Memory:	512K

Professional Master Key

You can run the UnFormat program, one of the *Professional Master Key* utilities discussed in Chapter 4, as a stand-alone program in your AUTOEXEC-.BAT file or other frequently used batch file. It creates a file called UNFOR-

MAT.PMK that contains the necessary information to restore the hard disk. You use the same UnFormat program to recover a formatted hard disk. The program will not recover an unprotected hard disk after formatting.

<table>
<tr><td>Product:</td><td>Professional Master Key
Utilities</td></tr>
<tr><td>Price:</td><td>$25.00</td></tr>
<tr><td>Category:</td><td>Shareware</td></tr>
<tr><td>Publisher:</td><td>RPG Software Farm</td></tr>
<tr><td>Address:</td><td>Post Office Box 9221
Columbus, Mississippi 39705</td></tr>
<tr><td>Phone:</td><td>Not Available</td></tr>
<tr><td>Notes:</td><td>The optional diskette set
includes a copy of this program.</td></tr>
<tr><td>Memory:</td><td>128K</td></tr>
</table>

Take Charge

The *Take Charge* format recovery program only works with protected disks. It will not recover a formatted unprotected hard disk. The format recovery program is only a small portion of the overall Take Charge package discussed in Chapter 5.

Operation   Format Recovery. The Take Charge format recovery program only works on protected disk. You protect a disk by running Format Recovery with a /S option. On the 20 Meg test disk, this created a 59K file called DSKIN-FOE.DAT on the A-drive. You cannot store this file on another drive. Running Format Recovery with the /R (recovery) properly recovered the hard disk.

Limitations   Before it started, it properly reported the date of the protection file as 3/11/89. However, after recovery, it reported the drive was restored to its state as of 12/12/86.

Conclusion   The Take Charge format recovery program is adequate protection against accidentally formatting your hard disk unless you are running DOS 4.0. It is just a small portion of the overall Take Charge package. Chapter 5 covers Take Charge in more detail.

<table>
<tr><td>Product:</td><td>Take Charge</td></tr>
<tr><td>Price:</td><td>$99.95</td></tr>
<tr><td>Category:</td><td>Commercial</td></tr>
<tr><td>Publisher:</td><td>Departmental Technologies, Incorporated</td></tr>
<tr><td>Address:</td><td>Post Office Box 645
Andover, New Jersey 07821</td></tr>
<tr><td>Phone:</td><td>(201) 786-6878</td></tr>
<tr><td>Notes:</td><td>A new version of Take Charge was shipped to late to include in this book. This new versions adds the ability to sway non-Take Charge utilities into memory over other applications using the Take Charge menu. These applications can be stand-alone or well behaved memory resident programs. This works very similar to Headroom.</td></tr>
<tr><td>Memory:</td><td>20K</td></tr>
</table>

8
Disk Optimization Software

The smallest chunk of data that DOS can read or write to a disk is a sector. A sector is always 512 bytes or .5K. As you can imagine, keeping track of 40,000 sectors on a 20M hard disk would be time consuming for DOS. To reduce this overhead, DOS sometimes combines several sectors into a cluster. The size of a cluster depends on the version of DOS used and the size of the disk. The 1.2M floppy diskettes used in the IBM AT have one sector clusters while a 30M AT hard disk has four sector clusters.

Small clusters have an advantage, they waste less space. A file one byte long will always occupy one cluster. As a result, one sector clusters would waste 511 bytes. Four sector clusters would waste 2047 bytes ($512*4-1$). If files are of random length, on average each file will waste one half of one cluster. With large clusters and a lot of files, this waste can be large. This unused space is called slack. Large clusters also have an advantage. With larger clusters the file allocation table (FAT) is smaller, so DOS will be faster anytime it accesses the FAT.

WHY A DISK MIGHT NOT BE OPTIMUM

Consider an empty disk with four sector (2,048 byte) clusters. First copy a 1,900 byte file to the disk. Since the file is less than 2,048 bytes, DOS places the file entirely in the first cluster. Now copy a 4,000 byte file to the disk. DOS places the first 2,048 bytes of the file in the second cluster and places the remaining 1,952 bytes in the third cluster. The disk looks like:

Cluster 1: File 1, 1,900 bytes used, 148 bytes free.

Cluster 2: File 2, 2,048 bytes used, 0 bytes free.
Cluster 3: File 2, 1,952 bytes used, 96 bytes free.

Now use the word processor to add 149 bytes to the first file. The file will no longer fit in the first cluster. It cannot spill over into the second cluster because that cluster is in use. There are three things DOS can do:

1) Find two free clusters that are together on the disk and move the file to those clusters. This could prevent a file from being written to a disk with plenty of free space simply because there were not enough free clusters together. It would also slow down writing large files to disk since DOS would have to write the entire file to a new location.
2) Move the second file to make room for the first file. This would not be a problem with this example. However, it would dramatically slow down writing to the disk if DOS has to move a 1M file to make room for the extra cluster.
3) Spill the file into cluster 4.

DOS takes the third option, so the disk now looks like:

Cluster 1: File 1, 2,048 bytes used, 0 bytes free.
Cluster 2: File 2, 2,048 bytes used, 0 bytes free.
Cluster 3: File 2, 1,952 bytes used, 96 bytes free.
Cluster 4: File 1, 1 byte used, 2,047 bytes free.

In the above example, DOS stores file 1 in two disjoint areas. This is file fragmentation. It slows down DOS. DOS must wait for the disk drive to move the heads to different locations to read or write the file. The more you use your disk, the worse the file fragmentation becomes. You erase small files, creating holes of free space surrounded by data. When you add a large file to the disk, it must fill several of these holes at different locations.

WHAT CAN BE DONE

The process of correcting the above problem is disk optimization or disk condensing. A program moves the clusters around until files are together. The steps to optimizing the above disk are:

1) Read cluster 1. It contains the first file in the directory, so it is ok where it is.
2) File 1 need to have data in cluster 2, so copy the existing data to a new location. The result is:

Cluster 1: File 1, 2,048 bytes used, 0 bytes free.
Cluster 2: Empty.
Cluster 3: File 2, 1,952 bytes used, 96 bytes free.
Cluster 4: File 1, 1 byte used, 2,047 bytes free.
Cluster 5: File 2, 2,048 bytes used, 0 bytes free.

3) Move the rest of file 1 to cluster 2. The result is:

Cluster 1: File 1, 2,048 bytes used, 0 bytes free.

Cluster 2: File 1, 1 byte used, 2,047 bytes free.
Cluster 3: File 2, 1,952 bytes used, 96 bytes free.
Cluster 4: Empty.
Cluster 5: File 2, 2,048 bytes used, 0 bytes free.

4) File 2 is the next file in the directory and needs to start in cluster 3, but cluster 3 has other data, so move that data to another location. The result is:

Cluster 1: File 1, 2,048 bytes used, 0 bytes free.
Cluster 2: File 1, 1 byte used, 2,047 bytes free.
Cluster 3: Empty.
Cluster 4: File 2, 1,952 bytes used, 96 bytes free.
Cluster 5: File 2, 2,048 bytes used, 0 bytes free.

5) Move the beginning of file 2 to cluster 3. The result is:

Cluster 1: File 1, 2,048 bytes used, 0 bytes free.
Cluster 2: File 1, 1 byte used, 2,047 bytes free.
Cluster 3: File 2, 2,048 bytes used, 0 bytes free.
Cluster 4: File 2, 1,952 bytes used, 96 bytes free.
Cluster 5: Empty.

6) Read cluster 4 and verify that it contains the correct data.

The result is a disk that has each file all together. COPY A:*.* B: will produce a copy of the diskette in the A drive that is not fragmented. It is difficult but possible to optimize a hard disk without a special program. If you back up the hard disk, format the hard disk, then restore the hard disk, you will have an unfragmented hard disk. For most users, it is not worth the trouble.

A typical hard disk will get much more benefit from the first optimization than from subsequent optimizations. That is because your hard disk contains a lot of files, like .COM and .EXE files that DOS never writes to. They can be fragmented when you first copied them to the disk if the disk had a lot of holes. Once they are together, they will not be split up again so subsequent optimizations will not affect them.

Disk optimization programs typically use the order of the files in the directory to determine the order on the disk. This means that the optimizer can move files around just because their order has changed in the directory. For this reason, it is always best to use a utility program to sort your directories before optimizing them. You should use the same sort keys each time.

THE ADVANTAGE OF AN OPTIMUM HARD DISK

An optimum hard disk has three advantages:

1) The hard disk is faster. A fragmented file causes the heads on the hard disk to have to move all around to read or write the file. As a result, it takes longer.

2) File recovery is easier. If you accidentally erase a file, you will have an easier time recovering it from an optimum hard disk. This is especially true if you have to manually recover the file. Once you find any cluster in the file you know were to look for the rest of the file. The directory entry for a file points to the first cluster and is not deleted if another file occupies that cluster. Therefore, you always have a clue to the remaining portion of the file even if a file occupies that first cluster. If the file was fragmented, the remaining clusters could be anywhere on the disk and you do not have a clue to their location.

3) Format recovery is easier. Most format recovery programs have little trouble recovering protected hard disks regardless of the fragmentation. On an unprotected hard disk, the probability of a successful format recovery is much higher on an optimum hard disk.

You may also find that you have a little more space after optimizing your hard disk. When you create a subdirectory, DOS allocated 2K for the subdirectory. That is room for 64 entries. (2,048-bytes divided by the 32-bytes DOS uses for each directory entry.) DOS uses two of those spaces for its own purposes. That leaves 62 free entries. Once you exceed this, DOS adds space to the subdirectory file in 2K increments. However, if you later delete these extra files, DOS does not reduce the directory space. Since you cannot recover erased files after disk optimization, some optimizers will reduce the size of these large subdirectory files. That is the only file reduction performed by disk optimizers. If you have no oversized subdirectory entries, the space on your hard disk will not change.

THE DANGER OF OPTIMIZATION

There are several additional things to consider when optimizing a disk. The optimizer cannot move certain DOS and copy protection files. These files are position sensitive. The program must update the FAT as it remaps the disk. If there is a power failure while files are being moved, the FAT may not agree with the actual location of the files on the disk.

Frequent updates are safer but more time consuming. Finally, you will not be able to recover files erased before the optimization. Erasing a file removes part of its information from the FAT and frees the disk space, but does not remove the data from the disk. In the process of moving clusters around to optimize a disk, it is likely that the cluster containing erased data will be overwritten.

Disk optimizers can give you a good scare if you are using the DOS FASTOPEN program (FASTOPEN was introduced with DOS 3.3). FASTOPEN stores the disk location of files when DOS first accesses files. This saves time because the next time DOS needs a file it does not have to look for it. Since disk optimizers move files around, they are not where FASTOPEN expects them. When this happens, DOS will give you a 'File not found' error message. The solution is to reboot the computer. Some of the disk optimizers, like the Mace Utilities, force you to reboot. Others, like the Norton Utilities, give you a choice.

You should always reboot immediately after optimizing your hard disk. If the program does not give you that option, then reboot manually after you exit the program. An additional, and major, consideration is format protection. The optimizer has moved your files around to such an extent their location does not come close to your protection file. If your format protections program is in your AUTOEXEC.BAT file, then it will update your protections as you reboot.

THE TESTING

I performed the testing using a 40 Meg Plus Development Passport hard disk divided into two identical 20 Meg partitions. One stored the fragmented structure and the other was optimized for the testing.

1) I created a single subdirectory on the Passport drive.
2) I created a file on my regular (C-drive) containing one byte.
3) I wrote a batch file to successively copy this single byte file to the subdirectory on the Passport drive. (I had to use a subdirectory because the capacity of the root directory is limited. Unlike the root directory, the directory for a subdirectory is stored in a file that can expand as required.) It first copied it to a file named "1", the "2" and so on.
4) After step 3, I had over 10,000 on the D-drive. (The capacity of the hard disk was slightly over 20 Meg. Even though each file only contained a single byte, DOS allocated 2K (2,048-bytes) to each file.) I placed that list of names into a batch file, sorted in random order. The batch file would erase enough small files to fit a larger file and then immediately copy the larger file. Since the files were in random order, the erased clusters were usually not contiguous. (A few were, of course. That is why the fragmentation was not 100%.) Therefore, DOS copied the larger file to non-contiguous clusters. Hence, the file fragmentation.

Step 4 continued until all the small files were replaced with larger files.

One problem I ran into was Plus Development does not distribute an image copy routine with the Passport drive. That is really not unusual. Very few users would have a use for such a utility. However, without an image copy program, there was no way for me to transfer the fragmentation on one hard disk to another. My second approach was to use a tape drive to produce an image backup to restore. However, the Irwin drive I had only supported file-by-file transfers. Again, that is not unusual. File-by-file is a far superior method of operation for a tape drive. Luckily, Charles Guzis at Sydex came to my rescue. He wrote a program for me to image copy one hard disk to another. He even did it for free. Thanks Charles!

A few of these programs would not run under DOS 4.x. However, I found I could boot off a DOS 3.3 floppy disk and still use the Passport Drives so this did not present a problem.

Most of these programs were smart enough not to optimize an already optimized hard disk. In other words, if you optimize the disk once and then immediately run the program again it takes only a few seconds the second time. However, most of these programs would grind away if you optimized the hard disk, sort the directories into a different order and ran the optimizer again. With the single exception of Vopt, all of the optimizers actually put the files together with the clusters in the proper order. DOS can read the clusters in any way but the purpose of an optimizer is to put them in sequential order.

Other chapters cover the non-optimization functions of these programs. This chapter only covers their ability to optimize a hard disk. Table 8-1 shows the performance of each program. It also lists any important notes. Most disk optimization programs perform other functions as well. As a result, you should look at the overall value of the package rather than just the performance of the optimization program. If optimization takes too long on your system, you can always optimize at lunch or at night.

DJ: Disk Jockey

DJ: Disk Jockey is a collection of twelve utilities. One of those utilities is a disk optimization program. This chapter covers the disk optimization of DJ: Disk Jockey. Chapter 4 covers the remaining utilities.

Installation   DJ: Disk Jockey does not have an installation program. The manual has complete instructions for installing DJ: Disk Jockey for a floppy or hard disk system.

Operation   The optimizer, called Reorg, runs from the command line. Its only parameter is the disk to optimize. It begins by displaying a screen with technical information on the disk to optimize. Figure 8-1 shows this. If you elect to continue, it displays an estimate of the completion time at the bottom and the percent complete.

Limitations   The README file warns about using Reorg with memory resident programs. As a solution, it suggests you boot off a DOS diskette. This will work with some systems. However, a good many systems require commands in the CONFIG.SYS or AUTOEXEC.BAT files to operate properly or to access certain drives at all. The Plus Development Passport drive requires a device driver. The Compaq DeskPro 286 requires a device drive when the hard disk is partitioned into multiple drives. DOS 4.x requires a SHARE command in the AUTOEXEC.BAT file for large hard disks, and so on. All of these computers could run improperly when booted from a DOS disk.

In addition, the Reorg program is slow. As the table at the beginning of the chapter shows, it is one of the slowest disk optimizers available.

Manual   The manual for DJ: Disk Jockey is very brief. Inexperienced users will have trouble using DJ: Disk Jockey solely because of the manual.

In addition to the manual, DJ: Disk Jockey includes an extensive README file on the disk. Unlike many other programs, it does not leave you to your own devices to read the file. DJ: Disk Jockey includes a README.COM program that displays the README file on the screen.

Table 8-1. **Disk Optimization Times.**

Program	Time	Notes
DJ: Disk Jockey	1:25:46	1,2
DS Optimize: Fast	14:16	
DS Optimize: Protected	15:43	
Mace Utilities Gold	29:03	3,4
Norton Utilities	11:40	5,6
PC Tools Deluxe	1:55:05	

All times on an IBM Model 70 running at 16 MHz
Using a Plus Development Passport removable drive with a "standard" set of fragmented files

[1]DJ: Disk Jockey is not DOS 4.0 compatible.

[2]The DJ: Disk Jockey estimate for its completion time was remarkably accurate. It was never off more that 4%.

[3]Mace runs CHKDSK and reports of fragmented files before optimizing the disk. The 2:15 required for those operations is included.

[4]Mace forces a reboot once the optimization is complete.

[5]Complete Optimization.

[6]Norton gives you the choice to reboot once the optimization is complete.

Program	Time	Notes
Optune: Normal Optimization	9:33	1
Optune: Packed Optimization	9:41	2,3
Optune: File Realignment	9:38	4,5
Take Charge: Sequential Order	24:49	6
Take Charge: Minimize Future Fragmentation	24:52	7,8
Vopt	0:11	9

All times on an IBM Model 70 running at 16 MHz.
Using a Plus Development Passport removable drive with a "standard" set of fragmented files

[1]This method only places the pieces of each file together. There will be holes between the files and the files will not be in directory order.

[2]Pieces of files are placed together with no holes in between. However, they are not placed in directory order.

[3]In normal operation, the normal mode is much faster than the packed mode. The times are close together in this test because the test disk is far more fragmented than you are likely to see in actual operation.

[4]This places the files together, removes the holes in between and places the files in directory order.

[5]In normal operation, the normal mode is much faster than the packed mode. The times are close together in this test because the test disk is far more fragmented than you are likely to see in actual operation.

[6]Not DOS 4.0 compatible.

[7]Not DOS 4.0 compatible.

[8]Place read only files first, then directories, then program files and then the remaining files in directory order.

[9]This did not completely defragment the test hard disk. Total disk fragmentation was reduced from 67% to 63% so significant fragmentation remained.

```
TEST       BAT       42    3-19-89    1:09p
COMMAND    COM    25307    3-17-87   12:00p
PLUSDRU    SYS     8918    6-30-88    1:00a
CONFIG     SYS       42    3-14-89    5:15p
AUTOEXEC   BAT       42    3-18-89    7:59p
IMAGECOP   EXE    10313    2-23-89   11:43p
JUNK                12489    3-19-89    1:51p
        22 File(s)      855552 bytes free

A:\DJ>reorg d:
DJ Version 1.5 · Revolution Software, Inc. · 201-366-4445

Drive D has:

  267 total files
    6 of those files have exactly one cluster
  261 of those files have more than one cluster
    3 of the multi-cluster files have all contiguous clusters
  258 of the multi-cluster files have non-contiguous clusters

IMPORTANT NOTE: You should NOT reorg your disk unless you have a
COMPLETE backup of your disk.  Also, you should NOT run reorg if
any RAM-resident programs are currently loaded.

Do you wish to continue?  Please press Y to continue or N to quit.
```

Fig. 8-1. Before optimizing a disk, DJ: Disk Jockey displays technical information about the disk and gives you the option to stop the optimization.

Conclusion   The Reorg disk optimizer in DJ: Disk Jockey is very slow. In addition to disk optimization, DJ: Disk Jockey includes 11 other programs. Chapter 4 covers these.

Product:	DJ: Disk Jockey
Price:	$59.95
Category:	Commercial
Publisher:	Revolution Software, Incorporated
Address:	715 Route 10 East
	Randolph, New Jersey 07869
Phone:	(201) 366-4445
Notes:	Two memory resident programs are included. These require 5K each
Memory:	256K

DS Optimize

DS Optimize is a commercial disk optimization program. In addition to unfragmenting disks, it has a serviceable DOS shell, unerasing routine and hard disk unformatter.

Installation   DS Optimize comes with an automatic installation program. The program lets you enter any name for the subdirectory to install DS Optimize into. However, it expects to run from the A-drive. ASSIGN A=B corrects this.

Operation   DS Optimize loads with a menu very similar to the main menu for DS Recovery. Figure 8-2 shows this. The menu has options to show drive and subdirectory fragmentation. Figure 8-3 shows subdirectory fragmentation.

DS Optimize has two major types of optimization, fast and protected. Fast optimization is not interruptible. Design Software recommends you use the test option to verify that your computer is compatible with this mode. The protected optimization is slower than the fast optimization but you can stop it at any point. With either method, you can optimize the entire hard disk or a single subdirectory.

Within an optimization, you can specify a "most read" and "most written" subdirectory and file specification. During the optimization, DS Optimize places the "most read" files at the beginning of the data space near the file allocation table. This allows the hard disk to access this information rapidly. It places the "most written" files at the end of the data nearest the free space. This minimizes future fragmentation.

```
      DS OPTIMIZE Version 2.00a (c) Copyright 1988 by Design Software

\                      1234-1.PC1    1234-2.PC1    1234-3.PC1    1234-4.PC1
 ├─DBASE              DELTA-1.PC1   DELTA-2.PC1   DELTA-3.PC1   DELTA-4.PC1
 ├─GRAPHICS           FLASH-1.PC1   FLASH-3.PC1   FREE-1.PC1    FREE-2.PC1
 ├─LOTUS              FREE-3.PC1    FREE-4.PC1    FREE-5.PC1    FREE-6.PC1
 └─WORD               GIRL2.PC1     SURF-4.PC1    SURF-5.PC1    TAB-3.PC1
                      TECH-5.PC1    1.PCX         10.PCX        11.PCX
                      12.PCX        1234-1.PCX    1234-2.PCX    1234-3.PCX
                      1234-4.PCX    13.PCX        14.PCX        15.PCX
                      16.PCX        17.PCX        18.PCX        19.PCX
                      2.PCX         3.PCX         4.PCX         5.PCX
                      6.PCX         7.PCX         8.PCX         9.PCX
                      DELTA-1.PCX   DELTA-2.PCX   DELTA-3.PCX   DELTA-4.PCX
                      FLASH-1.PCX   FLASH-3.PCX   FREE-1.PCX    FREE-2.PCX
                      FREE-3.PCX    FREE-4.PCX    FREE-5.PCX    FREE-6.PCX

Optimize      :E:\*.*

# of Subdirs : 0      Backed Up : No    File Exclude: No    Sort : Ext    A
# of Files   : 82     Subdirs   : On    Att. Exclude: HSR   Type : Protected

Drive  Subdirectory  most Read   most Written  Toggle subs  Exclusions
Select drive to optimize
```

Fig. 8-2. The main menu for DS Optimize is used to configure the optimization and to explore the extent of fragmentation.

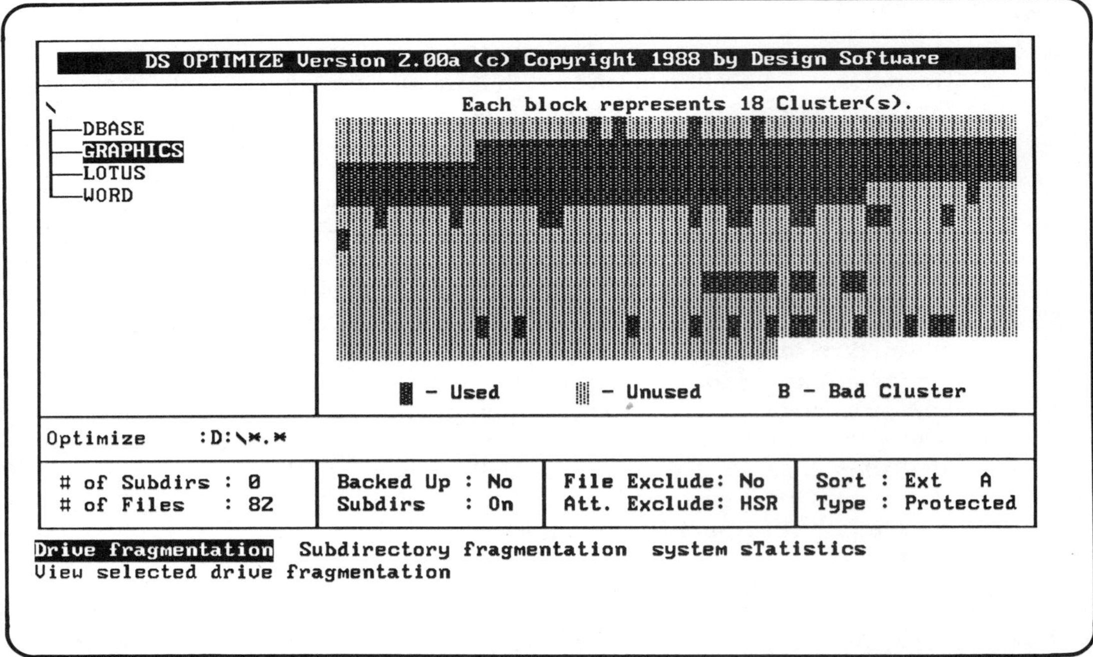

Fig. 8-3. DS Optimize can display the fragmentation for a single subdirectory.

In addition to optimizing hard disks, DS Optimize includes a DOS shell and a program to recover formatted hard disks. Chapter 3 covers the DOS shell and Chapter 7 covers the format recovery program.

Limitations   DS Optimize does not work with large hard disks. When I tried to run it on the 130 Meg hard disk on my IBM Model 70 DS Optimize would crash. DS Optimize only works with a total of 5,000 files and subdirectories. It does not work under DOS 4.x either. Instead of reporting an invalid media or some other error message, after about five seconds it reports the disk has been successfully optimized.

Manual   The manual is small, only about five inches square. The type in the manual is small enough that it is hard to read. Otherwise, the manual does a good job of explaining how to use DS Optimize.

Conclusion   DS Optimize works with DS Recovery to give the pair many of the features available in either the Norton Utilities Advanced Edition or the Mace Utilities Gold. The DS pair has not yet been upgraded to work with DOS 4.x, a distinct disadvantage. The unerasing is less powerful than in Norton or Mace but yet is serviceable for many applications. The unformatting routine works well on protected disks.

```
Product:      DS Optimize
Price:        $59.95
Category:     Commercial
Publisher:    Design Software, Incorporated
Address:      19808 Nordhoff Place
              Chatsworth, California 91311
Phone:        (800) 231-3088
              (818) 885-9000
Notes:        Not DOS 4.x Compatible
Memory:       256K
```

Mace Utilities Gold

The disk optimization program is only a small portion of the *Mace Utilities Gold,* discussed in Chapter 4.

Operation   You can run the optimization program for the menu or as a stand-alone program. First, it runs CHKDSK. Next, it lists all the fragmented files and their degree of fragmentation. Finally, it optimizes the hard disk.

Limitations   At first, the Mace optimizer reads disk information into memory and then it spends a good deal of time performing calculations on that data. During this time, the screen is not showing anything and the hard disk light is not on. It does the same thing just before performing the actual optimization. Both times the delay was so long I was afraid the program had locked the computer. It had not but the program should display some message to let you know it is thinking. I ran these tests on a 16 MHz IBM Model 70. Users with slower computers are much more likely to get the impression of a hung computer.

```
Product:      Mace Utilities Gold
Price:        $99.00
Category:     Commercial
Publisher:    Paul Mace Software
Address:      400 Williamson Way
              Ashland, Oregon 97520
Phone:        (503) 488-0224
Memory:       256K
```

Norton Utilities Advanced Edition

The disk optimization program is a small portion of the *Norton Utilities Advanced Edition,* discussed in Chapter 4.

Operation   The Norton Utilities offers a lot of flexibility for how you arrange the files on the hard disk. It will let you:

- Specify the order to place the directories on the disk.
- Specify the order to place the files on the disk. By specifying the location of files and subdirectories you can maximize the speed of the hard disk. You can also minimize future fragmentation by placing files that never change, like program files, at the front of the hard disk.
- Select the optimization method. The Norton Utilities offer four optimization methods:

    1) Complete Optimization. This moves all subdirectories (and any files you specify) to the front of the hard disk. After that, it lines the files up one at a time with no holes in between. This is the slowest, but most complete method.

    2) File Unfragment. This method unfragments as many files as possible without major file movement. It is much faster than a complete optimization. It leaves some holes between files and may not unfragment all files.

    3) Only Optimize Directories. This method simply moves subdirectories to the front of the hard disk.

    4) Quick Compress. This moves data forward to fill in any existing holes. Many files are left fragmented. However, any new files added to the hard disk will be unfragmented since no holes exist.

Limitations   Only the Norton Utilities Advanced Edition has the disk optimization program.

Conclusion   The disk optimization program that comes with the Norton Utilities Advanced Edition is an excellent disk optimizer. Even better, it comes as part of the excellent Norton Utilities Advanced Edition.

<table>
<tr><td>Product:</td><td>Norton Utilities Advanced Edition</td></tr>
<tr><td>Price:</td><td>$150</td></tr>
<tr><td>Category:</td><td>Commercial</td></tr>
<tr><td>Publisher:</td><td>Peter Norton Computing, Incorporated</td></tr>
<tr><td>Address:</td><td>2210 Wilshire Boulevard
Santa Monica, California 90403</td></tr>
<tr><td>Phone:</td><td>(213) 453-2361</td></tr>
<tr><td>Notes:</td><td>The Norton Utilities consists of a number of separate utilities each with its own memory requirements. With 256K, you will be able to run any of the utilities</td></tr>
<tr><td>Memory:</td><td>256K</td></tr>
</table>

Optune

Optune, as discussed in Chapter 7, is a disk optimization program with the ability to perform other hard disk "tune-ups" as well.

Operation   Most of the menus in Optune are three levels deep. You select the main area from the top menu. That brings up the second menu where you select the option you want to change.

Optune offers three types of optimizations:

1) Normal. This puts all the files together and sorts the directories. It does not pack all the files together. That means there can be holes between the files. This is the fastest form of optimization.
2) Packed. This performs a normal optimization plus it packs all the files together so there are no holes. It takes longer than a normal optimization.
3) File Realignment. This performs a packed optimization plus it places the files in the order they are in the directory.

While the optimization is running, Optune displays information about the process. It shows the drive, optimization mode, the file it is currently processing, percent complete, file sorting method select, status of verification and the time elapsed since the optimization began. Figure 8-4 shows this.

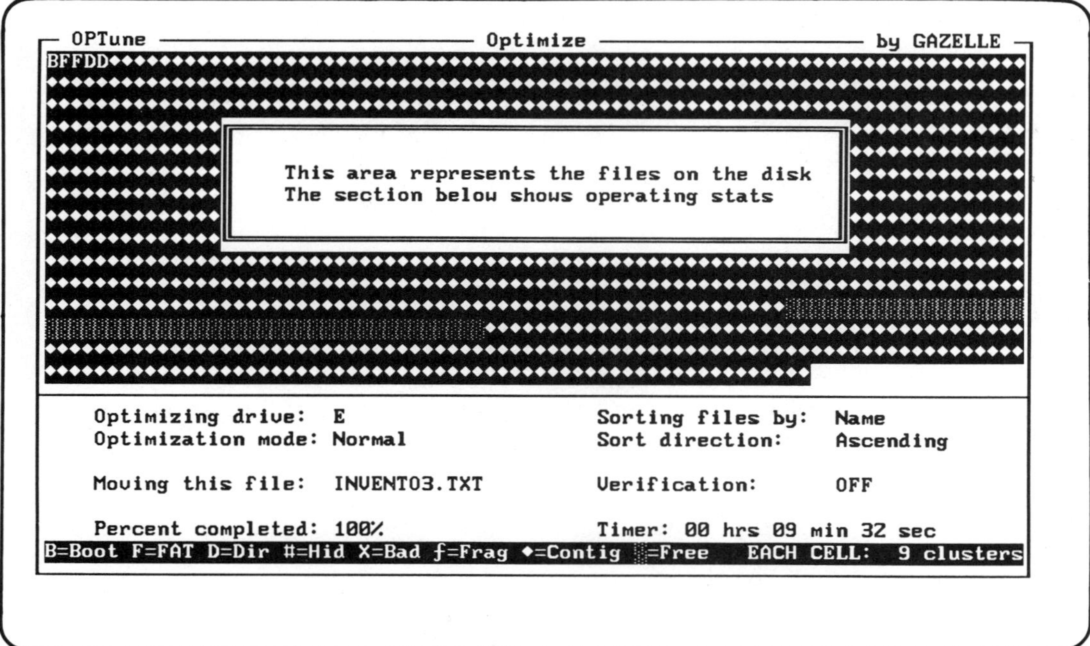

Fig. 8-4. Optune shows a wealth of information while it is optimizing a hard disk.

In addition to disk optimization, Optune offers a wealth of disk testing features. Optune can also recover from a formatted hard disk. Chapter 7 discusses these.

```
Product:      Optune
Price:        $99.95
Category:     Commercial
Publisher:    Gazelle Systems
Address:      42 North University Avenue
              Suite 10
              Provo, Utah 84601
Phone:        (800) 233-0383
Memory:       256K
```

PC Tools Deluxe Compress

The *Compress* program is the disk optimization portion of PC Tools Deluxe, discussed in Chapter 5. Compress was one of the slowest optimizers tested. Compress is more than an optimization program. It includes options to test the hard disk for problems.

Operation   Like the other PC Tools Deluxe programs, Compress uses pull down menus and has full mouse support. The Compress has an Analysis menu that you use to test the hard disk. The three menu options are:

1) Disk Analysis. This analyzes the hard disk and displays summary information. Figure 8-5 shows this.
2) File Analysis. This displays technical information about each file on the hard disk. Figure 8-6 shows this.
3) Surface Analysis. This runs a complete check on every cluster on the hard disk. If it finds one that is bad, it marks it so DOS will not use it. If the bad cluster contains data, it will try to recover the data and move it to a safe location. A nice option lets it run continually so you can run it overnight and see the results the next morning. It can send error reports to a printer or to another disk.

Compress has a sorting directory that lets you define how it sorts the directory entries. This sorts all the directories during the compression. The compression menu gives you three modes of compression:

1) Unfragment only. All this does is place all the current files in contiguous clusters. It will leave holes in the hard disk. New files being written to the disk will fill these holes and will be very fragmented.
2) Full compression. This places all the existing files together in contiguous clusters. This places all the empty space at the end of the hard disk.
3) Full compression and clear. This clears the empty clusters of any existing data. As a result, no file unerasing is possible. However, because of all the file moving during any optimization, file recovery after any optimization is very doubtful.

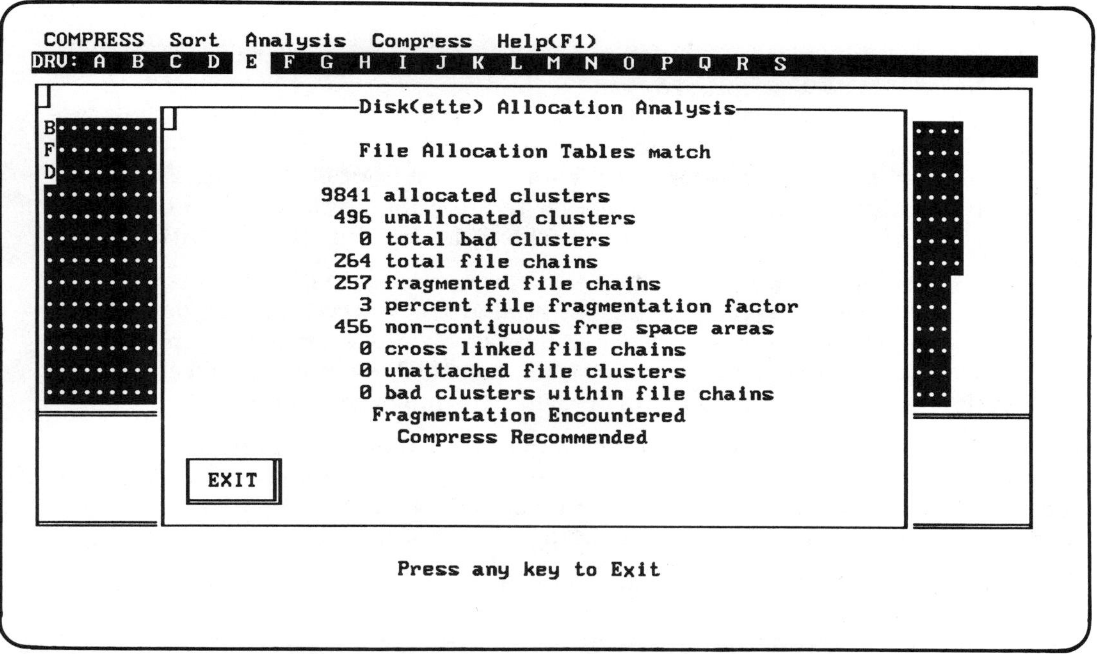

Fig. 8-5. Compress can display technical information on the amount of file fragmentation on a hard disk.

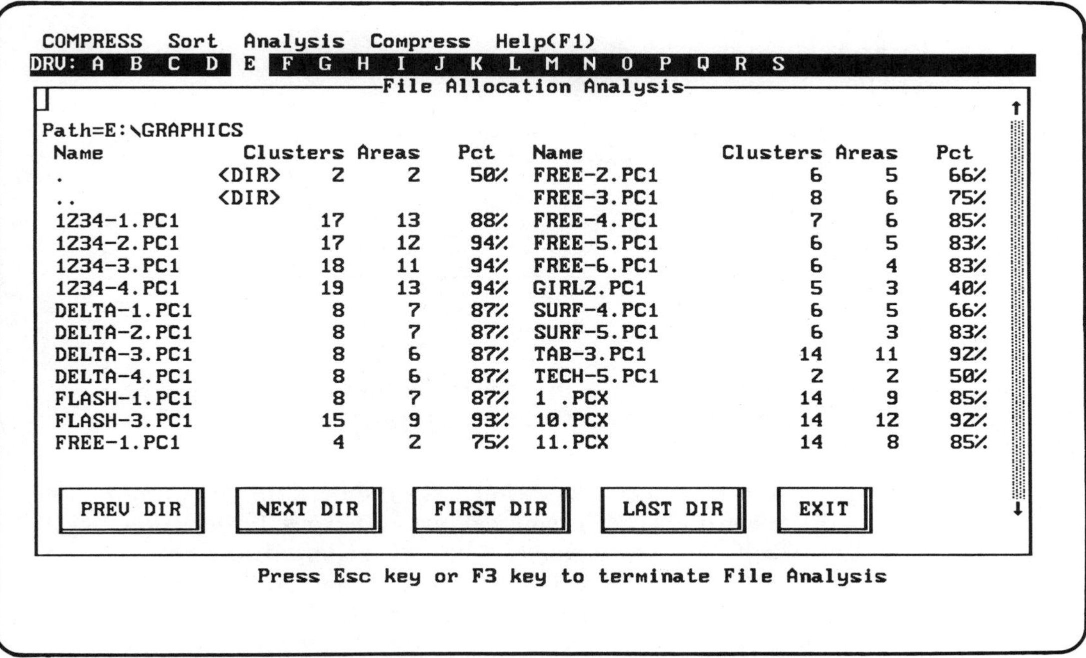

Fig. 8-6. For each file on the hard disk, Compress can show the number of clusters the file contains, the number of different areas containing clusters from this file, and the percentage of fragmentation.

There are three file ordering options:

1) Standard. This lets Compress place the files in whatever order it decides will lead to the fastest optimization.
2) DOS. This places the files in the order specified in the directories, e.g., the order you see the files when you get a DIRectory.
3) Programs first. This places all the programs at the front of the disk. They rarely change so placing them together reduces the chunks of files that DOS has to arrange other files around. This reduces future fragmentation.

The actual optimization takes place with the usual flashing squares. These flashing squares represent the files on the hard disk that are being moved around. Compress has an elapsed time clock and a percent complete indicator. As it moves each file, Compress displays the file name, the old cluster and the new cluster. Few programs provide this much information.

Limitations   The Compress program is much slower than other optimization programs. This does not make much difference if you are planning on running it at night or over the weekend. However, if you will be running the optimizer and then waiting on it to finish, you should select another program.

Conclusion   Compress is a slow but competent disk optimizer. If your primary purpose is to purchase a disk optimizer, then you should consider another package. However, you run disk optimizers infrequently and you can run them over the night or even over the weekend. Therefore, you should not reject PC Tools Deluxe simply because it has a slow disk optimizer.

Product:	PC Tools Deluxe
Price:	$129.00
Category:	Commercial
Publisher:	Central Point Software, Incorporated
Address:	15220 NW Greenbrier Parkway
	Suite 200
	Beaverton, Oregon 97006
Phone:	(503) 690-8090
Memory:	512K

Take Charge

Take Charge is a commercial disk and file maintenance program. The disk optimizer is just a small portion of the overall program, discussed in Chapter 5.

Operation   The disk optimizer first asks if you have removed all copy protected software. It will not continue unless you respond with a yes. It then runs the DOS CHKDSK and tells you to escape if CHKDSK reported any cross-linked files. However, if CHKDSK is not available and does not run the optimizer will not abort. After running CHKDSK, the optimizer shows its single menu. Figure 8-7 shows this. The optimizer can place files in five different orders. They are:

```
╔══════════════════════════════════════════════════════════╗
║              Optimization Menu                           ║
╠══════════════════════════════════════════════════════════╣
║                                                          ║
║   Disk Drive to be Optimized  :                 D        ║
║   Number of files on the disk :                267       ║
║   Number of occupied clusters :              10002       ║
║   # of non-contiguous clusters:               7576       ║
║   Percentage of fragmentation :                 75       ║
║                                                          ║
╚══════════════════════════════════════════════════════════╝

╔══════════════════════════════════════════════════════════╗
║         Disk Optimizer Alignment Methods                 ║
╠══════════════════════════════════════════════════════════╣
║                                                          ║
║  ==> 1. Sequential Order (fastest)                       ║
║      2. Read Only, Directories, Dir Entries              ║
║      3. Read Only, Directories, FIFO Files               ║
║      4. Read Only, Directories, File Size                ║
║      5. Read Only, Dirs, Exe/Com Files, FIFO             ║
║                                                          ║
║ ↑↓—Move Arrow    1-5 or ←┘—To Make Selection   ESC—Abort ║
╚══════════════════════════════════════════════════════════╝
```

Fig. 8-7. The only menu in the Take Charge disk optimizer is the one where you select the method of optimization. You cannot change the information shown at the top of the screen.

1) Directory order. That is the order you see them in when you list files with a DIR command.
2) Read-only files first, then subdirectories, then files based on their physical order on the disk.
3) Read-only files first, then subdirectories, then the files in directory order.
4) Read-only files first, then subdirectories, then files in size order.
5) Read-only files first, then subdirectories, then .EXE and .COM program files then files in directory order.

The optimizer has the normal hard disk map that shows its progress. However, rather than showing the optimized files as a different color, it shows them as little happy faces. It was cute the first time I saw it but it quickly got old.

Limitations   After running the optimizer, I would receive a "Load error code = 7. Press any key" error message any time I tried to load the Disk Services menu. I received this error message even if I exited to DOS without unloading Take Charge and later tried to run Disk Services. Pressing any key only caused Take Charge to display the same error message again. There proved to be no way out of this other than rebooting.

Conclusion   The disk optimizer is a slow but serviceable optimization program. It is, however, only a small portion of the overall Take Charge package. Take Charge is covered in Chapter 5.

Vopt

Vopt is primarily a commercial disk optimization program. However, it comes with several other handy utilities. Chapter 4 covers these.

Operation   Vopt does not reorganize the hard disk in the same sense as the other programs in this chapter. After running Vopt, your hard disk will still have significant fragmentation. Running Vopt again will not reduce that fragmentation.

Vopt has no menu, it is strictly a command-line program. You enter: VOPT E: to optimize the E-drive. Two command-line switches are available. /N suppresses the normal display and /F causes Vopt to automatically delete lost cluster chains.

Vopt ran very fast, taking only eleven seconds on the test disk. Figure 8-8 shows the normal Vopt display. Vopt did not do much reorganization on the test hard disk. The test hard disk was 67% fragmented, meaning there are 9,831 fragmented clusters. Vopt only moved 51 clusters. These were part of 22 files. After running Vopt, the test hard disk was 63% fragmented and 9,780 fragmented clusters. Running Vopt again caused no improvement. Even after I deleted a 3 Meg file to give Vopt plenty of free space, it did not show much improvement. It ended up 56% fragmented with 8,030 fragmented clusters.

In addition to disk optimization, the Vopt package contained several other programs. These are covered in Chapter 4.

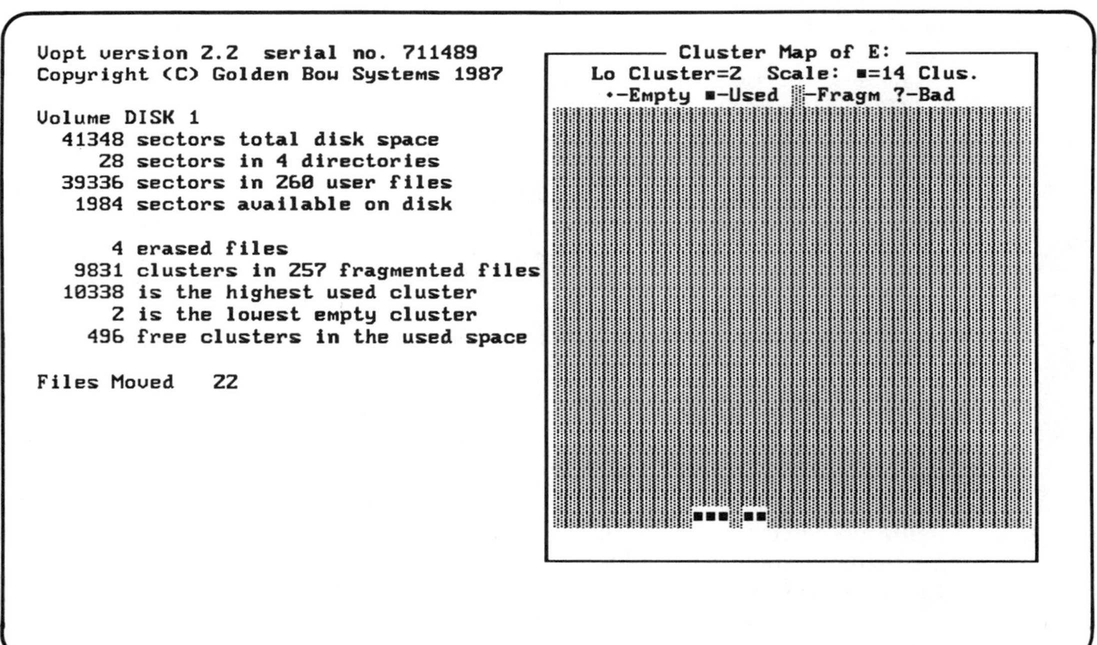

Fig. 8-8. Vopt displays technical information on the hard disk while it is running.

Limitations   Vopt is added to your AUTOEXEC.BAT file so it cleans up your hard disk every time you boot. It could probably keep your hard disk fairly free of fragmentation if you started with an optimized hard disk. However, once a hard disk develops fragmentation no amount of running Vopt will correct the problem.

I tried running Vopt on the 130 Meg hard disk on the IBM Model 70. Each time, it reported "Crosslinked Files" and did nothing. The DOS CHKDSK program and the Norton Disktest program found no problems. The Vopt CHKDSK program refused to run.

The manual claims Vopt will force the computer to reboot if you are using the DOS program FASTOPEN. I was and it did not. Vopt will only work with 10,000 files and 500 subdirectories.

Conclusion   For correcting serious disk fragmentation, Vopt proved to be inadequate. Vopt refused to run on a standard PS/2 hard disk. Any of the other disk optimization programs would do a better job.

<table>
<tr><td>Product:</td><td>Vopt</td></tr>
<tr><td>Price:</td><td>$49.95</td></tr>
<tr><td>Category:</td><td>Commercial</td></tr>
<tr><td>Publisher:</td><td>Golden Bow Systems</td></tr>
<tr><td>Address:</td><td>2870 Fifth Avenue
Suite 201
San Diego, California 92103</td></tr>
<tr><td>Phone:</td><td>(619) 298-9349</td></tr>
<tr><td>Memory:</td><td>512K</td></tr>
</table>

9
Console Speed-Up Programs

Depending on its usage, the computer console is either the keyboard or the screen. For example, the command:

COPY CON EXAMPLE

will copy everything you type on the keyboard (the CONsole) into a file called EXAMPLE. You stop sending text to the file by pressing the F6 key. However, the command:

COPY EXAMPLE CON

will copy the contents of the file EXAMPLE to the screen.

DOS uses very conservative methods of controlling the console. These conservative methods mean the computer runs slower than it can. Programmers have long bypassed DOS for screen updating because they can write routines to update the screen much faster than DOS updates the screen. However, all DOS programs and many less expensive programs depend on DOS for screen handling. Some of the programs in this chapter will give those types of programs a speed burst by improving the way DOS writes to screen.

When processing keystrokes from the keyboard, DOS is equally conservative. DOS only allows you to type twelve characters ahead of the computer. (This is called the type-ahead buffer.) Many of these programs increase the size of the type-ahead buffer. They also improve the way DOS handles keystrokes. Three characteristics are important:

1) If you press down a key and hold it down, how long does it take before that key begins repeating. DOS takes a long time, and that can be annoying when you are trying to move around a document or worksheet.

2) As you continue to hold down the key, how rapidly does it repeat. The faster it repeats, the faster you can move around your documents. DOS repeats slowly.

3) Once you take your finger off the key, how soon does it stop repeating. This can be a special problem with a program that increases the type-ahead buffer and slow software. If the software is processing the keystrokes slower than DOS is sending them, the type-ahead buffer has keystrokes in it. Once you take your finger off the key, these stored keystrokes will cause the cursor to act as though you still had your finger on the key.

Screen and keyboard speedup are the major features of these programs. However, like the "grab-bags" at a flea-market, you will find a number of additional features in these programs. Some blank the screen after a set period on inactivity (to prevent burning an image into your monitor) and others will let you control the shape of your cursor.

Cruise Control

Cruise Control is a small and inexpensive commercial cursor control program.

Installation   Cruise Control comes with an automatic installation program that runs from any drive. It lets you install Cruise Control in any subdirectory. However, it installs Cruise Control improperly if you select a subdirectory not on the boot disk.

Operation   The primary function of Cruise Control is to speed up your cursor when you hold down a key. This is most useful for the cursor movement keys. It does not do this the same way most programs do. You do not select a set speed from a menu or enter one at the command line. Rather, Cruise Control figures out how fast your program can accept keystrokes and sends its keystrokes at just that speed. A few programs, like WordStar 3.31, will actually get keystrokes slower than the standard repeating rate on the keyboard.

Like similar programs, Cruise Control auto-stops. When you quit pressing a key, it immediately stops. However, it works a little differently. Other programs stop by purging the type-ahead buffer when you stop pressing a key that is auto-repeating. On the other hand, Cruise Control senses the speed the program can accept keystrokes. It never lets repeated keys into the type-ahead buffer any faster than the program can take them. As a result, when you release a key there are no additional key-presses pending in the type-ahead buffer.

Cruise Control has a couple of other nice features. They are:

- Pressing 5-T inserts the time into the current application.
- Pressing 5-D inserts the date into the current application.
- Pressing 5-Delete instantly blanks the screen. Pressing any key restores the screen.

- It will blank the screen after a preset period of inactivity. You set this value on the command line when you start the program. Pressing any key restores the screen.

Cruise Control uses the 5-key on the number pad with the numlock off as its command key. Normally, if you press the 5-key with the numlock off nothing happens. It uses this rather than a Control or Alt combination to reduce conflicts with other programs.

Limitations The installation program installs Cruise Control improperly if you select a subdirectory not on the boot disk. I installed Cruise Control on a hard disk partitioned into two drives, the C-drive and D-drive. The computer boots off the C-drive and only uses the AUTOEXEC.BAT file on the C-drive. I told the installation program to install Cruise Control on the D-drive. It created its own AUTOEXEC.BAT file in the root directory of the D-drive.

Cruise Control interferes with normal operation if you hold down a key while DOS is executing a command. I issued a DIR command for a large subdirectory. As soon as files started scrolling by, I began to hold down the 1-key. When the directory finished, there were only two 1's in the type-ahead buffer. So far that is what you would expect. Cruise Control figured out that the computer could not accept any more commands and stopped accepting them. However, it does not beep to warn the user. In addition, when DOS was finally able to accept commands, Cruise Control began sending a series of returns. It did this even though I was still holding down the 1-key. This behavior was not unique to the DIR command or the 1-key. It does, however, only apply to repeated keys. If you type in another command while DOS is displaying the directory, it buffers that command properly.

The manual and installation program talk about selecting either A, B or C Cruise Control strategy. However, neither the manual nor the installation program explains what this means. However, a readme file on the disk explains it. Basically, strategy-A is everything except Microsoft Access (B) and WordStar 3.31 (C).

Manual As discussed above, the manual tells you to select a Cruise Control strategy without explaining the strategies. Otherwise, it does an adequate job of explaining how to use the program. Once you get the program installed and running to your liking, you will probably never need to use the manual again.

Conclusion Cruise Control offers automatic configuration of the cursor speed and most of the other features of NoBlink/Accelerator. For controlling the cursor, it does a good job. However, it does not give you any control over screen color.

Product:	Cruise Control
Price:	$59.95
Category:	Commercial
Publisher:	Revolution Software, Incorporated
Address:	715 Route 10 East
	Randolph, New Jersey 07869
Phone:	(201) 366-4445
Memory:	5K

FANSI-Console

FANSI-Console is a shareware console speed-up program. The FANSI stands for Fast ANSI. You pronounce it "Fancy". The ANSI stands for American National Standards Institute. FANSI-Console completely replaces the DOS ANSI.SYS program.

Installation   There is no installation program and the process is not well explained in the manual. The manual merely instructs you to copy the files to a subdirectory or to a scratch diskette.

FANSI-Console is a DOS device driver. That means it is loaded into memory when the computer boots. It also means that loading FANSI-Console requires a device statement in your CONFIG.SYS file. The manual explains the statement but will not add it automatically. Appendix F explains more about DOS device drivers.

Finally, you must modify your PATH statement so you can use the programs that come with FANSI-Console. The manual does a very poor job of explaining this and even has an error in the example.

Operation   FANSI-Console has a number of functions. However, its more important function is speeding up screen writing for any program or DOS command that uses the BIOS to write to the screen. It does this very well. For example, my FANSI-Console directory has 206 files in it. The DIR command takes 15.05 seconds under DOS. It takes 6.37 seconds under FANSI-Console in show (monitor has show) mode. It only takes 4.18 seconds in fast (no show) mode. FANSI-Console does not affect programs like Lotus 1-2-3 that write directly to the screen memory.

In text mode, FANSI-Console can store lines as they scroll off the screen for you to recall later. This requires additional memory, about 160-bytes per line. If you have expanded memory, FANSI-Console can use it to store this text. This buffer also allows you to print the text and even use it as keyboard input after it scrolls off the screen. That allows you to use the text buffer to recall DOS commands.

FANSI-Console can blank the screen after a selected period of inactivity. You can set the period for up to one hour. However, its default mode is not to blank the screen.

FANSI-Console includes a program to remap the keyboard. You must first create a template. A FANSI-Console utility displays a map of the keyboard on the screen. You move the keys around to build your custom layout. The top of each key shows its normal setting and the bottom shows the remapped setting. Once you have created your custom utility, you run a program to load it into memory.

FANSI-Console expands the type-ahead buffer to 255-characters. It also adds a special Control-F command to flush the type-ahead buffer without affecting the program that is running. FANSI-Console can change the keyboard repeat rate to any rate you specify. This is the speed that keys repeat as you hold a key down. Like similar programs, FANSI-Console auto-stops. When you quit pressing a key, it immediately quits repeating rather than repeating until the type-ahead buffer is empty.

FANSI-Console replaces the normal print-screen handling with its own routine that handles problems like no printer without long delays.

Normally, you configure FANSI-Console with switches in your CONFIG.SYS file. It would be unusual to need to change them. However, FANSI-Console has the capacity to change many of them by running a program. However, you cannot change options that allocate memory. You make these changes through a nice menu-driven program.

Limitations   Some of the functions of FANSI-Console use environmental space. If you have not expanded your environmental space, you can easily run out of room. The manual only explains how to expand the environmental space under DOS 3.0 and 3.1.

FANSI-Console lets you redefine keys as macros. For example, you could define the F1 key as "DIR *.BAK" so you would get a list of all your *.BAK files when you pressed F1. However, this requires sending complex escape sequences to FANSI-Console. A keyboard macro program like SuperKey is much easier to use.

Manual   FANSI-Console comes with two manuals, a user manual and a technical manual. Both are complete and completely explain how to use FANSI-Console. However, both are technical in nature and difficult to use. A new user would have trouble understanding these manuals.

Conclusion   If you normally load ANSI.SYS, FANSI-Console is a much better choice. It is much faster than ANSI.SYS, offers more features and lets you change many of its operating parameters without rebooting. However, if you just want to speed up your screen writes, then another program would be a better choice.

Product:	FANSI-Console
Price:	$75
	$25 for a demo version
Category:	Shareware
Publisher:	Hersey Micro Consulting, Incorporated
	No Smoking Software
Address:	Post Office Box 8276
	Ann Arbor, Michigan 48107
Phone:	(313) 994-3259
Memory:	42K

NoBlink/Accelerator

NoBlink/Accelerator (*NoBlink* for short) is a commercial program to control the shape and speed of your cursor.

Installation   NoBlink has an installation program that automatically copies the program file to the root directory of your boot disk. It also adds the command to start the program as the last line in your CONFIG.SYS file. Even though the program is a .COM file, you must load it as a device driver. The installation program will run from any drive.

Operation   NoBlink works like a memory resident program. You press Control-Shift-$ to pop up its menu. This menu lets you select a number of operating parameters. They are:

- The cursor shape. There are eight shapes, from a tiny underline to a full-size block.
- A blinking (normal) or nonblinking cursor.
- The color of the cursor.
- The speed the cursor repeats when you hold down a key. Only four speeds are available. When you select any of the three faster than normal speeds, NoBlink adds an auto-stop mode. When you quit pressing a key, it immediately quits repeating rather than repeating until the type-ahead buffer is empty.
- EGA and VGA colors. You can select the foreground and background colors. The screen changes to show your choice as you toggle through the selections. Unlike many color setting programs, these colors are "sticky." Many times, when you set screen colors with a program they are reset to white on black after a DOS CLS (CLear Screen) command. NoBlink stays in effect after a CLS command.
- Blank the screen. NoBlink does not work like a normal screen blanking program. It does not wait in memory counting seconds until the computer has been inactive for a specified time. Rather, you select a blank screen from the NoBlink menu. The screen stays blank until you press any key. This is less useful than a normal screen blanking program. However, it does let you blank the screen if you are working on sensitive information (or playing games) and someone walks in on you.

Limitations   NoBlink lets you configure a number of cursor parameters from its menu. However, it has no way to save these parameters. As a result, you must reset them each time you run the program. NoBlink slightly slows down screen writes. A directory of 206 files that took 15.05 seconds to display without NoBlink loaded took 15.82 seconds with it loaded.

NoBlink is supposed to stop the computer from beeping when you reach the end of the type-ahead buffer. However, NoBlink did not perform consistently. When you enter a command, you enter different keys one after another. In this mode, the computer beeps when the type-ahead buffer is full. If you hold down one key and let it repeat, the computer does not beep when the type-ahead buffer is full. This also causes all the type-ahead buffer to lose all the keystrokes you enter.

Manual   The program is very easy to use and it is not likely you will need the manual much. However, the fifteen page manual does a good job of explaining how to use the program.

Conclusion   NoBlink is a small and inexpensive program that gives you excellent control over the cursor and screen colors.

```
Product:     NoBlink Accelerator
Price:       $49.95
Category:    Commercial
Publisher:   Nostradamus, Incorporated
Address:     4525 South Wasatch Boulevard
             Suite #335
             Salt Lake City, Utah 84124
Phone:       (801) 272-0671
             (801) 272-0675 (Fax-Office
             Hours)
             (801) 272-0675 (BBS-After
             Hours)
Memory:      6K
```

PC-Kwik Power Pak

The *PC-Kwik Power Pak* is primarily an extremely easy to use and fast commercial caching program. However, the package also includes two console speed up programs. They are a keyboard and screen speed up programs.

Installation　　PC-Kwik Power Pak comes with an automatic installation program. The manual also has instructions for users who want to install the program manually.

Operation　　You load the two console speed up programs in PC-Kwik Power Pak from the command line or in your AUTOEXEC.BAT file. The keyboard accelerator takes 3K and the screen accelerator takes 4K.

You use Alt-Plus to speed up the keyboard repeat rate and Alt-Minus to slow it down. You use Alt-Control-Plus to cause it to start repeating sooner. You use Alt-Control-Minus to delay when it starts repeating. The left and right cursor movement keys go twice as fast as the remaining keys. The program has a spreadsheet mode to turn this off.

The screen speed up program only works with programs that write to the screen through the BIOS. For these programs, it speeds them up more than any other program I have ever seen. A directory that took 2.06 seconds under DOS took less that 0.45 seconds with the screen accelerator program loaded.

The screen accelerator program stores screens for later recall. It uses the Super PC-Kwik cache memory for this. For it to work, the cache must be active before loading the screen accelerator.

Limitations　　The keyboard speed up program suffers from severe cursor run-on in Lotus 1-2-3. After you stop pressing a cursor key, it may be two hundred cells later before the cursor stops.

Manual　　The manual is excellent. It is well written and easy to understand.

Conclusion　　Both the screen and keyboard accelerator programs are excellent programs. I was especially impressed with the screen accelerator. These programs are only a small portion of the PC-Kwik Power Pak package.

```
Product:      PC-Kwik Power Pak
Price:        $129.95 For Package
Category:     Commercial
Publisher:    Multisoft Corporation
Address:      15100 SW Koll Parkway
              Suite L
              Beaverton, Oregon 97006
Phone:        (800) 288-5945
              (503) 644-5644
Notes:        The PC-Kwik Power Pak includes a RAM disk
              and a print buffer that both use memory
              allocated to the cache. As a result, they do not
              require their own memory. The screen
              accelerator uses cache memory to store
              screens for later recall. It will speed up screens
              without cache memory but you will not be able
              to recall past screens.

              The memory requirements below are for the
              program. The memory allocated to the cache
              itself is an additional memory requirement.
Memory:       Expanded Memory/Full Features
              16K    Super PC-Kwik
              16K    Spooler
              8K     Screen Accelerator
              2K     Keyboard Accelerator
              Expanded Memory/Minimum Configuration
              8K     Super PC-Kwik
              5K     Spooler
              6K     Screen Accelerator
              2K     Keyboard Accelerator
              Extended Memory/Full Features
              40K    Super PC-Kwik (Small Buffer)
              52K    Super PC-Kwik (Large Buffer)
              16K    Spooler
              8K     Screen Accelerator
              2K     Keyboard Accelerator
              Extended Memory/Minimum Configuration
              23K    Super PC-Kwik (Small Buffer)
              33K    Super PC-Kwik (Large Buffer)
              5K     Spooler
              6K     Screen Accelerator
              2K     Keyboard Accelerator
```

RONNY'S PICKS

If you normally load ANSI.SYS, FANSI-Console is a much better choice. It is much faster than ANSI.SYS, offers more features and lets you change many of its operating parameters without rebooting. If you do not use ANSI.SYS, then the screen accelerator in PC-Kwik Power Pak is an excellent choice to speed up your screen. It has an additional advantage of being only a small part of an excellent package that includes a RAM disk, disk cache and print buffer. I was less impressed with the PC-Kwik Power Pak keyboard accelerator. It suffered too much from cursor run-on. Cruise Control is a much better keyboard accelerator.

10
Speeding Up Your Hard Disk

Disk caching uses the memory in your computer to speed up hard disk operation. Some cache programs will even speed up your floppy drives. A disk cache program sets aside a portion of memory for its own use. Every time DOS requests information from the disk, the cache program intercepts that request. It checks its memory and if the data DOS requested is in its memory it supplies it to DOS. In this case, DOS never reads the disk drive at all. This is where the caching speeds up the computer. The speed increase is a function of how fast both the computer and hard disk are. The faster the computer, the faster the cache program can check its memory for the data. The faster the hard disk, the less time the cache saves.

If the cache program does not find the data in its memory, it allows DOS to read the disk. In this case, the cache grabs a copy of the data for itself as DOS reads it off the disk. By taking time to check its memory and grab a copy of the data, the cache actually slows down the computer.

As you can see, a cache is a balancing act. It balances the longer times it takes to read new information off the disk against the time savings when supplying data that DOS has already read once. Different applications on the same computer have different relationships between these two forces. For example, as you write and edit a document, WordStar will frequently read portions of its code off the disk. As you move around the document, it will occasionally read portions of the document from disk and write other portions back to disk. This is why you can edit a document much larger than your available memory. A cache will speed up this a lot. Now consider running Lotus 1-2-3 on the same machine. Lotus loads entirely into memory. The only program information it reads off the disk are its help files if you press F1. If you do not use the help function, the program never accesses the disk. When you load a worksheet into memory, it loads the entire worksheet. The entire worksheet remains in memory. Lotus does not write it back to disk until you save it. A cache will not speed up this operation and may even slow it down.

IMPROVING THE ODDS

There are a couple of things the cache program can do to improve its speed. They are:

1) Working smarter.
2) Improving the odds of having the data requested by DOS.

Working smarter is the generic sort of thing any program can do to get a speed improvement. Only with a cache program it is more important. For each request, the cache has to search through a lot of memory, often in the megabytes. Even a small increase in the speed of this operation can make a significant difference in cache performance.

There are a number of things cache programs do to improve the odds of having the data requested by DOS. They include:

1) Reading in more information than DOS requests. The theory is that when DOS requests data from a sector, it is likely to soon need data from surrounding sectors. However, in practice the theory has some difficulty. After use, the caching memory will be full of data with no more room.

2) Figuring out which data to purge from the cache after it fills up. All caches use some for latest requested last purged algorithm. The cache drops data that has waited the longest since being used. This makes sense. If you run WordStar for awhile, then its overlay files will make it into the cache. When you leave WordStar to use Lotus, the cache has no way to know it can purge the WordStar data. However, as you use Lotus, the computer does not access the WordStar data. As this continues, the purge algorithm will finally realize it can drop the WordStar data.

3) Making DOS disk writes more intelligent. When you save your Lotus worksheet, DOS writes the entire file to disk even if you have changed only one byte in one sector. DOS will even write the entire file to disk if you have not changed it since the last time you saved it. Some caches will check the data being written to disk against its own version and only allow the write if the data has changed. This feature is not effective with many programs and most word processors. Many programs write the data you save to a new address and only then delete or rename the old version. Since the data is going to a new location, the cache will not stop it. Still other caches will multi-task the disk writing so the computer can go on to something else. A few will hold the data in memory without writing until the computer is idle.

CONFIGURING YOUR CACHE

Your first choice is where the cache is to get the memory it uses to store its data. Your three choices are conventional memory, extended (LIM or Lotus/Intel/Microsoft) memory or expanded (AT-memory) memory. These days, the combination of large programs and useful memory resident programs make conventional memory a poor choice. It is a rare user who can spare 128K or more of the available 640K for a cache.

Many other users do not really have a choice as their machine only has extended or expanded memory and not both. If you have a choice, extended memory generally works slightly faster since the processor must switch to protected mode to use expanded memory. However, the difference is generally within one percent. In fact, it was so close in my testing I only reported extended memory times. The choice can be even more confusing if you are using a memory manager like 386^{Max} or CEMM (Compaq Enhanced Memory Manager). These programs simulate extended memory using expanded memory.

A second question you face with a cache is the size of the memory to allocate to the cache. If you are using expanded memory, then memory allocated to the cache reduces the space available for Lotus worksheets and other applications using expanded memory. I experimented and found that if you have the memory, you should allocate a minimum of 512K to the cache. Below that, and performance suffers. Above 512K, the cache overhead gets large enough that you only get minor improvements. A few programs even start to lose performance as the cache grows above 512K.

A few of the caches give you an extra speed boost by changing the way DOS writes to the disk. Only writing changed data back to the disk is fairly safe. Some caches go beyond that and either multi-task the writes or save them till the computer is inactive. These are more dangerous as your data is not safe until it reaches the disk. If you lose power, lock up or reboot then you have lost all the data still in the cache. All of Norton's horses cannot get it back.

REMOVABLE DISKS

A few of the caching programs will also cache data going to and from a floppy drive. This improves operations more than caching the hard disk because the floppy drive is much slower on both reads and writes. However, it is also more dangerous. If you change the disk without the cache noticing, it can supply DOS with information from the cache that was on the first disk while DOS is requesting information from the changed disk. If the cache has the FAT and directory from the first disk and uses that to aid DOS in writing to a changed disk then you can destroy all the data on the disk. AT-class machines have a built-in changed disk detection method. However, PC and XT machines do not. The cache has to check the disk itself. If you combine floppy diskette caching with a cache program that waits to write to the drive, then you have the makings of a real disaster.

NEVER, EVER. . .

Use a disk optimizer (Chapter 8) with a caching program active. It will not help much since most programs read and write each cluster only twice when moving it. In addition, some disk optimizers only periodically write the FAT back to the disk. They keep it in memory between writes. As a result, the FAT the cache and disk optimizer are using can be different.

DOS has a small caching program called BUFFERS built in. You load it with a BUFFERS= statement in your CONFIG.SYS file. If you do not have a CONFIG.SYS file or it does not have a BUFFERS= statement, then DOS starts with default value. In most cases, you should set the BUFFERS= statement to a very small number when using a cache.

DOS 3.3 introduced a second and entirely separate cache called FAST-OPEN. You load FASTOPEN with a command like "FASTOPEN c:=40" statement in your AUTOEXEC.BAT file. Unlike the BUFFERS= statement, DOS has no default for FASTOPEN if you do not run the program. FASTOPEN stores the location of the files you access on a hard disk. In the above example, it stores the location of forty files. If you do not use a cache program, FASTOPEN can speed up your hard disk a significant amount. However, my tests showed it did not help at all while using a cache. It turns out that FASTOPEN is even more dangerous than a cache when you run your disk optimizer. FASTOPEN does not update its location as the disk optimizer runs. When you finish, if DOS tries to access a file through FASTOPEN and the disk optimizer moved that file, then FASTOPEN cannot find the file. At that point, DOS gives you the very scary "file not found" error message. For this reason, you should always reboot after running a disk optimizer.

THE TESTING

I tested the caches on a number of different programs. For a lot of applications, they did not matter. However, they made a measurable difference in database performance and document spell checking so I settled on those to benchmark the programs. For database testing, I constructed a database with six fields. Three fields contained randomly arranged character data and three contained randomly arranged numeric data. I performed two benchmarks on this data, the time to sort it on three keys and the time to index it on three keys. For spell checking, I recorded the time to check a 147K document with 18,600 words that contained no errors. Both of these applications read the same portions of the disk over and over. Therefore, you will realize most of the benefits of the first time through. To be sure, I ran the benchmarks a second time. Generally, the incremental improvement the second time through was fairly small. Table 10-1 shows the results.

The Vcache caching program includes a benchmarking program called Database. This program creates, reads, writes and updates a database on your hard disk. The manual suggests you use this to figure out the proper BUFFERS= statement for your CONFIG.SYS file. I also ran this program to compare the performance of the various caching programs. Table 10-2 shows these results.

Table 10-1. **Disk Caching Program Timing Results.**

Program	Database Sort[1]	Database Index[2]	Microsoft Word Spell Check[3]
DOS: BUFFERS=3	11/10	18/20	3:47/3:43
DOS: BUFFERS=20	12/8	18/19	2:53/2:51
DOS: BUFFERS=99	11/9	18/19	1:59/1:57
Super PC-Kwik	8/8	17/18	1:08/1:07
Vcache	10/7	18/17	1:08/1:07

All times on an IBM Model 70 running at 16 MHz

[1]Time (in seconds) to sort a 270K database with 5,000 records on three keys.

[2]Time (in seconds) to index a 270K database with 5,000 records on three keys.

[3]Time (in minutes) to check the spelling in a 147K 18,600 word document using Microsoft Word.

Table 10-2. **Disk Caching Program Timing Results for Databases.**

	DOS BUFFERS=3	DOS BUFFERS=20	DOS BUFFERS=99
Create Database	8.7	11.3	11.3
Forward Read 1000 Records	8.7	8.7	8.7
Backwards Read 500 Records	12.4	12.5	12.5
Random Read 1000 Records	20.9	20.2	20.2
Random Write 1000 Records	20.5	10.1	9.9
Random Update 500 Records	20.7	10.5	10.4

	Super PC-Kwik	Vcache
Create Database	1.8	2.9
Forward Read 1000 Records	.8	0.6
Backwards Read 500 Records	.9	0.8
Random Read 1000 Records	1.5	1.8
Random Write 1000 Records	3.9	6.2
Random Update 500 Records	5.2	6.6

All times on an IBM Model 70 running at 16 MHz

DOS

DOS allows you to specify a BUFFERS= command in your CONFIG.SYS file.

Installation   BUFFERS is an internal DOS command. All you do to install the BUFFERS is add the BUFFERS= statement to your CONFIG.SYS file and reboot the computer.

Operation   The number of allowable buffers is one to ninety-nine. Each buffer requires about .5K so a BUFFERS=99 statement in your CONFIG.SYS file requires about 49.5K of conventional memory. Increasing the buffers increased the speed of the spelling checker a great deal but it had very little impact on the database.

Limitations   The optimum setting for the BUFFERS= statement varies on your application and your system. You will have to experiment to find the proper setting.

Manual   The DOS manual only devotes two pages to the buffers command and gives very little information on the optimum setting for your computer.

Conclusion   The speed increase for some applications is large enough that it is worth while to experiment to find the proper setting.

PC-Kwik Power Pak

Super PC-Kwik Disk Accelerator (*Super PC-Kwik* for short) is an extremely easy to use and fast commercial caching program. It is part of the PC-Kwik Power Pak package.

Installation   Super PC-Kwik comes with an automatic installation program. The manual also has instructions for users who want to install the program manually.

Operation   Super PC-Kwik is a program you load from the command line or in your AUTOEXEC.BAT file. You use command line switches to configure the program and tell it how much memory to use.

The cache checks writes and only writes to disk when the data has changed. It will also buffer and multi-task writes to floppy disk drives. You will be able to return to your program well before the cache finishes writing to the floppy diskettes.

The cache includes many useful features. You can:

- Select which drives to cache and which to ignore. This is useful if you have multiple drives or have a cartridge drive you switch a lot.
- Flush all the data from the cache. This might be useful in some cases when you switch applications.
- Temporarily disable the cache. This is useful for applications where the cache slows down the operation. It is also useful for operations like disk optimization where it is dangerous to use a cache.

Super PC-Kwik works well with Bernoulli drives. It will also work with extended memory managers like 386^{Max}. When the program loads, it can test the computer and drives and figure out the best settings.

Super PC-Kwik is one of five programs in the PC-Kwik Power Pak. The rest of the packages in the PC-Kwik Power Pak are:

- Print buffer. The print buffer stores data in RAM. You do not set up a special area in RAM for the print buffer, it "borrows" the memory it needs from the caching program. Chapter 20 covers the print buffer in more detail.
- RAM disk. Unlike other RAM disks, you do not set up a special area in RAM for the disk. Rather, it borrows memory as it needs it from the caching program.

- Keyboard accelerator. This lets you control the repeat rate for your keyboard. Chapter 9 covers the keyboard accelerator in more detail.
- Screen accelerator. This speeds up some screen writes. It also lets you scroll the screen back to see what scrolled off. Chapter 9 covers the screen accelerator in more detail.

The RAM disk and the print buffer (see Chapter 20 for more details) both use the same memory as the cache program. They borrow memory from the cache when they need it and return extra memory to the cache as they finish with it. You load the RAM disk using a DEVICE= statement in your CONFIG.SYS file. That means the computer loads it before the cache, which you would load in the AUTOEXEC.BAT file or from the command line. If you forget to load the cache and try to access the RAM disk, you get an "invalid drive" error message.

The RAM disk defaults to a paltry maximum size of 128K with room for 64 entries in its root directory. You can change these using switches on the DEVICE= line in the CONFIG.SYS file. Increasing the size of the RAM disk has no negative impact on the cache because the RAM disk does not grab memory until it needs it. When grabbing memory, it gets the smallest amount it needs.

The RAM disk functions much like a cache where you control what stays in the cache. For example, you might use your word processor a lot but leave it often to do other tasks. Under that situation, you should copy your word processing files to the RAM disk. The cache might purge the word processing files while you are performing other tasks but they remain in the RAM disk. One major disadvantage to the RAM disk is you lose data saved to the RAM disk when you turn the computer off, reboot or lock up the computer. However, data write to a cache is almost immediately written to the disk. Therefore, it is probably best to reserve the RAM disk for the programs you run a lot.

PC Tools Deluxe (see Chapter 5) comes with a stripped down version of the Super PC-Kwik caching program. It does not include the other programs in the PC-Kwik Power Pak. The performance of the PC Tools Deluxe version of the program is very similar Super PC-Kwik.

Limitations   Super PC-Kwik requires far more memory when loaded into extended memory than expanded memory. A 512K buffer in extended memory required 43K while it required only 16K in expanded memory.

Manual   The manual is excellent. It begins with a clear explanation of what a disk cache is. It then explains how to use Super PC-Kwik. However, many users will not need this explanation since Super PC-Kwik can configure itself for optimum performance in most environments.

Conclusion   Super PC-Kwik is the overall faster cache program I tested. Beyond that, it is well thought out and genuinely easy to use. Being able to share its memory with a RAM disk and a print buffer adds a great deal to its usefulness. (For ordering information, see page 251.)

Vcache

Vcache is a fast and compact caching program.

Installation   There is no installation program. The manual does not tell you how to copy the files to the hard disk. About all the manual tells you is to add the command to your AUTOEXEC.BAT file.

Operation   Vcache comes with three hard disk caching programs. There are separate programs for conventional, expanded and extended memory. Vcache included a fourth conventional memory caching program for floppy disk drives. All of these caches are command-line programs.

The default configuration of Vcache will delay writes for one second to group multiple writes together. You can use a switch to set this to zero or two seconds. You can also configure the cache to grab additional data when reading the disk. This is useful if you use programs that spend a lot of time reading the disk sequentially. The default setting is 2-4K depending on the type of machine you have. You can configure Vcache to grab up to 32K at a time. This will slow down random reads but greatly speed up sequential reads.

Vcache will cache any hard disk device, including those that require a device driver. It works with up to four device drivers. It will also cache a Bernoulli drive, however, not on the same system as a hard disk.

Vcache includes two additional programs. One lets you set the keyboard repeat rate and the other will speed up some screen writes.

Limitations   Vcache includes a program called Vkette to cache floppy disk drives. This program requires 256K of conventional memory. When I tried to use it, my computer locked up every time it tried to access the A-drive. After several failed attempts, I checked the A-drive with CHKDSK. It found 655 lost chains. The system date on Vkette is 6-30-87 so this is most likely either a 1.44 Meg drive or DOS 4.x incompatibility.

Manual   The manual is very short and only devotes a couple of pages to the cache program. However, it is fairly simple to use so most users will find the manual adequate.

Conclusion   Vcache is a simple to use and effective hard disk caching program. It was ineffective at caching floppy disk drives.

Product:	Vcache
Price:	$59.95
Category:	Commercial
Publisher:	Golden Bow Systems
Address:	2870 Fifth Avenue
	Suite 201
	San Diego, California 92103
Phone:	(619) 298-9349
Notes:	Conventional memory usage is a function of the cache size
Memory:	20K Conventional Memory Typical

RONNY'S PICK

All of these cache programs speed up your computer. If you do not have any extended or expanded memory, then you should not be using a cache. Their performance is poor when you can only allocate a few kilobytes of conventional memory. However, with only conventional memory you should take the time to experiment and find the optimum setting for your BUFFERS= statement in your CONFIG.SYS file. Its value makes a lot of difference with some operations as the charts clearly show.

If you have the extended or expanded memory to allocate to a cache, then the choice is clear. Super PC-Kwik is by far the best available cache program. In many of the tests it was the fastest program. When it was not the fastest, it was near the top. Beyond speed, Super PC-Kwik offers an intelligent and flexible design. It easily shares its memory dynamically with a RAM disk and print spooler that comes with Super PC-Kwik.

11
Hard Disk Drive Enhancement Utilities

DOS sets very exacting limits on what you can do with your hard disk. After low-level formatting the hard disk (not a DOS function) DOS takes over with two programs, FDISK and FORMAT. Both have well defined and very conservative limits. While Microsoft and IBM have played it very conservative with DOS, other vendors have rushed in to provide additional functions.

The programs in this chapter are definitely not for everyone. In fact, you should probably skip this chapter unless you know a lot about computers. (For that very reason, I will not be making comments about inexperienced users understanding the manuals. These are very technical products and technical manuals are acceptable.)

Disk Manager: Hard Disk Installation

Disk Manager: Hard Disk Installation (*Disk Manager* for short) is a commercial hard disk installation program.

Installation   Disk Manager has no installation program and the manual does not explain how to install the program. Since some of the programs are destructive, I ran it from a DISKCOPY of the distribution diskette.

Operation   Disk Manager is almost completely automated. It first tests the system to make sure it can communicate with the hard disk. Then it prompts you to select the model from a list it presents on-screen. If you have a list from the manufacturer, you can enter a list of defects. Finally, you tell Disk Manager

DOS format. Disk Manager can even transfer the system files for you. Disk Manager supports drives up to 512 Meg. However, the drive you use to boot from must be 32 Meg or smaller.

Disk Manager allows you to select the interleave for the hard disk. You can also use Disk Manager to mark partitions of your hard disk as read-only. It allows you to select the number of entries allowed in the root directory.

Manual   Disk Manager comes with a twelve page printed manual and extensive disk-based reference material. In addition, Disk Manager has on-line help available while operating. All of the reference material is on adequate quality.

Conclusion   Disk Manager gives you automated installation and large hard disk partitions.

Product:	Disk Manager
	Hard Disk Installation Utility
Price:	$124.95
Category:	Commercial
Publisher:	Ontrack Computer Systems
Address:	6222 Bury Drive
	Eden Prairie, Minnesota 55344
Phone:	(800) 752-1333
	(612) 937-1107
Memory:	128K

HTest/HFormat

HTest/HFormat is a set of machine-level utilities for hard disks. It allows exhaustive testing for and locking out of bad sectors at the controller level. It will low-level format most hard disks. It can change the interleave without reformatting the hard disk. It includes a performance test. It will work with standard MFM or RLL controllers. The hard disk can have up to 16 heads and 1024 cylinders.

Installation   HTest/HFormat has no installation program and the manual does not explain how to install the program. Since some of the programs are destructive, I ran it from a DISKCOPY of the distribution diskette.

Operation   HFormat is a low-level formatting program. It can low-level format the entire hard disk or any portion down to a single track. You can run it in non-destructive mode. As the manual points out, no sane person would do this without a current backup. After formatting the hard disk, HFormat will test the hard disk for errors.

HTest performs surface checks of a formatted hard disk that is in working order. This is an extremely thorough test that took over an hour on a 20 Meg hard disk.

HPerf measures the performance of your hard disk. It measures:

1) Track to track seek time. This is the time it takes to move from one cylinder to the next.

how to partition the hard disk. Once configured, Disk Manager performs a low-level format, partitions the hard disk as specified and performs a high-level

2) Average seek time. This is the time it takes to move from one cylinder selected at random to another.

3) Test track transfer rate. This is the rate the hard disk can transfer data stored in sequential tracks to computer memory.

4) Random transfer rate. This is the rate the hard disk can transfer data stored in randomly selected tracks to computer memory.

HOptimum can test your hard disk to find its optimum interleave rate. Once found, HOptimum can convert the hard disk to that interleave without losing any data on the hard disk.

XFDisk is a partitioning program and is a direct replacement for the DOS FDISK program. XFDisk saves a copy of the master boot record. You can use this later if you need to replace a damaged master boot record. In addition, XFDisk will not destroy any existing file allocation table [FAT] or directory information on the partitions it works with.

Limitations   Does not work with PS/2 ESDI controllers.

Manual   The manual is excellent. It includes extensive clear coverage on using these programs to recover from a hard disk disaster. In addition, the manual has a number of appendices to explain the areas and terms beginners are going to find confusing.

Conclusion   While not quite as extensive as Disk Technician Advance, HTest /HFormat performs a number of disk tests. In addition, HTest/HFormat can low-level format many hard disks. HOptimum allows you to change the interleave to its optimum value without losing data.

<table>
<tr><td>Product:</td><td>HTest/HFormat</td></tr>
<tr><td>Price:</td><td>$89.95</td></tr>
<tr><td>Category:</td><td>Commercial</td></tr>
<tr><td>Publisher:</td><td>Paul Mace Software</td></tr>
<tr><td>Address:</td><td>400 Williamson Way
Ashland, Oregon 97520</td></tr>
<tr><td>Phone:</td><td>(503) 488-2322
(800) 523-0258</td></tr>
<tr><td>Memory:</td><td>64K</td></tr>
</table>

SpeedStor

SpeedStor is a commercial program that completely automates preparing your hard disk for use. It performs everything for you, the low-level format, the partitioning and the DOS formatting.

Installation   There is no installation program and the manual does not discuss installing SpeedStor. Since the main purpose of SpeedStor is configuring unformatted hard disks, it is not likely you will be installing SpeedStor. I ran my copy from a DISKCOPY of the distribution disk.

Operation   Type install, answer a couple of questions and SpeedStor takes care of the rest. It performs a low-level format. The low-level formatting program performs several tests. This includes controller, seek and read/write tests. Next, SpeedStor partitions the hard disk. It can divide the hard disk into a number of small partitions or a single partition up to 2048 Meg, you decide. However, the drive you use to boot from must be 32 Meg or smaller. If you need to store very large files, SpeedStor can combine two or more physically separate drives so DOS treats them as a single drive. Finally, it performs a DOS format. All automatically. All you have to do is transfer the DOS system files to the hard disk using the DOS SYS command.

If you have an AT-type computer, SpeedStor will automatically store the proper drive parameters in the CMOS memory. You do not even have to run the Setup program. And SpeedStor will use the full drive capacity even if your AT BIOS does not directly accommodate your drive parameters.

Several different versions of SpeedStor are available, including a special version for PS/2 computers. Some versions only work with certain types of hard disks. There is also a universal version. Make sure you purchase the proper one when you go to purchase SpeedStor.

Manual   The manual has a lot of technical information including jumper settings for some hard disks. This is not a program for a beginner and this is not a manual for a beginner.

Conclusion   If you configure a lot of hard disks, this is the program for you. It automates one of the most boring and confusing tasks in setting up any computer.

<table>
<tr><td>Product:</td><td>SpeedStor</td></tr>
<tr><td>Price:</td><td>$99.00</td></tr>
<tr><td>Category:</td><td>Commercial</td></tr>
<tr><td>Publisher:</td><td>Storage Dimensions</td></tr>
<tr><td>Address:</td><td>981 University Avenue
Los Gatos, California 95030</td></tr>
<tr><td>Phone:</td><td>(408) 395-2688</td></tr>
<tr><td>Memory:</td><td>256K</td></tr>
</table>

Vfeature Deluxe

Vfeature Deluxe is a copy-protected commercial program to low-level format and partition a hard disk. It also has rudimentary data security.

Installation   The first step to installing Vfeature Deluxe is ''locking'' the master disk to the disk controller. This lock causes Vfeature Deluxe to only work with this controller. However, there is a switch to relock Vfeature Deluxe if you change controllers. You may also enter an optional password. If you use a password, Vfeature Deluxe requires that you enter the password each time you run Vfeature Deluxe.

After locking the master disk, the manual instructs you to copy the master disk onto a blank system disk. Vfeature Deluxe includes its own program to do this. Since you can copy the disk, this is not true copy-protection. However, you can only use the copied disk on the original computer you locked it to.

Operation   You enter a single command to run Vfeature Deluxe. It begins reading the CMOS (AT) or ROM (XT) to decide on the drive type. Next, it asks you a series of questions. After this, Vfeature Deluxe performs a low-level format on the hard disk. When that finishes, it brings up a partitioning menu. This works very much like the DOS FDISK program except it allows disk partitions up to 1,024 Meg. However, the drive you use to boot from must be 32 Meg or smaller. It also allows you to connect two physically separate drives so DOS treats them as a single logical drive. Vfeature Deluxe also allows you to password protect the hard and floppy drives.

Limitations   Vfeature Deluxe is copy protected. In addition, it will not run under DOS 4.0 or under DOS 3.3.

Manual   The manual is very brief. This is acceptable for the installation portion of Vfeature Deluxe since the program is for technically advanced users. It is less acceptable when explaining how to use the security features of the program. Users are likely to have to experiment to use the security.

Conclusion   The main function of Vfeature Deluxe is to provide partitions larger than 32 Meg under DOS 3.x and 2.x. It does that. The security part is operational but cumbersome. The copy-protection is really minor since you are not likely to run the program very often.

Product:	Vfeature Deluxe
Price:	$120
Category:	Commectial
Publisher:	Golden Bow Systems
Address:	2870 Fifth Avenue
	Suite 201
	San Diego, California 92103
Phone:	(619) 298-9349
Notes:	Sort of copy protected. See the text for details
Memory:	384K

_____________Part Three_____________

Protecting Your Data

____

12
Backup Software

Backup systems are new to the many computer users. They may be buying their first computer or adding a hard disk to an existing computer. When you work with floppies, backups are not very difficult. You usually have your software on one floppy and your data on another. You only need to back up the software once, when you purchase it. You back up data using COPY A:*.* B: or DISKCOPY A: B:.

Backups are more difficult when you have a hard disk. First, you usually have the software "mixed in" with data files. You have two alternatives. One, spend a lot of time copying your data to floppies one file at a time. Or two, spend a lot of time backing up the entire hard disk to floppies.

You can speed up the process of copying data onto floppies by segregating data files into separate subdirectories, a good idea in any case. With this structure, you can use batch files to move between subdirectories and copy your data to floppy diskettes. However, the process is slow. The basic reason is that the DOS COPY command is slow. It reads one file, then writes the file, then reads a second, and so on . . . The DOS 3.2+ XCOPY command can sometimes speed up the process, but not by much. XCOPY reads as many files as it can, then writes all those files.

Hard disk backup programs transfer data much faster and do not require custom batch files. As a result, most hard disk users will end up using a backup program. You have three alternatives:

1)   Use the backup and restore programs that come with DOS.
2)   Use one of the commercial backup programs.
3)   Use a more expensive hardware backup device.

THE REASON FOR BACKUP

Back when everyone used floppies, the most damage you could do with one "dumb mistake" was 360K. Like dumb mistakes, bad disks or defective hardware rarely damaged more than 360K. Large hard disks now give us the ability to damage 70M or more with one command or as the result of defective hardware. 70M is over 200 diskettes!

Many small businesses maintain all their records on a single microcomputer. All the payroll records, all the tax information, all the bid information, and so on. Imagine the impact to that business if they lost all those records. I know of one company that had their three computers stolen. Naturally, they did not have backups. They were so desperate for the data that they ran ads saying the thieves could keep the computers, and they would not press charges. All they wanted was to get their data back. They never did, and they ended up going out of business.

I know of a Fortune 100 company that maintains a lot of their legal information on microcomputers. One of the analysts tried to format a floppy with (you guessed it): FORMAT

He was lucky. There was a recent backup and he lost only a few hours work. The manager told me that losing the files on that hard disk would have delayed a billion dollar legal case. They know how important their data is. They make daily backups.

I have about 20 articles in progress, a year's worth of work on my dissertation and a lot of tax information on my hard disk. I make a daily incremental backup and two full backups weekly. I store one backup at home and the other at my office.

Is this carrying backing up too far? I do not think so. An incremental backup takes about two minutes and the two full backups take less than half an hour. So I spend less than an hour per week on backups. This time is like insurance. It would take an experienced typist over twenty hours to rekey just my dissertation. It would take me thousands of hours to redo the research if I lost the hard disk copy and could not locate a printed copy. Even my notes are on the hard disk. Now add in the time to redo all the other files, and you begin to see why I make backups.

I learned this lesson the hard way. The first hard disk I purchased was a piece of junk. In less than two months it crashed four times. The first time I lost most of my data files. Of course I had the software diskettes so I did not lose the software. I was lucky, I had been using the hard disk only a few weeks so I did not lose much. I started making infrequent backups. The next crash (luckily) cost me only a few day's work. After that, I began making daily backups and never went back to taking the risk of going without a backup. Stop and think how long it would take you to replace every bit of data on your hard disk.

HARDWARE ALTERNATIVES

At some point, backing up by swapping a lot of floppies becomes very arduous. This is especially the case in a LAN environment with its large hard disks and shared files. Disk-based backups are also impractical to engineers and designers who are creating huge CAD/CAM designs. Luckily, software backups to floppy diskettes are not the only backup alternative. A tape drive is an especially nice piece of hardware for performing backups. I discuss one tape drive at the end of this chapter.

SOFTWARE FEATURES

Backup software, like automobiles, varies. Cars vary from economy cars like the Honda Civic to luxury cars like the Rolls Royce to sports cars like the Porsche 944. Similarly, there is a wide range of features available in backup software. As a minimum, all the programs offered:

1) Full backup. The programs were able to back up an entire hard disk.
2) Incremental backup. The programs were able to back up only those files that had changed since the last backup.
3) User specified files. The programs were able to back up files meeting a user supplied specification like *.DOC.
4) User specified subdirectory. The programs were able to back up a specific subdirectory.

These features are enough to meet the needs of the majority of hard disk users. In fact, you can have a very powerful backup methodology using just these four features.

YOUR APPROACH TO BACKUPS

You have copies of most of your software on the original distribution diskettes so you do not need to back up these files very often. In fact, you could back up these just after installing them and safely never back them up again. However, when you have them mixed in with other files, this strategy is difficult. This is a good reason to strictly segregate programs and data into separate directories.

Except during installation, software files do not change. The software is "tied together" with system files that do not change very often. These include batch files, AUTOEXEC.BAT, CONFIG.SYS, and subdirectories. You can safely go a long time between these files as well. They generally change only when you install new software or remove existing software.

If damaged, you can replace these system files from an old backup, the distribution diskettes, or a local software store. However, things are not that simple with your data files. You create them and only you can replace them. You do not measure their value in purchase price or size, but in the human capital invested in their creation. It is important to back up these files frequently.

Your first backup should be a full backup. This gives you a good copy of installed software and system files. It also gives you a copy of your data files. When you change a data file, DOS automatically changes a flag it maintains with the file name to indicate that a current backup no longer exists. At the end of the day, or week if you want to live dangerously, you make an incremental backup. The backup software looks through your hard disk for files with the archive flag set on. The software backs up that file and resets the flag, then looks for the next file.

This process is fairly painless since incremental backups are very quick. As you continue backing incremental backups, the diskettes begin to pile up. If you are constantly updating a 300K database, then you will create a new copy of this file to diskette every day. Another problem is that files you have erased from the hard disk still exist on the backup diskettes. Files that have been renamed will exist on the backup diskettes under both names. If you have to restore from backup diskettes, you can end up with a lot of extra files this way.

You can resolve these minor problems using the following batch file:

```
cd \
dirsort en/s
filefind *.* > c:\bat\listing.txt
```

The first line goes to the root directory. The second line is optional. It sorts all the directories in extension order with file name as the tie breaker. Dirsort is one of the programs that come with the Norton Utilities. The third line uses another Norton Utilities program to find all files (*.*) on the hard disk. DOS piping (>) sends the output to the file c:\bat\listing.txt, or any other file name you choose. If the file does not exist, DOS creates it automatically. If it does exist, DOS erases it before writing to it. If you do not have the Norton Utilities, you can replace the last line with:

```
chkdsk/v>c:\bat\listing.txt
```

All this batch file does is create a file containing a list of all the files on the hard disk. By running it before backing up, your program will back up this file—even by an incremental backup. If you must restore, you can compare the files that exist after the restore to listing.txt. You can erase or rename any files on the hard disk but not in listing.txt. Therefore, you can delete them after the restore.

This takes time. Depending on the type of system you have it can take half as long as a full backup with the fastest program. In addition, all this is cumbersome. At some point you have so many diskettes from incremental backups that it is time to erase them and make another full backup.

These types of backups will protect you from hardware problems and dumb mistakes. It does not protect you from theft, fire, or other types of damage. For that, you need a second backup set stored off site.

Off-site backups are especially critical for smaller facilities that are more prone to breakins. Some time ago, the Atlanta papers carried a series of articles on breakins at local churches. In one breakin, in addition to office equipment, the thieves took 20 floppy disks. These disks contained five years of work by the pastor. All his sermons, his master's thesis, and all his notes from his prison ministry. He cannot replace most of this data at any price. An off-site backup would have required 20 disks (about 15 dollars) and one hour of work.

You must maintain this off-site backup set as strictly as the on-site set. In order to create a second incremental backup, your backup program must give you the option of not resetting the archive flag. Not all of them do. The rating indicates which ones lack this very useful feature.

Many organizations with very critical files maintain their three or so newest incremental backups. These are called the grandfather, father, and son. The purpose of these multiple backups is being able to recreate changes to important files.

If you need multiple backups for only a few files, there is a better way. I have a subdirectory just for "old" copies of files. Every time I make a major change to a file, I first copy it to this subdirectory with a number extension. So the first version of this chapter is BACKUP.001, the second is BACKUP.002, and so on. This way, I can always go back to an earlier version if I decide I do not like the changes.

MORE FEATURES

In addition to the above features, other useful features were available on only a limited number of programs. These include:

1) Choice on archive flag resetting. This makes it easy to maintain multiple incremental backups. If the program does not have this but uses standard DOS format diskettes, you can make the second incremental backup by DISKCOPYing the first incremental backup.
2) Automatic diskette formatting. This prevents you from having to prepare diskettes first. If the program formats diskettes to a non-DOS format, it should be smart enough not to format diskettes with files without confirmation.
3) File exclusion. Since you know that programs never change, it would be useful to exclude all *.EXE files.

Tables 12-1 through 12-7 at the end of this chapter give a complete feature-by-feature comparison of all the programs.

RESTORING

No one ever wants to restore a file. Restoring a file means you either have a hard disk problem or you have damaged or erased a file accidentally. In addition, while you back up frequently, you only infrequently restore. You will spend the majority of your time using the backup program. Therefore, you should give it the majority of the weight when you select program. However, a backup program is worthless without its restore program.

Speed is not the primary consideration for restoring. Speed is of such minor concern that my benchmarks do not even include restore speed. What is important for the restore program is ease of use. If you use the backup program frequently, you will learn the command structure. Because you will rarely use the restore function, it must be easy to use.

In addition to being easy to use, the restore program must never trash a good file. That is, it must not overwrite a good file with an earlier version without warning you first and giving you the chance to stop it.

BENCHMARKS

I performed all backups using a 16 MHz IBM Model 70 with a 130 Meg hard disk. I created a 10 Meg partition just for this chapter. That way, I was able to fill it with files and leave it constant for the entire process. The total space used by the 252 files was 9,676,146 bytes. Since DOS allocates file space in even clusters, these files occupied 10,000,384 bytes of disk space. That represents three percent slack or unused space.

The largest file was 3,319,659 bytes and the smallest was 42 bytes. There were several major categories of files:

1) Word processing files. There were 59 files requiring 1,851,392 bytes.
2) Lotus worksheet files. There were 19 files requiring 1,739,496 bytes.
3) Small system files, e.g., batch files and small utilities. There were 139 files requiring 194,127 bytes.
4) Graphic files. There were 21 files requiring 381,402 bytes.
5) Program files. There was one file requiring 253,952 bytes.
6) dBASE database and index files. There was 12 files requiring 1,936,118 bytes.
7) Straight ASCII files. There was one file requiring 3,319,659 bytes.

Unless otherwise indicated, I performed all backups to a single 1.44 Meg 3.5 inch floppy disk drive. To see if any of the programs had problems with inferior disks, I used only disks certified as double sided/double density. These are 720K disks.

I worried that doing all the benchmarks on a very fast machine would bias the results. To test this, I repeated some of the tests on a 4.77 MHz PC Clone. While not as extensive, they indicate that a program that is fast on a fast computer will also be fast on a PC. Just not as fast. If program A is faster than program B on a fast computer, the A will be faster than B on a PC.

I tested the restore program by restoring back to the hard disk. I then compared the restored files to an identical copy stored in another subdirectory. I used a program to compare each set of files byte-for-byte. That allowed me to spot a restore error as small as a single byte in 10 Meg. I repeated this backup then restore three times for each program. I checked each restore for errors by comparing them with the duplicate files. I timed each backup and used the average in the tables.

I have tried to clarify the major backup alternatives using a consistent methodology. There are two sets of tables at the end of the chapter to help you select the best backup method for you personally.

1) A review of each program. That emphasizes the strengths and weaknesses of that program. These are in alphabetical order by program name.

2) A set of charts comparing the features and performance of each method.

Back-It

Back-It is a flexible commercial backup program. While not the fastest backup program, its speed is acceptable. The user interface may seen overwhelming at first.

Installation   Back-It comes with a program that handles installation. You can run the installation program from either drive. In addition to installing Back-It, it lets you modify the colors of Back-It and test your DMA [Direct Memory Access] chips.

Backups   The main menu configures Back-It for both backups and restores. Figure 12-1 shows this. You select subdirectories to back up from a graphical tree. Figure 12-2 shows this. There is also a menu where you can enter ten file specifications to include and ten to exclude. The specifications cannot include subdirectories. Back-It constantly updates its screen as you develop the backup definition. You can save the configuration to disk for reuse. However, you can only save one configuration.

Restores   Restores work similarly to backups. There is a graphical tree where you select subdirectory to restore. However, the subdirectories shown

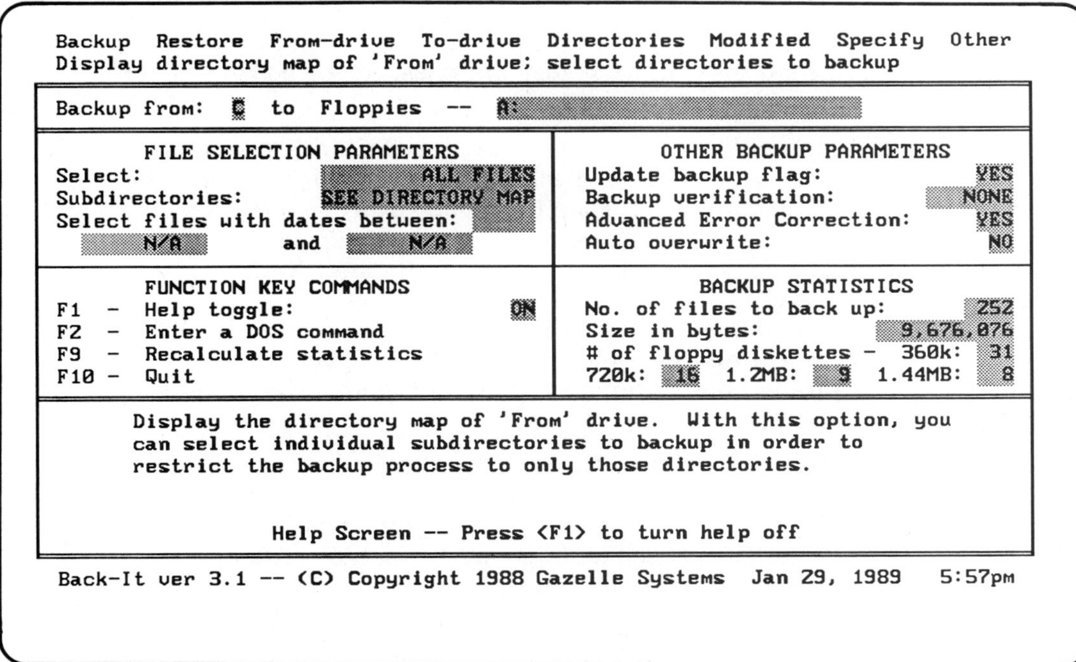

Fig. 12-1. The Back-It main menu is used to configure the program for both backups and restores.

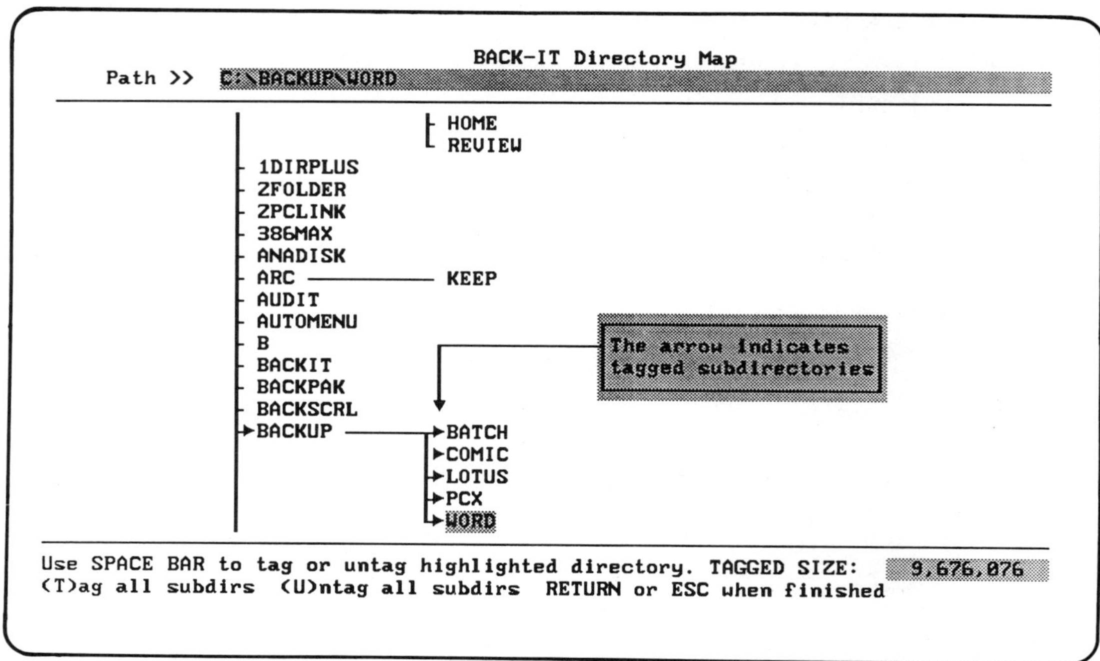

Fig. 12-2. Back-It uses a graphical tree to select subdirectories to include in the backup.

are from the entire hard disk and not just the ones processed during the backup.

Limitations   Back-It is only significantly faster than DOS with verification turned off. With DOS verification on, Back-It and DOS run at comparable speeds. Back-It is significantly slower than DOS when using its super verification mode. (Using Back-It super verification, every byte of information written to a target disk is read back and compared to the source data.) See Appendix F for more information on DOS verification.

You can only tag subdirectories to include in the backup when Back-It is showing its graphical tree display. Unfortunately, that display could not display all the subdirectories on my hard disk. Its limit is about 200 subdirectories.

Manual   The manual is clear and well written. Inexperienced users will have no problem understanding the manual or learning how to use Back-It. The manual does suffer from more than its share of self promotion. It often brags about its features and compares itself to unnamed competitors. After awhile, I found that to be very annoying.

Conclusion   Back-It is a very flexible backup program. However, it lacks file compression and forces you to choose between file verification and reasonable speed.

```
Product:    Back-It
Price:      $129.95
Category:   Commercial
Publisher:  Gazelle Systems
Address:    42 North University Avenue
            Suite 10
            Provo, Utah 84601
Phone:      (800) 233-0383
Memory:     256K
```

Backpak

Backpak is a backup program that produces backup files that are directly usable by DOS. Backpak is very slow, on some operations it is even slower than DOS.

Installation   There is no installation program. The manual explains how to copy its files to an existing directory but not how to create a subdirectory just for Backpak.

Backups   Backpak is essentially an enhanced copy command. During a backup, Backpak copies files to the floppy disks using exactly the same file format as the DOS COPY command. It places files in subdirectories on the diskette that correspond to their subdirectory name on the hard disk. Unless a file is too large to fit on a single disk, it is never split across two diskettes. As a result, you can restore files using the COPY command if you do not have access to Backpak. In addition, you can run files on a backup disk just like a regular file.

The first disk in the backup set has the volume label BACKREST001, the second is BACKREST002 and so on. When Backpak encounters a file too large to fit on a single disk, it drops this labeling scheme. Instead, it begins creating labels based on the file name and a sequence number. It writes the large file sequentially to as many diskettes as it needs. Back-It processes large files at the end of the backup.

Backpak is a command line program. For those not wanting to use this mode of operation, Backpak has a menu interface. Basically, you work through this menu to construct the command line prompt required to run Backpak.

The first time you use Backpak to perform a complex backup, you can use the graphical tree to tag subdirectories. Figure 12-3 shows this. This creates a non-ASCII file that you can include in later command-line entries to specify which subdirectories to back up. You cannot tag specific files within a subdirectory.

Restores   You can easily restore every file from a set of backup disks or a single file from the command line. You use the menu program to develop a more complex restore. Backpak reads the subdirectory information off the first backup disk. It uses that to construct a listing of backed up subdirectories.

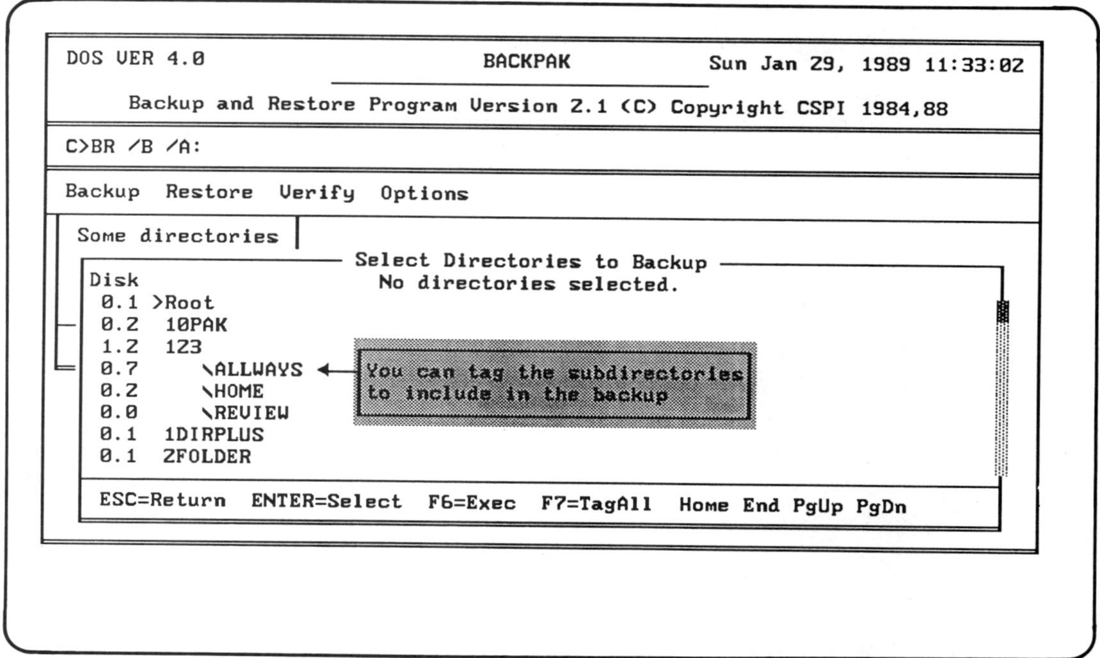

Fig. 12-3. Backpak uses a graphical tree to tag specific subdirectories to include in a backup.

Figure 12-4 shows this. From this information, you select specific subdirectories to back up. You can even enter a file specification for each subdirectory. However, it limits you to a single file specification for each subdirectory.

Limitations   Backpak tracks the backup disks using the volume label. Any disk you use during a backup must either have the volume label it expects or have no volume label at all. As a result, the user must either manually reformat each set of disks before making a new backup or painstakingly track volume labels.

Backpak makes tracking volume labels very difficult. It labels files too large to fit on a single diskette using a different sequence than the regular backups. All this results in it being very difficult to make sure you feed the proper disk to Backpak at the proper time.

When there are a lot of files on a disk, performing a new backup to the same disk can take an incredible amount of time. One disk took about three minutes when it was unformatted, including the time to format the disk. That same disk took well over six minutes to rerun the backup. Since you usually recycle older backup sets as you replace them with newer ones, this represents a significant speed penalty. In fact, it is far faster to format the disks using DOS and then perform the backup. The speed penalty was not so severe when there were fewer files on the disk.

Some system messages and most error messages were simply flashed to the screen then almost immediately replaced with something else. At one

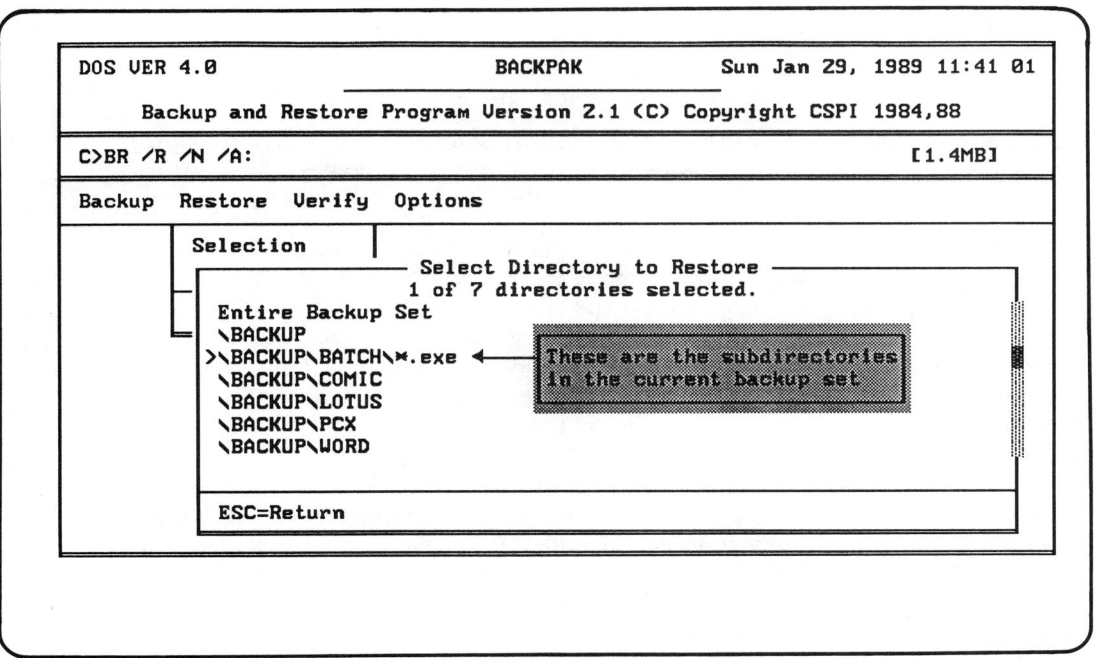

Fig. 12-4. Backpak can read the first backup disk and show the user a list of all the backed up subdirectories. This information can also be used to construct a custom restoration.

point it wrote all the files to go on eight disks to the screen without pausing. I was then asked if the proposed backup was ok! I expect that was caused by the speed of the 16 MHz IBM Model 70 I was using. However, you should be able to read error messages no matter how fast your computer is.

Manual   Because of the complex way Backpak operates, explaining how to use Backpak is fairly difficult. An experienced user will be able to read the manual and understand how to use the program but an inexperienced user will not.

Conclusion   The files Backpak produces on the backup floppies are just like the ones on the hard disk unless a single file is too large to fit on a floppy. That would be a very useful arrangement if Backpak was acceptably fast, but it is not. Backpak was even slower than DOS. In addition, the complex tracking required to meet its volume label requirements are extremely complex. All this serves to make Backpak a very difficult and cumbersome program to use.

Product:	Backpak
Price:	$99.00
Category:	Commercial
Publisher:	California Software Products
Address:	525 North Cabrillo Park Drive
	Santa Ana, California 92701
Phone:	(714) 973-0440
Memory:	384K

Diskpack

Diskpack is a fairly small and simple commercial backup program. While small, Diskpack does offer data compression and is much faster than DOS.

Installation   There is no installation program. Diskpack consists of four programs. The manual explains how to create a subdirectory, copy these four programs to that subdirectory and add that subdirectory to your PATH statement.

Backups   Think of the DOS BACKUP program as an overweight middle-aged man doing his best to jog around a track. Now think of Diskpack as a young agile sprinter running rapidly around the same track. That image is the best way to think of Diskpack. It works almost identically to DOS. Both are command line driven. Both eschew menus. They even have similar command-line switches, only Diskpack has more. The real difference between them is backup time (Diskpack is a screamer) and the number of disks required (Diskpack offers excellent file compression).

Diskpack has all the advantages and disadvantages of a command line interface. On the plus side, it is easy to incorporate Diskpack into batch files. In addition, you do not have to wade through a lot of menus to get started. On the negative side, you can only back up those directories you can specify in a single PATH statement. (Of course, you can make multiple backups, backing up one path each time. You can even automate this with a batch file.) In addition, you either have to remember complex command-line syntax or write a batch file to remember it for you.

You can specify the following options when starting Diskpack:

?	Display help.
1	Do not prompt for the first diskette.
A	Do not reset the archive bit.
B	Beep when prompting for another diskette.
C	Create catalog of backed up files on hard disk. It will not add the catalog to the floppy diskettes.
D	Back up only those files created after the date specified following the /D switch.
H	Include hidden files in the backup. Normally, Diskpack excludes these from a backup.
I	Display registration information if you have an unregistered copy of the shareware program.
M	Back up only files modified since the last backup.
P	Prompt before backing up each file.
S	Include subdirectories in backup.
V	Display additional information during the backup. This information is the sectors of the floppy diskette being written to and additional technical information.
W	Prompt the user before reading source files.

Restores   Like the backup program, the restore program is a command line program. You cannot select files to back up from a listing, you must list the files on the command line. Since each restore allows only one file specification with wildcards, restoring several files can take time. You either restore everything with ***.*** or you spend a lot of time specifying individual files to restore.

The switches available in the restore program are:

?	Display help.
1	Do not prompt for the first disk.
B	Beep when prompting for a disk.
D	Display file names without restoring. Because of the data format used by Diskpack, it must decompress the data to show the names. As a result, this takes a long time. You should create a catalog to avoid this.
I	Display registration information.
P1	Prompt before restoring a hidden or archive file.
P2	Prompt before restoring each file.
R	Restore files. Without this, Diskpack will just compare the files on the backup disks to the ones on the hard disk.
S	Include subdirectories.
V	Display additional technical information about the restore.

Limitations   Requires formatted diskettes. Diskpack requires completely error-free diskettes. It first checks the file allocation table and will reject any diskettes with any sectors marked as bad. The purpose of DOS marking bad sectors is so you can use good diskettes that happen to have a bad spot. By rejecting these diskettes, Diskpack makes it harder to find backup diskettes.

Compared to the backup program, the restore program is slow. It took Diskpack over nine minutes to restore one file from the test backup back onto the hard disk. At several points it took so long I thought the computer had locked up.

Manual   The manual is brief but adequate. Diskpack has a fairly simple command line interface and it does not take the manual long to explain it.

Conclusion   Diskpack is fast making backups. Only Fastback Plus and PC Backup Plus were faster. It is very slow restoring files. If you are looking for a fast backup program and you only infrequently restore files, Diskpack is an excellent choice.

Product:	Diskpack
Price:	$89.00
Category:	Commercial
Publisher:	Biologic
Address:	11982 Coverstone Circle
	Suite 1622
	Manassas, Virginia 22110
Phone:	(703) 368-2949
Memory:	320K

DS Backup+

DS Backup+ is a commercial backup program. It offers a DOS compatible mode and a faster custom format mode. Both modes offer file compression. It is extremely easy to use. You will not need the manual. It offers the ability to stop a backup now and pick up at exactly the same point later. That is a great feature if someone is always interrupting you with urgent tasks.

Installation   DS Backup+ comes with an installation program that automatically handles installing the software. It only runs from the A-drive but an ASSIGN A = B statement corrects that. The program allows you to install DS Backup+ on any drive in any subdirectory.

Backups   DS Backup+ has two backup modes. The first mode is a DOS mode. It creates DOS compatible files using a DOS formatted diskette. This method is slower and requires formatted diskettes. The second mode uses a proprietary format and will format diskettes as required. This mode is faster. DS Backup+ has an optional file compression mode you can use in conjunction with the DOS and high-speed backup modes.

Figure 12-5 shows the main menu for DS Backup+ in DOS mode. The non-DOS mode looks and operates identically. You use a menu on the right to select the options for the backup. The panel on the left reflects most of the changes. The "Media Needed" calculation does not reflect any data compression you have selected. The panel at the bottom lists the files currently in the backup. If there are a lot of files or multiple subdirectories, you will have to scroll to see all the files. It does not show multiple subdirectories on the same screen.

The DOS mode program requires formatted disks, it cannot format them automatically. However, the prompt you get between each disk gives you the

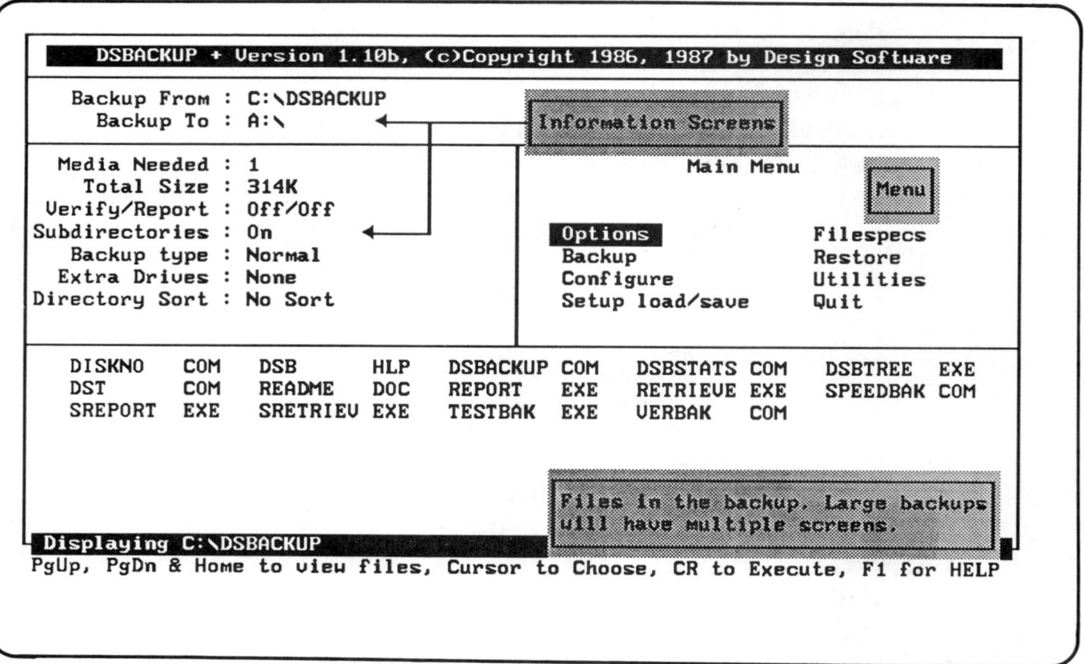

Fig. 12-5. The DS Backup + main menu shows how many disks are needed, the size of the backup, the status of DS Backup + and the files to be backed up.

option of formatting the next disk. It stores files on the disk in a format where DOS can read the disk. Only DS Backup+ can restore the files.

Other   DS Backup+ comes with several useful programs. They are:

- TESTBAK.COM. This program checks how many files on your hard disk need backing up. This is a great way to decide if you need to perform a backup. It runs from the DOS prompt so you can add it to your AUTOEXEC.BAT file.
- VERBAK.COM. This program is a more detailed verification of a backup that the program can perform. It is useful for critical information.
- REPORT.EXE. This program produces a report for your backup. Report only works with DOS format backups.
- RETRIEVE.EXE. This program recovers damaged or missing DS Backup+ files.
- DISKNO.COM. This program shows the volume number for a non-DOS format disk.
- DS Timer. This is a memory resident program that can stay in the background and perform DOS commands which you specify. You can, of course, use this to make unattended backups as long as they will require no more than a single diskette.

Restores   The restore works just like the backup program. You select files the same way. In fact the backup and restore programs run from the same menus.

Limitations   The non-DOS mode cannot calculate percentage complete when compressing backups. It displays a percentage of filled disks divided by the number of disks that it would require without compression. The DOS mode program cannot automatically format disks as required. It does not sense when you change disks, forcing the operator to respond to many prompts.

The non-DOS mode would not automatically use my 3.5 inch drive at 1.2 Meg. Rather, it tried to use it as a 720K disk. I had to use a command line switch to force it into the proper mode.

Manual   The manual for DS Backup+ is very good. It contains examples on using DS Backup+. It also explains terms and procedures clearly.

Conclusion   DS Backup+ is fairly flexible and easy to use. It is not, however, very fast. In addition, its data compression is ineffective. DS Backup+ is a good choice for small to moderate backups.

Product:	DS Backup+
Price:	$79.95
Category:	Commercial
Publisher:	Design Software, Incorporated
Address:	1275 West Roosevelt Road
	West Chicago, Illinois 60185
Phone:	(800) 231-3088
	(312) 231-4540
Memory:	256K

Fastback Plus

Fastback Plus is an extremely fast backup program with excellent data compression. No other backup program even comes close to its speed or data compression. The backup program is also extremely flexible. You can back up one file or just about any combination of files. Its restore function is far less flexible than earlier versions of the program.

Installation   Fastback Plus comes with an installation program to automatically install the program. Earlier Fastback Plus installation programs were very inflexible. You had to go through this long process that tested your disk drive(s) and Direct Memory Access chip(s). The entire process takes twenty minutes and requires a blank floppy disk for each drive it tests. While that option is still available, it is no longer necessary.

In addition to testing the hardware, the new menu-driven installation program lets you easily change which drives you are using for backups. With the old version of Fastback Plus, changing from the 1.2 Meg A-drive to the 360K B-drive on an IBM PC/AT required working through the entire installation program. With Fastback Plus it is a snap.

Backups   You use the main menu to configure how you want the backup to work. Figure 12-6 shows this. First, you select the hard disk to back up. The next step is to select files to include. To do a full backup, you would select the

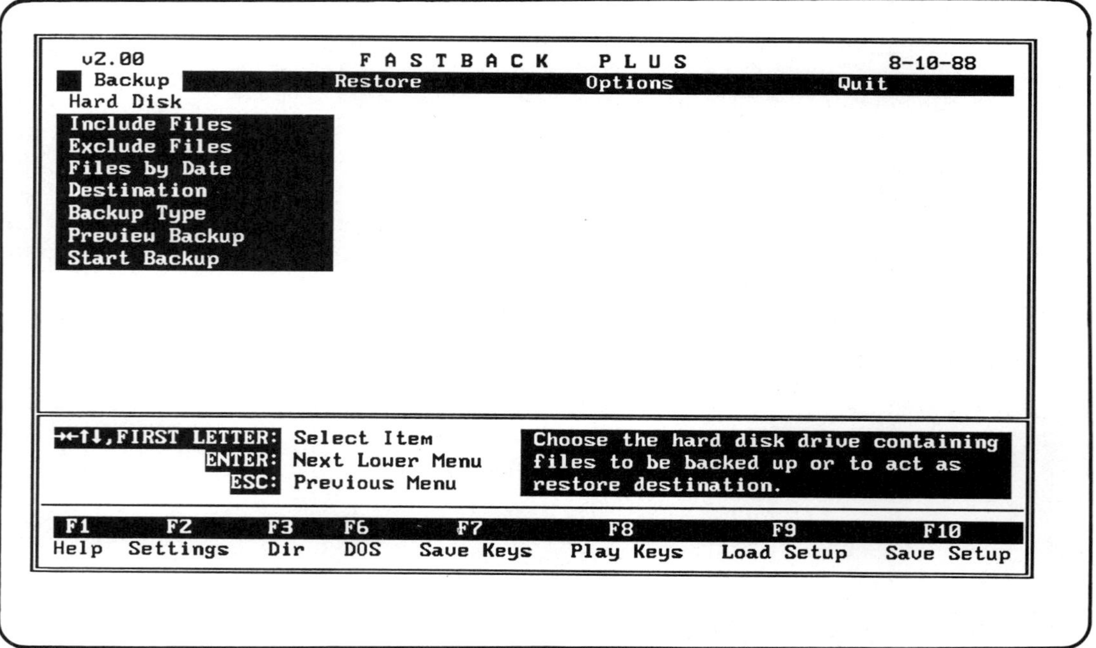

Fig. 12-6. The main Fastback Plus is used to select either backing up, restoring or configuring the program.

root directory with the include subdirectories option. To be more selective, you can list up to twenty individual subdirectories to include in the backup.

While you could enter each subdirectory manually, Fastback Plus has a better way. When you press F3, you get a screen like the one in Fig. 12-7. You move the cursor around between the files and subdirectories and press insert for each entry you want to include. Fastback Plus automatically pastes that information into the listing of files to include.

After selecting include files, you can exclude some of those files from the backup using the "Exclude Files" option. With this option, you select files just like the "Include Files" option. This is useful for excluding backup (*.BAK) and scratch files from the backup. You can also select files by date. Fastback Plus allows you to select the earliest and latest date to backup.

Fastback Plus lets you perform a full backup with or without resetting the archive bits. You can also perform an incremental backup with or without resetting the archive bit. You can add the incremental backups to the end of an existing disk or started on a new disk.

Once you get to the backup screen, shown in the screen shot below, you have only two options, estimate and start the backup. The estimating procedure tells you:

- How many of the files are on the disk it will back up.
- The total size of the files it will back up.
- The number of disks it will require.

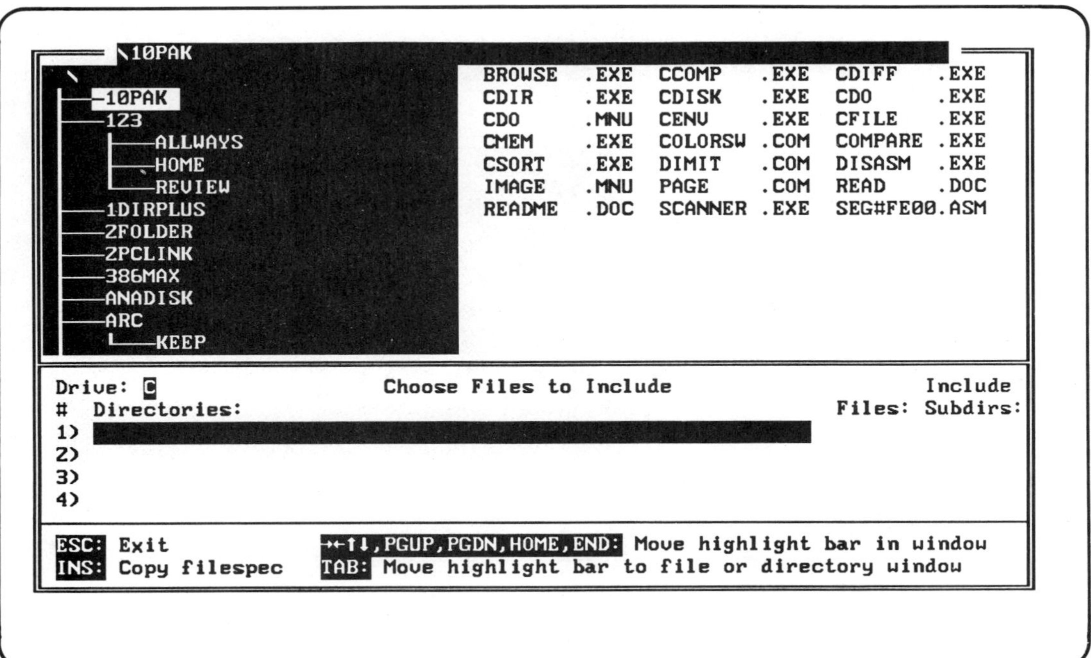

Fig. 12-7. With Fastback Plus you can select files and subdirectories to include and exclude from a graphical tree.

- The time required for the backup.
- The expected transfer speed.

As Fastback Plus is running, it constantly updates these figures. Figure 12-8 shows this.

Fastback Plus stores its files in DOS format. It stores all of the data in a single file. It requires Fastback Plus to restore the data to the hard disk. If a disk is unformatted, Fastback Plus will format it automatically.

Restores   The restore program works very much like the backup program. You select a history file matching the set of backup disks you plan to use. The "Include Files" option reads that history file and lets you select the files on the backup to restore to the hard disk. There are "Exclude Files" and "Files by Date" options as in the backup program. You can control when files are over-written and even confirm each overwrite.

Limitations   As a test, I selected a premium disk and formatted it using DOS. I used a batch file to continually test the disk for four hours using the Norton Utilities. After doing that, I backed up a single subdirectory to that disk using Fastback Plus. After all that, the restore program found problems with the disk.

When Fastback Plus estimates the time and number of disks required to perform a backup, it does not take into account file compression. It will not consider file compression even if you have selected it. On all the machines I

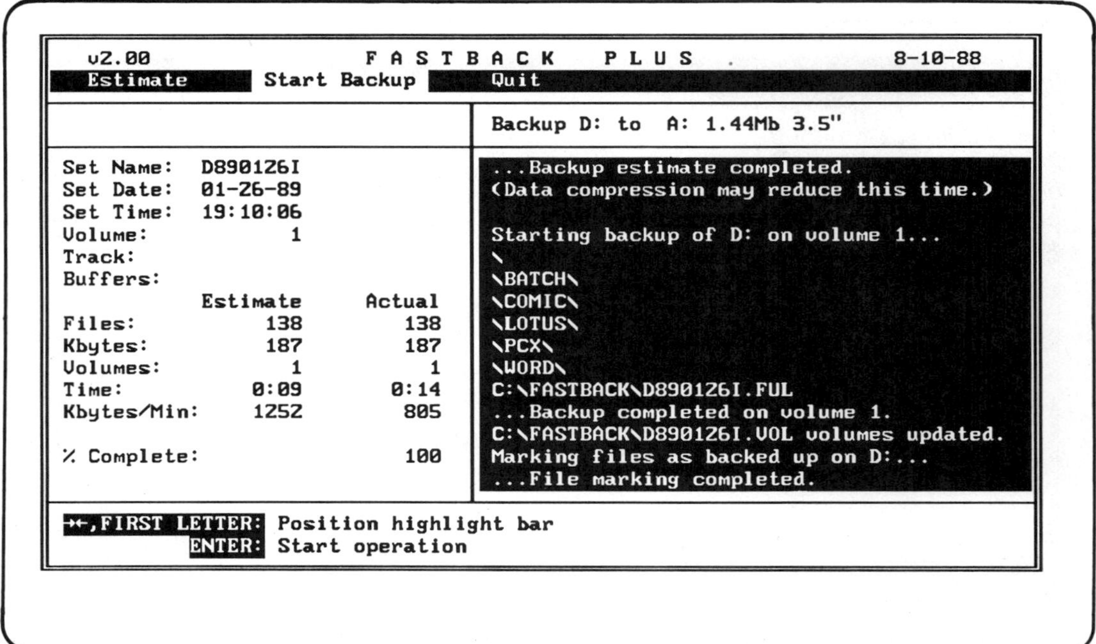

Fig. 12-8. As Fastback Plus performs the backup, it displays summary information and compares that information to its estimate.

tested, disk compression substantially reduced both, leaving the estimates way off mark.

Using the graphical tree representation of the hard disk to select files and subdirectories to include or exclude from the backup is a very easy way to make this selection. However, Fastback Plus has limited memory for displaying this information and could only display about two hundred subdirectories on my hard disk. When you request a graphical tree while selecting files to exclude, Fastback Plus does not list all the files you have selected to back up. Rather, it lists every single file on the hard disk, even those not selected using the include function. This makes it far more difficult than necessary to develop complex backup.

Fastback Plus has a "Preview Backup" option that tries to make designing complex backups easier. It does not simply show a graphical tree representing the backup. Rather, it shows the entire hard disk and individually marks the files and subdirectories that it will back up. You have to manually hunt through the entire hard disk to find them.

Manual   The manual is excellent. It explains everything in clear, easy to understand language. Warnings and important information is in highlighted boxes. There is a reference section and a separate section explaining how to use Fastback Plus.

Conclusion   Fastback Plus has a very fast and highly flexible backup program. I have nothing but praise for the backup side of Fastback Plus. However, I had continual problems with the restore program in Fastback Plus. A backup program that cannot reliably restore data is as bad as no backup program at all. I cannot, in good faith, recommend Fastback Plus.

Product:	Fastback Plus
Price:	$179
Category:	Commercial
Publisher:	Fifth Generation Systems
Address:	11200 Industriplex Boulevard B-350 Baton Rouge, Louisiana 70809
Phone:	(800) 225-2775
Memory:	448K

Fastback: An Historical Perspective

I began using Fastback a long time ago. Back then, Fastback was about the best backup program around. In fact, it got me out of several bad jams. My first computer had a "flaky" hard disk. It would work properly for about six months and then quit working. The only way to get it going again was a low-level format, which erases all the data. After the low-level format, the disk would work fine for about another six months. These failures occurred suddenly, without warning, so I learned to make frequent backups. I always made these with Fastback, and I was always able to restore every file properly.

Unfortunately, Fastback has been "upgraded" to the point the program is no longer dependable. My experiences with Fastback Plus have all been terrible.

In early 1988, I was upgrading from an 8088 clone to an IBM Model 80. The Model 80 came with an external 5.25-inch 360K drive from IBM. I wanted to do two things. First, transfer all the files from the clones to the Model 80. Second, install any software that needed installation to work with the VGA display.

I expected the first step to be easy. I began by setting up the Model 80. After formatting the hard disk and installing the DOS files, I also installed Fastback 5.13. Next, I made two Fastback backups of the 8088. Then, I used Fastback to restore the files on to the Model 80. Or at least I tried . . .

Every time I would start to restore on the Model 80, it would crash after about two disks. When it crashed, it gave an "Internal Stack Failure" error message. This locked the machine up so completely I had to turn it off to restart it. I would increase the STACKS= command in the CONFIG.SYS file, reboot, and try again. This continued until I had the STACKS= command at its highest possible values. (There are two values, one for number of stacks and one for the size of each stack. Both were at their maximum value.) Even at this, Fastback failed after only four or five disks. I finally finished with all the files intact. It would have been quicker, however, to use DOS backup and restore.

In all fairness to Fastback, I was not using the latest version of Fastback. There had been one minor and one major upgrade since the version I was using. In spite of this, it is reasonable to expect your software to continue to work when you change machines.

I finally got through to Fifth Generation technical support. That was an experience in itself. It was over a twenty minute wait on a toll line. I expect toll calls and I will even accept long waits for cheap software. However, Fastback is not cheap. In fact, it is about the most expensive backup program on the market. For the price they get, they could have 800-lines or call the customer back when there will be a long wait.

Their answer to the above problem was that Fastback is not PS/2 compatible and I would have to upgrade to Fastback Plus. I am not sure I buy that answer. What I suspect is that Fastback is not DOS 3.3 compatible, however, I have no way to verify this. If they are right, then Fastback is the only program I know of that is not PS/2 compatible.

Fifth Generation kindly sent me a copy of the new Fastback Plus. When I received Fastback Plus, I found that could not handle the original Fastback disks. All it did was run the original Fastback restore program. That was the program that would not work.

When I began writing this book, it was clear I would need more RAM and disk space than was available on the IBM Model 80 I had. I called IBM and asked for another computer. They kindly sent me a 16 MHz Model 70. They also sent DOS 4.01. The Model 70 was easy to set up and I had it up and running with the hard disk formatted in under half an hour.

IBM did a really excellent job of making this computer easy to set up. There are no cards to plug in. There are no switches to set. All you do is:

1) Plug the computer into the wall outlet.
2) Plug the monitor into the wall outlet and into a jack on the computer.
3) Plug the keyboard into the computer. It is no more difficult than connecting the turntable and speakers to a stereo.
4) Boot off a floppy and format the hard disk, much like running a test record to set your equalizer.

The only way it could be easier is to ship the computer with the hard disk already formatted.

After setting the computer up, I needed to transfer all my data and programs. My first attempt was making a complete backup of the old Model 80 using Fastback Plus. I also copied all the Fastback program files onto a floppy so I could run them from the other machine. After copying Fastback onto the Model 70, I tried to restore my programs. Fastback choked on the final tracks of the first disk. It also choked on the second, third and fourth disks. I aborted the restore figuring something was wrong with the disks. First I formatted them with DOS. DOS found no problems with the disks. Rather than take that as the final opinion, I also ran Norton's disk testing program several times. It also failed to find any problems. Clearly Fastback was choking on something other than the disks.

At this point, I swore off Fastback, in addition to swearing in general. My real concern here was not so much all the work but the fact I had been using Fastback as my only backup medium. I wondered what I would do if instead of needing to transfer intact files between two computers I was depending on Fastback to recover damaged or lost files! After all, a backup program that cannot restore from its own backups is worthless. I ended up using another backup program and transferring the files without any problems.

I have been a Fastback fan and supporter (both word of mouth and in print) but this was the last straw. The last two times I had needed Fastback, it had refused to work. Even if these were random problems or simply PS/2 incompatibilities, how could I depend on a backup program that had failed me twice?

File/Saver

File/Saver is a shareware program for managing the DOS BACKUP program.

Installation   File/Saver has an installation program that creates a directory and automatically copies the files. It will run from any drive and can install the program on any drive in any subdirectory.

Backups   File/Saver consists of four programs that combine to control the DOS BACKUP program, maintenance, backup, history and a setup program to set colors.

The maintenance program configures File/Saver to work with your system. Figure 12-9 shows a typical screen. The subdirectory \BACKUP is on the C-drive. File/Saver backs it up every day. File/Saver last backed it up on 01/29/89. Another program will compare this date to the current date to flag this subdirectory if it needs backing up. You can create as many entries as you like.

The backup program compares the date of the last backup for each subdirectory with the current date and the specified backup interval. It then flags those it needs to back up. Figure 12-10 shows this. You flag those that you want to back up using the F2 key and then press Return to back them up. File/Saver feeds that information to the DOS BACKUP program to back up one subdirectory at a time. You could add this program to your AUTOEXEC.BAT file to check for required backups every time you boot the computer.

File/Saver tracks each backup and stores some information about that backup in a database. It uses that database to generate this report.

Restores   File/Saver only manages the DOS BACKUP program. It will not manage the RESTORE. Incredibly, the manual does not even mention how to restore backups created with File/Saver.

Limitations   When configuring subdirectories for File/Saver to back up, you must rely on your memory or on detailed notes. File/Saver has no way to list the subdirectories on the hard disk. You must also configure your hard disk

```
                          DATA MENU                          1/29/89
    _________________________________________________________________

        Source drive:                        C:

        Level 1 name(path):                  BACKUP

        Level 2 name(path):

        Level 3 name(path):

        Backup cycle:                        Day(s)

        Number of  Day(s)  between cycles:   1

        Date of last backup:                 01/29/89


                          Mode: MODIFY
 Accept with ↵
 Esc to File List
 F2  Months/Days                               ←↑↓→ + Edit Keys
```

Fig. 12-9. The File/Saver configuration program is used to tell the program which subdirectories to back up and how often.

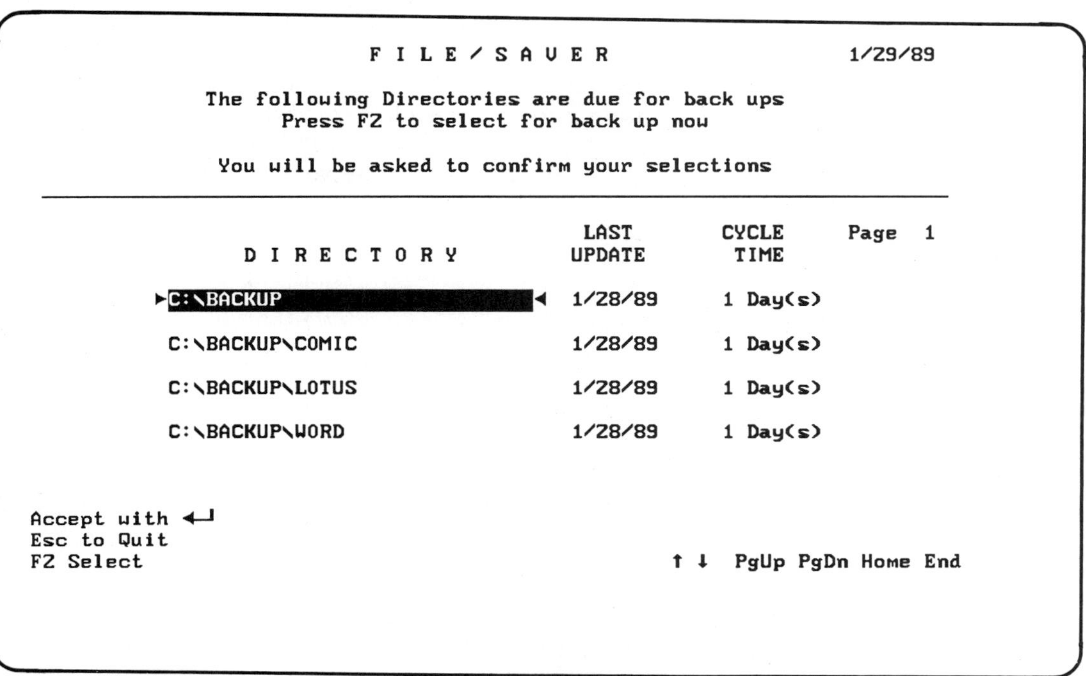

Fig. 12-10. The File/Saver backup program pops up to tell you which subdirectories are due to be backed up.

with three or fewer subdirectories as that is all File/Saver can handle. In addition, File/Saver cannot handle subdirectory names longer than eight characters. Including the period and three character extension, DOS allows names as long as twelve characters.

You can remove outdated information but it is difficult. The program prints the field displaying the date to delete all records before the date you input in one location on the screen. You enter the new date in the same area but due to a programming error the data entry location is actually offset one position. Thus, as you enter the new date, it skips automatically over what should be "/" 's but are actually numbers because of the single character offset. The result is that it is impossible to read the date once you enter a new one.

Manual   The manual adequately explains how to use File/Saver. However, I find it impossible to give a passing grade to a manual that tells you how to create a backup but never once tells you how to use it.

Conclusion   File/Saver has a somewhat difficult and outdated user interface and it is difficult to configure since it does not display subdirectories. However, once configured the backup control program is easy to use. In addition, it is handy to have a program pop up and tell you a subdirectory needs backing up. If you use DOS BACKUP to make backups and took the time to configure File Saver to back up data subdirectories frequently and on a staggered basis and program subdirectories less frequently but also staggered, it would be a useful program.

The optional diskette set includes a copy of File/Saver. I received a major upgrade to File/Saver too late to include it in this analysis. However, the diskette set contains the new version. The author tells me that this upgrade will handle restores, and that it is significantly faster than the version reviewed here.

Product:	File/Saver
Price:	$30
Category:	Shareware
Publisher:	Marcor Enterprises
Address:	8857 Commerce Park Place
	Suite D
	Indianapolis, Indiana 46286
Phone:	(317) 876-9376
Notes:	A copy of File/Saver is included on
	the optional diskette set
Memory:	128K

IBM DOS 4.01

Although the Backup and Restore functions of DOS have improved over the years, other programs have improved more. As a result, the DOS programs are adequate for only small hard disks with relatively simple needs.

Installation   DOS now comes with an installation program to install DOS files on a hard disk. It runs automatically and without problems. (Users of some non-IBM versions of DOS have reported problems upgrading to IBM DOS 4.x. This problem is likely to disappear as DOS 4.x becomes available from sources other than IBM.) It installs all the DOS programs, including Backup and Restore, in a single subdirectory, the normal arrangement.

Backups   DOS has a well earned reputation for being SLOW! It is far slower than the other programs in this chapter. In addition to being inflexible, Backup uses a complex command line syntax that many users find difficult. With only a command line interface, you cannot specify complex lists of subdirectories to back up or skip. Backup has room for only one path on the command line. Your only choice is if you want to back up all subdirectories off this single path.

Over the years, Microsoft has made small improvements to the Backup program. Earlier Backup versions wrote each file to disk individually. You could perform a directory on a backup disk and see what files you had backed up to that disk. To gain speed, Backup currently backs up files to one target file. Backup disks will only have two files. One contains data and another contains control information. Since you cannot perform a directory to see the contents of a disk, Microsoft has added a /L switch. This switch creates a log showing the name of the files and their backup disk.

Backup (and Restore) now work with floppy disks as well as hard disks. You can now restore files you backed up from a hard disk to a floppy disk, a major advantage for DOS. You can also back up from one floppy drive to another. This is useful if you need to share information on a large capacity 3.5 inch disk with someone else using low capacity 5.25 inch disks.

Restores   Restore uses the same command line interface used by Backup to extract files. Like Backup, it limits you to specifying a single path and a single file specification. If you did not produce a log file, you cannot tell what files you backed up or what disk they are on.

Limitations   During one of the backup timing tests, I accidentally pressed Return when it was pausing for a disk change without actually changing the disk. Backup went ahead and wrote over that disk with more files, effectively making the entire backup session useless.

When you insert a non-formatted disk, Backup will automatically format it for you. It does this by running the DOS formatting program. The program intercepts the DOS message to insert the disk and press any key. As a result, it skips this step. It also skips the step where it displays the summary information on the disk and requests a volume label. (DOS 4.x automatically prompts you for a volume label.) However, you still must answer no and press Return to the "Format another" prompt. This effectively doubles the keystrokes required to perform a backup. (Backup requires you to press any key after switching disks, it does not monitor the status of the disk drive and get this information automatically.)

The new version of Backup does not beep after each disk is full. It also does not beep when prompting you if you want to format another disk as described above. As a result, you have to keep your eyes glued to the screen during a backup.

Manual   Backup does not have a manual. Rather, it has three pages in your DOS manual. The Restore program gets two more. Because of the limited flexibility of Backup and Restore, three pages is adequate to explain how to use the program.

Conclusion   Backup and Restore are free with the purchase of DOS, their major advantage. Their slow operation and inflexibility make them inadequate for large hard disks or for users with complex backup requirements.

Intelligent Backup

Intelligent Backup is a very flexible commercial backup program. It easily performs complex backups on large hard disks. It can easily consolidate multiple incremental backups. It is, however, fairly slow and limited to 200 sub-directories.

Installation   Intelligent Backup comes with an installation program that automatically installs Intelligent Backup. The installation program asks for permission to modify your CONFIG.SYS file but never indicates what modifications are being made. (It increases the number of buffers in the BUFFERS = statement of the CONFIG.SYS file if it is too low. This change does not take effect until you reboot the computer.)

Intelligent Backup has a "nag" mode. With the proper code installed in the AUTOEXEC.BAT file, it will compare today's date with the date of your last backup. Depending on program settings, it will either perform a backup when the dates do not match or it will ask first. The installation program will install this for you, or the manual shows how to add it yourself. This is a nice feature when the computer is being set up by a knowledgeable person for someone else.

Backups   Intelligent Backup lives up to its name. In fact, if it were faster, Intelligent Backup would clearly be the best software backup option. Normally, you perform periodic full backups followed by many incremental backups. Eventually, you have to perform another full backup because the incremental backups have grown so numerous as to be unmanageable.

Intelligent Backup has an incremental backup feature that manages them so well you may never need to do a full backup after doing the first. For files you have erased from your hard disk, it removes them from the backups and recycles the space. This combined with a wealth of features to control file selection for backup make this a strong contender.

When you begin a backup, Intelligent Backup displays a list of subdirectories for you to use to select the ones to back up. After selecting to start the backup, Intelligent Backup displays a summary showing the three types of backups it can make. You select the type of backup to make and Intelligent Backup begins the process.

Restores   Intelligent Backup makes it easy to restore either the current version of a file or a prior version. It can show a complete list of backed up files. If you need more information on a file, Intelligent Backup can provide it. To select a file to restore, you simply move the cursor through this list and tag the files you want. If you like, you can narrow the list of files by specifying a beginning and ending date and time. It does not restore files outside this time frame.

Other   Intelligent Backup includes a full screen ASCII editor. You select it from the menu just like the other options. It is perfect for editing batch and other system files.

Intelligent Backup also includes a very simple DOS shell. It is really no competition for the stand-alone DOS shells in Chapter 3. It starts up with a list of subdirectories. While in subdirectory mode, you can . . .

- Switch to file mode. This displays all the files for only the currently highlighted subdirectory.
- Choose files in the currently highlighted subdirectory based on file attribute.
- Print a subdirectory list. When I selected print without a printer attached, I had to reboot to recover.
- Make a new subdirectory.
- Rename a subdirectory.
- Delete a subdirectory.
- Sort the subdirectories.

In file mode, you can . . .

- Edit an ASCII file using the built-in editor.
- Print a file. This too locks up the computer without a printer.
- Rename a file.
- Move a file or tagged files.
- Delete a file or tagged files.
- Change the file attributes.
- Copy a file or tagged files.
- Locate a file matching a file name.
- Sort the file listing.

While it has a number of features, the Intelligent Backup file management program lacks a graphical tree and other features that make the stand-alone shells easy to use.

Limitations　Intelligent Backup displays a list of subdirectories for you to use to select the ones to back up. It was only able to handle about 200 subdirectories. If the hard disk exceeds this amount, Intelligent Backup gives you an error message and tells you to press any key to try again. When you do, the machine locks up.

Intelligent Backup locked up my computer yet another time. During one backup, I gave it a defective floppy disk that would not format. After responding "Abort" to the "Ignore, Abort or Retry" error message, Intelligent Backup locked up.

Intelligent Backup depends on the DOS FORMAT.COM program to format its disks. Anytime you supply it with an unformatted disk is asks you if you want to format it. You then have to answer the DOS prompt on placing a disk in the A-drive and pressing any key. When DOS finishes, you have to enter a volume label (DOS 4.01 always prompts you for one). You then have to answer the "format another" DOS prompt. When you return to Intelligent Backup, it requires you to press any key to begin. That is a lot of prompts to go through.

Many times, Intelligent Backup was not able to spot an unformatted disk. Rather, it restored to the DOS "Ignore, Abort, Fail or Retry" error message. When that happened, it proved to be impossible to format a disk using Intelligent Backup. As a result, I did not perform the timing test using unformatted disks.

Manual　The manual is very good. In addition, the program supplements it with over three hundred context sensitive help screens in the program. Between the two, you always know what to do.

Conclusion　Intelligent Backup makes it very easy to manage large complex backups. Perhaps even more important, its restore program is extremely easy to use. If it were faster and offered file compression and automatic disk formatting, Intelligent Backup would be perfect. As it is though, it is still a very nice program.

```
Product:      Intelligent Backup
Price:        $149.95
Category:     Commercial
Publisher:    I Track Corporation
Address:      710 East Park Boulevard
              Suite 204
              Plano, Texas 75074
Phone:        (214) 578-8104
Memory:       256K
```

KeepTrack Plus

KeepTrack Plus has a very strong backup program. However, its recovery program is not nearly as powerful.

Installation KeepTrack Plus does not come with an installation program and the manual improperly tells how to install KeepTrack Plus. The manual illustrates how to install it in the root directory. In fact, you should install it in a subdirectory.

Backups KeepTrack Plus allows you to maintain a file in the root directory with both a list of files not to back up and a list of files to back up even if unchanged. While not as flexible as on the fly marking, this method is easier to use over the long term.

You select subdirectories and files to back up using a graphical tree. Figure 12-11 shows this. You can move around the display tagging files to back up. The back up menu then gives you the option of backing up all tagged files or only those that have changed since the last backup. You can also elect to ignore the tagged files and either backup all files or all files that have changed since the last backup.

Restores While the backup program is very flexible, the restore program is not. You can only restore files matching wildcards, no includes or excludes list. It prompts for each file to restore so you can specify to restore all files and answer yes to only those files you want. You can use a Control-Y to automatically select the remaining files if you do not need the prompting.

If a file is not split across disks, it stores in the file in an unmodified DOS format. Therefore, so you can also use the DOS COPY command to restore files.

Limitations It does not label shifted function key assignments on the screen. Some of these have important functions, like restoring, so this is an important omission. The main menu contains no command to restore and the manual gives the wrong steps. The manual says use Shift-F2 followed by a restore command. The actual command is Shift-F10 followed by a restore command.

Manual The manual does a good job of explaining how to use KeepTrack Plus. However, small but important small errors plagued the manual. For example, giving the wrong command to restore data. KeepTrack Plus includes a second manual that explains how to configure your hard disk. It does a good

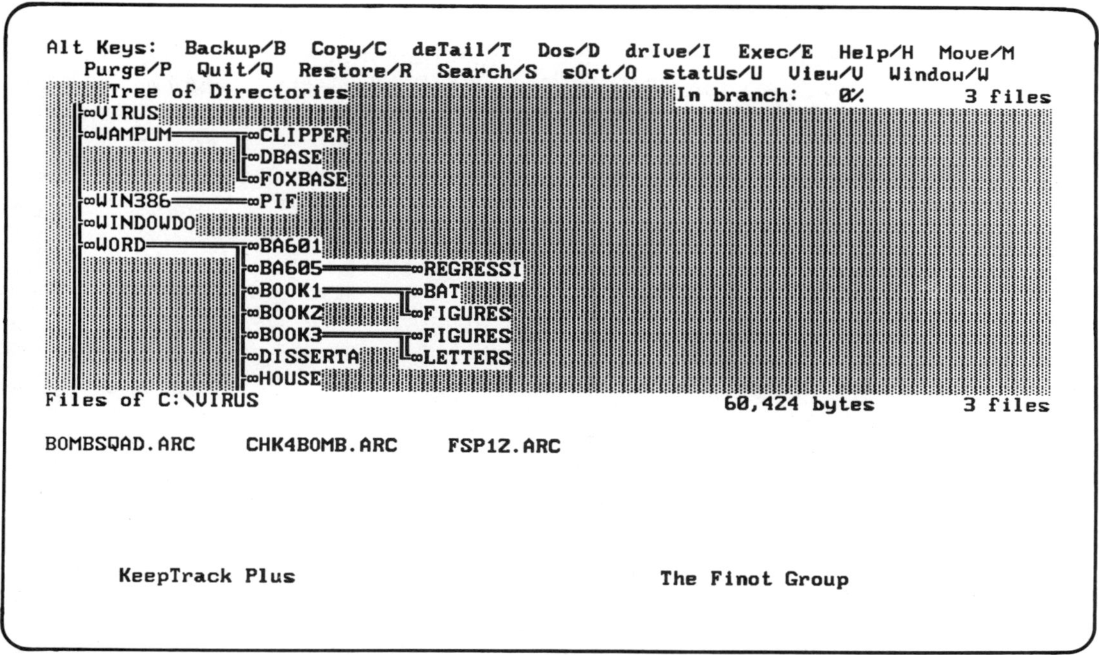

Fig. 12-11. KeepTrack Plus lets you select files to back up using a graphical tree.

job but it is printed in very small type and many readers will find it hard to read.

Conclusion   KeepTrack Plus is a flexible backup program with a limited restore program.

Product:	KeepTrack Plus
Price:	$99.00
Category:	Commercial
Publisher:	Finot Group
Address:	2680 Bayshore Parkway
	Suite 101
	Mountain View, California 94043
Phone:	(415) 966-1900
Memory:	384K

PC Backup

PC Backup is a small portion of the PC Tools Deluxe package. Chapter 5 discusses the remainder of the package. PC Backup is a good commercial backup program. However, the restore program is flawed and will not always restore files.

Backups   PC Backup uses a common menu for backups and restores. Figure 12-12 shows this menu. PC Backup uses a common menu for backups and restores. This menu displays the structure of the hard disk using a graphical tree. It also lists all the files in the currently highlighted directory.

PC Backup gives you two ways to select files to back up, manual and include/exclude. Using the manual method, you tab to the graphical tree display to activate it. The default for PC Backup is all files selected. You can move around the graphical tree and/or file lists tagging files to deselect. Deselecting a subdirectory deselects all the files in the subdirectory along with all the subdirectories and files branching off that subdirectory. If you prefer to manually select files to include, you can deselect the root directory which deselects everything. You then move around tagging files to include.

If you prefer to define your backup using include and exclude lists, you select that from the backup menu. That brings up a dialog box where you enter the files to include and exclude. This box has room for up to sixteen entries. PC Backup processes it from top to bottom. You enter includes and excludes in the same box with excludes preceded by a negative sign. Using either method, PC Backup updates the information at the bottom of the screen as you change the configuration.

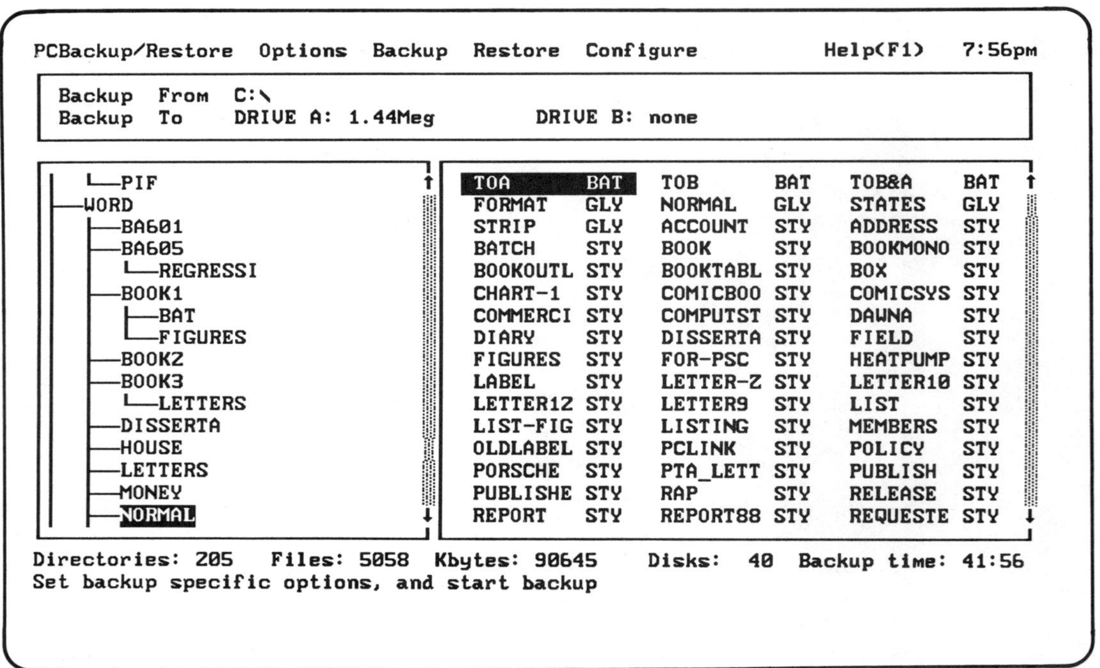

Fig. 12-12. PC Backup uses a common menu for backups and restores. This menu displays the structure of the hard disk using a graphical tree. It also lists all the files in the currently highlighted directory.

The Options menu lets you:

- Save the current configuration to a file and later reload it.
- Turn data compression on and off. There are two modes of data compression. One saves disk, e.g., maximum compression. The other compresses data only when it will not slow down the backup. This is the Quick Compress mode. On relatively fast computers, the computer is much faster than the disk drives. The program has ample time to compress data without slowing down the computer. Therefore, I did not time the Quick Compress mode.
- Turn verification on and off. The default setting is off.
- Turn the overwrite warning on and off.
- Turn on and off the elapse time display.
- Exit the program.

The Configure menu lets you:

- Set the drive type. It allows all four floppy disk sizes (360K, 720K, 1.2 Meg and 1.44 Meg) as well as backups to hard disks and removable hard disks.
- Program colors.
- Save the selected values as the system defaults.

The backup menu lets you:

- Select the hard disk and subdirectory to back up from.
- The drive or drives to back up to. If the back up is DOS mode, the backup can be to any DOS device that DOS addresses with a drive letter.
- Backup type. This lets you select full or incremental backup with or without resetting the archive bit. It also lets you select between DOS and High Speed DMA backups. The DMA backups are faster but the disks are not readable by DOS. You must restore the disks produced by the DOS backup before you can use them. As a result, the only advantage of being DOS readable is if you have to perform disk-level maintenance on the floppy disk.
- Move to manual file selection mode. You can also do this by tabbing to the graphical tree window or by clicking on that window.
- Selecting a subdirectory also selects the files in that subdirectory.
- Enter files to include and/or exclude.
- Select if it backs up files with hidden, system or read-only attributes.
- Enter the earliest and latest date to include in the backup.

Once you start the backup, PC Backup works very fast. In all modes it is as fast or faster than every other program. Its moving cursor goes through the graphical tree and file list indicating which files and subdirectories are being processed. It indicates the time and percent complete at the bottom of the screen.

Restores   The restore program is less flexible than the backup program. While backing up, PC Backup does not store any information about the backup on the hard disk. You can select files to restore by tagging the files. If you select this method, PC Backup reads the files you backed up from the last diskette in the backup set. Alternatively, you can enter subdirectories to include and exclude but only if you remember them. In general, you are flying blind using this method as PC Backup does not verify the include/exclude list.

The Restore menu lets you:

- Select where to restore the files to.
- Where to read the backup set from.
- Type of backup set, DOS or DMA. PC Backup cannot figure this out automatically. However, it does automatically adjust for data compression.
- Move to manual file selection mode. You can also do this by tabbing to the graphical tree window or by clicking on that window.
- Selecting a subdirectory also selects the files in that subdirectory.
- Enter files to include and/or exclude.
- Select if PC Backup includes hidden, system or read-only files in the restore.
- Select if it restores up files with hidden, system or read-only attributes.

Once you have configured a restore, PC Backup processes the list. It then requests only those disks it needs to perform the restoration. PC Backup will warn you before it overwrites a file. However, you can tell it to stop doing that and either skip or automatically overwrite existing files.

Limitations   When it first starts or when you change the source of the backup, PC Backup rereads the hard disk to calculate its statistics and display the graphical tree. On large hard disks, this can take a long time. In some cases, this time exceeded one minute. PC Backup attempts to estimate the number of disks required for a backup using data compression, however, the estimates were not close. PC Backup is supposed to abort the backup/restore if you press Escape. However, on my PS/2 computer pushing Escape while the program was running locked up the computer.

After finishing my initial review of PC Backup, it looked like a wonderful program. In fact, I selected PC Backup to use as my own backup program. The backup program worked wonderfully. Every few days it quickly made my backup without fuss or complaint. Then, one Saturday I was testing a program to edit the file allocation table (FAT). As always, I made a backup before undertaking such a dangerous activity. It turned out that the FAT editor had a major bug that caused it to crash and wipe out half my hard disk in the process. Because of my recent backup, that did not worry me. I dug out my DOS disk and reformatted the hard disk. Then I installed PC Backup and started to restore the data.

The first thing the restore program does is request the last backup disk. It reads the directory information on this disk so it can display a directory tree of the files in the backup. Once it finished reading this disk, it would process the information for several minutes then give me the error message "Nonremovable disk full." This was in spite of the 130 Meg hard disk being almost empty. I tried most of that weekend to restore my files. I did not succeed in restoring a single file. Monday, I called Central Point Software technical support for help. I spent well over an hour on the phone (at my expense) and they were not able to resolve the problem.

At one point they told me PC Backup would not work on a Model 70 or Model 80 computer. They seemed genuinely surprised I had succeeded in making a backup at all. Later, they told me PC Backup did not work with Sony 1.44 Meg drives. At another point they claimed the problem was the result of the disks I was using. I pointed out the program was not reading the disk when the problem occurred. Finally, they told me to send them the backup disks and they would see if they could recover any files. Central Point Software was unable to restore any significant files either.

This sort of problem should worry anyone with a hard disk. No amount of rotating backups will protect you from a restore program that will not work. The only copies of hundreds of hours of my work exist in PC Backup format backups. My equipment will not restore those backups so I lost the work on those backups forever.

Users with large partitions running under DOS 4.x should be especially concerned. In my tests of PC Backup, I backed up a 20 Meg subdirectory and then restored that subdirectory. PC Backup worked perfectly using the same machine and disks. It was only when I needed to restore more than 32 Meg that I had any problems.

I was only able to finish this book on time because I had a copy on a second computer. After this, my advice is to use two different backup methods for absolutely critical data. You should also occasionally try to restore files with your backup program to make sure that works. After all, so much is riding on your backup program.

Conclusion   The restore portion of PC Backup worked properly in my 20 Meg test. When I needed to restore my entire hard disk, the restore program would not restore a single file properly. A backup program with a non-functioning restore program is worthless. Central Point Software claims this problem only exists on some PS/2 computers. If you are using PC Backup, I highly recommend you test the restore program on your computer before you need it to make sure it will work. PC Backup is only a small part of the PC Tools Deluxe package.

```
Product:      PC Backup
Price:        $129.00
Category:     Commercial
Publisher:    Central Point Software, Incorporated
Address:      15220 NW Greenbrier Parkway
              Suite 200
              Beaverton, Oregon 97006
Phone:        (503) 690-8090
Notes:        PC Backup is only one small portion of
              the PC Tools Deluxe package.
Memory:       512K
```

Point & Shoot Backup/Restore

Installation   *Point & Shoot* comes with a batch file that automatically installs the program. The batch file expects to run from the A-drive. An ASSIGN A = B statement corrects that. It automatically installs the program in the \P&S subdirectory. The manual instructs the user not to change this.

Backups   The first Point & Shoot menu is basically a commercial for the program, because it is shareware. It does let you select between backup, restore, configuring the program and exiting. There are nine additional screens just like this one for defining ten backup sets. You move between them using the page-up and page-down keys.

When you enter the backup source paths, you can enter up to ten different subdirectories to include in the backup. You do not enter the subdirectories by typing them in. Rather, you select them from a graphical tree as shown in Fig. 12-13.

Point & Shoot stores files on disks just like the DOS COPY command would, unless the file has to be split across two disks. Unlike Backpak, Point & Shoot fills up each disk so one file usually ends up being split.

Restores   The Point & Shoot restore program is very inflexible. There are only two ways to select files to restore. You can either automatically restore every file in a backup or to have the program ask you if you want to restore each file individually.

Limitations   Point & Shoot is slow overall, but it is painfully slow with small files. The subdirectory with 139 small system files took over three minutes to back up to a formatted diskette.

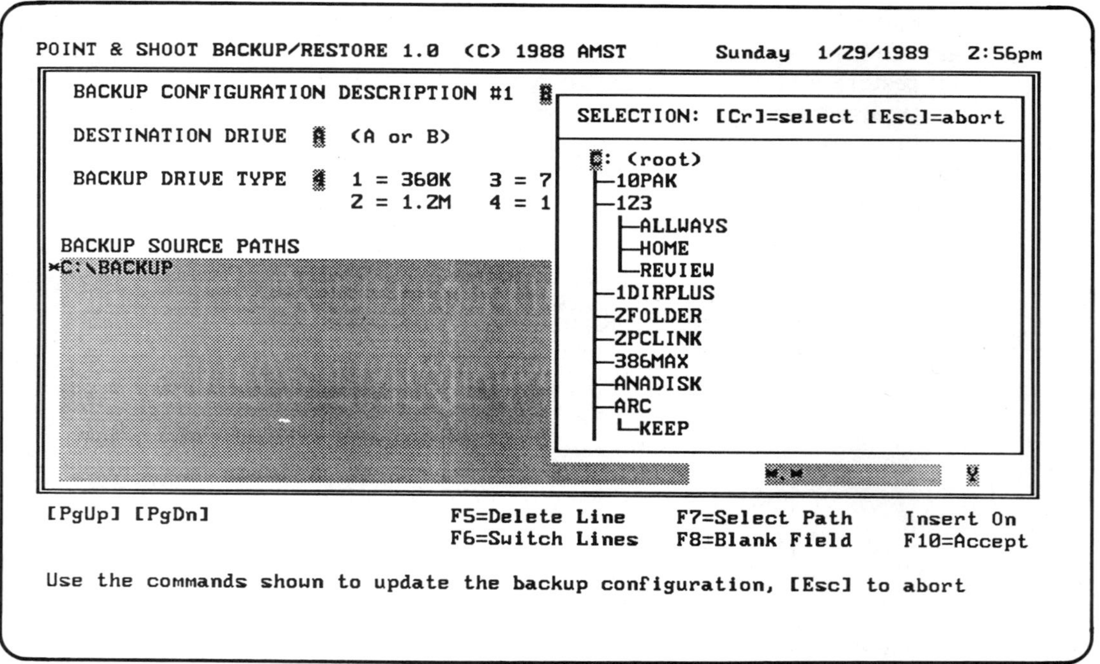

Fig. 12-13. With Point & Shoot Backup/Restore, you construct a backup set by selecting subdirectories from a graphical tree display.

Point & Shoot has a menu option to format disks. However, the disks used during a backup must be either preformatted or you must configure the program to format every single disk even formatted diskettes. Point & Shoot cannot automatically format only those disks that need formatting.

Point & Shoot would sometimes fail to format disks properly under DOS 4.01. On some of these occasions, it finished the formatting but crashed when it tried to update the file allocation table. On other occasions, it simply reported it was unable to format the disks. I checked all the disks using the DOS formatting program and the Norton Utilities and they were good.

Point & Shoot was unable to load all of my subdirectories into memory. It succeeded in loading only the first 200 or so. As a result, I could not include some of the subdirectories in the backup specification.

Manual   Like most shareware, Point & Shoot has its manual as an ASCII file on the disk. The manual is very brief and devoted only a few pages to explaining how to use the program.

Conclusion   Point & Shoot Backup/Restore is painfully slow, much slower even than DOS. Its only advantages over DOS are its menu driven operations and you can use most of the backed up files directly by copying them off the backup floppy.

<table>
<tr><td>Product:</td><td>Point & Shoot Backup/Restore</td></tr>
<tr><td>Price:</td><td>$35</td></tr>
<tr><td>Category:</td><td>Shareware</td></tr>
<tr><td>Publisher:</td><td>Applied Micro Systems Technology</td></tr>
<tr><td>Address:</td><td>Post Office Box 1596
Welch Avenue Station
Ames, Iowa 50010</td></tr>
<tr><td>Phone:</td><td>(515) 292-0426
(800) 537-7417</td></tr>
<tr><td>Memory:</td><td>256K</td></tr>
</table>

TakeTwo

TakeTwo is a commercial backup program. It has a flexible but extremely difficult to use backup program. In contrast, the restore program is very flexible. TakeTwo Manager includes a DOS shell.

Installation   TakeTwo comes with an installation program that automatically installs TakeTwo. It lets you change the name of the TakeTwo subdirectory and certain files as it runs. After copying the necessary files, it gives you the option of installing TakeTwo to the operating parameters of your system. If you select yes, it takes you to the System Configuration Menu.

Under the System Configuration Menu, you set . . .

- Floppy drive type.
- Drives to use. TakeTwo can use two different drives but they must be the same kind.
- Default backup classification for subdirectories. There are three classes; regular, once-only and never. It always backs up regular class subdirecto-

ries during a full backup or whenever you have modified it. It only backs up once-only class subdirectories during the first backup or anytime you have modified the file. It never backs up never class subdirectories.

- Default backup frequency. On change means make a backup whenever a file has changed. You can also specify the number of days between a backup.
- Number of days between full backups. TakeTwo intelligently manages the backups so restoring from incremental backups is not as difficult as it is with other programs. Occasionally, you will want to make a new full backup anyway. This lets you specify how often to make a full backup.
- Format program. This lets you specify a formatting program to use other than the DOS FORMAT.COM.
- Tone of the beeper when signaling for a disk change.
- The printer port to use.
- If verify is on or off.

You can also use this menu anytime you are using the backup program through the menu.

If you are going to use TakeTwo on a hard disk with more than one partition, then you must run the installation program once for each partition. Only one copy of the program is needed. However, TakeTwo requires a configuration file and catalog on each partition. The manual does not explain how to use TakeTwo with multiple drives. A "readme" file on the disk only briefly explained the process.

Backups   You begin by defining a file configuration. Figure 12-14 shows the File Configuration menu. The default for this display is showing subdirectories. You can display the files in any subdirectory and change their attributes individually. When you start a backup, TakeTwo computes statistics on the backup before beginning. Figure 12-15 shows this. It updates this screen as the backup proceeds.

Restores   It stores files in standard DOS format on the floppy disks. If they are not split across disks, you can restore using the COPY command. However, TakeTwo uses a unique subdirectory structure on each floppy disk so locating your file using DOS will be difficult.

Selecting files to restore is a snap! The initial display lists all the subdirectories on the backup. Pressing the "D" displays files one level deep. Pressing the "U" key reduces the display by one level. At any level, you move around and press the F9 key to mark files and/or subdirectories to restore. TakeTwo checks its list and only requests those disks it needs. You do not have to cycle through all the disk.

Other   TakeTwo Manager is a copy of TakeTwo that includes a full DOS shell. The manager starts with a graphical display of the hard disk structure. The display only shows one layer at a time. You move down one layer with the "N"ext key and up one with the "P"rior key. Pressing the F4 key while in the

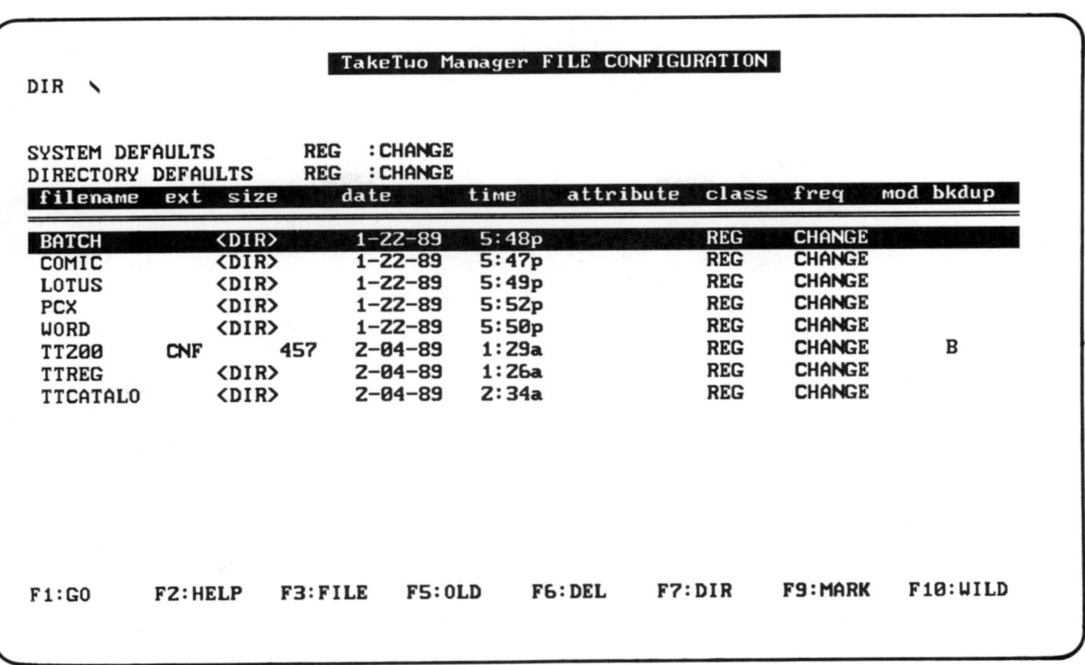

Fig. 12-14. The TakeTwo file configuration menu is used to override global defaults set in the System Configuration Menu for specific subdirectories and files.

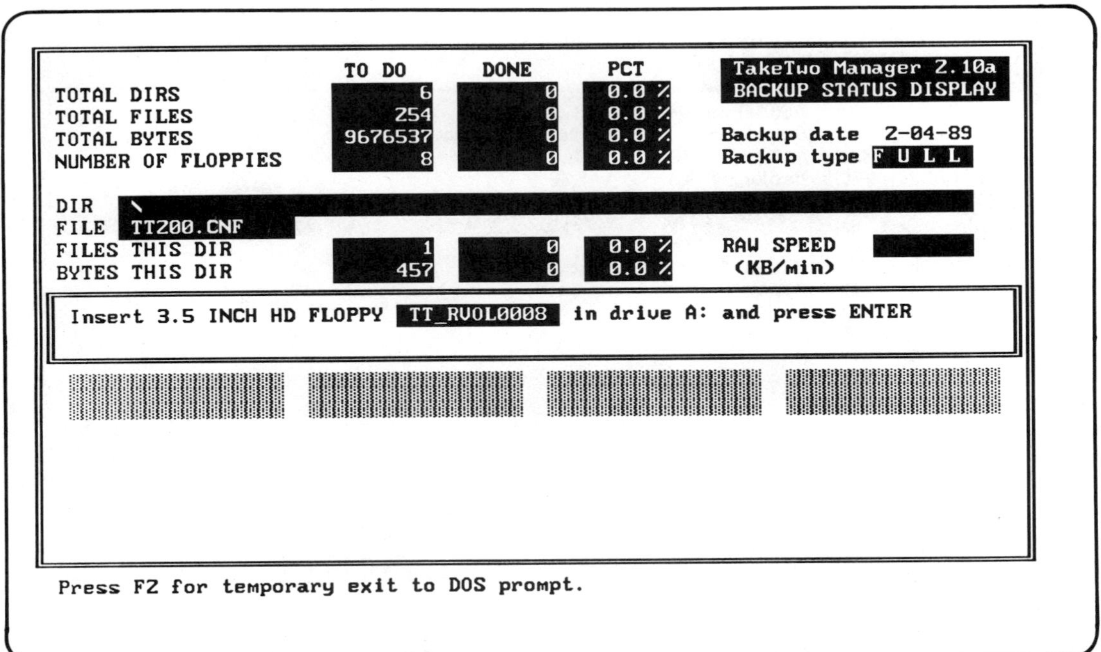

Fig. 12-15. When you start a backup, TakeTwo computes statistics on the backup before beginning.

graphical tree display pops up a subdirectory menu. This menu allows you to:

- Change subdirectories.
- Rename a subdirectory.
- Make a new subdirectory.
- Remove a subdirectory and any files in the subdirectory.
- Print a copy of the graphical tree.

Pressing Return lists all the files in the currently highlighted subdirectory. This screen also lists the size and creation time and date. It also lists the TakeTwo backup classification. By pressing the right arrow, you move to a display with only the file name, extension and space for a 50-character footnote. Figure 12-16 shows this.

With a file highlighted, you can pop up the file maintenance menu and perform the following activities:

- Change a file attribute.
- Copy a file.
- Delete a file.
- Find files matching a file specification on the hard disk.
- List the file on the screen.
- Move a file to another subdirectory.
- Overwrite a file with zeros and then erase it. That prevents the file from being recovered by someone else.

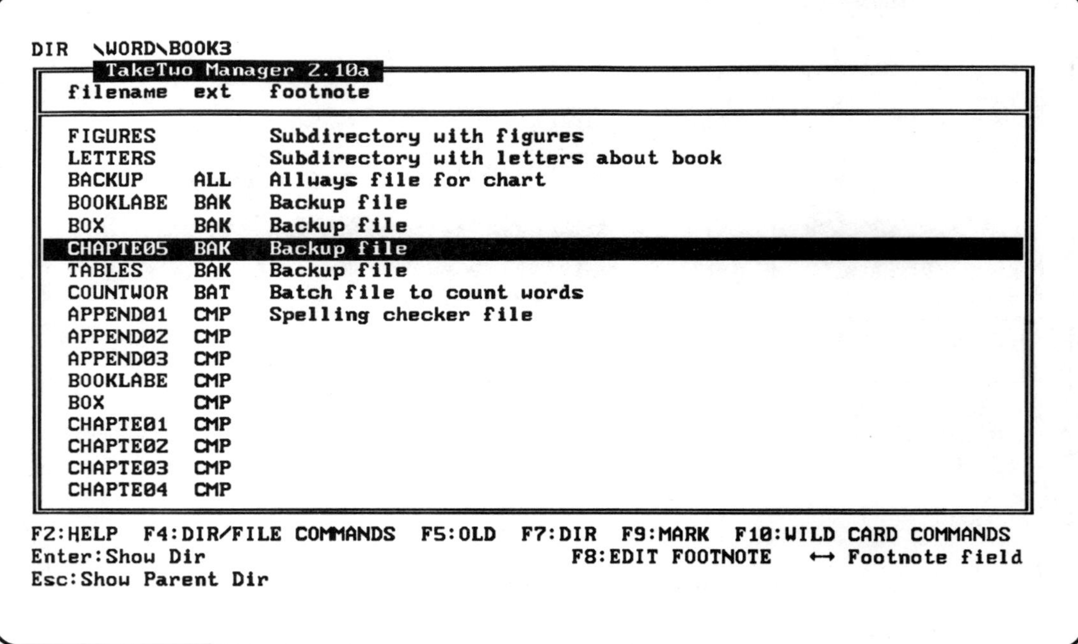

Fig. 12-16. The TakeTwo Manager lets you add a 50-character footnote to individual files. This footnote can only be viewed while in TakeTwo Manager.

- Print a file.
- Rename a file.
- Restore a file from a backup.
- Undelete a file.

You can run the manager from the DOS prompt. You can also load it as a memory resident program. However, the memory resident mode requires 268K. That is far too much to routinely load the DOS shell as a memory resident program.

Limitations   The user interface is difficult to use in the backup program. No data compression is available and TakeTwo is not especially fast. TakeTwo and TakeTwo Manager use the F2 key for help. This is an unusual key that many will have difficulty getting used to.

Manual   The manual is very difficult to read and understand. I had to read it three times before I felt comfortable using TakeTwo. Critical information, like how to run TakeTwo on multiple drives, is missing.

Conclusion   Except the complexity of configuring the backup program, using TakeTwo is fairly easy. Luckily, you only have to configure the backup program once. TakeTwo does not offer file compression.

<table>
<tr><td>Product:</td><td>TakeTwo</td></tr>
<tr><td>Price:</td><td>$99.00</td></tr>
<tr><td>Category:</td><td>Commercial</td></tr>
<tr><td>Publisher:</td><td>United Software Security, Incorporated</td></tr>
<tr><td>Address:</td><td>8133 Leesburg Pike
Suite 380
Vienna, Virginia 22182</td></tr>
<tr><td>Phone:</td><td>(800) 892-0007</td></tr>
<tr><td>Memory:</td><td>256K</td></tr>
</table>

HARDWARE BACKUP

All of the backup programs covered so far in this chapter have one thing in common, they back up to floppy disks. That means that you have to sit there and feed them disk after disk after disk. As a result, backups take longer than they should.

The real issue is not time. It does not matter if a hardware backup is faster or slower than backing up to floppy disks. The issue is user time. With a tape drive, for example, you can start the backup and leave the machine alone while it performs the backup. You can perform some useful task that does not require the computer while backing up. However, if you back up using floppy disks, you must stay with the computer during the procedure.

Now to drive this point home with a few calculations. First, assume you have a PC with a 30 Meg hard disk that is almost full. That is 28,000,000 bytes. Without data compression that requires a minimum of 78 (28,000,000/360,000) 360K disks. (A 360K diskette actually stores 362,496 bytes but I'll stick with whole numbers. Besides, you still need 78 disks.) If you keep one set near the computer and one set off-site that doubles your requirements to 156 disks. You really should keep more than one set of backups at each site. The experts recommend cycling through three sets. That brings you up to 468 disks.

Now purchasing 47 boxes of ten diskettes is not that expensive. The local computer store sells disks for about $5.00. So you can purchase all the disks for about $235. You can even buy name brand disks for under $500. That is cheaper than most tape backups. It is also cheaper than most other hardware backup systems.

However, switching 468 disks in and out of the computer will take a lot of time and patience. Since backing up to floppy disks requires more from the user, you are likely to perform the backup less frequently and is therefore less protection. On the other hand, you can sometimes automate hardware alternatives to the point that they require no user intervention.

The situation is getting better with the new computers. A typical AT with its 1.2 Meg disks would reduce the 468 disks down to about 140 disks. Because they cost more, the price of the disks will actually stay about the same. However, the user will spend a lot less time swapping disks.

If you own a PS/2 computer or any other computer with the new 1.44 Meg 3.5 inch floppies, things look better still. You can get by with about 118 disks. These disks are more expensive. You end up paying about $600 for these disks at the local computer store.

Of course, hard disks are getting bigger. One thing you notice about big hard disks is there is not a lot of empty space. Just as your bills expand to match (or exceed) your budget, software expands to fill your hard disk. Currently, I am using an IBM Model 70 with a 130 Meg hard disk. It has over 110 Meg of software on it. That means a full backup without data compression requires 77 1.44 Meg disks. The best I can do with data compression is 45 disks. And that is just for one backup.

While it was beyond the scope of this book to look at all the hardware available to perform backups, I did want to give you a taste. My experience with these products told me that the Irwin tape drives was about the best. Therefore, I have included two Irwin tape drives in this chapter. The first is the tape drive for an AT machine. The second is the tape drive for the IBM Model 70 PS/2 computer. They use the same software so the features are the same. Therefore, there is only one chart entry. I did not time the Irwin connected to the AT because its slower operation would distort the results. I also included performing a backup to a second hard disk.

Irwin Internal Tape Drive

Irwin internal tape drives are an excellent way to back up a hard disk without the fuss of having to swap disks. The Eztape software that comes with the drives is both easy to use and extremely flexible.

Installation (AT)   The Irwin tape drive is a superior product with a lot going for it. However, ease of installation is not one of them. The tape drive I reviewed was an external drive. In addition to the drive, it required a card inside the computer. Both the tape drive and the card came with an installation manual. The steps turned out to be the same, but the manuals looked so different that it took me some time to realize that.

The basic installation procedure is fairly straightforward. The steps are:

1)   Remove the computer cover.
2)   Plug the card into the computer.
3)   Disconnect the floppy drive from the controller and connect it to the Irwin card.
4)   Run a cable between the Irwin card and the floppy controller.
5)   Unplug the power cord from the B drive.
6)   Plug that cord into a special Irwin Y-cable.
7)   Plug the other ends of the Y-cable into the B drive and the Irwin card.
8)   Replace the cover.

This leaves a connector on the back of the computer that the portable tape drive plugs into. By installing this card on multiple computers, a single tape drive can service a number of computers.

My problem with the installation was two-fold. The major problem was only partially the fault of the Irwin manual. I was installing the drive on a Compaq DeskPro 286.

Two hints for Compaq owners. First, the cable from the Irwin card to the floppy controller is installed with the ribbon pointing up. This cable is keyed and cannot be installed wrong. The cable between the Compaq floppy drive and the Irwin card looks exactly like the Irwin cable, but is not keyed. My problem was that I assumed it was installed with the ribbon pointing up, just like the Irwin cable. That is wrong. Install the Compaq cable with the ribbon pointing down. Second, the Irwin manual says to install the Irwin card and then connect the cables to it. There is not enough room to connect the cables once the card is in the computer. You must connect the cables first. I expect this is the case with most computers.

Unlike almost every other computer, the Compaq does not have keyed floppy connectors. So you can plug them in one of two ways. The Irwin installation manual does not warn about this, and you guessed it, I plugged mine in the wrong way.

When I turned the computer on, both the A and B drives spun constantly. The computer would run off the C drive but would not recognize either the A or B drives. In addition, the Compaq refused to recognize the setup stored in its EPROM memory as valid. The first thing I did was check the Irwin installation manual for troubleshooting hints. There were none.

Luckily, I guessed the problem right away. With the Irwin installed correctly, the Compaq EPROM was erased when I turned it on. I do not know if that was from installing the Irwin drive incorrectly or if it is always the case when you install a tape drive.

A second problem was the manuals themselves. They are written in a short, technical manner as though Irwin expects the reader to have a lot of experience installing computer equipment. There are photographs, but only for an IBM XT/AT. I have seen similar manuals with photographs from Compaqs and several other major computers. Clearer instructions, more photographs, a "when things go wrong" troubleshooting section, and consistent manuals between products would do wonders. Better yet, let your dealer install it.

The software to run the tape drive comes on a 5.25 inch floppy and comes with the drive. It comes with an installation program that you must use since the software is compressed to fit onto one disk. The software is not copy protected. In fact, the license gives you the right to install the single software package on every computer you use the Irwin drive with. This is a very logical license.

Installation (PS/2)   On the IBM PS/2 computers, you cannot connect both the external 360K 5.25 inch disk drive and the internal Irwin drive.

(This is a limitation of the computer, not the backup drive. If you need a 360K drive, Irwin makes an external drive that uses the 5.25 inch floppy controller. You normally have the controller connected to the drive. When you want to make a backup, you switch the cable from the disk drive to the tape drive.)

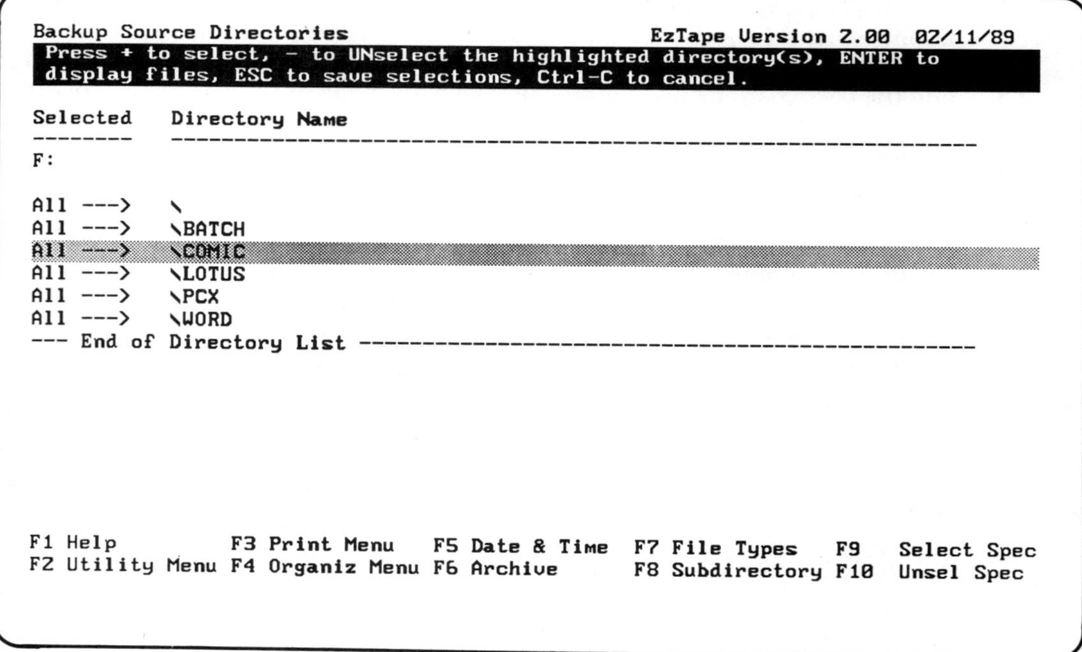

Fig. 12-17. After you have selected a hard disk, Eztape takes you to a panel that lists all the subdirectories on this hard disk. Here you can tag specific subdirectories to include.

The steps to install the drive on the IBM Model 70 are:

1) Unscrew the two thumb screws on the back that hold the cover on.
2) Slide the cover off.
3) Slide out the plastic spacer IBM places in the second internal drive slot.
4) Bolt the Irwin installation plate onto the Irwin drive.
5) Slide the Irwin drive into the drive slot.
6) Replace the blank drive cover on the case with the Irwin cover.
7) Slide the case back onto the Model 70.
8) Tighten the thumb screws on the back.
9) Boot off the IBM reference disk you created when you set up the computer. This reconfigures the computer to access the tape drive.

It sounds easy and it is. My total installation time was less than one half hour.

Backup You use the Irwin software program (EzTape) to select the files to back up or restore. The first backup menu gives you the options to . . .

1) Back up the entire default drive.
2) Develop a custom backup, called a parameter file.
3) Load a parameter file created earlier.
4) Edit an existing parameter file.

```
Backup Source Files                          EzTape Version 2.00   02/11/89
Press + to select, - to UNselect the highlighted file(s), ESC to save
selections, Ctrl-C to cancel.

Selected     File Name       Size        Date        Time    Archive    File Type
--------     ---------       ----        ----        ----    -------    ---------
F:\BATCH

  --->       CHECK.BAS       9216     11/18/87     20:31     Off       -  -  -
  --->       FASTSCRN.BAS    2560     11/27/87     20:30     Off       -  -  -
  --->       SCREEN.BAS       729      9/24/87     14:26     Off       -  -  -
  --->       SWEEP.BAS       5376     11/27/87     11:58     Off       -  -  -
  --->       1.BAT             28     10/11/87     16:14     Off       -  -  -
  --->       2.BAT             23     10/11/87     16:14     Off       -  -  -
  --->       2-2.BAT          256     12/15/87     10:40     Off       -  -  -
  --->       2-3.BAT          384     12/15/87     10:52     Off       -  -  -
  --->       2THINGS.BAT       28      7/28/87     16:15     Off       -  -  -
  --->       3.BAT             33     10/11/87     16:15     Off       -  -  -
  --->       4.BAT             25     10/11/87     16:15     Off       -  -  -
  --->       5.BAT             19     10/11/87     16:16     Off       -  -  -
  --->       6.BAT             24     10/11/87     16:16     Off       -  -  -
  --->       A.BAT              8      7/27/87     16:36     Off       -  -  -

F1 Help          F3 Print Menu    F5 Date & Time   F7 File Types   F9    Select Spec
F2 Utility Menu  F4 Organiz Menu  F6 Archive       F8 Subdirectory F10   Unsel Spec
```

Fig. 12-18. Eztape can list every file in a subdirectory. You can move around this list tagging files to include in the backup.

Eztape begins by listing all the hard disks on your system. This list includes all the pseudo-hard disks created with the DOS SUBST command. Eztape shows a lot of hard disks on my system. The C, D and E-drives are physical drives. I created the remaining drives using the DOS SUBST command to shorten my PATH statement. Eztape only lets you select one hard disk. You cannot select multiple hard disks, even when both are SUBSTed off the same physical disk.

After you have selected a hard disk, Eztape takes you to a panel that lists all the subdirectories on this hard disk. Here you can tag specific subdirectories to include. Figure 12-17 shows this. If you press Return on any subdirectory in this listing, Eztape gives you a list of files in that subdirectory. In this list, you can tag specific files to include in the backup. Figure 12-18 shows this. Once you have specified all the files, you can save the setup in a parameter file for repeated use. You can have as many parameter files as you like.

You can run the backup program right away or run a memory resident program to cause the backup to take place at any time you specify. The 40 Meg tape will hold an entire hard disk without swapping on many systems. Therefore, the backup can easily take place at night or during lunch without anyone being there.

The backup was faster than most of the programs that backed up to disks. However, Fastback Plus was much faster. While Fastback Plus performs a faster backup, the Irwin drive will run unattended. That way, you can do something else while the computer is performing a backup.

Restores   The restore program is absolutely incredible. You have the option of restoring every file from a backup onto any hard disk. If you need to be more selective, Eztape will read the list of files off the tape. It then presents you with a list of files like the one in Fig. 12-19.

Limitations   One of the preformatted tapes Irwin sent me was defective. Eztape backed up to about half the tape and then seemed to "hang." It spent over one hour trying to back up a small batch file before I stopped the backup program. Irwin sells their tapes pre-formatted and Eztape does not have a formatting option. Therefore, I was not able to re-format the tape to mark over the bad spot.

The Irwin drive is extremely easy and flexible for most hard disks. However, users with a hard disk too large to back up to a single tape will find it more difficult to use. It takes around 15 minutes for Eztape to fill a tape. It then waits for you to swap tapes. Although you can take a break, you cannot exactly run Eztape unattended (see Fig. 12-20).

If your hard disk exceeds 40 Meg, you will want to develop several parameter files where each one contains less than 40 Meg of data. That way, each backup can run unattended. You can include critical subdirectories in each parameter file and divide less critical ones among parameter files.

You cannot use the PS/2 internal tape drive on a machine with an external 360K drive. This is a limitation of the PS/2 computer and not the Irwin drive.

```
Restore Source Files                      EzTape Version 2.00  02/11/89
Press + to select, - to UNselect the highlighted file(s), ESC to save
selections, TAB to change target, Ctrl-C to cancel.

Selected    File Name        Size      Date      Time    Archive    File Type
--------    ---------        ----      ----      ----    -------    ---------
1:\BACKUP\BATCH

   --->     CHECK.BAS        9216    11/18/87   20:32    Off        - - -
   --->     FASTSCRN.BAS     2560    11/27/87   20:31    Off        - - -
   --->     SCREEN.BAS        729     9/24/87   14:27    Off        - - -
   --->     SWEEP.BAS        5376    11/27/87   11:59    Off        - - -
   --->     1.BAT              28    10/11/87   16:15    Off        - - -
   --->     2.BAT              23    10/11/87   16:15    Off        - - -
   --->     2-2.BAT           256    12/15/87   10:41    Off        - - -
   --->     2-3.BAT           384    12/15/87   10:53    Off        - - -
   --->     2THINGS.BAT        28     7/28/87   16:16    Off        - - -
   --->     3.BAT              33    10/11/87   16:16    Off        - - -
   --->     4.BAT              25    10/11/87   16:16    Off        - - -
   --->     5.BAT              19    10/11/87   16:17    Off        - - -
   --->     6.BAT              24    10/11/87   16:17    Off        - - -
   --->     A.BAT               8     7/27/87   16:37    Off        - - -

F1 Help          F3 Print Menu    F5 Date & Time   F7 File Types    F9   Select Spec
F2               F4 Backup Info   F6 Archive       F8 Subdirectory  F10  Unsel Spec
```

Fig. 12-19. When you go to restore data from a tape, Eztape can list every file on the backup tape along with its size and creation time and date. You can then move around this list tagging files to restore.

Nevertheless, it is a significant limitation if you need 5.25-inch compatibility. Irwin makes a second PS/2 drive that uses the same controller as the IBM external drive. To back up, you unplug the cable from the drive and plug it into the tape unit. When you finish the backup, you reconnect the floppy drive. Unfortunately, this unit was not available for testing.

Manual   The installation manual for the Compaq was difficult to follow. Part of that is no doubt because installing the drive on a Compaq is far more difficult. The manual for the PS/2 computer was better but still needed some improvement. The manual for Eztape was very good and easy to follow.

Conclusion   The backup tapes are very small, smaller than a deck of cards. This makes storing off site, or even mailing, easy. If you feel uncomfortable installing the drive yourself, have the dealer do it for you. That way you have the advantage of a tape drive while avoiding the most difficult part.

```
Product:     Irwin Model 2040 AT Tape Drive
Price:       $699    Internal drive
             $799    External drive
                     Including Model 8425 installation kit
             $140    Connector card for external drive
             $35     Preformatted 40 Meg Tapes
Category:    Commercial
Publisher:   Irwin Products Group
             Cipher Data Products, Incorporated
Address:     2101 Commonwealth Boulevard
             Ann Arbor, Michigan 48105
Phone:       (800) 348-6242
Notes:       PC's with a 37-pin floppy disk connector on
             the back do not require the connector card.
Memory:      640K for EzTape
```

```
Product:     Irwin Model 2040 PS/2 Tape Drive
Price:       $699    Internal drive
                     Including Model 8470 installation kit
             $35     Preformatted 40 Meg Tapes
Category:    Commercial
Publisher:   Irwin Products Group
             Cipher Data Products, Incorporated
Address:     2101 Commonwealth Boulevard
             Ann Arbor, Michigan 48105
Phone:       (800) 348-6242
Notes:       PS/2 computers do not require a card.

             This drive can not be used on a PS/2 that has a
             360K external drive attached.
Memory:      640K for EzTape
```

Sy-TOS

For reasons that are not important here, I was not able to do a full review of
Sy-TOS. However, I was impressed with the product and did want to briefly discuss it.

Tape drives usually come with their own software for making backups.
Some of it, like Eztape for the Irwin drives, is very good. However, some other
drives come with software that is difficult to configure and difficult to use.
What you may not know is there are alternatives. You do not have to use the
software that came with your tape drive.

One such after-market tape backup software package is Sy-TOS from
Sytron. Sy-TOS stands for Sytron Tape Operating System. Sy-TOS is so good
that IBM has adopted it as the software for their 6157 tape drive. That means
IBM has also adopted the data format Sy-TOS uses to store the data on the
tape. Unlike DOS, there is no standard format for storing data on tape. Most
vendors use their own format. That is why you cannot restore a tape created by
one vendor's software using another vendor's restore program. In addition to

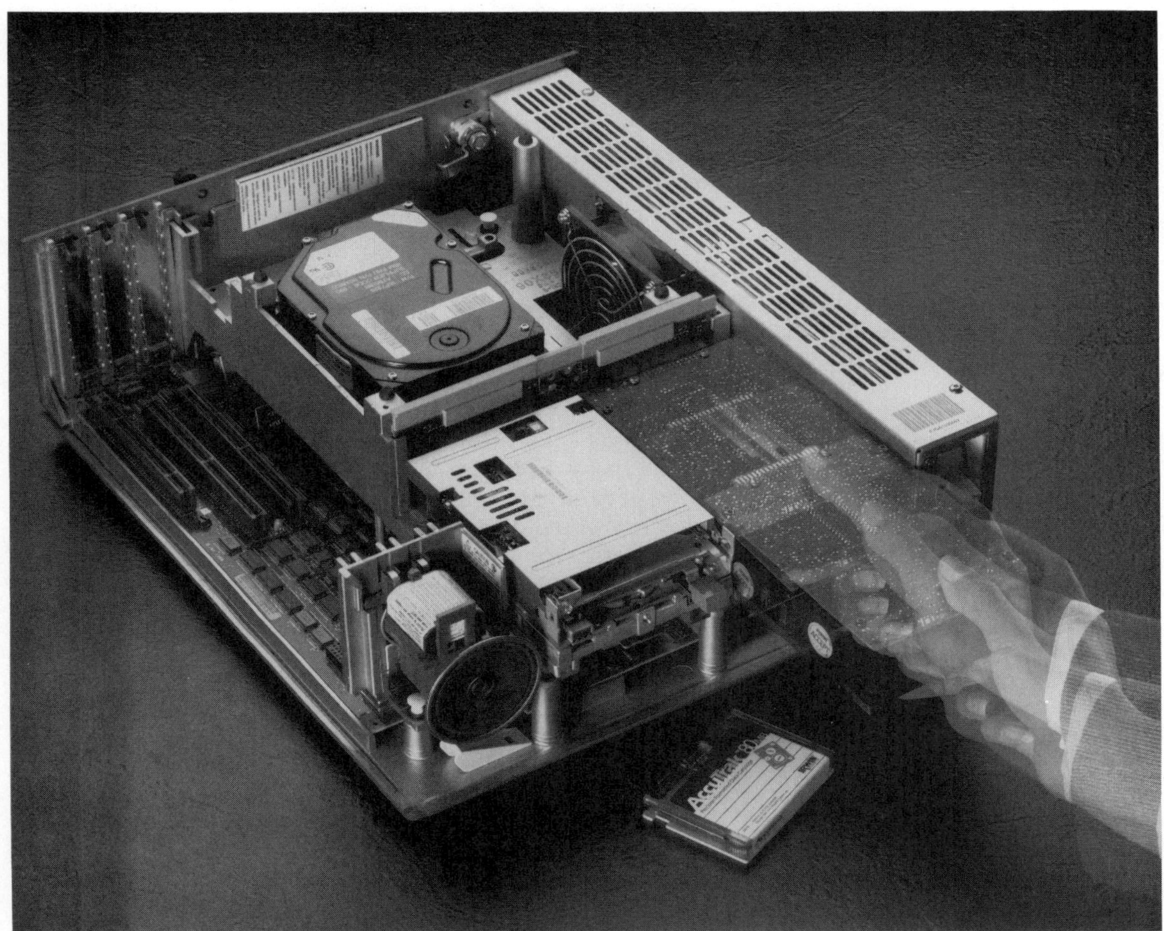

Fig. 12-20. Slide-in tape backup for a PS/2.

IBM, several other companies use Sy-TOS. They include Cipher Data Products, Incorporated, Kennedy Company, Tandberg and Wangtek, Incorporated.

XCOPY to Second Hard Disk

Although expensive, copying all the files to a second hard disk is the single most reliable way of performing a backup. Its big disadvantage is it is difficult to store backups off-site.

Installation   For this test, I backed up to an external Plus Development Passport removable hard disk. Installing this system is more difficult than installing a second hard disk. However, you have the advantage of being able to remove the drive for secure or off-site storage.

The steps to install the external Passport drive are:

1) Remove the cover from the Passport drive housing.
2) Install the connector that the drives plug into inside the Passport housing.
3) Replace the housing cover.
4) Remove the cover from the computer.
5) Install a card inside the computer.
6) Replace the computer cover.
7) Connect the card to the Passport drive.
8) Because I was installing the drive on a PS/2 computer, I had to boot off a reference disk and run the IBM installation program. I also had to add a device driver to my CONFIG.SYS file.
9) Format the drives.

Backups   To copy all the files from the C-drive to the D-drive, you issue the command: XCOPY C:\ D:\ /S/E

You can perform an incremental backup by adding a /A parameter. However, this runs so fast you will probably want to skip this. If the capacity of your primary hard disk exceeds the target, you will need to write a custom batch file to only back up those subdirectories containing important data.

Restores   You perform all restore using the DOS COPY or XCOPY commands.

Limitations   This is a fairly cheap form of hardware backup if you use an inexpensive hard disk, like a Plus Development Hardcard. However, in order to store multiple backups both on and off-site, you need an interchangeable drive. Both the Passport drive or a Bernoulli drive are excellent choices for this. Both are much more expensive than a tape drive and their media cost more than tapes. Both do, however, give you added functionability. You can also use them to store data while you are working on it. Tape drives cannot do this.

Manual   The Passport drive came in several boxes. One contained the removable media. Another contained the drive housing. Others contained the drive connector and the cabling. Each package had its own documentation. The installation manual was not clear and at one point had me jumping between manuals.

Conclusion   Backing up to a second hard disk is extremely fast. When that second hard disk has an interchangeable media, you have all the convenience of a tape backup. You also have the additional flexibility of being able to use the drive for other tasks in addition to performing backups.

RONNY'S PICKS

After using all these floppy disk backup programs and the Irwin tape drive, I am sure that a tape drive is much better than even the best floppy system. If you have a choice, go with a hardware alternative.

I had planned to leave the Irwin drive in my system permanently for my personal backups until I ran into the 5.25-inch incompatibility problem discussed above. Since much of my review software is on 5.25-inch disks, I reluctantly removed the Irwin drive.

My normal backup involves backing up to forty 3.5-inch 1.44 Meg floppies, and that is with data compression. My only concerns are speed recoverability. Prior to reviewing the software for this chapter, I had been using Fastback Plus. As you read above, it has a lot of problems. However, I had not found anything anywhere near as fast. So basically, I was keeping two sets of backups and hoping that if disaster struck I could get back everything between the two backups.

Fastback Plus has the speed but not the recoverability and constantly worrying about your ability to recover your files is no way to back up. One of my main goals while writing this chapter was to find a better backup program. One fast enough I could live with making frequent backups and one that would consistently recover all the files from the backup.

The very last program I tested was PC Tools Deluxe. Its backup program, PC Backup, really impressed me. It was only a few seconds slower than Fastback Plus. I immediately converted all my backups to PC Backup. As I discussed above, after using PC Backup for about a month, I suffered a hard disk crash. PC Backup was unable to restore any files after the crash.

After ruling out Fastback Plus and PC Backup, none of the rest of the programs has enough problems for you to avoid any of them. Based on the charts, you should be able to select the backup program with the best set of features to meet your specific needs.

Table 12-1. **Results of Timing Backup Programs.**

Program	Unformatted Time[1]	Formatted Time[2]	Number of Disk[3]
Back-It: No Verification	15:28	4:34	8
Back-It: DOS Verification[4]	19:22	8:18	8
Back-It: Super Verification[5]	21:10	10:06	8
Backpak: New Backup	20:13	10:01	8
Backpak: Updating Backup	N/A	17:10	8
Diskpack	N/A	4:15	3
DOS 4.01	20:27	8:57	7
DS Backup+: DOS Mode, Base[6]	N/A[7]	8:51	7
DS Backup+: DOS Mode, Verification On	N/A	14:27	7
DS Backup+: DOS Mode, Compression On	N/A	8:35	6
DS Backup+: Non-DOS Mode, Base[8]	17:15	6:03	7
DS Backup+: Non-DOS Mode, Verification On	21:02	9:54	7
DS Backup+: Non-DOS Mode, Compression On	16:44	5:31	6

All times on an IBM Model 70 running at 16 MHz.

---

[1]Time required to perform a backup with unformatted disks.

[2]Time required to perform a backup with formatted disks.

[3]The files used in this test were not representative of a normal hard disk. They were better suited for compression than the "average" file. As a result, backup programs using data compression reduced the number of disks more than they would on an average system.

[4]Every sector on every DOS disk has an associated cyclical redundancy check [or CRC] number associated with it. The CRC is computed mathematically from the data stored in that

Table 12-1. **Continued**

sector. A CRC value is not unique to that data, different data sets can have the same CRC. So the SRC is a good but not perfect check. When DOS VERIFY is on during a copy or backup, DOS does not compare actual source to target data. Rather, it checks target data against its CRC and compares source and target CRC's to make sure they are the same.

[5]Using Back-It super verification, every byte of information written to a target disk is read back and compared to the source data.

[6]The DOS mode has several different options that can affect backup time. This is the base case with all these options turned off. Each option will be tested alone and not in conjunction with other options.

[7]DS Backup+ has a menu option to format disks. It will not automatically format them during backup.

[8]The non-DOS mode of DS Backup+ has several different options that can greatly affect backup time. This is the base case with all these options turned off. Each option will be tested all and not in conjunction with other options.

Program	Unformatted Time[1]	Formatted Time[2]	Number of Disk[3]
Fastback Plus: No compression	12:36	8:57	8
Fastback Plus: Save Disks	4:48	2:30	3
Fastback Plus: Save Time	4:53	2:30	3
File/Saver[4]	20:27	8:57	7
Intelligent Backup	N/A[5]	8:22	7
Irwin Tape Drive	N/A[6]	6:20	N/A[7]
Keep Track Plus	N/A	7:25	7

All times on an IBM Model 70 running at 16 MHz

[1]Time required to perform a backup with unformatted disks.

[2]Time required to perform a backup with formatted disks.

[3]The files used in this test were not representative of a normal hard disk. They were better suited for compression than the "average" file. As a result, backup programs using data compression reduced the number of disks more than they would on an average system.

[4]Times are identical to DOS because File/Saver manages the DOS backup program but depends on DOS to perform the actual backup.

[5]Many times, Intelligent Backup was not able to tell that a disk was not formatted. Rather, it restored to the DOS "Ignore, Abort, Fail, or Retry" error message. When that happened, it proved to be impossible to format a disk using Intelligent Backup. As a result, I did not perform the timing test using unformatted disks.

[6]You purchase the tapes pre-formatted.

[7]It required a single 40 Meg tape.

Program	Unformatted Time[1]	Formatted Time[2]	Number of Disk[3]
PC Backup: No Compression/DOS	NA[4]	8:29	7
PC Backup: Compression/DOS	NA	5:39	2
PC Backup: No Compression/DMA[5]	11:19	4:40	7
PC Backup: Compression/DMA	4:09	2:38	3
Point & Shoot Backup/Restore	27:14	13:42	7
TakeTwo	N/A[6]	7:53	7
XCOPY to Second Hard Disk	N/A	1:58	N/A

Table 12-1. Continued

All times on an IBM Model 70 running at 16 MHz

[1]Time required to perform a backup with unformatted disks.

[2]Time required to perform a backup with formatted disks.

[3]The files used in this test were not representative of a normal hard disk. They were better suited for compression than the "average" file. As a result, backup programs using data compression reduced the number of disks more than they would on an average system.

[4]PC Backup in DOS mode gives you the option of formatting each disk as you change them. However, automatic formatting is built into the program. Therefore, the unformatted disk test was not included for PC Backup in DOS mode.

[5]Faster backup method that does not use DOS format on the disks.

[6]TakeTwo simply runs the DOS FORMAT program to format disks. Since it does not use an internal formatting program, there is no advantage to letting it format disks. Therefore, this was not calculated.

Table 12-2. Backup Program Features.

	Back-It	Back-pak	Disk-Pack	DS Back-up+	Fastback Plus	File/Save
Abort Backup Anytime	Y	Y	Y	Y	Y	Y
Backup to 1.2 Meg Disk	Y	Y	Y	Y	Y	Y
Backup to 3.5 Inch Disk	Y	Y	Y	Y	Y	Y
Backup to 360K Disk	Y	Y	Y	Y	Y	Y
Erases Target Disk	Y	Y	Y	Y	Y	Y[1]
Alternate Between Two Drives	Y	N	N	Y	Y	N
Command Line Backup	Y	Y	Y	Y	Y	Y
Control Over Archive Flag[2]	Y	N	Y	Y	Y	N
Estimates Disks Required	Y	Y	N	Y	Y	N
Estimates Time Required	N	N	N	Y	Y	N
Pause Backup Anytime	Y	N	N	Y[3]	Y	N
Requires Formatted Disk	N	N	Y	Y[3]	N	Y
Uses DOS Format on Disk	Y	Y	Y[4]	Y[3]	Y	Y
Warns Before Overwriting Disk	Y	Y	N	Y	Y	Y
Data Compression	N	N	Y	Y	Y	N

	IBM DOS 4.01	Intelligent Backup	Irwin Tape	Keep-Track	PC Backup
Abort Backup Anytime	Y	Y	Y	Y	Y
Backup to 1.2 Meg Disk	Y	Y	NA	Y	Y
Backup to 3.5 Inch Disk	Y	Y	NA	Y	Y
Backup to 360K Disk	Y	Y	NA	Y	Y
Erases Target Disk	Y[1]	Y	N	Y	Y
Alternate Between Two Drives	N	N	NA	Y	Y
Command Line Backup	Y	Y	Y	Y	N
Control Over Archive Flag[2]	N	Y	Y	Y	Y
Estimates Disks Required	N	Y	NA	Y	Y
Estimates Time Required	N	Y	N	N	Y
Pause Backup Anytime	N	Y	N	Y	N
Requires Formatted Disk	Y	Y	Y[5]	Y	N[6]
Uses DOS Format on File	Y	Y	NA	Y	Optional
Warns Before Overwriting Disk	Y	Y	Y[7]	Y	Optional
Data Compression	N	N	N	N	Y

Table 12-2. Continued

¹Root directory only.

²Will the program make an incremental backup without resetting the archive flag. This is critical if you maintain more than one set of backups. After the archive flag is reset, all you can make is a full backup.

³DSBackup+ has two modes, high-speed and DOS. This option works only in DOS mode.

⁴Diskpack uses DOS to prepare its disks for use. However, the method it uses to write to the disk causes problems for DOS programs. DOS can still read the disk and perform a DIR. However, the file size and available space calculations are incorrect. DOS CHKDSK objects to the arrangement of the files on the disk.

⁵Tapes must be formatted before use.

⁶Non-DOS or DMA mode formats automatically as required. DOS mode requires you to select the format option from the dialog box as you change disks.

⁷The backup program will not overwrite a tape, that must be performed using a separate utility. That takes about one minute.

	Point & Shoot Backup Restore	Take-Two
Abort Backup Anytime	N	Y
Backup to 1.2 Meg Disk	Y	Y
Backup to 3.5 Inch Disk	Y	Y
Backup to 360K disk	Y	Y
Erases Target Disk	Y	Y
Alternate Between Two Drives	N	Y
Command Line Backup	N	Y
Control Over Archive Flag[1]	N	N
Estimates Disks Required	Y	Y
Estimates Time Required	N	N
Pause Backup Anytime	N	Y
Requires Formatted Disk	N	N
Uses DOS Format on Disk	Y	Y
Warns Before Overwriting Disk	Y	Y
Data Compression	N	N

¹Will the program make an incremental backup without resetting the archive flag. This is critical if you maintain more than one set of backups. After the archive flag is reset, all you can make is a full backup.

	Back-It	Back-pak	Disk-Pack	DS Back-up+	Fastback Plus	File/Save
File Names	Y	Y	Y	Y	Y	Y
Exclude File Names[1]	Y	N	N	Y	Y	N
Archive Flag	Y	Y	Y	Y	Y	Y
File Creation Date	Y	N	Y	Y	Y	Y
File Creation Time	N	N	N	Y	N	N
Multiple Subdirectories[2]	Y	Y	N	Y	Y	N
Exclude Subdirectories[3]	Y	N	N	Y	Y	N
File Size	N	N	N	N	N	N

	IBM DOS 4.01	Intelligent Backup	Irwin Tape	Keep-Track	PC Backup
File Names	Y	Y	Y	Y	Y
Exclude File Names[1]	N	Y	Y	Y	Y
Archive Flag	Y	Y	Y	Y	Y
File Creation Date	Y	Y	Y	N	N
File Creation Time	N	Y	Y	Y	Y
Multiple Subdirectories[2]	N	Y	Y	Y	Y
Exclude Subdirectories[3]	N	Y	Y	Y	Y
File Size	N	N	N	N	N

	Point & Shoot Backup Restore	Take-Two
File Names	Y	Y
Exclude File Names[1]	N	Y
Archive Flag	Y	Y
File Creation Time	N	N
File Creation Date	N	N
Multiple Subdirectories[2]	Y	Y
Exclude Subdirectories[3]	N	Y
File Size	N	N

[1]For example, can you back up all the files on a hard disk except the *.BAK files.

[2]For example, can you back up the \DATA and \TAXES subdirectories with one backup session.

[3]For example, can you back up all the subdirectories except \OLDDATA and \DISCARD

Table 12-4. **Backup Program Displays.**

	Back-It	Back-pak	Disk-Pack	DS Back-up+	Fastback Plus	File/Save
Color Display	Y	Y	N	Y	Y	Y
Time During Backup	N	N	N	Y	Y	N
Percent Complete	Y	N	N	Y	Y	N
Time to Switch Disks	N	N	N	N	N	N
File Name During Backup	Y	Y	Y	Y	Y	Y
Subdirectory During Backup	Y	Y	Y	Y	Y	Y
File Date During Backup	N	N	N	Y	N	N
File Size During Backup	N	N	N	Y	N	N
File Time During Backup[1]	N	N	N	Y	N	N
Warns When Disk has Flaws	Y	N	Y[2]	Y	N	N
Summary Report of Backup	Y	N	N	Y	Y	N

	IBM DOS 4.01	Intelligent Backup	Irwin Tape	Keep-Track	PC Backup
Color Display	N	Y	Y	Y	Y
Time During Backup	N	Y	N	Y	Y
Percent Complete	N	Y	N	N[3]	Y
Time to Switch Disks	N	N	NA	N	N
File Name During Backup	Y	Y	Y	Y	Y
Subdirectory During Backup	Y	Y	Y	Y	Y
File Date During Backup	N	N	N	Y	N
File Size During Backup	N	Y	N	Y	N
File Time During Backup[1]	N	N	N	Y	N
Warns When Disk has Flaws	N	N	N[4]	N	N
Summary Report of Backup	N	N	N	N	Y

	Point & Shoot Backup Restore	Take-Two
Color Display	Y	Y
Time During Backup	N	N
Percent Complete	N	Y
Time to Switch Disks	N	N
File Name During Backup	Y	Y
Subdirectory During Backup	Y	Y
File Date During Backup	N	N
File Size During Backup	N	N
File Time During Backup[1]	N	N
Warns When Disk has Flaws	N	N
Summary Report of Backup	N	Y

[1]File creation time.

[2]Diskpack rejects all disks with flaws.

[3]Reports number of files backed up and total number of files to back up.

[4]Tapes are purchased already formatted with the bad spots marked.

Table 12-5. **Restore Program.**

	Back-It	Back-pak	Disk-Pack	DS Back-up+	Fastback Plus	File/Save
Abort Restorations Anytime	Y	Y	Y	Y	Y	NA
Catalog on Hard Disk[1]	Y	N	Optional	N	Y	NA
Command Line Restoration	N	Y	Y	Y	N	NA
Pause Restoration Anytime	Y	N	N	Y	Y	NA
Restore to Different Place[2]	Y	N	N	Y	N	NA
Restore to Floppy Diskette	N	Y[3]	N	Y	Y	NA
Search For File[4]	Y	N	N	Y	Y	NA
Search For Subdirectory	Y	N	N	Y	Y[5]	NA
Warns Before Overwriting	Y	N	N	Y	Y[6]	NA

	IBM DOS 4.01	Intelligent Backup	Irwin Tape	Keep-Track	PC Backup
Abort Restoration Anytime	Y	Y	Y	Y	Y
Catalog on Hard Disk	N	Y	N	N	N
Command Line Restoration	Y	Y[6]	Y	Y	N
Restore to Different Place[2]	N	Y	Y	N	Y
Restore to Floppy Diskette	Y	N	N	N	Y
Search For File[4]	N	N	Y	N	Y[7]
Search For Subdirectory	N	N	Y	N	Y[7]
Warns Before Overwriting	N	Y	Y	Y	Y

	Point & Shoot Backup Restore	Take-Two
Abort Restoration Anytime	N	Y
Catalog on Hard Disk[1]	N	Y
Command Line Restorations	N	N
Pause Restoration Anytime	N	N
Restore to Different Place[2]	N	N
Restore to Floppy Diskette	Y[3]	N[3]
Search For File[4]	N	N
Search For Subdirectory	N	Y
Warns Before Overwriting	Y	Y

[1]This speeds up searching and file selecting when restoring to the same hard disk as the backup.

[2]For example, restore the contents of the \DATA subdirectory to the \OLDDATA subdirectory.

[3]Since disks use DOS format for files, the files can be copied to any DOS device.

[4]Search prior to starting backup to either see if the file exists on the backup or to see what version it is.

[5]Depends on program settings.

[6]Entire hard disk only.

[7]PC Backup allows you to scroll through the list of all the backed up files tagging files to backup.

	Back-It	**Back-pak**	**Disk-Pack**	**DS Back-up+**	**Fastback Plus**	**File/Save**
File Creation Date	N	N	N	Y	Y	NA
Exclude Specific Files[1]	Y	N	N	Y	Y	NA
Exclude Subdirectories[2]	Y	N	N	Y	Y	NA
Multiple Subdirectories[3]	Y	Y	N	Y	Y	NA
File Names	Y	Y	Y	Y	Y	NA
File Size	N	N	N	N	N	NA
File Creation Time	N	N	N	Y	N	NA

	IBM DOS 4.01	**Intelligent Backup**	**Irwin Tape**	**Keep-Track**	**PC Backup**
File Creation Date	N	Y	Y	N	Y
Exclude Specific Files[1]	N	Y	Y	N	Y
Exclude Subdirectories[2]	N	Y	Y	N	Y
Multiple Subdirectories[3]	N	Y	Y	N	Y
File Names	Y	Y	Y	Y	Y
File Size	N	N	N	N	N
File Creation Time	N	Y	Y	N	N

	Point & Shoot Backup Restore	**Take-Two**
File Creation Date	N	N
Exculude Specific Files[1]	N	Y
Excluse Subdirectories[2]	N	Y
Multiple Subdirectories[3]	N	Y
File Names	N	Y
File Size	N	N
File Creation Time	N	N

[1]For example, can you recover all the files on a hard disk except the *.BAK files.

[2]For example, can you recover all the subdirectories except \OLDDATA and \DISCARD.

[3]For example, can you restore the \DATA and \TAXES subdirectories with one backup session.

	Back-It	Back-pak	Disk-Pack	DS Back-up+	Fastback Plus	File/Save
Price	$129.99	$99.00	$62.00	$79.95	$179.00	$30.00
DOS Access	Y	N	N	N	N	Y
Copy Protected	N	N	N	N	N	N
Error Correction	Y	N	N	Y	Y	N
Length of Free Technical Support	Limit Limit	Not Stated	Not Stated	No Limit	No Limit	Not Stated
Version	3.1	2.1	2.1	1.106	2.00	1.0

	IBM DOS 4.01	Intelligent Backup	Irwin Tape	Keep-Track	PC Backup
Price	$0.00	$149.95	$939[1]	$84.00	$79.95[2]
DOS Access	N	Y	N	Y	N
Copy Protected	N	N	N[3]	N	N
Error Correction	N	Y	Y	Y	Y
Length of Free Technical Support	NA	No Limit	No Limit	No Limit	No Limit
Version	4.01	2.1d	1.1	1.2	5.0

	Point&Shoot Backup Restore	Take-Two
Price	$35.00	$165.00
DOS Access	N	Y
Copy Protected	N	N
Error Correction	N	N
Length of Free Technical Support	Not Stated	1 Year
Version	1.2	1.10

[1]The exact price depends on what type of computer the drive is installed in.

[2]PC Backup is only a small portion of the PC Tools Deluxe package. The entire package sells for $79.95.

[3]Software license allows you to copy the software to any machine using the Irwin drive.

13
Document Indexing Programs

Backups, by their very nature, protect you from losing current data. A WORM [Write Once Read Many/Mostly] device cannot be erased so any backups can be recovered later. Other backups cannot help you recover data you erased six months ago because you did not think you would ever need it again. I had that happen a few times when I began using computers and I resolved never to have that problem again.

My solution was to create a subdirectory on my hard disk called \DIS-CARD. Anytime I felt I no longer needed a data file, I would copy it to the \DISCARD subdirectory. I continued to erase programs, after all, I could restore them from the original disk if I needed to. I also continued to erase small files that were easily recreated, like batch files.

When a lot of files began to accumulate, I would copy them to a floppy diskette and erase them from the hard disk. In the beginning that worked well. I found myself going back to these disks often. That convinced me it was worth-while to continue with this system. After a year or so, I had accumulated so many floppy diskettes that I began having trouble locating a specific file. My solution to that problem was to index the files on these floppy diskettes using a document indexing program.

In its simplest form, a document indexing program lets you avoid this problem. You feed it your documents, the program converts them to a set of indexes. Later, you can use an associated search program to find a document by searching on words you remember from the document. If you are looking for a letter to Fred Jones, then search on Fred Jones.

As useful as they were to me in tracking my growing pile of diskettes containing discarded data, indexing programs have the potential to do much more. For one thing, they can speed research. Consider the following three examples.

A lawyer is defending a case where his client ran a red light and hit a car. His office has two types of index files. The first are indexes of all the briefs his firm has filed. The second are indexes of major briefs filed by other firms. They read them into the computer with an optical scanner and then index them. They have so many indexes, they store them on multiple cartridges for a Bernoulli Drive. Before writing this brief, he searches all index sets for (red light AND (wreck OR accident) AND ticket). This lets him rapidly retrieve similar briefs. That reduces the time it takes him to prepare his brief.

A doctor has a patient with very unusual symptoms. The patient has a cough and his hair is falling out. This doctor gets his medical journals in both printed and in ASCII format on a disk. He knows he has read an article that mentioned those symptoms in passing. So he searches on (cough AND hair). This lets him rapidly find an article discussing his patient's problem.

A professor at a large university wants to write a paper on cycle time in fast food restaurants. Like the lawyer's office, this university scans and indexes journal articles. All the professor has to do to start his article is search on (cycle AND time AND restaurants).

All three of these examples share a common thread. Each individual is using indexing software much like we use the index to a book, to quickly home in on specific information. The difference is that the book index limits searches to the items the author considered important. (Technically, what the indexer at the book company thinks is important. This author has nothing to do with index production.) On the other hand, indexing software can find any information the user feels is important.

In general, there are two very broad categories of information users will want to index. The first category is information that will never change. The three examples above, along with my discarded floppy diskettes, are all of information that will never change. The other type of information is information that changes. For example:

The training department for a large utility maintains the training manuals for over five-hundred jobs. They update each training manual at least every six months. This training department indexes the manuals for easy locations of specific tasks, for example, resealing a residential electric meter. When the method changes, they must update the training manual for every job that involves resealing a residential electric meter. These include the meter reader, the reconnect man, the trouble man, and the special investigator. Without the index it would be difficult for them to locate every affected job for every procedure change.

This distinction between changing and non-changing information is not just cosmetic. If the information never changes, having to convert it to a specific format or add special internal markings is not a major problem. If you periodically update the information, then converting it after each update is time-consuming. Converting five-hundred manuals to ASCII, for example, is a big, but manageable, job. Converting five-hundred manuals to ASCII every six-months is a career.

Ize

Ize is a complex commercial document indexing program. It is much more difficult to learn to use than the other indexing programs. Ize does not index entire documents; rather, it indexes on a few keywords. Ize uses a limited number of keywords.

Installation   Ize comes with a fully automated installation program that will install Ize from any drive. The installation program leads you easily through the process of selecting the types of documents you will work with and the printers you will use.

Operation   Ize is much like a database for text. In fact, it calls its databases textbases. Its equivalent to database records are its text units. These are generally a single document and Ize limits them to 32K. Ize does not have an equivalent to database fields. With Ize, the entire 32K in the text unit is a single field. Its equivalent to database indexes are keywords. Just as some databases will only search on indexed fields, Ize will only search on its keys.

Ize can get its information from three sources, the built-in word processor, importing data directly into Ize and "hot-linking" to external files. Ize includes a very simple built-in word processor. It is acceptable for brief memos and not much else. It does have a template feature so you can structure data entry. Otherwise, it lacks features found on even simple word processors. As you create text with this word processor, you mark keywords by placing the cursor in that word and pressing the F4 key.

The second way to get information into Ize is to import it from another source. This works very much like importing a document into your word processor. In fact, Ize has a translation routine for many word processors. You cannot import data directly from a Lotus *.WK1 file. If the imported text exceeds the 32K limit on Ize text, Ize will automatically split the document into sections that do not violate this limitation.

There are two ways to mark imported text with keywords. The first is to scroll through the document after you have imported it and manually tag the keywords. This will be difficult if the document exceeded the 32K size limits. Ize splits the document very near the 32K break-point and tagging keyword takes up space in the document. As a result, you will have to delete text to tag keywords. A second way is to define a list of keywords in Ize before importing the text. Ize will then automatically tag all the words in the imported text that are in this keyword list.

A third way to get information into Ize is with a hot-link. With a hot-link, Ize does not actually load the document into its database. Rather, it loads its keywords and some working information on the document. If the document is larger than 32K, Ize only scans the first 32K for keywords. Ize has trouble scanning some types of files and will not catch all the keywords. It seemed to have particular trouble with worksheets.

When you hot-link to a file, Ize gives you a summary sheet on the screen. You can use this summary sheet to write yourself notes about the document or enter keywords. If you take the time to use this summary sheet, the summary sheet itself can give you enough information about the document during a search to see if it matches your needs.

When you want to look at a hot-linked document, Ize shells to DOS, loads the application program and then loads the hot-linked document. While shelling to an application program, Ize retains about 46K of memory. Ize retains enough of itself in memory to allow you to pop up an Ize window and modify the keywords associated with a document. This is especially useful if you do it while editing that document.

The major task is selecting keywords. Ize uses the keywords to group the documents that match a search request into an outline. Choose your keywords poorly and this feature is useless. For example, pick keywords that are too common and Ize will not be able to group matches on those words. Pick keywords that are too infrequent, and Ize will not be able to construct an outline at all. Even if you choose your keywords well, the Ize outline is not going to be very insightful. I expected that. Ize generates the outline by counting keywords.

Limitations   Ize would occasionally lock up my computer. That never happened while I was in Ize. However, it occasionally happened when I tried to start another application after exiting Ize. The problem seemed to depend on what I was doing in Ize and what application I was starting. Even at that, it did not happen consistently. The computer always locked just as I was starting a program so I never lost any data.

Importing large amounts of data into Ize is extremely slow. A single 75K file took about ten minutes. The importing time seems to be a function of how much formatting Ize has to strip out.

The first time I defined a number of files to hot-link to, Ize spent over fifteen minutes processing them. It then deleted all the information because the Ize file I was working with did not have a name. It also told me it could not process several Microsoft Word documents because I had not created them with Word. I carefully examined the files with Word and the Norton Utilities and they were perfect examples of Word files.

Ize lets you view Lotus files with hot-links into Ize. It tries to get around Lotus's inability to accept files on the command line by stuffing keystrokes into the keyboard buffer. However, this method will not work if you have an AUTO123.WK1 worksheet configured with your own menu. Many users do this to easily select the subdirectory they will be working with. Ize allows you to define your own hot-links. You could use this feature to bypass the AUTO123.WK1 problem.

Ize has the ability to run as a memory resident program. However, this mode requires more than 300K and does not use expanded or extended memory. That leaves so little room that running most programs with Ize loaded is neither practical nor often even possible. If you do run Ize in memory resident mode, it can pop-up over an application. Once activated, it can capture the data on the screen for its own use. Ize really needs a hard disk. Even a 1.44 Meg floppy disk drive limits its functions.

Manual   Persoft did a good job writing the manuals. They are well written and easy to read. They also have a lot of illustrations. There are actually three manuals, the tutorial, the reference manual and a manual on printers and hot-links. Ize has on-line, context-sensitive help. It is excellent in places and poor in others. It even occasionally gave unrelated information.

Ize comes with a tutorial to get you started using the program. As part of the tutorial, Persoft included a textbase that contained about 150 indexed business letters. The manual suggests you use these as the bases to write your own letters. I was not that impressed with their quality. Nevertheless, they would get you started if you were drawing a complete blank. Persoft did a good job of indexing the letters so finding an appropriate one is fairly easy. The tutorial itself leads you through the basics of Ize. It does not get into advanced topics like hot-links.

Conclusion   Ize works different than the other indexing programs in this chapter. All of the other programs index all of the words in a document except a few noise words. On the other hand, Ize only indexes those words you tell it to index. With the other programs except WordCruncher, indexing a document is almost no work at all. With Ize, indexing is a great deal of work. The payoff with Ize is that searching for documents is somewhat easier than with the other program if you select the keywords properly. Otherwise, you may not be able to find the document you want without a lot of work.

The clear manual and tutorial will get you started. However, Ize has a steep learning curve. Once you finish these, it will take you a great deal of time before you can perform complex, real-world work with Ize.

Rather than thinking of Ize as a business tool for managing information, you should think of Ize as a research tool. In fact, it is very much a better implementation of WordCruncher.

```
Product:     Ize
Price:       $445
Category:    Commercial
Publisher:   Persoft, Incorporated
Address:     465 Science Drive
             Madison, Wisconsin 53711
Phone:       (608) 273-6000
Memory:      512K   In Stand-Alone Mode
             320K   In Memory Resident Mode
             46K     When Running Another Program
```

Memory Lane

Memory Lane is a commercial memory resident document indexing program that monitors your work to decide what to index.

Installation   Memory Lane comes with an automatic installation program. This program creates a subdirectory called ML, copies the files to the hard disk, and modifies your AUTOEXEC.BAT file. If you have more than one hard disk, you can select the hard disk to install the program to. You have no control over the name of the subdirectory. It will optionally modify your AUTOEXEC-.BAT to include a SET variable required by Memory Lane and the command to load the program.

The installation program also has you select those drives and subdirectories you want Memory Lane to watch.

Indexing   The other programs in this review are able to determine which files have changed without being memory resident. Memory Lane cannot. In order to determine the files needing to be reindexed, Memory Lane must be memory resident when you modify those files. When Memory Lane is resident and you modify a file, Memory Lane adds that file to a list of files requiring reindexing.

Memory Lane uses a file to track the files it should schedule to reindex when you modify them and which ones to ignore. This is the privacy list. With prior versions of Memory Lane, you had to modify this file with an ASCII word processor. That was a time consuming and error prone method. Memory Lane now includes a utility that lets you select subdirectories to include and exclude from a graphical tree. Memory Lane constructs a privacy list automatically from your selections.

Memory Lane remains in memory and tracks those files it needs to reindex. However, it does not reindex them until you tell it to. That is a good approach, it keeps Memory Lane from taking up too much memory at an inappropriate time. To begin indexing, you press Alternate-S then F9. You can index files not in the reindex list by entering a complete path to the files. You might want to do this if you had to remove Memory Lane from memory to get extra RAM and you modified files without it loaded.

Memory Lane tracks any indexed files that you modify and prompts you to reindex them. It automatically removed deleted files from the index. That makes keeping your indexes up to date very easy.

Memory Lane has a clear speed advantage over every other program in this review. It was much faster at indexing documents than the other programs.

Search   Memory Lane allows you to search for a text string up to 15-characters long and there is room for about 10 character strings. While you cannot use any logical grouping in the search, the multiple text strings function like OR statements. You can search all files, the same group you searched last time, or a list of files. The files can be restricted further by the creation date and time and by the application program that created the file.

Memory Lane has two searching modes, indexed and non-indexed. The indexed mode is fast. A search through the indexed files took less than 10-seconds. That is slower than ZyIndex or OCRS but very respectable. You can also search non-indexed files. In this mode, it functions much like GOfer. The same search took 3-minutes and 13-seconds in non-indexed mode.

When it finds a match, the search program will let you browse through the file or print it. It also has numerous options for moving through the file while browsing. If you are inside another application, Memory Lane will list marked portions of text to import into your current document. Memory Lane will handle the format conversion for you.

Manual   The manual is short and not nearly enough to explain how to use the program. The writing is confused and often leaves out critical information. For example, while explaining the installation process, the manual failed to explain what it meant to build a privacy list. The manual did explain this elsewhere in the manual.

Limitations   Memory Lane would only partially run on under DOS 4.x. It would perform non-indexed searches without a problem. It would not select modified files for indexing. Every time I tried to index a file, Memory Lane locked up. Certain functions display a graphical tree of your hard disk. The 200 subdirectories on my hard disk were too many for Memory Lane. It shows a programming error message complete with variable names and then shows a partial tree.

Memory Lane maintains a privacy list to know what files to watch. You can (and should) use Memory Lane to modify this list. If you make modifications to this ASCII file outside of Memory Lane and you make a mistake, Memory Lane may well lock up when you try to load it. This is not necessarily a flaw since Memory Lane does provide adequate tools within the program to modify the privacy list.

Memory Lane is memory resident without adding much additional functionality for being memory resident. The only thing Memory Lane can do that ZyIndex cannot is search for text while running another program. It is unlikely that many users can spare the memory to run Memory Lane.

Conclusion   For the life of me, I do not understand why Memory Lane is memory resident. There is little it will do that ZyIndex will not do better. The only thing that Memory Lane does differently is let you search in the middle of another application. That is not an advantage that is worth the memory required by Memory Lane. Other than that, it is a good light-duty indexer.

Product:	Memory Lane
Price:	$99.00
Category:	Commercial
Publisher:	Group L Corporation
Address:	481 Carlisle Drive
	Herndon, Virginia 22070
Phone:	(703) 471-0030
	(800) 672-5300
Memory:	90K

Office Correspondence Retrieval System (OCRS)

OCRS offers fairly quick indexing and retrieving. OCRS only supports a limited number of word processing formats. You must convert others to ASCII. It will search on synonyms.

Installation   OCRS comes with an automatic installation program. This program will create the subdirectories as required and copy the files to the hard disk. It will also check your CONFIG.SYS file and make sure it has a FILES = 11 or greater statement. It runs from any drive.

Installing OCRS does not automatically install the indexes. It creates those as it needs them. When indexing files, if you enter an index name that does not exist, it creates it automatically. The indexes are much smaller than ZyIndex indexes.

Indexing   Unlike ZyIndex, which runs from a series of batch files, all the OCRS options run from a single program. OCRS has only one index mode, menu driven. You cannot use batch files or any type of script files to automatically index multiple sets of files. The only shortcut is using a single set of wildcards (e.g., *.DOC). However, I was able to construct a SuperKey macro to index successive sets of files.

The indexing screen of OCRS has three lines. On the first line you enter the name of the summary (index) file. If it does not exist, OCRS will create it for you. It can be in the current directory or you can specify a complete path. There is no limit to the number of summary files that can exist in one directory. OCRS maintains the entire database in a single file so the index file can become very large.

The second line specifies the input file(s). This line can specify the full path and can use wildcards. If the file has not changed since the last time you indexed it that file is not reindexed. However, if you included a note, it updates the note entry for each file. You must specify files with names and/or wildcards. OCRS does not have the ability to display files so you can tag them to include in the index.

The third line specifies a summary note of up to 128 characters. This note can include spaces. The note has two usages. You can use it as a reminder of location or content. OCRS indexes the note as well as the file so the note can also be a list of important keywords.

As OCRS indexes files, it displays four pieces of information:

1) The file name.
2) The percentage of the file completed.
3) The number of files it has already processed.
4) The number of files remaining to process.

OCRS handles only a few word processing formats. See Table 13-1. You must convert other formats to ASCII, a time-consuming operation. OCRS cannot automatically sense document format. When using a non-ASCII format, you must attach a special "loader" file. The process is menu driven and not difficult.

Table 13-1. **File Formats Directly Supported by Text Searching Programs.**

	Gofer	Ize	Memory Lane	OCRS	Word Cruncher	Zyindex
ASCII	Y	Y	Y	Y	Y	Y
Bank Street Writer	Y	N	N	N	N	N
Compressed Display Write 2	N	N	Y	Y	N	Y
Compressed Display Write 3	Y	N	Y	Y	N	Y
Compressed Display Write 4	Y	N	Y	Y	N	Y
dBASE II[1]	N	N	Y	N	N	N
dBASE III[2]	Y	N	Y	N	N	N
DIF	N	N	N	Y	N	N
EasyWriter	N	N	N	Y	N	Y
Framework	Y	N	N	N	N	Y
Guru	N	N	Y	N	N	N
IBM DIA/DCA Final Form	N	N	N	N	N	Y
IBM DIA/DCA Revisable Form	N	N	N	N	N	Y
Lotus 1-2-3[3]	Y	Y	N	N	N	N
Microsoft Word[4]	Y	Y	Y	N	N	Y
Multimate	Y	Y	Y	N	N	Y
Multiplan (SYLK)[5]	N	N	N	Y	N	N
Office Writer	Y	Y	N	N	N	Y
Palantir Word Processor	Y	N	N	N	N	Y
Paradox	N	N	Y	N	N	N
PCWrite	Y	Y	Y	N	N	N
Personal Editor	N	N	N	Y	N	N
Peach Text	N	N	N	Y	N	N
Pfs:Professional Editor	Y	Y	N	Y	N	N
Pfs:Write	Y	Y	N	N	N	Y

[1].DBF database files.

[2].DBF database files.

[3]This category will be especially important to those of you using Lotus or Lotus add-in products like 4Word to create letters and memos right in Lotus. Converting to ASCII or DIF is often not a good option. In that format, you store not only your document but numbers and formula. Formula entries like +AB17-CA5 can give document indexing programs problems or at least inflate the size of the index file(s).

[4]Microsoft Word stores the actual text in ASCII format. However, that ASCII text is surrounded by non-ASCII formatting information. This is a common word procession format. Some of these programs, like OCRS, will ignore the formatting information and successfully index the ASCII text. If your word processor creates this type of text (TYPE it to the screen to check) and if your document indexing program claims it requires ASCII text, you may want to try this trick to see if it works.

[5]SYLK is a special Multiplan file format used to exchange information between Multiplan and other programs.

	Gofer	Ize	Memory Lane	OCRS	Word Cruncher	Zyindex
Samna Word	N	N	Y	N	N	N
Smart Word Processor	N	N	N	N	N	Y
Spellbinder	N	N	Y	N	N	Y
Symphony	Y	Y	N	N	N	N
Volkswriter	Y	Y	Y	N	N	N
Volkswriter Deluxe II	Y	Y	N	N	N	Y
Wang Word Processor	N	N	N	N	N	Y
Word Perfect	N	Y	Y	N	Y[1]	Y
Word Plus	N	N	N	N	N	Y
Word Proof	N	N	N	Y	N	N
WordStar	Y	Y	Y	Y	N	Y
WordStar 2000	Y	N	Y	N	N	Y
Writing Assistant	N	N	N	Y	N	N
XyWrite II	Y	Y	Y	N	N	Y

[1]You must purchase Word Perfect from Electronic Text Corporation or pay them extra for help in configuring WordCruncher to work with Word Perfect. It is not explained in the manual.

OCRS worked well when set to ASCII on almost-ASCII files like Microsoft Word. Almost-ASCII files are word processing files that have non-ASCII information at the front of the file and ASCII text after that.

Search   Like the index option, the search option is also menu driven. The OCRS search program does not have all the logical options available with ZyIndex. The only available option is if you enter a search word twice in a row OCRS will count it more in the search.

After searching, OCRS displays a list of files. This list also includes the score, where a higher score indicates a better match; the file creation date, from DOS; the complete path; and part of the summary note.

The search program will let you:

- Browse through the documents that match. To do this, the document must be available to OCRS. If you indexed it from a floppy or you have erased or moved it, OCRS would not have access to the document.
- Print the document, if it is available.
- Change certain parameters. You can change the name of the document (useful if you have renamed it or moved it to a different location), change the summary note, or change the word processor associated with the document.
- Remove the document from future searches. The space is not reclaimed.
- Return to the main menu.
- Get help.

Unlike ZyIndex, OCRS does much more than just match words. OCRS comes with a large synonym file based on the American Heritage Dictionary Data Base, Roget's II, The New Thesaurus. It stores this information in a special file called WP.SYN. If you do not need this feature, you can erase this file and save 163K.

Other   OCRS allows you to delete a file from the index. To do this, you must perform a search that locates the file you want to delete. You then highlight that file name and select the remove option. That removes the file name from the database but does not reclaim the space. OCRS has no way to remove the space. Since the search summary shows the file data and note, OCRS, unlike ZyIndex, gives you some information to base the delete decision on. However, the need to find the file in a search first makes this feature difficult to use and its inability to reclaim the space greatly reduces its value.

OCRS will not automatically remove outdated files and in fact has no way of ever reclaiming the space used to store the index for an outdated file. You can, of course, delete the index and reindex only the current files.

Manual   IBM is not known for their user-friendly manuals. The OCRS manual is an exception. The manual explains the things, like creating a subdirectory, that most computer manuals automatically assume you know.

Limitations   There is no batch mode. To automatically process multiple sets of files, you must use keyboard macros. The file removal program requires you to first successfully search for a criteria to match that file. The file removal program cannot reclaim the space used by the index of a deleted file. It only supports a limited number of word processors.

Conclusion   If OCRS supports your word processor or you deal primarily with ASCII files, OCRS is a good document indexing program. While it is slower than ZyIndex and it has limited search logic, it has several advantages. The index files are much smaller, the speed is respectable, and the menu driven program is easier to use.

```
Product:     Office Correspondence Retrieval System
Price:       $295
Category:    Commercial
Publisher:   International Business Machine
Address:     900 King Street
             Rye Brook, New York 10573
Phone:       (914) 934-4822
Memory:      192K
```

WordCruncher

WordCruncher is not a generic document index program. It is designed to handle large ASCII documents that never/rarely change. Learning to use WordCruncher was more difficult than the other programs. In addition, document preparation time is non-trivial. Businesses or individuals looking for a program to manage the paperwork they produce should look elsewhere. Scholars or universities looking for a tool to aid them in literary research will find WordCruncher to be an acceptable tool.

Installation   WordCruncher comes with an automatic installation program. The program will create the subdirectories you specify for installation. The program will verify that your CONFIG.SYS file has a FILES=20 or greater statement. If not, it will modify your CONFIG.SYS file and reboot the computer. The installation program has nice graphics with overlapping windows to show you what is taking place.

The installation program will not run under DOS 4.x. It reads the disk in a nonstandard way to verify you have inserted the proper disk and DOS 4.x does not support that. As a result, it always tells you that you have inserted the wrong disk. The only way out is to reboot. WordCruncher will not run unless copied with the installation program. Both the indexing and searching programs suffer this same problem and will not run under DOS 4.x.

Indexing   WordCruncher is really two separate programs, IndexETC and ViewETC. Electronic Text Corporation (A company formed by Brigham Young University, the authors of the software) has separated these two programs to a larger extent than any other vendor. You can even purchase them separately. This keeps with the general philosophy of WordCruncher. Indexing is a mundane chore best assigned to a central staff or assistant. Searching and studying the document is the sexy part, best left to the researcher. The two programs even reflect this philosophy. The indexing program has a boring monochrome screen while the search program has a sexy color screen with windows.

The first step toward indexing a document does not involve WordCruncher at all. You must first convert the document to ASCII. Then you edit the document to place markers in the text. WordCruncher uses these markers to subdivide the text into meaningful sections, like chapters and paragraphs. WordCruncher will work without this set, but it is less useful.

WordCruncher does not allow you to use your own document extensions. You must use .BYB for a book file, .BYC for a character file, .BYD for a dictionary file, and so on. Each type of file has specific types of marker codes it expects.

One problem not well addressed by the program is the (quite likely) problem of mis-marked files. The program has no functions designed to verify the logic of the markings and no shortcuts to aid the user in verifying the markings himself.

Once you have a properly marked ASCII file, the next step is to run Index-ETC. The program has blanks for you to queue up to twenty files for processing. It does not allow wildcards. You must enter the full path for each file. Make sure you type the name in correctly. If the file does not exist, you get an error message and WordCruncher removes the entry without your having a chance to edit it. In addition, the only editing key before you press Return is the destructive backspace.

If you have more than twenty files, you must wait till it processes the first twenty before entering additional files. It does not support batch file processing, wildcards, or any other short-cut. WordCruncher has no facility for listing all the available files for you to pick from so you must have the names recorded. Next, it prompts you for the language. You have a choice of English, French, German or Spanish. Finally, it prompts you for an index file.

Once you have entered the file names, the indexing program goes to work. As it processes each file, it produces an estimate of the processing time for that document. It will not estimate the time required for all queued documents. As an indication of the type of documents it expects, the blank for estimated time has room for a time just short of ten hours!

The bottom line is that the indexing program is difficult and time consuming to use. Electronic Text Corporation has recognized that fact and will index files for you for $35 per hour. Since this saves you from purchasing the indexing half of the program, it could be a wise investment if you plan on using WordCruncher to research only a few documents.

Search   The search program only allows you to search one document file at a time. Once you have created an index file individually for each document, the next step is to individually attach those index files to WordCruncher. As with the indexing program, you must enter the drive and subdirectory manually. WordCruncher does let you select the index file from a list. However, this list does not indicate index files you have already selected and does not prevent you from adding the same file twice.

The first step is to select the single index to use. A pop-up window lists all the indexes that are available. A screen at the bottom lists the first 10 lines of the highlighted index. Another window displays summary information on the highlighted index. Figure 13-1 shows this.

The next step is to enter the word to search for. Instead of simply entering a word to search for, the program presents you with an alphabetical list of every word in the document, less a few noise words. You select the word(s) you want from the menu. You can speed-find a word in the menu by typing the first few letters of the word. The program will show each word in context, showing several lines with each word. Figure 13-2 shows this. Once you select a word and press return, WordCruncher will highlight the first few occurrences of that word. Figure 13-3 shows this.

The search program does have an option to link several documents so you can search more than one document at a time. The manual states Word-Cruncher limits this to works by the same author. However, the program does nothing to enforce this requirement. When you link several documents, the search program treats them as one large document.

Once you have found the word(s) you are looking for, you can extract them to a separate file. You can also print or index them separately.

Other   Blind and limited-sight individuals can use WordCruncher. You can customize it to play a separate tune for each section of the program. It also

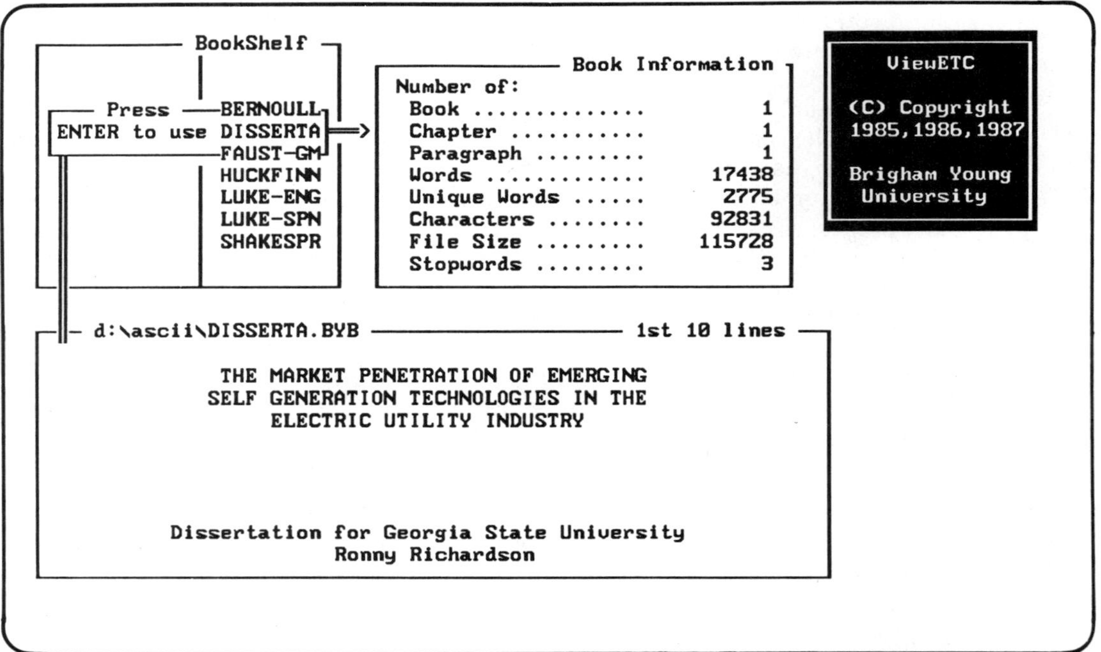

Fig. 13-1. The first step to running the WordCruncher search program is selecting the file to search. WordCruncher displays information on the highlighted file to help you make that decision.

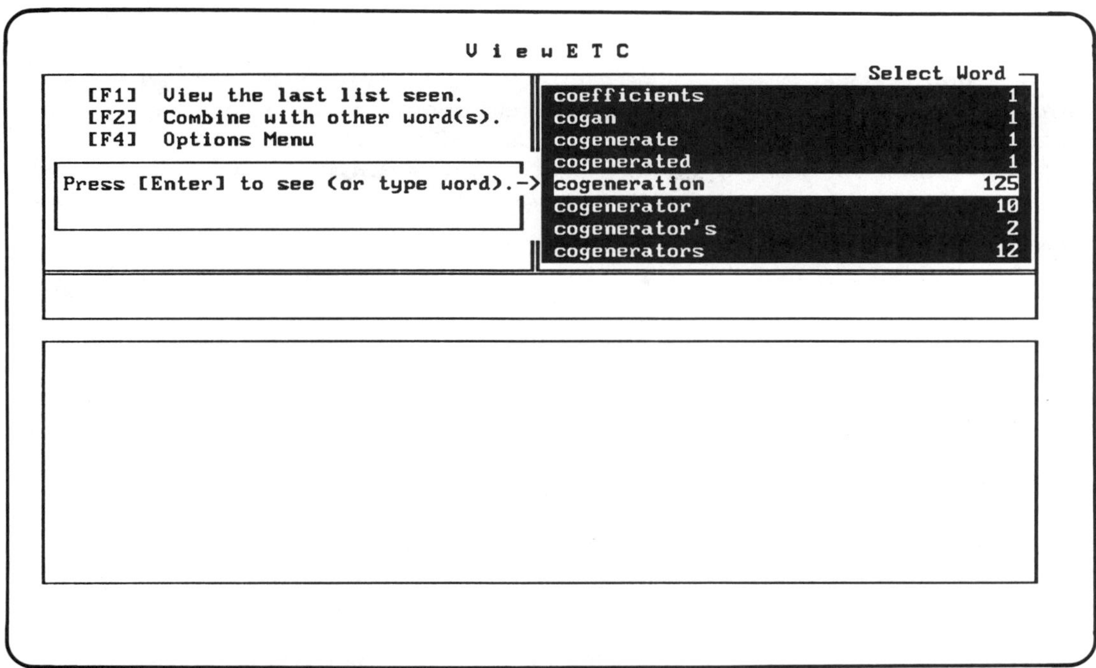

Fig. 13-2. The WordCruncher search program automates selecting words to search on by displaying a list of all the non-noise words in the file.

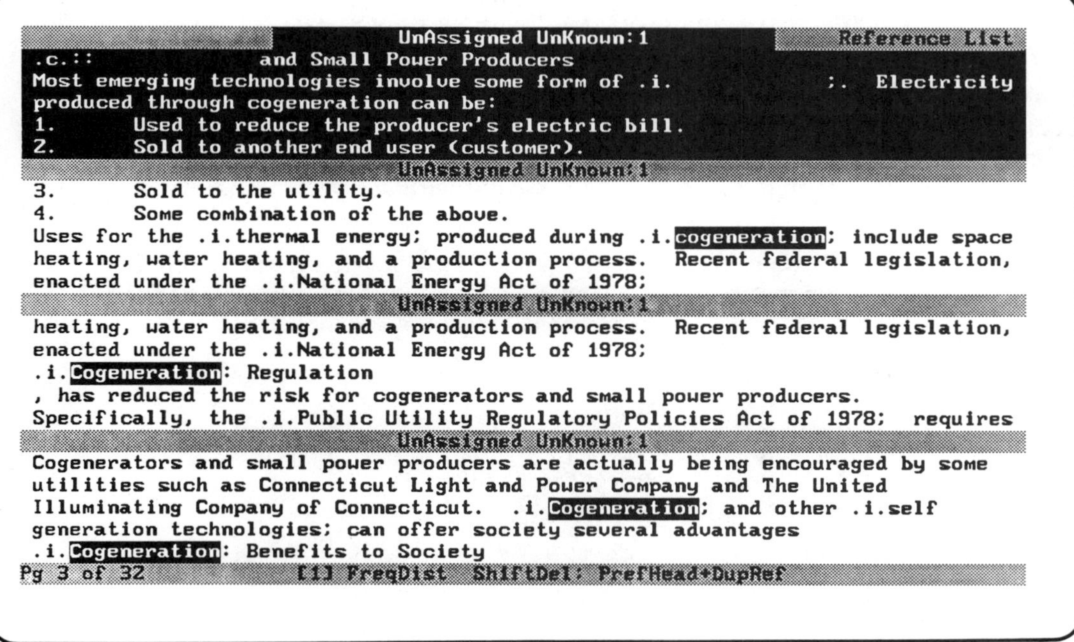

Fig. 13-3. After you select the file and word to search, WordCruncher displays the first few occurrences of that word.

works with different speech synthesizers. (These "read" the contents of the screen and "say" them in English.)

Electronic Text Corporation sells several sets of pre-indexed text sets to go with WordCruncher. You can purchase the Constitution Papers, the complete works of Shakespeare and the Utah State Code. The Constitution Papers include Mayflower Compact, the Monroe Doctrine, the United States' and most state Constitutions and other significant documents.

Manual The help screens are very poor. It is impossible to use Word-Cruncher without the manual, period. The help screens give only limited information and often you cannot even understand the help screens without the aid of the manual. With the other programs in this review, I was able to scan the manual once and productively use the software. Not so with WordCruncher. It took me carefully reading the manual several times to become productive. If you select WordCruncher, plan on spending a good deal of time getting up to speed.

This would be bad enough, but it gets worse. The manual is extremely poor. It is difficult to read, confusing, and has many screen illustrations no larger than a penny. In addition, the manual uses a large number of different typefaces in the manual. The user is supposed to remember which typeface stands for a shifted or alternated key and respond accordingly.

The search program allows you to reassign keys. The manual takes this into account and rarely refers to the default keystrokes to perform an operation. Instead, keystroke functions are referred to by name, like Print.

In addition to English, WordCruncher will work with French, German, and Spanish. It will work with the Duke University Language Toolkit to display the special characters these languages require, provided you have an EGA display.

Limitations WordCruncher is not DOS 4.x compatible. It has an extremely poor manual and the program itself has poor help screens. This is much worse because of the cumbersome user interface. However, the biggest limitation of all is the requirement that files be in ASCII format with special internal markings.

Conclusion WordCruncher is a somewhat useful tool for literary research. It is a very poor tool for managing the flow of documents for an individual or business.

```
Product:     WordCruncher
Price:       $299
Category:    Commercial
Publisher:   Electronic Text Corporation
Address:     778 South 400 East
             Orem, Utah 84058
Phone:       (801) 226-0616
Memory:      512K
```

ZyIndex

(*ZyIndex* comes in three versions, Personal, Professional, and Plus. My review is based on the Plus version which is the most powerful and the most expensive.)

ZyIndex is the best known of all the indexing programs. It offers rapid indexing and retrieving. Its nicest feature is it will index documents using their native format. You do not have to convert the documents to ASCII format before indexing them. ZyIndex is a no-frills package. It works, and does several things well. However, it often leaves you with the feeling that a little more is needed.

Installation   ZyIndex comes with an automatic installation program. When it prompts you for a disk, it checks to make sure you have given it the correct disk. If not, it asks you again for the disk.

While installing the program, it prompts you for the free memory the program will have available. That is the amount of memory after loading COM-MAND.COM and all your memory resident programs. The program suggests using 384K if you are not sure.

The Plus and Professional versions of ZyIndex allow you to install more than one set of indexes. When you do this, it stores the main program in one location and stores multiple sets of the index files in separate subdirectories. This feature is very useful, but very poorly explained in the manual. One of the things ZyIndex does very poorly is remove the information from its database on files that no longer exist. One way around this problem is to index all the files that will be rapidly outdated using one special index set. Instead of periodically "cleaning up" this list, you can erase it and reindex the few remaining files. You index more stable files using a different index set.

When you install ZyIndex, it creates a series of batch files with the default disk drive embedded. You use these batch files to control ZyIndex. They become especially important when you have more than one index set installed.

Indexing   ZyIndex has three modes of indexing, menu driven, auto-indexing and command line (or batch file) driven. Using the menu, you start with the ZYI command. ZyIndex first prompts you for the path to the files to index. Then it prompts you for the name for the disk. The path can contain wild-cards, so C:\WORD\REVIEWS*.DOC is a valid path. The name of the disk must not contain any spaces and ZyIndex limits it to 30-characters. Normally, you would only give a disk a name when using floppy diskettes or a removable hard disk.

After entering this information, ZyIndex gives you a list of all the files in the path you specified. You move the cursor around marking files for ZyIndex to index. Figure 13-4 shows this. After you have marked all the files, ZyIndex indexes them. One nice feature of ZyIndex is that it will automatically skip files that have not changed since the last time you indexed them. It then returns you to the menu to make more selections or to exit the program.

Another very nice feature is that ZyIndex can index word processing files using their native format. You do not have to convert them to an ASCII file

```
F1:Select new files     F2:Begin Indexing     F3:Change WP     F9:Help     F10:Exit

Select files to index: move cursor to filenames and press <enter>
RELEASE.ALL *       COUNTWOR.BAT        DOWN.BAT            UP.BAT
APPEND01.CMP        APPEND02.CMP        APPEND03.CMP        APPEND05.CMP
APPEND06.CMP        BOOKLABE.CMP        BOX.CMP            CHAPTE02.CMP
CHAPTE03.CMP        CHAPTE04.CMP        CHAPTE05.CMP        CHAPTE06.CMP
CHAPTE08.CMP        CHAPTE09.CMP        CHAPTE10.CMP        CHAPTE11.CMP
CHAPTE12.CMP        CHAPTE13.CMP        CHAPTE14.CMP        CHAPTE15.CMP
CHAPTE17.CMP        CHAPTE18.CMP        CHAPTE19.CMP        CHAPTE20.CMP
CHAPTE22.CMP        CHAPTE23.CMP        CHAPTE24.CMP        CHAPTE25.CMP
CHAPTE27.CMP        INTRO.CMP           OLDLABEL.CMP        TABLES.CMP
APPEND01.DOC        APPEND02.DOC        APPEND03.DOC        APPEND04.DOC
APPEND05.DOC        APPEND06.DOC        BOOKLABE.DOC        BOX.DOC
CHAPTE01.DOC        CHAPTE02.DOC        CHAPTE03.DOC        CHAPTE04.DOC
CHAPTE05.DOC        CHAPTE06.DOC        CHAPTE07.DOC        CHAPTE08.DOC
CHAPTE09.DOC        CHAPTE10.DOC        CHAPTE11.DOC        CHAPTE12.DOC
CHAPTE13.DOC        CHAPTE14.DOC        CHAPTE15.DOC        CHAPTE17.DOC
CHAPTE18.DOC        CHAPTE19.DOC        CHAPTE20.DOC        CHAPTE22.DOC

* Indicates file has not been changed since it was last indexed


Current Word Processor Is: Microsoft Word
```

Fig. 13-4. In menu mode, you select files to index with ZyIndex by moving the cursor through a file list and tagging files to index.

before indexing them. The only thing it will not do is automatically sense the word processor format and adjust itself. You have to tell it which format to use. Automatically sensing the file format is not as difficult to do as it sounds. Several packages do that now, most notably RightWriter. Table 13-1 shows the word processing formats supported by ZyIndex and other indexing programs. Table 13-2 compares the indexing programs on several other criteria. Table 13-3 compares the performance of these programs.

Using the menu has two major limitations. First, you can only select 64-files at any one time to index. If you have more than 64, you must process the first 64 and then the rest. The second limitation is that you can only process documents created with a common word processor at any one time. If you have two document formats, you must process the first then switch word processors to process the remainder.

Using the command line or auto-indexing method overcomes both these limitations, but adds their own complication. To index from the command line, you enter a command like: ZYI A:\ *.PRG/01 OFFICE_DISK_1

The ZYI runs the program. The A:\ *.PRG specifies all the files to be processed. There is no arbitrary limit on the number that it can process. The /01 specifies the word processor, in this case ASCII. It still takes one command per word processing format. The OFFICE_DISK_1 is the optional name of the disk. I use underscores in place of the spaces that ZyIndex does not allow.

Table 13-2. **Other Features of Text Searching Programs.**

	Gofer	Ize	Memory Lane	OCRS	Word Cruncher	Zyindex
Automatic Removal of Deleted Document[1]	NA	Y	N	N	N[2]	N
Automatic Sensing of Document Format[3]	Y	N	N	N	N/A	N
Browse Hits[4]	Y	Y	Y	Y	N/A[5]	Y
Document Summary Sheet[6]	N	Y	N	N	N	N
Hit Score[7]	N	Y	N	Y	N	N
Manual Removal of Deleted Document[8]	NA	Y	N	Y	Y	Y
Matches Highlighted[9]	N	N	Y	N	Y	Y
Multiple Indexes[10]	NA	Y	N	Y	Y	Y
Multiple Indexes Created on Fly[11]	NA	Y	N	Y	Y	Y

[1]When you index on C:\WORD\MEMO*.DOC will the program sense which files are missing and automatically remove them from the index.

[2]Since each document is stored in a separate file, removing the document and reclaiming the space is as easy as erasing the index files.

[3]Can the indexing program sense that a document was created with WordStar, for example, and automatically switch into WordStar format without the operator telling the program to expect WordStar format.

[4]Does the indexing program allow you to browse through all the documents it finds that match a search. (Assuming those documents are available to the program.)

[5]WordCruncher allows you to browse any document but searching is limited to a single document.

[6]Does the program have the facilities to use a document summary sheet for each document to uniquely identify that document.

[7]Does the index program assign a score to documents that match a search criteria. This allows you to judge how well a document matches your criteria.

[8]Can you manually remove documents from the index.

[9]When browsing through the documents on the hit-list, does the indexing program highlight portions where the document matches the search criteria.

[10]Can the program maintain multiple indexes. The alternative is storing all the information in a single index.

[11]Does the program let you create a new index without running an installation program.

	Gofer	Ize	Memory Lane	OCRS	Word Cruncher	Zyindex
Must Documents be Indexed in Advance[1]	N	Y	Y	Y	Y	Y
Notes[2]	NA	Y/N[3]	N	Y	N	Y
Note Length (Characters)	NA	32K	N/A	128	N/A	30[4]
Note Indexed[5]	NA	Y	N/A	Y	N/A	N
Search on Meaning of Word[6]	N	N	N	N	N	N[7]
Wildcard Indexing[8]	NA	N	Y[9]	Y	N	Y

[1]Can the search program search a document without first indexing that document.

[2]Does the program allow you to attach a note to documents being indexed.

[3]You can add notes to hot-linked files but not to other files.

Table 13-2. Continued

[4]No spaces.

[5]Does the program index the summary note along with the document. If so, this allows you to place keywords that do not appear in the document in the summary note.

[6]Will a search on the word "bug" find a file containing a list of insects. This is useful when you do not remember the exact wording of the file but do remember the subject.

[7]An optional package called ZyFeatures allows you to "almost" search on the meaning of terms. See the text for additional information on ZyFeatures.

[8]Can you summarize all documents by summarizing *.DOC.

[9]See text for more information.

You can make indexing even simpler using batch files, however, batch files are very poorly explained in the manual. To complicate matters even further, ZyIndex runs from the batch file ZYI.BAT. If you write a batch file under DOS 3.2 or earlier to call ZYI.BAT, it never passes control back to the calling batch file. The result is that only the first line of your original batch file ever runs. The solution is to include all the syntax required in your batch file and never call ZYI.BAT. The manual does not explain this. Figure 13-5 shows a sample batch file.

Auto-indexing consists of a ZyIndex list of files to include in the index and files to exclude. With the proper commands, ZyIndex reads and processes this list automatically. Figure 13-6 shows a sample auto-index list. Maintaining this list is difficult. ZyIndex objects anytime files in the exclude_files list do not exist. Not only does it object, it aborts processing the list. That means you have to edit the list every time you delete a file that you specifically excluded from the indexing.

Table 13-3. Indexing Results.

Package	Time	Index Size
Ize	16:07[1]	NA[2]
Memory Lane	3:24[3]	230K
OCRS	24:08	170K
WordCruncher	32:14[4]	1,747K
ZyIndex Plus	14:31	333K

All tests were performed on a 16 MHz IBM Model 70

---

[1]Some of the files were very large. These files were accessed by hot-links. However, Ize only searches the first 32K of large files for keywords. Therefore this index is incomplete.

[2]These were accessed in Ize using hot-links. As a result, Ize does not store a complete copy of the text or even a complete copy of the index.

[3]Memory Lane has two mutually exclusive indexing modes, fast and slow. Fast indexes much faster but the resulting indexes take more room. The slow mode takes longer to index and search, but the resulting index files take up less than half the space of the fast mode. I used the fast mode for all testing. You would only use the slow mode if your hard disk space was tight.

[4]Does not include the time required to convert the documents to WordCruncher format.

```
echo off
REM First make sure we are in the correct subdirectory
cd\zyindex
REM I number my disks as DISCARD #1, DISCARD #2, and so on
REM The next line makes sure I enter the number of the disk.
REM If I forget, it skips the indexing and displays an error message.
if  /%1==/  goto end
if exist a:*.doc ZYINDEX C:\ZYINDEX\ A:\*.DOC/03 OFFICE_DISCARD_DISK_%1
REM if exist a:*.doc skips over Microsoft Word section if there are no Word files
REM ZYINDEX calls the main program without the ZYI.BAT batch file.
REM C:\ZYINDEX\ is the path to the index files and must be the first entry
REM A:\*.DOC is the path to the files and must be the second entry
REM /03 selects Microsoft Word format and is optional
REM OFFICE_DISCARD_DISK_%1 is the optional disk name. %1 is replaced by the
REM number I enter
REM This is repeated for other types of files and word processing formats
if exist a:*.txt ZYINDEX C:\ZYINDEX\ A:\*.TXT/15 OFFICE_DISCARD_DISK_%1
if exist a:*.prg ZYINDEX C:\ZYINDEX\ A:\*.PRG/01 OFFICE_DISCARD_DISK_%1
if exist a:*.tlb ZYINDEX C:\ZYINDEX\ A:\*.TLB/01 OFFICE_DISCARD_DISK_%1
if exist a:*.wrk ZYINDEX C:\ZYINDEX\ A:\*.WRK/01 OFFICE_DISCARD_DISK_%1
REM Now skip over error messages since no errors
goto done
:end
cls
echo add disk number
echo add disk number
echo add disk number
echo add disk number
echo add disk number
echo add disk number
echo add disk number
echo add disk number
echo add disk number
pause
:done
```

Fig. 13-5. Batch file used to run ZyIndex.

```
.include_files
c:\benchmar\native\*.asc -c "ASCII files"    -w1
c:\benchmar\native\*.doc -c "Word files"      -w3
c:\benchmar\native\*.txt -c "Wordstar files" -w15

.exclude_files
c:\benchmar\native\chapt*.doc

.exclude_type
*.exe
*.com
*.bat
```

Fig. 13-6. Auto Index file used to run ZyIndex.

ZyIndex allows you to control "noise words." These are words like "and." Authors use them so much that including them in the database just wastes space. With ZyIndex, you can edit the noise word list and add or delete words to fit your applications. For example, in my writings about computers, "RAM" and "installation" are likely candidates as noise words.

Search   The search program lets you find information from indexed files. The search program is menu driven. You begin by entering the search criteria. ZyIndex allows you to enter this criteria using very powerful logic. You can use the logical operators AND, OR, NOT, and W/N (with in). Figure 13-7 shows this.

Entering Ronny AND Richardson would require both words to be in the file. Entering Ronny OR Richardson would match any file containing either of these words. Entering NOT (Ronny AND Richardson) would find those files that contained neither word. And entering Ronny W/N 10 Richardson would find the files where Richardson started within 10-characters of Ronny. You can group complex searches using parentheses as I did above. You can also use the DOS wildcards ? and *. "NOT?" is equal to "NOTE" and "NOT*" is equal to "NOTE" and "NOTICE". Finally, the search program can also use the DOS file name, file date, and file time to narrow the search. The search program is extremely flexible in allowing you to narrowly specify your search criteria.

After specifying the search criteria, ZyIndex computes a "hit list" that lists all the files that meet your criteria. If the file is still on the hard disk, you can easily view the files, with the matches to the criteria highlighted. Figure 13-8 shows this. If the file is on a floppy, ZyIndex does not tell you which floppy to insert. You must insert any floppy. When it fails to find the file, then it gives you the name of the floppy to insert.

The only real drawback to the search program is it only matches words. One of my test files contained a long list of insects. The search program did not match this file when searching for "bug". However, ZyFeatures corrects this.

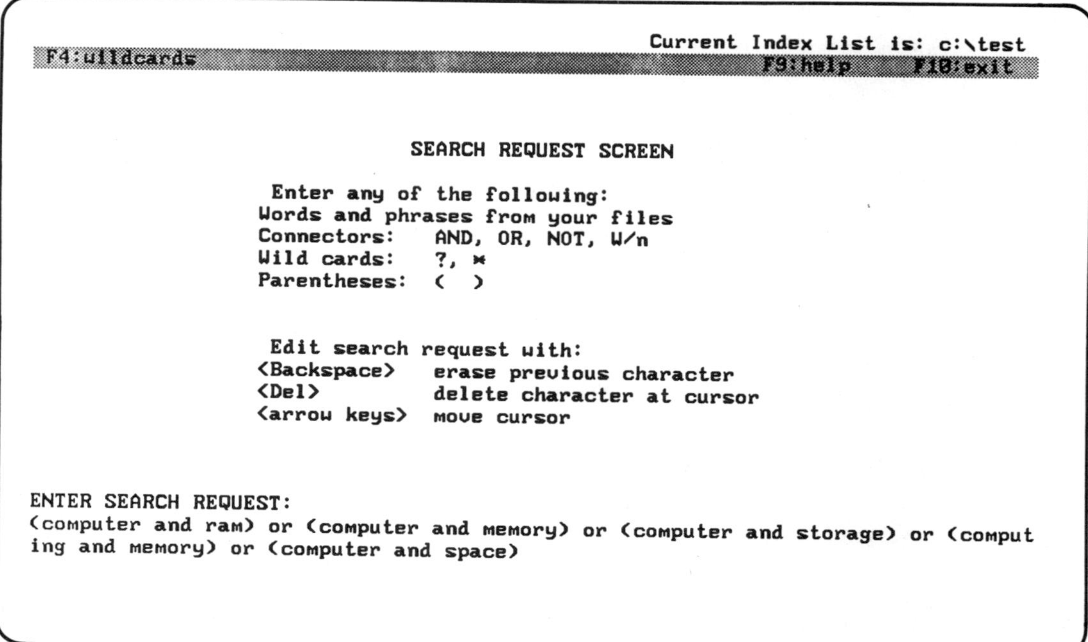

Fig. 13-7. ZyIndex allows you to enter complex search requests using complex logic.

```
F3:Previous file  F4:Next file  F5:Find  F6:Save  F7:Mark  F8:Unmark  F10:Exit
                                                    Page  1, Line    1
                              Displaying File: c:\benchmark\native\COMPAQS.DOC
Comment (F2 to edit): Compaq Portable III and DeskPro 286 12 MHz and De

Compaq Portable III and
DeskPro 286 12 MHz and DeskPro 386 16 MHz
Reviewed by Ronny Richardson
Introduction
Of all the clone makers, Compaq is in a very unique position.  Like IBM, Compaq
has positioned its computers as quality machines.  Like IBM, Compaq does not
compete on price.  In fact, the price of Compaq computers is second only to IBM.
 Compaq has such a good reputation in the market that it was able to bring out
an 80386 machine before IBM.  The DeskPro 386 was such a hit that other
companies soon began producing "Compaq clones."  By the time IBM announced a
80386 machine, the market was flooded with them.
But the DeskPro 386 is only one computer in the Compaq line.  This article will
take a look at the three most powerful members of the Compaq line; the
Portable III a 12 MHz 80286 portable machine, the DeskPro 286, a 12 MHz 80286
desktop machine, and of course the DeskPro 386, a 16 MHz 80386 desktop machine.


(computer and ram) or (computer and memory) or (computer and storage) or (comput
ing and memory) or (computer and space)
  33   Files Retrieved
```

Fig. 13-8. If the file is still on your hard disk, ZyIndex can display the file for you and highlight the words that match the search.

Other   ZyIndex (Plus and Professional) also comes with a utility program. This program is far weaker than the search and index programs. It performs the following functions:

1) List all indexed files.
2) Remove an indexed file, discussed below.
3) Change configuration. This is a fairly new utility to ZyIndex and one that was badly needed. In older versions of ZyIndex, changing most of the options you set when you install the program required installing the program again and reindexing all your files. This option makes most of those same changes easy. It lets you:

   a) Switch between full-featured and file-only indexing. In full-feature indexing, ZyIndex stores the exact location of each word so you can perform position sensitive searches. In file-only mode, ZyIndex only stores the words that occur in each file.
   b) Change the group for the index in the network version.
   c) Change the default word processor.
   d) Change the display mode. ZyIndex has three modes, normal—which shows 64 files, path—which shows 14 files and the complete path and comment—which shows 14 files and their commands.
   e) The memory allocated to the dictionary. You can set this 16K and 64K. It controls how may files you can index.

f) Change the special characters, like wildcards, to alternative characters so they will not interfere with searches you need to make on characters in a document.

g) The color used for the display and other minor operational parameters.

4) Move the index to another location.

5) Move text to another location. You would use this if you were transferring a document from your hard disk to an archive floppy. By updating the location, you would not have to reindex the file.

6) Change the name of a disk.

7) Install a new index.

8) Delete an existing index.

To see why you would want to remove an indexed file, consider a manager using Microsoft Word to write business memos in the C: \ WORD \ MEMO subdirectory. Once a month the manager indexes all the *.DOC files in this subdirectory. Once every six-months he discards memos that are over six-months old. The next time this manager indexes all the *.DOC files, ZyIndex is not able to figure out that some of the files in its database no longer exist. They remain in the database taking up space and showing up as "false finds" for every search. The only way to remove them is with the utility program.

Using it, it gives you a list of all the file names that you have indexed and no other information. You must decide which files to delete without being able to see the creation date or time and without being able to see the disk name. The file name is the only information you have to make your decision.

Deleting the name does not remove the file from the database. All it does is mark it as an undesired file. At this point it still takes up space, but it will no longer show up on a search.

To remove the information completely, you must run another program, the clean-up program. The clean-up program is the poorest program in the package. I used it on a large (over 2M) set of index files on an 8088 machine. The manual does not warn that clean-up requires disk space almost equal to the size of the existing set of index files. What the program does is copy the existing files to new files in another directory. During the copy, it deletes information on files you have removed using the utility program. When it finishes, it copies these new files back on top of the existing files.

As I explained above, you can avoid most of the problems associated with the clean-up program. You do this by keeping multiple index sets and simply deleting a set and reindexing the remaining files in place of running clean-up. This problem is a very good reason to avoid the Personal version unless your needs are very simple. The Personal version does not allow multiple indexes. At any time, you can upgrade to a higher version by paying the price difference and a $50 handling fee, a nice touch.

Manual   The manual is sometimes more technical than necessary. In order to use some of the more advanced features like auto-indexing, you are going to have to experiment because the manual does not explain this clearly.

Table 13-4. **Differences Between Different Versions of ZyIndex.**

Feature	Plus	Professional	Personal
Maximum Number of Files	15,000	5,000	325
Total Files per Hard Disk	Unlimited	Unlimited	325
Multiple Indexes	Yes	Yes	No
Number of Unique Words	500,000	125,000	125,000

Limitations   The file removal program does not give you the file dates, times, or disk name to help you make your decision. The clean-up program takes a LONG time to run. It limits disk names to 30-characters with no spaces. This is not nearly enough room to name disks. Handling of indexed files on floppies is cumbersome.

Conclusion   ZyIndex does a good job of indexing and locating files. It offers some very powerful commands for entering the search criteria. The programs you use to maintain the index set are simply not in the same league as the indexing and searching programs.

ZyIndex comes in three versions, Personal, Professional and Plus. Each higher version handles more files and more indexed words. Table 13-4 shows the major differences. In addition, the Plus version will work on a network.

```
Product:     ZyIndex
Price:       $95 Personal
             $295 Professional
             $695 Plus
             $2,595 Network Server
Category:    Commercial
Publisher:   ZyLab Corporation
Address:     3105-T North Frontage Road
             Arlington Heights, Illinois 60004
Phone:       (312) 632-1100
Notes:       ZyIndex will use all available memory
             only if configured for that amount of
             memory.
Memory:      448K
```

ZyFeatures

ZyFeatures is an add-in product for ZyIndex. It adds free-form database capabilities, limited macros, and a limited thesaurus to ZyIndex.

Installation   ZyFeatures comes with an automatic installation program that runs from any drive.

Free-Form Database   The free-form database option allows you to limit a search for a word or phrase to a restricted area of a document. For example, if your document contained data in the following arrangement:

First: Ronny
Last: Richardson

Area: PC
Magazine: Uptime Magazine Business Edition

you could tell ZyIndex that these were fields and then use ZyIndex to search for all the Uptime Magazine Business Edition authors who write about PC's. You would define the field "Magazine" as "Magazine to Area." Every occurrence of magazine in the document would begin the magazine field. That field would continue until the end of the file or the occurrence of the word area. It would define the field "Area" as "Area to First." For the above search, you would search on "(in magazine (Uptime) AND in area (PC or IBM or MS-DOS))."

While I do not see a lot of uses for this in general document indexing, I can see a lot of specialized uses for it. When paired with a word processor, you have most of the functions of a flat-file manager database. You print from your word processor and search from ZyIndex. This would be especially useful if your major use of a database was as an input for mail-merge printing.

Macros   The macro feature of ZyFeatures allows you to store a complex search criteria under a short name and easily recall it for later use. For example, "CS: (in magazine (Computer Shopper) AND in area (PC or IBM or MS-DOS))" would store the above, complex search criteria under the name CS. To use it again, just enter "@CS." This is very useful if-and-only-if you often search on the same criteria.

Thesaurus   The thesaurus is not a full-fledged, integrated thesaurus like the one in OCRS discussed below. With OCRS, you enter a word in the search criteria and OCRS automatically searches on its alternative meanings. With ZyFeatures, you enter the word and press F3. ZyFeatures gives you a list of alternative words to select from. You then select the additional word(s) to use in the search. This is less useful than the OCRS thesaurus. It does have one advantage that other thesauri would do well to adopt. The user can add words and alternate words to a special file and the thesaurus will use those words first.

Conclusion   ZyFeatures is a useful addition to ZyIndex. Note that it does not work with the Personal version.

```
Product:      ZyFeatures
Price:        $95.00
Category:     Commercial
Publisher:    ZyLab Corporation
Address:      3105-T North Frontage Road
              Arlington Heights, Illinois 60004
Phone:        (312) 632-1100
Memory:       448K
```

SEARCH ONLY PROGRAMS

All of the above packages have one thing in common, they require you to index documents before searching for text in those documents. In fact, you do not search the actual documents. Rather, you search through the indexes. This has the distinct advantage that you can search for text in documents not physically present on the disk. After indexing, you can archive the disks. You can even index files belonging to someone else.

The following packages do not require you to index the documents. Rather, they search the actual documents. The main advantages of this method is you do not have to spend a lot of time indexing documents. In addition, you waste a lot of disk space storing the indexes with the indexing programs. As you have seen above, indexing takes a long time. The main drawback is you cannot search for files that do not physically exist on the hard disk at the time of the search.

GOfer

GOfer is a text search program that can operate in either memory resident or stand-alone mode. For a text searching program, being memory resident has little advantage over being non-memory resident. It has the unique advantage among indexing programs of being able to search dBASE and Lotus 1-2-3 files.

Installation　　The cover of GOfer is illustrated with a very cute drawing of a GOfer. The manual refers to installation as "training your GOfer." This cuteness is carried on throughout the manual. I found it to be a refreshing change from stale computer manuals. It would quickly become obnoxious if you had to continually refer to the manual, but GOfer requires very few glances at the manual.

To "train" GOfer, the manual tells you to make sure the installation "disk is in the logged drive." At that point you run the installation program, which only configures GOfer for your screen display and types of programs to search. It does not transfer the files to the hard disk, it does not even tell you how to add the commands to start GOfer from your AUTOEXEC.BAT file. In an effort to be cute and short, the manual omits important information.

Search　　Pressing the GOfer hot-key brings up the main menu. Alt-G is the default but you can change it. From here, you enter the test to search for including AND, OR, and NEARBY. You also enter the drive, directory(s), and files to search and the VIEW. The view controls if you see the matches on screen or if GOfer sends them to a disk file, a printer, or to your current work.

Once you enter the search criteria and the files and directories to search, GOfer scours your hard disk looking for the text. Every time it finds a match, it displays the file name, the matching text and 16 lines of the text around the match. You can then have GOfer search for the next match or you can work with this match. GOfer can print the text, send it to a DOS file or bring it into your current application if you are running GOfer in memory resident mode. It took GOfer 3 minutes and 45 seconds to perform a test search through the test database. This is about the same as Memory Lane in non-indexed mode.

GOfer has the unique advantage of working with several non-word processing programs, including dBASE and Lotus 1-2-3, a feature not offered by most other programs. In addition, it works with any program supporting ASCII or EBCDIC.

GOfer can run as either a memory resident or stand-alone program. As a memory resident program, it requires between 94K and 167K. The exact memory requirements depend on how you configure GOfer. The more memory you give it, the faster it runs.

Other   GOfer has a browse mode that lets you look through documents created by any of its supported programs, including Lotus and dBASE. If it's running as a memory resident program, you can do this while in another application.

GOfer can compress (and decompress) files by about 50% to reduce storage requirements. There are many programs that do a better job of compressing files but GOfer can continue to search files it compresses.

Manual   Sections of the manual blend humor (e.g., training your GOfer) and necessary information well. This makes reading the manual unusually easy. Unfortunately, the manual leaves out necessary information, like using GOfer with a hard disk. These omissions mean you need some experience to get GOfer up and running.

Limitations   GOfer's main limitation is a generic limitation shared by all search-only programs. As explained above, you have to have continuous access to your files to find information in them.

GOfer does not allow you to define a set of files to search unless you can do it in a single file specification. For example, I might want to search all the *.DOC files in my \BOOK1, \BOOK2 and \BOOK3 subdirectories. With GOfer, I would either have to perform three different subdirectories or search all *.DOC files.

Conclusion   For me, GOfer does not do enough to be worth 79K of my already crowded RAM so I would not run it in memory resident mode. However, in stand-alone mode GOfer is an excellent search-only program. If you need to search either dBASE or Lotus files, then GOfer is your only choice.

<pre>
Product: GOfer
Price: $79.95
Category: Commercial
Publisher: Microlytics, Incorporated
Address: One Tobey Village Office Park
              Pittsford, New York 14534
Phone: (800) 828-6293
              (716) 248-9150 in New York
Memory: 256K   Stand-Alone
              79K   Memory Resident
</pre>

Hunter

Hunter is a shareware text searching program. The optional diskette set has a copy of Hunter.

Installation Hunter comes with an installation program. However, this batch file simply copies the two program files to the C-drive. If you want the files in a subdirectory, you will have to do that yourself.

Search Hunter can perform two types of searches, file name and file content. To find a file name, you tell it as much of the name as you know and fill out the rest with DOS wildcards. Hunter searches the disk drive and reports all the files that match the input specification.

Hunter can also search files for text and report all the files containing that text. It will prompt you for the file specification of the files to search. You can leave that blank to have Hunter search all files.

Limitations Hunter only searches for ASCII text and a single text string at that. You cannot do complex logical searches and it will not search non-ASCII text, such as WordStar. Many word processors store text in ASCII but surround it with non-ASCII characters. Hunter works with some of this type of file. Hunter is not compatible with DOS 4.x. It will try to search and abort without an error message after trying to access the first file.

Manual The manual is very brief. However, Hunter is also very easy to use so the manual gives you all the information you need.

Conclusion If you need a simple program to search ASCII files for a single text string, Hunter will do the job very fast and easy. The optional diskette set has a copy of Hunter.

<table>
<tr><td>Product:</td><td>Hunter</td></tr>
<tr><td>Price:</td><td>$25</td></tr>
<tr><td>Category:</td><td>Shareware</td></tr>
<tr><td>Publisher:</td><td>Thinking Software, Incorporated</td></tr>
<tr><td>Address:</td><td>46-16 Sixth Fifth Place
Woodside, New York 11377</td></tr>
<tr><td>Phone:</td><td>Not Available</td></tr>
<tr><td>Notes:</td><td>The optional diskette set includes a copy of this program.</td></tr>
<tr><td>Memory:</td><td>256K</td></tr>
</table>

Norton Utilities

The biggest use in most offices for a document indexing program is to find documents based on a few words you can remember from the document. For that you may not need a special program. The Norton Utilities include a program called TEXTFIND. This program will search the files you specify for the text you specify without the need to index the files in advance. It is very fast and extremely easy to use.

If your word processor does not create ASCII files, TEXTFIND may not work. However, many word processors store your text in ASCII but surround it with non-ASCII characters. TEXTFIND works with some of this type of program. Many other disk utility sets include a program similar to TEXTFIND. Check your set before you purchase a special ASCII search program.

```
Product:     Norton Utilities
Price:       $100
Category:    Commercial
Publisher:   Peter Norton Computing, Incorporated
Address:     2210 Wilshire Boulevard
             Santa Monica, California 90403
Phone:       (213) 453-2361
Notes:       The Norton Utilities consists of a number
             of separate utilities each with its own
             memory requirements. With 256K, you
             will be able to run any of the utilities
Memory:      256K
```

Text/File Handling Utilities

The *Text/File Handling Utilities* are a set of four shareware utilities. The main utility searches for ASCII strings in text. A second utility will replace one ASCII string with another. The third utility displays ASCII files on the screen. A final program replaces the DOS DEL command.

Installation   There is no installation program and the manual does not explain how to install the software. All you need to do is have the program files in a directory in your PATH statement. Otherwise, you must change to the program subdirectory before running the software.

Searching   Text/File Handling Utilities is a command-line driven program. In its simplest form, you enter: HUNTSTR "string" FILES

. . . where *string* is the ASCII characters you want to find and FILES are the files you want the program to search. Figure 13-9 shows sample output from the program. Text/File Handling Utilities is fast. A search through the test set of files took 1-minute and 7-seconds. That is much faster than GOfer or Memory Lane in non-indexed mode.

There are several switches you can use with Text/File Handling Utilities to improve its operation. The major ones are:

/C   This forces the search to be case sensitive.

/W   This tells Text/File Handling Utilities how many of the lines above and below the matching line to display on the screen. The default is to show three above, three below and the matching line. For the figure above, I set it to zero before and after. The maximum is ten before and ten after.

/M   This lets you enter multiple phrases. The default is an "OR" search where a line matches if it contains any of the multiple phrases. You can

```
HUNTSTR - Hunt for Text Strings V1.0
Copyright (C) 1988 RT Computer Consultants

***** file name = c:\benchmark\ascii\CERTIFIC.ASC
***** file name = c:\benchmark\ascii\COMPAQS.ASC
***** file name = c:\benchmark\ascii\COMPILE1.ASC
-----------------------------------------
[490] demonstration compiler identical to the full compiler except
-----------------------------------------
[494] This demo compiler is also useful to the programmer to
-----------------------------------------
[496] demo compiler is one of the major advantages of Quicksilver
-----------------------------------------
[590] Quicksilver was the only compiler that had this problem.
-----------------------------------------
[824] handle that yourself.  Clipper has no demo compiler so you
-----------------------------------------
[1000] Neither compiler uses meta commands.  These are instructions
-----------------------------------------
[1001] for the compiler to execute at compile time.  A common
-----------------------------------------
[1008] would enter INCLUDE<filename> in the code.  The compiler
-----------------------------------------
[1010] Meta commands could also be used to instruct the compiler to
-----------------------------------------
[1077] Quicksilver demo compiler $75 ($25 applies to full
-----------------------------------------
number of occurrences: 10
***** file name = c:\benchmark\ascii\COMPILER.ASC
-----------------------------------------
[622] demonstration compiler identical to the full compiler except
-----------------------------------------
[626] This demo compiler is also useful to the programmer to
-----------------------------------------
[628] demo compiler is one of the major advantages of Quicksilver
-----------------------------------------
[718] Quicksilver was the only compiler that had this problem.
-----------------------------------------
[1040] handle that yourself.  Clipper has no demo compiler so you
-----------------------------------------
[1256] Neither compiler uses meta commands.  These are instructions
-----------------------------------------
[1257] for the compiler to execute at compile time.  A common
-----------------------------------------
[1264] would enter INCLUDE<filename> in the code.  The compiler
-----------------------------------------
[1266] Meta commands could also be used to instruct the compiler to
-----------------------------------------
[1333] Quicksilver demo compiler $75 ($25 applies to full
-----------------------------------------
number of occurrences: 10
***** file name = c:\benchmark\ascii\COMPRESS.ASC
***** file name = c:\benchmark\ascii\COPYWRIT.ASC
***** file name = c:\benchmark\ascii\DBASE3.ASC
-----------------------------------------
[103] speed would be using a compiler like Clipper or Quicksilver, or
-----------------------------------------
number of occurrences: 1
***** file name = c:\benchmark\ascii\DHINT1.ASC
***** file name = c:\benchmark\ascii\DHINT2.ASC
***** file name = c:\benchmark\ascii\DISSERTA.ASC
```

Fig. 13-9. Results of running Text/File Handling Utilities.

also use "AND", "NOR" and "NAND". The AND forces the line to contain all the phrases. The NOR displays all the lines that contain none of the phrases. The NAND displays all the lines that contain exactly one of the phrases.

/I   This switch causes Text/File Handling Utilities to use the file listed after the switch as the list of file names to search. That way, you can easily search a lot of files in a single pass even if they are not in the same location.

/O   This causes Text/File Handling Utilities to list the matching file names in the file listed after the /O. I did not use this to create the figure above because it only lists the file name and not the text. Instead, I used DOS redirection to pipe the output to a file.

The Text/File Handling Utilities contains a program very similar to the text search program. Only this program will replace the text with something else once it finds matching text. You can have it make the replacements automatically or ask you about each one.

Another program included in the Text/File Handling Utilities is a file viewing program. This works exactly like the DOS TYPE command except you can use a /P switch to pause the screen after each screen full of information. The final program is a replacement for the DOS DEL command. It will ask you if you want to delete each file if you use the /Q switch.

Limitations   The Text/File Handling Utilities are command-line driven. Since DOS limits a command line to 127-characters, the length limits the number of strings you can search for. The file deleting program defaults to the same operation as the DOS DEL command. You must use a /Q switch to cause it to query you about each delete. That should be its default mode since otherwise it works just like the DEL command.

Manual   The manual does a very good job of explaining how to use the Text /File Handling Utilities. There are a number of examples of how to use the programs and what to expect from specific commands. There is even a complete list of error messages.

Conclusion   The Text/File Handling Utilities package is an excellent ASCII text searching program.

Product:	Text/File Handling Utilities
Price:	$25.00
Category:	Shareware
Publisher:	RT Computer Consultants
Address:	129 Shewell Avenue
	Doylestown, Pennsylvania 18901
Phone:	(215) 345-7867
Notes:	Multiple purchases results in discounts up to 40%. A copy of Text/File Handling Utilities are included on the optional diskette set.
Memory:	64K

RONNY'S PICKS

For business or personal use, my selection would depend on the word processor(s) I used. If your format is supported by OCRS, then select OCRS. It creates multiple indexes on the fly and improves your chances of finding the file you want by searching on synonyms.

If I had to support word processors that OCRS does not support, I would go with ZyIndex. It supports far more word processors than any other document indexing program on the market. This makes it an excellent "standard" for companies looking to standardize on a single program. However, it is missing the following features:

1) A summary sheet. Here I could enter key words, the document's author, its current location, and any special notes. None of these programs has this feature.

2) Easy (or automatic) deleting of outdated files. The only programs that currently have this feature are the ones that reduce functionality by creating a separate index for each document.

3) The ability to handle non-word processor files. All of these packages except GOfer are "word processor document handling program." What is really needed is an "information handling program." Such a program would index dBASE and Lotus documents at a minimum. GOfer does this but requires 79K of RAM. It should handle most other major documents with "unique" file formats. With all the word processors and even spelling checkers available for Lotus, we are seeing a real need for this right now. Currently no package fills that need. I personally have much more data in *.WK1 and *.DBF files that I need to track than I do in document files. GOfer comes the closest but is memory resident and I cannot afford the RAM.

If you just want to search through ASCII files that exist on your hard disk, then an indexing program is overkill. In addition, the indexes will take up a lot of space. For ASCII searches, the Text/File Handling Utilities are easy to use and very fast.

14
Data Translation Utilities

One of the more unfortunate facts of life is that almost no two programs use the same file format. That means that without help, most programs can only read the files they create. For example, Lotus can read *.WK1 files and dBASE can read *.DBF files, but they cannot read the other's files directly.

Many programs include a facility to translate the file formats of other programs, the so-called foreign format. For example, Excel can translate Lotus *.WK1 files as can VP Planner. That works well for most users. However, a few users need to translate between less popular or older formats. For them, a stand-alone translate program supporting many file formats may be just the answer. In addition, many programs can only import a few file formats and can export even fewer. Microsoft Word can convert WordStar files but cannot create them. WordStar cannot read files created by any other programs unless they are straight ASCII. The list goes on and on.

BridgeWorks

BridgeWorks is a powerful program for converting Lotus worksheets to and from comma delimited ASCII, Basic, Turbo Pascal, and dBASE III.

Installation   There is no installation program. The manual instructs you how to create a subdirectory and copy the files to it.

Operation   BridgeWorks is a set of stand-alone programs for transferring data to and from Lotus. It will work with comma delimited ASCII, Basic, Turbo Pascal, and dBASE III. The best way to illustrate its operation is with some examples.

Figure 14-1 shows a Lotus worksheet with some data in a range name called "Import." To transfer that data to a comma delimited ASCII file, we run a program called READ123, shown in Fig. 14-2. Figure 14-3 shows the resulting comma delimited ASCII file being typed to the screen.

You could, of course, import this comma delimited file into a number of other languages/packages since many support that file format directly. Some packages, like dBASE, have a procedural language that allows you to automate the process. Figure 14-4 below shows a dBASE program that will import data from a worksheet into its database file. Figure 14-5 shows the dBASE program running and Fig. 14-6 shows the resulting database file. Note the use of the program DEL_RC to remove the first line of the comma delimited file. That line contains nothing but a record count and number of fields per record.

Figure 14-7 shows a dBASE program for taking data from a dBASE database file and inserting it into a Lotus worksheet.

BridgeWorks is not a dBASE or Pascal utility. It consists primarily of two programs, READ123 and WRITE123. READ123 reads a Lotus worksheet and converts a range name into comma delimited format. WRITE123 takes a comma delimited file and inserts it into an existing Lotus worksheet in a specified range name. It also saves that worksheet under a new name. READ123 and WRITE123 can be used from any language that works with comma delimited files and has a procedural language capable of running external programs.

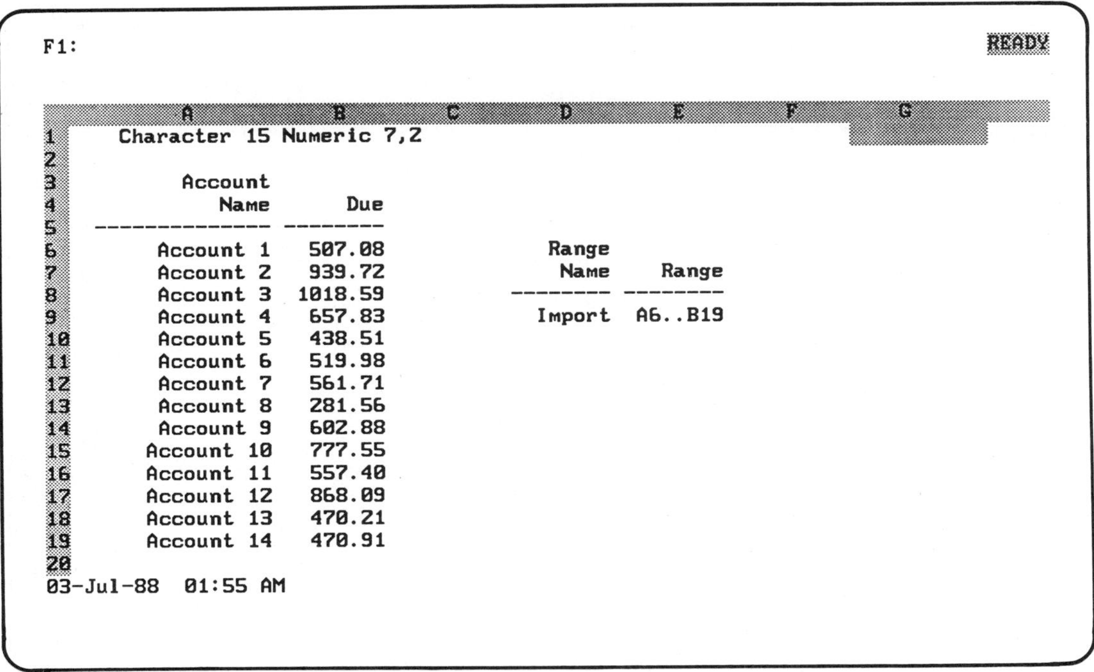

Fig. 14-1. The original Lotus worksheet containing data to be transferred to other programs.

```
C>READ123

BridgeWorks! Read123 version 2.45
Copyright (C) GreyMatter International, 1987

Source Worksheet [.W??]:  test.wk1
Range Name:               import
Data File [.BWA]:         test.bwa

C>
```

Fig. 14-2. The conversion program running from DOS. This program will convert the data into a comma delimited file.

```
C>type test.bwa
14,2
"Account 1",507.08
"Account 2",939.72
"Account 3",1018.59
"Account 4",657.83
"Account 5",438.51
"Account 6",519.98
"Account 7",561.71
"Account 8",281.56
"Account 9",602.88
"Account 10",777.55
"Account 11",557.4
"Account 12",868.09
"Account 13",470.21
"Account 14",470.91

C>
```

Fig. 14-3. The resulting comma delimited file being typed to the screen from DOS.

```
NOTE Close all databases for safety
CLOSE DATABASES
NOTE Run the program
RUN READ123 TEST.WK1 IMPORT TEST.BWA
NOTE Strip the first line with the record information
RUN DEL_RC TEST.BWA
NOTE Import the data
USE Account
SET SAFETY OFF
APPEND FROM TEST.BWA DELIMITED
USE
```

Fig. 14-4. A dBASE program for importing data from a Lotus worksheet into a dBASE database file.

Limitations/Manual   I have incorporated these two sections because the only major limitation of BridgeWorks is its manual and disk-based documentation. The manual never actually says what BridgeWorks does!

It tells how to run READ123 and WRITE123 but there is never any statement of purpose. Something like, "running READ123 creates a file in a format that many languages can operate on. Now here is an example of how to use that file with dBASE."

The sample programs included on the disk contain a number of errors. For example:

- Several programs refer to a README file that does not exist.
- The dBASE example opens a database file but never closes it.

```
dBASE III+>do example
YES

BridgeWorks! Read123 version 2.45
Copyright (C) GreyMatter International, 1987




DEL_RC version 2.00
GreyMatter International, Inc.
(c) copyright 1987

Deleting row/column count ...  Deletion Completed


dBASE III+>
```

Fig. 14-5. A dBASE program to import the data from a Lotus worksheet into a dBASE worksheet while running.

```
dBASE III+>use account
dBASE III+>list all
Record#   NAME                  DUE
      1   Account  1          507.08
      2   Account  2          939.72
      3   Account  3         1018.59
      4   Account  4          657.83
      5   Account  5          438.51
      6   Account  6          519.98
      7   Account  7          561.71
      8   Account  8          281.56
      9   Account  9          602.88
     10   Account 10          777.55
     11   Account 11          557.40
     12   Account 12          868.09
     13   Account 13          470.21
     14   Account 14          470.91

dBASE III+>
```

Fig. 14-6. The resulting dBASE database file.

```
NOTE First, open the file with the data
USE Account
NOTE Next, create a comma delimited file
COPY TO TEST2.BWA DELIMITED
NOTE Close the database
USE
NOTE Add the row header required by WRITE123
RUN ADD_RC TEST2.BWA
NOTE Now combine the original comma delimited file and the results of ADD_RC
RUN COPY ROWCOL.BWA+TEST2.BWA TEST3.BWA
NOTE Run WRITE123 to put the data into Lotus
RUN WRITE123 TEST.WK1 IMPORT TEST3.BWA TEST3.WK1
```

Fig. 14-7. A dBASE program for exporting data.

- The dBASE example erases every data record in the database before importing the Lotus data. This is rarely what you want to do.
- The dBASE example in the book imports the data with the record header intact and just notes that you must remove this record. My example runs DEL_RC first to strip the header before importing into dBASE.

I must point out that BridgeWorks is not for an inexperienced user. Anyone programming in a supported language can overcome the multiple problems in the documentation without a lot of difficulty.

Conclusion   BridgeWorks is a powerful, but poorly documented, program. It would be useful to anyone needing to incorporate information in Lotus and any compatible language.

<table>
<tr><td>Product:</td><td>BridgeWorks</td></tr>
<tr><td>Price:</td><td>$59.95</td></tr>
<tr><td>Category:</td><td>Commercial</td></tr>
<tr><td>Publisher:</td><td>Grey Matter International, Incorporated</td></tr>
<tr><td>Address:</td><td>100 North Country Road
Setauket, New York 11733</td></tr>
<tr><td>Phone:</td><td>(516) 689-7682</td></tr>
<tr><td>Memory:</td><td>256K</td></tr>
</table>

ConvertaCalc

ConvertaCalc converts worksheet files between a number of formats. It translates labels, formula, values, and most formatting properly.

Installation   ConvertaCalc comes with a program to install it on a hard disk. You must use this program because ConvertaCalc is one of the few utilities in this book that is copy protected.

Operation   Running ConvertaCalc is easy. You enter:

1) The source file type.
2) The target file type.
3) The source file including full path if needed.
4) The target file name including full path if needed.
5) Where ConvertaCalc should send the error messages. It can send them to screen, printer or a disk file.

ConvertaCalc will accept wildcards and give you a list of files matching that criteria, however, it will not accept wildcards as file names. You must run the program once per file. Table 14-1 shows the formats supported by ConvertaCalc.

Operation is fairly rapid. I used five benchmark worksheets to test it. They were:

1) ADDITION.WK1, with 5,000 addition operations.
2) SUBSTRACT.WK1, with 5,000 subtraction operations.
3) MULTIPLY.WK1, with 5,000 multiplication operations.
4) DIVIDE.WK1, with 5,000 multiplication operations.
5) POWER.WK1, with 5,000 exponential operations.

The average time to convert these files from Lotus Release 2 to Lotus Release 1A was 2-minutes and 50-seconds. I used an IBM Model 70 at 16 MHz.

Limitations   Warning: ConvertaCalc is copy protected. It includes a program to transfer that copy protection to your hard disk. You can also insert the key disk in the A-drive each time you run ConvertaCalc. It does not support the SuperCalc 4 format. However, it does support the 2, 3, and 3.1 formats.

Conversion From
Comma Separated
Data Interchange Format (DIF)
Lotus Formulae Print (*.PRN)
Lotus Release 1A
Lotus Release 2
Lotus Release 2.01
MultiPlan Symbolic Link
SuperCalc contents report (*.PRN)
Symphony
VisiCalc, Advanced
VisiCalc, Regular
Conversion To
Comma Separated
Data Interchange Format
Lotus Release 1A
Lotus Release 2
Lotus Release 2.01
MultiPlan Symbolic Link
SuperCalc 2 Data Format
SuperCalc 3 Data Interchange
SuperCalc 3.1 Spreadsheet
Symphony
VisiCalc

Table 14-1. **Formats Supported by ConvertaCalc.**

ConvertaCalc will not accept wildcards for file names, however, it can use them to list files. As a result, to convert ten files, you must work through the menus ten times rather than converting all the files at once with *.WK1.

ConvertaCalc has a very primitive, TTY-style user interface. A TTY interface is the type you get when you enter: DIR

The text scrolls from the bottom of the screen to the top. That is not necessarily bad, it just seems out of place given the slicker interfaces most of the other programs have.

Manual   The manual does a good job of explaining the various @functions and such that are not universally supported by different spreadsheets and how ConvertaCalc handles those. While you do not need a manual to run the program, the manual does a good job of explaining its usage.

Conclusion   Because ConvertaCalc is copy protected, I cannot recommend it.

Product:	ConvertaCalc
Price:	$245
Category:	Commercial
Publisher:	Micro Decision Systems
Address:	Post Office Box 1392
	Pittsburgh, Pennsylvania 15230
Phone:	(412) 854-4070
Memory:	192K
Copy Protected:	Yes

Data Junction

Data Junction is a combination of a data entry program and translation program. As a data entry program, it is easy to use but more difficult to use well than it should be. As a translation program, it has no equal.

Installation   Data Junction comes with an installation program that automatically installs it. For the most part, it is a very intelligent program. It asks you about each major package and gives you a chance to skip those packages you do not need to support. That lets you save disk space. When it finishes, it asks for your serial number and name and "brands" the software. The belief being that you will not provide pirated copies of software branded with your name. Its one problem is it insists on running from the A-drive even when the A-drive is the wrong type of drive. An ASSIGN statement cures that.

Operation   Data Junction has two functions, data entry and data transfer. Data Junction has a unique way of defining fields. You simply begin entering data, as shown in Fig. 14-8. Data Junction knows that when you press Return, one field ends and another begins. For the first record, Data Junction knows that when you press Return twice, you have entered all the fields are ready to start a new record. Figure 14-9 shows the Data Junction screen after entering several records.

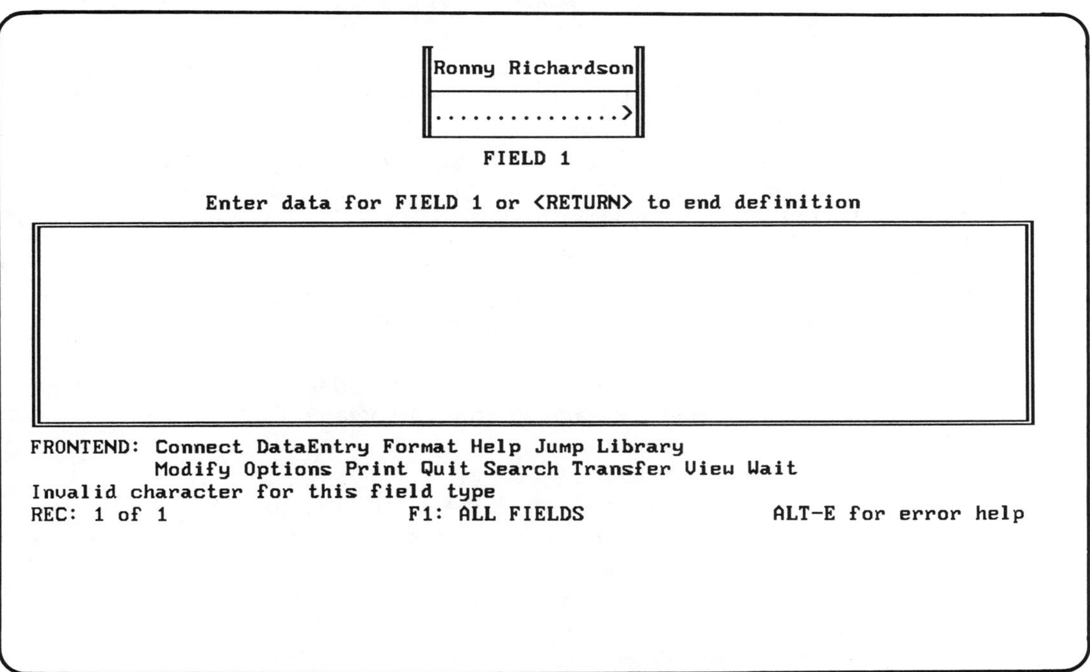

Fig. 14-8. Data Junction does not require any complex field definitions before entering data. When you are ready to enter the date, you simply begin typing.

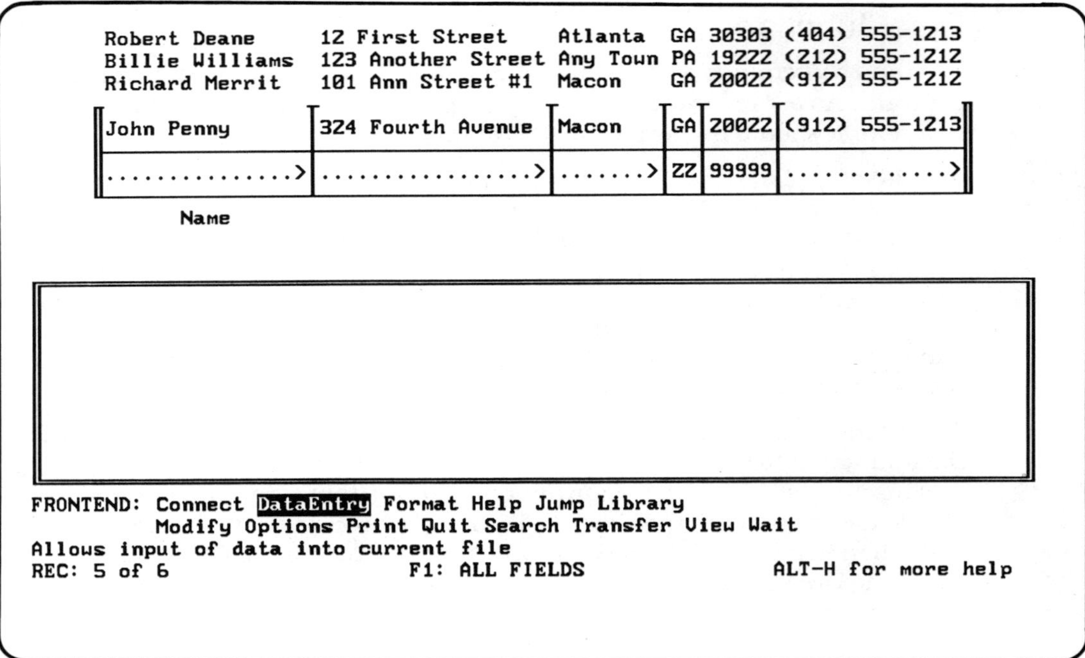

Fig. 14-9. Data Junction allows you to enter as many records as you like, so it can be used as a simple data entry program.

Because Data Junction can transfer data to a number of programs, it can function as a common interface to all these programs. If you have a data entry clerk that needs to enter data into Lotus, dBASE, and WordStar, they do not have to learn three packages. Instead, they can learn Data Junction and enter all the data into it. Table 14-2 lists the packages supported by Data Junction. It provides the following features to aid in data entry:

- It can require you to fill an entire field with data. This is useful for social security numbers, zip codes, and phone numbers that only have one correct length.
- You can add a message of up to 64-characters for each field to explain what to enter. It will only display that message when its associated field is highlighted for data entry.
- You can set a default entry for a field.
- You can use a shortcut list. When a shortcut list is attached to a field, as soon as you enter a single character, Data Junction searches the list for the first match and suggests it as the default. You can press Return to accept it or type another character to narrow the search. As you type more characters, Data Junction continues to narrow the search.
- Set valid ranges for numeric data so it only allows data within that range.
- You can use lookup tables to set the value in one field based on the value in another field. These lookup tables work just like Lotus lookup tables.

Table 14-2. **Packages Supported by Data Junction.**

ASCII (Delimited)	ASCII (Fixed)	Binary
Catamount	dBASE II	dBASE III
DIF	FoxBase	FoxBase 386
FoxBase Plus	Framework II (Database)	Framework II (Spread)
Lotus 1-2-3	Microsoft Word	Multiplan 2.0 (List)
Multiplan 2.0 (Spread)	Overland	Paradox
Reflex	Supercalc 4	Symphony
VP Info	VP Planner	WordStar

Data Junction can transfer data between any of the packages supported. The transfer is not direct. You move the data between its native format and Data Junction. Two examples will make this clearer.

The first example is converting the data entered above into Lotus format. Since it is already in Data Junction, I can transfer it directly to Lotus. Using the transfer menu, you select Lotus, as shown in Fig. 14-10. After supplying a file name, you tell Data Junction to execute the transfer. Figure 14-11 shows Lotus with the resulting worksheet file loaded.

The second example shows converting data from dBASE to Lotus. Figure 14-12 shows the data in dBASE using a BROWSE command. This data is loaded into Data Junction and translated to Data Junction format. Next, I select Lotus as the output file and the Data Junction format data is translated

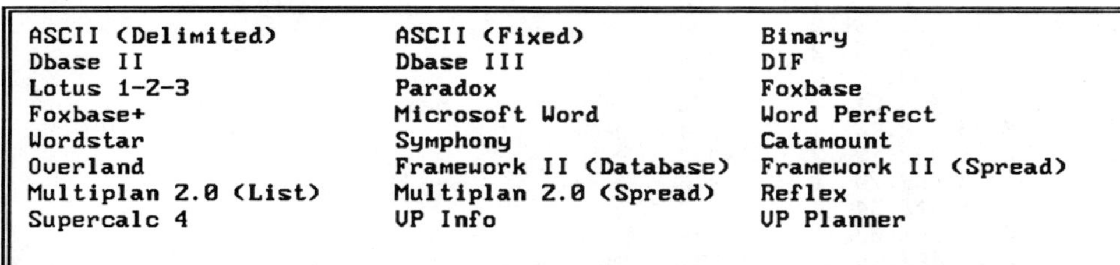

Fig. 14-10. Selecting the native format for Data Junction to transfer data to.

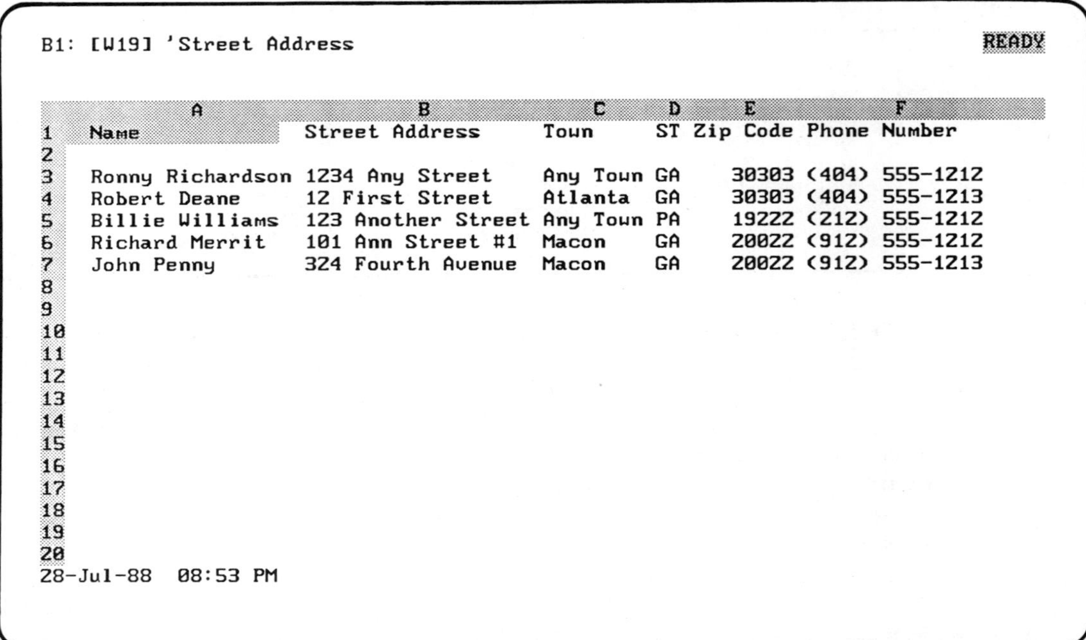

Fig. 14-11. A Lotus file that was created by Data Junction to receive translated data.

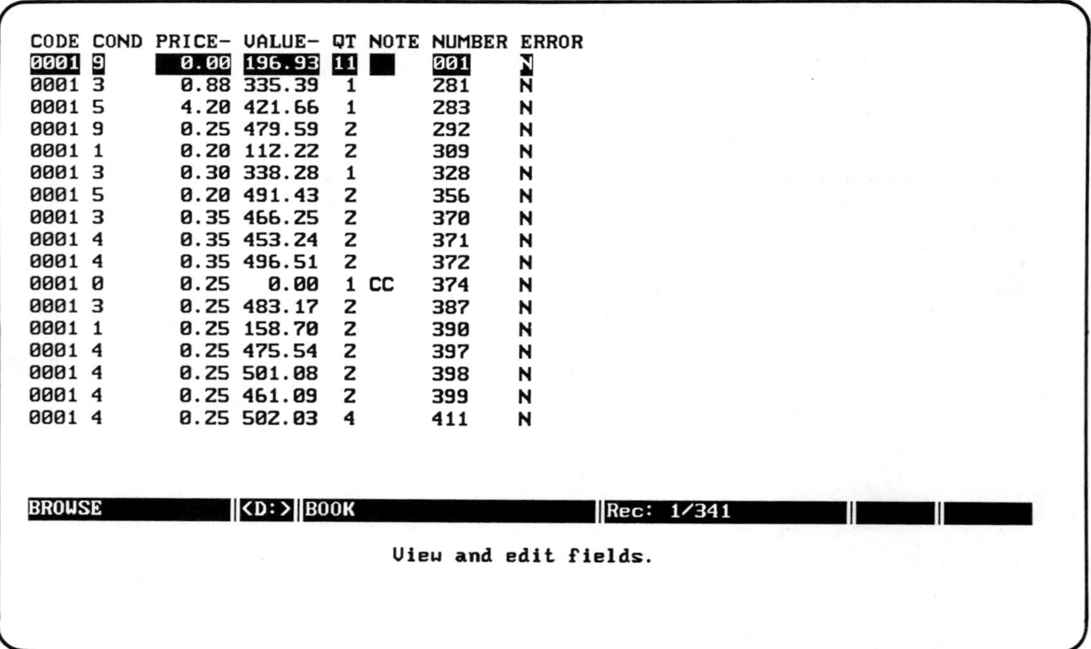

Fig. 14-12. Data in a dBASE file to be translated to Lotus.

```
B1: [W5] "COND                                                              READY

        A      B       C         D       E   F    G       H      I       J
1    CODE  COND      ICE       LUE     QT NOTE NUMBER  ERROR
2
3       1    9     0.00    196.93     11            1 N
4       1    3     0.88    335.39      1          281 N
5       1    5     4.20    421.66      1          283 N
6       1    9     0.25    479.59      2          292 N
7       1    1     0.20    112.22      2          309 N
8       1    3     0.30    338.28      1          328 N
9       1    5     0.20    491.43      2          356 N
10      1    3     0.35    466.25      2          370 N
11      1    4     0.35    453.24      2          371 N
12      1    4     0.35    496.51      2          372 N
13      1    0     0.25      0.00      1 CC       374 N
14      1    3     0.25    483.17      2          387 N
15      1    1     0.25    158.70      2          390 N
16      1    4     0.25    475.54      2          397 N
17      1    4     0.25    501.08      2          398 N
18      1    4     0.25    461.09      2          399 N
19      1    4     0.25    502.03      4          411 N
20      1    5     0.25    424.80      2          413 N
28-Jul-88   09:02 PM
```

Fig. 14-13. Data in a Lotus file after being translated from dBASE.

to Lotus format. Figure 14-13 shows the resulting Lotus file. Even with the two step process, the entire process was quick and painless.

Limitations   The data entry part of the program does not let you have calculated fields. This is where it calculates the contents of a field based on the contents of one or more other fields. You can set acceptable ranges for number, like between five and ten. However, this range is not dynamic. You cannot set a range like between five and ten for color = red and between six and forty for color = blue.

However, the biggest problem with the data entry portion is you have to work through so many menus to set anything. I found this approach confusing and difficult to work with. A much better approach would be to pop up a screen for each field where you set everything related to that field.

Manual   The manual is very good. It covers all the aspects of Data Junction. It has numerous examples and screen shots.

Conclusion   Data Junction is a very good, bordering on excellent, data entry program. If it were easier to set the defaults for fields, it would be excellent. The translation portion is quick, easy to use, and supports more formats than any other package. What more could you ask for?

Product:	Data Junction
Price:	$149
Category:	Commercial
Publisher:	Tools & Techniques, Incorporated
Address:	1620 West 12th Austin, Texas 78703
Phone:	(512) 482-0824
Memory:	512K

Fetch.*

*Fetch.** is a program that makes it easy to transfer data to and from Lotus. In addition to simply importing (or exporting) all data, it has the ability to selectively import (or export) data.

Installation   Fetch.* comes with an installation program that automatically installs Fetch.*. Unfortunately, it has two major problems:

1) It assumes it is running from the A-drive. I tried to install Fetch.* from the external B-drive of my Model 80. The program tried to read files from the A-drive. I ended up with the DOS "Abort, ignore or retry" error message. There was no way to overcome this problem from within the installation program. This is an all-too-common problem. The solution was to exit to DOS and issue an ASSIGN A=B command.

2) The program insists on installing the add-in driver even if you have already installed it for another Lotus add-in. This has the potential to cause serious problems. These can arise when the driver on the disk being installed is older than the one currently in use and another program requires the more recent driver.

Operation   Fetch is a program that makes it easy to move data between your database and Lotus. Fetch is not a bridging program. It does not allow Lotus to access data stored in an external database. Rather, it acts as transfer program. Tell it where the data is and it will go and get it. Alternatively, it will export data from Lotus to the file of your choice. Table 14-3 below lists the packages supported by Fetch. If that list does not include a package important to you, you can use the file description table of Fetch to define your own file format.

The manual does a poor job of explaining how to use Fetch. Once you get past the manual, importing data into Lotus using Fetch is easy. I have explained the steps below:

1) Select "Setup" from the main menu to define a file description table.
2) Select "Create" to create a new table.

ASCII	Comma-Delimited	Cyma Accounting
Dataease	dBASE III	DIF
Lotus 1-2-3	Paradox	PC-FIle
Quicken	Rbase	Reflex
Symphony	Timeslips	Word Perfect

Table 14-3. **Packages Supported by Fetch.**

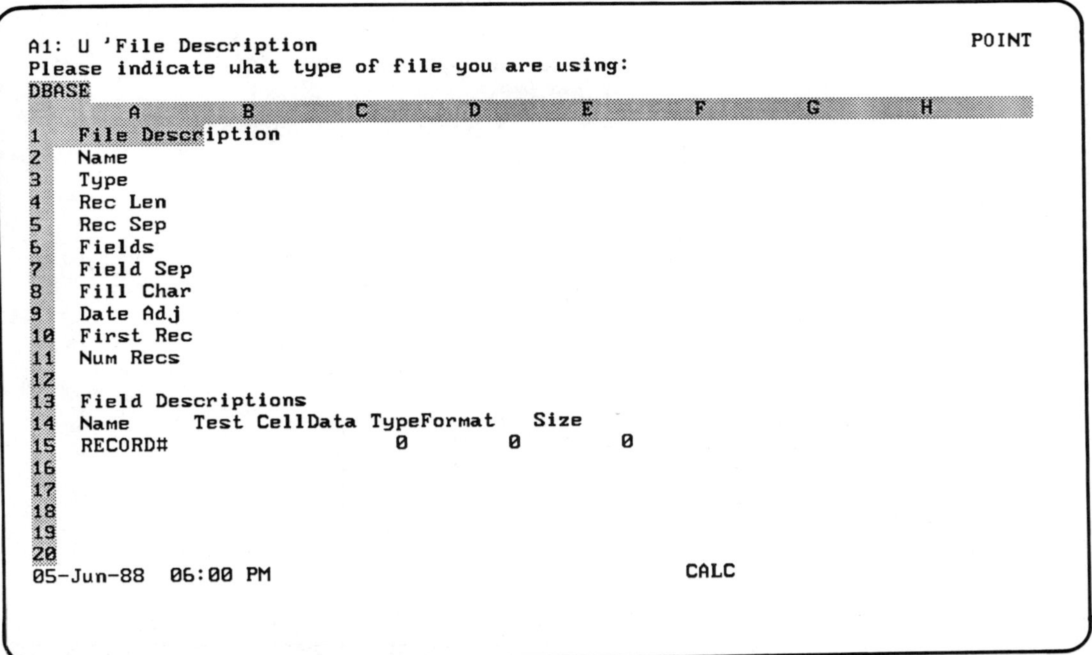

Fig. 14-14. Fetch screen shot showing user working through Fetch importing menu, and some of the information added to the worksheet by Fetch.

3) Tell Fetch where to place this information in the worksheet.

4) Tell Fetch what type of file you will be using. Figure 14-14 illustrates the progress so far. Notice that at this point Fetch has already added information to the worksheet. Before beginning this operation, the worksheet was blank.

5) Select either importing or exporting.

6) Select the database to use.

7) Return to the main menu and select "Import" to bring data into Lotus. You can also select "Export" to transfer a copy of the data from Lotus to the disk-based data file.

8) Select "Auto" to import all records or "Manual" to flag the records yourself using a criterion. The criterion can even include Lotus commands. Figures 14-15 and 14-16 show the data from the test database after using Fetch to import it. The first screen shot shows the information inserted into the worksheet by Fetch. The second shows the top of the data transferred from the dBASE *.DBF into Lotus.

In addition to its ability to transfer data between Lotus and other programs, Fetch.* expands the ability of Lotus to work with foreign files. Fetch.* provides several new @functions that allows Lotus to perform database functions on external files without importing them into Lotus. These include @functions equivalent to Lotus's @AVG, @COUNT, @MAX, @MIN, @STD,

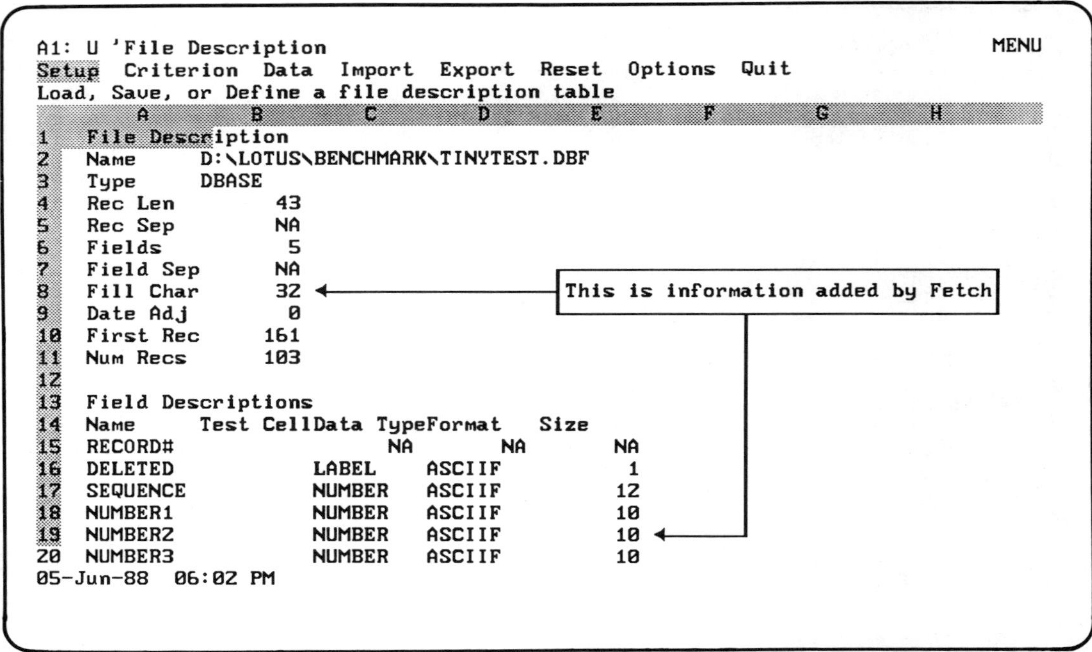

Fig. 14-15. Fetch screen shot showing top of worksheet with Fetch information after importing dBASE file.

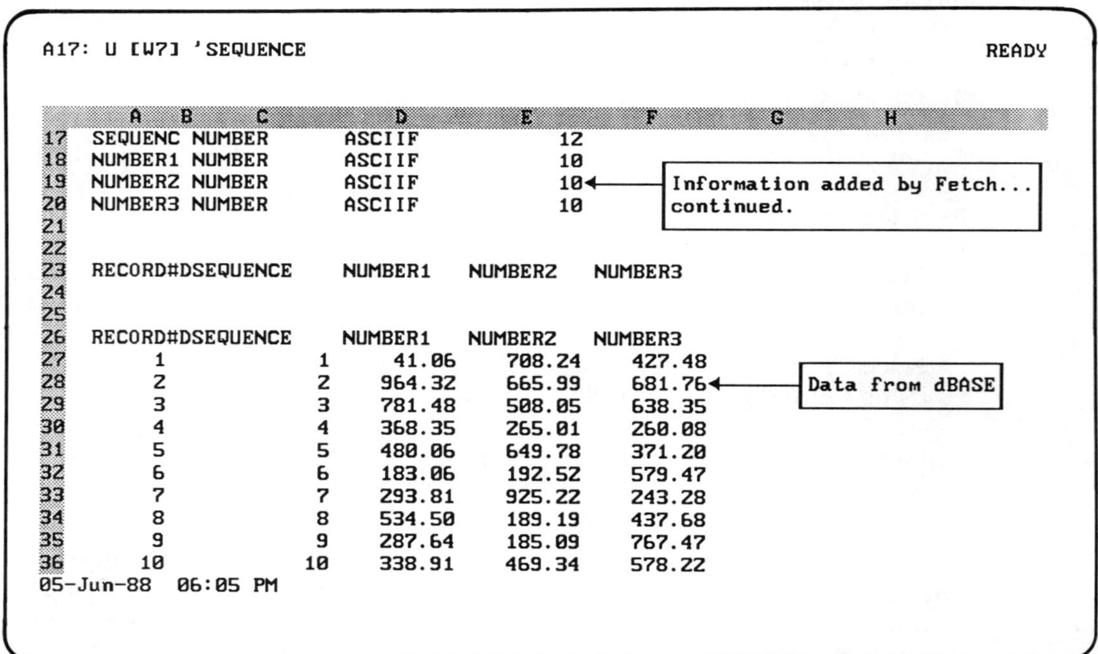

Fig. 14-16. Fetch screen shot showing dBASE data after using Fetch to import a dBASE*.DBF file.

@SUM, and @VAR. Fetch.* adds two new commands, @FFIND, which returns the current record number, and @FRECORD, which return the current record's content.

Manual   The manual is too short and does not spend enough time how to work with common data files. The program is easy enough to use that experienced users will have only a few problems figuring it out on their own. Novices may find it difficult to learn to use. After learning Fetch, it is easy to use.

Conclusion   Fetch makes it fairly easy to move data to and from Lotus worksheets.

Although their primary function is not data conversion, many of the Lotus database programs will also convert data to and from Lotus and a stand-alone database, usually dBASE.

<table>
<tr><td>Product:</td><td>Fetch.*</td></tr>
<tr><td>Price:</td><td>$99</td></tr>
<tr><td>Category:</td><td>Commercial</td></tr>
<tr><td>Publisher:</td><td>Manusoft Corporation</td></tr>
<tr><td>Address:</td><td>8570 West Washington Boulevard
Culver City, California 90232</td></tr>
<tr><td>Phone:</td><td>(800) 292-6123</td></tr>
<tr><td>Memory:</td><td>80K</td></tr>
</table>

HiJaak

The advent of desktop publishing has made the translation of graphic formats much more necessary. Many users want to construct documents that contain graphs from Lotus, drawing from a paint program, and screen shots captured from the display into a single document along with text from their word processor. To do this, you must convert all these images to one of the formats understood by the desktop publishing program.

Summary   HiJaak converts graphic files between a number of formats. It will convert Lotus *.PIC files to any supported format but will not convert other formats to Lotus *.PIC format. HiJaak includes a separate Capture program to capture graphic and text screens and to intercept the output of non-supported formats as output is sent to a printer.

Installation   HiJaak does not include a program to copy its files to the appropriate place, you must do that manually. The manual explains the process. Once in place, you must run a setup option from the main menu to define your screen and printer type and configure the hot-key.

Operation   HiJaak is really two programs in one. The first program is a screen capture program. The second is a graphic file conversion program.

The screen capture program, called Capture, is a model of simplicity. First, you must load Capture into memory. Capture is a memory resident program and is always available once loaded. You can load it using the HiJaak

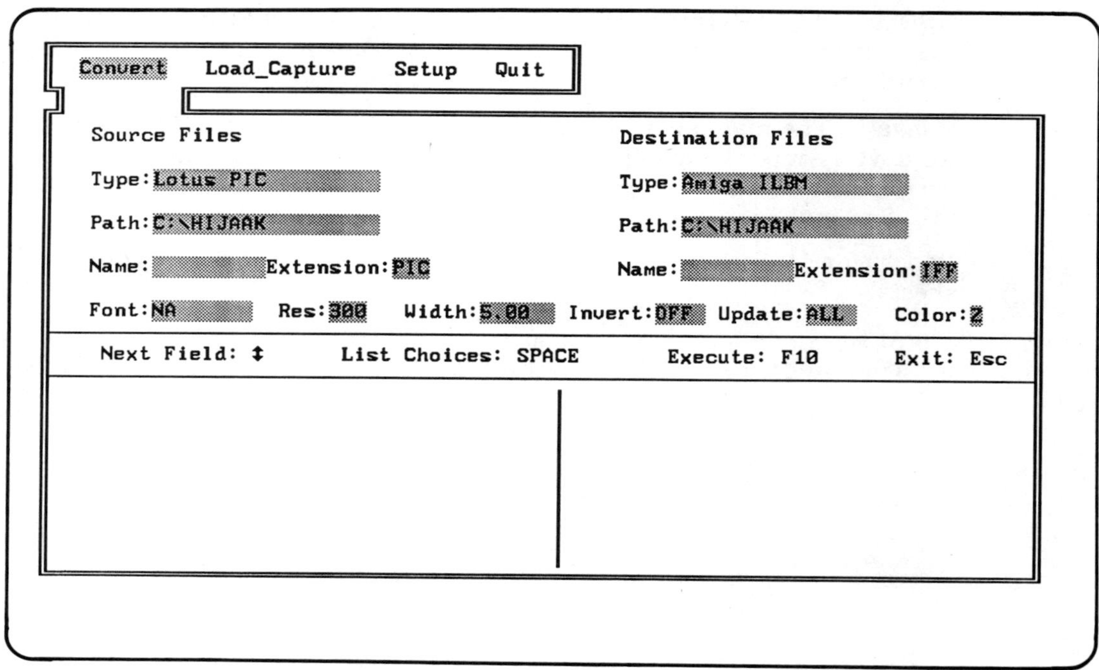

Fig. 14-17. The main menu for converting graphic files using HiJaak.

main menu or from the DOS prompt. The best place to load it is, of course, with your AUTOEXEC.BAT file. Once loaded, you invoke it with its hot-key. A simple menu pops up that gives you the choice of saving the screen to a file or printing it on a printer. In addition, pressing Escape will cancel the operation. It saves screens in a proprietary format, however, HiJaak can convert them to any supported format. Color screens will have to be gray-scaled with Inset (a separate program by the same company) before conversion by HiJaak. Once saved to a file and gray-scaled (if color), you can translate the file using HiJaak.

You start HiJaak from DOS prompt. When you select file translation, you see the fill-in-the-blank screen shown in Fig. 14-17. HiJaak supports wildcards for file names, so it can translate a group of files from a single format to a new single format with one command. The translation process itself is fast and does not require user intervention. Table 14-4 lists the formats supported by HiJaak.

Limitations   I could not get Capture to work while I was running Windows. In addition, HiJaak will not convert to the Windows Clipboard format.

Manual   The manual is clear and well written.

Conclusion   HiJaak does a good job of both capturing screen images for further use and converting between different graphic formats. It is especially powerful when combined with the InSet program.

```
Product:    HiJaak
Price:      $89.00
Category:   Commercial
Publisher:  Inset Systems
Address:    12 Mill Pond Road
            Danbury, Connecticut 06811
Phone:      (203) 794-0396
Memory:     49K
```

Table 14-4. Graphics Formats Supported by HiJaak.

Format	**Source**	**Target**
Amiga[1]	Yes	Yes
CompuServe[2]	Yes	Yes
Dr. Halo Cut Files[3]	Yes	Yes
GEM Images	Yes	Yes
HP LaserJet[4]	Yes	Yes
InSet/HiJaak	Yes	Yes
Lotus[5]	Yes	No
Macintosh[6]	Yes	Yes
PC Paintbrush[7]	Yes	Yes

[1]The Amiga source file is limited to 16 colors. Any additional information is lost.

[2]The interlaced GIF format is not supported for output files. Multiple Image GIF files are not supported.

[3]Black and white images only. Two color CUT files are supported.

[4]Supports any sources of HP LaserJet images. HiJaak can translate only raster images while the LaserJet printer supports several additional printing modes. LaserJet text and Line commands are not supported.

[5]The default width is 5.0 inches and the number of colors created is controlled by the color option.

[6]MacPaint images are limited to 576×720 pixels. When used as a source file, any dots outside this range are lost.

[7]The files created are for PC Paintbrush V3.0 or later. For older versions of PC Paintbrush you must use Debug to modify the file.

Format	**Source**	**Target**
PostScript	No	Yes
Scanner TIFF	Yes	Yes
Text	Yes	Yes
Unison NewsMaster[1]	Yes	Yes
Unison PrintMaster[2]	Yes	Yes
Windows Paint[3]	Yes	Yes

[1]Black and white images only. NewsMaster files are clipped to 2040 columns by 255 rows.

[2]Black and white images only. PrintMaster files are clipped to 88 by 52 pixels.

[3]Black and white images only.

R-Doc/X

R-Doc/X is an excellent commercial word processing document translation program.

Installation   There is no automatic installation program. The manual contains detailed instructions on copying the appropriate files. There is a list of overlay files and the manual explains that you can erase the overlay files for the formats you do not use.

Operation   When you start R-Doc/X, it first lists all the formats it supports and asks you to select the input format. Next, it prompts you for the output format after displaying a list of supported formats. After that, it asks for the file names of the files to convert. You can use DOS wildcards to specify multiple files. You must remember the file names as R-Doc/X has no way to show you the directories or files on the hard disk. Finally, it asks you for the output file name. After answering these four prompts, R-Doc/X goes off and converts all the documents. It shows a gauge for each file as it converts it. When it finishes, you have the option of converting more files or quitting. Table 14-5 lists all the formats supported by R-Doc/X.

Limitations   As part of the installation instructions, the manual spends a great deal of time explaining how to install ANSI.SYS on your system. However, R-Doc/X runs the same with or without ANSI.SYS loaded. All of the R-Doc/X prompts scroll by in Teletype fashion. This is a much cruder user interface than users are use to. It works but looks terrible. To make matters worse, the document formats have different numbers on each menu. R-Doc/X has no user definable conversion format. R-Doc/X does not support Microsoft Word style sheets.

Conversion To and From
ASCII
Displaywrite 3
Freestyle
IBM DCA/RFT
Leading Edge WP (Convert From Only)
Lotus Manuscript
Microsoft Word
Multimate
Officewriter
Palantir
PC-Write
PeachText 5000
PFS:Professional
PMate
PSF: Write
Spellbinder
Volkswriter
WordMarc Composer
Wordperfect
WordStar
Writing Assistant
XyWrite

Table 14-5. **Formats Supported by R-Doc/X.**

Manual   The manual is nothing more than a collection of typed pages stapled together. It is hard to read but contains all the information necessary to use the program. The manual is even harder to read because each section has a number, with the number going three deep at times. For example, one section may be numbered 1:4:2 and the next 1:5:1. It has a section on using R-Doc/X in batch mode. However, this section uses advanced topics like DOS piping so inexperienced users will have problems understanding it.

Conclusion   No word processing file translation program converts documents perfectly and R-Doc/X is no exception. However, its conversions are close enough for most users.

Product:	R-Doc/X
Price:	$149.00
Category:	Commercial
Publisher:	Advanced Computer Innovations
Address:	30 Burncoat Way
	Pittsford, New York 14534
Phone:	(716) 383-1939
Memory:	128K

Trans for 1-2-3

You are probably wondering why anyone would pay for a program to translate ASCII files when Lotus can load them directly. It does this using the /File Import (Text/Number) commands. If you import the ASCII text as text, then you can use the /Data Parse command to convert it to column form.

For many users, these commands work well, and are all they will ever need. This approach does have a couple of limitations:

- It assumes all the data has common columns. Many mainframe data actually has a set of titles at the top of each page. As a result, you must manually parse each page separately.
- Lotus will only import lines of 256 characters or less. If your file exceeds this limit, then you must edit it first with a text editor.
- Unusual numeric formats; like $100, 9 1/2, or 45%; confuse Lotus to such an extent that they require extensive manual editing.

Back in 1984, I had the job of converting more than 300K of ASCII data from a mainframe database into a Lotus worksheet. Each line was about 400 characters long. There were headers on each page. Each page was slightly different because each page represented a different company. It took me four days of editing that file manually using WordStar, Lotus, and SuperKey to finish it. I went back and found the original ASCII file. Trans for 1-2-3 did the same job in under a minute.

Summary   Trans for 1-2-3 is a program to intelligently convert ASCII files to worksheet files. It supports all releases of Lotus as well as Symphony.

Installation   There is no installation program. The manual explains how to install the software. The disk consists of only two files, TRANS.EXE and SAMPLE.TXT. You simply copy them to your Lotus directory or any subdirectory in your path.

Operation   There is nothing to using Trans for 1-2-3. At the DOS prompt, you enter: TRANS FILENAME /WK1

. . . with a few options and Trans for 1-2-3 does the rest. The options are:

- /WK1. Create a Lotus Release 2 worksheet.
- /WKS. Create a Lotus Release 1A worksheet.
- /WRK. Creates a Symphony Release 1 worksheet.
- /WR1. Creates a Symphony Release 1.1 worksheet.
- /Columns. Trans for 1-2-3 uses a complex algorithm to decide on column placement. This option allows the user to preempt Trans for 1-2-3.
- /Fractions. Normally, Trans for 1-2-3 treats 9 1/2 as a label. This flag causes it to convert fractions to their numeric equivalent, e.g., 9.5.
- /Output. Lets you specify the name of the output file. If not specified, it will have the name of the input file with the appropriate extension.
- /Skipfirst. Some mainframe data contains printer control information in the first column. This causes Trans for 1-2-3 to skip the first column.
- /Zerolabels. Causes Trans for 1-2-3 to treat numbers with leading zeros as labels. Useful when account numbers start with zeros.

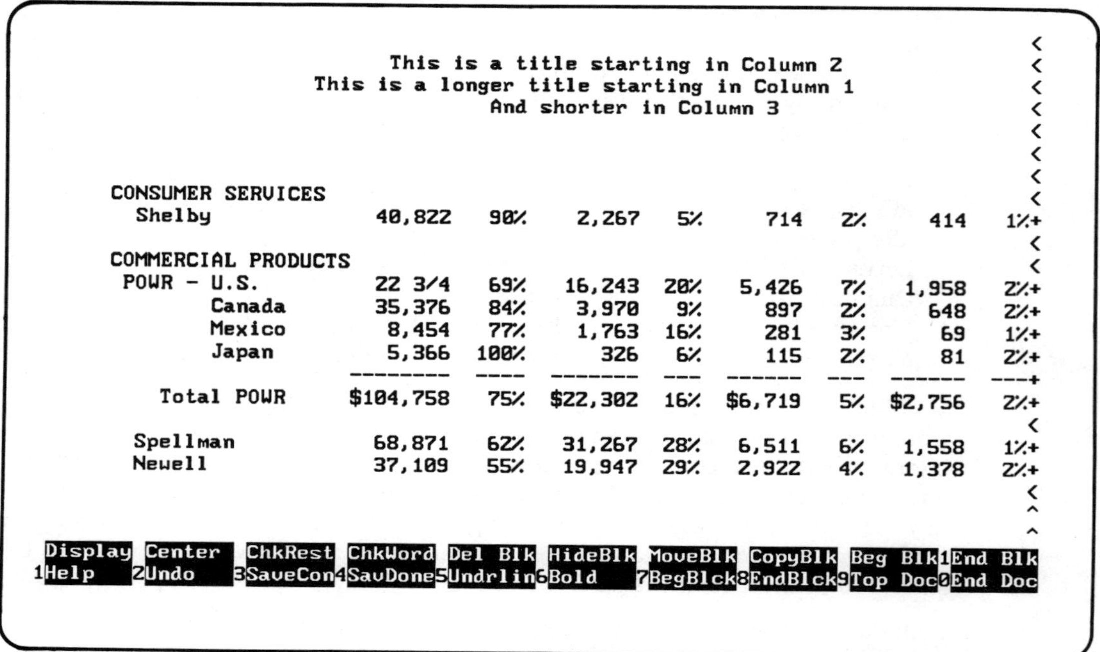

Fig. 14-18. A WordStar non-document listing of the ASCII file Trans for 1-2-3 will be translated into a Lotus*WK1 file.

```
A7: [W25]                                                              READY

       A                    B      C        D      E        F      G
 1
 2                          This is a title starting in Column 2
 3                     This is a longer title starting in Column 1
 4                          And shorter in Column 3
 5
 6
 7
 8       CONSUMER SERVICES
 9         Shelby          40,822   90%     2,267   5%       714   2%
10
11       COMMERCIAL PRODUCTS
12         POWR - U.S.      22.75   69%    16,243  20%     5,426   7%
13              Canada     35,376   84%     3,970   9%       897   2%
14              Mexico      8,454   77%     1,763  16%       281   3%
15              Japan       5,366  100%       326   6%       115   2%
16                         --------  ----  -------  ---   ------   ---
17         Total POWR     $104,758   75%  $22,302  16%   $6,719   5%
18
19         Spellman       68,871    62%    31,267  28%     6,511   6%
20         Newell         37,109    55%    19,947  29%     2,922   4%
25-Jun-88  06:57 PM
```

Fig. 14-19. The Lotus*.WK1 file resulting from the translation by Trans for 1-2-3.

Figure 14-18 shows an ASCII file being displayed using WordStar non-document mode. Note there are several items that make the file difficult to import with Lotus:

- Commas, dollar signs, and percent signs included with some numbers.
- Fractions included after some numbers.
- Different column format in different parts of the document.

Figure 14-19 shows this same file in Lotus after being translated using Trans for 1-2-3.

Limitations   Trans for 1-2-3 is limited to:

1) 500 characters on each line.
2) 50 worksheet columns on each line.
3) 1,000 lines per file.
4) Available memory.

Manual   The manual is short, but explains using Trans for 1-2-3 adequately.

Conclusion   Trans for 1-2-3 is a niche product. However, if you need to import irregularly formatted ASCII files into Lotus, Trans for 1-2-3 makes it painless.

```
Product:      Trans for 1-2-3
Price:        $95.00
Category:     Commercial
Publisher:    Intex Solutions, Incorporated
Address:      161 Highland Avenue
              Needham, Massachusetts 02194
Phone:        (617) 449-6222
Notes:        The amount of memory required
              depends on the size of the file to be
              processed. A 100 line file requires
              200K while a 1,000 line file
              requires 550K
Memory:       200K-550K
```

Word for Word Professional

Word for Word Professional is a commercial word processing document translation program.

Installation   Word for Word Professional has an automatic installation program. It will ask you which word processing formats you plan to use and then install just those formats. Each format only requires 50K so you should be able to fit all you need on your disk.

Operation   You begin by selecting the source and target formats from a common menu. Figure 14-20 shows this. Word for Word Professional offers two

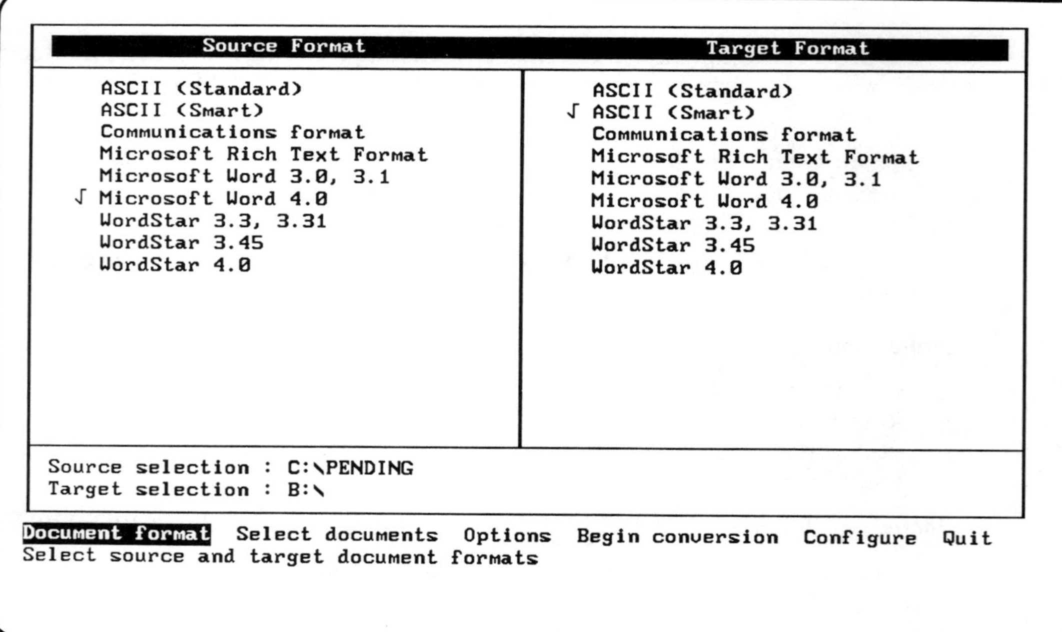

Fig. 14-20. With Word for Word Professional , the first step in translating a document is selecting the source and target formats.

unique formats. The first is COM(munications). This format converts files for asynchronous transmission while retaining all the formatting. The receiver must also have Word for Word Professional to convert the file back to its original format. A second unique format is Smart ASCII. When translating to Smart ASCII, Word for Word Professional figures out the formatting instructions from the original format. It then tries to use ASCII characters to produce a similar format. For example, if you have a left margin of 10 and a bottom margin of 5 then Word for Word Professional will add ten spaces to the beginning of each line and add five returns at the bottom of each page.

After selecting the format, you work through a series of Lotus-like menus to select the files to translate. First, you select the source subdirectory. At that point, Word for Word Professional lists all the files in that subdirectory. You have the option of selecting the files with wildcards, e.g., *.DOC, or moving through the subdirectory and tagging the files to process. Figure 14-21 shows this.

Finally, you tell Word for Word Professional the target subdirectory and names to use. As it processes the files, Word for Word Professional shows a gauge of its progress. Figure 14-22 shows this.

You can also run Word for Word Professional in command-line mode without using its menus. Using that method, you must give it four parameters, source name, target name, source format and target format. This is fairly easy and means you can run Word for Word Professional from a batch file.

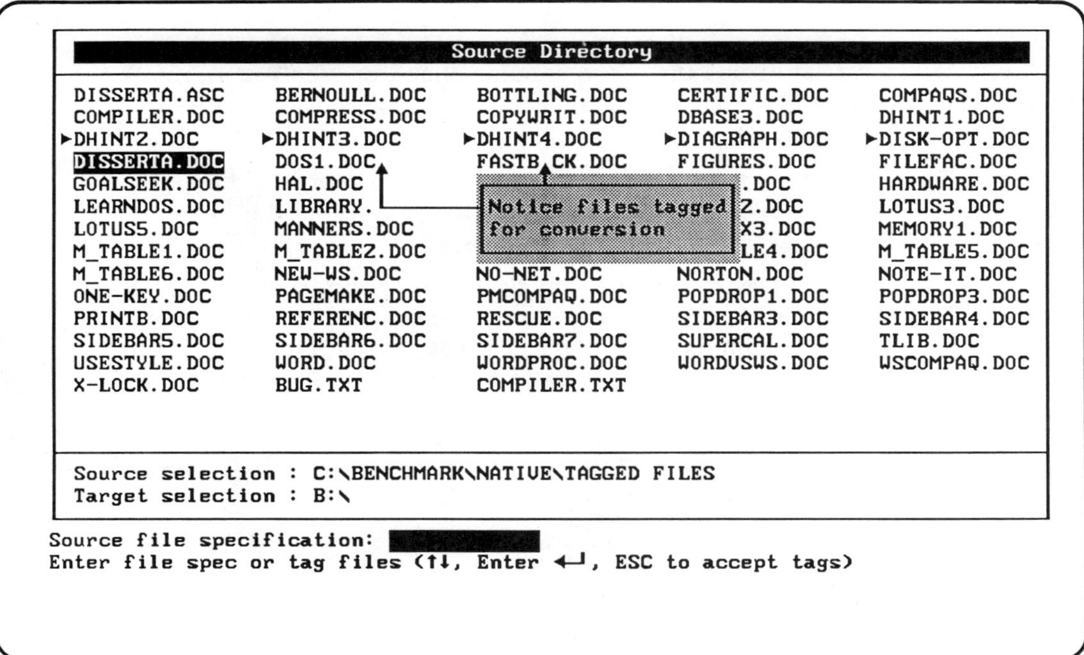

Fig. 14-21. Word for Word Professional lets you select files to translate from a listing of all the files in the subdirectory you select.

```
                        Converting Documents
    FROM:   File name =     C:\BENCHMARK\NATIVE\DISSERTA.DOC

            File format = Microsoft Word 4.0


            >.................................................<
            0%           25%          50%          75%         100%

    TO:     File name =     C:\TEMP\DISSERTA.ASC

            File format = ASCII (Smart)


            >............                                    <
            0%           25%          50%          75%         100%

 Source selection : C:\BENCHMARK\NATIVE\TAGGED FILES
 Target selection : C:\TEMP\*.ASC

 0 of 1 documents complete
 Press the ESC key to interrupt conversion after current sequence, please wait.
```

Fig. 14-22. Word for Word Professional displays a gauge showing its progress as it translates files.

Limitations   Word for Word Professional supports far less formats than does R-Doc/X; however, it supports the more popular one. Word for Word Professional does not support Microsoft Word style sheets. It does not have a design-your-own conversion format.

Manual   The manual is crowded and hard to read. It does contain the necessary information and Word for Word Professional is easy enough to use that you can skip the manual altogether.

Conclusion   No word processing file translation program converts documents perfectly and Word for Word Professional is no exception. However, its conversions are close enough for most users. It is easy enough to use that the average user will not have any trouble even if they only use it infrequently.

Product:	Word For Word Professional
Price:	$149.00
Category:	Commercial
Publisher:	Design Software, Incorporated
Address:	19808 Nordhoff Place
	Chatsworth, California 91311
Phone:	(800) 231-3088
	(818) 885-9000
Memory:	256K

RONNY'S PICKS

Worksheets   It really is no contest. Data Junction is far-and-away the best general translation program of the lot. It is easier to set up and use than either Fetch, ConvertaCalc or BridgeWorks and it supports more native formats. For translating ASCII files to Lotus, it is more powerful than Trans for 1-2-3. If you only have one translation program, it should be Data Junction. However, Data Junction does not translate word processing or graphics formats.

Word Processing   I tested the word processor conversion programs by creating a complexly formatted document in Microsoft Word. I translated that document into WordStar. I then translated the WordStar document in Multimate and the Multimate document in WordPerfect. Finally, I translated the WordPerfect document back into Microsoft Word. By comparing the before and after Microsoft Word documents, I was able to gauge how well the programs worked.

Most of the character formatting such as bold, underlining and the like, translated well. The real problems turned out to be margins, tabs and headers/footers. Neither program did a very good job on these. Fortunately, these are usually global setting so they are easy to correct. Other than the headers/footers, neither program lost any text. And in no case did the cleanup take very long.

Word for Word Professional has a easier to use user interface and does a slightly better job than R-Doc/X. However, the programs are close enough you can buy the cheapest one unless you need support for a less popular format. In that case, you should check the charts as R-Doc/X supports more formats.

Graphics   For graphics formats, HiJaak is about the best translation program you can buy.

15
Preventing Unauthorized Access to Your Data

Normally, you think of protecting your data as making frequent backups as explained in Chapter 12. According to an American Office Dealer study, over 40% of the businesses that lose their data to theft or damage go out of business within six months.

While backups are a major part of data protection, it may not be enough. The American Bar Association estimates that computer crime, not counting computer theft, costs American business four billion dollars a year. This is only an estimate because most victims never report computer crimes. In fact, the FBI estimates that victims report less than 20% of all computer crimes. The reasons vary, but a major one is the firms do not want the public to see them as having weak security.

The crimes range from employees raising their own salary and students raising their grades, up to employees stealing millions of dollars. For exam-ple . . .

Caltech students used a computer to print out over one million entries in a fast food contest. They ended up winning a car.

In 1973, employees at the Equity Funding Corporation used a computer to print up over 60,000 fake insurance policies. These were resold to other companies for over two billion dollars.

It is not likely that the data on your PC is worth that much. However, stop and think what could happen to you and your business if it became public knowledge. Bidding policies getting out might destroy your ability to bid on jobs. Employee information getting out might result in a liability suit against you or a competitor stealing a valuable employee. The thief may turn accounting information over to the IRS. They might sell new product designs and strategies to competitors. The list goes on and on.

There are three ways to protect the data on your microcomputer:

1) You can remove the data from the computer and lock it up. You can do this using either floppy disks, a removable hard disk or a Bernoulli Box. You can copy information to floppy disks and erase it off the hard disk. However, you must make sure that none of the information can be recovered from the hard disk using a file unerasing program such as the Norton Utilities.

2) You can encrypt it, using an encryption program such as the one that comes with SuperKey. Using this method you must make sure that the password remains secure but not forgotten. You must also make sure that all copies of the data, including any .BAK files, are encrypted.

3) You can prevent unauthorized users from using your computer. AT's and clones use a lock and key to prevent unauthorized usage. Some vendors offer hardware cards that make unauthorized access to the computer difficult.

The method you select depends on both the type of data you store on your computer and on how accessible your computer is. If you have no sensitive data on your computer, then it makes little sense trying to prevent access to that data. If your computer is in an area with controlled access, then you do not need complex computer security. However, if you have sensitive data on a computer in a public area, you need to safeguard that data.

REMOVING DATA FROM THE COMPUTER:
Plus Development Passport Removable Hard Disk

There are several removable hard disk drives available. The Passport from Plus Development is one of the best. The advantage of a removable hard disk drive for security is you do not have to do anything special. You work with your software all day long as you normally would. At the end of the day or whenever you want to secure your data, you remove the hard disk from the computer and lock it up.

The Passport drive from Plus Development is a removable hard disk. The housing stays in the computer permanently but you can remove the drive itself. This has three major advantages:

1) You can carry the drive to another computer and use it if that computer has a Passport drive. This lets you easily transport 20 or 40 Meg. Base units are available for PC's, AT's and PS/2 computers so you can connect the Passport to a number of different types of computers.

2) When one cartridge fills up, you can replace it with another. This gives your machine unlimited capacity.

3) You can lock the hard disk up when not in use for the ultimate in data security.

Installation   The version I installed was a two-drive external case with a PS/2 adapter. I installed it in an IBM Model 70. It came in several different boxes . . .

1) The external case.
2) The controller card.
3) The drive.
4) The drive connector to go inside the housing.
5) The cables.

Each box had its own installation manual. Getting everything coordinated was a little difficult.

After I got everything figured out, installation proved to be fairly easy. Open up the IBM Model 70. Insert the controller card into an empty slot then close the computer back up. Open up the external case and install the connector that attaches to the drive then replace the cover. Insert a drive into the case. Connect the cable between the controller and case and plug the case into an outlet. That was it for hardware installation. It took me less than an hour.

There is a switch on the back of the removable drive that controls if the computer boots off the Passport drive or another drive. That switch is especially useful if you run off different operating systems. Just install one system per cartridge and boot off the operating system of your choice. There is a second switch that write-protects the drive. In these days of viruses that is a handy feature.

The next set was software installation. The Passport comes with software to lock and unlock the drive. This disables and enables the external eject button. There is also a program to eject the cartridge. Finally, you have to add a device driver to your CONFIG.SYS file. PS/2 owners have to boot off your "reference disk" to update the CMOS in the PS/2 computer. The computer uses the reference disk to update the internal memory whenever you change the hardware.

The Passport drive consists of a couple of components. The first part is a half-length controller card. The second part is the mounting bay. There are two types, a half-height internal unit or an external casing. The external case has room for two drives. The final part is the drive itself. These come in 20 or 40 Meg versions. You can use them interchangeably.

The drive itself is a 40-millisecond [ms] drive with a run-length-limited controller with a 1:1 interleave. It has full-track buffers and other speed enhancements to give the drive the performance of a 28 ms drive. Figure 15-1 shows the Passport drive installed in an AT.

The Passport is essentially a sealed Winchester drive. It has a shock rating of 150 g's. While I did not test this, Plus Development claims it will withstand a drop onto a hard surface from one foot away or more. However, rapid deceleration stresses the bearings and other components. It is not likely this drive could take repeated shocks. Plus Development ships each drive with a custom padded carrier to reduce the stress on the drive.

Fig. 15-1. This shows the Passport drive installed in an AT.

Winchester drives are prone to hard disk head crashes. A head crash is when the heads bump into the surface of the hard drive. At a minimum, this grinds some of the magnetic material off the hard disk platter. At its worst, it can leave the drive inoperative. Plus Development has designed the Passport with automatic head parking and head locking to minimize this problem.

Operation   Once installed, the Passport functions exactly like any other hard disk.

Limitation   The only really significant limitation to the Passport drives specifically is the cost. Adding a second 40 Meg cartridge costs $795 or almost $20 per Meg. That is more than most other ways of adding capacity to your system.

Manual   The Passport suffered from too many manuals. Plus Development includes an installation manual with each component. A much better approach would be to have one single manual. The manuals themselves were not well written and were difficult to follow. However, installation is a one time difficulty. After that, the Passport drives do not require a manual.

Conclusion   The Passport removable hard disk is a pricy but effective way of transporting large amounts of data between different computers.

ENCRYPTION SOFTWARE

I did not review any dedicated encryption/decryption programs for this book. Data encryption/decryption is such a small aspect of security that vendors usually combine it with other programs. In fact, several of the programs in this book, including DS Tools and PC Tools Deluxe, offer encryption/decryption.

PREVENT ACCESS TO THE COMPUTER

Some AT's and clones use a lock and key to prevent unauthorized usage. If your computer has such a lock, using it regularly offers strong protection against unauthorized use of your computer. If your computer lacks a lock, you need to add one. Even if your computer has a lock, some of these products may add additional security.

Lockerup

Lockerup is a tiny, memory resident, public domain program for locking up your computer until you press the proper keystroke.

Installation   There is no installation program and the documentation does not discuss how to install the program. All you must do to install Lockerup is copying LOCKERUP.EXE to a subdirectory in your PATH.

Operation   Lockerup is a tiny memory resident program. It requires only about 1K of RAM so the best way to use Lockerup is to add it as the first command to your AUTOEXEC.BAT file. However, first rename the program to something like SETCLOCK.EXE or STARTUP.EXE so no one will know what it is supposed to do. Be creative with the name, however, the extension must be .EXE.

Lockerup locks out all keystrokes including Control-Alt-Delete. A locked computer cannot be rebooted. However, you can turn the computer off and reboot from a floppy diskette.

Lockerup will immediately lock out the keyboard. However, it does not lock out the batch file so your AUTOEXEC.BAT file will continue to run until it finishes. You will have to press Alt-Left/Shift-U to unlock the keyboard. Later, if you are going to be away from the computer and want to relock it, just press Alt-Left/Shift-L.

For a little more security, use the batch file in Fig. 15-2. You know to press Alt-Left/Shift-U to unlock the computer and then any key to restart after the PAUSE. However, any other user will think the computer is defective.

Limitations   You can change the locking and unlocking keystrokes that Lockerup uses and you probably should. However, you must use Debug (a program

```
echo off                                    <--- Turns ECHO off
lockerup                                    <--- Rename command and program to startup (see text)
echo Internal Error                         <--- Fake error message
echo Error Number 1771:NTC                  <--- Fake error message
echo Contact XYZ Computer Corporation       <--- Fake error message
pause>nul                                   <--- Stop the batch file. The ">nul" pipes the "press any key"
                                                 DOS message
```

Fig. 15-2. Lockerup batch file to fake a problem.

that comes with DOS) and know keyboard scan codes. This is likely to prove difficult or impossible for beginners. (You will still be able to use the program without this, you just cannot change the locking and unlocking keystrokes.)

You can call Lockerup from multiple batch files and it does exactly what it should. However, rather than accessing the original copy already in memory it loads a new copy. As a result, every time you load Lockerup from a batch file, you reduce memory by 1K. This is not a problem if you load it once in your AUTOEXEC.BAT. However, it prevents you from writing batch files to automate the locking.

Manual   The documentation does a good job of explaining how to use Lockerup. However, its explanation of changing the locking and unlocking codes is so brief that only an experienced user will understand the instructions.

Conclusion   Adding Lockerup as the first command of your AUTOEXEC.BAT file offers good low-cost security. It will not stop an experienced user but often that is not the type of user you are looking to lock out.

Product:	Lockerup
Price:	Free
Category:	Public Domain
Publisher:	Warren E. Fuller
Address:	1211 HolmeWood Drive
	Pasadena, Maryland 21122
Phone:	Not available
Notes:	A copy of lockup is included
	on the optional diskette set
Memory:	1K

PC Password

PC Password is an 8-bit card that simply prevents the computer from booting without a password. Unlike the X-Lock card, PC Password has only one password and no function other than restricting access to the computer.

Installation   Installing PC Password is easy. The steps are . . .

1) Open the cover and slide the card into any empty slot.
2) Add a device driver to your CONFIG.SYS file.
3) Boot to make sure everything works properly. If you have problems, you have to adjust the switch settings on the card.
4) Bolt everything back together.

The manual explains this poorly. I ended up guessing till I got a setting that worked.

Once everything is working, you can take the "ultimate" installation precaution. They include two special screws with the card. You can screw these screws in but not out. By using one to bolt in the card, removing the card is much more difficult. Of course, it will also be more difficult for you if you ever have to work on the computer. I do not recommend using this screw. If someone is willing to take the time to disassemble your computer to get to your data, all they have to do is steal the hard disk and look at it later at their convenience.

Operation   Because PC Password is a card and not a program, it is not possible to defeat it by booting off the A drive. PC Password requests the password very early in the boot process, before the computer processes CONFIG.SYS file. It allows you an unlimited number of attempts to enter the correct password. PC Password also kicks in and requests a password each time the computer is rebooted. At the DOS prompt, you can lock up the computer by entering LOCK. This will cause PC Password to request a password before releasing the computer for additional work.

PC Password includes a proprietary encryption/decryption program that accesses the PC Password board as part of the algorithm. As a result, files encrypted using this method can only be decrypted on that computer. That offers maximum file protection but introduces the danger of losing data if the PC Password board should fail. Also included is a public domain DES Encryption program from Jim Gillogly and Lauren Weinstien.

Limitations   Although the X-Lock card will perform many additional functions, such as timing users and collecting billing information, PC Password will not. It functions as a gate to the computer, a gate with a single key. Once the gate is open, the computer functions normally in every way. The advantage of this reduced functionality is a lower price.

Manual   The manual is adequate in most respects. It does not do a good job of explaining how to set the switches for different configurations, a one-shot problem. It also fails to warn of the problems you might have encrypting a file on a PC Password machine and then expecting to be able to decrypt it on another machine.

Conclusion   For users with sensitive data on their hard disk and no computer lock, PC Password is cheap and effective protection.

<table>
<tr><td>Product:</td><td>PC Password</td></tr>
<tr><td>Price:</td><td>$199.99</td></tr>
<tr><td>Category:</td><td>Commercial Hardware</td></tr>
<tr><td>Manufacturer:</td><td>Computer Commodities USA</td></tr>
<tr><td>Address:</td><td>7127 Shady Oak Road
Minneapolis, Minnesota 55344</td></tr>
<tr><td>Phone:</td><td>(612) 942-0992</td></tr>
<tr><td>Notes:</td><td>For the device driver that allows communication between the software and the card once the computer has booted</td></tr>
<tr><td>Memory:</td><td>1K</td></tr>
</table>

X-Lock 100 Card

The *X-Lock 100* card from A-O Electronics, Incorporated is a sophisticated way to control access to any IBM PC, XT, AT, or clone. It requires anyone turning on the computer or rebooting it to have a password. You can bypass it without removing it from the computer.

Installation   The steps to installing the card are:

1)   Remove the computer cover.
2)   Remove the rear cover plate to the slot for the card.
3)   Remove a yellow tab on the card (used to protect the battery) and insert the card in the appropriate slot. At this point the manual indicates that you should reinstall the cover, however, that is not necessary if you are careful.
4)   Turn on the computer. The card will perform a diagnostic test.
5)   Turn the computer off, remove the card and change the setting on dip switch 8.
6)   Reinstall the card.
7)   Reinstall the cover.
8)   Turn on the computer. The first time you turn the computer on, the card will ask you to enter a "superuser" password. This allows you to access all devices as well as assigning and changing passwords.

The entire installation took me less than 10 minutes.

The card also comes with a lock to prevent unauthorized removal of the computer cover. This lock is a metal tube with a small hole in one end and a large hole in the other end. You insert one of the cover screws into the large hole to where it protrudes through the small hole. You then screw this into one of the cover screw holes. Then you fill the large hole with a lock. Once installed, if you grab the metal tube and pull while unscrewing, you can remove the whole assembly without even using a screwdriver.

Operation   The X-Lock 100 is a short card that forces anyone trying to use the computer to enter a password. Anytime you turn the computer on or reboot, it presents you with a log-on screen. You then get ten attempts to enter a correct password. After ten tries, the computer "locks up." A-O Electronics says there are 5,072,820,000,000,000,000,000 trillion possible passwords, so random guessing is not likely to be successful. Because it is a card and not a program, it is not possible to defeat it by booting off the A-drive.

The card does more than prevent access by unauthorized users. Each of 72 passwords has associated attributes. The superuser can give each password access to any parallel port and to any hard disks. The card records the time each password uses the computer. It makes that available in a database. So you can assign different passwords to different projects and the card will track time for billing. It also tracks all printer usage.

Once you have entered your password, the card is completely transparent unless you try to access a device not authorized by your password. The card comes with software that allows each user to check his time on the system and allows superusers to check everyone's time. The software is not copy protected.

Limitations   When you enter the initial password, the card does not display it on the screen. In addition, you are not asked to verify it and there is no way to correct a typing mistake. It is common for password software to ask for the password twice and require a match before continuing but the card does not. In addition, the backspace key does not remove typing errors. Rather, the card reads it as one of the characters of the password.

The X-Lock 100 card leaves the A-drive spinning while asking for a password. After ten incorrect passwords, it locks the computer, but leaves the A-drive spinning. This means that an undetected unauthorized entry attempt could cause your A-drive to spin forever.

In addition to these two major problems, the card has several minor problems or deficiencies. You must either give a user no access to the hard disk or unrestricted access, you cannot give limited access to only a few subdirectories. There is no way to lock out destructive commands like ERASE*.* or FORMAT C:. The only way to switch users is to turn the computer off or reboot it.

Manual   The manual is brief but adequate.

Conclusion   The X-Lock 100 offers a simple effective way to restrict computer access and to track computer usage. Any computer with sensitive information stored in it that is accessible by unauthorized personnel would benefit from the card. The card is more effective if combined with a more effective lock than the one provided with the card. If you rent computers or computer time, the combination of passwords and tamper proof timing is an unbeatable combination.

<table>
<tr><td>Product:</td><td>X-Lock 100</td></tr>
<tr><td>Price:</td><td>$495.00</td></tr>
<tr><td>Category:</td><td>Hardware</td></tr>
<tr><td>Publisher:</td><td>Infosafe Corporation</td></tr>
<tr><td>Address:</td><td>2137 Flintstone Drive
Tucker, Georgia 30084</td></tr>
<tr><td>Phone:</td><td>(404) 491-8044</td></tr>
<tr><td>Notes:</td><td>Infosafe Corporation manufacturers several cards very similar to the X-Lock 100 card. They are...

X-Lock 10. It has nine individual passwords plus the administrator. It sells for $299 for an AT/PC or $399 for a PS/2.

X-Lock 20. It has nine individual passwords plus the administrator. Has on-board data encryption. It sells for $495.

X-Lock 50. It has 130 individual passwords plus the administrator. Allows encryption of entire hard disk and floppy disks used with the system. Key stored on the card. It sells for $595.</td></tr>
<tr><td>Memory:</td><td>0K</td></tr>
</table>

RONNY'S PICKS

I have been using the Passport drive and the PC Password board for several months now and both offer excellent security with minimal hassle. Either one would go a long way toward making your computer more secure. They both also have a major advantage over other systems. Encryption and other such security schemes require time to learn and operate. They intrude enough that they lower productivity and frustrate users. Neither the Passport or the PC Password devices do that. A worker can learn either in about five minutes and neither interferes with proper users.

16
Dealing with Copy Protection

With regard to copy protection, users today are far luckier than they were a few years ago. Today, almost no major business programs are copy protected and the vast majority of entertainment programs are not copy protected. It is not only possible, but quite easy to fill all your software needs without purchasing copy protected software.

Users were not so lucky a few years ago. The major database, dBASE, was copy protected. The major spreadsheet, Lotus, was copy protected until just recently. Many major word processors, like WordStar, were never copy protected. However, others like Microsoft Word were.

THE PROBLEMS WITH COPY PROTECTED SOFTWARE

Copy protected software leads to a couple of major headaches/risks for users. The largest risk for the user is the failure of the protection scheme. Some methods require the user to insert a "key" floppy diskette into the computer to start the application. Floppy diskettes are prone to failure and easy to damage. Because the copy protected application will not run without the key disk, the vulnerability of the floppy diskette meant the application was as vulnerable. If the key disk fails, the user cannot use his program until he arranges to have the key disk replaced. If the software firm was out of business or has discontinued the program, the user might never get the application to run again. This has proved to be a major headache. In fact, many companies sold their protected programs with a backup key disk or allowed registered users to purchase one for a small fee.

Still other copy protection schemes allow the user to install the program and key on the hard disk. This method does not require a key diskette. However, it does depend on hidden files with special characteristics that it places on the hard disk. If these files are damaged, or in some cases even moved, the application fails. One of the major problems disk optimizing software vendors face is making sure their programs leave copy protection files alone. At least one copy protection method I know of would fail to run if installed on a hard disk and you backed up the hard disk. The only way a user with this program can make a backup was to first uninstall the copy protection, run the backup then reinstall the copy protection.

Computer users literally revolted against copy protection. This revolt took three forms. First, many users simply refused to purchase copy protected software. Second, technically experienced users began to explore the copy protection schemes and methods to defeat them. The user community, especially bulletin boards, had hundreds of text files explaining how to remove the protection on specific programs. Third, a few vendors began to sell hardware and especially software to defeat copy protection. These were boards and programs that the average user could understand and operate.

It was this third category that spelled the defeat of copy protection. Almost every user had either had a problem with copy protection or knew someone who had. Users were primed to remove copy protection. For a while, the vendors of copy protection and "copy busting" programs engaged in warfare. A new copy protection method would come out and a few days later a program would be out to defeat it. However, the battle was short-lived and most major vendors have dropped copy protection entirely.

I started not to include this chapter since copy protection is rare today. My advice to anyone is not to purchase copy protected software unless you have absolutely no alternative. I decided to include it for those of you with no choice and those who own copy protected software and are happy with it. Keep in mind, however, that sooner-or-later the disk with the files required by the protection scheme will fail. When that happens, you need an alternative. Programs to unprotect or copy protected programs give you that alternative.

Copy II PC

Copy II PC is the most famous and most effective of the PC "copy busting" programs. It will let you make backup copies of most copy protected programs. Of course, it also allows the pirates to do the same.

Installation   There is no installation program and the manual does not explain how to install the software.

Operation   Copy II PC is really several programs in one. The main copy program, called Copyiipc, does not defeat the copy protection at all. Rather, it reproduces a copied disk that is identical to the original disk in every way. If the original was copy protected, then the copy is copy protected.

A second program, called Nokey, is a memory resident program you run before using programs that check for a key disk. It watches the copy protected program. When it tries to check the A-drive for the key disk, Nokey sends it information indicating the key disk is there.

A third program, called Noguard, will copy SUPERlok disks. In the process, Noguard actually removes the copy protection from the disk. Copyiipc will usually tell you if Noguard can remove the protection from a disk it is copying.

Manual   The manual is brief and difficult to use. All the information is there but you will have to read the manual a couple of times first.

Conclusion   Copy II PC does an excellent job of copying or even removing the copy protection from most copy protected packages.


```
Product:      Copy II PC
Price:        $39.95
Category:     Commercial
Publisher:    Central Point Software, Incorporated
Address:      15220 NW Greenbrier Parkway
              Suite 200
              Beaverton, Oregon 97006
Phone:        (503) 690-8090
Notes:        The Copy II PC program will use all
              available memory to speed the copy
              process.

              Some non-standard computers, like the
              PC Junior and Tandy 1000's, require
              256K.

              Some Tandy 1000 computers do not have
              a DMA (direct memory access) chip.
              These require a memory expansion board
              containing a DMA chip.
Memory:       64K
```

Copy II PC Option Board

The *Copy II PC Option Board* is a floppy disk controller replacement that turns your computer into a disk duplicating machine.

Installation   The basic installation procedure is fairly painless. You insert the board into an empty slot. This slot must be next to the floppy disk controller. You disconnect the cable from the floppy disk controller and connect it to the board. Finally, you run a cable from the board to the floppy disk controller. Effectively, you are placing the Copy II PC Option Board in between the floppy disk drives and their controller.

That sounds easy, and it was on the Compaq I used to test the board. However, it can be very difficult on some computers. You should check your computer or check with Central Point Software before purchasing the board. This is especially important if you have a nonstandard clone.

Operation   The Copy II PC Option Board uses the same technology found in professional disk duplicating machines. The board does not remove copy protection. Rather, it copies every single byte from one disk to another. It does this no matter if the disk is laid out in a nonstandard pattern. In fact, it allows you to duplicate Atari, Kaypro, Amiga and Apple format disks on your PC.

All you do to make a copy is enter: TC A: B:

The TC stands for transition copier and runs a special copy program. It is not the standard Copy II PC copy program. If you like, you can enter TC alone and work through a menu. There are a couple of switches that are easy to use and explained in the manual.

Although I did not test it, the manual explains how to use the Copy II PC Option Board to transfer data files between the IBM and Macintosh computers.

Limitations   There is no PS/2 version of the Copy II PC Option Board.

Manual   The manual does a very good job of explaining how to install and use the Copy II PC Option Board.

Conclusion   Unless you have a PS/2 computer, the Copy II PC Option Board is the easiest and most flexible method available for copying copy protected software.

Product:	Copy II PC Deluxe Option Board
Price:	$159.00/$259.00 (See Note)
Category:	Hardware
Publisher:	Central Point Software, Incorporated
Address:	15220 NW Greenbrier Parkway
	Suite 200
	Beaverton, Oregon 97006
Phone:	(503) 690-8090
Notes:	The Copy II PC Option Board can not copy disks whose protection relies on physically damaged disks. However, Central Point Software sells an advanced version of the board for $259.00 that will copy damaged disks. This sort of copy protection is extremely rare today.
	The Deluxe Option Board enables sharing of Macintosh files using the PC's internal 3.5 inch disk drives. Files may be read from or written directly to Macintosh data diskettes.
	Requires one half-size PC/AT (ISA) compatible expansion slot.
Memory:	256K

CopyWrite

CopyWrite allows you to make copies of a number of popular copy protected software packages. When copy protection was more popular, the vendor updated CopyWrite monthly to keep it abreast. As copy protection has become less popular, the frequency of updates has decreased. Registered users can upgrade anytime for $15.00.

Installation   There is no installation program. The manual does not explain how to install the program. It tells you to make a backup copy but does not tell you how.

Operation   CopyWrite is really several separate programs, CopyWrite, Unguard, and Ramkey. CopyWrite will copy the contents of a diskette, including the copy protection, onto another diskette. Unguard will create a completely unprotected copy of a diskette. You can copy this unprotected version with the DOS COPY program. You can also copy the unprotected version to a hard disk. Ramkey is a memory resident program that prevents some copy protected programs from verifying that the correct diskette is in drive-A.

CopyWrite will copy many common copy protection methods. Unguard will produce unprotected copies of most SoftGuard SUPERLoK protected programs. RAMKEY will allow copies of some software to run. You must load RAMKEY first. A complete list of software that will work with the CopyWrite software is available from Quaid Software.

CopyWrite and Unguard are menu driven programs, with no parameters to set. Using them is as easy as typing CopyWrite or Unguard and following the directions on the screen. Since the programs cannot deal with defective target disks, you should format the target disk first to make sure it has no bad spots. If you only have one floppy disk drive, the program will tell you when to switch disks. Unguard will also copy to and from a hard disk. If the resulting program requires RAMKEY, the copy program will tell you. You then simply include RAMKEY in your AUTOEXEC.BAT file.

Limitations   CopyWrite will not work with some ProLock copy protection methods. Quaid Software stated that they were not covering that method because Vault Corporation, makers of Prolock, was in bankruptcy and they did not expect it to be popular. Vault Corporation has filed a law suit against Quaid Software for producing a program to copy Prolocked software.

Manual   My major concern in using CopyWrite is a statement on page 9 of the manual: "Whenever possible the authors of CopyWrite have inserted '*booby traps*' into CopyWrite in an effort to thwart those who attempt to use it for illegal purposes." (emphasis mine) The manual does not state what those booby traps are and a call to Quaid Software yielded no additional information.

The CopyWrite manual briefly explains how to use the software and some of the technical terms associated with copy protection. The 32 page manual has a table of contents but no index. This is not a major flaw since you can run the program without the manual. CopyWrite is not copy protected. Their customer service is free but the call is a toll call to Canada.

Conclusion   CopyWrite represents a good buy for $50.00. It allows you to make backup copies of most of your copy protected software. Some of these copies will then be unprotected. My only concern is the unspecified "booby traps" that Quaid Software builds into the program. I would feel much better if I knew what those booby traps were and more importantly, if I knew they would not damage my software or computer.

```
Product:      CopyWrite
Price:        $55.00
Category:     Commercial
Publisher:    Quaid Software Limited
Address:      45 Charles Street East, 3rd Floor
              Toronto, Ontario
              Canada M4Y 1S2
Phone:        (416) 961-8243
Notes:        Upgrades cost $18.00
Memory:       128K
```

RONNY'S PICKS

The best thing you can do is not purchase copy protected software. If you have older software packages, check for upgrades. Many programs have released unprotected versions. If you must use copy protected software, then Copy II PC is a cheap and effective way to copy it and perhaps unprotect it in the process. If your software uses an exotic method that Copy II PC does not support, then most likely the Copy II PC Option Board will copy it.

17
Anti-Viral Software

There has been much publicity lately about troublesome computer programs, often labeled "viruses." Much of that publicity has been in the popular press and has been wrong. Television, weekly magazines and broadcast news have shown a great deal of misunderstanding of what viruses are and how they threaten computers. In this chapter, I will not tell you how to write a virus or give you a detailed technical explanation of how they work. Rather, I will explain viruses and related problems generally. Then I will tell you what you can do to protect yourself.

THE HISTORY

In the beginning . . .

The late Jim Hauser developed the first known computer virus in 1982. His self-replicating program gave a "guided tour" of Apple II computers. Jim Hauser insisted that his virus was harmless, but he acknowledged the potential for great harm presented by self-replicating programs.

Fred Cohen developed the first intensively studied virus in late 1983 as an experiment for a weekly seminar on computer security. The basic idea of a virus was very simple, and very similar to the biological organism from which it derives its name. The virus would be a program that would reproduce itself and infect other programs with copies of itself. Mr. Cohen wrote his original virus on a VAX 11/750 computer. He inserted the completed virus into a program called VD, a program that displays details about the Unix operating system. He distributed the modified version of VD using a system bulletin board. It infected all of the users using VD. Even users who knew about the experiment were unable to protect themselves. After the experiment, he removed all traces of the virus from the system. The results of the experiment were so threatening that the administrators of the computer system would not allow any more viral experiments.

(Fred Cohen, *Computer Viruses*, Ph.D. dissertation, University of Southern California, 1985. Copies of Dr. Cohen's dissertation and his other works can be obtained from Dr. Cohen c/o Advanced Software Protection; Post Office Box 90069; Pittsburgh, Pennsylvania 15224.)

Fred Cohen's concerns about the possible threat of viruses and his willingness to discuss these possibilities brought him into conflict with various computer security experts. His critics argued that it was safer to keep silent about such computer hazards and that making such hazards known to the public was dangerous. The counter-argument was that an informed computing public was a better defense against malicious programs.

THE LEHIGH VIRUS

The name comes about because the virus was first discovered at Lehigh University in Pennsylvania. The Lehigh virus was an MS-DOS virus first noticed in late November of 1987 when Lehigh University users reported many floppy disk failures. It hid in an area of COMMAND.COM called the stack space. It loaded from the stack space into memory every time the computer booted. It would attempt to infect other disks inserted into the infected computer. After four replications, it would destroy all the data (and programs) on the original computer. All the while, similar counters were ticking on other infected computers. The incubation period was long enough that it infected backup disks as well. As users restored the damaged computer from backup, the counter began once again. This virus hit many users more than once.

Fortunately, the creator of the Lehigh virus made a major mistake. Once the virus came to light, this mistake made it easy to spot infected disks. When the virus infected COMMAND.COM, it changed the file date to the current date. (This is easy for the author of a virus to prevent so do not use this method as your only technique for spotting infections.) All a user had to do was check the date of COMMAND.COM to see if the virus had infected his computer. Removing the virus proved to be easy as well. The virus was completely contained in the stack space of COMMAND.COM. This space is normally all zeros on the disk. All that was necessary to remove the virus was a short program to write all zeros to the stack space. In all, university staff treated more than 600 infected disks in this fashion.

ISRAELI VIRUS

The Israeli virus was discovered in late 1987. The discovery of .COM and .EXE files that were growing in size was the first major clue that something was amiss on some of the Hebrew University's MS-DOS computer systems. The virus would attach 1808 bytes containing the virus code to the file's beginning. The virus would also write the five character string "MsDos" to the

.COM file's end. The initial infection would cause the .EXE files to grow by 1808 bytes and the .COM files by 1813. You might overlook that if it was not for a major programming flaw in the virus code. The virus would not infect .EXE files just once. Instead the virus would keep adding 1808 bytes to the .EXE files each time the computer executed an infected program. As a result of such growth, some .EXE files would become too large to load.

When experts at the University isolated the virus and studied it, they discovered several other characteristics. On Fridays and on the 13th day of a month, the virus would slow down the computer system. More disturbing was what the virus would do on a Friday the 13th. It would destroy any accessible executable file. The next Friday the 13th was May 13, 1988, the day before the State of Israel's 40th Birthday. This date and the Middle East location of the case led some reporters to attribute a political motive for the virus. No one has discovered hard evidence to substantiate this theory, and the case has been extremely out of character for Middle Eastern terrorism. As emphasized by Y. Radai of the Hebrew University and by others, the virus was most likely developed by a prankster.

The University's computer specialist did develop a cure for this virus that stopped the virus before its destructive target date. There were several variants of this virus reported in Israel and a couple possible cases in other countries.

BRAIN VIRUS

Basit Farooq wrote the original MS-DOS Brain. Basit Farooq is a nineteen-year-old software vendor from Pakistan. Mr. Farooq sold pirated software in Pakistan, which has no copyright protection for software. He wrote the brain virus to place on copies of his pirated software being purchased by Americans because they do have copyright protection on software. In that respect, the brain virus may be the first attempt to replace copy protection with viral protection.

The name for this virus comes from its distinctive trait of writing the volume label "(c) BRAIN" on floppy disks without volume labels. The original Brain virus was, though annoying, relatively mild; but several copycat versions of the Brain have been developed. They bear names such as "Ashar" and leave their own labels. Some of these versions are very destructive.

PEACE VIRUS

This MacIntosh virus bears mention in an MS-DOS utilities book because it exemplifies that even shrink-wrapped commercial software is not 100% safe from the viruses. In early March of 1988, many users of Aldus Publishing's FreeHand, a graphics program for the Macintosh, were greeted with the message, "We would like to take this opportunity to convey our universal message of peace to all Macintosh users around the world". (P. Honan, *Beware: It's Virus Season*, Personal Computing, July 1988, page 36.) The virus was designed by the editors of a MacIntosh magazine reportedly to demonstrate the extent of software piracy and to extend a greeting to MacIntosh users on the first anniversary of the release of the MacIntosh II. It is believed that a sub-contractor for Aldus infected his machine with the virus when he played a game from a disk he had obtained from a Canadian computer users group. Although the virus was designed to be benign, several FreeHand users reported that the virus damaged data on their systems.

The biggest damage caused by the virus was its tarnishing of Aldus Publishing's excellent reputation. Also Aldus had to recall about 5,000 copies of FreeHand.

TERMS

The popular press picked up on the term ''virus'' and now applies it to every sort of purposeful damage to a computer. There are actually several different types of problem programs. (Many computer security experts have debated the definitions of the various troublesome programs. The definitions given here are what can be called the classical technical definitions.) They are:

Virus

A virus is a short program that hides in computer systems. It will always have a self-replicating routine which will copy the virus into other files. A virus lives only to reproduce and spread until some event occurs to cause some other action. The very nature of a virus makes it hard to detect. Because it usually hides inside other programs, you cannot perform a: DIR VIRUS.COM. . . and expect to see a dangerous program. In fact, the existence of just such a program would defeat the very purpose of a virus. If it existed as a separate program, it could only run and reproduce when you entered the command to its own program. By hiding in other programs, the virus gets to run when they run. Generally, the virus only hides in specific types of programs. As a result, it is often very good at hiding. The size of the program file may not change. The date and time of the program may not change. Usually, the program will appear to run normally.

The most commonly infected programs are three special DOS files called IBMBIOS.COM, IBMSYS.COM and COMMAND.COM. (The names of the first two systems files may vary with the type of DOS one uses.) The first two files are hidden (you do not see them when you type DIR) and system (entering their name will not run the program) files. It loads all three every time you start your computer. A virus will only infect other files if its code executes. For this to happen, you or another program you run must use the infected program. Once a virus successfully infects a system program, it knows it will get to run any time the computer operates. The lack of an immediate problem is the most critical threat of a virus. When you contract a cold virus, the virus hides and begins reproducing right away. However, you do not get sick right away. You probably infect a number of people before getting sick. A computer virus works the same way. Every time you insert a floppy disk into an infected computer, the virus is going to try to get on that disk. If it succeeds, it is going to try to get into every computer anyone uses that disk in. All before you even know your computer has a virus.

After the incubation period, the virus may begin to perform whatever other actions its programmers built into it. A benign one may simply display some message on the screen. Others may format your hard disk. However, it is the ones in the middle that cause the largest problems. The benign message usually causes no real problem. Major destruction of data is easily detectable and generally the data can be reconstructed from a backup. However, the virus may begin changing only a few bytes of data at a time. That sounds minor, but what if the few bytes that get changed are in tax or payroll records?

Worse yet, this slow creeping damage is likely to be undetected until long after modified backups have replaced the unmodified ones.

Trojan Horse

The original Trojan Horse was "a huge, hollow wooden horse filled with Greek soldiers and left at the gates of Troy: when it was brought into the city, the soldiers came out at night and opened the gates to the Greek army, who destroyed the city." (Footnote: *Webster's New World Dictionary,* David B. Guralnid, Editor in Chief, Simon and Schuster, 1982.) In short, it was a desirable item that enticed the recipient to let down defenses, but inside it was the recipient's destruction.

Like a computer virus, the computer Trojan horse behaves much like its noncomputer counterpart. A Trojan horse is a program that is suppose to do something useful but it also damages the computer. Trojan horses are typically small, easy-to-write programs such as games or utilities. Some Trojans are legitimate programs that someone has "hacked" (modified) to include a destructive routine.

One notable case is the hacked version of Ross Greenberg's FluShot antiviral program. Somebody took FluShot's documentation text file and made it into a text displaying executable file that would also destroy the contents of the disk. Not only did the Trojan damage data, it also hurt Mr. Greenberg's reputation. This and other cases are a good reason for getting software from reliable sources. An advanced version of the FluShot program is reviewed later in this chapter.

Most Trojan horses do their damage immediately upon execution. There are some Trojan horse programs ("logical bombs") which will only do their damage when certain conditions are met. For example, a Trojan horse version of a tax accounting program might format its victim's disks the first time the program runs in April.

The major difference between a Trojan horse and a virus is the Trojan horse does not infect other programs or other machines. The only way to transmit a Trojan horse is by copying the program containing it to another system. Removing a Trojan horse is as easy as erasing the infected program. The difficult part is, of course, knowing if you have a virus or a Trojan horse. (The Dirty Dozen listing by Eric Newhouse is a list of Trojan horse programs and other "bogusware." This listing is available from many computer bulletin board systems, including Mr. Newhouse's at (617) 498-8448.)

Worm

A worm is generally a program that burrows through a computer system or a network. It may do this by moving itself to different locations on a system or by making copies of itself. Even when a worm makes copies of itself, unlike a virus, these copies are separate, distinct files. The worm does not copy its code into another program. The much reported "ARPANET Virus" which jammed up the Federal Advanced Research Projects Agency computer network was a worm. The two most publicized "virus" cases of 1988 were not viruses by the classical definition. As mentioned here, the "ARPANET Virus" was a worm. The Burleson "virus" case in Texas was a case of outright computer sabotage involving a "logic bomb" type of Trojan horse. In neither case was there any danger of the programs infecting other software.

PREVENTING VIRAL INFECTION

Your two strongest defenses against viral infection are the write protect tab and common sense. A virus cannot come into your computer through the power lines. It cannot come into your computer over the signal going to your modem, although you can download infected programs over your modem.

There was a prank message going around awhile back that claimed 2400 baud modem could be infected over the phone line. That is simply not true. You can use a modem to download infected software. However, the act of downloading infected software does not infect your system. To infect your system, you must run the infected program. The only way a virus can get into your computer is by your running an infected program in your computer. That infected program can come from a disk, a network, or over the modem.

If you have a good write-protect tab on a floppy disk, it is physically impossible for a normal floppy drive to write to the disk. Therefore, it is physically impossible for a write-protected floppy disk to become infected. Whenever you take data from your computer to another computer for printing, your disk should be write-protected. Anytime you take a program to run on another computer, your program disk should be write-protected.

In addition to the write-protect tab, the following guidelines will help you minimize the chance of infection.

1) Limit viral access to your computers. Only run commercial software that you purchased from a known source. Avoid pirated software like the plague. Likewise, be cautious about "borrow-ware or borroware" or software rentals. Only run shareware or public domain software if you download it from a reliable network like PC-Link or CompuServe, you purchased from a reliable shareware distributor.

   Many shareware authors will send you a disk with the latest version of their program for five to ten dollars. You still have to register if you like the program but this makes sure the software is clean. All of the software included on the optional diskette set that goes with this book was obtained directly from the software author.

Never run a program if you do not know where it came from. "Know thy software!" If your computer is accessible by anyone you do not completely trust, turn it off and lock it up when you are not around. If it does not have a lock, install a card like the PC-Lock card. Even with trusted people, it may be wise, especially in corporate settings, to control the software used on the systems.

Self-extracting files which are popular on some networks present a special hazard. These files contain a collection of files in a compressed format along with a routine to decompress them. Unlike the more common archived files, which require a separate utility to decompress them, the self-extracting files are themselves executed. A Trojan horse or a virus infected program can masquerade as a self-extracting file. When run, the file would do its damage. Unlike the regular archived files, you cannot examine the contents of the self-extracting files before running any untested program. Users have reported that one utility that can make self-extracting files can include hidden files. This feature makes it harder for one to know exactly what was in the self-extracting file. The only software that really has a legitimate reason for being distributed as self-extracting files are the archiving utilities themselves.

2) On your own computer, never run from the original program disks. If a virus ever infects your computer, you will need these original disks to restore the system to a clean state. When you buy software, the first thing you should do is write-protect the software disks. That way, they cannot become infected even if your computer is infected when you install the software.

3) Make regular backups. When you go to make a backup, cold-boot (e.g. turn the computer off for thirty seconds) off a write-protected DOS disk. Then run your backup program off a write-protected floppy diskette. That way, there is no chance of your backup being infected. If you think there is any chance the data files in your backup are infected, restore them to another system and verify their structure. If your backup program has a verify option, use that to check the structure. Keep two or three sets of backup disks instead or writing all backups on the same set of disks This gives a better chance of finding clean backups if your computer is infected.

4) Anytime software gives you an error message because it wants to write to a write-protected disk, assume a virus is trying to infect the disk. If you think the software may legitimately need to write to the disk, say during an installation, call technical support first. Verify that the software does indeed write to the disk and when that writing takes place. You can successfully install most non-copy protected software with write-protect tabs in place. In fact, many vendors sell their software with a permanent write-protect tab. This not only protects you from viruses but also from the more common accidental overwrites.

5) The favorite file for viral infection is COMMAND.COM since it executes when the computer starts and is accessed many times while the computer

is running. Never place COMMAND.COM on a disk unless you need to boot from that disk. Format most disks without the system. Write-protect your disks that have COMMAND.COM on them. Boot from those disks then put a program disk without COMMAND.COM into the computer to run. The computer may occasionally ask you to insert the disk containing COMMAND.COM in the A-drive. This is normal. However, it will never need to write to that disk so leave the write-protect tab on the COMMAND.COM disk. You can also use a utility, like the Norton Utilities or the DOS ATTRIB.COM program, to make COMMAND.COM a "read-only" file. On my system, I have gone so far as to make every executable (.EXE and .COM files) read-only. This prevents some viruses from writing to the files. However, a virus can bypass this so making a file read-only is not 100% effective against viral attack.

6) Besides hiding the COMMAND.COM and other executable files, changing filenames of certain programs can give an extra measure of protection from viruses and other malicious programs. FORMAT.COM is a prime candidate for a name change. (I have renamed FORMAT.COM on my system and use a FORMAT.BAT to use the renamed FORMAT program. The .BAT file allows only drives A and B to be formatted.) If you are familiar enough with DOS, you can rename COMMAND.COM and set up your system to find the program under its new name. However, do not rush out and change the name of every file. Some programs refer to other files and won't be able to find them if you have changed their names.

7) A warm reboot (Control-Alternate-Delete) does not remove everything from memory. Some viruses are able to stay in memory during a warm reboot. To be safe, when using another computer, turn it off for thirty seconds before using it. While the computer is off, insert your own write-protected boot disk in the A-drive. That way, even if the COMMAND.COM on the hard disk is infected you should be protected.

8) If you must ever run a program of unknown origin, run it on a machine without a hard disk. Boot and run that machine from a write-protected DOS disk. Store any data produced by the program on a disk containing only data, no program files. Program files end with the extensions .COM, .EXE or .SYS. Only transport the data disk to another machine. If you have an anti-viral software package, use it while running this program.

9) Keep in touch with your system and with its files. Once in a while, look at the file directories, preferably using a method that also displays hidden files. (CHKDSK /V is one means of doing this.) If you see unexplained new files, check them out. Watch for .COM and .EXE files with the same name. While this might be caused by a malicious program, you definitely run the risk of executing the wrong program. (In a case of .COM and .EXE files with the same name, DOS will run the .COM file and not touch the .EXE file. One common cause for this copying different versions of the same software. Sometimes an upgraded version may switch to a different extension.) Drastic changes in file sizes or dates may point to trouble.

DETERMINING WHETHER YOU WERE ATTACKED

We all lose files occasionally. We enter DEL ∗.BAT when we meant DEL ∗.BAK. Just because you lose a file does not mean a virus has infected your computer. Because of the publicity surrounding viruses, almost everything that goes wrong with a computer these days is being blamed on a viral attack. For the average user, the chances of accidentally formatting your hard disk or your hard disk crashing for mechanical reasons are far greater than a viral attack.

When you find files missing or damaged, the first thing to do is to decide if you have been doing anything that could have caused the problem. Did you have to reboot while editing that file because the computer locked up? Have you been cleaning out the hard disk? Could you have entered a DEL command wrong? If the answer is yes, your best bet is to restore the missing file from a recent backup and go on about your business. To be safe, you will want to cold-boot from your write-protected DOS disk. You will also want to run your restore program from a write-protected disk. As a final precaution, you should write-protect your backup disks. You cannot, of course, do this during your backups but most programs will allow it during a restore.

You may be more worried if you turn your computer on one day and cannot access the hard disk or you find many files missing from the hard disk. However, the cause is still far more likely to be nonviral. I once owned a computer with a flaky hard disk that would quit working about once every six months. It took a low-level format, FDISK and a DOS format to get it working again for another six months. The problem was not a virus, it was a mechanical problem. Your best bet is to have any total system failure looked at by a qualified service person. If, however, you find out you have a virus, then you will have to rebuild your system. The steps are:

1) If you can still access the system, get off any data files of which you do not have a recent backup. As above, cold-boot of a write-protected DOS disk and run your backup disk from a write-protected disk. Data files cannot carry viruses. (The virus can, of course, change the data in a data file or erase it altogether. So while you can assume the data file does not contain a virus you cannot be sure it is undamaged.) So you can use data files from an infected system. Do not backup any files with a .COM, .EXE or .SYS extension.

2) Perform a low-level format of the hard disk. Many hard disks do this using the DOS program called DEBUG. Only run DEBUG from a write-protected DOS disk. Check your manual or contact your drive manufacturer for low-level formatting instructions.

3) Run FDISK and FORMAT. These are both DOS programs and you should only run them from a write-protected DOS disk.

4) Restore your software from the original disks.

5) Restore your data from your most recent backup, running the restore program from a write-protected disk. Do not restore any files with a .COM, .EXE or .SYS extension. Extend this caution to other files that contain exe-

cutable code. They include files with the .OVR and the .OVL extension. In fact, if you can restore a current version of a particular file from an original program disk, do not restore it from any other disk regardless of its extension.

DETERMINING WHETHER YOU NEED ANTI-VIRAL SOFTWARE

Unless you have followed the steps outlined above, anti-viral software is going to be ineffective on your system. Write-protect tabs, common sense and frequent backups are far more important than anti-viral software. Even the companies producing this software will tell you that.

If you are using these steps, then anti-viral software makes sense if . . .

1) You are using your computer in an academic environment. So far, viruses have been far more common on personal computers at our universities. These computers, more than any others, need additional protection. This warning also applies if you have a corporate computer system and any of your employees is taking computer courses at a college or a university. These employees, among the best resources of a corporation, have sometime unwittingly carried troublesome programs from the university to their workplace.

2) You frequently use different computers. Again, this is most common in the academic environment where the student goes to a PC laboratory and uses any one of dozens of computers in a common pool. This is especially dangerous when you must also share a common pool of software. Most university PC laboratories allow you to check out software from a pool of available software. Since the software is of unknown origin, there is no way to verify you have a clean copy. PC support people and consultants face a similar risk because their work will take them and their disk from one computer to another. Placing a write-protect tab on an already infected disk offers no additional protection. In this situation, anti-viral software is a must. Also consider purchasing your own software and write-protect it.

3) Your computer is accessible by others. Anti-viral software gives you an extra layer of protection since you do not know what these other individuals are doing while using your computer. Some anti-viral software is bundled in with general data security software.

4) You have your computer connected to a network, especially when you do not know everyone else on the network.

5) You download software from bulletin boards where you are not sure they take the time and effort to ensure they have only clean copies of software.

6) You run copy protected software. Generally, you cannot install copy protected software with the distribution disks write-protected. With many packages, you cannot even run the software off a write-protected disk. As a result, it is far easier for a virus to infect the copy protected disk.

7) You run pirated software. You really should avoid pirated software. It comes from individuals who have already shown they have little regard for

the law or the rights of others. Given the criminal nature of pirated software, it is hard to believe the pirates make sure they sell only clean copies of their stolen software.

8) You develop software for others, especially if you sell your software. Getting a virus on your system means far more than damaged data, it can ruin your reputation or expose you to legal action. (In the wake of the Peace virus case, Aldus Publishing was considering legal action against the authors of the virus and the subcontractor with the infected computer.) Although computer law is still in its infancy, the ability to show that you have taken reasonable precautions may help your defense against accusations of negligence. You will still need to take extra precautions with your system, but the anti-viral software does help.

THE ANTI-VIRAL PACKAGES

Mr. Glath points out that like write-protect tabs, common sense and backups, an anti-viral package is not 100% protection. "Any security system can be broken by someone dedicated and knowledgeable enough to put forth the effort to break the system." (Computer Viruses: A Rational View, an unpublished paper by Raymond M. Glath, President of RG Software Systems, Incorporated.)

Mr. Glath also points out that the level of protection you need depends on several things, including:

1) The sensitivity of the data on your computer.
2) The number of personnel having access to your computer.
3) The security awareness of computing personnel.
4) The skill levels of computing personnel.
5) Attitudes, ethics, and morale of computing personnel.

A key point to remember in anti-viral software is software that monitors what your system does and occasionally interferes when the actions of the system appear to be actions a virus would take. Even if they never have to alert you to danger, their actions are not free. Every check the program makes requires computing time and that time reduces the time available to your computer to perform other tasks. There are several things that anti-viral software can do to protect your system:

1) Signature checks. The anti-viral program derives a signature for every key file on the computer. The signature is a number mathematically derived from the contents of the file in such a fashion that different files will have different signatures. When the signature of a file changes the anti-viral program knows that something, possibly a virus, has altered that file.

Other things can change a program file as well. For example, the configuration program for SideKick writes your changes back directly into the program file SK.COM. An anti-viral program performing a signature check would not know that, all it would know is the file SK.COM has somehow been changed. Fortunately, many software authors are getting away from configuration schemes that modify the executable files, opting instead for schemes such as separate configuration files.

Usually, the software stores the results of the signature checks in a data file. That data file may not be encrypted. Encrypted signature data files are safer. Some anti-viral packages run checks against the data file only upon booting up the system or when you issue a special command. Such infrequent checks may allow too wide of a gap on systems which are not re-booted for hours or even for days. Other anti-viral packages will run more frequent checks. Signature checks will not prevent primary virus infection, that is, the first infection of one or more files. What signature check will do is alert you of the possible presence of a virus and, thus, help to prevent secondary infections.

2) Write-protection. Important files are write-protected by changing their attributes to read-only. You can do the same thing with the Norton Utilities or the DOS ATTRIB program. This protection is software-based and can be bypassed.

3) Constant watching. The anti-viral program stays in memory and watches for behavior that appears to be viral behavior. The memory-resident approach is an attempt to intercept any infection, including primary infections. This method suffers from varying degrees of false alarms. For example, on its highest level of protection one older package will object twice every time you format a disk using the DOS program FORMAT.COM. One objection is for the actual formatting and the other is when DOS writes the volume label. Most programs require you to confirm the virus-like behavior before it allows the command to execute. As a result, this method can actually prevent infection. Of course, if there are too many false alarms, then users will quit using the software. Besides the false alarms, there is the challenge of interpreting the warning messages. Even experts may have a difficult time determining if an intercepted disk writing attempt was the result of a valid program or of a virus.

4) Access restriction. Several anti-viral software packages are actually access and data security packages with anti-viral features as an added feature. Most of these packages will not allow you to run any new software on the computer system unless a system administrator has "authorized" that program. The anti-viral bonus provided by this feature is that it ensures the system of using only tried and tested software. A couple of these security packages will encrypt files, including program files, to give extra protection. Some security packages will prevent anybody from bypassing their defenses by booting from floppy disks. Access restriction is not particularly useful for a system used by only one person. It is important for systems, such as ones in offices, where many people share a few computers.

5) Recovery helps. Although this is not really an anti-viral feature, the recovery utilities provided by some anti-viral software provide added protection. Usually, such software will make special backups of critical disk information such as the boot sector and the File Allocation Table (FAT). Such backup can make system restoration much easier.

Most anti-viral packages use some combination of the first three methods. A few packages use only one method, usually the software packages designed for other purposes and that added anti-viral capabilities as a selling feature.

With anti-viral software, there are many issues to consider. Some of these issues affect the actual usefulness of the software; others affect the usefulness of the software on a particular system. Before purchasing an anti-viral program, you need to consider the following (This list was expanded from the excellent list of "special considerations for virus protection packages" Raymond M. Glath lists in his unpublished paper reference.):

1) Effect upon operation: How will the program effect the normal operation of your computer? If it only checks files when you boot, does that take a long time? If it is memory resident, does it take up a lot of RAM? Does its operation use so many clock cycles that the computer runs noticeably slower?

2) Ease of use: How easy is it to use? The user most likely to be infected is a fairly new or inexperienced user. They must be able to use the program and, unless there is a technical systems administrator, to install the program. Any messages displayed by the program must both be a clear enough warning that the user does not overlook them. They must offer enough of an explanation that the new user understands the message. The messages should be concise and not misleading. An often neglected but vital factor for ease of use is the documentation. Is it clear but thorough? Does it discuss troubleshooting? What technical support does the vendor have?

3) False alarms: The software must minimize false alarms. The software should be like an ejection seat in an airplane: You know it is there when you need to know, but it should not go off too often in normal operation. Some older anti-viral software will give multiple warnings to a routine procedure such as formatting a floppy disk. Sometimes, such interference can make routine tasks, such as programming and compiling programs, almost impossible. Many of the newer anti-viral packages allow fine tuning of these interruptions.

4) Probability of continued use: This is really a combination of the first three issues. Users will simply not use a program that slows down their computer or constantly badgers them with false alerts. They especially will not use a program that is hard to use or displays messages they do not understand. Nor will they continue to willingly use the software if it intimidates them by giving an impression that Big Brother is watching.

5) Effectiveness: How effective is it, or stated another way, does it work? After all, it does little good for you to use an easy to use program that does not slow down your computer if it does not work.

This factor was an important consideration in the review and testing of the software listed in this chapter. While no anti-viral software could be considered 100% effective against any virus present or future, the better the software resists various systems attacks, the better are your chances against catastrophic virus damage.

A related consideration is what types of files the program protects. Some anti-viral software limit their protection to only the systems files and files with a .COM or .EXE extension. Other anti-viral software allow you to select the protected files.

6) Detection of primary infection: Does the software detect a virus before or after it has infected a program or made its attack? (e.g.: Does it catch the primary infection?) Before is much better. However, detecting the infection soon after it happens usually allows you to recover all your data.

7) Indication of suspect files: If an infection does get past the anti-viral program, can it help you spot which files the virus infected? That way, you can erase those files without having to reformat the system. Of course, you would want to cold-boot from a write-protected DOS disk before erasing the infected files. You would also want to completely erase them using a program like the WIPEFILE program included with the Norton Utilities.

8) Compatibility: Is the anti-viral program compatible with your current hardware, software and especially your memory resident software. Also consider the major uses of your computer. A computer used almost exclusively for word processing presents a different situation for an anti-viral package than a computer used for developing Pascal programs. The stability of the computer system is a major factor to consider. Some systems undergo very few changes; they run the same software for years. Other systems are constantly being updated and upgraded. (This is especially true of the power users' computers.) The anti-viral package should be able to adapt. If you are using the computer in a local area network (LAN), check if the anti-viral software will work with a LAN. I was not able to fully answer this question because MS-DOS LAN systems are extremely varied. Make sure that you can return the software if it is incompatible with your system.

9) Implementation costs: How much does it cost to buy the package for all the systems that you want to protect? How much training/learning does the program require? How much user time does operating the anti-viral program take? Will it require hiring a technician? If a program takes up too much time or money, you are going to end up not using it.

10) Maintenance considerations: Does the anti-viral package require a dedicated technician to administer the system? If so, does it allow for alternatives in case the systems administrator is unavailable? Can you update the system easily as you install new programs?

11) Security/accessibility balance: Does the anti-viral package carry the possibility of making your data secure from everybody . . . including you? A few packages are capable of doing this if their own files are damaged. Some of these packages lose the ability to unencrypt files if an encryption key file is damaged. Others will lock out the ability to boot from floppy drives. Normally, this is a great security feature, but if the anti-virus software is damaged or something happens to the systems files, recovery will be extremely difficult. Unless your computer use requires a high degree of security, the software should allow some way of recovering

the system if it is damaged. Yet any route of access into a computer carries a risk of unwelcome access. The better programs give you a choice.

12) Extra benefits: Does the anti-viral package have any benefits beyond its anti-viral function. We are in the age of multi-function software. Disk optimization packages also offer file unerasing. File-unerasing packages also offer anti-viral software. The more useful features any program gives you the higher its value.

BEFORE YOU INSTALL ANTI-VIRAL SOFTWARE . . .

There are several general recommendations to make it easier to install the software and to protect your system. I have learned many of these recommended things through hard experience. They are the following:

1) If you have heard it once, you have heard it a thousand times, but it is so critical—BACK UP YOUR DATA. It is good computing practice and it will give you a safety net if, by some accident, the disk crashes. Also keep a backup DOS floppy disk handy. If you have favorite utilities such as a text editor, keep them available on a floppy disk. You may need them in an emergency.

2) Read the documentation. Although many power users tend to first experiment and then read the instructions, this is very dangerous with any software that affects the way DOS stores and processes files. Such software includes disk sector editors, disk optimizers, and, of course, many anti-viral software packages. Again, take the time to read and to digest the documentation.

3) Make sure that you have read ALL the documentation. Many of the anti-viral software packages include documentation update text files on the disks themselves. Often the printed material will make no mention of such files. Yet they often contain very useful and, sometimes, critical information. Look at each disk's directory for files that look like text files and examine them. Common clues are filenames such as READ.ME and UPDATE.DOC. Look for .TXT or .DOC extensions.

4) Make sure that you have the required equipment, software, hardware, and disk space. Some of the more extensive anti-viral packages require up to 1M of hard disk space. Not having these prerequisites could cause the installation to fail and possibly lock you out of your own system. It is possible to regain access but it takes much time, effort and skill.

5) If you have previously made your AUTOEXEC.BAT or CONFIG.SYS files into hidden or read-only files, change them so the installation program can modify them. Some anti-viral software will add commands to these files. Often, the installation programs will not tell you that they could not modify these files. Also keep a backup of these files and compare these files with their backups after installation. This will give you an idea of what changes the installation program made. Although none of the reviewed software did this, some installation programs will overwrite the existing CONFIG.SYS file. If the original CONFIG.SYS contained instruction for the use of various device drivers, you may find that your system

will not work properly. In such a case, add the instructions from the backup copy of CONFIG.SYS.

6) Allow enough time to do the job right. Haste is a tremendous pitfall when installing anti-viral software. Allow time to properly configure the system. Also, you will need a couple of days or even weeks until you are sure that the system is fine tuned. If you can avoid it, do not install anti-viral software just before a big important rush project involving your computer.

7) Have someone you can call for technical help just in case. That person could be the anti-viral software's technical support staff, your local PC expert, or a user's group.

Certus (version 2.1 tested)

(Anti-viral software is changing rapidly. For that reason, I have included the version number in these reviews.)

FoundationWare's *Certus* is a comprehensive anti-viral software package. It will run signature checks on selected files. Certus will provide the selected files with software write protects and block the execution of any unauthorized software. It will also intercept suspicious disk access attempts. It provides an assortment of utilities to give extra protection for certain circumstances and to assist you in working with Certus. If you want to, Certus will keep system audit logs.

Installation   There is an installation program. The manual has two sets of installation instructions. The regular installation instruction and the section "Installing FoundationWare Certus for Those Who Refuse to Read Manuals." Use the regular installation instructions. They give steps that will save much potential aggravation later on. Certus allows you to select what programs will be both protected and approved to run on the system by selecting their extension. In few cases, this can give a nasty surprise if a program uses data files that have extensions also used by protected programs. I discovered this when I included .FON (font) extensions as protected ones. One of my telecommunication packages uses a telephone log file with a .FON extension. Certus interpreted the routine update of the phone log as an attempt to modify a protected file.

During installation, you have the option of making a "Critical Disk." Use that option. The Critical Disk is a great recovery feature. Even if the boot sector and the FAT are completely scrambled, Certus can restore the system from the Critical Disk.

Operation   Except for the various maintenance and special utilities, there is little to run once you have Certus set up. You run the memory resident disk access watching program from the AUTOEXEC.BAT. During boot up, it runs signature checks on the protected files. After boot up, the memory resident software checks each program being executed. If the program is not one of the approved programs, Certus will display a warning prompt similar to the one shown in Fig. 17-1. Depending upon the security level chosen during installation, it might not allow it to run. To add the program to the approved and

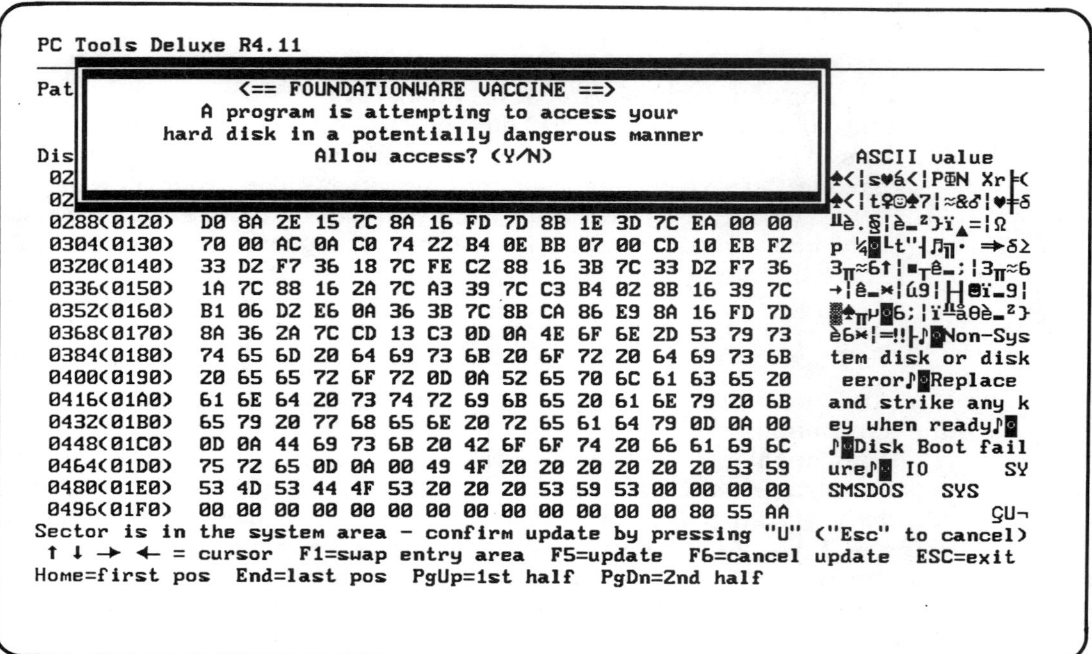

Fig. 17-1. Here, Certus gives a warning when program code files not previously approved are being accessed.

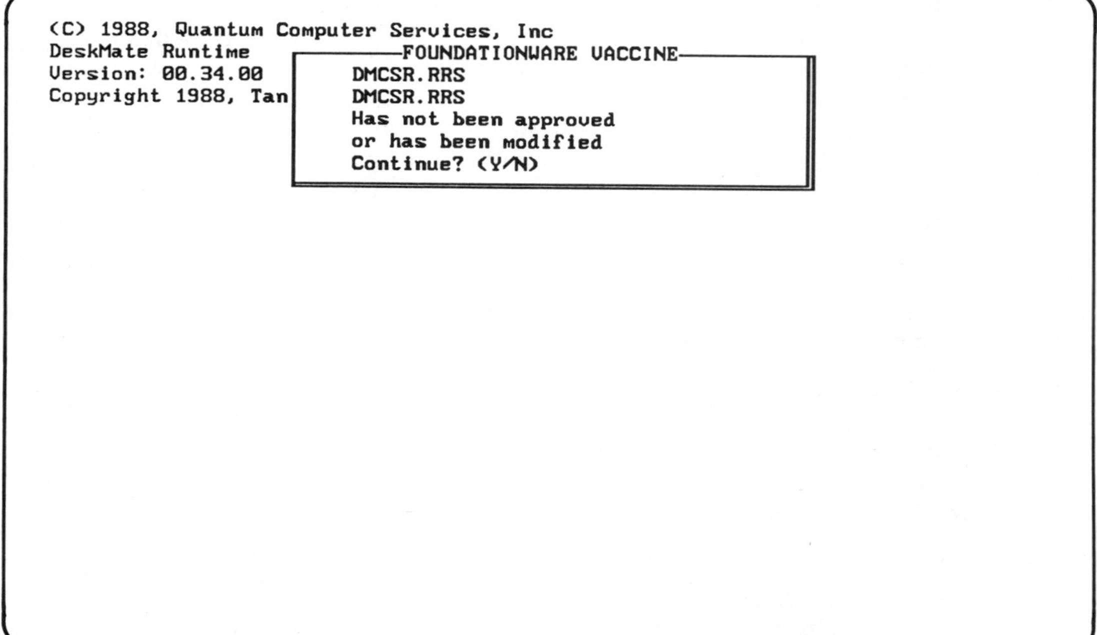

Fig. 17-2. An attempt to modify the book sector is intercepted by Certus.

protected software list, you can use either the QUICK or QUICKVAC utilities. If a program attempts to modify critical areas such as the boot sector, Certus will intercept it and display the warning in Fig. 17-2.

Limitations   The biggest drawback is the difficulty in setting it up and properly configuring it. To get the most out of the stringent protection while not hampering regular work, you will need to take the time to fine-tune the Certus configuration on your system. Such complexity will be intimidating to novice computer users.

Manual   The manual has been upgraded from a thick booklet of the earlier FoundationWare Vaccine packages to a loose-leaf "DOS Manual" style book. With this change, the manual has greatly improved. It now provides trouble-shooting instructions for the program. For most questions that arise out of using Certus, the answer will be somewhere in the manual's 151 pages.

Conclusion   Strict and thorough are the first two words that come to my mind to describe Certus. Although the price is on the high end, it provides good protection for computer systems which need not only general protection from virus, but also need control of their use. As the name implies, Certus is best suited for corporate systems which need a way of administering PC's. Also, Certus is the only anti-viral package reviewed that has addressed the question of local area networks. It will on workstations connected to LANs. There is a version called Certus FS for protecting LAN file servers.

Product:	Certus
Price:	$189.00
Category:	Commercial
Publisher:	FoundationWare
Address:	13110 Shaker Square
	Cleveland, Ohio 44120
Phone:	(216) 752-8181
Notes:	Corporate discounts are available.
	Requires 512K to install, 7K to run.
Memory:	7K

Data Physician (version 1.5 tested)

Data Physician is a set of anti-viral utilities. The main program, DATAMD provides signature checks of selected files. PADLOCK and DIKSLOCK intercept disk accesses. The NOVIRUS utility works with DATAMD to provide frequent signature checks of files. There is the ANTIGEN utility to attach self-checking routines to individual programs. VIRALERT is intended to spot virus activity before an infection occurs.

Installation   There is no installation program, but the manual offers clear step-by-step instructions. You must manually copy the individual program to the hard disk. You have to modify the CONFIG.SYS file to use the PADLOCK utility.

Operation   For the main Data Physician program, run DATAMD. It will give you several options. You can designate which files it will protect by the signature check. You can run the signature checks. If need be, you can attempt to remove a virus but success is not guaranteed. PADLOCK works in the background, acting as an "intelligent" write protect challenging disk writes.

If you use NOVIRUS, it can be adjusted for how many signature checks you want it to run whenever you run any executable file. This allows for constant signature checks of the files.

VIRALERT, unlike PADLOCK, will intercept write attempts only to .COM, .EXE, .SYS file or to the boot sector. If you are willing to accept increased false alarms, you can make VIRALERT detect other disk activities.

Limitations   The DATAMD virus removal option sounds good, but usually it is safer to restore the file from clean backups.

Manual   The manual consists of a thick bundle of loose leaf pages. Each component software package of Data Physician has its own section. At first glance, the thickness of the manual is intimidating, but it is well laid out. The program diskette had extra documentation in a text file.

Conclusion   Data Physician provides several useful anti-viral utilities.

<table>
<tr><td>Product:</td><td>Data Physician</td></tr>
<tr><td>Price:</td><td>$149.00</td></tr>
<tr><td>Category:</td><td>Commercial</td></tr>
<tr><td>Publisher:</td><td>Digital Dispatch, Incorporated</td></tr>
<tr><td>Address:</td><td>55 Lakeland Shores Road
Lakeland, Minnesota 55043</td></tr>
<tr><td>Phone:</td><td>(800) 221-8091</td></tr>
<tr><td>Memory:</td><td>128K</td></tr>
</table>

Disk Watcher (version 2.0 tested)

Like SoftSafe, *Disk Watcher* is another data protection package that recently added virus protection. Disk Watcher started as a software package to guard people from accidental destruction of data. Later, the software upgraded to include anti-viral capabilities.

Installation   There is an installation program. When run, the program provides a detailed menu for configuring Disk Watcher. For each option, it gives a brief explanation. Two of the most interesting settings are the power user option and the learn options. The power user option allows you to select whether you have to hit Enter after keying the option letter or not. It is safer to have to hit Enter, giving you a second chance. The learn option allows you to adjust the security level on your system. You can set Disk Watcher to allow you to approve a challenged program for now and future sessions or you can set it to allow the approval of a program for the current session. The strictest setting would always deny a challenged program. During installation, you can select the hot-key combination to bring up the Disk Watcher menu.

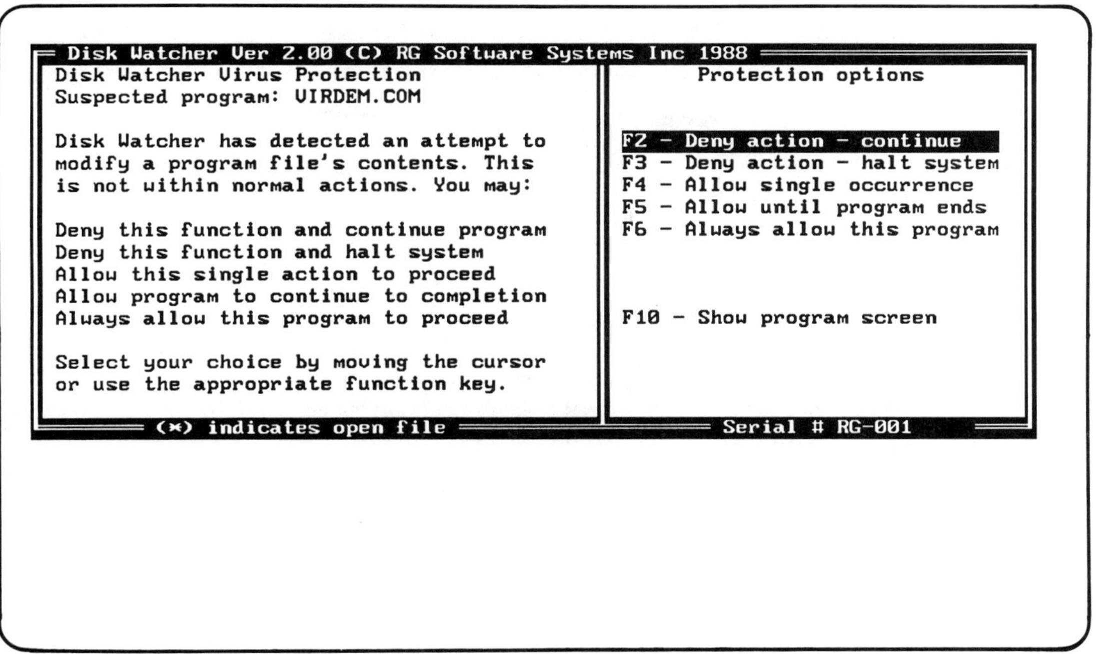

Fig. 17-3. The Disk Watcher warning prompt displayed when it intercepts a suspicious disk access.

Operation You bring up the main Disk Watcher menu by using the hot-key combination you selected during installation. The menu does not offer any explicit anti-viral option. Instead, it provides a number of hard disk and file management utilities.

If Disk Watcher finds a suspicious disk access, it will display a warning prompt like the one in Fig. 17-3. Disk Watcher also keeps track of the number of hidden files on the disk and it will give a warning if the number changes.

Limitations Disk Watcher did allow me to erase COMMAND.COM. It lacks some of the anti-viral features, such as signature checks, found in many other packages.

Manual It includes two manuals in the form of thick booklets. One is the manual for Disk Watcher version 1.02. The other is the supplement for Disk Watcher version 2.0. The earlier manual has no mention of viruses at all. Although the manuals do present quite a bit of reading, they clearly explain how to use Disk Watcher. The manuals explained how to decide your response to warning messages.

Conclusion Disk Watcher does provide a number of safeguards against common data damage due to mistakes. It will protect the system from changes to the boot sector and to the system files. It also provides a hard disk manager. However it could use several other anti-viral features to improve the protection.

```
Product:     Disk Watcher
Price:       $99.95
Publisher:   RG Software Systems
Address:     2300 Computer Avenue
             Willow Grove, Pennsylvania 19090
Phone:       (215) 659-5300
Memory:      47K
```

Dr. Panda Utilities

Dr. Panda Utilities are a set of anti-viral utility programs. They offer an anti-viral toolkit. The core utilities are the PHYSICAL signature check utility, the LABTEST file examining utility, and the MONITOR memory resident disk access checker. Other utilities include a program which tells you if the program is becoming memory resident, a program to detect and remove the Brain virus, and a memory resident program mapper.

The LABTEST and the MONITOR programs bear a resemblance in function to the CHK4BOMB and BOMBSQAD utilities often seen on computer networks. This is not a coincidence. CHK4BOMB and BOMBSQAD, which were accidentally premature releases are the ancestors of LABTEST and MONITOR. The authors have removed these programs from shareware distribution and request networks not to carry the CHK4BOMB and BOMBSQAD programs. In addition, the programs in the Dr. Panda Utilities have greatly improved upon the two premature releases.

Installation   For the PHYSICAL utility, run the PINSTALL program. Have a copy of DOS on a floppy disk. The installation program uses the DOS floppy disk as a basis of checking your system files. For extra security, you are able to rename the PHYSICAL signature data file. PINSTALL allows you to select the files it will check.

You must manually copy the other utilities to the hard disk. There is no special setup required for these utilities. You may want to modify your AUTOEXEC.BAT and some of your other batch files so they run the appropriate utility. For example, have the AUTOEXEC.BAT run PHYSICAL each time you boot up the system. Some of the batch files can be modified so they set the MONITOR options.

Operation   You run the PHYSICAL utility by simply entering PHYSICAL. It will check against the signature records in the PHYSICAL data file and display the test results as in Fig. 17-4. Also it lists any hidden files on the disk. If you are installing new software, you can either run PINSTALL again or use PHYSED editor for the PHYSICAL data file.

To run LABTEST, just enter LABTEST with or without the name of the file to test. If you do not specify a filename, LABTEST will prompt you for it. LABTEST will scan the file for any suspicious disk activities and display a warning if it finds any such activities. Figure 17-5 shows this. Then it will display a screen such as the one shown in Fig. 17-6 with any embedded ASCII test found in the file.

```
A:\>physical
PHYSICAL V3.1
Copyright (C) 1988  All rights reserved.
PANDA SYSTEMS
Wilmington, Delaware

All System Files Check OK!

Hidden Files.  Be Alert for any suspicious names:
\IO.SYS
\MSDOS.SYS

Checking Other Files:
File Checks OK  C:\PC-CACHE.COM
File Checks OK  C:\DOS\ASSIGN.COM
File Checks OK  C:\DOS\BACKUP.COM
File Checks OK  C:\DOS\CHKDSK.COM
File Checks OK  C:\DOS\COMP.COM
File Checks OK  C:\DOS\DISKCOMP.COM
File Checks OK  C:\DOS\DISKCOPY.COM
File Checks OK  C:\DOS\EDLIN.COM
File Checks OK  C:\DOS\FDISK.COM
```

Fig. 17-4. The results of PHYSICAL's check of files. Note, also, the listing of the hidden files on the system.

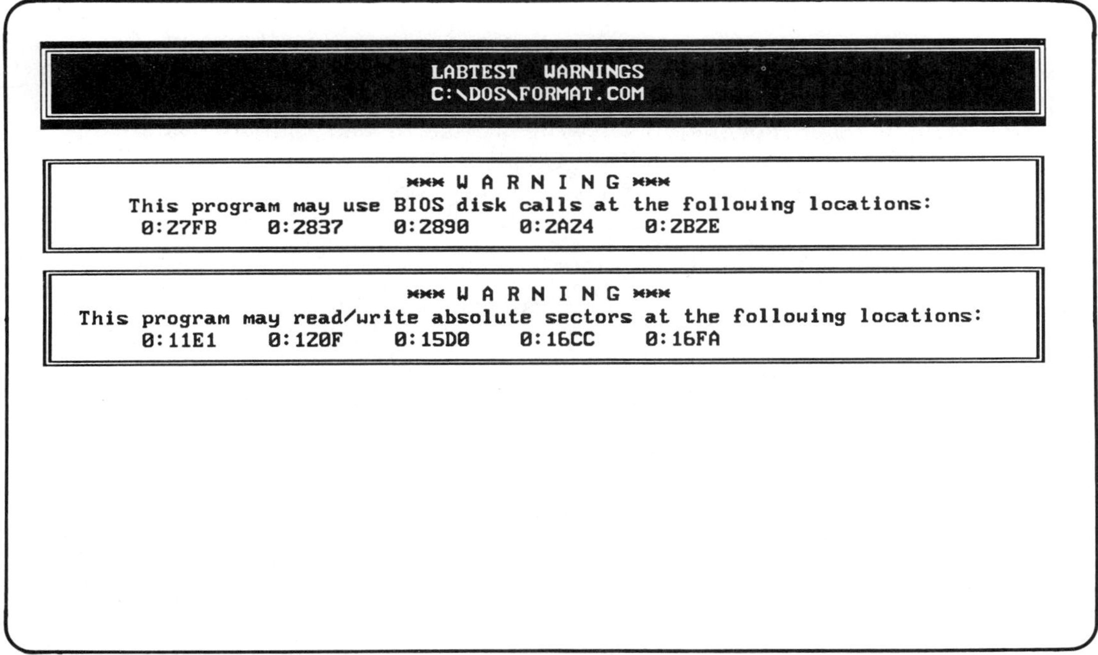

Fig. 17-5. LABTEST displays warnings about potentially dangerous routines within the tested program.

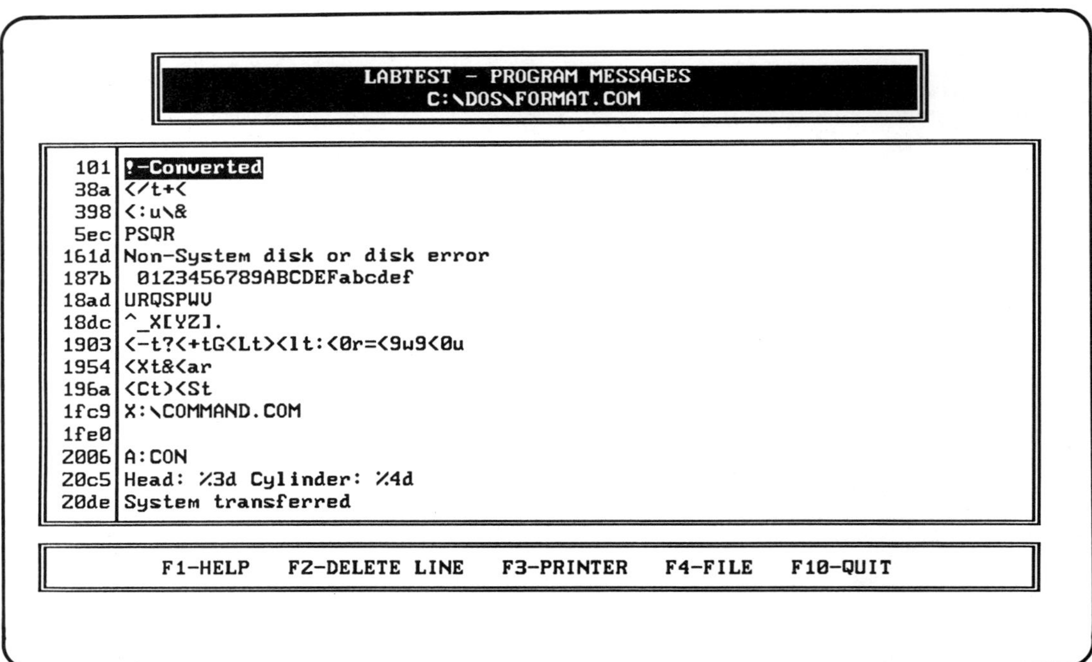

Fig. 17-6. LABTEST displays the ASCII text embedded within the tested file.

You run MONITOR by entering MONITOR along with any combination of several options. MONITOR will detect attempts to format disks and to change critical disk areas such as the boot sector. Depending upon the options chosen, MONITOR will intercept attempts to write to disks, to read from disks or to verify disks. With any interception, MONITOR gives an option of continuing or aborting the activity. For certain activities, such as formatting floppy disks, you can deactivate MONITOR by entering MONITOR X.

Limitations   There is no overall installation program other than for PHYSICAL. The coordination of the utilities will depend upon how you incorporate them with your software.

Manual   The manual comes in a text file on the disk. It provides clear instructions for using most of the programs on the disk. The manual does not mention a few new additions, such as DRHOOK. However, these new additions are self-explanatory with help screens.

Conclusion   As I said above, Dr. Panda Utilities provides an excellent anti-viral toolkit. Some of the utilities, such as LABTEST and NOBRAIN, have no equivalents in the other reviewed packages. Whether or not you get Dr. Panda Utilities, it is helpful to know that company not only sells anti-viral software but recovers damaged systems.

Product:	Dr. Panda Utilities
Price:	$79.95
Publisher:	Panda Systems
Address:	801 Wilson Road
	Wilmington, Delaware 19803
Phone:	(302) 764-4722
Memory:	3K

Flu_Shot Plus (version 1.52 tested)

Flu_Shot Plus is a shareware anti-viral software package that offers three major modes of software protection. It offers signature checks of selected files, software write protection, and a memory-resident disk access watcher. Flu_Shot is driven by a table file, giving it tremendous flexibility. You can obtain it from various computer networks, shareware distributors, or directly from Ross Greenberg's computer bulletin board system.

Installation   You must manually copy the Flu_Shot files to the hard disk or to another floppy. The manual text does not explain which files have to be copied, but if one has a rudimentary understanding of DOS, it will be easy. There is the main program file FSP.COM plus a sample copy of the Flu_Shot configuration table FLUSHOT.DAT. To run Flu_Shot, these are the only files required. There is an additional program, FLU-POKE.COM, to modify FSP.COM so Flu_Shot can use a different name for FLUSHOT.DAT. Make sure that you keep a backup copy of the Flu_Shot files.

The next step in installing Flu_Shot is to edit FLUSHOT.DAT to customize it for your system. You enter the protection option for a given file in the form of COMMAND = FILENAME OPTION. The command is a single letter specifying how Flu_Shot is to handle the specified file. There are a variety of command options. If you want more than command to apply to a file, you will have to enter a new entry for each command. For most of the commands, it allows DOS wildcards (* and ?). To write protect all your .COM files, you would have the line P = *.COM in FLUSHOT.DAT. Although the manual does not mention this, using a file listing of all your files will make it easier to make a comprehensive FLUSHOT.DAT. To make such a file, you can enter: CHKDSK C: /V >
FLUSHOT.DAT

Then you can edit the resulting FLUSHOT.DAT file to fit the proper format. If you get stuck, you can check back to the FLUSHOT.DAT on the original copy. As you edit FLUSHOT.DAT, check the manual for details about the commands and options. Ross Greenberg explains the advantages and disadvantages of the various commands. Be sure to approve any memory resident programs that you use.

Flu_Shot stores the correct signature value on the same command line which tells Flu_Shot to run signature checks on the file. Therefore, you must enter the correct signature value for each file to be thus checked into FLUSHOT.DAT. How do you know what is the signature value for each file? You do not. The first time through, enter a dummy value such as [12345] for each file. Run Flu_Shot. As it goes through the initial checks, it will find that the actual signature values do not match the dummy values you entered (unless you made a one-in-a-million lucky match). Flu_Shot will give a warning message such as Fig. 17-7 for each failed signature check along with the correct signature value. Jot these correct values and replace the dummy values in FLUSHOT.DAT with the correct ones.

If you want Flu_shot to be active upon booting up, you will need to edit your AUTOEXEC.BAT to include the FSP command. If you have included read protection for your AUTOEXEC.BAT in FLUSHOT.DAT, you will need to use the -Sn switch. This will allow Flu_Shot to wait for eighteenths of a second before becoming active, thus allowing the AUTOEXEC to finish without a warning message.

Operation   Once you have configured the FLUSHOT.DAT table, using Flu_Shot is easy. Figure 17-8 shows the message you receive when you run the FSP command, either by your AUTOEXEC.BAT or by you. This message appears after Flu_Shot has run all the signature checks. It uses the upper right corner of the screen to display a status indicator. A "+" means that it is active and a "-" means it is inactive. You can toggle between active and inactive states by hitting the Alt key three times. If you want indicator hidden, e.g. a program you use displays its information in that spot, hitting the Control key three times will toggle the display.

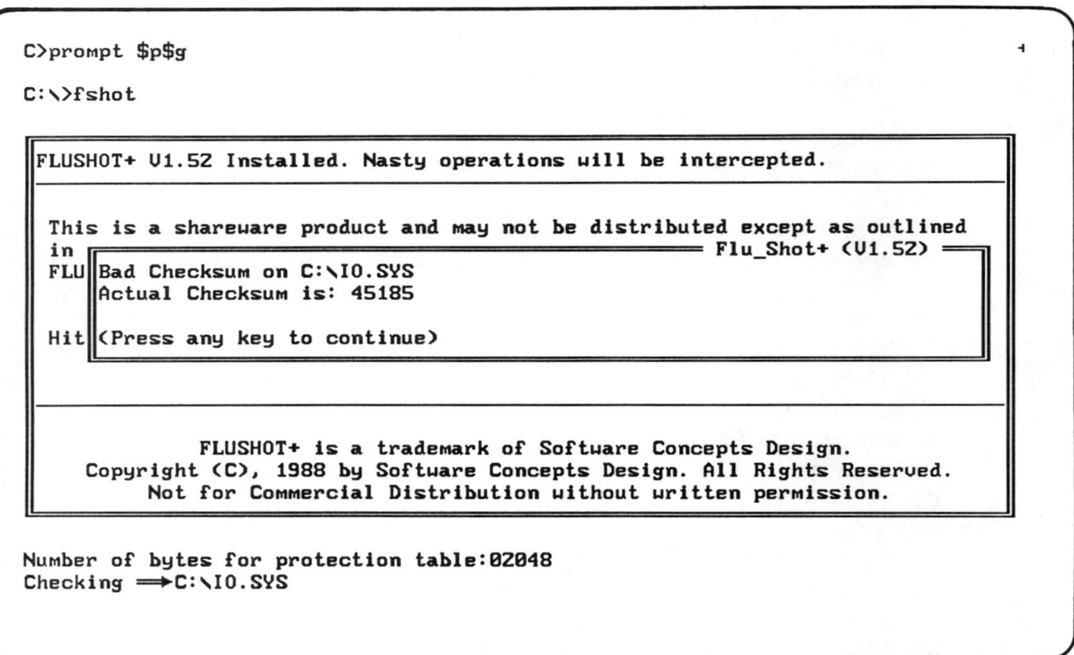

Fig. 17-7. This signature check warning prompt appears when a file designated to have a signature check fails the test.

```
C:\>fshot -s52                                                          G+

┌──────────────────────────────────────────────────────────────────────┐
│ FLUSHOT+ V1.52 Installed. Nasty operations will be intercepted.        │
├──────────────────────────────────────────────────────────────────────┤
│                                                                        │
│ This is a shareware product and may not be distributed except as outlined │
│ in the accompanying documentation. To download the most recent release of │
│ FLUSHOT+, call the RamNet BBS at: (212)-889-6438, 2400/1200/N/8/1 (24hr)  │
│                                      -- Ross M. Greenberg (02/01/89)    │
│                                                                        │
│ Hit Alt  three times to toggle FLU_SHOT+ triggering.                   │
│     Ctrl three times to toggle activity display indicator.             │
│                                                                        │
├──────────────────────────────────────────────────────────────────────┤
│                                                                        │
│         FLUSHOT+ is a trademark of Software Concepts Design.            │
│   Copyright (C), 1988 by Software Concepts Design. All Rights Reserved. │
│       Not for Commercial Distribution without written permission.      │
└──────────────────────────────────────────────────────────────────────┘

Number of bytes for protection table:02048

C:\>
C:\>
```

Fig. 17-8. This is the screen that you get when you run Flu_Shot. Note the " + " or a "-" there indicating whether or not Flu_Shot is active.

If Flu_Shot detects an attempt to modify a vital area of your disk, it will give the warning prompt in Fig. 17-9. As with most situations challenged by Flu_shot, you have the option to continue with the activity or to exit it. If you attempt to delete a protected file, Flu_Shot gives you the error message in Fig. 17-10. The only case where Flu_Shot does not give an option to continue with an activity is when an unapproved memory-resident program is loading into memory. Flu_Shot takes no chances here. It displays the message in Fig. 17-11 and aborts the loading of the memory resident program. Should you want to run that program, you will have to either inactivate Flu_Shot or edit FLUSHOT.DAT to approve the program.

Limitations   The main limitation is that Flu_Shot requires a bit of work to get started. To update Flu_Shot to protect new files requires you to edit FLUSHOT.DAT. You must enter the signature checks manually into the FLUSHOT.DAT file after running Flu_Shot once to see the correct checksum in the warning messages. The signature check data is not protected by encryption. If you do not have a printer, using the electronic manual is tedious.

Manual   The 32-page manual supplied in a text file (FSP.DOC) is thorough. It does assume some rudimentary knowledge of DOS and the ability to edit text files. Aside from that, the explanations are good, guiding you through setting up FLUSHOT.DAT and using the program. The manual takes the time to

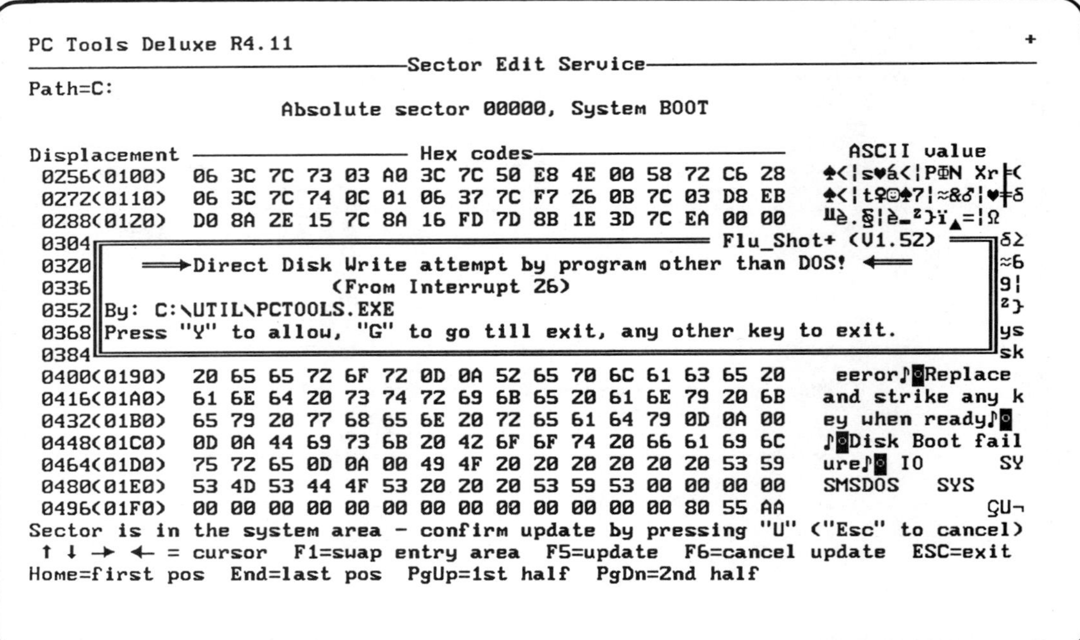

Fig. 17-9. Flu_Shot gives this warning if it detects an attempt to change a critical area of the disk such as the boot sector.

```
C:\PUB>del command.com




                                                    Flu_Shot+ (V1.52)
   Delete being attempted on:
   C:\PUB\COMMAND.COM
   By: C:\UTIL\PCTOOLS.EXE
   Press "Y" to allow, "G" to go till exit, any other key to exit.
```

Fig. 17-10. Flu_Shot will respond to an attempt to delete a protected file with this message.

```
C:\>dosedit

Alias List:


                                            =========== Flu_Shot+ (V1.52) ==========
  ? WARNING! TSR Request from an unregistered program!
  Number of paragraphs of memory requested (in decimal) are: 01295

  (Press any key to continue)
```

Fig. 17-11. Flu_Shot will challenge any unapproved memory resident program that tries to load into memory. Unlike the other warning prompts, this one gives no option of continuing.

explain how to decide how to answer the warning prompts and how to use various special options.

The manual has an interesting style. Sometimes, it is fiesty as Ross Greenberg chews out the "worms" who write viruses and Trojan horses. At other times, it talks as a friendly teacher. Ross Greenberg, at the end of the manual, emphasizes that the best defense against virus damage is not his program but good backups.

Conclusion Considering the low price, the ability to try it before paying for it, and the tremendous flexibility, Flu_Shot is a good anti-viral option for many power users. Flu_Shot resisted attempts to modify the boot sector and the system files. If you have properly configured FLUSHOT.DAT, the program will provide a great measure of protection.

Product:	Flu_Shot Plus
Price:	$10 plus $4 handling fee
Publisher:	Ross M. Green/Software Concepts Design
Address:	594 Third Avenue
	New York, New York 10016
Phone:	(212) 889-6431 - Voice
	(212) 889-6438 - Bulletin Board
Memory:	256K

Mace Vaccine (version 1.1 tested)

Mace Vaccine is the anti-viral software from the people who brought us the Mace Utilities. The Mace Vaccine consists of a single memory-resident program, VACCINE.COM which will intercept suspicious disk activity. When it intercepts such activity, it provides a warning message with an option to continue the activity or not. You can select two levels of protection. The Mace Utilities Gold programs includes a copy of Mace Vaccine.

Installation   The software has no installation instructions or program Mace Vaccine. You copy VACCINE.COM from the original disk to either your hard disk or to another floppy disk. The manual suggests adding the VACCINE command to your AUTOEXEC.BAT file.

Operation   There are only three VACCINE command options. Entering VACCINE by itself will give the default level 1 protection. Figure 17-12 shows the message Mace gives you. At level 1, Mace Vaccine will protect the drive against access to systems files and COMMAND.COM. Entering VACCINE 2 will increase the protection to level 2 by further restricting access to the disk. With either option, Vaccine takes up about 5.5K. Should Vaccine run into conflicts with other programs, you can deactivate it but not remove from memory by entering VACCINE OFF. Just enter VACCINE or VACCINE 2 to reactivate

At either protection level, Mace Vaccine will give a warning prompt when it encounters certain disk activities. Each warning prompt gives you the option to allow the activity to continue or to abort it. It may repeat the warning

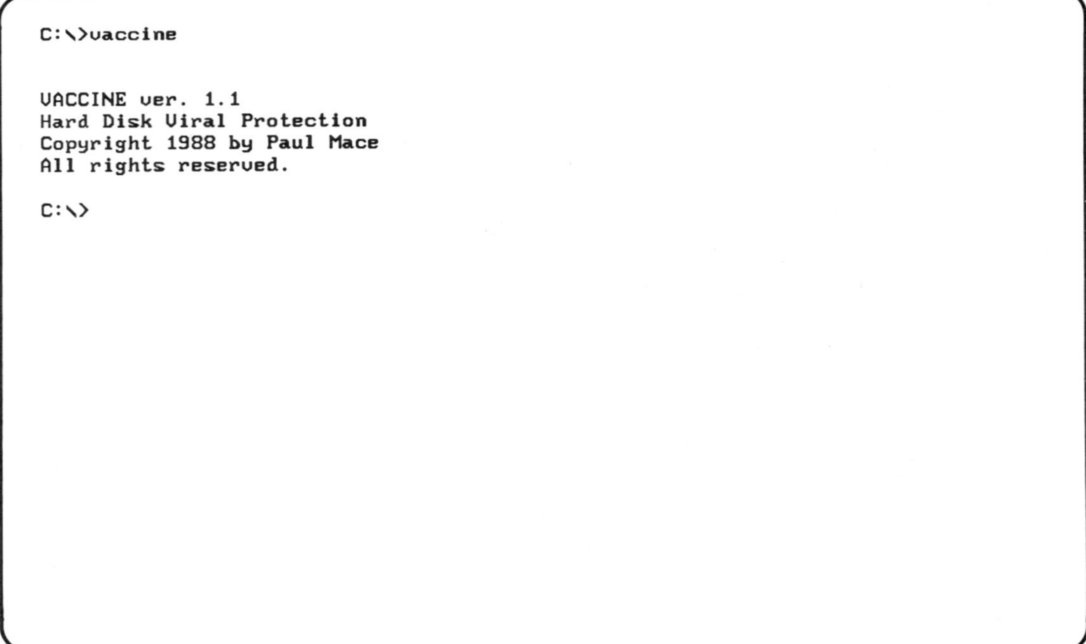

Fig. 17-12. This is the initial message given by Mace Vaccine when it is first run.

prompts several times before the computer returns to the DOS prompt. Figures 17-13 and 17-14 show two warning prompts given when Vaccine challenged a floppy disk format.

Limitations   The two warnings for a routine floppy disk format is a nuisance. Mace Vaccine does not check for changes in files; it will detect only certain disk access activities. If a virus or something else changes any file while Vaccine was not active, it would never detect it.

The biggest limitation is the way Vaccine will abort an attempt to modify COMMAND.COM or the systems files. It challenges attempts to modify these files and gives the option of aborting the modification. It takes several "no" replies to get back to DOS. Everything seems normal until it is time to reboot. The reboot fails because although the modification was aborted, other damage to the file occurred. Repairing damaged COMMAND.COM is simple. Just copy COMMAND.COM from original DOS disk. Repairing the damaged system files with the DOS SYS command would not work. This repair takes either reformatting the hard disk or doing some advanced DOS work. This protection can be compared to a car that protects you from injury in a collision by exploding just before it hits anything.

Manual   The manual is a card with operation instructions on one side and a brief introduction to viruses on the other. What the operation instructions say

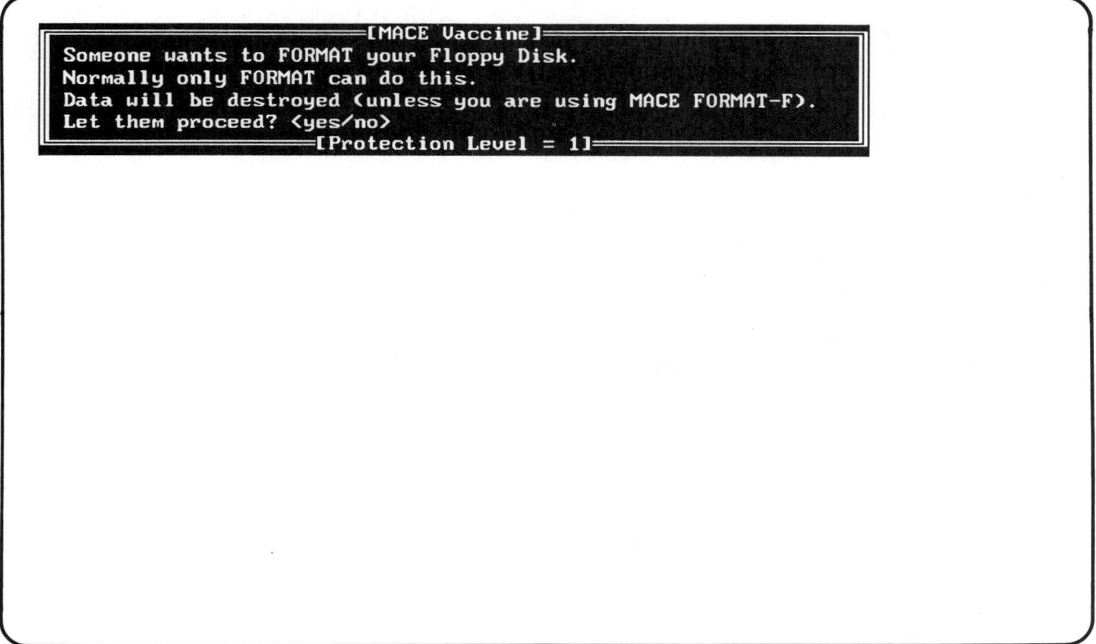

Fig. 17-13. Mace Vaccine will give two warning prompts during a routine format of a floppy disk. This is the first warning.

Fig. 17-14. This is the second warning prompt given by Mace Vaccine while formating a floppy disk.

is clear and simple. However, they leave a lot out. There is no explanation of exactly what activities are challenged by Vaccine nor any explanation of how to decide what answer to give the warning prompt. Should it detect a real virus, the manual card tells nothing about data recovery. Of course, the Mace Utilities Gold manual has a wealth of data recovery information; however, none of it is specific to viral recovery.

Conclusion   Mace Vaccine is the simplest and the least expensive commercial anti-viral package reviewed here. In fact, it is too simple. It gives little protection for it to be a reliable virus safeguard. The lethal trait of wrecking COMMAND.COM and the system files under certain conditions is a major flaw. Mace Vaccine lacks the quality of the Mace data and disk recovery utilities. If you need low cost anti-viral software, consider Flu_Shot Plus.

Product:	Mace Vaccine
Price:	$20
Publisher:	Paul Mace Software
Address:	400 Williamson Way
	Ashland, Oregon 97520
Phone:	(503) 488-2322
Notes:	Mace Vaccine is included at
	no additional charge in the
	Mace Utilities Gold.
Memory:	5.5K

SoftSafe

SoftSafe is a general computer security package that includes an anti-viral system file comparison feature. SoftSafe requires the system's users to logon with passwords as they would on a computer network. Up to eight separate users' ID's can be used on the system. It will encrypt selected data files, allowing only the files' owner to have access to their unencrypted versions. SoftSafe will prevent circumventing its defenses by booting up from a floppy and modifying the hard drive. There is also a lock-out feature to hide the contents of the screen display and to prevent others from tampering with the system.

Installation An installation program is provided along with a "Quick Start Card" explaining the installation procedure. To run the program, enter A:INSTALL. Most of the installation steps are explained by the installation program. It has been well designed. The program will ask if the system has been backed up. If not, it will exit the installation process. If you answer "yes" to the backup question, the installation program will continue and store recovery information on a floppy disk. The next step gets a bit noisy as SoftSafe updates the hard disk. Then, the installation program will ask for the serial number printed on a label affixed to the software's manual. Next, you are asked for the name of the "Safe" directory which will store the encrypted files. Remove the SoftSafe disk's write protect tab so that the installation program can update the disk. Then, the installation program will create several subdirectories on the hard disk and copy the SoftSafe files to the hard disk. After all this, the program tells you to reboot and logon.

When you reboot, you will be greeted with a logon menu asking for your ID and password. Logon with the default ID and password given in the manual. If they are entered correctly, SoftSafe will ask if you want to check for viruses. After that, you will be at the DOS prompt. Essentially, the basic installation is complete. You can, by using the SOFTSAFE.EXE, change your password, add more user ID's, and customize SoftSafe. Generally, the person who installs SoftSafe would be considered its Owner or systems administrator. Be sure to change the OWNER password to prevent others who have read the manual from gaining access to the system.

Operation Using Softsafe is relatively simple once you get used to its unique environment. When the system is booted up or someone else has logged off the PC, SoftSafe will present a logon screen. Just enter your ID and password. If they are valid, you will be asked if you want to check for viruses. If you answer "yes," SoftSafe will compare your system files and COMMAND.COM with copies stored elsewhere on the disk with encrypted names. If a difference is detected, SoftSafe will ask what you want to do with the file that failed the test. Your options are Kill, Ignore or Save. Kill will use the copy to overwrite the suspect file. Ignore will use the suspect file. Save will replace the test copy with the questioned file. This option is used in cases where a legitimate change was made to the system file.

If you have the OWNER ID, you can add more users and make other changes. To do this, enter C:\SOFTSAFE\SOFTSAFE OWNER. You will get a menu like the one shown in Fig. 17-15.

The lock-out option can be used at anytime by hitting the Control, Alt and L keys at the same time. The current display will be hidden by the logon display. To get back to the system, either you or the OWNER has to logon.

Limitations   Only the system files and COMMAND.COM are checked. No option for checking other files. There is a hazard of losing the ability of unencrypting encrypted files if SOFTSAFE.SYS is deleted, modified, moved or renamed. Only the Owner can run DOS CHKDSK.

Manual   The SoftSafe manual is a small hard cover book. A "Quick Start Card" with installation instructions is included. The manual does a favor to the reader by explaining its terminology. The procedures are clearly explained.

Conclusion   SoftSafe's main asset is its ability to control access to the computer system. The special virus protection feature appears to be an addition to comfort virus-wary customers. For some systems, good access control is all that is needed to greatly reduce the virus risk and SoftSafe will do that job well. On some other systems, SoftSafe, supplemented with another anti-viral software package, such as Dr. Panda Utilities or Flu_Shot, will do the job. But as a full-fledged anti-viral software, it falls short.

```
                          SoftSafe Control Panel                    Ver S1.15
  Add UserID     Change Password      List Encrypted Files    Remove UserID    Exit

     Safe Word:   SAFE                      Virus detection file:   XXXXXXX

  +------------------------+-----------------------------+-----------------------+
  |      User Name         |    Password last changed    |    Encrypted files    |
  +------------------------+-----------------------------+-----------------------+
  |      OWNER             |          4/30/89            |           0           |
  |                        |                             |                       |
  |                        |                             |                       |
  |                        |                             |                       |
  |                        |                             |                       |
  +------------------------+-----------------------------+-----------------------+


                              Add a new UserID
  +,+ To HiLite Menu Option                       [Esc] to exit [Enter] to select
  t,+ to select user              (C)opyright 1988, Software Directions, Inc.
```

Fig. 17-15. SoftSafe Owner Change Panel allows the user with OWNER ID to add more users and to perform other tasks.

(The newer version of SoftSafe is reported to include a signature check program for examining all executable files. This version was not available for review.)

```
Product:     Soft Safe
Price:       $99.00
Publisher:   Software Directions, Inc.
Address:     1572 Sussex Turnpike
             Randolph, New Jersey 07869
Phone:       (201) 584-8466
Memory:      40K
```

Virusafe (version 1.52 tested)

Virusafe offers three types of protection. It has a signature check program, a program that checks the memory for virus code and a memory resident that will warn you of suspicious disk accesses.

Installation   An installation batch file is provided. The manual does not mention that you have to access the A drive before running INSTALL.BAT. This omission along with a programming error in the batch file would result in a program not being run if INSTALL is run from any other drive. Also, the Virusafe disk must be in the A drive during installation. If you have to use another drive, you will either have to edit INSTALL.BAT or use the DOS ASSIGN command.

While installing Virusafe, you will be given a menu to configure the Program Integrity Check (PIC) signature checking program. Although it may be a bit confusing at first, follow in the instructions on the menu and you should be able to learn quickly how to navigate around the PIC configuration menu and select the files to be checked.

Operation   To use PIC to check the signatures of the selected files, enter PIC /n from the DOS prompt.

To run the memory resident disk access watcher, run WS.EXE. The manual gives a list of various options that can be used with it. When VS runs into a suspicious activity, it will present the message in Fig. 17-16.

Limitations   The flaw with the INSTALL.BAT program could cause some trouble. PIC only allows .COM and .EXE files to be selected for signature checks, leaving other files vulnerable. The warning message given by VS memory resident program claims that certain relatively common activities, such as a program becoming memory resident, are rare. This can be misleading.

Manual   The manual was the one for an earlier version and several references did not apply to the Virusafe version on the disk. There is an update documentation text file on the disk, but nowhere in the packaging was there any hint to go looking for the text file. The manual was adequate in most parts but more details about the various options could have been given.

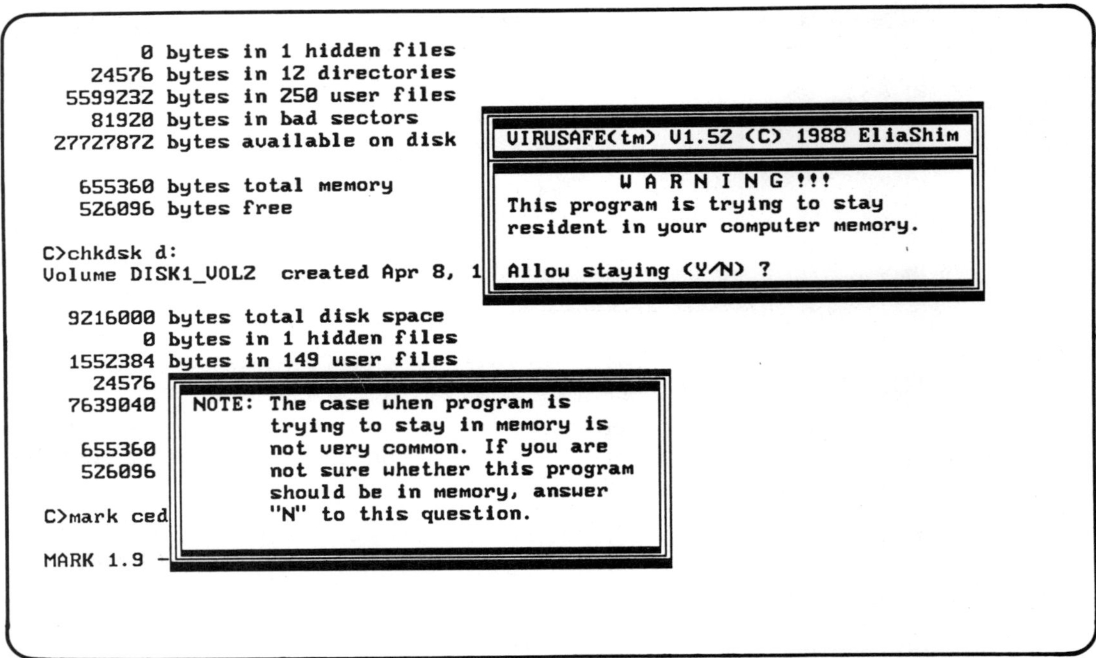

Fig. 17-16. A warning message given by VS.EXE when it encounters a program becoming memory resident.

Conclusion   Virusafe is serviceable anti-viral package but considering its price and some of its shortcomings, it is not the prime choice.

Product:	Virusafe
Price:	$150.00
Category:	Commercial
Publisher:	COMNETCO, Incorporated
Address:	2475 Laminton Road
	Badminster, New Jersey 07921
Phone:	(201) 781-7940
Notes:	The price is for Version 1.6
Memory:	7K

Virus Guard

Virus Guard is a two-part signature check program. One part, SigGen, will both generate the signature values and check the signature values of all .COM, .EXE and system files against their earlier values. The other part, RamWatch, is a memory resident program that will perform a signature check upon any program being executed. A hard disk is required.

Installation   Virus Guard has an installation program and the manual's instructions are clear. The installation program allows you to install Virus Guard on a hard disk other than C:. The installation program will create a

\VG subdirectory on the specified hard disk and copy the SigGen and RamWatch files to that subdirectory. Also, the installation will insert commands to run the two programs at the beginning of the AUTOEXEC.BAT file. (If the AUTOEXEC.BAT is read-only, this won't happen and the installation program won't notify you.) Then, the installation program will run SigGen to set up the signature data file. This must be done before using RamWatch, otherwise every program would fail the signature check.

Operation   RamWatch is run with the RW command. There are no options. Once it is run, it remains in memory. There is no inactivation option. To inactivate RamWatch, the manual suggests either removing the RW command from the autoexec.BAT and rebooting or deleting RW.COM from the \VG subdirectory and rebooting. When RamWatch encounters a program about to be executed that is not listed in the signature data file, it will give the message in Fig. 17-17. Should the program about to be executed fail the signature check, RamWatch will indicate this with the message in Fig. 17-18. With either warning, you get the option to continue or to abort the program.

To run SigGen, you have to go to the \VG subdirectory and enter SIG-GEN. SigGen will give you the menu in Fig. 17-19. It allows to you to derive signature data for all .COM, .EXE and system files on the disk or to run signature checks on the programs on your disk. If the SigGen signature checks encounter a file that failed the check, indicating that it was changed, it displays the message in Fig. 17-20.

```
                        File not found

IO.SYS does not exist in Signature file for comparison.

Rebuild the Signature file with SigGen or add IO.SYS now.

F1 - Add IO.SYS to the Signature file now.
F2 - Run IO.SYS without adding it to the Signature file.
F3 - Abort---don't run IO.SYS
```

Fig. 17-17. If RamWatch does not find the program about to be executed in the signature data file, it will give this message.

```
ANSIDRAW.COM has failed comparison

ANSIDRAW.COM has been modified and no longer matches the
copy in the Signature file.   There are three possible causes:

     A program has crashed previously, corrupting ANSIDRAW.COM
     A virus has damaged ANSIDRAW.COM
     ANSIDRAW.COM has modified itself intentionally.

If ANSIDRAW.COM is corrupted by a previous program crash,
abort the program and restore it from your backup.

If you think that a virus has damaged ANSIDRAW.COM, use SigGen
to compare the Signatures of all the other files known to SigGen.

If you are sure ANSIDRAW.COM modifies itself, then
disable Signature checking.

F1 - Build new Signature for ANSIDRAW.COM
F2 - Disable Signature checking for ANSIDRAW.COM
F3 - Abort---don't run the program.
```

Fig. 17-18. RamWatch will give this message if the program about to be executed fails the signature check.

```
                    SigGen Main Menu

F1 - Build signatures for all programs

F2 - Check signatures for all programs

F3 - Exit



     Make selection with function keys -
```

Fig. 17-19. This is SigGen's main menu.

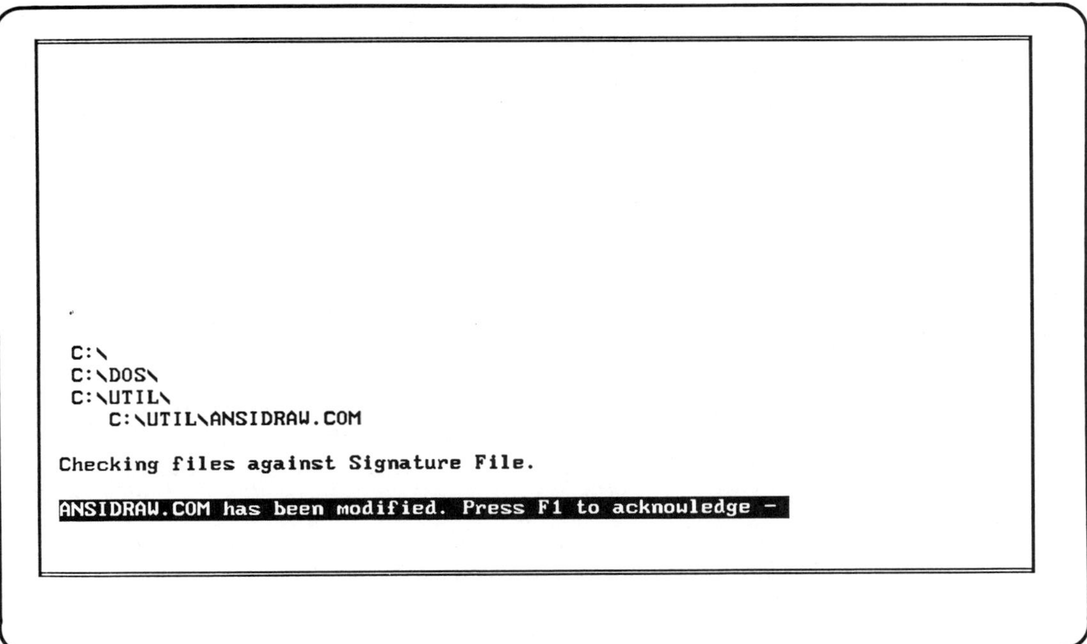

Fig. 17-20. This is how SigGen indicates that it has found a file that has been changed.

A special problem occurs if RamWatch gives a warning while you have a graphics display. The message will not be displayed. Instead you will get stray lines and the system appears to be locked up. But if you respond with one of the acceptable RamWatch responses, the screen will clear up and the computer will unlock. This is a common problem with many memory resident anti-viral software.

Limitations   Virus Guard offers only one type of protection (e.g.; signature checks). It will detect changes in .COM and .EXE files after they happen, not before or during the changes. The signature checks are limited to .COM, .EXE and the system files. There is no way of protecting other files, such as .OVL, that contain executable code. Ironically, although SigGen will not generate signature values for these other files, but RamWatch did challenge the use of the files by their associated programs.

Manual   The manual is a small 13-page booklet containing brief explanations of viruses and the Virus Guard SigGen and RamWatch programs. It is clear and concise. The explanations of the various RamWatch messages are very helpful. The instructions about what to do if a virus is found were inadequate.

Conclusion   Although the RamWatch provides a more frequent signature check of files than do many other programs, it relies upon only one protection method.

```
Product:     Virus Guard
Price:       $24.95
Publisher:   IP Technologies
Address:     1575 Corporate Drive
             Costa Mesa, California 92626
Phone:       (714) 549-4284
Memory:      128K
```

Watchdog and Watchdog Armor Watchdog

Watchdog and Watchdog Armor Watchdog is another data security package that has moved into the anti-viral category. It restricts activities on a computer system, Like SoftSafe, Watchdog requires users to logon with a password. Watchdog can restrict access to the hard disk when booting from floppy. With Watchdog Armor, the system can be prevented from booting from a floppy disk. There are many other features such as DES encryption and a mail option.

Installation   Watchdog software has its own installation program. Follow the instructions given by the program and by the manual. The installer becomes the de facto systems administrator.

Watchdog Armor also has an installation program. Because it is possible to lock yourself out of your own system, follow the instructions closely. When installing the Armor board into the PC, be sure to discharge all static electricity before touching the board.

Operation   When the computer boots up, you will get a logon screen. Enter your ID and password. Then you will get a menu similar to the one shown in Fig. 17-21. You can run various Watchdog functions from this menu, go to systems administrator's menu (if you have the systems administrator's ID and password), or go out to DOS. There is no explicit anti-virus program to be run. But Watchdog will intercept attempts to modify the systems files or to do other damage and abort them.

Limitations   Watchdog is a complex security package that requires a great deal of effort to set up properly.

Manual   Be prepared for a lot of reading, especially if you are going to be the systems administrator. The Watchdog software comes with three manuals— a thin installation manual, a medium sized users guide and a thick systems administrator's guide. The manuals take a bit of effort to read, but overall their explanations of Watchdog procedures are clear. Watchdog Armor comes with a thin installation manual which explains the procedures clearly except for one item. The Armor installation manual does not explain how to decide the memory address setting to use.

Conclusion   Watchdog even without the Armor is the most expensive of the anti-viral packages reviewed here. Its anti-viral capabilities are primarily the result of the stringent access security and data control Watchdog provides.

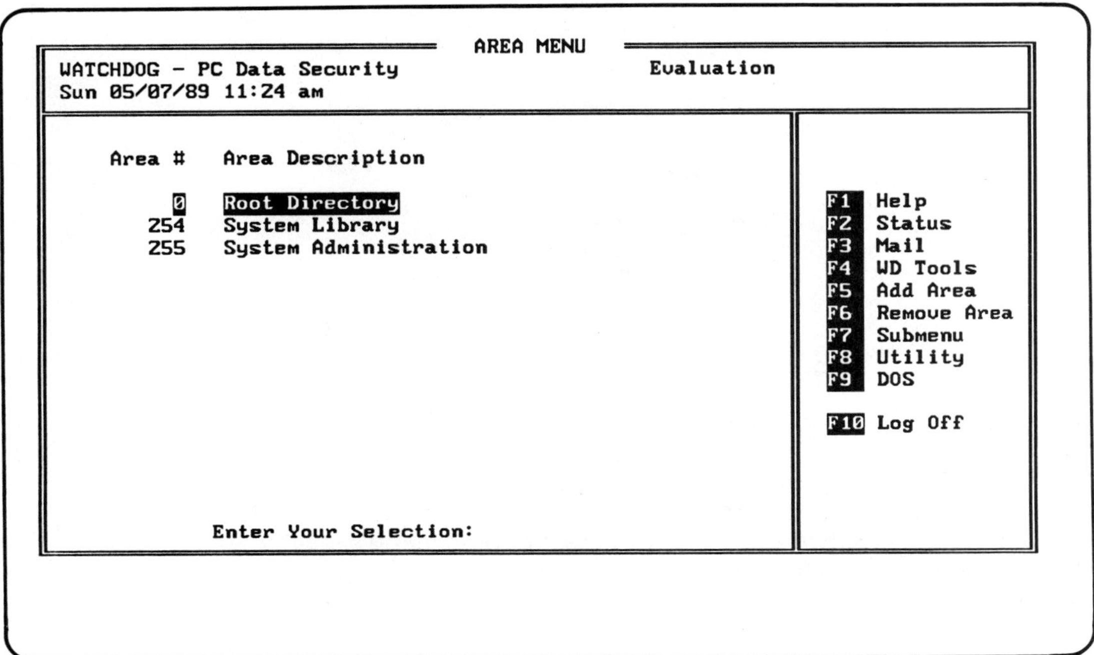

Fig. 17-21. The initial Watchdog menu.

The security features make Watchdog a good choice for installations needing a high degree of security. For most computer users, good protection can be obtained more economically from other packages.

Product:	Watchdog
Price:	$295.00
Category:	Commercial
Publisher:	Fisher International Systems
Address:	Post Office Box 9107
	4073 Merchantile Avenue
	Naples, Florida 33942
Phone:	(800) 237-4510
	(813) 643-1500
Notes:	Due to Watchdog's use of DES encryption, export of Watchdog outside of the United States is restricted by Federal law.
Memory:	384K

```
Product:      Watchdog Plus Armor
Price:        $445.00
Category:     Hardware and Software Combination
Publisher:    Fisher International Systems
Address:      Post Office Box 9107
              4073 Merchantile Avenue
              Naples, Florida 33942
Phone:        (800) 237-4510
              (813) 643-1500
Notes:        Due to Watchdog's use of DES
              encryption, export of Watchdog outside
              of the United States is restricted by
              Federal law.
Memory:       384K
```

RONNY'S AND JOHN'S PICKS

If you need high security, either Certus or Watchdog are the better packages. For the user with less demanding requirements, Dr. Panda's Utilities or Flu_Shot is an excellent choice. For all users, the general guidelines in this chapter should always be the first thing to protect your system. None on this software replaces common sense.

CHAPTER ACKNOWLEDGMENTS

Much of this chapter was written by J. D. Abolins, who works for the New Jersey State Department of Environmental Protection as a PC support specialist. He graduated from Monmouth College with a B.S. in Environmental Sciences. John D. Abolins has worked with computers since 1981. He has written articles about various computing topics, including computer viruses and defenses against malicious programs.

Datavue loaned me a Datavue Snap computer to use to work on this chapter. The Snap computer proved to be an excellent computer and a big help.

## Part Four

Memory Resident Aids

18
Adding Notes to Files

One problem with DOS is it only gives you eleven characters to describe a file. That is eight for the name and three for the extension. Some programs further restrict you. For example, Microsoft Word expects document files to end with a .DOC extension. dBASE III+ expects database files to end with a .DBF extension. Lotus 1-2-3 expects worksheet files to end with a .WK1 extension. Many other programs have similar restrictions on the extension. Oh sure, you can override this expectation with some programs and assign your own extension. However, it makes it harder to work with the program.

To further complicate matters, the eight characters DOS gives you for the file name is further restricted. DOS does not allow a name like "My Work." First, DOS does not allow spaces in file names (see note below) and second, DOS converts all characters in a file name to uppercase. The real problem is: it is very difficult to develop eight-character file names that you will understand in six months. Just exactly what do the files "PROJ1223.DOC" or "LETR-2JBC.DOC" relate to anyway?

File noting programs let you solve this problem by attaching notes to files. These notes can be long enough to explain what the file relates to in detail. There are two types of file noting programs: memory resident, and non-memory resident. (When working with files directly from DOS, you can add what appears to be spaces. When you are entering the file name and want to enter a space, hold down the ALT-key and type 255 on the number pad. That enters an ASCII character into the file name that appears on the screen as a space. Not all programs support this, however, so you will need to experiment with the ones you use. You can use this same trick when creating subdirectories to make them harder to get to. Just add a single ASCII code 255 as the last character of the subdirectory name. That way, you cannot tell it is there when you perform a DIRectory, but you must add it to change to that subdirectory.)

MEMORY RESIDENT FILE NOTING PROGRAMS

As the name implies, a memory resident (or TSR) file noting program sits in memory all the time. (TSR stands for Terminate and Stay Resident. That is a commonly used fancy name for memory resident programs.) Any time you want a file but do not remember its name, you can pop up the TSR file noting program. Then you search through the description for the file you want. Because they stay in memory, they can monitor what you do to your files and adjust when you move or rename a file. Of course, because they sit in memory they reduce the memory available to other programs.

Smart Notes

Smart Notes is a memory resident program that allows you to attach notes to applications in text mode. It remembers where to display those notes by storing the text on the screen when you attach a note. It displays the note when that same text reappears. It has a special Lotus mode that allows you to attach notes to specific cells.

Installation   Smart Notes does not have an installation program, but installation is straightforward. You must add the command to load Smart Notes to your AUTOEXEC.BAT file if you want the program loaded automatically. If you use several memory resident programs, you must find a loading order that avoids conflicts. The Smart Notes manual offers realistic suggestions for a number of programs. RamLord, covered in Chapter 1 can also help.

Operation   Smart Notes is a memory resident program. You can use it to attach notes to most any application, including DOS, that runs in TEXT mode. You cannot attach a note to any program that requires a graphics adapter. So you could not, for example, attach a note to a Lotus graph.

When you attach a note, Smart Notes "remembers" the text surrounding the note. Any time Smart Notes sees that same text, it assumes it is time to display the associated note. It stores notes attached to a file called <filename>.<extension> in a file called <filename>.SNS. If you modify text after attaching a note, you can cause the note to become "unattached." Smart Notes still has the note, it just does not know to display it.

Smart Notes has a special Lotus mode. That allows you to attach notes that remain attached to specific cells regardless of how you rearrange the worksheet. The first step is to attach a special worksheet containing the formulae used by Smart Notes to track notes. The location of these cells is not important. After that, you can attach notes to any cell.

This Lotus mode overcomes a major problem with text-matching note program. When you attach a note to a formula and it is recalculated to a new value, the note becomes unattached.

Table 18-1 compares the add-in note programs across a number of features and Table 18-2 compares the memory resident ones.

Table 18-1. **Note Programs Comparison for Lotus Add – Ins.**

Feature	Note-It+	Noteworthy
Block deletes	Yes	Yes
Block moves of text	Yes	Yes
Can notes be linked together	Yes	No
Change the size of a note	No	Yes
Copy text	Yes	Yes
Help	Yes	Yes
Import text	No	Yes
Maximum note size (in characters)	500	8,000
Maximum notes per file	250	No Limit
Move text	Yes	Yes
Move the note around	No	Yes
Print notes	Yes	Yes
Search and replace	No	Yes
Search through notes	Yes	Yes
Search through worksheet	Yes	Yes
Uses expanded memory	No	Yes
Uses extended memory	No	No

Table 18-2. **Note Programs Comparison for Memory Resident.**

Feature	Smartnotes	Cell Noter
Block deletes	No	No
Block moves of text	Yes	No[1]
Can notes be linked together	No	No
Change the size of a note	Yes	No
Copy text	No	No[2]
Help	Yes	No
Import text	No	No
Maximum note size (in characters)	230	530
Maximum notes per file	125	513
Move text	No	No
Move the note around	Yes	No
Print notes	Yes	Yes
Search and replace	No	No
Search through notes	Yes	Yes
Search through worksheet	Yes	No
Uses expanded memory	No	No
Uses extended memory	No	No

[1]The entire contents of one cell can be moved to another cell.

[2]The entire contents of one cell can be copied to another cell.

Limitations   Smart Notes can store fifty notes in each file. This file is separate from the application and does not alter the application file in anyway. Smart Notes can store as many files as you like.

Smart Notes remembers the location of a note by storing the text around the note. Change the text and the note becomes unattached. You can still look at it and even reattach it, that is if you remember where it goes.

In general, using a general product causes problems for a specific application like Lotus and Smart Notes is no exception. Each time you move to a new area of the screen, Smart Notes scans that area to see if it should display any notes. If it finds any, Smart Notes displays all its notes for that screen at one time. This can lead to "over-crowding" when you try to attach a number of notes to a worksheet. In addition, because Smart Notes is not an add-in, you cannot detach it from within Lotus if you need the memory. You can, however, remove it from the DOS prompt. Finally, Smart Notes has a more general limitation. It will not work in graphics mode.

Manual   The manual is clear and well written.

Conclusion   Smart Notes offers you a way to attach notes to any application running in text mode.

```
Product:      Smart Notes
Price:        $79.95
Category:     Commercial
Publisher:    Personics Corporation
Address:      63 Great Road
              Maynard, Massachusetts 01754
Phone:        (800) 445-3311
Memory:       85K
```

Cell Noter

Cell Noter is a good memory resident Lotus note program. You cannot purchase Cell Noter. However, it comes free with the Spreadsheet Auditor package.

Installation   There is no installation program. The manual does explain how to install the program. For some reason, the installation instructions are in an appendix.

Operation   Cell Noter is memory resident. You must load it before starting Lotus. If you use it a lot, the best place to do that is in your AUTOEXEC.BAT file. Cell Noter has a command to unload it from memory if you need to reclaim the memory it uses. To do that it must be the last one loaded and you must be at the DOS prompt.

To edit an existing note or create a new note, you move the cursor to the cell to attach the note to and press Alt-F1. Figure 18-1 shows the main menu. The built-in editor is simple, but effective for short notes.

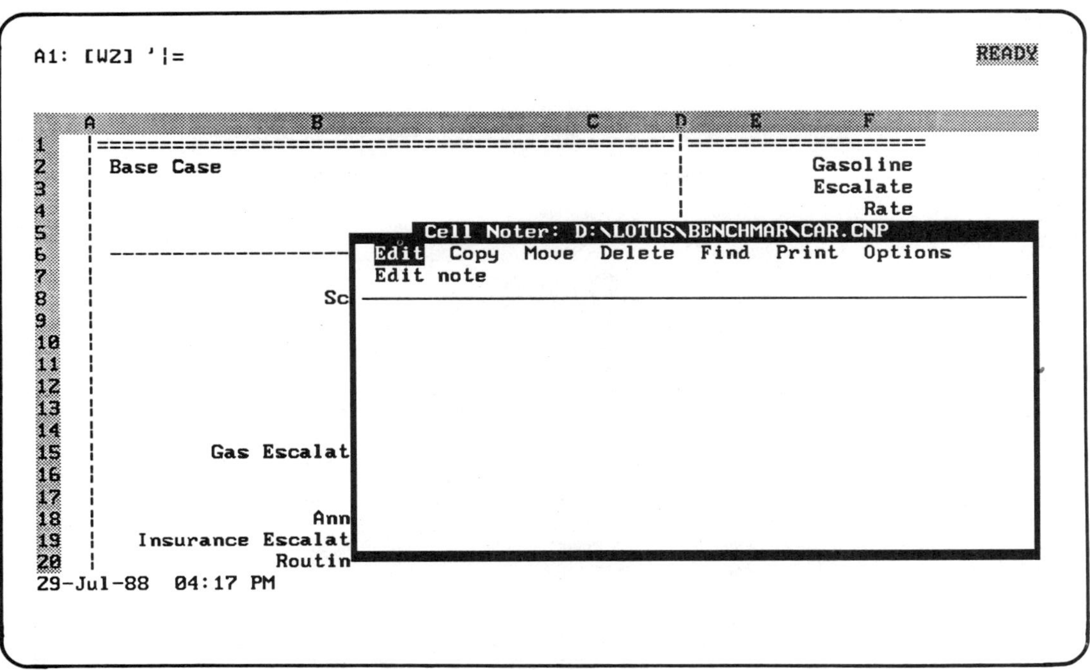

Fig. 18-1. The Cell Noter lets you attach notes to important cells in your worksheet.

Cell Noter will highlight each cell on the current screen that has a note attached when you press Alt-F2. Figure 18-2 shows this. Cell Noter also lets you attach notes to file names and subdirectories when Lotus is performing a /File Retrieve or /File Save command.

Cell Noter has commands to:

- Copy the contents of a note from one cell to another cell.
- Move the contents of a note from one cell to another cell.
- Delete a note.
- Find a note containing a word or phrase you supply.
- Print notes to the printer or to an ASCII file.

It saves notes automatically when you save your worksheet. If you exit without saving, Cell Noter will ask if you want to save the notes.

The real power of the Cell Noter program is evident when you use it with the Spreadsheet Auditor program. Cell Noter can attach notes while you are looking at a worksheet in either program. That way, when you find an error you do not have to take notes manually. You just attach an electronic note to the problem cell.

Limitations   Cell Noter can lose information anytime you modify a worksheet without it attached. In addition, it also loses information when you sort a range that has notes attached to cells in that range. It sometimes loses information when a macro inserts rows or columns into a worksheet.

```
F9: (P2) @IF($GAS_RATE="Low",H9,@IF($GAS_RATE="Medium",I9,@IF($GAS_RATE="HiREADY
```

```
     A              B                        C      D   E        F
1  |=================================================|====================
2  | Base Case                                       |         Gasoline
3  |                                                 |         Escalate
4  |                                                 |           Rate
5  |                       INPUTS       VALUE        | Year      Used
6  |  ---------------------------------  ---------   | ----      ----
7  |                  Run Number:                1   | 1988     0.00%
8  |             Scenario Number:                0   | 1989     6.83%
9  |               Discount Rate:          12.00%    | 1990     6.82%
10 |               Miles to Keep:          50,000    | 1991     6.85%
11 |                   Car Make:  Gamma              | 1992     6.33%
12 |                   Car Model:        1441502     | 1993     6.81%
13 |                       Cost:         $19,935     | 1994     6.06%
14 |                   Gas Cost:           $0.89     | 1995     6.49%
15 |  Gas Escalate Rate to Use:  Medium              | 1996     6.84%
16 |                Gas Mileage:               21    | 1997     6.04%
17 |               Life (miles):          70,000     |====================
18 |            Annual Insurance:          $1,031    |
19 | Insurance Escalate Rate to Use:  Medium         |
20 |         Routine Maintenance:          $203      |
   29-Jul-88   04:21 PM
```

Fig. 18-2. When you press Alt-F2, Cell Noter highlights every cell on the current screen that has a note attached.

Manual   The manual is well written and contains numerous screen illustrations.

Conclusion   Cell Noter is a good cell noting program. However, other programs in this chapter are better. That does not mean you should buy them. Cell Noter uses less memory than Note-It or Smart Notes. If you use the Spreadsheet Auditor, Cell Noter is the only note program to consider for two reasons. First, it is free. Second, it can attach notes while auditing the worksheet.

Product:	Cell Noter
Price:	Included with Spreadsheet Auditor
Category:	Commercial
Publisher:	Computer Associates
Address:	1240 McKay Drive
	San Jose, California 95131
Phone:	(408) 432-1727
Memory:	58K

Note-It Plus

Note-It Plus gives you the ability to attach notes to your worksheet. These notes are useful for documenting your work, assumptions, or work remaining.

Installation   Note-It Plus does not have an installation program. The manual explains the installation process.

Operation   To edit an existing note or create a new note, the first thing you do is move the cursor to the cell where you attach the note. You then invoke Note-It Plus using the menu-key you assigned when you attached it. Figure 18-3 shows the Note-It Plus main menu. You then select the edit option from the menu. The note editor is simple, but effective for the short notes. Figure 18-4 shows using Note-It Plus to edit a note.

The menu has a browse option. This lets you browse through all the notes attached to a worksheet. If someone has documented the worksheet, this is an excellent way to acquaint yourself with the worksheet or to look for specific information.

Note-It Plus has options to . . .

- Print a single note.
- Print a note and part of the associated worksheet.
- Print all the notes.
- Print all the cells with attached notes.

The search option is one of Note-It Plus's more powerful features. It lets you search either the notes attached to the current worksheet or all notes in a sub-directory.

```
A12: [W32] 'Number of pedestrians buying                              MENU
Edit  Browse  List  Mark  Clipboard  Delete  Search  Goto  Print  Options  Quit
Edit or create a cell note
                     A                         B          C              D
 1  LEMONADE STAND LOCATION ANALYSIS   06-Jun-88              Note-It Plus
 2
 3  Location                         Swimming Pool   Bus Stop
 4  Hours stand open                     1-5 p.m.    3-6 p.m.
 5  Number of hours open                    4           3
 6  Pedestrian traffic per hour                               +--------------+
 7     Kids                                90          30     | Note-It Plus |
 8     Adults                              15         160     | main menu    |
 9  % of pedestrians buying lemonade                          +--------------+
10     Kids                               55%         18%
11     Adults                             32%         28%
12  Number of pedestrians buying
13     Kids                               50           5
14     Adults                              5          45
15  Price per glass                     $0.50       $0.50
16  Revenue per day
17     Kids                            $24.75       $2.70
18     Adults                           $2.40      $22.40
19     TOTAL                           $27.15      $25.10
20  Revenue per average hour            $6.79       $8.37
06-Jun-88   07:51 PM
```

Fig. 18-3. Note-It Plus Main Menu.

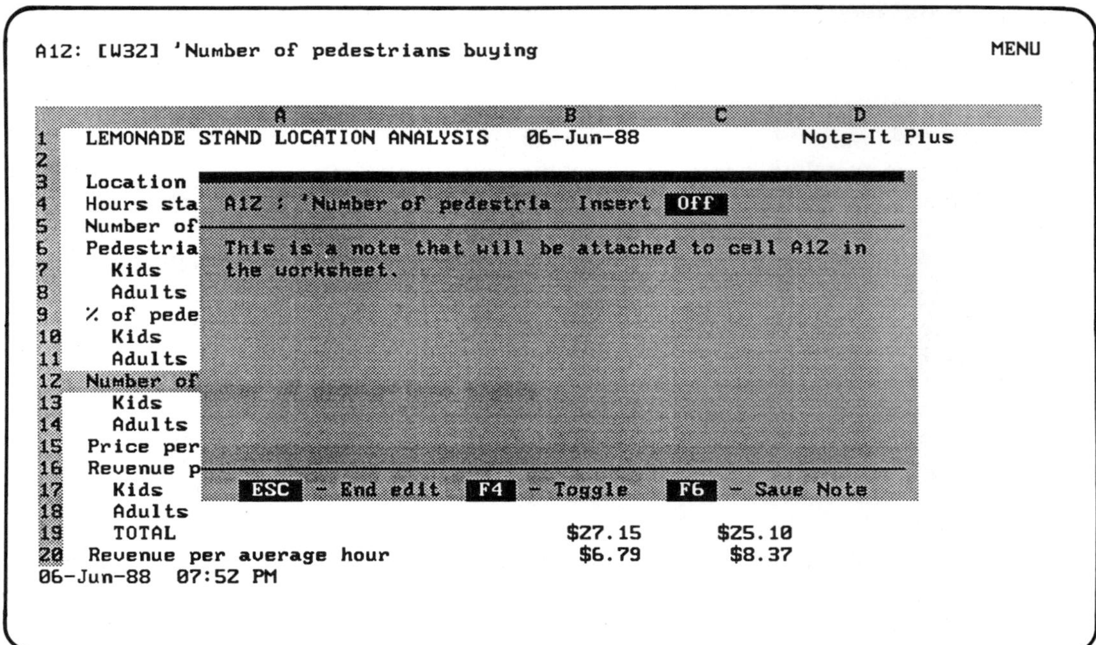

Fig. 18-4. Editing a note using Note-It Plus.

You can search for a phrase, a word, or any other type of information you have entered into a cell. Until document indexing programs are able to index worksheets, this is your best bet for locating a particular worksheet. Especially long after you have forgotten what the cryptic eight-character file name stands for.

In addition to 250-cell notes, Note-It Plus lets you attach a single file note to a worksheet. It stores the file note in a <filename>.WNT file. It stores the cell notes in a <filename>.NTS file. <Filename> is the name of the worksheet. These two files must have the same file name as the worksheet. If you use DOS to rename the .WK1 file, you must rename these files as well.

Note-It Plus includes a clipboard. The clipboard is useful for transferring data to different locations of Lotus. It is especially useful for making a copy of formulae without changing the cell references.

Limitations   Note-It Plus can only have 250-individual cell notes per worksheet. Each note can have up to 500-characters. This results in a 125,000-character (250x500) limit on notes. The 250-individual cell notes are not an important limitation since Note-It Plus allows you to link notes together. Linked notes form a chain. After you see one note, you see the next, then the next, and so on.

When you attach a note, Note-It Plus creates a range name with a name like "|NOTE1|". If you have referenced that cell in a formula, e.g. +A1, after the program creates the range name, Lotus automatically changes that reference to +|NOTE1|. If you delete the range names, your formula may end up as

+ERR. Not only do these range names alter the formula (but not the underlying calculations) they can cause problems for worksheet auditing programs. Some auditing programs insist on flagging single cell range names as errors. A final drawback is that attaching Note-It Plus requires almost 75K. If you need to, you can get this space back by detaching it.

Manual   Like all Turner-Hall products, Note-It Plus has a very good manual.

Conclusion   At $79.95, Note-It Plus is an excellent product for Lotus 1-2-3 users. It easily lets you overcome the "where did I get that number" problem.

Product:	Note-It Plus
Price:	$79.95
Category:	Commercial
Publisher:	Turner Hall Publishing
Address:	10201 Torre Avenue
	Cupertino, California 95014
Phone:	(408) 253-9600
Memory:	70k

Noteworthy

Like Note-It Plus, *Noteworthy* gives you the ability to attach notes to your worksheet. These notes are useful for documenting your work, assumptions, or work remaining. Noteworthy requires less memory than Note-It Plus.

Installation   Noteworthy comes with two semi-automatic installation programs. One copies the files you need to run Noteworthy if you have already installed the Lotus add-in manager. The other copies and installs the add-in manager. You run the second program only if needed.

Operation   To edit an existing note or create a new note, the first thing you do is move the cursor to the cell that has the note attached. You then invoke Noteworthy using the menu-key you assigned when you attached it. The note editor is simple, but effective for the short notes. Figure 18-5 shows using Noteworthy to edit a note.

Noteworthy has a map mode. This mode highlights every cell in the worksheet with a note attached. You can use the standard cursor keys to move around the worksheet to find cells with notes. Figure 18-6 shows this. In addition, Noteworthy has a flag that appears at the bottom of the screen any time the cursor is on a cell with a note.

Noteworthy has options to print a single note, print all the notes in a worksheet and a list of all the notes in a worksheet. The search option lets you search the notes attached to the current worksheet.

Noteworthy includes a clipboard. The clipboard is useful for transferring data to different locations of Lotus. It is especially useful for making a copy of formulae without changing the cell references.

Limitations   Each note can contain up to 8,000 characters. There is no limit to the number of notes that you can attach to a worksheet. Like Note-It Plus,

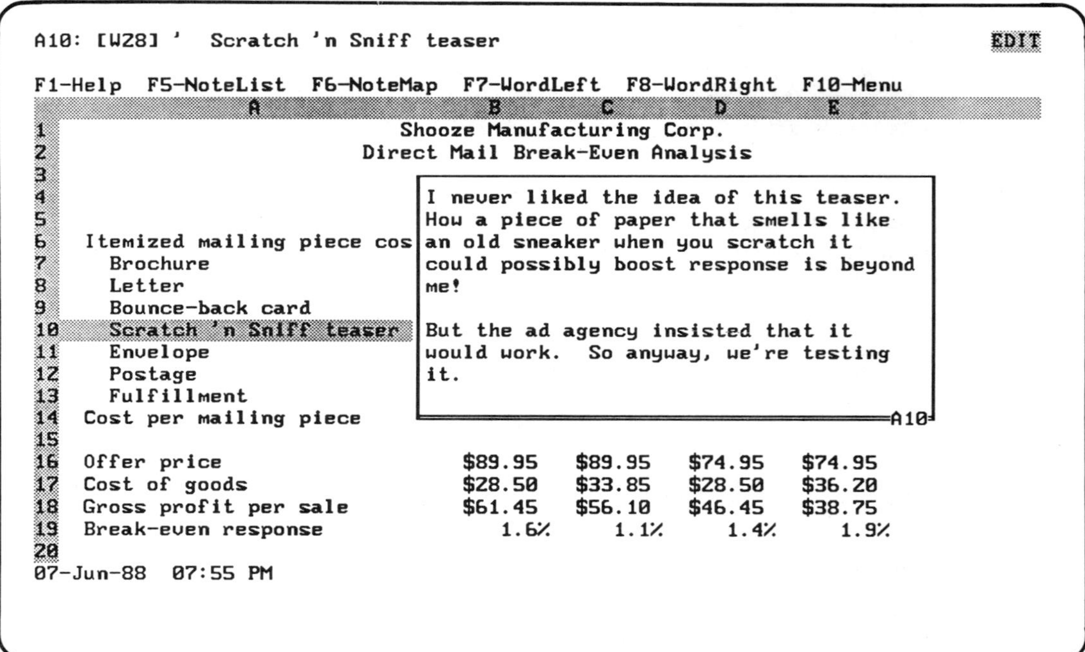

Fig. 18-5. Entering a note with Noteworthy.

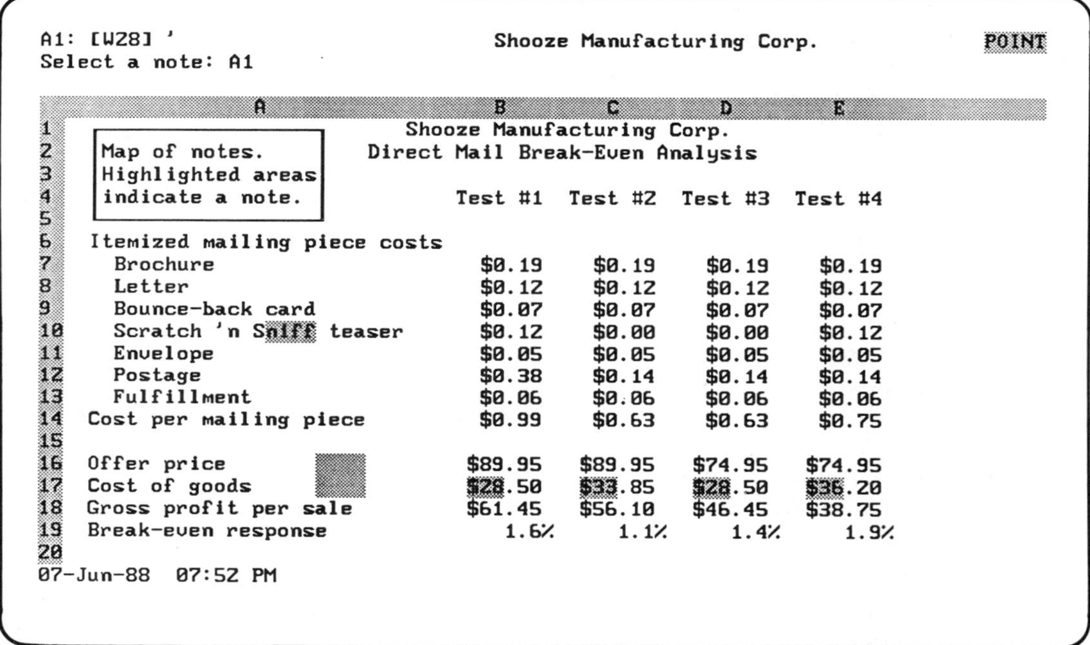

Fig. 18-6. Noteworthy can display a map of the worksheet showing cells with notes attached.

Noteworthy uses range names to track the placement of notes. This creates all the problems discussed above.

Manual   Noteworthy has a very good manual.

Conclusion   Noteworthy costs the same as Note-It Plus, yet it has fewer features. It makes up for that by requiring slightly more than half the memory. The big consideration in deciding between the two is do you want the extra features or want to save the memory.

```
Product:      Noteworthy
Price:        $79.95
Category:     Commercial
Publisher:    Funk Software
Address:      222 Third Street
              Cambridge, Massachusetts
              02142
Phone:        (617) 497-6339
Memory:       50K
```

NON-MEMORY RESIDENT FILE NOTING PROGRAMS

Non-memory resident file noting programs are stand-alone programs. Since they are not in memory, they do not reduce the memory available to other applications. However, you pay for that by only being able to use them when you are at the DOS prompt and not running another application. If you need to find a file in the middle of a Lotus session, you must exit to DOS to use one of these programs. In addition, since they are not in memory, they cannot watch for changes to the files. If you rename, delete or move a file you must remember to "tell" the programs yourself or they will not have the current information.

Norton Utilities

The Norton Utilities are a collection of helpful stand-alone programs. One of these utilities is a program called File Info. File Info is a non-memory resident way to attach a 65–character comment to file names. It stores the existing file name and the comment in a database file called FILEINFO.FI. Each time you enter the FI command, the program matches file names to display with comments. It has commands to add and modify comments and to remove comments for files that no longer exist. Since the program is not memory resident, it cannot update the file automatically when you delete, rename, or move files. Figure 18-7 shows an example.

Also See . . .

ClassiFILE, the DOS shell covered in Chapter 2, lets you add a 35-character description to each file and subdirectory.

```
fa          exe       9,304    11-15-88    4:50p   Set, reset, and scan file attributes
fd          exe      10,294    11-15-88    4:50p   Set a file's date and time stamp
fi          exe      18,438    11-15-88    4:50p   Attach and view filename comments
fs          exe       9,218    11-15-88    4:50p   List or total file sizes
ld          exe       9,548    11-15-88    4:50p   Graphic display of directory tree
lp          exe      13,564    11-15-88    4:50p   Print files with formatted output
ncc         exe      51,388    11-15-88    4:50p   Set colors, ports, keyboard and more
tm          exe       7,504    11-15-88    4:50p   Automatic timing with 4 stopwatches
si          exe      16,484    11-15-88    4:50p   Report computer technical info
ts          exe      19,130    11-15-88    4:50p   Locate text in files or disks
vl          exe      11,120    11-15-88    4:50p   Controls disk volume labels
wipedisk    exe      13,410    11-15-88    4:50p   Overwrite disk, for maximum security
wipefile    exe      13,180    11-15-88    4:50p   Obliterate files for security
fileinfo    fi        3,217    11-15-88    4:50p   Contains all of the file comments
mary                  1,145    11-15-88    4:50p   "Mary had a Little Lamb" for BE BEEP
bedemo      bat         659    11-15-88    4:50p   Demonstration of Batch Enhancer (BE)
bedemo      dat       7,640    11-15-88    4:50p   Data file used by BEDEMO.BAT
menu        dat         850    11-15-88    4:50p   Menu example, used in BEDEMO.BAT
rtdemo2     exe      79,079    11-15-88    4:50p   Program used by TUTORIAL.BAT
tutorial    dbd     169,639    11-15-88    4:50p   Database used by TUTORIAL.BAT
tutorial    bat         166    11-15-88    4:50p   This runs Norton Utilities Tutorial

39 files found     46,157,824 bytes free

C:\NORTON>
```

Fig. 18-7. The Norton Utilities File Info program lets you add a 65-character comment to each file without resorting to a memory resident program. Of course, you can only see this comment while using the Norton Utilities.

NAME NOTING PROGRAMS

Name noting programs are a fairly recent development. These are programs that insulate you from the tiny name restriction of DOS. Using these programs, you enter a long descriptive name. These memory resident programs match that long name with a DOS-legal name. Depending on the package, you can also enter the DOS name or the package may even do that for you.

All DOS sees are normal names like MY-PROJ.WK1. However, what you see is quite different. The memory resident name noting program translates MY-PROJ.WK1 into a more descriptive name like "Converting 123 Lakeshore Drive to Total Electric." You select from a list of names like this. Once you make your selection, the programs looks up the DOS-legal name in its database. It then feeds that name to DOS.

Extend-A-Name

Extend-A-Name is a memory resident program that separates the user from the eight-character DOS file names. You enter long descriptive file names and Extend-A-Name remembers which DOS file it applies to.

Installation   There is an installation program. I could run it from the A-drive. An ASSIGN A=B cured that. The installation program firsts asks for your name. After that, it gives you a list of programs and you select which ones you use. You move the cursor around pressing "Y" for each program you have. This selection automatically configures Extend-A-Name to work with those programs.

You can select a maximum of thirteen "trigger slots." Some programs, like DisplayWrite 3, only require one trigger slot. Others, like DisplayWrite 4, require as many as seven. After I selected Lotus and Microsoft Word, I did not have room to select any other of the programs I used. Table 18-3 below lists the products supported by Extend-A-Name and the number of trigger slots they use.

It then asks for your initials. It uses these to automatically generate DOS-legal file names if you choose to let the program do this. You then tell it if you have a color monitor. Finally, you select which version of Extend-A-Name to use. Table 18-4 lists the different versions.

The installation program adds the command to start Extend-A-Name as the next to last command in the AUTOEXEC.BAT file. It is one of the few programs to use that slot, most of them use either the first or last position. The last position is a bad position. If the command before that (the old last command) calls a menu or shell program, DOS may skip the new last command (to load the software.) So the next to last position makes sense. Extend-A-Name makes a cardinal error, however. When it modifies the AUTOEXEC.BAT file it does not save a copy of the unmodified version.

Table 18-3. **Programs Supported by Extend-A-Name, with the Number of Trigger Slots They Require.**

Program	Trigger Slots
Agenda	2
DisplayWrite 3	1
DisplayWrite 4	7
Enable Version 2	7
Lotus 1-2-3 Version 1A	2
Lotus 1-2-3 Version 2	5
Microsoft Word Version 4	5
Multimate WP I	2
Multimate WP II	2
Peachtext	2
PC-Write	2
PFS:Write	1
Q&A Write	6
Quattro	6
Samna IV Version 2	1
Sprint (Adv UI)	4
Smart DB	2
Smart SS	5
Smart WP	6
Symphony	5
Volkswriter 2	2
Volkswriter 3	6
WordPerfect 4	6
WordPerfect 5	6
WordStar 2000	6
WordStar Version 4	6
WordStar Version 5	4
XyWrite III+	4

For This Many Files	Extend-A-Name Uses This Much Memory
100	39K
175	46K
250	52K
325	59K
400	65K
400	5K Regular Memory and 66K Expanded Memory

Table 18-4. Memory Usage by Extend-A-Name.

The manual says it will install Extend-A-Name in the root directory of a hard disk and must remain there. It actually installed it in a subdirectory called \XNAME.

Operation   Most likely, you are going to want to use Extend-A-Name with both new and existing files. To do that, you must tell Extend-A-Name what the DOS names, locations and expanded names are. You do that by working through a fairly simple set of menus. The process follows these steps:

1) Set the path to the data files. The Path command is to enter a new path.
2) Enter the data file extension. Extend-A-Name can only work with one extension entry at a time. It may be possible to actually describe more than one of the extensions you use using wildcards.
3) Tagging the files to use. After you enter the extension, Extend-A-Name lists all the matching files on the screen. You tag the ones you want to work with. The files you select go into an unassigned library. A library in Extend-A-Name is just a grouping of common files. They do not have to be from the same program. For example, one folder on a project might have Lotus data files, memos written in WordStar and database files from dBASE.
4) Adding Extend-A-Name names. You move the cursor to the unassigned files entry and press Return. There is a menu at the top and a list of file names and Extend-A-Name names at the bottom. Initially, the two are the same. Using the rename command, you can change the Extend-A-Name to more descriptive names. Once you have assigned the names, this screen is quite informative. Figure 18-8 shows this.
5) Assigning to a meaningful library. The final step is to copy files from the unassigned library into meaningful libraries. You do this by tagging the files and issuing an "Assign" command. Figure 18-9 shows the results.

Using Extend-A-Name requires a modification in the way you work with subdirectories. The normal way is to have a separate subdirectory for each activity. If you are working on ten different projects, you might have ten subdirectories for the associated Lotus files. Extend-A-Name can only work with one subdirectory at a time. It creates a separate listing for each subdirectory and only shows the listing for the subdirectory that is currently active.

With Extend-A-Name, you would have a single Lotus directory for all your Lotus files. You would separate them by project by creating an Extend-A-Name library for each project.

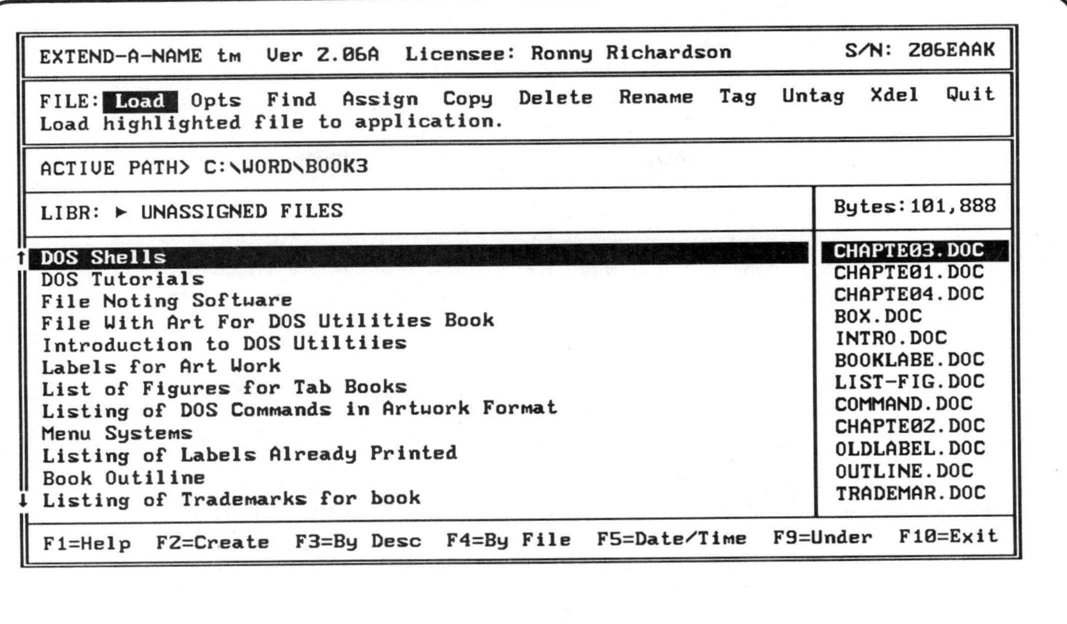

Fig. 18-8. Once the extended names have been assigned, the Extend-A-Name display can be quite informative.

Fig. 18-9. Extend-A-Name allows files to be grouped into meaningful sets of files called libraries. The files in these libraries do not have to be in the same subdirectory.

Once you have your computer configured, working with Extend-A-Name is a model of simplicity. Any time you go to save or load a file, Extend-A-Name pops up and you select the file from a sixty-character explanation and Extend-A-Name supplies the DOS name automatically. If you like, you can configure Extend-A-Name to allow you to enter the DOS name.

Limitations   The limitation of 13 triggers is a significant limitation. There are certain combinations of only two programs that exceed the number of available triggers. A read-me file explains how to set up complex batch files to run Extend-A-Name with more than thirteen triggers. However, a maximum of thirteen triggers can be active at once. This is likely to be too complex for inexperienced users.

I also found it difficult to use Extend-A-Name with some programs. You cannot configure the program from the installation program to work with programs that do not go through a menu to obtain files. For example, with Basic you enter 'Load "file"' without a prompt and in dBASE you enter "Do File" at a dot prompt. You can enter either of these commands at any point on the screen. You can manually capture a trigger for this type of program. However Extend-A-Name expects it to always be on the exact same point of the screen.

I tried to enter DO at the dot prompt and manually popped up Extend-A-Name to select the file name. Extend-A-Name erased the DO and the file name alone was fed into dBASE. Of course, that resulted in a dBASE error. At least the file name was on the screen so I could enter it manually.

Extend-A-Name adds a hidden file called XNAME.LIB to each subdirectory where you pop it up. This may cause some confusion especially when using a DOS shell that shows hidden files. Extend-A-Name will not work properly if you delete this file. The manual does warn about this file.

Manual   The manual is excellent. It explains the program in great detail. It uses a number of screen shots to illustrate to the reader what to expect when using the program. There were a number of minor differences between the manual and the way the software worked. This could have been due to my receiving an upgrade to the program without receiving an upgrade to the manual. In addition to the manual, Extend-A-Name comes with a tip sheet that explains how to use the program with a number of programs.

Conclusion   Extend-A-Name is a great way to insulate new users from the difficulty of the eight character limit on DOS names. If I were setting up computers for new users, I would add it to each one especially if expanded memory were available to reduce its impact on conventional memory. I think experienced users have adjusted to the eight-character limit and will get much less use from the program. I know I have completely adjusted. As I was configuring the program to work with my existing files, I was able to identify almost every one from their names.

If you use Extend-A-Name, you should provide the DOS name yourself. It seems likely that at some point you are going to have to do something with a file that Extend-A-Name cannot help you with. At that point, you are more likely to be able to identify a file with a name that you selected, such as LETR-2MOM.DOC, than with a name like RLR00001.DOC. If you use a DOS shell to manage your files, you must assign your own meaningful names since Extend-A-Name cannot provide you with a descriptive name while using a DOS shell.

Product:	Extend-A-Name
Price:	$49.95
Category:	Commercial
Publisher:	World Software Corporation
Address:	124 Prospect Street
	Ridgewood, New Jersey 07450
Phone:	(800) 962-6360
	(201) 444-3228
Notes:	Exact memory usage depends on the number of files with extended names.
Memory:	39K for 100 files
	46K for 175 files
	52K for 250 files
	59K for 325 files
	65K for 400 files

NameTag

NameTag is a pop-up utility that lists all the files in a directory along with any 40-character descriptions you have added.

Installation   NameTag comes with a program to automatically install Name-Tag. The installation program lets you install NameTag from either the A- or B-drive and install it on any drive and in any subdirectory. It gives you the option of starting NameTag automatically by adding it to the AUTOEXEC.BAT file or starting manually.

Operation   Operating NameTag is more straightforward than Extend-A-Name, partially because NameTag does less. Anytime you press its hot-key, NameTag pops up with a display like Fig. 18-10.

This NameTag display shows . . .

- The DOS file name.
- The DOS extension.
- The file size.
- The file creation date.
- Any 40-character comments entered using NameTag.

You can scroll the cursor around and easily edit the file comments. Editing file comments is easier than with Extend-A-Name where you must work through a menu.

As you scroll through the files, you can even peak into the contents of a data file. Figure 18-11 shows this. This feature is only useful for ASCII and near-ASCII files like word processing files as NameTag performs no formatting

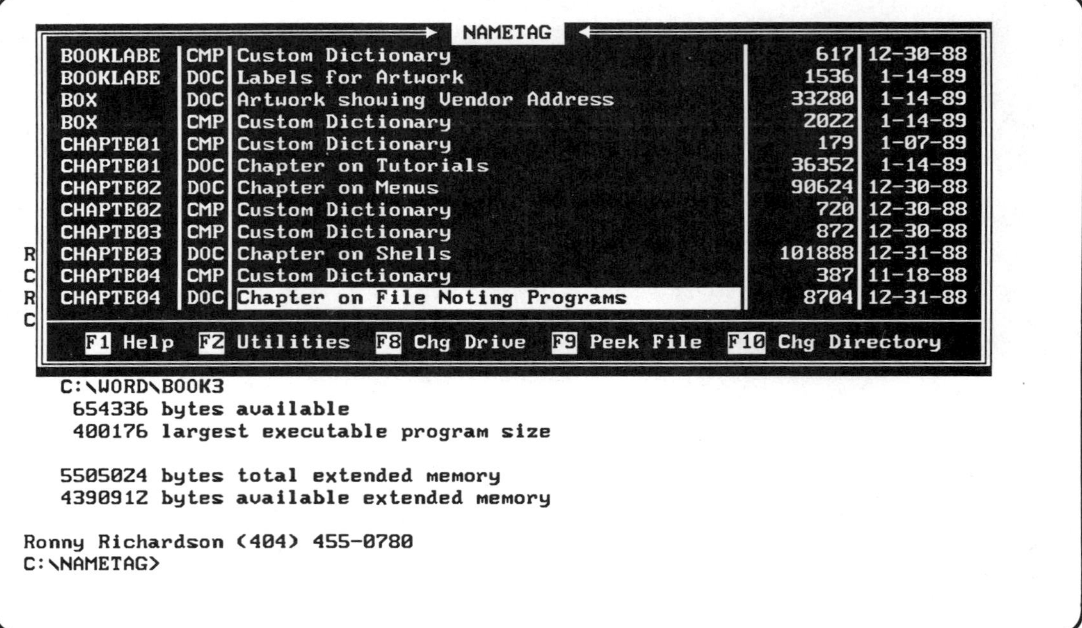

Fig. 18-10. The NameTag display shows the DOS file name and extension, the 40-character comment added using NameTag, the file's size and the file creation date.

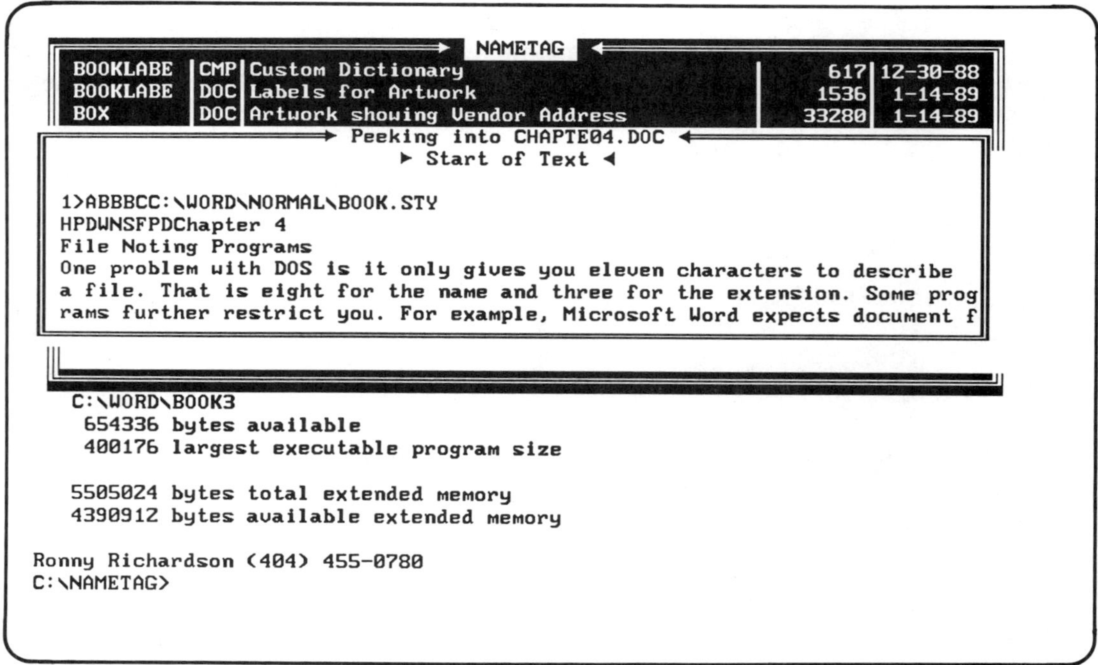

Fig. 18-11. NameTag lets you peak into the contents of your datafile.

for display other than stripping out high order ASCII characters. There is a pop-up menu to let you . . .

- Copy.
- Erase.
- Rename files.
- Display disk information from within NameTag.

Limitations   NameTag cannot supply the DOS file names to your application. Because it shows the file name on its display, this is at best a minor problem.

Manual   While not nearly as good as the Extend-A-Name manual, the Name-Tag is adequate. You can read it in only a few minutes and it will explain how to use NameTag.

Conclusion   NameTag is useful for adding comments to file names. It does not automatically pop-up so it is never in the way. You only use it when you want to use it.

```
Product:      NameTag
Price:        $39.95
Category:     Commercial
Publisher:    Mastersoft, Incorporated
Address:      4621 North 16th Street
              Phoenix, Arizona 85016
Phone:        (800) 624-6107
              (602) 277-0900
Memory:       66K
```

RONNY'S PICKS

For using file names longer than eight characters, Extend-A-Name is slightly better than NameTag. However, the differences are so slight that you should purchase the cheaper of the pair. For adding notes to files, I prefer the Norton FileInfo program. It lets you add reasonable size notes without taking up memory and getting in the way.

19
Memory Resident Managers

MS-DOS 2.0 first introduced the terminate and stay resident [TSR] interrupts for PC's. In addition to the interrupts, DOS 2.0 included the first memory resident programs for the IBM PC. These were:

- PRINT.COM. It allows background printing of ASCII files.
- GRAPHICS.COM. It allows screen prints of graphics.
- ASSIGN.COM. It allows DOS to treat one drive as another.

Beyond these TSR programs, Microsoft provided very limited information on using these interrupts. Microsoft did not provide this documentation for a reason. They were afraid if they documented the interrupts they would have to support them with all future releases of DOS. That was something they wanted to avoid.

The lack of documentation forced software developers to "reverse engineer" these three TSR programs. This lack of documentation and support from Microsoft was one of the major factors leading to the lack of standardization in TSR programs.

Software developers were busy developing two types of TSR software. The first type were extensions to DOS. These included RAMdisks, print spoolers and interfaces between memory board clocks and software. This type of software makes no DOS function calls once installed, therefore they are not likely to interfere with any other software. The second type uses function calls once installed. These generally have a "hot-key." Examples of these are keyboard macros and pop-up notepads. These are generally the TSR software that causes problems.

A TSR program that causes no problems is called well-behaved. Misbehaved TSR programs can cause all sorts of problems. These include trashed files, locked computers and even trashed hard disks. These problems have led to a new class of TSR programs designed to manage existing applications.

LOADING AND UNLOADING MEMORY RESIDENT SOFTWARE

The programs in this section are primarily for freeing up memory. They let you load a lot of TSR software into memory at the start of a computing session. You can later release these packages when you need more memory. They will let you release TSR software even when a package does not have the ability to release itself.

Releasing TSR software is all Mark/Release and PopDrop do. Referee adds some limited management functions.

Mark/Release

Mark/Release is a memory resident program manager. It forms layers between various programs. Using these layers, the program is able to remove memory resident programs from memory even when the programs lack internal method of being removed. Mark/Release is a set of public domain programs. The optional diskette set includes a copy of Mark/Release.

Installation   Mark/Release does not have an installation program. All you have to do is to copy the executable program files to a subdirectory in your PATH.

Operation   Mark/Release is a set of public domain programs designed by Kim Kokkonen to install and uninstall memory resident software. You run Mark between each layer of memory resident software. It uses about 1.5K to record the current state of the system. Using Mark, you can create as many layers as you need. Running Release restores the system to its state the last time you ran Mark. You can run Release several times to peel away memory resident layers. You can only safely run Release and other programs to drop memory resident software from the DOS prompt. Many programs let you exit to DOS. For example using the Lotus /System option or the WordStar run a program option. Running any program to drop TSR software from within an application will create a hole in RAM that will cause unpredictable results.

The package includes several other programs. Mapmem displays the layers created by Mark along with the associated TSR program names if you are using DOS 3.#. Ramfree displays the remaining RAM much quicker than CHKDSK. Eatmem uses up RAM, useful for testing software in reduced RAM or for very old programs that do not recognize memory above 512K.

Limitations   The current virus scare associated with downloaded software means you must be very careful about how you obtain your copy of Mark/Release. However, I obtained the copy on the optional diskette set directly from the author of the program. It is therefore safe.

Manual   Mark/Release does not include a manual. It does include a read-me file on the disk that does an adequate job of explaining how to use Mark/Release.

Conclusion   Mark/Release is a public domain program. The author does not request a donation so you can use the program free for noncommercial purposes. It is an excellent program with an unbeatable price. The optional diskette set includes a copy of Mark/Release.

<table>
<tr><td>Product:</td><td>Mark/Release</td></tr>
<tr><td>Price:</td><td>Free/$20.00 See Note</td></tr>
<tr><td>Category:</td><td>Public Domain</td></tr>
<tr><td>Publisher:</td><td>TurboPower</td></tr>
<tr><td>Address:</td><td>Post Office Box 66747
Scotts Valley, California 95066</td></tr>
<tr><td>Phone:</td><td>(408) 438-8608</td></tr>
<tr><td>Notes:</td><td>The optional diskette set includes a copy of this program.

There is no charge for the program; however, TurboPower charges a $20 handling fee if you order the program from them.</td></tr>
<tr><td>Memory:</td><td>1.5K</td></tr>
</table>

PopDrop

A memory resident program manager. It forms layers between various programs. Using these layers, the program is able to remove memory resident programs from memory even when the programs lack internal methods of being removed. In addition, PopDrop allows you to activate and deactivate various memory resident programs manually from its menu.

Installation   PopDrop does not include an installation program. All you must do is to copy the executable program files to a subdirectory in your PATH.

Operation   PopDrop is essentially a slicker version of Mark/Release that you must pay for. Like Mark/Release, PopDrop allows you to place layers between memory resident programs and then later to peel away those layers. Unlike Mark/Release, PopDrop includes everything in one program.

POPDROP starts the program and places the first layer.

POPDROP UP places a new layer after you load a memory resident program.

POPDROP CLEAR removes all memory resident programs but does not disturb the bottom PopDrop layers.

POPDROP STOP removes everything including the bottom PopDrop layer.

POPDROP # removes everything down to that layer.

POPDROP VIEW shows a map of the memory resident software was in memory. This is similar to Mapmem. Figure 19-1 shows this. Finally,

POPDROP BOOT performs a warm boot of the computer.

```
              654336 bytes total memory    356272 bytes free
    ___________________________________________________________________

    298064   PopDrop layer  4  SIDEKICK
                71600 bytes
    ___________________________________________________________________

    226464   PopDrop layer  3  HS
                61872 bytes
    ___________________________________________________________________

    164592   PopDrop layer  2  GRAB
                26912 bytes
    ___________________________________________________________________

    137680   PopDrop layer  1  SUPERKEY
                64064 bytes
    ___________________________________________________________________

     73616   DOS 3.30, DOS extensions, and programs loaded before PopDrop
                73616 bytes
    ___________________________________________________________________

PopDrop Commands:
   Up        Clear      View       Activate     Boot    1-3 for layers to keep
   Down      Stop       Hooks      Inactivate   Quit    ?   for help

Enter first letter, digit(s) or the enter key:
```

Fig. 19-1. PopDrop Main menu. Notice it shows SuperKey, Grab, HotShot, and SideKick loaded in separate layers. Each layer can be removed individually, in order, beginning with SideKick—or they can be removed in blocks.

Limitations   PopDrop includes a special program so you can issue PopDrop commands from a batch file. Sometimes, issuing a STOP or CLEAR command with this program causes DOS to lose track of its batch file. The vendor is aware of the problem and says it is due to a limitation of DOS.

Manual   PopDrop comes with an excellent manual and the best disk-based tutorial I have ever seen for any software program. Their technical support is first rate. I have called several times with problems and they have sent out a correction disk right away.

Conclusion   Given its similarity to Mark/Release, which is free, you may be wondering why you should pay for PopDrop. PopDrop comes with a slick visual tutorial explaining memory resident software and its associated problems. In addition, PopDrop comes with a small manual (Mark/Release has a manual on disk), and telephone support (even though you will not need it). In addition, PopDrop has none of the risk associated with the Trojan horse and virus programs. Of course, the version of Mark/Release on the optional diskette set is safe.

```
Product:    PopDrop
Price:      $54.95
Category:   Commercial
Publisher:  InfoStructures, Incorporated
Address:    Post Office Box 32617
            Tucson, Arizona 85751
Phone:      (602) 299-5962
Memory:     1.5K
```

Referee

Referee is a memory resident program manager. It forms layers between various programs. Using these layers, the program is able to remove memory resident programs from memory even when the programs lack internal methods of being removed. In addition, Referee allows you to activate and deactivate various memory resident programs as you run different applications.

Installation   Referee does not include an installation program. The manual does explain how to copy Referee to your hard disk.

Operation   Like Mark/Release and PopDrop, Referee will allow you to peel away layers of memory resident software. It also does much more than the other programs. Referee allows you to enable and disable memory resident programs at will. In addition, you can create RAM Teams. These are combinations of memory resident programs that you turn on and off together.

You begin by loading Refwatch. Refwatch requires 22.5K, far more than the other two programs. A pop-up menu to replace its command driven mode requires an additional 15K. Unlike Mark/Release and PopDrop, you do not have to form the layers between programs because Refwatch automatically performs that function. You unload programs using Referee by selecting their names from a menu. If the program you select has TSR programs loaded after it, these are also automatically deleted. If Referee did not delete these additional programs, the single deleted program would create a hole of free memory between TSR programs with unpredictable results.

In addition to unloading a program, Referee allows you to deactivate any program. Unlike delete, deactivate does not require you to deactivate other programs first. Once deactivated, Referee will allow you to reactivate the program. This function is useful when a specific TSR program, like WordPop, conflicts with a specific application program, like Spread 8 – 9 – 0. When you want to use Spread 8 – 9 – 0, just deactivate WordPop. It is also useful when a spreadsheet TSR, like NewNum, conflicts with a word processing TSR, like WordPop. You can deactivate WordPop when using your spreadsheet and NewNum when using your word processor. You can automate this process by creating RAM-Teams. Using a RAM-Team, Referee automatically deactivates WordPop when you start your spreadsheet. It would also automatically deactivate NewNum when you start your word processor.

Limitations   Requires far more memory than PopDrop or Mark/Release. It requires almost as much memory as RamLord without providing the features of RamLord.

Manual   The manual does a good job of explaining its many features. It does a poor job of explaining how to install Referee.

Conclusion   Referee is far more powerful than either Mark/Release or Pop-Drop but not nearly as powerful as RamLord or 386^{Max}. Mark/Release and Pop-Drop simply let you drop memory resident programs at will while Referee also allows you to control which programs are active when. All this extra power comes at the cost of about 18K, depending on how many layers you create.

Product:	Referee
Price:	$69.95
Category:	Commercial
Publisher:	Persoft, Incorporated
Address:	465 Science Drive
	Madison, Wisconsin 53711
Phone:	(608) 273-6000
Memory:	22.5K

MANAGING TSR SOFTWARE

The programs below take TSR management much further than just letting you easily unload TSR software. These packages control how the program actually runs. They swap images of TSR software to and from disks so it is all not in memory at once.

If this sounds confusing, consider the following example:

When you want to show slides, you use a slide projector. Most slide projectors can only show one slide at a time. The machine holds the rest in a tray until needed. When you tell it to display a given slide, it is dropped into a slot in the projector. If another slide was already in the slot, it removes it first.

RamLord operates just like this slide projector. It has a slot for only a single TSR package. However, its tray has room for twenty. You can fill the tray as full as you like, until all twenty slots are full. You then use hot-keys like a remote control to tell *RamLord* which "slide" to drop into the "slot." Just like you can only view the one slide in the projector, you can only use the one TSR package loaded by *RamLord*. This ability to manage TSR software makes these packages more powerful than the unloading programs.

When you start these programs, they generally:

1) Loads each memory resident program, one at a time.
2) Copy an image of its place in memory to disk or to extended or expanded memory.
3) Unload that program.
4) Load the next and repeat the process.

This continues till there is a disk image of each memory resident program. They reserve enough memory for the largest program. At your command, they will swap any one memory resident program into the hole. That way, you can have as many memory resident programs available as you like while using only the amount of space required by the largest one plus the memory required by the manager.

Extra

Extra is a commercial memory resident program for managing other memory resident programs.

Installation   Extra comes with an installation program that automatically installs Extra on your hard disk. It will run from any drive. After installing the software on the hard disk, the installation program automatically displays the 'Readme' file. This file gives you last minute tips that are not in the manual. Automatically displaying the file is a nice touch.

Operation   After installation, Extra requires configuration before you can use it. The best thing to do first is to print a copy of your AUTOEXEC.BAT file. The Extra configuration program presents you with a TSR software definition screen.

Using this screen, you enter the name of each TSR program, the commands needed to load it, and an Extra hot-key. The names are just for your information so you can make them descriptive. The loading commands are the same as you would enter from DOS, including any switches or file names. Extra comes preconfigured for many TSR software packages. For these, you

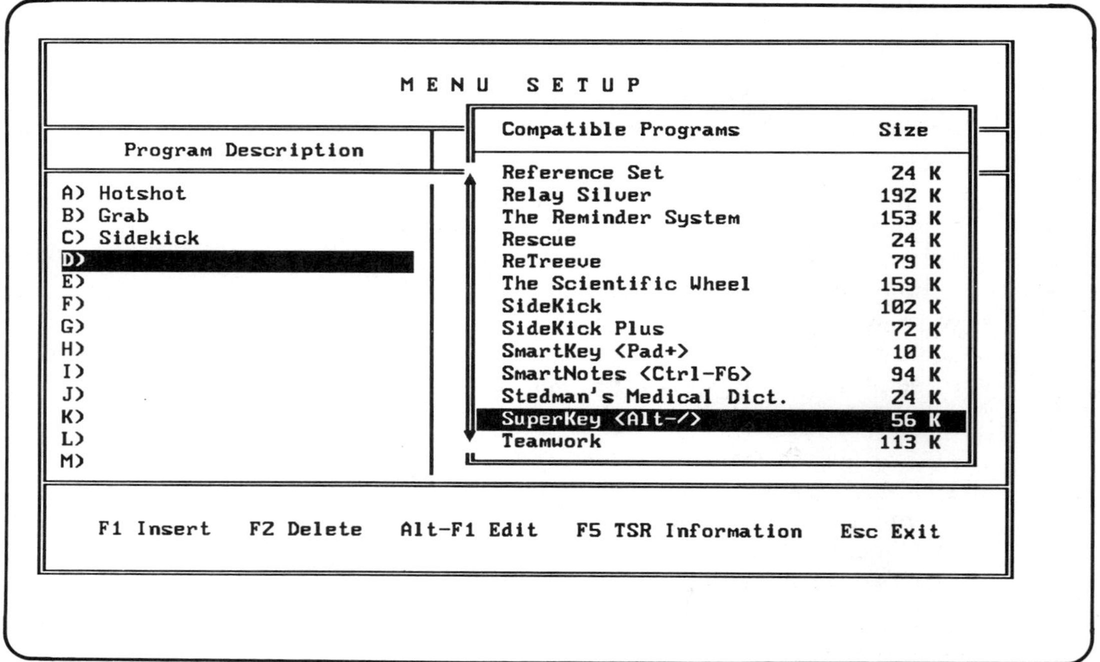

Fig. 19-2. Extra comes with a list of preconfigured software packages. To install these, all you have to do is select them from the menu. Extra will automatically search your hard disk for the proper files.

just select their name from a menu. Figure 19-2 shows this. After you select the package, Extra will automatically search your hard disk for the program.

Each line represents a separate memory image and only one image will be in memory at any time. Since only one TSR image is in memory, you do not need to worry about the loading order. I have SideKick first, SuperKey last, with other programs in the middle. That would lock up my computer if I tried it from DOS. If you have programs that must be in memory together, you can specify their loading on a single line separated with '+ +'. That way, Extra will load them together.

After configuring Extra to load your software, you complete one file screen that defines how Extra will operate. When you exit the configuration program, Extra brags on how much memory it saved you by showing the memory requirements with and without Extra.

You do not load your memory resident software (either manually or in the AUTOEXEC.BAT file) when you start your computer. Rather, you start Extra. It reads its configuration file and loads each piece (or set) of software individually. It creates a disk image of the RAM as configured by each package. It can also store this image in extended or expanded memory. That makes it run much faster.

It then creates a hole in RAM big enough to hold the largest package, or set of packages when two or more must be loaded together. When you need to load a memory resident package, you press Control-Spacebar. That brings up the Extra menu where you select the TSR package to load into memory. Extra removes the current package from its RAM hole, saves it to disk and loads the requested TSR package into the same RAM hole. It first copies the package to disk so you do not lose any work-in-progress. Extra does not "pop-up" the TSR package. To do that, you use the standard hot-key for the TSR package you want to run.

Limitations   Extra is not compatible with Windows. Every time I started Windows without unloading Extra, the computer locked up. Fortunately, you can remove Extra from memory. Extra proved to be somewhat unstable. It would occasionally lock up after loading a memory resident program for no apparent reason. I tested Extra only with programs it is supposed to be compatible with so this must have been a problem with Extra itself.

In addition, Extra switches individual packages in and out of memory. You cannot use it to control programs like RAM disks that need to remain in memory constantly.

Manual   The manual is very well written and extremely easy for a beginner to understand.

Conclusion   Extra is an excellent way to manage TSR software. This is especially true if you load two or more pop-up TSR packages and the total of all their RAM requirements excluding the largest is more than 35K.

Product:	Extra
Price:	$99.00
Category:	Commercial
Publisher:	Delta Technology International
Address:	1621 Westgate Road
	Eau Claire, Wisconsin 54703
Phone:	(715) 832-7575
Notes:	In addition to 35K, Extra requires enough additional memory to load the largest TSR package.
Memory:	35K

Headroom

Headroom is a memory resident program for managing programs. It is better than Extra or RamLord because it also works with stand-alone applications.

Installation There is an installation program to copy the Headroom files onto your hard disk. It expects to run from the A-drive and an ASSIGN A = B statement will correct that if you must run from the B-drive.

Operation Headroom is a cross between RamLord (see below) and Software Carousel (see Chapter 25). It lets you swap memory resident software into and out of memory in a fashion similar to RamLord. It also lets you swap stand-alone applications into and out of memory.

Headroom can swap programs to either disk or extended or expanded memory. Swapping to disk is the slowest. With stand-alone applications it can be faster to actually load the software than to swap it from a slow hard disk. However, even on a slow machine it is faster to swap the applications if you use either extended or expanded memory.

Swapping a stand-alone application to memory (or disk) is easy. At any point in your program, you press the Headroom hot-key of Alt-Enter. That brings up the Headroom menu. You press F4 to go to another menu and select swap. Headroom will ask you where to swap the program to. Headroom understands modern screen displays. Unlike many TSR software packages, it will properly restore the screen on EGA and VGA monitors. If you are swapping to memory, you return to the DOS prompt or a previously swapped out program very rapidly. You also have all of your previously available conventional memory free for the next application. The manual recommends you only swap out an application when it is safe, e.g. when rebooting would not cause you to lose any work.

Swapping another program is even easier. When you swap a program out of memory, Headroom prompts you for the program name. To return that program to memory, you press the Headroom hot-key and select that program from a menu.

Swapping memory resident software is even easier. You load the TSR software into memory and return to the DOS prompt. Then you run a Headroom program called SWAPOUT. It automatically creates an image of the TSR software in memory (or on disk) that you can swap in and out of memory. In doing this, it frees the conventional memory used when it loaded the TSR software. In addition, since multiple TSR programs are not in memory at once, you do not have to deal with conflicts. You can even configure Headroom to automatically pop up the TSR package when you press the hot-key for the TSR package.

Headroom allows you to build a custom configuration and save it to disk. You can define all the TSR software you want available and even all the stand-alone packages you want loaded and Headroom will load them all automatically. However, you must have the exact same memory configuration each time you load this configuration as you did when you created it. Change anything, including something as simple as increasing your BUFFERS= statement, and you have to recreate this configuration.

Limitations   The Headroom arrangement for loading TSR packages limits their ability to interact with the program you are running when you pop them up. With Headroom, you work within the TSR software while without any problem. However, when you exit the program, Headroom unloads it from memory. That means your keyboard macro program cannot pass keystrokes to your application. You can, of course, load any TSR packages that must interact with your software before loading Headroom. That way, they are always available.

A few programs do not run properly when you are using Headroom to swap programs into and out of memory. I loaded three programs into memory and then tried to run a simple DOS batch file. DOS looked like it was doing something but the batch file did not run.

Manual   The manual is terrible. I read it several times and still did not understand it. I finally had to just sit down and learn Headroom by using it. The manual reads like a programmer wrote it. They should completely rewrite it. Fortunately, between reading the manual and playing with Headroom for awhile, you can learn to use it.

Conclusion   If you do not have extended or expanded memory, then Headroom really has nothing to offer you over RamLord or Extra. However, if you do have extra memory, Headroom will increase your productivity. You can rapidly switch between applications, even while running an EGA or VGA display. In addition, you can reclaim much of the memory used by your TSR software.

<table>
<tr><td>Product:</td><td>Headroom</td></tr>
<tr><td>Price:</td><td>$95.00</td></tr>
<tr><td>Category:</td><td>Commercial</td></tr>
<tr><td>Publisher:</td><td>Helix Software Company, Incorporated</td></tr>
<tr><td>Address:</td><td>83-65 Daniels Street
Briarwood, New York 11435</td></tr>
<tr><td>Phone:</td><td>(718) 262-8787</td></tr>
<tr><td>Memory:</td><td>61K</td></tr>
</table>

RamLord

RamLord is a memory resident program for managing other memory resident programs.

Installation   RamLord does not have an installation program to copy the files to your disk, you must do that manually. The manual explains the process.

After you copy the files, RamLord requires a complex installation before you can use it. The best thing to do first is to print a copy of your AUTOEXEC .BAT file. You begin by removing all memory resident [TSR] programs from memory. You cannot install RamLord while any TSR programs are in memory. The easiest way to do this is to boot from your DOS disk.

The RamLord installation program presents you with a TSR software definition screen. Using this screen, you enter the name of each TSR program, the commands needed to load it, and a RamLord hot-key. (More on the RamLord hot-key later.) The names are just for your information so you can make them descriptive. The loading commands are the same as you would enter from DOS, including any switches or file names. You specify one line as the default line. This is the TSR package that is first available when RamLord loads.

Each line represents a separate memory image and only one image will be in memory at any time. Since only one TSR image is in memory, you can forget loading order problems. I have SideKick first, SuperKey last, with other programs in the middle. That would lock up my computer if I tried it from DOS. If you have programs that must be in memory together, you can specify their loading on a single line separated with Control-N. That way, they will load together.

Operation   You do not load your memory resident software (either manually or in the AUTOEXEC.BAT file) when you start your computer. Rather, you start RamLord. It reads its configuration file and loads each piece (or set) of software individually. It creates a disk image of the RAM as configured by each package. It can also store this in extended or expanded memory. That makes RamLord run faster.

It then creates a hole in RAM big enough to hold the largest package, or set of packages when it must load two or more together. It loads the default package into this hole. When you need to use another memory resident package, you press the RamLord hot-key assigned to that package. RamLord removes the current package from its RAM hole, saves it to disk and loads the requested TSR package into the same RAM hole. It first copies the removed package to disk so you do not lose any work-in-progress.

The RamLord hot-key does not "pop-up" the TSR package. To do that, you use the standard hot-key for the TSR package you want to run. Rather, the RamLord hot-key is a command to RamLord to change the TSR package it has loaded in memory.

Limitations   RamLord is not compatible with Windows. Every time I started Windows without unloading RamLord, the computer locked up. Fortunately, you can remove RamLord from memory by popping up its main menu and pressing F1.

In addition, RamLord switches individual packages in and out of memory. You cannot use it to control programs like RAM disks that need to remain in memory constantly.

Manual   The manual is well written and complete.

Conclusion   RamLord is an excellent way to manage TSR software. This is especially true if you load two or more pop-up TSR packages and the total of all their RAM requirements excluding the largest is more than 35K.

<table>
<tr><td>Product:</td><td>RamLord</td></tr>
<tr><td>Price:</td><td>$99.95</td></tr>
<tr><td>Category:</td><td>Commercial</td></tr>
<tr><td>Publisher:</td><td>Waterworks Software</td></tr>
<tr><td>Address:</td><td>913 Electric Avenue
Seal Beach, California 90740</td></tr>
<tr><td>Phone:</td><td>(213) 594-4768</td></tr>
<tr><td>Memory:</td><td>25K</td></tr>
</table>

OTHER MEMORY MANAGEMENT: 386^{Max}

386^{Max} is an extremely powerful commercial memory management software for 80386-based machines. It performs the following:

- Remaps extended memory to fill "holes" in conventional memory.
- Remaps memory where the computer uses the fastest memory as conventional memory
- Moves BIOS routines into fast memory.
- Converts the remaining extended memory into expanded memory. This is optional.

Installation   There is no installation routine, you must install 386^{Max} manually. The complete installation requires you to modify your CONFIG.SYS and AUTOEXEC.BAT files. The manual explains this. However, you should be technically inclined or have help. In addition, before you begin, you should prepare a bootable diskette with all the software you would need to correct any problems.

Operation   It is important to realize that 386^{Max} is not like all the other programs in this section. 386^{Max} will help you manage TSR software. Unlike the other programs, that is not its primary function. Its primary function is to manage the memory on a 80386 machine.

You load 386^{Max} as a device driver in your CONFIG.SYS. That means DOS loads it into memory before any other software, except other device drivers. It is even loaded before COMMAND.COM. This gives it unparalleled ability to control memory.

The biggest feature of 386^{Max} is memory filling. Here, it performs three functions:

1) Back-filling. If the machine does not contain a full complement of conventional memory, 386^{Max} will "fill-up" 640K by emulating conventional memory using extended memory. This is especially useful for the Intel 80386 motherboards that only have 512K of 32-bit conventional memory but support 32-bit extended memory cards. With 386^{Max}, you can avoid having to add a slower 16-bit conventional memory card to obtain the full 640K.

2) Low memory-filling. Depending on the type of display adaptor you have, you may have usable conventional memory space above 640K. DOS reserves 256K directly above the 640K limit for use by the display adaptor. Not all display adaptors use all this memory space. 386^{Max} can reclaim any available space for use as conventional memory by DOS. EGA and VGA displays gain nothing as their displays use all available space. CGA displays gain 96K. So CHKDSK with 386^{Max} filling this memory with a CGA adaptor will show 736K available to DOS. Monochrome adaptors gain 64K. Hercules gains 64K. This additional memory is directly available to DOS as conventional memory and is directly supported by most DOS programs.

3) High memory-filling. Depending on the display adaptor, there is conventional memory space above the display adaptor and below the 1024K limit on conventional memory. 386^{Max} can make this available for loading memory resident software. With EGA and VGA, you gain 176K. With CGA you gain 192K. With Monochrome you gain 240K. And with Hercules you gain 192K. To use this memory, you must run a special program (385MAX. COM) with a /LOADHIGH command. This closes low memory so only high memory is available for loading. When you finish loading into high memory, you run 386MAX.COM with a /LOADLOW command. This closes high memory and opens low memory. You cannot store a single program across both areas. However, you can load separate programs in both locations. To load a program into high memory, it must fit entirely into high memory. You can load more than one TSR program into high memory if they will fit. Some TSR software is not well behaved enough to load into high memory.

386^{Max} performs a number of additional functions:

- It can swap any memory with any other memory. Many 80386-based accelerator cards contain memory but require you to use some or all of your slower 16-bit memory on the original motherboard as low memory. Many users overcome this by removing as much of their 16-bit memory as possible. 386^{Max} allows you to swap the memory. Therefore, you can use the 32-bit accelerator card memory as low memory and use the slower 16-bit memory as less frequently accessed extended memory. 386^{Max} can automatically decide which is the slower memory.
- LIM [Lotus/Intel/Microsoft, or just Lotus] memory version 4.0 support. You can use all or part of your remaining extended memory as Lotus memory.
- It can map slower 8-bit or 16-bit ROMs into fast 32-bit memory for faster operation.

Finally, 386^{Max} comes with a program that can visually display memory usage for your computer.

Limitation Is not compatible with any protected-mode software. This includes Windows 386 and DESQview. The high loading feature of 386^{Max} is incompatible with the RamLord program discussed below. Otherwise, the two programs work well together.

Manual The manual contains all the information you need to install and operate 386^{Max} It is not written for a beginner. That is acceptable. I would not expect a neophyte to be using this type of software. If you need its features but are not sure you can install 386^{Max} get help.

Conclusion 386^{Max} is an extremely powerful software package for 80386-based machines. If your machine meets its memory requirements then 386^{Max} should be in your CONFIG.SYS file, period. It requires 1 Meg of conventional memory and a minimum of 256K of extended memory.

Product:	386^{Max}
Price:	$74.95
Category:	Commercial
Publisher:	Qualitas, Incorporated
Address:	8314 Thoreau Drive
	Bethesda, Maryland 20817
Phone:	(301) 469-8848
Notes:	386^{Max} requires 3.5K of conventional memory and 60K of extended memory for its code. To run, it requires an 80386-based computer, a minimum of 256K extended memory starting at 1 Meg or the equivalent amount of recoverable shadow RAM such as found on a Compaq DeskPro 386, and DOS 3.0 or higher.
Memory:	3.5K Conventional Memory
	256K Extended Memory

RONNY'S PICKS

If you have an 80386 machine and meet the memory requirements, then you should be loading 386^{Max}. Its numerous features make it extremely valuable.

If you do not have extended or expanded memory, then RamLord should be the only TSR software management program you consider. This is especially true if you meet the requirements where RamLord will save your memory. The requirement that you must meet for RamLord to save your memory is the RAM requirements of all your memory resident pop-up programs except the largest, must exceed the 25K required by RamLord. That way, when RamLord adds its 25K and reserves enough RAM for your largest TSR program, it will reduce the total memory requirements.

You might want to consider RamLord even if you fail this test. Since different TSR programs are never in memory at the same time unless you tell RamLord to load them together, RamLord can cure memory resident conflicts. For example, the Microsoft Word thesaurus will not work with SuperKey loaded. Because I always loaded SuperKey, I could never use my thesaurus. Now, I can easily use the thesaurus by making sure SuperKey is not in the RAM hole when I need the thesaurus. Finally, RamLord also means you can add new TSR programs without guilt.

However, if you do have extended or expanded memory, then Headroom will give you all the functions of RamLord and more. In addition to swapping TSR software into and out of memory, Headroom will swap your stand-alone applications. All that adds up to one powerful package. Headroom is a very new product and still has kinks they need to work out. As they do this, Headroom will become an extremely powerful utility.

20
Print Buffers

Typically, your printer is the slowest part of your system. When you print, the slow printer slows down even the fastest computer. When you print, the following takes place:

1) The computer sends a character to the printer. (This is a slight simplification. Some printers have a few kilobytes of built-in memory. They can use this to store a little text before printing. Once this buffer is full, the printer behaves just as described.) If that is the last character, the computer quits printing. Otherwise, it continues to step 2.
2) The computer starts asking the printer if it can accept another character.
3) Finally, the computer answers yes. The computer loops back to step 1.

Because the delaying factor is the printer, a faster computer will not print any faster than a slower one. Because many programs, including Lotus, do not have background printing, you lose all use of your computer while the above is going on.

A print buffer is a solution to the delays caused by a slow printer. The print buffer accepts output from the computer as fast as the computer can send it. All the while it is doling the output to the printer as slowly as required. That way, the computer finishes before the printer does and you get back control of the computer much faster.

There are three types of print buffers:

1) Hardware. This is a box of memory and a power supply. You connect your printer cable to the buffer and its printer cable to the printer. The advantage of a hardware buffer is it does not use any computer RAM. Its disad-

vantage is you must allocate expensive RAM to nothing but printing. This type of print buffer was once quite popular but is being replaced by the third type of buffer.

2) RAM Buffers. This is a memory resident program that causes part of the RAM in the computer to emulate a hardware print buffer. The RAM requirements of modern programs combined with the usefulness of other memory resident software has made these uncommon. New versions are available that use extended or expanded memory in place of main memory. These are popular and vendors usually bundle them with their memory boards.

3) Disk-based Buffers. These buffers are like the RAM buffers in that they use a memory resident kernel to intercept print instruction. Unlike the RAM buffers, they do not buffer the intercepted printing in RAM. Rather, they buffer it in one or more disk files. This gives the disk-based buffers almost unlimited capacity.

In addition to buffering the printing, disk-based buffers offer a host of additional features. This is possible because they store the entire print job as a file which they can manipulate. Most disk-based buffers will allow you to send jobs to the printer in a different order than you printed them. They will also allow you to delay printing by capturing the data to disk for later printing.

Table 20-1 shows how fast each of the buffers will free a computer that printed an 83 page report using Microsoft Word. Generally, you want the faster buffer. However, flexibility can also be important. As a reference point, the table also shows the time for an older Quadram Microfazer hardware buffer. This buffer has 512K of RAM which was more than enough to store the entire document.

Duet

Duet is a disk-based print buffer that works with almost any software package. It has several features especially for laser printers. In addition to intercepting and buffering print streams, Duet can directly print Lotus files with-

Table 20-1. **Printer Buffer Timing Tests.**

Program	Time	Notes
Duet	1:54	
LaserTORQ Buffering to Disk	1:10	
LaserTORQ Buffering to Memory	1:10	
PC Kwik Print Spooler	1:10	
PrintQ	2:58	
Quadram Microfazer	1:53	[1]

All times are for an IBM Model 70 running at 16 MHz and printing to an HP LaserJet Plus.

All times are for the time required until the computer was free.

[1]This is a stand-alone hardware buffer with 512K of RAM.

out the need for Lotus. Duet's ability to print Lotus *.WK? files exceeds Lotus' ability.

Installation   Duet includes an installation program that will automatically install Duet. The program lets you select things like the type of printer(s) you have from menus. It does not let you change the hot-key. You can install the program in four versions requiring between 60K and 128K. You can save 38K off the full configuration by either not being able to print Lotus files directly or by not being able to print sideways. You can save an additional 30K by skipping both options.

If Duet does not support your printer, you can send a copy of your manual to the company. They will write a driver especially for your printer.

Operation   Duet is a memory resident print buffer. It captures printing the computer thinks it is sending to the printer and stores it in a disk file. One file per printout. Duet sends the printing to the printer as slowly as the printer requires. Except for using one file per printout rather than one large file, this part of Duet is very similar to PrintQ.

Where Duet really shines is working with Lotus (or Symphony and close clones of either) files. Duet can read the file from disk and print a range without loading Lotus. Duet does not show the file but it does list the range names so you will want to assign printing range names while in Lotus. Once you have specified this information, you can go directly back to other operations. When printing directly from a worksheet, Duet does not buffer the printing directly. Rather, it reads the worksheet information as the printer needs it. As a result, it does not need disk space to buffer Lotus printing by Duet.

Not only can Duet print Lotus worksheets directly, it can do it better than Lotus. Lotus limits you to 100 lines per page and 240 characters per line. Duet's limits (999) are much more generous and you are far less likely to exceed them. These larger limits make Duet perfect for printing with extra small laser fonts. Once you have designed the printout the way you want, you can save the settings for later use.

You can use Duet to perform simple printer controls such as advancing the paper or selecting fonts. You can stop the printer temporarily if you get an important call and the printer is too loud. You can have Duet queue the printing and wait to print to a specified time. If you have installed Duet for more than one printer or more than one font cartridge, you can use a Duet menu to easily select between different printers. Of course, you must take care of the mechanics of switching cables, turning switches, or whatever to actually switch printers.

When using a laser printer, you can use Duet to download fonts, select the paper tray, select between landscape and portrait mode, and send printer macros.

Limitations   Duet is not compatible with RamLord. When I tried to load Duet using RamLord the computer locked.

Manual   The manual is excellent. It has a tutorial and a number of hints. It is written in an enjoyable and chatty style.

Conclusion   Duet is a very good disk-based print buffer. For laser printers and heavy Lotus printing, it is a better buffer than PrintQ. For other uses they are roughly equivalent. If you manage your memory resident software with RamLord, which is an excellent manager, you must use PrintQ.

Product:	Duet
Price:	$89.95
Category:	Commercial
Publisher:	Consumer Software, Incorporated
Address:	736 Chestnut Street
	Santa Cruz, California 95060
Phone:	(800) 645-5501
	(800) 556-6699 in California
Notes:	Three alternative installation configurations are available that can reduce memory down to 60K. 38K can be saved by either not being able to print Lotus files directly or by not being able to print sideways. An additional 30K can be saved by skipping both options
Memory:	128K

LaserTORQ

LaserTORQ is a commercial print buffer program that can buffer to disk or memory. It will use conventional, extended or expanded memory. Laser-TORQ is optimized to work with laser printers.

Installation   Installation is a two step process. First, you transfer the files to the hard disk. There is no batch file or installation program to do this but the steps are clearly explained in the manual. The second step is to configure LaserTORQ. There is a program to do this. You need to tell LaserTORQ what port to use, where to store the buffered data and how much memory or disk space to allocate to buffering.

Operation   LaserTORQ is a print buffer but without the integrated control features of PrintQ or Duet. Once installed and loaded into memory, Laser-TORQ does its work with little or no user intervention. There is only one simple menu. This menu lets you purge the buffer, pause printing and select the graphics optimization method used by LaserTORQ. It also shows you graphically how much space is available in the buffer.

LaserTORQ optionally optimizes graphics you send to the laser printer. It modifies the graphics in two ways. First, it removes the unnecessary data most graphics programs send to define white space. Second, it translates the graphics commands into a format that minimizes memory requirement. As a result, you can print almost any full-page of graphics on a 512K LaserJet Plus or clone. This also minimizes the data actually sent to the printer. That can significantly speed up printer if you are using an old serial interface LaserJet printer.

LaserTORQ has two forms of optimization, quick and full. Quick gets the printing started faster but full provides the maximum amount of optimization. You select either of these methods or no optimization from the LaserTORQ menu.

LaserTORQ is interrupt driven. Rather than continually checking the status of the printer port, it uses an interrupt signal to figure out when to send an additional character to the printer. That made LaserTORQ the faster print buffer when buffering to disk and tied for first place when buffering to memory.

Limitations   LaserTORQ does not have the queue control of PrintQ. With PrintQ, you can assign priorities to jobs to control printing order, rearrange jobs to print everything using a certain form and much more. With Laser-TORQ, all you can do is pause printing and clear the buffer.

LaserTORQ is flexible about where it stores its buffered data. It will spool to disk or to any type of memory. However, you must tell it how much space to use in advance. That makes sense with memory, especially extended memory which lacks an industry standard way to reserve memory. However, PrintQ easily grabs hard disk space as it needs it. Its buffer can be as small as a few kilobytes or as large as several megabytes and PrintQ will adjust it as necessary. With LaserTORQ, you must specify the size in advance. If you tell it 1 Meg, then LaserTORQ immediately grabs 1 Meg of hard disk space.

It gets worse. If you should fill up the available space, you cannot expand the buffer "on the fly." Once your buffer is full, you have to wait on your printer. LaserTORQ accepts one character for each character it sends to the printer. Dynamic allocation would cure this but LaserTORQ does not do that.

Once you pop up the LaserTORQ menu, you can clear the buffer by pressing Control-C. You cannot clear it one print job at a time. Rather, it is all or nothing. You either let every job print or you clear out the entire buffer. PrintQ will let you clear jobs one at a time. In addition, it clears the buffer as soon as you press Control-C. There is no warning prompt first.

PrintQ buffers its printing to disk. If there is a computer problem, like a power failure or rebooting, you can restart the printing near the spot where it left off. LaserTORQ cannot do that when buffering to memory since you lose the contents of your memory with most problems. It will not do that when buffering to disk. When LaserTORQ starts, it creates a new file using the same name. That erases the only file along with its contents.

Manual   The manual is one of the best computer manuals I have ever read. The manual begins by explaining the terms used in the manual. I point that out because it has the best explanation of interrupts I have ever read. The rest of the manual is just as good, except for one mistake. The manual shows the command to add to your AUTOEXEC.BAT file to start LaserTORQ as: \
LTORQ \ LTORQ

In fact, Microsoft added the ability to start programs not in your PATH by entering the full path to the program in DOS 3.0. This command will not work under 2.x series DOS. That is, however, the only nit I found to pick. Anyone writing software manuals should read this one.

Conclusion   LaserTORQ was the quickest stand-alone print buffer I tested. It also allows you to print full-page graphics on a 512K LaserJet, a significant advantage.

```
Product:      LaserTORQ
Price:        $99.00
Category:     Commercial
Publisher:    LaserTools Corporation
Address:      3025 Buena Vista Way
              Berkeley, California 94708
Phone:        (800) 346-1353
              (415) 843-2234
Notes:        A version of LaserTORQ, called
              TORQ, that is not optimized for
              laser printers is available for
              $79.00.
Memory:       21K
```

PC-Kwik Print Spooler

PC-Kwik Print Spooler is an extremely easy to use and fast print spooler. It is part of the PC-Kwik Power Pak package.

Installation   PC-Kwik Print Spooler comes with an automatic installation program. The manual also has instructions for users who want to install the program manually.

Operation   PC-Kwik Print Spooler is a program you load from the command line or in your AUTOEXEC.BAT file. You use command line switches to configure the program.

The print buffer uses the same memory as the PC-Kwik Power Pak cache program. It borrows memory from the cache when it needs it and returns extra memory to the cache as it finishes with it. The print spooler is a program you load either from the command line or in your AUTOEXEC.BAT file. You must load it after the cache program.

Limitations   Super PC-Kwik requires far more memory when loaded into extended memory than expanded memory. A 512K buffer in extended memory required 43K while it required only 16K in expanded memory.

Manual   The manual is excellent.

Conclusion   If you are already loading the Super PC-Kwik Disk Accelerator, then the PC-Kwik Print Spooler is a good choice. Otherwise, one of the print buffers that buffer to disk would be a better choice.

```
Product:      PC-Kwik Print Spooler
Price:        $129.95 For Package
Category:     Commercial
Publisher:    Multisoft Corporation
Address:      15100 SW Koll Parkway
              Suite L
              Beaverton, Oregon 97006
Phone:        (800) 288-5945
              (503) 644-5644
Notes:        The PC-Kwik Print Spooler is just a small part of
              the PC-Kwik Power Pak. It includes a RAM disk
              and a print buffer that both use memory
              allocated to the cache. As a result, they do not
              require their own memory. The screen
              accelerator uses cache memory to store screens
              for later recall. It will speed up screens without
              cache memory but you will not be able to recall
              past screens.
Memory:       17K (Print Spooler adds 17K to the normal
              requirements of the cache program.

              5K If used without pop-up activated using hot-
              keys.
```

PrintQ

PrintQ is a disk-based print buffer that works with almost any software
package.

Installation   PrintQ includes an installation program. This program brands
the software with your name and address. It shows this information each time
you load PrintQ into memory. It also prints this information out as a registration form for you to mail in. You must use the installation program to initially
install PrintQ; however, the program is not copy protected. The installation
program will copy the software to any drive; however, it always uses the
\PRINTQ subdirectory.

Operation   PrintQ's operation is simpler than Duet primarily because PrintQ
offers fewer features. Unlike Duet, PrintQ cannot print worksheet files itself. (It
can, of course, buffer the printing output of Lotus.) Unlike Duet, PrintQ cannot
print sideways.

Because all PrintQ does is buffer printing, its operation is fairly simple. It
has an informational screen, you do not change anything at this level. Submenus are used for changes. You use the primary submenu to control the
attributes of each print job.

From this menu, you can:

- Change the status of a print job.
- Change the priority of a print job. Normally, it prints each job in a first-
  come, first-served order. You can change this order by changing the relative
  priorities of the jobs. This is useful for grouping all the print jobs using the
  same form or downloadable fonts together.

- Form length.
- Form alignment. You can have PrintQ pause for alignment before printing each page or just before the first page. Pausing before the first page is useful for changing forms.
- Number of copies. You can specify up to 255 copies. PrintQ does not use the laser printer's built-in ability to print multiple copies at eight pages per minute once the first page is in memory. Rather, it simply sends the printing instructions to the printer over and over.

PrintQ can also save any print job to disk as an ASCII file.

PrintQ is also able to buffer serial output going to a plotter if your graphic program can either send plotter output to a parallel port or print to a file. To do this, you must first run the MODE command to set the baud rate to the same rate as the plotter. You set the graphic program to plot to parallel port. If it cannot do that, you can have it plot to a DOS file named "PRN". (PRN is a DOS reserve word that stands for the printer port. Anything that DOS sends to PRN automatically goes to the printer. You can print ASCII files by copying them to PRN. You can also use LPT1, LPT2 or LPT3 in place of PRN.) Finally, you configure PrintQ to receive input from LPT1 and output to COM1. I tested PrintQ in this configuration with several popular graphics programs and it worked wonderfully. I performed the test on a 12 MHz AT clone driving an HP 7550A eight pen plotter. PrintQ gave me back the computer in about 10% of the time it took if I waited on the plotter to finish.

Limitations PrintQ has several annoying but minor problems printing with a laser printer using downloadable fonts. PrintQ stores the fonts and actual printout as separate jobs. If you change the priority of one, you must remember to change the priority of the other. Sometimes PrintQ ejects several blank sheets between jobs when soft fonts are being loaded.

PrintQ has a more serious problem when its "buffer" is full. Duet stores each print job as a separate file. This prevents any one file from becoming extremely large. With PrintQ, the single file used to store all the print jobs can grow to several thousand kilobytes. Sometimes this file exceeds the internal limits set by PrintQ. When this happens, PrintQ does not automatically expand the limit. Rather, it pops up and asks you to do so.

If the file ever becomes so large that it exceeds PrintQ's maximum size, you have a serious problem. PrintQ will continue to expand the file size but only a few bytes at a time and only in response to a full buffer error message. Every time you get this error message, your only choice is to retry or expand. Retry simply checks to see if the buffer is still full. Expand adds a few bytes. You will continually get this error message as the current application continues to try and print. You must continually tell it to expand every few minutes. To be fair, this is an unlikely problem unless you print a lot of graphics or use a lot of downloadable fonts since the maximum file size is several megabytes.

PrintQ has an even more serious problem if the hard disk becomes full. It pops up with an error message requesting more space. There is no way to exit

PrintQ and stop the printing. You can enable printing from the PrintQ menu and wait to recover space.

Manual   The manual is very good. It explains using a PrintQ in a manner where even an inexperienced user will understand.

Conclusion   PrintQ is a very good disk-based print buffer. Its problems are either minor or problems that will rarely occur.

<table>
<tr><td>Product:</td><td>PrintQ</td></tr>
<tr><td>Price:</td><td>$89.00</td></tr>
<tr><td>Category:</td><td>Commercial</td></tr>
<tr><td>Publisher:</td><td>Software Directions</td></tr>
<tr><td>Address:</td><td>1572 Sussex Turnpike
Randolph, New Jersey 07869</td></tr>
<tr><td>Phone:</td><td>(201) 584-8466</td></tr>
<tr><td>Memory:</td><td>62K</td></tr>
</table>

AutoPLOT

AutoPLOT I and *AutoPLOT II* are commercial print buffers designed to work especially with plotters and printers being driven by AutoCAD version 2.5 or later. They will work in either serial or parallel mode.

Installation   There is an installation program that installs AutoPLOT on your hard disk. The installation program will prompt you for permission to add its start-up commands to your AUTOEXEC.BAT file. After installing AutoPLOT, you must run a configuration program to tell it what type of printer or plotter you are using. If you tell it to buffer a serial port, it will prompt you for the communications parameters.

Operation   Anyone who thinks printers are slow should have to wait on several complex drawings being plotted by a serial plotter. Even a fast plotter gives new meaning to the definition of slow.

AutoPLOT I sits in memory and takes the plotter information from AutoCAD as fast as AutoCAD will send it. It stores that information on disk and sends it to the plotter as slowly as the plotter needs it. Since it stores the information on disk rather than memory, AutoPLOT I can buffer as many drawings as your hard disk has room for.

With AutoPLOT II, you use AutoCAD to create plot files. AutoCAD prints these very fast because it does not have to wait on a plotter. In fact, it can create these files on a computer without a plotter. AutoPLOT II reads these print files and plots them in the background. Since these plot files are standard DOS files, you can create AutoCAD plot files on one computer (or several computers) and use another computer to print them. You only need AutoPLOT II on the computer that is driving the plotter.

I performed some testing on AutoPLOT II and found it freed up the computer in an average of eight percent of the time it took AutoCAD to finish plotting. It was, of course, somewhat cumbersome to stop using AutoCAD to queue up the print files. AutoPLOT I would avoid this for you by queuing the plots automatically. If you need to create drawings on one file and plot them on another, then AutoPLOT II is the better choice. If you do everything on one machine, AutoPLOT I is probably a better choice.

Limitations   I tried to configure AutoPLOT II to work with several programs that used the plotter including Lotus Freelance and Computer Support Picture Perfect. I was not able to get it to work properly.

Manual   The manual does a very good job of explaining how to use Auto-PLOT with AutoCAD. It does not discuss using AutoPLOT with any other programs.

Conclusion   AutoPLOT significantly speeds up serial plotting and parallel printing with AutoCAD.

Product:	AutoPLOT II
Price:	$179.95
Category:	Commercial
Publisher:	The Software Machine
Address:	2450 East 7000 South
	2nd Floor
	Salt Lake City, Utah 84121
Phone:	(801) 944-9212
	(800) 366-8949 Orders Only
Memory:	33K

RONNY'S PICKS

It is simply not possible to pick one best print buffer. Each of the three general print buffers had an important function it performed better than the others.

LaserTORQ is very fast and highly optimized to work with laser printers. That, combined with its ability to print full page graphics on LaserJet Plus printers with 512K, make LaserTORQ the best choice for some laser printer users. However, its inability to control the queue like PrintQ and its inability to dynamically allocate queue size means LaserTORQ is far less flexible than PrintQ. Duet is slower and slightly less flexible than PrintQ. However, its ability to print Lotus files without loading Lotus and with more options than Lotus make it very useful for some users as well.

## Part Five

Expanding DOS

21
Replacing or Enhancing DOS Commands and Functions

There are a number of packages available that essentially improve on the commands built into DOS. Some, like the *California 10 Pak,* are a set of commands that replace a number of DOS commands. Others, like *Quick Change,* replace only a single DOS command. This chapter collects all this software together and presents it in alphabetical order.

California 10 Pak

California 10 Pak provides a number of useful utilities. Most of these utilities perform the same function as a DOS command/program, only they do it better.

Installation   The manual explains how to install California 10 Pak in both the root directory or a subdirectory. You should install California 10 Pak in a subdirectory. The manual tells you to set up the PATH where it contains only the root directory and the directory containing California 10 Pak. This is incorrect. If you want California 10 Pak in the PATH, you should amend your PATH statement to contain the California 10 Pak subdirectory. The manual also gives brief directions on how to install California 10 Pak under OS/2. I did not test the program under OS/2.

Operation   California 10 Pak contains ten main programs. Each can operate as a stand-alone program and that is how you will use them most of the time. The set also contains a menu program that acts as a shell from which you can run any of the programs. Figure 21-1 shows this. The ten individual programs are:

1) BROWSE. You use this program to view ASCII files. Unlike the TYPE command, you can scroll forwards and backwards. Unlike LIST, BROWSE does not accept wildcards. Figure 21-2 shows this.

2) CCOMP. This program is similar to the DOS COMPARE command. It compares two different hex files. Unlike COMPARE, CCOMP highlights the differences for viewing. In addition, CCOMP can handle far more differences than COMPARE. Figure 21-3 show this.

3) CDIFF. This program is similar to CCOMP only it only works on ASCII files. Figure 21-4 shows this.

4) CDIR. This program shows a directory. It allows you to sort the directory in a number of different orders. These sorts only affect screen order, it does not change how DOS stores the information on the disk. You can also chain into CFILE and BROWSE from this display. Figure 21-5 shows this.

5) CDISK. You use this program to view disk information, including individual sectors and boot records. Figure 21-6 CDISK shows the file allocation table.

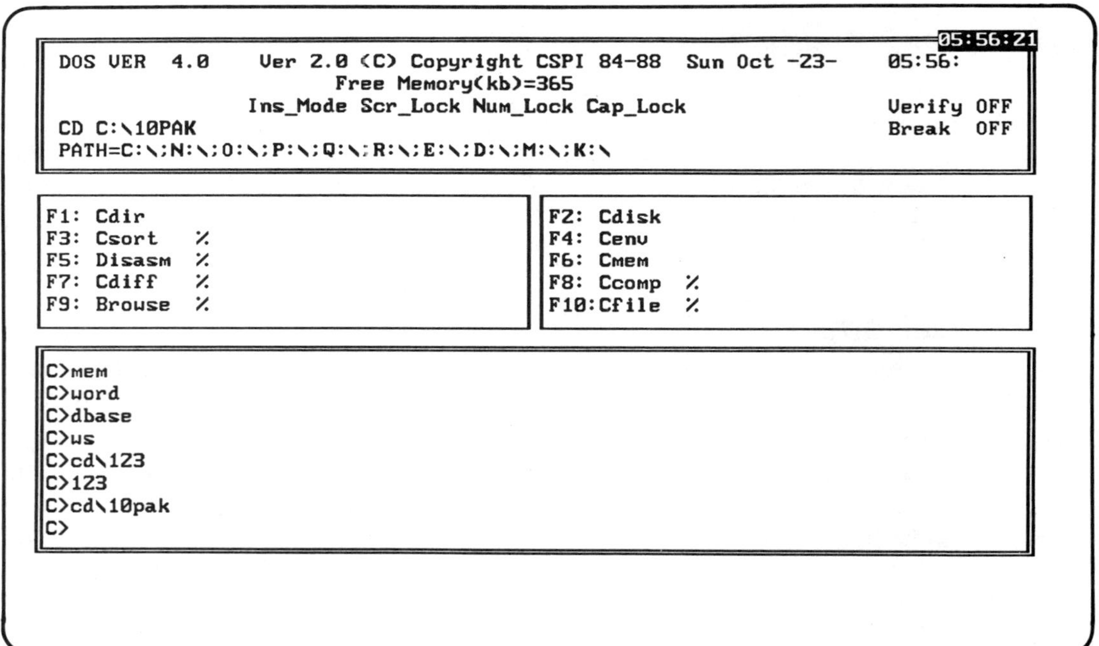

Fig. 21-1. The California 10 Pak Shell program lets you run any of the 10 programs from a main menu. This shell also displays your last few DOS commands.

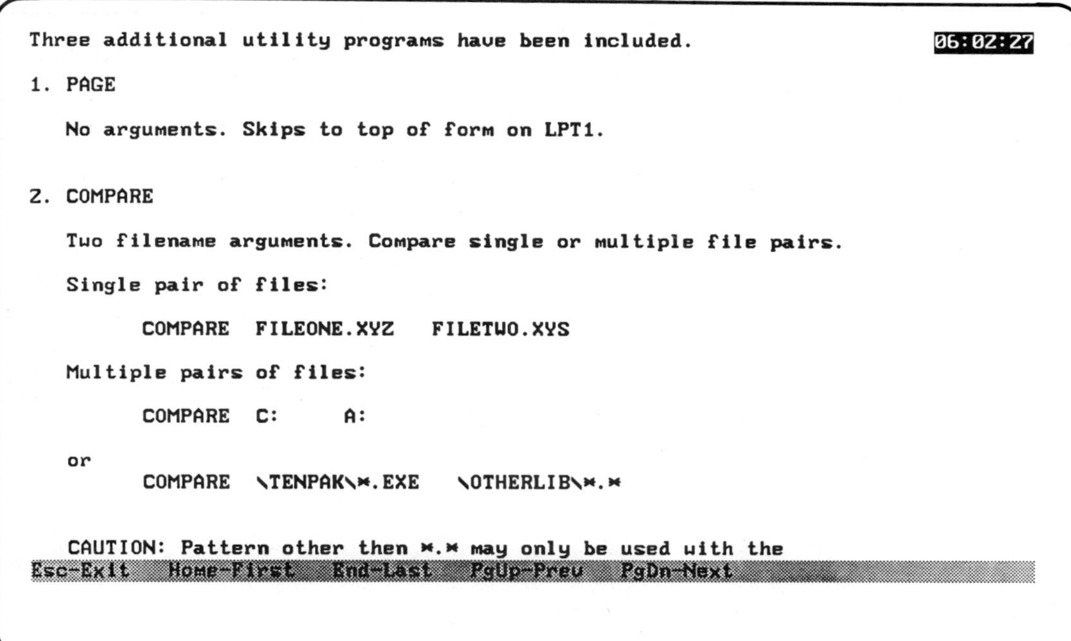

Fig. 21-2. Using the Browse program to look at the contents of an ASCII file.

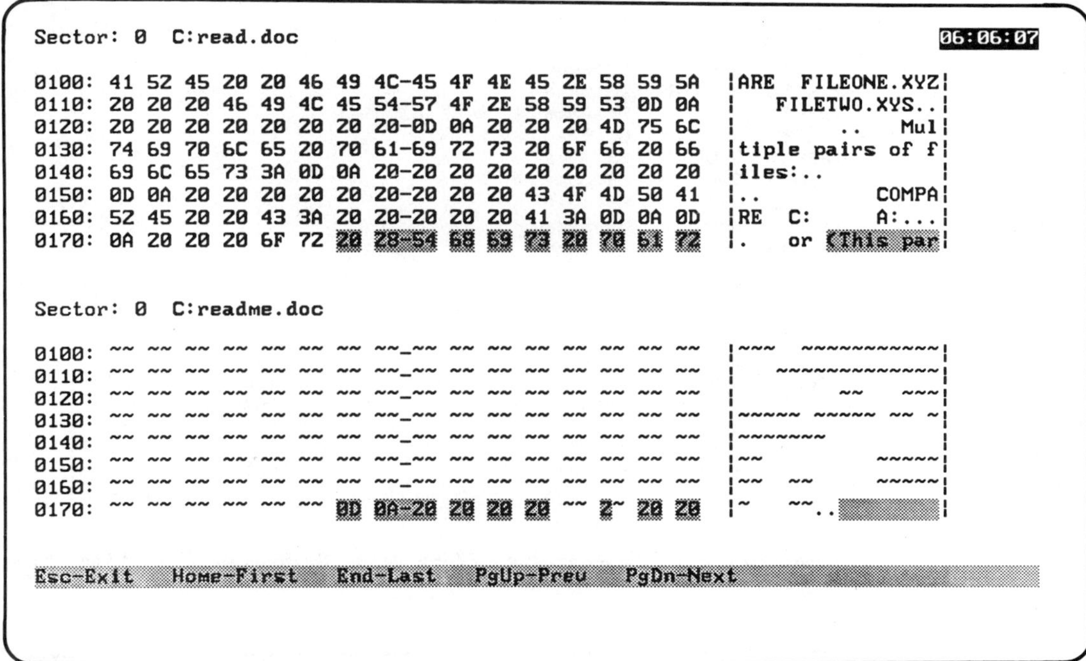

Fig. 21-3. Rather than just reporting differences, CCOMP actually highlights them on the screen.

```
CDIFF 'C:read.doc' vs 'C:readme.doc'                              06:08:24

1st File Line=20 vs 2nd File Line=20
   or (This part is different)
   or



Esc-Exit   Home-First   End-Last   PgUp-Prev   PgDn-Next
```

Fig. 21-4. Using CDIFF to compare two ASCII files for differences.

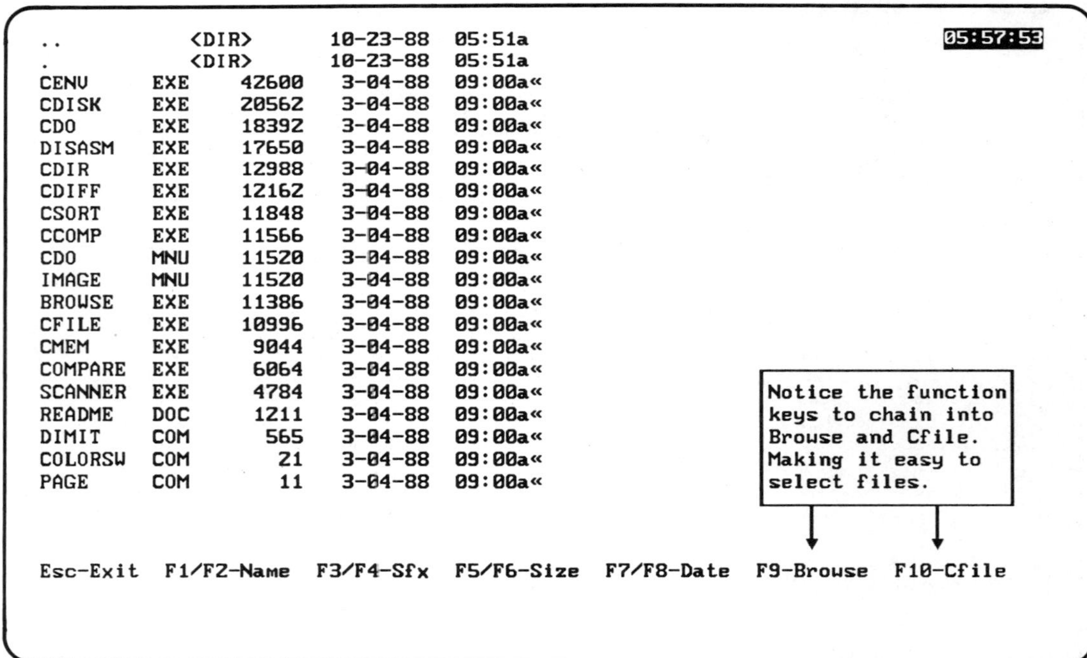
```
..              <DIR>        10-23-88   05:51a                              05:57:53
.               <DIR>        10-23-88   05:51a
CENV     EXE     42600       3-04-88    09:00a«
CDISK    EXE     20562       3-04-88    09:00a«
CDO      EXE     18392       3-04-88    09:00a«
DISASM   EXE     17650       3-04-88    09:00a«
CDIR     EXE     12988       3-04-88    09:00a«
CDIFF    EXE     12162       3-04-88    09:00a«
CSORT    EXE     11848       3-04-88    09:00a«
CCOMP    EXE     11566       3-04-88    09:00a«
CDO      MNU     11520       3-04-88    09:00a«
IMAGE    MNU     11520       3-04-88    09:00a«
BROWSE   EXE     11386       3-04-88    09:00a«
CFILE    EXE     10996       3-04-88    09:00a«
CMEM     EXE      9044       3-04-88    09:00a«
COMPARE  EXE      6064       3-04-88    09:00a«
SCANNER  EXE      4784       3-04-88    09:00a«          ┌──────────────────┐
README   DOC      1211       3-04-88    09:00a«          │ Notice the function│
DIMIT    COM       565       3-04-88    09:00a«          │ keys to chain into │
COLORSW  COM        21       3-04-88    09:00a«          │ Browse and Cfile.  │
PAGE     COM        11       3-04-88    09:00a«          │ Making it easy to  │
                                                        │ select files.      │
                                                        └──────────────────┘
                                                              ↓         ↓

Esc-Exit   F1/F2-Name   F3/F4-Sfx   F5/F6-Size   F7/F8-Date   F9-Browse   F10-Cfile
```

Fig. 21-5. Using CDIR to perform a directory. CDIR allows you to sort the files in a number of different orders and chain into CDISK and BROWSE.

```
DOS Ver  4.0   Drive=2  Media: Unassigned          06:09:35
Sector 0 Table Missing (Defaults used)

Root Dir Entries = 512
Sectors    Total = 20739
           Hidden = 1

No. of Cylinders = 305
           Heads = 4
      Secs/Track = 17
            Fats = 2
Secs per Cluster = 4
Bytes per Sector = 512

Sectors Reserved = 1
        for FAT(s) = 16
        Directory  = 32
  Total Overhead = 49




Esc-Exit  F1/F2-Hex  Home-First  End-Last  PgUp-Prev  PgDn-Next
```

Fig. 21-6. Using CDISK to view the file allocation table. It can be used to view any sector on the disk.

6) CENV. You use this program to display information about the environment. It can display:

   - Memory layout.
   - Equipment configuration and model.
   - Network information.
   - Performance.
   - CMOS information.
   - Interrupt vector table.
   - Program segment prefix for CENV.

   Figure 21-7 shows one of the CENV screens.

7) CFILE. You use this program to display non-ASCII files.

8) CMEM. This program displays the contents of a selected area of memory.
   Figure 21-8 shows CMEM displaying the contents of the ROM BIOS.

9) CSORT. A sorting program to replace the DOS SORT program. This is a
   memory only sorting program so it runs faster than DOS. It only works
   with files 60K and smaller.

10) DISASM. This program disassembles an area in the RAM or ROM. You
    can also use DISASM to disassemble .COM and .EXE files.

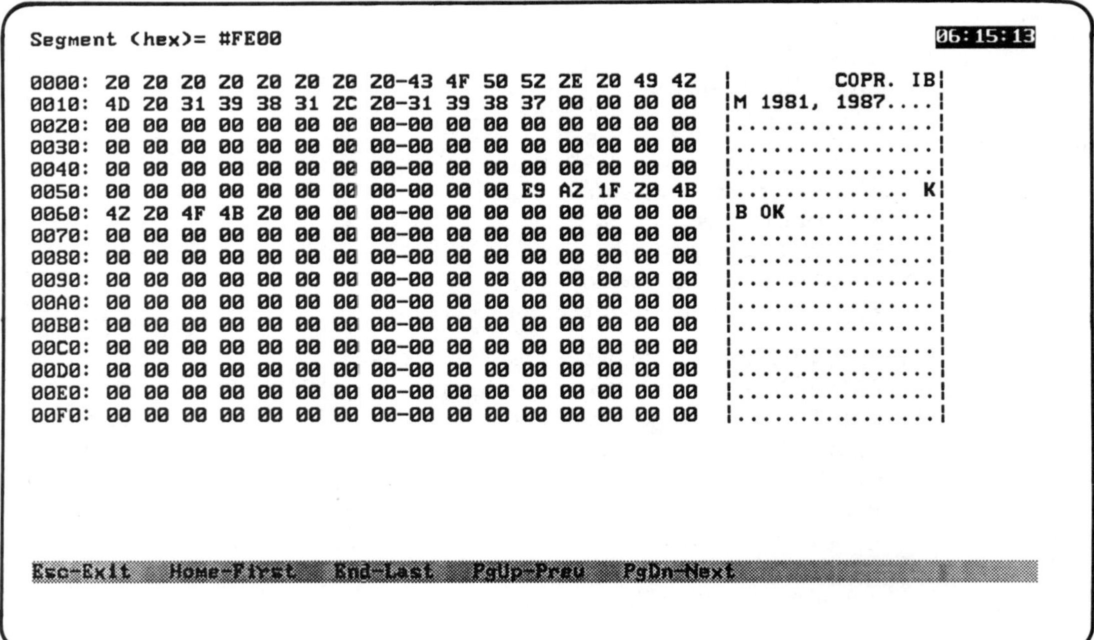

Fig. 21-7. CENV can be used to show a wealth of information about the environment.

Fig. 21-8. Using CMEM to display the contents of the ROM BIOS.

In addition to these 10 programs, California 10 Pak includes several additional programs that are especially useful in batch files. They are:

1) PAGE. This program sends a formfeed to the printer attached to LPT1.
2) COMPARE. This program compares two files and highlights their differences.
3) SCANNER. This program searches for a text string in a file or group of files.
4) DIMMER. This program is a memory resident program that blanks the video screen after eight minutes of inactivity. It will not work under OS/2.

Limitations A few of the programs, like CENV, have minor compatibility problems with DOS 4.0. These are relatively minor and do not greatly reduce their usefulness.

Manual The manual is very good. Not only does it explain how to use each program, it has a number of screen shots so you always know what to expect.

Conclusion California 10 Pak contains a number of very useful utilities, especially BROWSE and CDIR.

<table>
<tr><td>Product:</td><td>California 10 Pak</td></tr>
<tr><td>Price:</td><td>$99.00</td></tr>
<tr><td>Category:</td><td>Commercial</td></tr>
<tr><td>Publisher:</td><td>California Software Products</td></tr>
<tr><td>Address:</td><td>525 North Cabrillo Park Drive
Santa Ana, California 92701</td></tr>
<tr><td>Phone:</td><td>(714) 973-0440</td></tr>
<tr><td>Memory:</td><td>128K</td></tr>
</table>

Command Editor

Command Editor [CED for short] is a shareware DOS extension. It adds several useful internal commands to DOS. The optional diskette set contains a copy of CED.

Installation There is no installation program and the manual does not discuss installing CED. All you must do is copy CED.COM to your boot disk or a directory in the PATH on your hard disk. The first time you issue the CED command, CED loads completely into memory and does not need to access the disk again.

Operation You load CED into memory by typing CED. Generally, you would load CED while booting in your AUTOEXEC.BAT file. CED is primarily a DOS enhancement. However, it will also work with a few programs, like Edlin and Debug, that request buffered keyboard input through DOS function 0AH.

They are:

^End. Delete all the characters from the current cursor position to the end of the line. Note that ^ End means Control-End (hold down the Control key while pressing the End key).

^Left. Move the cursor one word to the left.

^Right. Move the cursor one word to the right.

Backspace. Destructively backspace one character.

Delete. This deletes the character over the cursor.

End. Move the cursor to the end of the last DOS command. This is equivalent to the F3 editing key under DOS.

Escape. Cancel the command.

Insert. Toggle between insert and overstrike mode, just like in a word processor.

Left. Move the cursor one position to the left. This is similar to editing with a word processor in that moving the cursor does not erase characters as it does in DOS.

Right. Move the cursor one position to the right.

CED records the DOS commands you enter into a 2K buffer. You can scroll through this buffer using the up-arrow and down-arrow. You can press return to execute an old command as is or use the editing keys built into CED to modify it. There are three types of commands CED does not add to its buffer. They are:

1) Commands with two characters or less. As the author of CED points out, it is more trouble to scroll back through the buffer to reuse these commands than to enter them again.
2) Commands you tell CED to ignore.
3) Commands you recall from the CED buffer and use as is. If you modify the command, then CED adds it to the buffer.

CED improves the way commands work with parameter recall. Anytime you enter a command, CED remembers the parameters you enter with that command. For example, if you entered the command: WORD CHAPTE06.DOC /G then CED remembers 'CHAPTE06.DOC /G' as the parameter associated with the command WORD. Every time you enter the command WORD without a parameter, CED adds the 'CHAPTE06.DOC /G' parameter automatically. If you enter WORD followed by a parameter different from 'CHAPTE06.DOC /G', then that parameter becomes the parameter CED adds to WORD.

CED does not use parameter recall for every command. That would be dangerous with commands like DEL or FORMAT. In addition, it would require a lot of memory. You tell CED which commands to use parameter recall with using the command: CED PCALL COMMAND where pcall is the keyword for parameter recall and command is the command to turn on parameter recall for. You can use parameter recall for multiple commands and you can use it for non-DOS commands like compilers and word processors.

CED lets you shorten many commands by using synonyms. A synonym is a short command that substitutes for a long command. For example, you tell CED that the command 'W' translates to 'WORD CHAPTE06.DOC /G' and every time you enter W<return> at the DOS prompt, CED substitutes WORD CHAPTE06.DOC /G. You assign these using the SYN keyword. For example: CED SYS W WORD CHAPTE06.DOC /G would assign the command discussed in the example above. You can have multiple assignments. In addition, a single assignment can execute multiple commands. CED also has a command to clear an assignment if that is necessary.

You can tell CED to ignore certain commands. The syntax is: CED IGNORE command.

CED will completely ignore these commands and pass them on to DOS. It does not store these commands in its buffer for recall. It is also not checked for aliases. If you had used a synonym to assign the name d as "C:" and had told CED to ignore the FORMAT command, then it would not convert the command: FORMAT D to FORMAT C:. For special cases, you can have CED ignore a single command by starting it with a Control-N. CED strips off the Control-N before passing it to DOS but otherwise ignores the command.

As you can imagine, CED is extremely useful for customizing DOS to work the way you want. However, it would be very difficult to issue all of the CED commands at the start of session even in your AUTOEXEC.BAT file. CED avoids this problem by letting you build a configuration file with your common assignments. CED reads this file when it starts. That configures it the way you want it.

CED includes the ability to add new commands to the CED language. In fact, there are a couple of shareware packages that do just this. However, adding commands to CED requires programming skills beyond those of the average user.

Limitations   CED synonyms allow you to assign multiple commands to a short name. You make this assignment as the DOS CED command followed by parameters. Since you issue the assignment through DOS, the entire command is subject to the DOS 127-character command line limit. This limits the number of commands you can assign to a single name.

Manual   The documentation does a good job of explaining how to use CED.

Conclusion   CED is a very powerful and extremely useful expansion to DOS. The optional diskette set contains a copy of CED.

Product:	Command Editor (CED)
Price:	$38.00
Category:	Shareware
Publisher:	The Cove Software Group
Address:	Post Office Box 1072
	Columbia, Maryland 21044
Phone:	(301) 992-9371
Memory:	14K

Con > Format

Con > Format is a shareware memory resident diskette formatting program. While it takes about the same time as DOS to format a disk, you can use the computer for something else while Con > Format is formatting diskettes.

Installation   Con > Format has an installation program to install the program automatically. It will install Con > Format from any drive and subdirectory to any drive and subdirectory. Optionally, the installation program will add a command to your AUTOEXEC.BAT file to automatically load Con > Format. The installation program also allows you to attach any hot-key and color configuration to Con > Format.

Operation   Con > Format is incredibly easy to use. Press the hot-key you assigned during the installation program and it pops up. You select the disk drive and format size then tell it to go. You can continue to use the computer while it formats a disk. When it finishes, it will either beep at you or pop up a window asking if you want to format another disk. This is user selectable. Con > Format required one minute and thirty three seconds to format a 3.5 inch disk at either 720K or 1,440K. DOS required one minute twenty four seconds and one minute thirty three seconds respectively.

Limitations   If you accidentally try to access the drive being formatted, Con > Format will lock the computer temporarily until it finishes formatting that diskette. It will not work with some less compatible computers including the Tandy 2000 and PCjr. Con > Format will only pop up in text mode, you cannot use it in graphic mode.

Manual   Like most shareware programs, Con > Format has its manual as an ASCII file on the disk. The manual does a good job of explaining how to use most of the features of Con > Format. I did find its explanation of using Con > Format to place a serial number on the disk to be confusing. This is the only aspect of the program a beginner is likely to have a problem with.

Conclusion   I do not format enough disks to include Con > Format in my AUTOEXEC.BAT file. However, there are occasions where I do format a lot of disks. From now on, I plan to load Con > Format to do this formatting so I can accomplish something during the formatting.

Product:	Con > Format
Price:	$15 Non Commercial
	$50 Commercial
	$4 Upgrade
Category:	Shareware
Publisher:	Sydex
Address:	153 North Murphy Avenue
	Sunnyvale, California 94086
Phone:	(408) 739-4866
Memory:	11K

CopyQM

CopyQM is a shareware disk duplication program. It is much faster than DISKCOPY when you are working with unformatted diskettes. It can make multiple copies while reading the source diskette only once.

Installation   CopyQM has an installation program to automatically install the program. It will install CopyQM from any drive and subdirectory to any drive and subdirectory.

Operation   CopyQM reads a source disk once. If it is too large to completely fit into conventional memory, CopyQM will use expanded memory, extended memory or the hard disk. CopyQM will then write as many target diskettes as you like. If you regularly copy a specific diskette, CopyQM can store an image of the diskette on your hard disk for easy retrieval.

CopyQM runs from the command line. There are command-line switches to place the portion of the source disk that will not fit into conventional memory in another location. You can use expanded memory, extended memory or the hard disk. You can specify a serial number for the disk, control verification and control formatting. If you specify quick mode, it does not format the portion of the target diskettes that do not contain data. If the source disk has a lot of free space, this will save considerable time. However, the user will not be able to store data on the disk and will not be able to copy the disk with DISKCOPY.

If you cannot remember the command-line switches, CopyQM has a prompt mode. In this mode, it will ask you a couple of questions. These questions are:

- The source and target drives.
- The verification setting.
- If you want to use the hard disk to store any portion of the file that will not fit into conventional memory.

No other options are available in prompt mode. If you enter help instead of command-line switches, CopyQM will display all its switches using several screens.

Once it is running, CopyQM requires keyboard input. It senses when you change diskettes. You first insert the source, or master, diskette. CopyQM reads that once. You then insert a series of blank diskettes for CopyQM to write to. It completely writes to each diskette before prompting for the next. It shows a bar graph at the bottom of the screen to indicate its progress.

CopyQM reads a disk slightly faster than DISKCOPY. It writes to an unformatted diskette much faster than DISKCOPY in either quick or normal mode. It actually takes CopyQM longer to write to a formatted disk than it takes DISKCOPY. However, the time difference is less than the time DISKCOPY wastes each time it rereads the source diskette.

Limitations   In prompt mode, CopyQM gives you the option of using the hard disk to store any portion of the file that will not fit into conventional memory. However, the prompts do not give you the option of using extended or expanded memory. CopyQM does not warn if the target diskette already contains data. CopyQM requires a master disk without any errors or bad spots. CopyQM will not work with a Tandy 2000 or PCjr computer.

Manual   Like most shareware programs, CopyQM has its manual as an ASCII file on the disk. The manual does a good job of explaining how to use most of the features of CopyQM. I did find its explanation of using CopyQM to place a serial number on the disk to be confusing. This is the only aspect of the program a beginner is likely to have a problem with.

Conclusion   CopyQM is the intelligent copying program DISKCOPY should be but is not. If you routinely make more than a few DISKCOPYs of the same disk, CopyQM will save you time. The optional diskette set contains a copy of CopyQM.

Product:	CopyQM
Price:	$15 Non Commercial
	$50 Commercial
	$4 Upgrade
Category:	Shareware
Publisher:	Sydex
Address:	153 North Murphy Avenue
	Sunnyvale, California 94086
Phone:	(408) 739-4866
Notes:	Exact memory requirements
	depend on the amount of data on
	the disk to be copied
Memory:	512K

DJ: Disk Jockey

DJ: Disk Jockey is a handy collection of stand-alone utilities that add additional DOS-like commands to your computer.

Installation   DJ: Disk Jockey does not have an installation program. The manual has complete instructions for installing DJ: Disk Jockey for a floppy or hard disk system.

Operation   DJ: Disk Jockey consists of thirteen program files. Each performs a different task. They are:

1) D.EXE. This is a specialized version of DIRSORT.EXE. All of the other DJ: Disk Jockey programs, including DIRSORT.EXE, display a help screen if you enter the program name without the necessary command line switches. However, D.EXE displays a directory when used without switches. It will use all the switches that are available with DIRSORT.EXE

2) DECRYPT.EXE. This is the opposite of ENCRYPT.EXE. It removes the file encryption. It is a command line program also and works just like the encryption program. It adds one additional switch, /V. This lets you see

the first few decrypted lines of each file to make sure you used the correct
key. It gives you the chance to abort the process if the key is wrong.

3) DIRSORT.EXE. This program is just like the DOS DIR command except it
sorts files according to the key you specify on the command. You can sort
files by name, extension, size or date. You can sort in either ascending or
descending order.

4) DISKTEST.EXE. This program tries to read each cluster on the specified
disk to make sure it is readable. It marks bad clusters.

5) ENCRYPT.EXE. This is a command line encryption program. It is a software implementation of the Data Encryption Algorithm [DEA] published
by the National Bureau of Standards. (*Federal Information Processing
Standards*, Publication 46, January 15, 1977.) The encryption
algorithm is public knowledge. However, it bases its exact action on the
key you select. This is a very tough method to crack.

(The National Bureau of Standards claims that if someone knows
nothing about the file then there is no way to crack the code other than
trying every possible key. The key is a 56-bit key. As a result, there are
over 70,000,000,000,000,000 (seventy quadrillion) keys. However, crack-
ing the code is much easier if the person trying to crack it knows any part
of the key or any part of the file.)

If you fail to enter all the appropriate information, it will not prompt
you for the information. Rather, it will abort and display a help screen.
You enter information in the following format: ENCRYPT /switch Password
File Name

There are two switches:

/B.   This causes Encrypt to process files differently. It not only processes
the files in the current subdirectory matching the file specification,
it also processes any matches in any subdirectories below (further
from the root directory) the current directory.

/Q.   This is a "quick" non-DEA approved encryption algorithm.

Password is any six, seven or eight character phrase. You can use almost
any ASCII character including high-ordered bits. You cannot include a
space or an escape character. It treats upper and lowercase letters differently. The encrypted file replaces the original file and uses the same
name. It completely replaces the original file so someone cannot use an
unerasing program to recover the unencrypted version. It had no problem processing files too large for memory and too large to create a second
copy of the file on the disk.

6) FINDDUPE.EXE. This processes all the subdirectories in a disk looking
for duplicate files and reporting matches to the screen. To qualify as a
duplicate, they must have the same name, extension, date, time and size.
There is a switch to perform a character-by-character comparison of
potential matches to verify that they are duplicates. There is also a
switch to compare only file names and extensions. This is useful to find
duplicates where you have modified one version.

7) FINDFILE.EXE. This finds all the files on a drive matching the file specifications you enter. It allows wildcards.

8)   PROTECT.EXE. This program will add and remove read-only and system attributes to files. It can also display hidden files. You use it to change files so users cannot accidentally erase them.

9)   README.COM. This is an electronic manual that explains the new features of DJ: Disk Jockey that are not in the printed manual. It allows you to page forwards and backwards and to go directly to a specific topic. It also has an option to print the manual in the background.

10) REDIRECT.COM. This is a 5K memory resident program that can direct printing from any parallel port to another parallel port or to a file. It does not work with serial ports.

11) REORG.EXE. This is a disk optimizer. Chapter 8 covers this.

12) SEARCH.EXE. This program looks for ASCII text inside files matching a file specification you enter. The searching is quick. As an unusual bonus, it allows you to use or/and/not in specifying the text to search for.

13) SETPRINT.COM. This is a printer setup program. You configure it by defining a printer escape sequence to attach to each letter. In addition to a letter, these sequences can have meaningful names. This is performed with command lines like: SETPRINT [027][015][016] A COMPRESSED

You can store up to twenty six (one per letter) escape sequences this way. To send one to the printer, you enter: SETPRINT A

You can also load Setprint into memory. It requires 5K that way. It will look for escape sequences being sent to the printer and will translate them according to the sequences you have loaded into the program. For example, if a program set an Escape-A to the printer, Setprint would substitute Escape-015-016. Note that the 027 in the definition is the ASCII code for Escape.

Limitations   None of the DJ: Disk Jockey functions are compatible with DOS 4.0. The DIRSORT.EXE program only displays the files in sorted order. It does not change the actual order on the disk.

Manual   The manual for DJ: Disk Jockey is very brief. Inexperienced users will have trouble using DJ: Disk Jockey solely because of the manual. Even experienced users will have trouble with the printer setup program because the manual explains it so poorly.

In addition to the manual, DJ: Disk Jockey includes an extensive README file on the disk. Unlike many other programs, it does not leave you to your own devices to read the file. DJ: Disk Jockey includes a README.COM program that displays the README file on the screen.

Conclusion   The encryption/decryption programs are very good. The disk optimizer is very slow but adequate. The other programs work well. Overall, DJ: Disk Jockey has a unique mix of utilities. Many of them are not utilities users commonly need. Therefore, you must closely match DJ: Disk Jockey's functions against your needs.

```
Product:     DJ: Disk Jockey
Price:       $59.95
Category:    Commercial
Publisher:   Revolution Software, Incorporated
Address:     715 Route 10 East
             Randolph, New Jersey 07869
Phone:       (201) 366-4445
Notes:       Two memory resident programs
             are included. These require 5K
             each
Memory:      256K
```

DOSUtils

DOSUtils is a collection of five useful programs and a central menu.

Installation   There is no installation program. The manual does not explain how to install the programs on a hard disk. In fact, it tells you to run them from the floppy. I copied them to a subdirectory on my hard disk and they worked properly.

Operation   DOSUtils is five utilities that run from a central menu. You can also run each program from the DOS prompt.

The disk look utility lets you look at any sector on the disk and even modify the sectors in either ASCII or hexadecimal. If you are technically inclined, you can use this utility to back up critical information on your hard disk. Later, if someone formats the disk, you can restore that critical information to unformat the disk. Of course, one of the commercial unformatting programs covered elsewhere is an easier way to do this.

The file look utility is similar to the disk look utility except it works directly with files rather than sectors on the hard disk.

You use the file recover utility to unerase files. It lists all the files available for unerasing at the top of the screen and menu options at the bottom. You can search through the files to find specific ASCII text if you are not sure which file you want to unerase. Figure 21-9 shows the main file recovery utility and the information it displays. Figure 21-10 shows the optional screen that is available for each file. I had no problems unerasing files.

The scan utility scans the hard disk testing for:

- Lost clusters.
- Cross-linked files.
- Invalid cluster assignments.
- Incorrect file sizes.
- Mis-matched file allocation table entries.
- Disk surface defects.

Figure 21-11 shows the result of running the disk scan.

The Diagnose-N-Analyze utility performs a number of tests and modifications on your hard disk. This program can:

- Display all disk parameters.

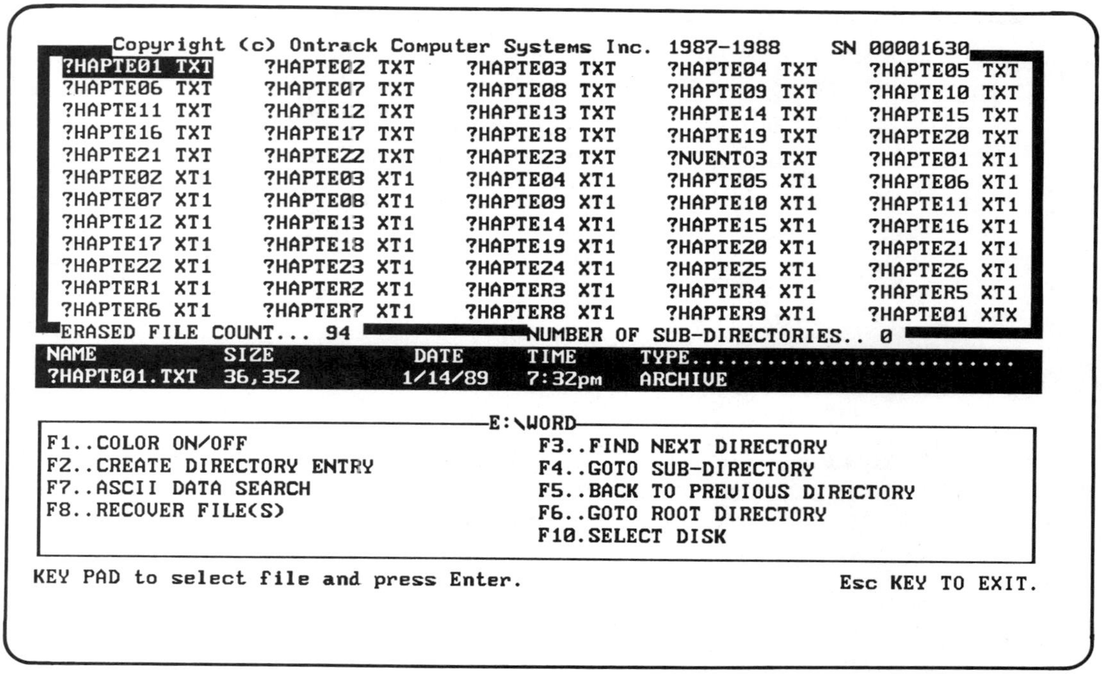

Copyright (c) Ontrack Computer Systems Inc. 1987-1988   SN 00001630

Fig. 21-9. With the file recovery utility of DOSUtils, you can unerase files.

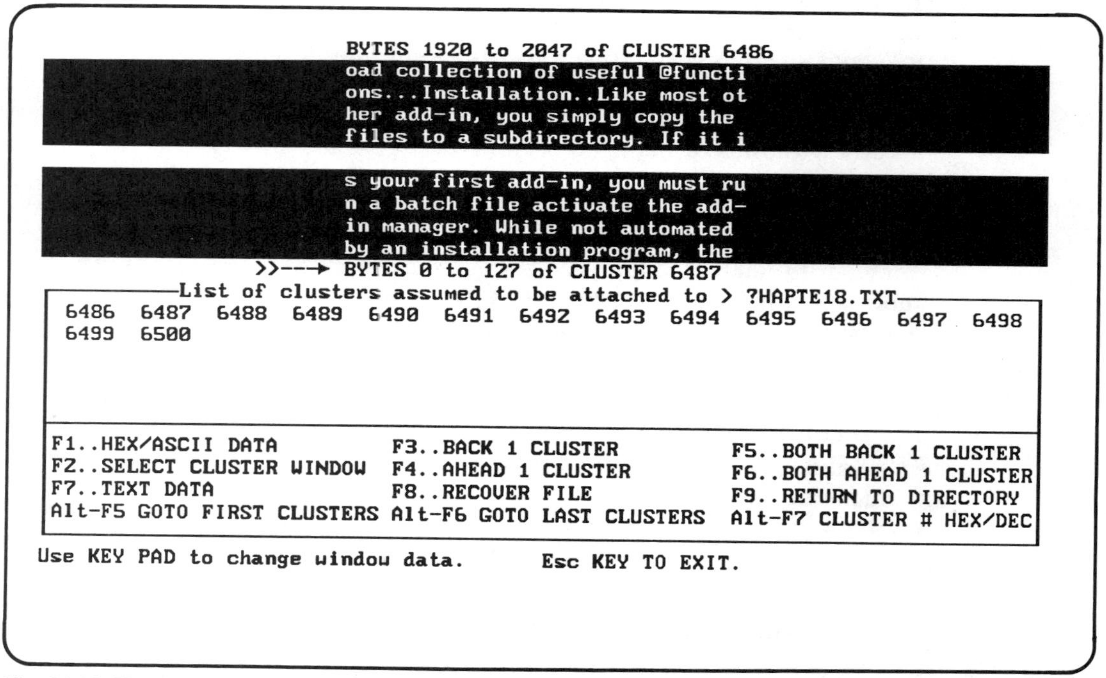

Fig. 21-10. The file recovery utility of DOSUtils can display a good deal of technical information on each file to be unerased.

```
        DISK SURFACE SCAN AND DATA INTEGRITY TEST

  Drive D: BPB statistics:          Drive D: is volume DISK 1
OEM Name...............IBM  4.0     It was created at  4:59am
Total Bytes...........21,229,056    On Monday, February 6, 1989
Bytes Per Sector.......512
Total Sectors..........41,463       21,170,176 bytes total data space
Sectors Per Track......17                    0 bytes total bad space
Tracks Per Cylinder....8             1,015,808 bytes available space
Root Directory Entries.512                   0 bytes in 1 hidden files
Sectors Per Cluster....4                14,336 bytes in 4 directories
Total Clusters.........10,337        20,140,032 bytes in 260 user files

                           MAIN MENU
F1...Check file structure (CHKDSK).  F2...De-allocate a cluster.
F3...READ scan used data areas.      F4...Re-examine previous error data.
F5...READ scan unused data areas.    F6...WRITE-READ scan unused data areas.
F7...READ scan all data areas.       F8...READ used, WRITE-READ unused.
F9...Turn color on/off.              F10..Select drive.
                                     Esc..TERMINATE

   Copyright (c) Ontrack Computer Systems Inc. 1987-1988    SN 00001630
```

Fig. 21-11. The disk scanning utility of DOSUtils checks out a hard disk for a number of problems.

- Display the contents of the system ROM and even make modifications.
- Perform a low-level destructive or nondestructive format over any given range. Using the nondestructive mode, you can dynamically change the disk interleave factor.
- Test the disk controller.
- Perform several seek tests.
- Test the disk subsystem error correction code circuitry.
- Verify the ability to read and write to selected tracks using both sequential and random mode.
- Measure transfer rates.

Limitations   When running from the C-drive, the file look utility would not allow you to edit files on the C-drive. Its first prompt is for the drive containing the file to edit. Entering C at this point returned you to the main menu with no error message. The file recover program refused to run from the C-drive at all. It also refused to operate on the C-drive. It worked fine with the D-drive hard disk. The scan utility refused to operate on the C-drive. Like the file recovery utility, it worked properly on the D-drive.

The Diagnose-N-Analyze test would not run on my C-drive and the Passport drives prevent low-level formatting so it would not run on them. It ran fine on an AT clone running DOS 3.3.

Manual   These are programs for technically advanced users and the manual reflects that. Nether the programs or manual are for beginners.

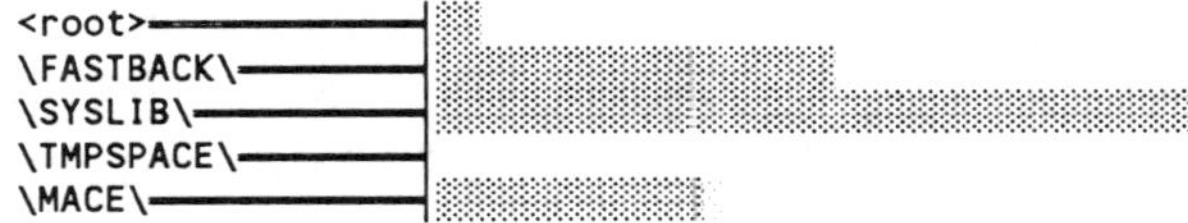

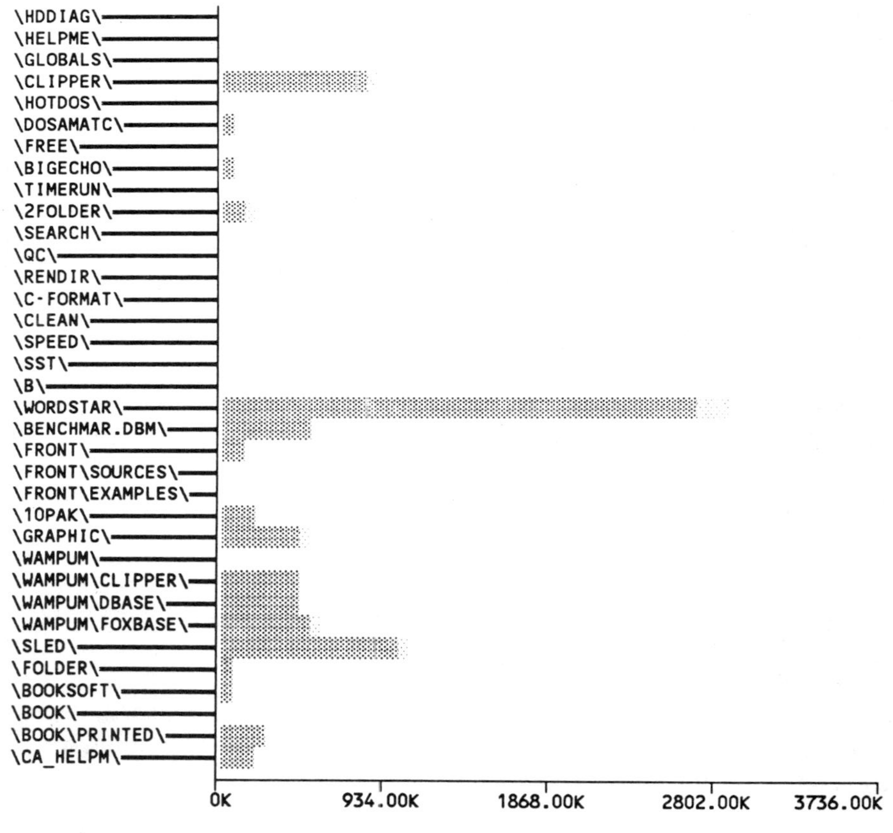

Fig. 21-12. A graphical representation of disk space by Dspace.

Conclusion   These programs are over-kill for the average user. However, the advanced user will find them helpful for locating and correcting specific problems.

```
Product:    Dosutils
Price:      $124.95
Category:   Commercial
Publisher:  Ontrack Computer Systems
Address:    6321 Bury Drive
            Eden Prairie, Minnesota 55346
Phone:      (612) 937-1107
Memory:     256K
```

Dspace

Dspace shows graphically how files and subdirectories use the space on your hard disk.

Installation Dspace consists of two files, DSPACE.DOC and DSPACE.EXE. All you must do to install Dspace is to copy these files to a subdirectory in your PATH. The disk-based documentation adequately explained the process.

Operation To run the program, you simply enter DSPACE at the DOS prompt. The program draws a stacked bar graph showing disk space usage by subdirectory. Part of the bar shows actual space used and the remaining part shows slack. Slack occurs because DOS allocates disk space in whole clusters regardless of the actual space required. Figure 21-12 shows this.

The /E switch gives you space allocation by file extension across subdirectories. This is useful to see how much space different types of files use. Figure 21-13 shows this. The /S switch causes the program to create the graphs using standard ASCII characters rather than high-ordered IBM ASCII characters.

Limitations The program suffers from a minor scaling problem caused by having to fit all the information on an eight-character wide screen. When the disk is very large and has a lot of files in one subdirectory that bar becomes very large. As a result, small subdirectories have bars so small they are not visible on the graph. The figures above show this.

Manual Dspace is so simple to use, you may never need any sort of documentation. However, the disk-based documentation does a good job of explaining how to use the program.

Conclusion Dspace is a very useful tool for visualizing how DOS is storing files on your hard disk. The optional diskette set has a copy of Dspace.

```
Product:    Dspace
Price:      $5.00
Category:   Shareware
Publisher:  Bob LaFleur
Address:    45 Ionia Street
            Springfield, Massachusetts 01109
Phone:      Not Available
Memory:     128K
```

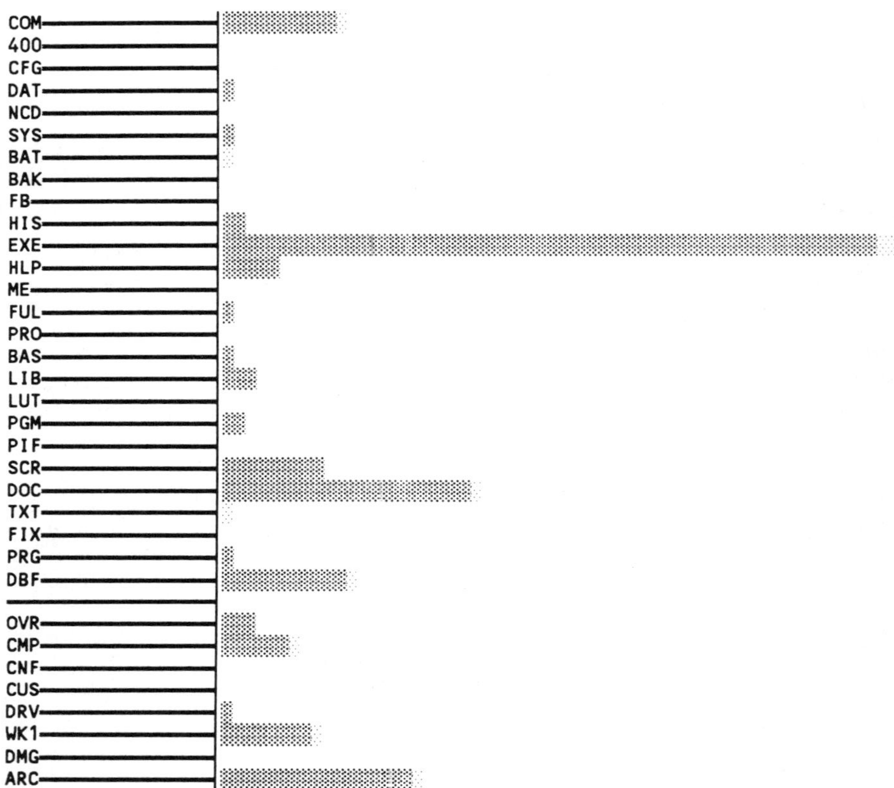

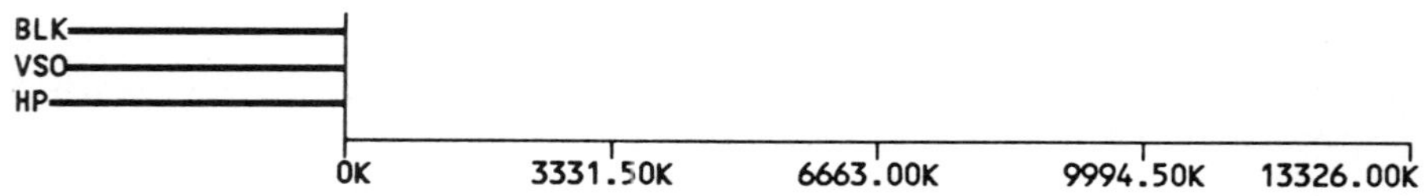

Fig. 21-13. A graphical representation of disk space by Dspace.

FastCopy

FastCopy is a speedier version of DISKCOPY for 360K disks only. You get only slight speed improvements when making only one copy. The real advantage of FastCopy is when you are making multiple copies since it only has to read the source disk once. The optional diskette set has a copy of FastCopy.

Installation   There are no installation instructions and the documentation file does not explain how to install FastCopy. All you must do is copy the program file to a subdirectory in your PATH. You would typically use the subdirectory that contains your DOS programs.

Operation   FastCopy works like DISKCOPY except there are more switches. The command to start FastCopy is: FASTCOPY A B C D E F where the parameters are:

A   The source drive.
B   The target drive. You must enter both even if they are the same.
C   The "force format" switch. An ON value forces FastCopy to format every disk. An OFF value reserves formatting for only unformatted disks.
D   The "set format only" switch. You can format disks rapidly with FastCopy by copying a fresh formatted disk to a number of unformatted disks. You do this by setting this switch to ON.
E   This is the "set verify" switch. To understand this switch, you must understand the DOS VERIFY function. Appendix F explains this. The set verify option in FastCopy works in just the same way.
F   This is the "set fast drives" option. Some computers are able to run even faster by setting this switch ON. Others must run slower and have this switch set OFF. You must experiment to see if you can use the ON option on your computer.

As a test, I compared DISKCOPY and FastCopy on a 360K drive on a 16 MHz IBM Model 70. Using FastCopy to copy a single disk to a formatted disk would take about the same time as DISKCOPY. When DISKCOPYing to an unformatted disk, FastCopy would be slightly faster. The real speed advantage of FastCopy comes in when you have to make multiple copies. Since FastCopy only has to read the source disk once while DISKCOPY reads it for every copy, you save time for every copy after the first.

Limitations   FastCopy takes slightly longer to write to a formatted disk than does DISKCOPY and it only supports 360K disks. The additional command-line switches make FastCopy slightly more difficult to use than DISKCOPY.

Manual   The documentation file is brief but adequately explains how to use FastCopy.

Conclusion   FastCopy is very useful if you make multiple DISKCOPYs of the same disk, for example, a programmer distributing copies of a program disk. FastCopy offers, on average, very little speed increases over DISKCOPY when making single copies.

```
Product:    FastCopy
Price:      $20.00
Category:   Shareware
Publisher:  Systems, Software, Support
Address:    Post Office Box 751022
            Houston, Texas 77275
Phone:      Not Available
Notes:      A copy of FastCopy is included
            on the optional diskette set.

            Source code in 'C' is furnished
            to registered users for a $2.50
            service charge.
Memory:     400K
```

FormatQM

FormatQM is a shareware disk formatting program. It is slightly faster than the DOS FORMAT program.

Installation FormatQM has an installation program to automatically install the program. It will install FormatQM from any drive and subdirectory to any drive and subdirectory.

Operation FormatQM is completely command-line driven. There are switches to control which drive it formats, the size of the formatting and the verification status. FormatQM can alternatively format between multiple drives as long as they are the same size. It senses when you change a disk. It also displays a bar graph at the bottom of the screen to show its progress.

Limitations FormatQM cannot install the system files on a diskette. However, you can use the SYS command to do that after formatting. FormatQM is only slightly faster than DOS.

Manual Like most shareware programs, FormatQM has its manual as an ASCII file on the disk. The manual does a good job of explaining how to use FormatQM.

Conclusion FormatQM is only slightly faster than DOS. Its major advantage will be for someone who has multiple drives that are the same size. The optional diskette set contains a copy of FormatQM.

```
Product:    FormatQM
Price:      $10    Non Commercial
            $40    Commercial
Category:   Shareware
Publisher:  Sydex
Address:    153 North Murphy Avenue
            Sunnyvale, California 94086
Phone:      (408) 739-4866
Notes:      The optional diskette set
            includes a copy of this program.
Memory:     24K
```

Global

Global is a small shareware utilities that lets you enter commands that take effect in all of the subdirectories at once. The optional diskette set has a copy of Global.

Installation   There is no installation program and the documentation does not mention how to install Global. All you must do is to copy GLOBAL.EXE to a subdirectory in your PATH.

Operation   On my computer, I end up creating a lot of files I have no desire to keep. To keep them straight, I start them with the name "JUNK". So there will be files like "JUNK.BAT", "JUNKER.DOC" and so on. When it is time to clean up the files, I would like to be able to issue a command like DEL JUNK*.* and have it take effect across all my subdirectories. Unfortunately, DOS does not have such a command. Some of the DOS shells I covered in Chapter 3 will do this, but loading a DOS shell just to delete all the "junk" files seems like overkill.

Issuing DOS commands across subdirectories is exactly what Global does. The form of the command is:

GLOBAL filter start "command %1"

where the additional information is:

- Filters. You separate these with semicolons. Global passes these to the command as replaceable parameters.
- Start. This is the directory to start in. It processes all child directories off this directory. If you leave this out, Global assumes the root directory.
- Command. The command must be in quotation marks and is any legal DOS command or program. It references the filters using DOS replaceable parameters.

A few examples will make the syntax clearer:

GLOBAL *.DOC \WORDSTAR "COPY %1 A:"

would copy all the .DOC files in subdirectories under the \WORDSTAR subdirectory to the A-drive. Another example is:

GLOBAL JUNK*.* \ "DEL %1"

This deletes all the JUNK*.* files on the hard disk. Finally,

GLOBAL *.BAK;*.OLD \ "DEL %1"

would delete all the backup and old files.

Limitations   The syntax is a little cumbersome. In addition, the program does not have error messages to help you figure out what went wrong if a command does not behave the way you expected.

Manual   The documentation does a good job of explaining how to use Global.

Conclusion   I have found Global to be an extremely useful command. However, like all powerful commands, it has its dangers. For example, inadvertently entering

GLOBAL *.BAT \ "DEL %1"

instead of "*.BAK" will delete all of your batch files. Use caution when using Global. This need for caution is not because Global is an imperfect program. Rather, it is because Global is a powerful program.

<table>
<tr><td>Product:</td><td>Global</td></tr>
<tr><td>Price:</td><td>$15.00</td></tr>
<tr><td>Category:</td><td>Shareware</td></tr>
<tr><td>Publisher:</td><td>Software Alternatives</td></tr>
<tr><td>Address:</td><td>5172 E. 65th Street
Indianapolis, Indiana 46220</td></tr>
<tr><td>Phone:</td><td>Not available</td></tr>
<tr><td>Notes:</td><td>A copy of Global is included on
the optional diskette set.</td></tr>
<tr><td>Memory:</td><td>128K</td></tr>
</table>

List

List is an extremely powerful program viewing ASCII files on your monitor. In my opinion, it is the most useful shareware program currently available. Every computer should have a copy of LIST.COM installed.

Installation   All you have to do to install List is copy LIST.COM to a directory in your PATH. The manual does not explain this.

Operation   You use List to look at, but not modify, ASCII files. In its simplest form, you enter:

LIST FILENAME.EXT

to look at a single file. If you want to look at a number of files, you enter:

LIST *.EXT

or some other file specification.

Figure 21-14 shows the standard List display. The standard cursor keys will move you around the file. If you specified a single file when you started List, then either Escape or Q will exit List. If you used wildcards to specify a number of files, then escape will load the next file in the file specification. Q will exit List without viewing the remaining files.

List can be used to view non-ASCII files as well using its hexadecimal mode. Pressing Alt-H switches List to "hex" mode. Half of the screen shows the ASCII value and half shows the hexadecimal value.

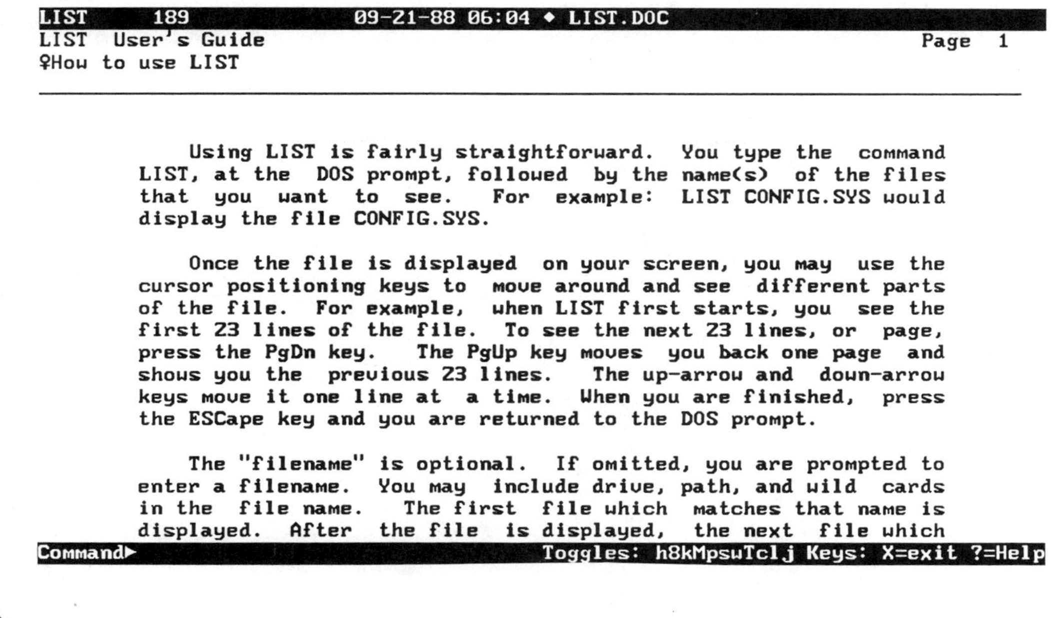

Fig. 21-14. List is an extremely useful program for viewing ASCII files.

List has a number of switches to control how it displays the file on the screen. For example, there are switches to:

- Replace non-text and control characters with blanks.
- Expand tab characters to a specified number of spaces.
- Display the high-order ASCII line and box drawing characters.
- Display WordStar files properly.
- Remove control characters and backspaces.
- Print what you screen to the printer.

List can search a file for specific text. The search can be case sensitive or insensitive. If you are running on a network, List has several alternative methods of dealing with file sharing.

You might think that all these options mean that you will have to keep the manual close by to effectively use List. That is not the case for two reasons. First, most of the time you will simply list the file and scroll through it using the cursor keys. The options and switches are for special cases. Second, when a special case arises, there is a comprehensive help screen to remind you what options and switches are available. Figure 21-15 shows this.

Limitations   List is extremely well written. I found no bugs or significant problems. I did, however, run into one minor problem. I am writing this book using the very fast IBM Model 70 running at 20 MHz. List has an option of continuous scrolling. Using this option, List continually moves the cursor down

```
LIST      484           09-21-88 06:04  ◆ LIST.DOC
              LIST      Version 6.4a         9/21/88
              (c) Copyright  Vernon D. Buerg  1983-88
              139 White Oak Circle, Petaluma CA 94952
              For personal use only. May not be sold.

F1   Display HELP info    a-B  mark Bottom line    T HOME   Top of file
F2   set FIND bg          a-C  Clone LIST.COM      B END    Bottom of file
F3   Find next text       a-D  copy to file        D PgDn   ahead one page
F4   set FIND fg          a-E  toggle EGA 25/43    U PgUp   back one page
F5   set text bg          a-F  get new Filespec    c-PgUp   list previous file
F6   set text fg          a-G  Goto DOS            c-PgDn   list next file
F7   set 1/25 bg          a-H  toggle Hex mode     c-left   go to col 1
F8   set 1/25 fg          a-J  Junk filter         7 or 8   strip/leave hi-bit
F9   Find prev text       a-M  Mark top line       *        star filter
F10  Exit to DOS          a-R  toggle Ruler        +/-/#    skip to line #

K    toggle Key ahead     a-S  toggle Sharing
P    toggle Printing      a-T  toggle Tabs         If you find LIST of value,
W    Wrap long lines      a-U  unmark lines        a gift of $15, or any amount,
/    Scan for exact text  a-W  freeze top window   would be greatly appreciated.
\    Find any case text   a-X  exit, restore scr
X    Exit to DOS, cls     a-Y  goto bookmark
                                                   Press ENTER to resume
Command▶                          Toggles: h8kMpswTclj Keys: X=exit ?=Help
```

Fig. 21-15. List has a comprehensive help screen to remind you of what all program switches and options are available.

for you. You can control its speed using the plus and minus keys. Because my computer was so fast, I was never able to slow List down enough to read the text.

Manual   The manual is very good, but most readers should skip a large part of it. The first part of the manual tells you how to use the program and what all the switches and special keys do. Read that part. The last part of the manual explains such technical features as how to use Debug to modify the code to reassign the keyboard. Skip that part unless you are very technically inclined. As the manual indicates, you do not need to know that to use List.

Conclusion   I originally downloaded LIST.COM about two years ago. Somehow, I only got LIST.COM, not the documentation. In addition, that version did not give the address for shareware payments in the program help screen. As a result, I had no idea where to send a payment or request the documentation. I easily managed to use the program and even came to depend on it without any documentation. When I found the newer version reviewed for this book, I immediately sent in the shareware payment of $15.

You will not find any better program for looking at ASCII files. In fact, I doubt you will find any better program for anything near the $15 registration fee for List. The optional diskette set has a copy of List.

```
Product:      List
Price:        $15
Category:     Shareware
Publisher:    Vernon D. Buerg
Address:      139 White Oak Circle
              Petaluma, California 94952
Phone:        (707) 778-8944
              (707) 778-8841
Notes:        A copy of LIST.COM is included
              on the optional diskette set

              Phone numbers are for a 24-hour
              bulletin board system. They are not
              voice numbers

              Exact memory requirements
              depend on configuration
Memory:       96K
```

MicroHelp Utility

MicroHelp Utility is a collection of utilities in an 11K memory resident package.

Installation   There is no program to install MicroHelp Utility on your hard disk. The manual does a very poor job of explaining how to install MicroHelp Utility.

Operation   You begin by loading MicroHelp Utility into memory. There are a number of command line switches to control what options it loads with. Entering TMU again after MicroHelp Utility is in memory brings up the configuration screen. Figure 21-16 shows this.

The features of MicroHelp Utility are:

- Screen size. For EGA and VGA users, there are two programs called 25.COM and 43.COM. These two 32-byte programs easily convert the screen between these two modes of operation. The MicroHelp Utility does not have to be in memory to use these two programs.
- Scroll lock. When DOS is displaying information that is scrolling off the screen, a long DIR for example, pressing the Scroll Lock-key will stop the scrolling. Pressing it again will restart scrolling.
- Command editing. Pressing the up and down arrows will cycle through prior DOS commands. You configure how many commands it stores. In addition, if you press the left arrow to edit the command on the command line, it does not erase the command as you move to the left.
- Scroll buffering. The MicroHelp Utility stores text that has scrolled off the screen in a text buffer. You can view this text by pressing the Page Up and Page Down-keys.
- Keyboard. You can configure how long it takes for the keyboard to start repeating once you hold down a key. You can also configure how fast the keys repeat.

```
 The MicroHelp Utility      (C) 1987 MicroHelp, Inc.      All Rights Reserved

        cUrsor            Scroll buffer        Color              Monitor

Blinking cursor   Solid   Buffer size  08   Foreground   Snow check       Off
Overstrike size   02 03   Alt monitor  Off  Background   Protection       Off
Insert size       06 13                                  Line 26/43       Off

        Keyboard                            Aliases

Buffer on/off     On      Buffer size  00
Start repeat      03      File name
Next repeat       00
PrtSc intercept   On                       Hot keys
Case filtering    Upper
                          Form feed
        Other             Multi command   '
                          Dupe screen
Auto screen dup   Off     Blank screen
Wake-up alarm     00 03
Redirect/piping   Off     Exit  Save  Configure  Remove
Command buffer    10      Press Enter to return to DOS, ?=Help
Errorlevel        On      or Tab, Shift-Tab, Rt/Lft arrows or caps letter.
```

Fig. 21-16. The MicroHelp Utility has a configuration menu you can use in place of command line switches. These values can be saved so they will become the program default.

- Alias. You can build a list of aliases for the MicroHelp Utility to use. For example, you could set "XX" equal to "\WORDSTAR\PROJECT1\LETTERS\HQ" and the two commands below would be the same.

CD\WORDSTAR\PROJECT1\LETTERS\HQ

CD XX

  It does not limit aliases to subdirectories. You can use them for anything you normally enter at the DOS prompt.
- Formfeed. MicroHelp Utility can send a formfeed to the printer using a single hot-key you define in the configuration menu.
- Print Screen. The MicroHelp Utility can turn off the print screen function to prevent problems if you hit the key accidentally and do not have a printer.
- Faster scrolling in DOS. This was the thing I noticed most. When you are in DOS, the screen seems to fly when displaying information from a DOS function such as DIR.

Limitations   Storing screen information as it scrolls off the screen takes a lot of memory to be useful. If you have expanded memory, the MicroHelp Utility will use it. Otherwise, the memory expense is probably not worth the benefit.

Manual   The manual is not well organized. The program features and how to use them are scattered throughout the manual rather than collected in a single location. The manual was occasionally hard to follow.

Conclusion   Most of the features of the MicroHelp Utility are very useful. However, I found I could not waste the space required for the scroll back buffer to be effective. Otherwise, the memory requirements of the program are minimal.

<table>
<tr><td>Product:</td><td>MicroHelp Utility</td></tr>
<tr><td>Price:</td><td>$59.00</td></tr>
<tr><td>Category:</td><td>Commercial</td></tr>
<tr><td>Publisher:</td><td>MicroHelp, Incorporated</td></tr>
<tr><td>Address:</td><td>4636 Huntridge Drive
Roswell, Georgia 30075</td></tr>
<tr><td>Phone:</td><td>(404) 552-0565</td></tr>
<tr><td>Notes:</td><td>The program requires 10K. The remaining space is user configureable and is used for buffers. If the machine has expanded memory, MicroHelp will store its buffers in the expanded memory.</td></tr>
<tr><td>Memory:</td><td>11K-75K</td></tr>
</table>

Palert

Palert warns you when free disk space on your hard disk is getting dangerously low. User of Palert will avoid problems caused when application programs are not able to save data before terminating. Palert also helps you make sure you have sufficient free space before beginning daily processing.

Installation   All you must do to install Palert is to copy PALERT.EXE to a subdirectory in your PATH. This is not explained in the manual.

Operation   Palert can operate from the DOS prompt to tell you the available space better and faster than a DIR or CHKDSK command. Figure 21-17 shows the results of running Palert.

However, its real power is when you combine it with a batch file. You can configure Palert to set the DOS ERRORLEVEL when there is less than a specified absolute or percentage of free space available. By testing on the ERRORLEVEL, the batch file can branch to an error handling routine when you run short of disk space. This is especially useful when you are running from floppy diskettes or you are running a program like dBASE that will crash if it runs out of disk space.

Manual   The manual is brief but it adequately explains how to use Palert. The only thing missing is a section on how to install the program.

```
C:\P>palert
PALERT    Version 1.6    Copyright 1987 by Norm Patriquin
----------------------------------------------------------
For HELP, enter PALERT /H

Space for drive C: --
    Free  space on drive is     909312   (0.9 Meg)
    Used  space on drive is   20346880   (20.3 Meg)
    Total space on drive is   21256192   (21.3 Meg)

0   ███████████████████████████████████████  100
            Percent of space used on disk -   95


C:\P>
```

Fig. 21-17. Palert warns you when your disk is almost full. It gives you both the space available and a graphical representation.

Conclusion   Palert is a useful utility especially if you are running from floppies or you tend to fill up your hard disk. The optional diskette set contains a copy of Palert.

Product:	Palert
Price:	$15/$30/$45
Category:	Shareware
Publisher:	Norm Patriquin
Address:	Post Office Box 8263
	San Bernardino, California 92412
Phone:	Not Available
Notes:	$15 to register a single copy
	$30 for single registration and manual
	$45 to register all utilities and manual
	Fees include future upgrades at no charge
	Included on optional diskette
Memory:	200K

Pattr

Pattr sets DOS attributes for the files you specify. You can use it to set or change the file attributes on any files.

Installation   All you must do to install Pattr is to copy PATTR.EXE to a subdirectory in your PATH. The manual does not explain this.

Operation   DOS files can have any or all of four attributes:

1)   Archive. This attribute flags files you have modified since the last time the file was backed up.
2)   Read Only. This attribute flags files that DOS cannot write to or modify.
3)   Hidden. This attribute flags files that do not show up when you perform a DIR. Hidden files are interesting because .COM, .BAT, and .EXE files operate normally even if they are hidden.
4)   System. This attribute flags files that have a special purpose for the operating system.

Pattr has a number of switches. Some of these select the files to operate on. For example:

- Filespec. You can select the files using a file name in conjunction with wildcards.
- /SA. This selects files having the archive attribute set.
- /SS. This selects files having the system attribute set.

Files can also be selected by their date. Once you select the file, you use switches to turn on or off any of the four attributes. There are also switches to select all files except those specified and to let you verify each file before processing. Figure 21-18 shows this.

```
C:\P>pattr palert.* /rn
PALERT.DOC     12053     ARCHIVE      -- UPDATED
PALERT.EXE     23072     ARCHIVE      -- UPDATED

Changed 2 of 2 files containing 35125 characters

C:\P>
```

Fig. 21-18. Using Pattr, you can change the file attributes of any file.

Limitations   Personally, I like command line programs like Pattr. However, new users often find them difficult to use. It would be nice to have an interface that showed all the files and their attributes where you could change them interactively.

Manual   The manual is brief but it adequately explains how to use Pattr. The only thing missing is a section on how to install the program.

Conclusion   Pattr is a useful program for managing file attributes. The optional diskette set contains a copy of Pattr.

Product:	Pattr
Price:	$15/$30/$45
Category:	Shareware
Publisher:	Norm Patriquin
Address:	Post Office Box 8263
	San Bernardino, California 92412
Phone:	Not Available
Notes:	$15 to register a single copy
	$30 for single registration and manual
	$45 to register all utilities and manual
	Fees include future upgrades at no charge
	Included on optional diskette
Memory:	200K

Pcopy

Pcopy is a greatly enhanced version of the DOS COPY command. Pcopy supports multiple input/output disks, copy by date, copy only newer files, copy without overlay, merge directories, directory creation, and multiple directory scanning.

Installation   All you must do to install Pcopy is to copy PCOPY.EXE to a subdirectory in your PATH. The manual does not explain this.

Operation   The DOS COPY command has a number of serious limitations. They include:

- It can erase large files. If you issue the command

```
COPY BIGFILE.DOC
```

DOS is intelligent enough not to try to copy the file on top of itself. However, change that command to

```
COPY \CURRENT\BIGFILE.DOC
```

and DOS will try to perform the copy. It will read part of BIGFILE.DOC into memory and then write that chunk on top of BIGFILE.DOC, erasing the remaining portion of the file in the process.

- It does not work properly when subdirectories do not exist. For example, if you issue the command

```
COPY *.DOC \NOTHERE
```

and \NOTHERE does not exist, DOS will copy all the files to a single file called NOTHERE in the root directory.

- DOS will copy an older version of a file over a newer version.
- There is no way to select files other than wildcards. For example, you cannot copy all files created after a given date.

The newer DOS XCOPY command overcomes some of these limitations. XCOPY is discussed later in this chapter.

As good as XCOPY is, Pcopy is even better. Pcopy has the same syntax as COPY. It is:

PCOPY FROM TO /SWITCHES

where:

- FROM is the DOS file specification for the source files.
- TO is the target for the copy command.
- /SWITCHES are the Pcopy command switches.

The switches are what sets Pcopy apart from either COPY or XCOPY. Those switches are:

/A. This selects only those files marked for backup by DOS.

/B. This causes Pcopy to reset the archive bit after copying the file. This is useful if you use Pcopy as your backup program for either a full or incremental backup.

/C. Copy only, do not delete after copying. This is the default condition so you can normally ignore this switch. However, it is useful for overriding switches built into batch files.

/D. Used to select files by date. You can select files before, after, or matching a specified date.

/D-. This deletes all files on the target drive before copying. This is also useful for backups but you should use it with great care.

/DC. You use this to copy all the files in a specified subdirectory to a subdirectory with the same name on another drive.

/E. This causes Pcopy to only copy files that exist on the target location. This switch is useful for refreshing data files on diskettes.

/F:file. This causes processing not to start until Pcopy encounters the specified file name. For example, if a DIR showed five files, FILE.001, FILE.002, FILE.003, FILE.004, and FILE.005 in that order, then the command /F:FILE.004 would process only the last two files.

/IFA:path. Pcopy will copy files only if they do not currently exist in the alternative path specified with this command.

/IFP:path. This is just the opposite of /IFA. Pcopy copies files only if they do exist in the alternative path specified with this command.

/L:file. This causes processing to stop after Pcopy encounters the specified file name. For example, if a DIR showed five files, FILE.001, FILE.002, FILE.003, FILE.004, and FILE.005 in that order, then the command /L:FILE.004 would stop processing after FILE.004.

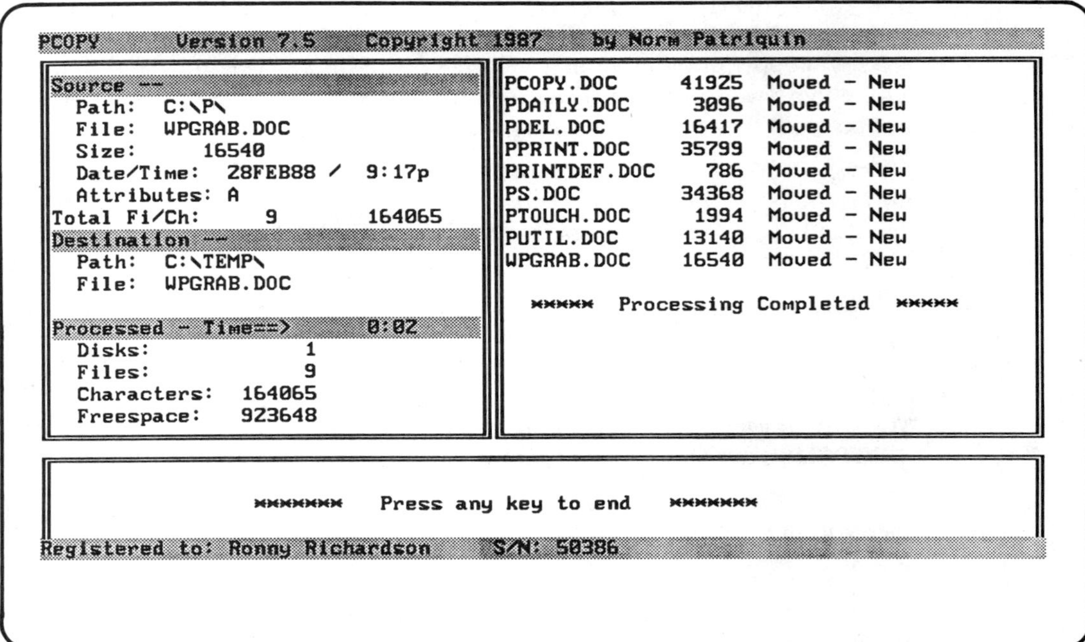

Fig. 21-19. Pcopy has a wealth of options. The options make it far more powerful than the DOS COPY or XCOPY commands.

/M. This causes the screen to pause every time the screen is full until you press a key. Figure 21-19 shows this.

/ME. It moves all the files in the FROM directory that are newer than the same file in the TO directory to the TO directory. It deletes all other files. This is useful for merging two directories.

/MU. You use this switch when you are copying from several floppies. After it processes each disk, it gives you the option of processing another disk or stopping.

/N. It only processes files that do not exist in the TO directory.

/NP. This causes Pcopy not to pause.

/NW. This turns off the Pcopy windows and causes Pcopy to use DOS facilities for all displays.

/O. This reverses the purpose of the file specification. It only processes files not matching the specification.

/P. This causes Pcopy to pause and ask permission before processing each file.

/R. This causes Pcopy to replace any duplicate files in the TO directory regardless of the file dates.

/RE. You use this once to register your copy of Pcopy. This requires a special number you receive when you register.

/RO. Normally, Pcopy skips read only files. /RO causes it to process them as well.

/S. This causes Pcopy to also process all the subdirectories of the directory specified. If you specify the root directory, then all subdirectories on the disk are processed.

/SA. This causes Pcopy to make a backup copy of any files before it overwrites them with a newer version.

/SF. Normally, Pcopy skips system files. /SF causes it to process them as well.

/SZ:size. This lets you select those files larger or smaller to the size specified.

/T. This tested the specified switches without actually processing the files.

/U. This processes only those FROM files that either do not exist in the TO directory or those FROM files that are newer than their TO directory counterparts.

/V. Causes Pcopy to use the DOS VERIFY = ON option while copying.

/WH. This causes Pcopy to tell you why it did not process each skipped file.

/X. This causes Pcopy to delete the file in the FROM directory after it is successfully copied to the TO directory. This switch is especially useful when moving files between subdirectories on a single disk. In this case, Pcopy does not actually copy the data, it simply updates the directory entry. That makes moving very fast, it can move a 2 Meg file as rapidly as a 2K file. It also lets you move files that are too large to copy then delete. For example, you copy move a 2 Meg file between directories when the disk has only 1 Meg of free space.

If there are switches you use every time you use Pcopy, then you can make them the default value by adding the command

```
SET PCOPY = /SWITCHES
```

to your AUTOEXEC.BAT file. This places these switches into the environment where Pcopy will read them.

Limitations   Pcopy is an exceptionally powerful replacement for the COPY command. Its only real limitation is the vast array of possible switches. However, that is also its power. This is one program you will definitely want to take the time to learn.

Manual   The manual is brief but it adequately explains how to use Pcopy. The only thing missing is a section on how to install the program.

Conclusion   Pcopy is extremely powerful, much more powerful than either COPY or XCOPY. Every DOS user should have a copy and should take the time to learn to use the program. Rarely will you find an inexpensive utility this powerful. The optional diskette set has a copy of Pcopy.

```
Product:      Pcopy
Price:        $15/$30/$45
Category:     Shareware
Publisher:    Norm Patriquin
Address:      Post Office Box 8263
              San Bernardino, California 92412
Phone:        Not Available
Notes:        $15 to register a single copy
              $30 for single registration and manual
              $45 to register all utilities and manual
              Fees include future upgrades at no charge
              Included on optional diskette
Memory:       200K
```

Pdaily

Pdaily is a simple utility that sets the DOS ERRORLEVEL to 1 the first time you run it each day and 0 every other time.

Installation   All you must do to install Pdaily is to copy PDAILY.EXE to a subdirectory in your PATH. The manual does not explain this.

Operation   You would normally only use Pdaily in a batch file. Pdaily sets the DOS ERRORLEVEL to 1 the first time you run it each day and 0 every other time. By testing on the DOS ERRORLEVEL after running Pdaily, you make sure that a task is only performed once each day. Figure 21-20 shows an example of how you could use Pdaily to perform an incremental backup first thing each day.

Pdaily performs its magic by creating a 0-length file with the current date and time. Each time you run it, it checks the system date against the date of this file. If they are the same, it sets ERRORLEVEL to 0. If they are different, it updates the date of the file and sets ERRORLEVEL to 1. That way, it works even if you reboot or turn the system off. There are a couple of switches to change the name of this file and reset Pdaily from "already done today" to " not done today." You can do the same thing yourself by erasing this file.

Manual   The manual is brief but it adequately explains how to use Pdaily. The only thing missing is a section on how to install the program.

Conclusion   Pdaily is one of those things that is a major time saver if you have a use for it but worthless otherwise. If you need to run something once a

```
ECHO OFF
PDAILY
IF ERRORLEVEL 1 GOTO BACKUP
GOTO SKIP
REM This complex jumping around is necessary because of how the ERRORLEVEL test works
REM For more information, see my book MS DOS Batch File Programming...Including OS/2
:BACKUP
BACKUP C:\ A: /S/M
:SKIP
REM Rest of AUTOEXEC.BAT
```

Fig. 21-20. Sample AUTOEXEC.BAT using Pdaily.

day, Pdaily works and works well. The optional diskette set contains a copy of
Pdaily.

Product:	Pdaily
Price:	$15/$30/$45
Category:	Shareware
Publisher:	Norm Patriquin
Address:	Post Office Box 8263
	San Bernardino, California 92412
Phone:	Not Available
Notes:	$15 to register a single copy
	$30 for single registration and manual
	$45 to register all utilities and manual
	Fees include future upgrades at no charge
	Included on optional diskette
Memory:	200K

Pdel

Pdel is a great hard disk maintenance tool. It is a greatly enhanced version
of the DOS delete command. In addition to normal delete functions, it can;
delete all occurrences of files across multiple directories, delete based on date,
delete until a specified amount of free space is available, and provide many
other options.

Installation   All you must do to install Pdel is to copy PDEL.EXE to a subdirectory in your PATH. The manual does not explain this.

Operation   The DOS DEL and ERASE commands are extremely limited. All
you can do is either erase one file at a time or erase all the files that match
some wildcard configuration. The Pdel command works similar to the DOS
erasing commands except it has a number of optional switches to increase its
power. They are:

/A.   Delete only those files marked by DOS as archived.

/D.   Used to select files to delete that are older, younger, or the equal to a
specified date.

/DI.   This is a very powerful and dangerous command. It will delete all
the files in a subdirectory as well as all the subdirectories that branch off that
subdirectory and it will remove the subdirectories.

/F:file.   This causes processing not to start until the specified file name is
encountered. For example, if a DIR showed five files, FILE.001, FILE.002,
FILE.003, FILE.004, and FILE.005 in that order, then the command
/F:FILE.004 would process only the last two files.

/FS:#.   This causes Pdel to delete files until there is #K free space available
and then stop. This is useful for erasing only those files necessary to get a certain amount of free space.

/L:file.   This causes processing to stop after the specified file name is
encountered. For example, if a DIR showed five files, FILE.001, FILE.002,

FILE.003, FILE.004, and FILE.005 in that order, then the command /L:FILE.004 would stop processing after FILE.004.

/M. This causes the screen to pause every time the screen is full until you press a key.

/N. This turns off color.

/O. This reverses the purpose of the file specification. Only files not matching the specification will be processed.

/P. This causes Pdel to pause and ask permission prior to processing each file.

/RE. If the file is a hidden, system or read only file, this resets the attributes so Pdel can process it.

/RO. Normally, Pcopy skips read only files. /RO causes it to process them as well.

/S. This causes Pcopy to also process all the subdirectories of the directory specified. If the root directory is specified, then all subdirectories on the disk are processed.

/SF. Normally, Pdel skips system files. /SF causes it to process them as well.

/SZ:size. This lets you select those files larger or smaller to the size specified.

/T. This tested the specified switches without actually processing the files.

/W. This physically erases all the disk area that contains the file rather than simply erasing the directory entry. This prevents unauthorized recovery of the file using an unerasing program.

Limitations Pdel is an exceptionally powerful replacement for the DEL/ERASE commands. Its only real limitation is the vast array of possible switches. However, that is also its power. This is one program you will definitely want to take the time to learn.

Manual The manual is brief but it adequately explains how to use Pdaily. The only thing missing is a section on how to install the program.

Conclusion Pdel is extremely powerful, much more powerful than either DEL or ERASE. Every DOS user should have a copy and should take the time to learn to use the program. Rarely will you find an inexpensive utility this powerful. The optional diskette set contains a copy of Pdel.

Product:	Pdel
Price:	$15/$30/$45
Category:	Shareware
Publisher:	Norm Patriquin
Address:	Post Office Box 8263
	San Bernardino, California 92412
Phone:	Not Available
Notes:	$15 to register a single copy
	$30 for single registration and manual
	$45 to register all utilities and manual
	Fees include future upgrades at no charge
	Included on optional diskette
Memory:	200K

Point 'N Shoot Pop Up Menus

Mouses (or is that mice) are becoming far more popular for MS-DOS computers. There are a couple of reasons. First, a mouse is useful especially when the software is written with the mouse in mind. Anyone who has used Microsoft Word combined with a mouse knows this. The mouse does not replace the keyboard, rather, it supplements it. Second, several programs that require or really need a mouse, like PageMaker and Ventura Publishing, have become very popular. Since users purchase a mouse for these programs, they naturally want to use that mouse with other programs.

Point 'N Shoot Pop Up Menus overcomes the lack of mouse support built into popular software packages. It is a set of menu programs that interface between your mouse and various software packages, including DOS. There is a separate menu program for interfacing with each software package.

Installation   The installation instructions are not clear but the vendor is willing to help you out over the phone if you cannot get things working. Originally, I could not figure out how to use Point 'N Shoot Pop Up Menus with my system. My problem came about because I install my mouse using a

DEVICE = MOUSE.SYS

statement in my CONFIG.SYS file and the documentation only talks about using the product when the mouse attached by running a program that comes with the mouse called MOUSE.COM. Only my mouse did not come with that program. It turns out that the package works the same with the MOUSE.SYS device driver but you could not find that out from the documentation.

There is really no installation necessary other than copying the programs to a subdirectory in your PATH and configuring your mouse properly. Chances are, if you have been using your mouse, you already have it configured properly.

Operation   You begin by selecting the proper command for the program you will be running from the documentation. For example, you use the mouse driver with Lotus, you enter MSLOTUS. You can simplify this by adding the proper command to a batch file. That is all it takes to get Point 'N Shoot Pop Up Menus up and running. They are memory resident programs. The DOS driver required 24K and the Lotus driver required 18K. Point 'N Shoot Pop Up Menus supports a number of programs in addition to DOS and Lotus.

Pressing the left mouse button brings up the main menu. Figure 21-21 shows this. Notice the five menu options beginning with a "?". These run a special utility called YDU included with the package. This program can also be run from the command line without going through the menu. Figure 21-22 shows this.

Many other of these selections lead to submenus. Each of these options runs a batch file you have to write. The manual does not explain this. You cannot change the names shown on the screen.

Several of the submenus contain multiple keystrokes. Computer users with the use of only one hand (or a mouth stick) will find this especially convenient. There is an "Edlin & Batch Utility" submenu. If you must use Edlin,

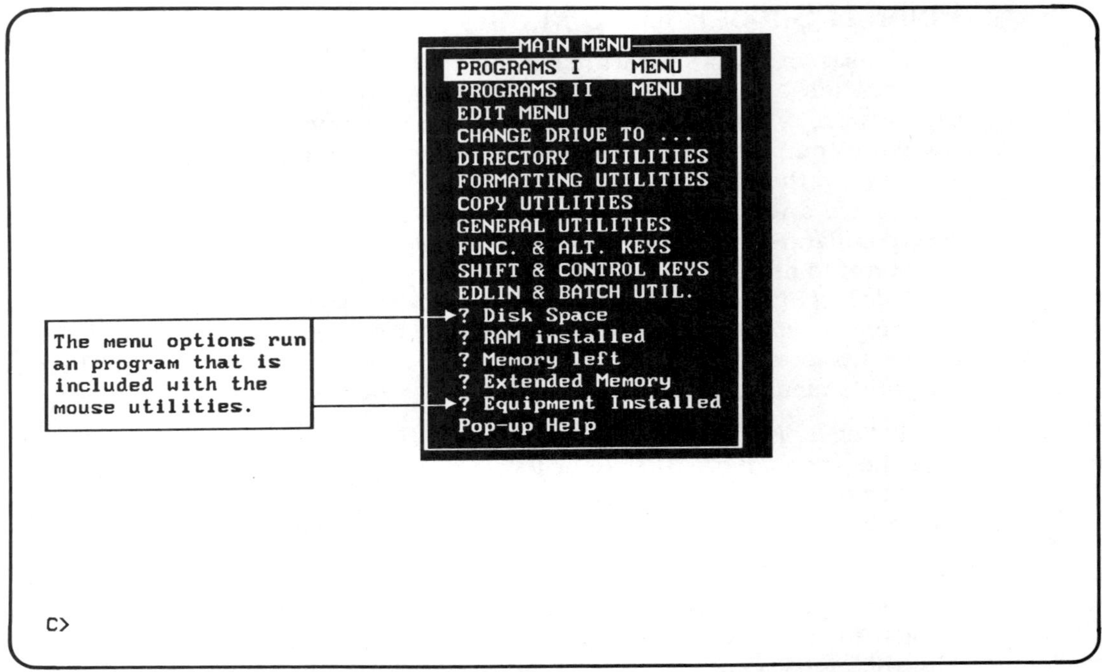

Fig. 21-21. The main menu for Point 'N Shoot Pop Up Menus. Notice that many selections lead to additional sub-menus.

this menu will save you from having to remember the commands. The batch file commands available are incomplete but useful.

Limitations   The real problem is not Point 'N Shoot Pop Up Menus. Rather, it is that DOS was never intended to work with a mouse. As a result, the interface always seems clunky. There are, however, some things Yolles Development could do to improve Point 'N Shoot Pop Up Menus. The big thing is add a utility to let you change the names of the programs that show up in the menu. The next thing would be to improve the manual.

Manual   Point 'N Shoot Pop Up Menus does not come with a manual. You get seven pages of typed instructions on installing the appropriate driver for your mouse and software and a single example in WordPerfect. These mouse drivers support a lot of software and each supported package deserves a page or two of documentation. As a result, I have to rate the documentation inadequate.

Conclusion   Point 'N Shoot Pop Up Menus is a good value. For one low price, you get a mouse interface for a number of popular programs. These are not great interfaces, but they are adequate for those who want to expand their use of the mouse. They are not good enough for you to rush out and buy a mouse in order to use them.

```
C>YDU DSKSPACE

          Yolles Development Disk Space Total Utility
- - - - - - - - - - - - - - - - - - - - - - - - - - - - - - - - - - - - - - - - - - - - - - -
Total clusters     = 354
Available clusters = 75
Sectors per cluster = 2
Bytes per sector   = 512
Free disk space    = 76800

C>YDU MEMSIZE

          Yolles Development Available Memory Utility
- - - - - - - - - - - - - - - - - - - - - - - - - - - - - - - - - - - - - - - - - - - - - - -
Memory Size = 640K bytes

C>YDU MEMLEFT

          Yolles Development RAM Memory Remaining Utility
- - - - - - - - - - - - - - - - - - - - - - - - - - - - - - - - - - - - - - - - - - - - - - -
Far heap memory left =  268608
Core memory left     =  32890
Bytes of RAM left    =  301498

C>YDU EXTMEM

          Yolles Development Available Extended Memory Utility
- - - - - - - - - - - - - - - - - - - - - - - - - - - - - - - - - - - - - - - - - - - - - - -
Available Extended Memory Size = 0K bytes


C>YDU EQUIPR

Number of printers = 1
Game adapter not present
Number of serial ports = 2
DMA present
Number of diskette drives installed = 2
Initial video mode = CGA 80x25 B/W text
Math coprocessor present
```

Fig. 21-22. This is the system information available through the use of the Pop 'N Shoot Pop Up Menus.

Product:	Point 'N Shoot Pop Up Menus
Price:	$39.00
Category:	Commercial
Publisher:	Yolles Development
Address:	124H Blossom Hill Road
	Suite 3200
	San Jose, California 95123
Phone:	(408) 270-0934
Memory:	24K

Pprint

Pprint is a generalized utility to print DOS text type files. Pprint is different from other utilities in that it provides support for many printers and print options. In addition to printing, Pprint can also select lines for printing based on their contents, print after skipping lines, print x pages, restart printing at any page, stop printing at any page, and use LASER fonts when printing. PPRINT also has many other options.

Installation   All you must do to install Pprint is to copy PPRINT.EXE to a sub-directory in your PATH and rename the appropriate printer driver to PPRINT-.DEF. Copying the files is not explained in the manual but selecting the proper printer driver is.

Operation   Pprint prints ASCII files, just like the DOS PRINT command. Unlike DOS PRINT, Pprint supports a number of printers and a number of command switches. While the switches are too numerous to list, the more interesting ones are listed below:

/CO:#.   Set the number of copies to be printed of each file.

/DB.   Set the printer to double strike.

/D:(date).   Select files to print based on date.

/F_.   _ is replaced with a specific letter code. You use this to select a font.

/G.   This starts special formatting for C source code.

/LC.   Compress all sets of spaces on a line to a single space.

/LD.   Configure the printer to use line drawing symbols.

/ND.   Ignore duplicate lines in the file.

/PD:x.   Specify an alternate DOS device for printing. This device can be LPT2 or a file name.

/PL.   Convert all text to lowercase.

/PU.   Convert all text to uppercase.

/P#.   This sets the printer to the point size specified by #.

/S.   Configure a laser printer to print on both sides of the paper (requires a second pass through the printer) in side-by-side format.

/2E.   Print only even numbered pages.

/2D.   Print only odd numbered pages.

To begin printing, you enter Pprint followed by the file name and appropriate switches. Figure 21-23 shows the Pprint display while printing. If you press any key, Pprint asks if you want to stop or pause printing. If you pause printing, you can return to where you left off later using the EXIT command.

Limitations   The DOS PRINT command was one of the first memory resident programs introduced. It begins printing and returns the use of the computer to the operator. Occasionally, it grabs a few fractions of a second to send more characters to the printer. While the computer runs slower, PRINT allows you to use the computer while printing. Pprint does not. While it is printing, you cannot use the computer for anything else.

Manual   The manual is brief but it adequately explains how to use Pprint. The only thing missing is a section on how to install the program.

Conclusion   If you tend to print a lot of ASCII files, then you will find Pprint far more flexible and powerful than the DOS PRINT command. However, you will pay for that by not being able to use your computer during printing. If that

```
--------------------------------------------------------------------------------
 PPRINT  V3.82  S/N: 50386  ---  Registered to: Ronny Richardson
--------------------------------------------------------------------------------
 PPRINT  Version 3.82
   File number 1
   Copy 1 of 1 being printed

 Printing PPRINT.DOC     version:  4JUL88  1:21p
   SIZE = 35799    Remaining:   29691   Page 5 of 32 (estimated)
 ===> Press any key to pause printing <===
```

Fig. 21-23. Although not memory resident like the DOS PRINT command, Pprint has a number of switches that give it far more power.

is important to you, you should read the chapter on print buffers. A copy of Pprint is included on the optional diskette set.

Product:	Pprint
Price:	$15/$30/$45
Category:	Shareware
Publisher:	Norm Patriquin
Address:	Post Office Box 8263
	San Bernardino, California 92412
Phone:	Not Available
Notes:	$15 to register a single copy
	$30 for single registration and manual
	$45 to register all utilities and manual
	Fees include future upgrades at no charge
	Included on optional diskette
Memory:	200K

Psearch

Psearch is a versatile file find/text search utility. It was developed to help users quickly locate and process files based on their name or contents. Psearch not only locates files, but also can issue DOS commands against them when they are found. Psearch is great for locating a specific word processing document that contains a word or string of words.

Installation All you must do to install Psearch is to copy PS.EXE to a subdirectory in your PATH. Copying the files is not explained in the manual.

Operation Psearch has two modes of operation, menu-driven and command line-driven. The menus are useful when you want to quickly find specific text in a file without having to worry about syntax. The command line mode is useful when you want to build batch files to perform the same operation over and over.

Psearch has a number of possible uses, including:

- Finding all the files that contain specified text.
- Finding all the files with a name that matches a specified file specification.
- Searching for text in Lotus files. When Psearch finds a match, it can show a small part of the Lotus worksheet. Figure 21-24 shows this.
- Perform any command on files matching the search criteria. This is especially useful. With Psearch, you can specify a DOS program or command to be executed on each match that is found. For example, you can copy the matches to another disk, delete them or even compress them into an archive file. If you specify the text to match as "*", then each file matching the file specification will be processed.
- Search through archived files.

Limitations The viewing text in a Lotus file only works with Lotus *.WKS files. Since the release of Lotus Release 2, Lotus has been producing *.WK1 files. Psearch will not let you view these. The author has fixed this in a later version.

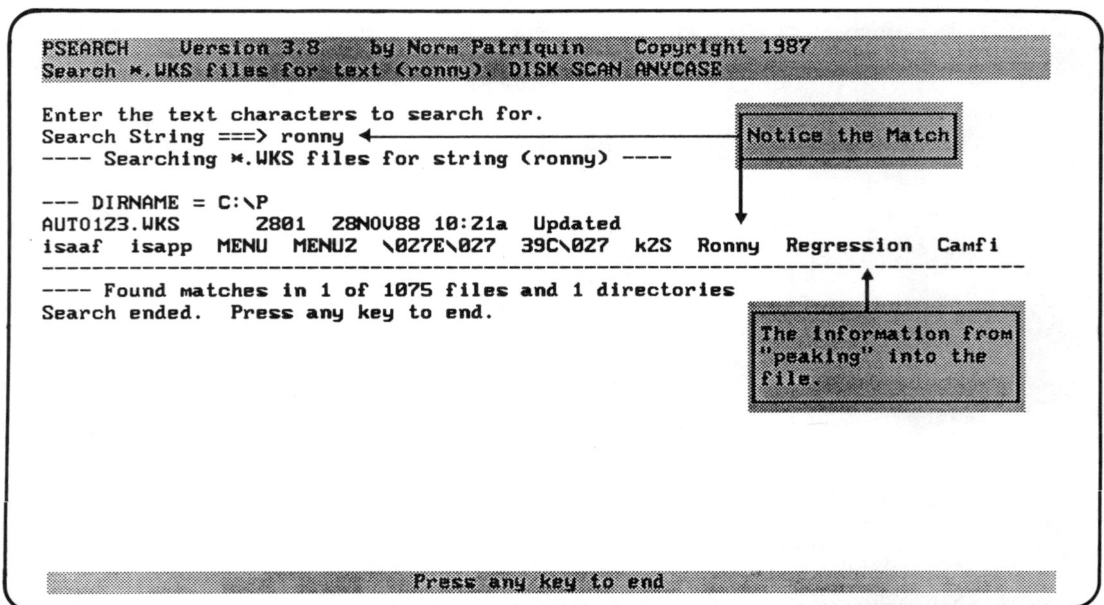

Fig. 21-24. Psearch can search through all the files on your hard disk looking for the text you specify. When it finds a match, it can automatically show you that match.

Manual   The manual is brief but it adequately explains how to use Psearch. The only thing missing is a section on how to install the program. There is one confusion, however. When the manual discusses the syntax for running an external program to produce archived files,

PS *.WKS/O:366/X:ARC A OLDSTUFF.ARC #

it read as though the entire command was Psearch syntax. It took me a good deal of time to realize that "ARC" was not part of the Psearch syntax but rather was an external program that Psearch was running. Since I do not own this specific archiving program, I had to change the command to run my program.

Conclusion   In my daily computer use, when I need to search for text, I use the Norton Text Find command. It has far fewer options than does Psearch but the additional options in Psearch make it harder to use. In addition, Norton can search through the erased area of the disk while Psearch cannot. For those reasons, I prefer Norton to Psearch. However, if you need a program more powerful than the fairly simple one in Norton or you do not want to buy Norton for this feature, then Psearch is a very good choice. You can improve its operations greatly by taking the time to figure out how you will use the program and writing one or more batch files with the syntax for your applications.

Product:	Psearch
Price:	$15/$30/$45
Category:	Shareware
Publisher:	Norm Patriquin
Address:	Post Office Box 8263
	San Bernardino, California 92412
Phone:	Not Available
Notes:	$15 to register a single copy
	$30 for single registration and manual
	$45 to register all utilities and manual
	Fees include future upgrades at no charge
	Included on optional diskette
Memory:	200K

Ptouch

Ptouch is a quick and simple way to change the date and time on some or all of your files.

Installation   All you must do to install Ptouch is to copy PTOUCH.EXE to a subdirectory in your PATH. Copying the files is not explained in the manual.

Operation   Ptouch will change the data and time on any files you select with the command line file specification. Figure 21-25 shows this. There are switches to:

- Select the new date and time to apply to the files. If you do not specify one, the current values are used.
- Select the first and/or last file to process in the subdirectory.

```
C>ptouch *.*
#  1 -- Changed   WPGRAB.1       from   1JAN86  12:31p to   7DEC88   12:31p
#  2 -- Changed   PPREADME.1ST   from   1JAN86  12:31p to   7DEC88   12:31p
#  3 -- Changed   PA123.BAT      from   1JAN86  12:31p to   7DEC88   12:31p
#  4 -- Changed   PS123.BAT      from   1JAN86  12:31p to   7DEC88   12:31p
#  5 -- Changed   PSFF.BAT       from   1JAN86  12:31p to   7DEC88   12:31p
#  6 -- Changed   PSFFS.BAT      from   1JAN86  12:31p to   7DEC88   12:31p
#  7 -- Changed   PSFIND.BAT     from   1JAN86  12:31p to   7DEC88   12:31p
#  8 -- Changed   PSFNDARC.BAT   from   1JAN86  12:31p to   7DEC88   12:31p
#  9 -- Changed   PSSELECT.BAT   from   1JAN86  12:31p to   7DEC88   12:31p
# 10 -- Changed   WPL.BAT        from   1JAN86  12:31p to   7DEC88   12:31p
# 11 -- Changed   WPS.BAT        from   1JAN86  12:31p to   7DEC88   12:31p
# 12 -- Changed   WPGRAB.DES     from   1JAN86  12:31p to   7DEC88   12:31p
# 13 -- Changed   PTOUCH.DOC     from   1JAN86  12:31p to   7DEC88   12:31p
# 14 -- Changed   PUTIL.DOC      from   1JAN86  12:31p to   7DEC88   12:31p
# 15 -- Changed   WPGRAB.DOC     from   1JAN86  12:31p to   7DEC88   12:31p
# 16 -- Changed   PTOUCH.EXE     from   1JAN86  12:31p to   7DEC88   12:31p
# 17 -- Changed   WPGRAB.EXE     from   1JAN86  12:31p to   7DEC88   12:31p
# 18 -- Changed   WPGRAB$$.BAT   from   1JAN86  12:31p to   7DEC88   12:31p

Selected 18 files.

C>
```

Fig. 21-25. Ptouch can easily change the date and time of files you select to any other date and time you specify.

- Select files by date and time for processing..
- Select file by the archive bit for processing.
- Prompt before processing each file.

Manual   The manual is brief but it adequately explains how to use Ptouch. The only thing missing is a section on how to install the program.

Conclusion   This is one of those utilities you do not really need but are occasionally nice to have around. There are ways to "trick" DOS into updating the date and time to the current values using the COPY command, but Ptouch is far easier.

Product:	Ptouch
Price:	No Charge
Category:	Shareware
Publisher:	Norm Patriquin
Address:	Post Office Box 8263
	San Bernardino, California 92412
Phone:	Not Available
Notes:	$45 to register all utilities and manual
	Fees include future upgrades at no charge
	Included on optional diskette
Memory:	200K

Quick Change

Quick Change (I will call it QC for short) is an intelligent subdirectory changer. It replaces the CD command and makes dealing with a complex directory structure easier.

Installation   Installing QC is more complicated than simply copying the three files to a subdirectory in your PATH. The real power of QC requires you to modify a file called QC.PTH. QC.PTH is an ASCII file containing a list of subdirectory "nicknames" and the PATH to each nickname. The QC.PTH for my system is shown in Fig. 21-26 below. In addition, you must issue the command SET QC = C:\QC\QC.PTH. This places a SET variable in the environment pointing to the subdirectory and file containing the list of nicknames for QC. You will probably want to add this command to your AUTOEXEC.BAT file. This installation process is adequately explained in the manual.

Operation   The basic command for using QC is:

QC 'nickname

where nickname is an easy to remember name you assign to a specific subdirectory. For example, on my system the command:

QC 'letters

is the same as the DOS command:

CD \ WORD \ BOOK3 \ LETTERS

So QC offers two major advantages over the DOC CD command. First, you use less keystrokes. Second, you enter names that you assign and make sense to you rather than cryptic DOS names. An additional, although minor, advantage of QC is the path assigned to a nickname can include a drive. So issuing the command:

QC 'takeoff

would be the same as entering the DOS commands:

A:
CD \ WORD \ BOOK3 \ LETTERS \ DISCARD

The easiest way to add and delete nicknames is with an ASCII word processor. However, QC has commands to let you do the same thing from the DOS

<table>
<tr><td rowspan="9">Fig. 21-26. The QC.PTH file for my system.</td><td>

```
root=C:\
dos=C:\SYSLIB
book=C:\WORD\BOOK3
letters=C:\WORD\BOOK3\LETTERS
takeoff=A:\WORD\BOOK3\LETTERS\DISCARD
school=C:\WORD\BA605
qc=c:\QC
backup=C:\FASTBACK
```

</td></tr>
</table>

prompt. Additionally, QC has a few other useful commands. Those additional QC commands are:

QC #**number.**   Change to the subdirectory associated with the supplied line number in QC.PTH.

QC **$nickname.**   Same as QC 'nickname.

QC +**nickname.**   Add the current subdirectory to QC.PTH using the supplied nickname.

QC /**A nickname** = **path.**   Add an entry to QC.PTH matching the supplied nickname and path.

QC /**D nickname.**   Delete the supplied nickname entry from QC.PTH.

QC /**H.**   Get help.

QC /**L.**   List all the entries in QC.PTH.

QC ~**nickname.**   Same as QC 'nickname.

QC . . .   Move back one subdirectory. This is the same as CD..

Limitations   There are two features that QC needs to be the perfect directory changing program. First, it needs a graphical display to select any subdirectory just like you get with the NCD program from the Norton Utilities. Second, it needs a command to list all the available nicknames so you can select one using some sort of moving cursor.

Manual   The electronic manual adequately explains how to use QC.

Conclusion   Quick Change is far superior to the DOS CD command. Once you get set up and get used to using nicknames, you will never go back to entering cryptic DOS change directory commands. A copy of Quick Change is included on the optional diskette set.

<table>
<tr><td>Product:</td><td>Quick Change</td></tr>
<tr><td>Price:</td><td>$5/$10/$20</td></tr>
<tr><td>Category:</td><td>Shareware</td></tr>
<tr><td>Publisher:</td><td>Steven Flores</td></tr>
<tr><td>Address:</td><td>11711 East 27th Street
Tulsa, Oklahoma 74129</td></tr>
<tr><td>Phone:</td><td>Not Available</td></tr>
<tr><td>Notes:</td><td>$5.00 is for a personal license

$10.00 is for a commercial or governmental license

$20.00 is for a program disk and printed documentation

A copy of Quick Change is included on the optional diskette set</td></tr>
<tr><td>Memory:</td><td>11.3K</td></tr>
</table>

SuperDuper

SuperDuper is a commercial rapid copying program for single or double-sided 5.25 inch 40-sector diskettes.

Installation   There is no installation program and installation is only briefly mentioned in the manual. All you must do to install SuperDuper is to copy SD.EXE to a subdirectory in your PATH. There are two additional files, however, these are just advertisements for additional Golden Bow Systems products.

Operation   Using SuperDuper is similar to and just as easy as using COPY. Like COPY, SuperDuper is a command-line driven program. You enter SD, the source drive, the target drives and the switches on the command line. There are switches to:

- Format all diskettes before writing to them. This is useful as an additional safety feature to verify the diskettes are good or to make sure they do not leave your system with existing data on them.
- Turn off DOS verification. If you have VERIFY=ON in your CONFIG.SYS file, then DOS checks the cyclical redundancy check [CRC] number for every block of data it copies. This slows down the copy. If you use good diskettes you can generally turn this off to save time.
- Turn on additional checking. This causes SuperDuper to physically check each byte of data it writes to the disk rather than just checking the CRC. This is useful for copying critical diskettes.
- Prompt for disk changes.
- Alternate copies between two disk drives without prompting.

Like other disk copy programs, SuperDuper is not really faster if you are only making one copy. In fact, depending on your switch setting it can be a few seconds slower. However, unlike DISKCOPY SuperDuper only reads the source diskette once. Therefore, you save that time for every copy you make after the first copy. (When using formatted diskettes, DISKCOPY spends half its time reading the source diskettes.) That also reduces the number of diskette swaps you have to make in half.

Limitations   SuperDuper cannot copy high capacity 1.2 Meg 5.25-inch diskettes or any 3.5-inch diskettes. SuperDuper cannot save an image of the source diskette on the hard disk for later use.

Manual   The manual is brief but adequate. SuperDuper works so similarly to DISKCOPY that you may really never need the manual.

Conclusion   SuperDuper is a useful copying program if you need to make multiple copies of the same source diskette on a 40-track 5.25-inch drive.

Product:	SuperDuper
Price:	$49.95
Category:	Commercial
Publisher:	Golden Bow Systems
Address:	2870 Fifth Avenue
	Suite 201
	San Diego, California 92103
Phone:	(619) 298-9349
Memory:	395K

Tmpspace

Tmpspace reports on how much space is allocated to files you define as being erasable.

Installation   Tmpspace consists of three files, TMPSPACE.DOC, TMP-SPACE.TXT and TMPSPACE.EXE. The first is the documentation, the second is an erasable file definition table and the third is the program. To install Tmpspace, you copy TMPSPACE.EXE to a subdirectory in your PATH and TMP-SPACE.TXT to the root directory. You then edit TMPSPACE.TXT so it contains a list of all the file types you consider erasable, e.g. *.BAK, *.TMP, *.$$$, and so on.

Operation   You enter TMPSPACE at the DOS prompt and the program reads the directory and reports the amount of space containing those file types listed in the TMPSPACE.TXT file both in space terms (e.g. 204K) and as a percentage (e.g. .18%). If you specify a /B switch, Tmpspace will also create a batch file to erase all the erasable files for you.

Limitations   Tmpspace will only work with TMPSPACE.TXT in the root directory. I strongly dislike having program files in my root directory. You should have the option of keeping TMPSPACE.TXT in the program subdirectory.

Manual   Tmpspace is so simple to use, you may never need any sort of documentation. However, the disk-based documentation does a good job of explaining how to use the program.

Conclusion   Tmpspace is an extremely useful utility for tracking and deleting erasable files. It is available on the optional diskette set.

```
Product:     Tmpspace
Price:       $5.00
Category:    Shareware
Publisher:   Bob LaFleur
Address:     45 Ionia Street
             Springfield, Massachusetts 01109
Phone:       Not Available
Memory:      128K
```

Wpgrab

Wpgrab builds a batch file to start any program with a specific data file specified. It can optionally start the program for you.

Installation   All you must do to install Wpgrab is to copy WPGRAB.EXE to a subdirectory in your PATH. Copying the files is not explained in the manual.

Operation   When you enter WPGRAB followed by a file specification, you see a menu of the most recent files matching your file specification. Figure 21-27 shows this. You move the cursor to the file you want and press return. Wpgrab

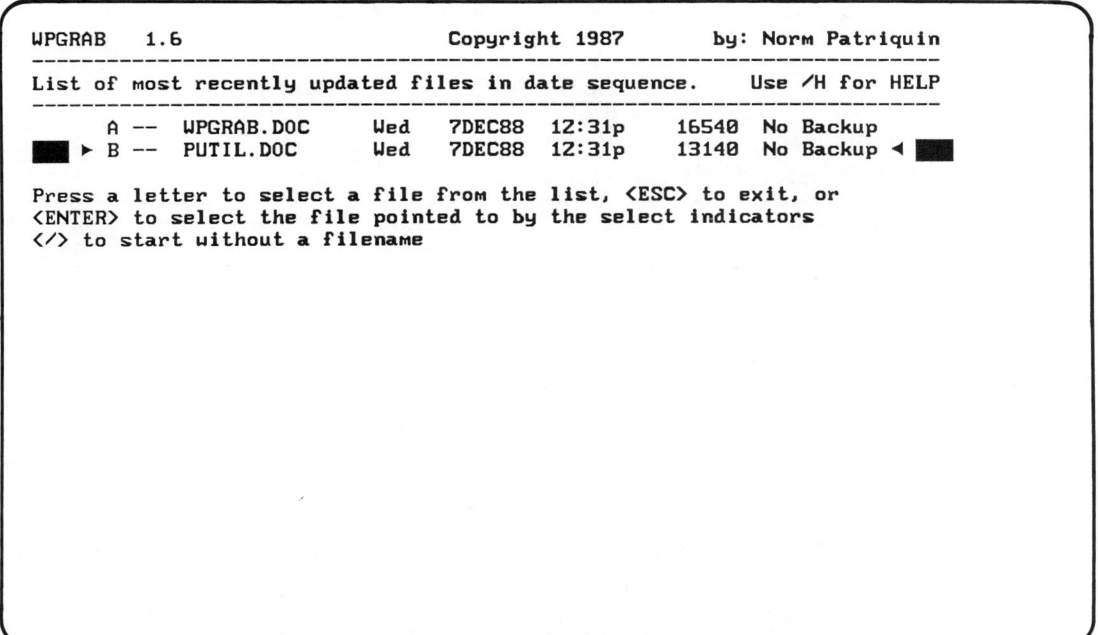

Fig. 21-27. When you start Wsgrab, it presents you with a list of the more recent files matching your file specification. You select the file you want by moving the light bar to the file you want and pressing Return.

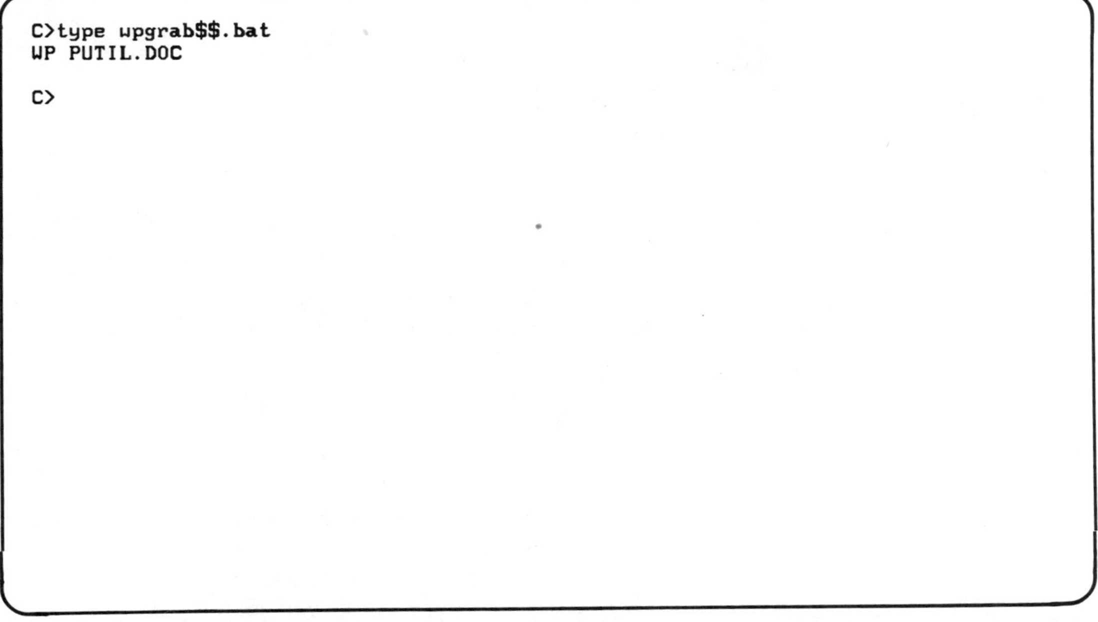

Fig. 21-28. The file you select is automatically incorporated into a batch file to start your application and supply it with the select file name.

automatically constructs the batch file shown in Figure 21-28. There are
switches to:

- Change the name of the program to be run to something other than "WP".
- Automatically select the most recent file.
- Automatically run the program without building a batch file. This method
  allocates 30K to Wpgrab while your other program is running.

Manual   The manual is brief but it adequately explains how to use Wpgrab.
The only thing missing is a section on how to install the program.

Conclusion   If your word processor accepts files on the command line and
cannot automatically select the last file you were working on, Wpgrab is a useful utility. Some word processors can do this automatically. For example, starting Microsoft Word with a /L causes it to automatically load the last file you
were editing and return you to the place the cursor was located when you
exited last.

<pre>
Product: Wpgrab
Price: $15/$30/$45
Category: Shareware
Publisher: Norm Patriquin
Address: Post Office Box 8263
             San Bernardino, California 92412
Phone: Not Available
Notes: $15 to register a single copy
             $30 for single registration and manual
             $45 to register all utilities and manual
             Fees include future upgrades at no charge
             Included on optional diskette
Memory: 200K
</pre>

VGA Dimmer

VGA Dimmer is a screen blanking program that works with most display
adapters up to VGA.

Installation   There is no installation program. The manual explains how to
install VGA Dimmer. It also explains how to modify your AUTOEXEC.BAT file
to include VGA Dimmer.

Operation   VGA Dimmer is very simple to use. You start the program with
the command:

```
dimmer/time
```

where time is the number of minutes of inactivity before the screen is blanked.
Once the screen goes blank, pressing any key brings it back. Entering a /H in
place of a time brings up a help screen. Figure 21-29 shows this. You can manually toggle VGA Dimmer on and off from the keyboard. You can also blank
the screen from the keyboard to protect sensitive information when someone
comes by your computer.

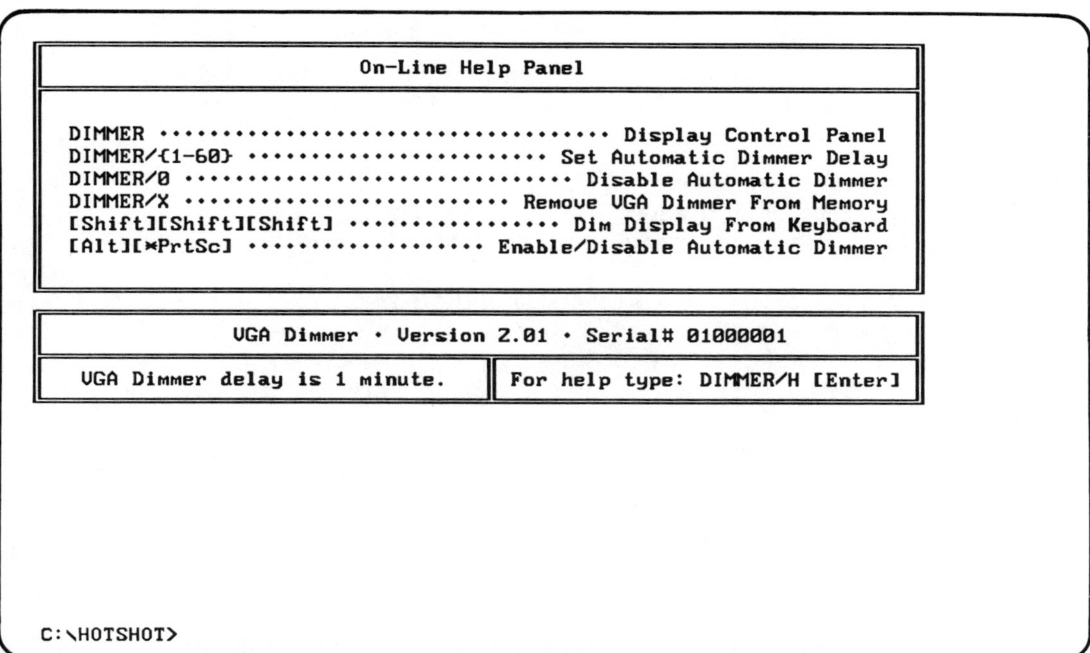

Fig. 21-29. When you start VGA Dimmer with a /H, it brings up a help screen showing the keystrokes VGA Dimmer uses and its current setting.

Limitations   VGA Dimmer conflicts with Microsoft Windows and Hayes Smartcom.

Manual   While VGA Dimmer is a fairly inexpensive program, it has an excellent manual. It is written in large, nice type. It is easy to read and does a good job of explaining how to use VGA Dimmer.

Conclusion   VGA Dimmer supports VGA, MCGA, EGA, CGA, monochrome and Hercules displays. It does an excellent job while using only 3K of memory. VGA Dimmer is an excellent program.

Product:	VGA Dimmer
Price:	$29.95
Category:	Commercial
Publisher:	Revolution Software, Incorporated
Address:	715 Route 10 East
	Randolph, New Jersey 07869
Phone:	(201) 366-4445
Memory:	3K

Vtools

There is no installation program for *Vtools.* The manual explains how to install the program.

Operation   Vtools is a collection of useful tools. The package includes:

Vdd.   This is a visual directory. It displays files using the same format as DOS. However, you can scroll the list up and down. While using this directory, you can also perform the following:

- Display the current file in ASCII mode by pressing the A-key.
- Display the current file in hexadecimal mode by pressing the B-key.
- Sort the listing by date/time, name, extension or size by pressing the appropriate key.
- Display only subdirectory entries by pressing the T key.
- Move to the currently highlighted subdirectory by pressing the plus-key.
- Move to the parent subdirectory by pressing the minus-key.
- Delete the currently highlighted file or subdirectory by pressing the Del-key.
- Get help by pressing the F1-key.
- Exit to either the currently highlighted subdirectory or the subdirectory you started in by pressing the appropriate key.

Vloc   This locates all the files on your hard disk matching the input file specification. Once the files are displayed, Vloc has all the features of Vdd covered above.

Vref   This compares files on two different drives or in two different subdirectories to see if they match. Figure 21-30 shows this. You can instruct Vref

```
Vref 1.01 Date/Size Compare   Copyright (C) Golden Bow Systems 1988
   BOOKLABE BAK      * not found
   CHAPTE05 BAK      * not found
   CHAPTE11 DOC      Dates differ:       2-19-89   vs.    12-31-88
   CHAPTE05 DOC      Dates differ:       2-19-89   vs.     2-12-89
   CHT-BACK DOC      compare
   CHAPTE08 DOC      Dates differ:       2-19-89   vs.     2-18-89
   CHT-INDX DOC      compare
   BOOKLABE DOC      Dates differ:       2-19-89   vs.     2-18-89
   CHT-MENU DOC      compare
   CHT-TEMP DOC      compare
   CHAPTE11 BAK      * not found
   OLDLABEL DOC      compare
   CHAPTE08 BAK      Dates differ:       2-19-89   vs.     2-18-89
   BOX      DOC      * Back dated:         2:18a   vs.       7:59p
   TABLES   DOC      Dates differ:       2-19-89   vs.     2-18-89
   TABLES   BAK      Dates differ:       2-19-89   vs.     2-18-89
```

Fig. 21-30. The Vtools Vref program compares files in two locations to see if they are the same.

to update the older files with newer versions. This is extremely useful if you often have to transport files back and forth between two different machines.

Vmov   This is a fast way to move files between two different subdirectories on the same disk. The files themselves are not moved or changed, only their directory entries are moved. As a result, a 1 Meg file can be moved as fast as a 1K file.

Vds   This sorts subdirectories by extension, date, name or size. Multiple sorting criteria can be used and all subdirectories below the current subdirectory can be included in the sort.

Vcd   This is a quick directory changer. To change to the C:\WORD-STAR\PROJECT1\LETTERS\HQ subdirectory, all you would have to enter is VCD HQ. Unlike the Norton NCD program, you must enter the entire name of the target subdirectory.

Vatt   This program displays the file attributes for a file or optionally changes the attributes.

Vdate   This program lets you change the DOS file date and time to the values you enter on the command line.

Vhex   This program converts numbers back and forth between hexadecimal and decimal. For example, entering the command VHEX 1Ah (1A in hexadecimal) would return the value 26d (26 in decimal.)

Limitations   The Vds sorting does not have a reverse sort option. You cannot, for example, sort files from largest to smallest or from newest to oldest. Vatt does not support wildcards.

Manual   The manual is well written and does a good job of explaining how to use these programs.

Conclusion   This is a great collection of utilities, especially the directory and moving utilities. I would, however, rename VMOV.EXE to MOVE.EXE.

Product:	Vtools
Price:	$59.95
Category:	Commercial
Publisher:	Golden Bow Systems
Address:	2870 Fifth Avenue
	Suite 201
	San Diego, California 92103
Phone:	(619) 298-9349
Memory:	256K

XD—Extended DOS

XD—Extended DOS (XD for short) is a collection of several useful commands under a central menu. For the most part, these commands replicate DOS commands, only they do a better job.

Installation   All that is required to run XD is to copy several files to a subdirectory in your PATH or to the floppy you wish to run them from. The process is adequately explained in the online documentation.

Operation   XD has two modes of operation, menu and command-line. In menu mode, you select the command from a menu and in command-line mode you enter the same command at the command line. The features available are:

- Changing the file attribute.
- Copying files. XD lets you specify more than one type of file to copy. For example, you could copy all .EXE and .COM files. In addition, once you enter a file specification or set of file specifications, XD lets you pick and choose among the matches.
- Deleting files. Like copying, you can specify more than one file specification and you can pick and choose among the matches.
- Deleting subdirectories and all the files in them, called "Killing." This is one stroke subdirectory removal. Like copying, you can specify more than one file specification and you can pick and choose among the matches.
- Listing files to the screen or printer. Like copying, you can specify more than one file specification and you can pick and choose among the matches.
- Moving files between subdirectories. This is like a copy followed by a delete. Like copying, you can specify more than one file specification and you can pick and choose among the matches.
- Renaming files. Like copying, you can specify more than one file specification and you can pick and choose among the matches. XD lists all the files with both their existing and new names for you to pick from.
- Searching for text in files. Like copying, you can specify more than one file specification and you can pick and choose among the matches.
- Changing the time and date stamp on files. Like copying, you can specify more than one file specification and you can pick and choose among the matches.
- Updating files. This searches the PATH for more recent versions of the files you specify. Where more recent versions are found, the older versions are updated. This is useful for backing up data files to floppies without using a backup program. Like copying, you can specify more than one file specification and you can pick and choose among the matches.

When you enter XD, you get the main menu. This menu lists all the commands and gives a brief explanation of each. You select a command by entering the first letter of the command. For example, I entered the attribute command.

The next screen prompts you for the file specification. You can enter a full path. You can also enter more than one file specification. Each file specification you enter will be combined into a joint set of files to be processed.

Depending on the command you select, there may be additional screens requesting information. With the attribute option, the next screen prompts for the switches to input how to set the attributes.

Once all this information has been entered, XD gathers a list of all the files that will be operated on. It presents that list on the screen and you can check yes or no for each file. The files you check no for will be skipped during processing.

You can avoid many of these screens by entering the information on the command line. For example, for the attribute command you would enter:

XD ATTR *.*

You cannot avoid all the screens, however. For each command you must check off the files from the file specification set to operate on. For the attribute command, you cannot enter the switches on the command line, you must wait for the program prompt.

Limitations   The program really needs a full command line mode. For example, for the attribute command above, I should be able to enter:

XD ATTR *.* -A /ALL

to completely skip the menus. That would make batch file operations easier.

Manual   The manual explains how to get XD up and running. It also gives a couple of examples on how to operate XD. That is probably enough if you only plan to use XD through the menu. It could use more examples of command line use.

Conclusion   XD—Extended DOS is a collection of a number of enhanced DOS commands. These enhancements are very useful, especially the ability to enter more than one file specification and to see and pick from a list of all the affected files. A copy of XD—Extended DOS is included on the optional diskette set.

<table>
<tr><td>Product:</td><td>XD - Extended DOS</td></tr>
<tr><td>Price:</td><td>$29.95</td></tr>
<tr><td>Category:</td><td>Shareware</td></tr>
<tr><td>Publisher:</td><td>Buttonware, Incorporated</td></tr>
<tr><td>Address:</td><td>Post Office Box 96058
Bellevue, Washington 98009</td></tr>
<tr><td>Phone:</td><td>(206) 454-0479</td></tr>
<tr><td>Notes:</td><td>Included on optional diskette set.</td></tr>
<tr><td>Memory:</td><td>128K</td></tr>
</table>

XCOPY

XCOPY is not a separate program, it is a part of newer DOS packages. I am including it in this book because there is a lot of misinformation about XCOPY in print.

Prior to DOS 3.2, the only way to copy files was the COPY command. DOS 3.2 changed all that by introducing the XCOPY command. The COPY command is an internal command. That means it is part of COMMAND.COM. The need to keep COMMAND.COM small (to save room for other programs) limits the "bells-and-whistles" that could be added to COPY. XCOPY avoided that problem by being an external command. To use XCOPY, XCOPY.EXE must be in the current directory or in the PATH.

Installation   XCOPY is part of DOS, which has no installation program. XCOPY must be in a subdirectory that is in your PATH.

Operation   When using wildcards, the COPY command reads one file, writes that file, then reads the next file. XCOPY reads all the files that will fit into memory, writes those files, and then reads the next batch of files. You would think that XCOPY would be faster. In fact, just after DOS 3.2 was released there were a number of magazine articles that said XCOPY was faster without much in the way of evidence. The writers just assumed that a method of operation that seemed more efficient must be faster.

Speed is a testable hypothesis, so the first thing I did was test the speed claims. First, I copied 49 files (974,987-bytes) from my hard disk to a 1.2 Meg floppy drive using a Compaq DeskPro 286 running at 12-MHz. It took 3 minutes and 10.28 seconds using the COPY command and 3 minutes and 24.9 seconds using the XCOPY command. Score one for COPY. OK, maybe XCOPY is faster if you use faster drives. So I copied the same files from one subdirectory to another subdirectory on the same hard disk. COPY took 33.75 seconds while XCOPY took 39.87 seconds. Score two for COPY.

Maybe XCOPY works faster with a single file. So I tried a 784,178 - byte file, first from the hard disk to the floppy drive. COPY took 59.18 seconds while XCOPY took 1-minute 8.15 seconds. Score three for COPY. Copying the same file between two subdirectories took 15.22 seconds with COPY and 15.97 seconds with XCOPY. Score four for COPY.

Maybe XCOPY is faster on slower computers. I tried similar tests on my 4.77 MHz 8088 clone. COPY won every test. Desperate for something XCOPY could do faster than COPY, I tried these tests on a 16 MHz 386 machine. Again, COPY was faster in every test. In fact, I failed to find one test where XCOPY was faster than COPY.

In spite of being slower than the COPY command and being unable to copy to non-file devices, XCOPY has enough additional features to make it very useful.

One of its most useful features are the numerous switches available with XCOPY:

/A.   This causes XCOPY to copy only those files that have been modified since the last backup. This is a good way to make an incremental backup as long as none of your files is larger than the capacity of your floppy diskette. Its advantage over BACKUP/M is that the resulting files can be used by any computer without first restoring the file, something you cannot even do if the second computer does not have a hard disk. This does not, however, reset the archive bit so DOS still sees the file as requiring backup. The syntax is:

XCOPY C:\WORK\ *.* A:/A

/M.   Identical to the /A switch except the archive bits are reset in the original directory as the files are copied so DOS sees the files as unmodified. The syntax is:

XCOPY C:\WORK\ *.* A:/S

/D. This switch lets you copy files created or modified after a given date. The syntax is:

XCOPY C:\ WORK \ *.* A:/D:01-01-1988

/S. This adds subdirectories to the copying process. For example, if you do all your work with a word processor in your C:\WORD subdirectory with the documents stored in child-subdirectories by project, you could copy all the modified files to the A-drive with the command:

XCOPY C:\ WORD \ *.* A:/M/S

Not only would this copy the files to the A-drive, it would create identically named subdirectories on the A-drive if they did not already exist. Notice that this command combines two switches.

/E. The /S switch will not create a A:\WORD\PROJECT9 subdirectory if the C:\WORD\PROJECT9 subdirectory is empty. Adding a /E after the /S will cause empty subdirectories to be created on the target drive. The syntax is:

XCOPY C:\ WORD \ *.* A:/M/S/E

/W. This causes XCOPY to wait for a keystroke before copying any files. This is useful in batch files where the user is to change disks. (Prompt him first with the ECHO command.) The syntax is:

XCOPY C:\ WORD \ *.* A:/M/S/E/W

/P. This causes XCOPY to prompt you before copying each file. This lets you decide on each file to copy. The syntax is:

XCOPY C:\ WORD \ *.* A:/M/S/E/W/P

/V. This causes XCOPY to ''sort of'' verify the copy process. From the name, you would expect that VERIFY causes DOS to check data it writes to a disk to make sure it was written properly. This is ''sort of'' what DOS does.

When DOS writes information to disk, it also includes a special checksum, called a Cyclical Redundancy Check or CRC. Writing the same data to disk will always cause DOS to write the same CRC to disk. By including the data and the CRC on the disk, DOS has two versions of the data.

When DOS reads the data from disk, it again computes the CRC and compares the computed CRC to the one read from the disk. If they do not match, DOS knows it has read the data incorrectly. When the two CRC's do not match, DOS tries several more times. If it cannot read the data where the CRC's match, it responds with the ''Abort, Ignore or Retry'' error message.

When using /V with XCOPY (or COPY from the DOS prompt with VERIFY ON) DOS does more than writing data to disk. After writing the data, it reads the data and computes a new CRC. If that new CRC matches the CRC stored with the data on the disk, DOS assumes the data was written properly. Note that DOS does not compare the data on the disk with the data in memory, which would be the best test. All it does is compare checksums.

There are occasions when a copy command can have more than one meaning. For example:

```
XCOPY C:\WORD\*.DOC A:\PROJECT
```

In this case, is A:\PROJECT a file or a subdirectory? If the directory A:\PROJECT exists, XCOPY will assume a directory. If the file exists in the root directory called PROJECT, XCOPY will assume a file. If neither exists, the command

```
\XCOPY *.BAT A:\OLDBAT
```

could indicate a file or a subdirectory. When in doubt, XCOPY will ask you.

A final advantage of XCOPY is it returns a ERRORLEVEL code to indicate how the copying process was completed. The codes are:

0   Normal completion.
1   No files to copy.
3   The user terminated the copying process with a ^C or ^Break or responded with an "A" to the "Abort, Retry, or Ignore" error message.
4   Any other error.

You can test for these ERRORLEVEL codes in batch files (not from the keyboard) using the batch IF command. For example:

```
IF ERRORLEVEL 4 ECHO OTHER ERROR
IF ERRORLEVEL 4 GOTO END
IF ERRORLEVEL 3 ECHO COPYING ABORTED IN PROCESS
IF ERRORLEVEL 3 GOTO END
IF ERRORLEVEL 1 ECHO NO FILES TO COPY
IF ERRORLEVEL 1 GOTO END
ECHO XCOPY SUCCESSFUL
:END
```

The GOTO END statement is required because the ERRORLEVEL test is a greater than or equal test, so the two following statements are the same (although both are invalid to DOS).

```
IF ERRORLEVEL = 0
IF ERRORLEVEL = 0
```

Limitations   With the COPY command, you can not only copy files, you can copy between logical devices. For example, you can create a simple batch file by copying the keystrokes from the keyboard to a file with the command:

```
COPY CON: SIMPLE.BAT
```

You press ^Z or F6 to stop sending keystrokes to the file. You can list a file on the screen by copying that file to the screen with:

```
COPY SIMPLE.BAT CON
```

You cannot do any of this with XCOPY. XCOPY will respond with a "Does con specify a file name or directory name on the target (F=file, D=Directory)?" message. When you respond, you will get a "Cannot XCOPY to a reserved device" error message.

Another limitation is that XCOPY cannot append files. With COPY, you can enter:

```
COPY FILE1 + FILE2 + FILE3 BIGFILE
```

to combine several files into one large file. If you try this with XCOPY, it will respond with an "invalid parameters" error message.

Manual   XCOPY has only a few pages in the DOS manual. That is, however, adequate to explain the usage of XCOPY.

Conclusion   Even though XCOPY is slower than COPY, requires an external file, and cannot replace some of the functions of COPY, the combination of powerful switches and ERRORLEVEL code reporting makes XCOPY a powerful command.

22
Batch File Aids

DOS batch files are nothing more than a method of saving keystrokes and automating operations. You can store any DOS command you can enter from the keyboard in a file with a .BAT extension and play it back later. DOS also lets batch files read information from the command line and replace entries %1–%9 with information from the command line. For example, if the batch file DIRA.BAT contained the following line:

```
DIR A:%1/P
```

and you entered DIRA *.DOC, then the batch file would execute the command DIR A: *.DOC/P.

While the DOS batch language is useful, it is not very powerful. It is very good at storing keystrokes, as illustrated above, but it has very limited branching ability. After three major upgrades (2.0, 3.0 and 4.0) and numerous minor upgrades (1.01, 1.1, 2.1, and so on) DOS still has only seven special batch commands. These, combined with the normal DOS commands, can still do a lot. For more information, see my book *MS-DOS Batch File Programming on the IBM PC . . . Including OS/2* from TAB BOOKS.

One very nice thing about the DOS batch language is it is very easy to expand the language. If you need a function not included in the language, just write a DOS program to perform that function. You can then run that program from within your batch file.

Batutil

Batutil is a program included in the shareware Stackey package. Batutil gives you far more power in your batch files and more control over the DOS environment.

Installation   The manual did not cover installation. All you must do is copy BATUTIL.EXE to a subdirectory in your PATH.

Operation   Batutil has commands to return the following information to the batch file:

- The current time, date and day of the week.
- The total free disk space.
- The total amount of memory.
- The CPU and type of coprocessor if present.
- Whether a file exists not only in the current directory.
- If a file has today's date.
- If one of two files is older than the other.

Batutil also has commands to:

- Have the user input a string and get it stored in the environment. This is a difficult task and requires the program use undocumented DOS functions.
- Have the user type in a user name or password.
- See if a password or user name matches a predetermined list and has each item.
- Allow you to put strings in the environment up to a length of 255 characters rather than the 127- character maximum that DOS allows. Your PATH string can be up to 250 characters rather than the 122 characters that you can enter with DOS. (The lower limits are because the "PATH =" statement takes up the first five characters.) While DOS doesn't care about long paths, you may have an application program that does and crashes if it finds a path over 127 characters. I did not find any and the vendor only found one, Techhelp from Flambeaux Software.
- Pop up a file name list for the user to choose from and have the answer stored in the environment.
- Easily add subdirectories to and delete subdirectories from your PATH.
- Allow full screen editing of your environment and PATH.
- Allow you to save the environment to a file, to load or merge a file into the environment and to kill the environment.

Batutil does menus in a big way. You can define menus with any shape and size. The menus can have different colors and even have shadows. You can add up to 80 characters of explanation for each menu option. While a menu is active, it fully supports the mouse for moving the cursor and making a selection.

There are about fifty commands that return a number from 0 to 199. If the command appears inside braces then it stores the return code in the environmental variable RC (short for "return code"). If the command appears in brackets, then BATUTIL will exit without running the rest of the command line and place this integer in the DOS errorlevel.

Three commands read information in from a file rather than just taking their commands from the command line. This gets them around the 127-character limit for command lines. The ECho command displays text on the screen in colors you set before the echo command. PRetty displays text in colors that you can adjust as part of the string displayed and MEnu displays a user defined menu.

Limitations   Batutil allows you to expand your PATH up to 250 characters. While this worked with all the programs I tested it with, there is an easier way. Using the SUBST command, you can replace long paths to subdirectories with drive letters. As a result, you can replace the subdirectory entry "C:\DOS\PROGRAMS\NON-IBM" with "E:\" and considerably shorten your PATH. This is a much better approach than the Batutil approach.

Manual   I review a beta copy of Batutil so the documentation and even the program features may change by the time they release it. The manual was very complete and covered all the Batutil commands in detail. The manual was a rough draft so I could not draw any conclusions as to its final quality.

Conclusion   From what I saw of the beta release of Batutil, it is an extremely powerful addition to your batch files. The author's plan to distribute Batutil as part of the Stackey package.

Beyond.Bat

Beyond.Bat is a powerful replacement for the DOS batch language. It can run as a memory resident or as a stand-alone application. While very powerful, it is difficult to learn and there is no compiler so every user must own a copy. Beyond.Bat tries to do much more than Extended Batch Language or Batutil. Rather than enhancing the DOS batch language, Beyond.Bat tries to replace it.

Installation   Beyond.Bat does not have an installation program. The manual explains how to install the program; however, it explanation is confusing.

Operation   At its simplest level, Beyond.Bat is one more enhancement for DOS batch files. You use Beyond.Bat commands to write Beyond.Bat batch files. That makes Beyond.Bat a programming language. Users of Relay Gold or Relay Silver will have a head start in learning this language. Beyond.Bat comes from the same company and its language is almost identical to the script language used in the Relay products.

Although not a memory resident shell, you can use the language to write one. In fact, one of the sample applications is a shell program the user can modify for his own purposes.

Beyond.Bat can read and write files. It can create and use variables far beyond the %0 – %9 and environmental (e.g.%PATH%) offered by DOS. The variable names can be up to nine characters. They can contain information with up to 255 characters. There are system variables (like &Date) for storing global information.

In addition to branching based on variable values, a la DOS, you can use mathematical or string operations on these variables. Before version 3.3, DOS could not branch from one batch file to another and return (without the COMMAND/C Branch trick). Beyond.Bat handles this and other types of branching with ease.

In addition to subroutines, Beyond.Bat allows you to collect all the batch files for a specific application into libraries for easy management. All this makes it easy to develop complex applications the way you should, in pieces.

Beyond.Bat makes it easy to develop screens. You can use these screens to provide the user with information or to request information from the user. Beyond.Bat can perform input validation on information requested from the user. One of the sample applications is a restaurant reservation system written in Beyond.Bat code.

Although not reviewed, VM Personal Computing sells an Advanced Development Kit for $25. This kit allows the user to:

- Add memory resident help to existing applications.
- Add a learn mode to Beyond.Bat.
- Use Beyond.Bat as a keyboard macro program.
- Access the editor in pop-up mode.

Beyond.Bat has three methods of operation:

1) Fully Memory Resident. Beyond.Bat loads everything it needs into memory so no command requires it to read the disk. This method requires 165K of RAM. That is enough to make this mode only useful for someone running Beyond.Bat from a floppy disk system.

2) Semi-Memory Resident. Beyond.Bat loads a 5K kernel into RAM. This small memory resident program examines every command entered at the DOS prompt. If it is a Beyond.Bat script it runs that script. Otherwise, the command is passed to DOS. Memory requirements for semi-memory resident are similar to stand-alone except for the additional 5K of RAM for the memory resident program.

3) Stand-Alone. In this mode Beyond.Bat is not active until called. To call Beyond.Bat, you precede the script file name with a BB. This mode requires 128K to run a script and an additional 65K to run an application.

Beyond.Bat reads the entire script into memory before executing it. That is much faster than DOS's method of reading the batch file one line at a time.

Documentation   The authors of the Beyond.Bat documentation failed to remember they were writing documentation for a programming language that is not documented anywhere else. Explanations include all the necessary information but are often brief with only a few examples. There is no quick reference card.

There is a sample application that converts your batch files to Beyond.Bat batch files. That helps make the conversion. It also goes a long way toward helping you learn the system because it gives you sample programs with a known purpose to study.

Limitations   Beyond.Bat applications are not compiled. That means that everyone you develop an application for must have Beyond.Bat to execute that application, an expensive proposal.

I had a problem with the full memory resident mode. When I loaded it into memory, my computer stopped working properly. DOS would run any .EXE or .COM program in the current directory but would not search the PATH. No amount of resetting the PATH would cause DOS to search the PATH. In addition, DOS refused to run any .BAT file regardless of its location or whether it had DOS or Beyond.Bat commands. These problems continued regardless of the loading order of my memory resident software and even when I loaded Beyond.Bat loaded.

The first time I called technical support, they would not help me because they had not yet received my registration. When I finally got through to them, they said they knew about the problem and offered to send me a fix (called a "zap") only if I first mailed them a disk. (They also had a bulletin board I could have downloaded the zap from.) I sent them a disk and they sent me a zap to fix the problem I reported and several additional problems as well.

Because of the attitude of the technical support department, the length of time it took to get a major bug corrected, and the fact that free technical support is available for only 30 days, I rate the support as unacceptable. VM Personal Computing offers extended support for Beyond.Bat. For $50.00, it adds one year of support and a newsletter.

Beyond.Bat memory resident applications would not run from a DOS memory resident DOS shell. The stand-alone applications ran without any problem. On some clones, running an application when Beyond.Bat is loaded as a memory resident program will cause the computer to lock and force a cold reboot.

Conclusion   Beyond.Bat is an extremely powerful replacement for DOS batch files. In fact, there is not a more powerful form of script file available for the PC. Its main drawbacks are the lack of a compiler so you can distribute applications to people without Beyond.Bat, poor documentation, and poor technical support.

<table>
<tr><td>Product:</td><td>Beyond.Bat</td></tr>
<tr><td>Price:</td><td>$99.00</td></tr>
<tr><td>Category:</td><td>Commercial</td></tr>
<tr><td>Publisher:</td><td>Microcom Software Division</td></tr>
<tr><td>Address:</td><td>Sales
500 River Ridge Drive
Norwood, Massachusetts 02062</td></tr>
<tr><td>Phone:</td><td>(617) 551-1999</td></tr>
<tr><td>Notes:</td><td>Exact memory usage depends on how you use Beyond.Bat.</td></tr>
<tr><td>Memory:</td><td>5K-150K</td></tr>
</table>

Bigecho

Bigecho is a copyrighted quasi-public domain program for displaying large characters on the screen.

Installation   There is no installation program and the documentation does not mention installation. Bigecho comes with a number of files including demonstrations and documentation. However, all you have to do to install it is copy BIGECHO.COM to a subdirectory in your PATH.

Operation   Bigecho can display ten characters per line and can show three lines per screen. You typically use Bigecho in batch files and you must have ECHO OFF for the screen to look right. Figure 22-1 shows the output of the batch file in Fig. 22-2. Control-A sends a happy face to the screen and Control-B sends a reverse happy face to the screen.

The distribution package also includes a program called Goodday. This program reads the system clock and displays the appropriate greeting in large Bigecho-like letters on the screen.

Limitations   You may have some difficulty finding Bigecho. The authors allow you to copy the software and give away the disks but not to sell them. Bigecho is on one of the optional disks.

Fig. 22-1. The Bigecho program displays three rows of up to 10 very large characters on the screen.

```
@echo off              <--- Turns off ECHO. Under DOS 3.3 and later, commands starting with @ do not ECHO
bigecho Hello From     <--- Sends first line to screen
bigecho     ^A         <--- Sends second line to screen. The ^A is Control-A and sends happy-face
bigecho  Tab Books     <--- Sends third line to screen
pause>nul              <--- Pauses batch file to read screen. The ">nul" keeps the "press any key" DOS
                            message from showing on the screen by piping it to nul.
```

Fig. 22-2. Sample Bigecho batch file.

Manual   Bigecho is extremely ease to use. The sample batch files and documentation that come with Bigecho do a good job of explaining how to use Bigecho.

Conclusion   Bigecho makes for interesting and entertaining batch files.

Product:	Bigecho
Price:	Free
Category:	Quasi-Public Domain
Publisher:	Ctrlalt Associates
Address:	Suite 133
	260 South Lake Avenue
	Pasadena, California 91101
Phone:	Not Available
Notes:	Bigecho can be freely copied
	and passed around as long as
	no fee is charged for the
	copies
Memory:	64K

Datetime

Datetime is a program to make it easier to set the time and date on computers without a clock.

Installation   There is no installation program and the documentation does not mention installation. Datetime comes with a number of files including demonstrations and documentation. However, all you have to do to install it is copy DATETIME.COM to a subdirectory in your PATH.

Operation   Normally, you would place the Datetime as a command in your AUTOEXEC.BAT file. The program clears the screen and displays the current date in large characters. If you do not have a clock, the power-on date is January 1, 1980. If that is the case, Datetime automatically displays the date of the last time it ran. That way, if you have rebooted, the date will be correct. Otherwise, the date will likely only be a day or two days off. You use the cursor control arrows to change the date.

After that, Datetime displays the time. Again, you use the cursor control arrows to set the correct time. When you press Return, Datetime first modifies the DATETIME.COM file to add the current date and then returns control to the batch file.

Manual   The documentation file does a good job of explaining how to use Datetime.

Conclusion   If you do not have a clock, Datetime makes it quicker to set the date. Its large eye-catching characters make it more likely you will really set the date and time.

```
Product:      Datetime
Price:        $5.00
Category:     Copyrighted Public Domain
Publisher:    Paul Burney
Address:      10800 Alpharetta Highway
              Suite 200-N8
              Roswell, Georgia 30076
Phone:        Not Available
Memory:       128K
```

Extended Batch Language

A 9K memory resident package called *Extended Batch Language* [*EBL* for short] greatly reduces the limitations of DOS batch files. EBL is a high level programming language.

Installation   EBL does not have an installation program and the manual does not explain how to install the software. EBL comes with a number of program files. You should copy these to their own subdirectory and add that subdirectory to your PATH.

Operation   There are two ways to run EBL. The first is to start each line of your batch file with the "BAT" command. This loads EBL and has it to process the rest of the line. For example, the batch line:

BAT READ Input your password > %0

prompts the user for a password and stores it in the %0 variable. That variable is available only for the rest of the batch file. You can also have EBL store the information in environmental variables if you need to use them after the batch file finishes.

The second way to run EBL is to load EBL into memory for the entire batch file with a "BAT/P" command at the beginning of the batch file. This mode makes it somewhat difficult to enter DOS commands. Once you load EBL, it expects to process all the batch commands. To enter a DOS command, you must use a "LEAVE" command to get out of the EBL processor. To reload the EBL processor again you must use the "BAT/P" command again. If you only want to enter a single DOS command, you can use the "SHELL" keyword at the beginning of the line. When it encounters a SHELL command, EBL turns the rest of the line over to DOS to process.

Although all the features are too numerous to mention, the major ones are:

- Call a subroutine.
- Change the colors.
- Check to see if a file exists.
- Four function mathematical operations.

- IF..Then..Else statements.
- Read a single character from the keyboard.
- Read characters from the screen. You would use this to read information placed on the screen by another program. This only works in text mode.
- Skip over a specified number of lines in a batch file. This is similar to a GOTO command.
- Stuff keystrokes into the keyboard buffer.

EBL includes several libraries of additional functions. These include:

- Booting the computer.
- Centering strings.
- Changing drives and subdirectories.
- Converting a string to uppercase.
- Converting characters to hexadecimal, decimal or ASCII.
- Executing an 8086 INT instruction.
- Reading a value from a specific memory location a la a Basic Peek statement.
- Returning the current date or time.
- Returning the current subdirectory.
- String manipulation.
- Writing a value to a specific memory location, like a Basic Poke statement.

Limitation/Manual   EBL is distributed as shareware. The purpose of shareware distribution is to give you a chance to try out a program before you buy it. However, the EBL distribution disk does not have a manual on the disk. To get documentation, you must register EBL. In any case, the printed manual is a very good manual.

Conclusion   EBL is essentially a DOS programming language. As such, it has the advantage of providing much more control and many more functions than the DOS batch language. It also has the drawback of being more difficult to learn to use. If you find yourself looking for ways to trick DOS or wishing for more DOS power, then Extended Batch Language is your answer. If you find it difficult to understand even simple DOS batch files, then EBL has nothing for you.

Product:	Extended Batch Language
Price:	$49.00
Category:	Shareware
Publisher:	Seaware Corporation
Address:	Post Office Box 1656
	Delray Beach, Florida 33444
Phone:	(305) 392-2046
Memory:	128K

Stackey

Stackey is a small, shareware program that will place keystrokes in your keyboard buffer. Typically, you would use Stackey in a batch file.

Installation   The documentation file for Stackey does not discuss how to install the program. All that you have to do to install Stackey is copy STAC-KEY.COM for a subdirectory in your PATH.

Operation   A number of programs require redundant keystrokes. For example, if you enter DEL *.*, then DOS will prompt you to see if you really mean it. Formatting a disk requires that you insert a disk and press any key. Many applications require you to press a key to get past a copyright screen.

Stackey is a memory resident program. The first time you load Stackey, it takes up about 640-bytes for code and storing keystrokes. You tell Stackey what keys to use on its command line and it loads those keys into the keyboard buffer as though you had pressed those keys. You generally use Stackey in a batch file so Stackey gives you a way to have a batch file "type" keystrokes for you.

For example, the batch file:

Stackey NPROJECT.BAT "CR"
Wordstar

loads Stackey into memory, starts WordStar, and automatically loads PRO-JECT.BAT for editing in non-document mode. Stackey replaces the "CR" with a Return.

The batch file:

Stackey N%| "CR"
Wordstar

would open any file you specified on the command line in non-document mode.

Stackey includes a number of special keystroke codes for characters that would be hard to include in a batch file. For example:

"+C"	Turning CapsLock on.
"+N"	Turning NumLock on.
"+S"	Turning ScrollLock on.
"-C"	Turning CapsLock off.
"-N"	Turning NumLock off.
"-S"	Turning ScrollLock off.
"^ ["	Pressing the escape key.
"CR"	Pressing the enter key.
"DA"	Pressing the down arrow.
"DE"	Pressing the delete key.
"DQ"	Pressing the double quote ["] key. You need this because this is a Stackey control key when entered directly.
"EN"	Pressing the end key.
"ES"	Pressing the escape key.
"HM"	Pressing the home key.
"IN"	Pressing the insert key.
"LA"	Pressing the left arrow.
"LF"	Pressing Control-enter.

"PD"	Pressing the page down key.
"PU"	Pressing the page up key.
"RA"	Pressing the right arrow.
"SQ"	Pressing the single quote ['] key. You need this because this is a Stackey control key when entered directly.
"TA"	Pressing the tab key
"UA"	Pressing the up arrow.
#3	Repeat the next character three times.
W#	Wait the indicated time. # is a number between 1 and 256 and represents the number of 55 milliseconds to wait. So W18 causes a delay of one second. You need this if a program clears out the keyboard buffer (called flushing) since the keystrokes after the W# command are not put into the buffer until after the delay.

This list is just a sample. The documentation lists a number of other special characters codes.

Manual   The documentation file does a good job of explaining how to use Stackey. It has a number of sample applications and explanations of what those applications do.

Conclusion   For most applications, Stackey is extremely easy to use. You figure out the keystrokes to stack and how to enter one or two special characters like escape or return. A more complicated application may require a delay because an application flushes the buffer. For these types of applications, you will find Stackey a practical and easy to use program. Stackey can handle more complicated applications but you are going to have to experiment with the keystrokes that Stackey sends.

Product:	Stackey
Price:	$39.00
Category:	Shareware
Publisher:	Ctrlalt Associates
Address:	Suite 133
	260 South Lake Avenue
	Pasadena, California 91101
Phone:	Not Available
Memory:	640-bytes

RONNY'S PICKS

Personally, I write fairly simple batch files. About the only enhancement I use is a program to get a single keystroke from the user. Norton includes this program in his utilities. The source code for the one I use is in my *MS-DOS Batch File Programming on the IBM PC . . . Including OS/2*. If I were going to use a high performance batch language, I would select Extended Batch Language. Both the language and the manual have an edge over Beyond.Bat. However, and this is a major however, you cannot share batch files you write with either EBL or Beyond.Bat with other machines unless you purchase a copy for each machine. That makes setting up complex batch files in a business environment an expensive proposition. Until a batch enhancement language offers some sort of compiler where I can use the resulting batch files anywhere, I plan to stick with DOS. (The keystroke program I use is in the public domain so I can use it on any machine. If you use Norton's, then you have this same problem.)

23
File Compression Software

Data files take up a lot of space on your hard disk. If your hard disk is getting full, some of that space can be reclaimed by using a file compression program. File compression programs use special algorithms to reduce the size of a file. Not only does file compression reduce the required storage space, it reduces the required telecommunication time. File compression software can run in one of two modes, memory resident and standard DOS program.

A simple example will show you how file compression works. Read over this chapter. Note I did not use the letter x very often but I used the words "SQZ Plus" frequently. To compress the file, first replace all the lowercase x's with ^x. This actually makes the file larger. Replace each occurrence of SQZ PLUS with a lowercase x. Replace all uppercase X's with ^X, then replace the period and space at the end of most sentences with an uppercase X. With 256 possible characters, these types of changes can reduce the overall size of many files. This is string compression. Each document is likely to have common phrases used over-and-over. The program replaces these with a short code like ^x. The more frequent and longer the strings, the greater the compression.

Another compression technique is run-length coding. Many applications, like simple word processors, line things up with a number of spaces in a row. Worksheets often contain a row of dashes under each column. The compression software can replace each of the multiple occurrences of the same character with the character once and its length of occurrence.

Some compression packages store common words, like "the", in a dictionary and automatically replace it with a shorter version. This is dictionary compression. Finally, digraph compression replaces common letter sets, like "ed" with shorter versions.

Most word processing files commonly use less than 64 characters for common upper and lowercase letters, numbers, spaces, punctuation, and formatting characters. You can code sixty four possibilities using only six bits instead of the normal eight, saving two bits per character. You can code any uncommon letter or other character not covered by this scheme using two sets of six bits. When most characters in a file are common characters, this will reduce file sizes 25%.

The type of translation used on the file is either fixed or variable. With fixed translation, the program compresses each file according to a fixed algorithm. This results in dramatic swings in compression rations. The algorithm compresses a file well matched to the translation algorithm to less than 25% of its original size. However, it compresses a file poorly matched to the translation algorithm poorly. The file can actually end up larger after "compression."

Some programs use a variable translation algorithm. They read the file or group of files to be compressed and produce a custom algorithm. A drawback to this method is that in addition to the compressed file, the program must also store a copy of the resulting translation algorithm. The additional overhead of storing this algorithm reduces the advantage of compressing files, especially small ones.

Some types of files cannot be compressed to any great extent. These are files that have a fairly even mix of characters. The file does not have to use all 256 ASCII characters. A mix of 129 randomly arranged characters will prevent using six or seven bit coding and the random nature of the file will prevent successful substitutions. While most files are not random in nature, the structure of most .EXE and .COM files is such that they appear random to the compressing program.

Worksheet files are excellent candidates for file compression. In addition to standard numeric and text compression, the worksheet file format lends itself to compression. Lotus stores information on all blank but formatted cells. (All comments apply to Symphony and other Lotus clones as well.) Stripping out this information has no impact on the working of the spreadsheet but it reduces the file size. It also permanently removes this information. Lotus also stores two pieces of data for formulae cells, the formula and the last calculated value of that formula. The compression program can strip this formula value from the file with no impact other than forcing a recalculation when your retrieve the file.

Cubit

Cubit is an excellent file compression program that will work with most data files including Lotus.

Installation   Cubit has an installation program that will automatically install it. The program worked flawlessly.

Operation   Cubit has two modes, memory resident and standard DOS program. Memory resident Cubit requires about 51K. It acts as a buffer between the disk and your application programs. When an application program accesses a Cubit compressed file, Cubit intervenes and uncompresses the file. If you use Microsoft Word to edit a Cubit compressed file, Cubit would create an uncompressed version on disk before it allowed Word to access the file. When you exit Word, Cubit would automatically recompress the file(s). Memory resident Cubit only works on previously compressed files so you must first compress your files using the stand-alone version.

Memory resident Cubit was indifferent to loading order. I load File Facility, Superkey, Sidekick, and several public domain memory resident programs in my AUTOEXEC.BAT file. Cubit successfully loaded and ran in any position. It even loaded and ran after Sidekick, and that is not an easy feat.

The non-memory resident DOS program version of Cubit compresses files for the first time. It can also decompress files. It asks for the names of the files to compress and the names to use for the compressed files. It accepts DOS paths and wildcards. It does not warn you if the output file names you have selected will cause a file to be overwritten.

Cubit has a new mode that recognizes Lotus files and gives excellent compression. It also has a stand-alone program to decompress files that you can legally distribute with compressed files for decompression. That is an extremely nice touch that greatly expands the usefulness of Cubit. Table 23-1 below shows how Cubit performed in compressing the benchmark Lotus files, along with several Microsoft Word (*.DOC) and dBASE III (*.DBF) files.

Cubit has a stand-alone program for compressing large groups of files from the DOS prompt. While running, the program displays a small block as it progresses through each file.

Table 23-1. **Cubit File Compression.**

File	Compressed Size	Normal Size	Reduction
ADDITION.WK1	12,717	146,727	91.3%
CAR.WK1	19,537	46,506	58.0%
DIVIDE.WK1	12,945	176,719	92.7%
MULTIPLY.WK1	12,949	176,721	92.7%
POWER.WK1	13,428	146,534	90.8%
SUBTRACT.WK1	12,719	146,728	91.3%
DISSERTA.DOC	75,301	134,528	44.0%
CHAPTER1.DOC	18,791	39,936	52.9%
CHAPTER2.DOC	30,886	66,560	53.6%
CHAPTER3.DOC	4,264	7,680	44.5%
CHAPTER4.DOC	17,041	37,376	54.4%
CHAPTER5.DOC	6,999	13,312	47.4%
CHAPTER6.DOC	11,802	23,552	49.7%
CHAPTER7.DOC	8,398	16,384	48.7%
CHAPTER8.DOC	10,132	22,016	54.0%
CHAPTER9.DOC	5,679	10,240	44.5%
BOOK.DBF	334,026	334,026	0%
NOTES.DBF	3,529	5,725	38.4%
PUBLISH.DBF	1,633	2,841	42.5%
TITLE.DBF	78,782	130,563	39.7%
TEST.DBF	540,311	540,311	0%

Limitations   Cubit did not perform well with some database files, failing to compress them at all.

Manual   The manual is good, but not nearly as good as the SQZ PLUS manual.

Conclusion   In the past, deciding on one file compression package was difficult. SQZ PLUS worked best with Lotus, Squish worked best with databases, and Cubit worked best with everything else. That has changed. Cubit works almost as well on Lotus files as does SQZ PLUS, and in less memory. That makes Cubit a serious contender for your only file compression package.

<table>
<tr><td>Product:</td><td>Cubit</td></tr>
<tr><td>Price:</td><td>$69.95</td></tr>
<tr><td>Category:</td><td>Commercial</td></tr>
<tr><td>Publisher:</td><td>SoftLogic Solutions, Incorporated</td></tr>
<tr><td>Address:</td><td>One Perimeter Road
Manchester, New Hampshire
03101</td></tr>
<tr><td>Phone:</td><td>(800) 272-9900</td></tr>
<tr><td>Notes:</td><td>The memory resident version of Cubit requires 48K. The stand-alone file compression program requires 128K</td></tr>
<tr><td>Memory:</td><td>48K/128K</td></tr>
</table>

DS Squeeze

DS Squeeze is a commercial, menu-driven file compression program.

Installation   DS Squeeze includes an installation program that automatically installs the software in the subdirectory of your choice. You must run the installation program from the A-drive. An ASSIGN A = B statement will allow you to run it from the B-drive.

Operation   DS Squeeze is not a typical file compression program. It does not place itself between the disk and an application program to compress files going to disk and decompress files going to the application. Rather, it is a stand-alone file compression program. In that respect, it functions much like the archiving programs many bulletin boards use to reduce file transmission times.

The DS Squeeze screen strongly resembles the screen from a DOS shell. Figure 23-1 shows this. You move the cursor on the graphical tree to select the subdirectory the files are coming from. When you tell DS Squeeze to begin compressing, it prompts you for the files to include in the archive. You select these by tagging them, just as you do in a DOS shell. You can include as many source files in a single archive file as you like. DS Squeeze then prompts you for the target directory and file name. Table 23-2 shows the results of using DS Squeeze to compress the benchmark programs.

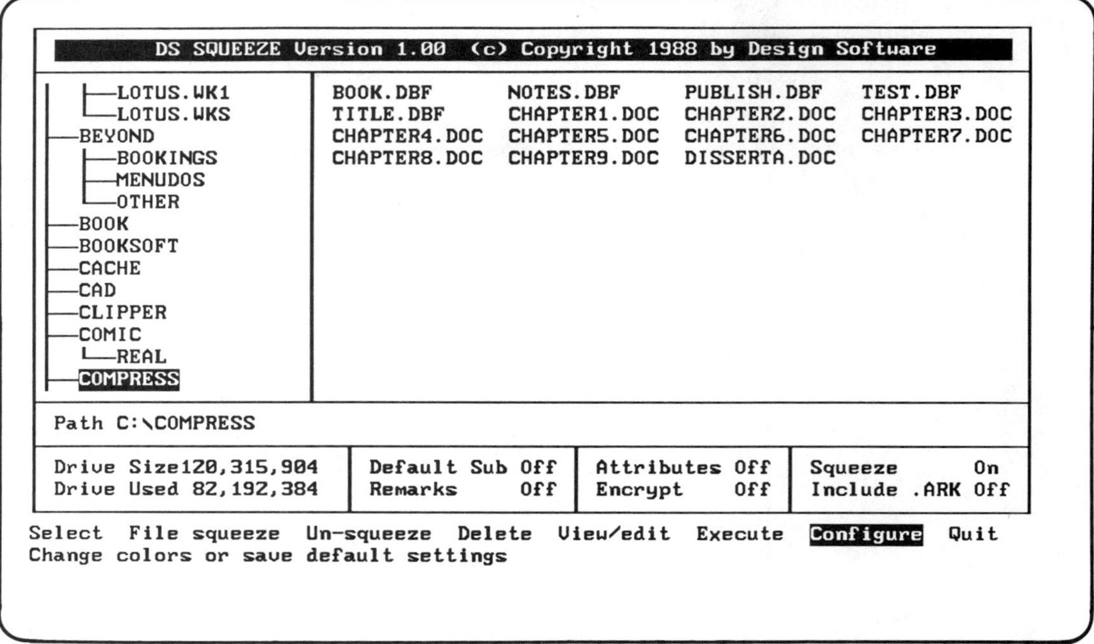

Fig. 23-1. With DS Squeeze, you use a graphical tree and file list to select the files to compress.

Table 23-2. **DS Squeeze File Compression.**

File	Compressed Size	Normal Size	Reduction
ADDITION.WK1	30,726	146,727	21%
CAR.WK1	24,678	46,506	53%
DIVIDE.WK1	78,366	176,719	44%
MULTIPLY.WK1	78,291	176,721	44%
POWER.WK1	27,327	146,534	19%
SUBTRACT.WK1	31,199	146,728	21%
DISSERTA.DOC	66,239	134,528	49%
CHAPTER1.DOC	19,014	39,936	48%
CHAPTER2.DOC	31,163	66,560	47%
CHAPTER3.DOC	4,357	7,680	57%
CHAPTER4.DOC	17,186	37,376	46%
CHAPTER5.DOC	7,003	13,312	53%
CHAPTER6.DOC	11,654	23,552	50%
CHAPTER7.DOC	8,804	16,384	53%
CHAPTER8.DOC	10,986	22,016	50%
CHAPTER9.DOC	5,834	10,240	57%
BOOK.DBF	73,197	334,026	22%
NOTES.DBF	2,779	5,725	49%
PUBLISH.DBF	1,338	2,841	47%
TITLE.DBF	37,080	130,563	28%
TEST.DBF	370,974	540,311	69%

Decompressing files works the same way. You first select the file to decompress. DS Squeeze gives you a list of all the files in that archive file and you select the ones you want to decompress by tagging them.

In both compression and decompression mode, you can have DS Squeeze erase the source file after processing it. In decompression mode that only erases the files you decompress, not the entire archive file.

DS Squeeze has an interesting feature that allows you to run a program inside an archive file without first decompressing it. You use the execute command and highlight the archived program you want to run. Using this feature, DS Squeeze retains 105K while the program is running. If the program requires supporting files inside the archive, it may not run properly.

DS Squeeze includes an unerase program. It works just like the Quick Unerase program in the Norton Utilities. You enter the subdirectory and file specifications and the unerase program recovers the file if it can do so without user intervention. If it cannot recover the file automatically, you must use another program because it does not have a manual mode. It is also not DOS 4.x compatible.

Limitations   DS Squeeze does not include a decompress program you can distribute with your files. As a result, you can only share files compressed with DS Squeeze with someone else who owns DS Squeeze. A small program that would only uncompress the files that you could include with compressed files without restrictions would greatly enhance the value of DS Squeeze.

If you try to run DS Squeeze without enough memory, it will appear to work. If you tell it to compress files, it will act as though it does just that. It does not give any error messages or warnings. However, it does not compress the files. That could cause you to delete files thinking you had saved them in an archive file. The decompression mode has the same problem.

Manual   The manual is complete and gives you all the information you need to run DS Squeeze. However, the writing is difficult to follow. That is not a major problem because DS Squeeze is easy enough to use you do not really need the manual.

Conclusion   DS Squeeze does a good job of compressing files and it is very easy to use. However, it cannot decompress files on the fly and you can only share the compressed files with a fellow DS Squeeze owner.

Product:	DS Squeeze
Price:	$69.95
Category:	Commercial
Publisher:	Design Software, Incorporated
Address:	19808 Nordhoff Place
	Chatsworth, California 91311
Phone:	(800) 231-3088
	(818) 885-9000
Notes:	DS Squeeze reduces this requirement to 105K while running a program inside an archive file.
Memory:	256K

Squish Plus

Squish Plus is an exceptionally easy-to-learn and easy-to-use file compressor. It offers maximum compatibility and minimal memory usage. Once installed, it requires virtually no user interaction.

Installation   Installing Squish Plus is a four-step process. The steps are:

1) Copying the files to your hard disk or boot floppy. Squish Plus's mode of operation make it perfect for floppy-drive only systems. The software has no program to automate this but the manual explains the process.
2) Adding a device statement to your CONFIG.SYS file. The manual explains the statement you must add but does not tell you how to add this statement. (You would use any ASCII editor.) The manual also fails to discuss where in your CONFIG.SYS file to add this command. That is important if other drives you use require a device driver. This is the only step an experienced user would have any trouble with.
3) Creating a "Squish Plus drive." You run a program that does this automatically. You only have to perform this once.
4) Attaching the Squish Plus drive. You have to do this every time you boot the computer. You can add the necessary command to your AUTOEXEC-.BAT file.

Operation   The device driver in your CONFIG.SYS file lets Squish Plus address a file as though it were a physical drive. This works similarly to the DOS SUBST command that lets DOS address a subdirectory as a physical drive. When you create the file during the installation, you tell Squish Plus how big to make the file. It goes out and grabs that much space using the file name you specify. You can optionally assign a password to the drive/file.

Each time you boot, you use the attach command to give Squish Plus access to the drive/file. If you created it with a password, the attach program will prompt you for that password. Once you enter the password, the drive/file is completely unprotected until you run the detach program.

Once attached, all your programs and utilities treat the drive/file as a physical drive. You can cache the drive, optimize the drive and even unerase files on the drive. To almost every program and utility you use, the drive/file appears as a physical drive. The only difference is Squish Plus compresses each file going to the drive.

The compression and decompression are completely automatic and fully transparent. Any file going to the drive gets compressed and any file leaving the file gets uncompressed. Squish Plus does all this in the background without the user ever doing anything.

If you like, you can configure to attach multiple Squish Plus drive/files. In addition, you can create multiple drive/files to attach at different times.

With Squish Plus loaded, DOS treats the file as a drive. So do backup programs so you will have no trouble backing up the Squish Plus drive/file. You can also back it up as a file without Squish Plus loaded.

You can log onto and work with the Squish Plus drive/file just like any other drive. The interface is so transparent that files show their normal non-compressed size with the DIR command. They are still compressed, Squish Plus just hides that from you. For that reason, I was not able to measure the individual compression on the files. The overall compress for all the files was 43%.

Limitations　　Squish Plus is not DOS 4.x compatible. When I tried to run it under DOS 4.01 it told me the file allocation table was damaged and suggested I run CHKDSK. I did and it did not report any problems. Booting off DOS 3.3 corrected the problem.

Squish Plus will not compress files to send to someone else. You could copy all the files to a single drive/file then send that file. However, that would require that the receiver have Squish Plus. It would also require you to decide on a drive size large enough to hold the files while small enough so it does not have a lot of empty space. That would be difficult.

Like the other file compression programs, Squish Plus has little effect on program and overlay files. In fact, the manual suggests that you do not use the Squish Plus drive/file for programs. They run fine. However, Squish Plus increases loading time because the file has to be decompressed before it can operate. Since Squish Plus is ineffective on programs, there is little point in waiting.

Manual　　The manual does a good job of explaining how to set up and use Squish Plus. Once it is operational, Squish Plus is easy enough to use that you will rarely need the manual.

Conclusion　　Squish Plus is close to being the perfect individual file compression program. Squish Plus automatically compresses and decompresses files without ever getting in the way. It is especially useful for portable computer users. It easily turns your 720K drives into 1440K drives and turns your 1440K drives into 3 Meg drives.

Product:	Squish Plus
Price:	$99.95 plus $5.00 shipping
Category:	Commercial
Publisher:	Sundog Software Corporation
Address:	264 Court Street
	Brooklyn, New York 11231
Phone:	(718) 855-9141
Notes:	Exact memory depends on how
	Squish is installed.
Memory:	36K
	20K if using EMS memory

SQZ PLUS

SQZ PLUS is a compression program that works with all releases of Lotus 1-2-3, Symphony files, and VP Planner. It comes in two versions, one is an add-in for working with recent releases of Lotus, the other is a memory resident program for working with other programs. Since it only works with one type of files, SQZ PLUS uses a very specialized translation algorithm.

Installation   SQZ PLUS comes with an installation program. It works perfectly.

Operation   SQZ PLUS works in both memory resident and add-in mode. While the add-in mode requires slightly more memory, it has the advantage of being detachable if you need to recover the memory. With the memory resident version, you must exit to DOS to recover the memory. In addition, the add-in version can create a history.

To run the memory resident version, you load SQZ PLUS. It automatically loads Lotus. Unlike most Lotus add-ons that use this loading method, SQZ PLUS can load other programs. You do this by adding their name after the SQZ PLUS command. For example:

SQZ PLUS C: \ HAL \ HAL @C: \ LOTUS \ 123

would load SQZ PLUS, Hal, and finally Lotus. DOS automatically removes SQZ PLUS, and any other programs loaded this way, from memory when you exit from Lotus. This is the best way to load Lotus add-ons since it prevents them from using precious RAM when you are not in Lotus. It also means that the programs must be compatible with other memory resident programs that expect you to load them last. SQZ PLUS worked well with all my memory resident programs including the difficult to get along with Sidekick.

You attach the add-in version using the Add-In Manager. Like other add-ins. You can configure it can to automatically attach each time you start Lotus. Appendix G gives more information on the Lotus Add-In Manager.

File Compression   Either version of SQZ PLUS acts as a buffer between Lotus and the disk. SQZ Plus intercepts and executes any calls to the disk by Lotus. Once you load and activate SQZ PLUS, you can only retrieve files compressed by SQZ PLUS. To load non-compressed files, you must turn SQZ PLUS off from its main menu or compress the file in stand-alone mode before entering Lotus. The SQZ PLUS main menu also lets you control how it compresses files. You can toggle on/off the squeezing action, the stripping of blanks, the stripping of values from formulae, the communications mode, and password protection.

The communications mode uses only ASCII characters between 20 and 127. This is useful for older transmission systems that do not allow binary transfers. Of course, the receiver must also have SQZ PLUS. The password mode allows you to assign a SQZ PLUS password. This mode is for users of Lotus version 1A, which does not have password protection. It is not compatible with the password protection mode built directly into later releases of Lotus.

There is also an annotate option. This lets you store a 50 character comment along with the file. It only displays this comment using the History option of the stand-alone program. You can save only one comment per session (/File Retrieve starts a session), however, you can add a new comment each session. The memory resident version does not support annotation. Figure 23-2 shows a History.

Table 23-3 shows the compressing obtained using SQZ PLUS on the benchmark programs. Figure 23-3 shows the SQZ PLUS main menu. In some

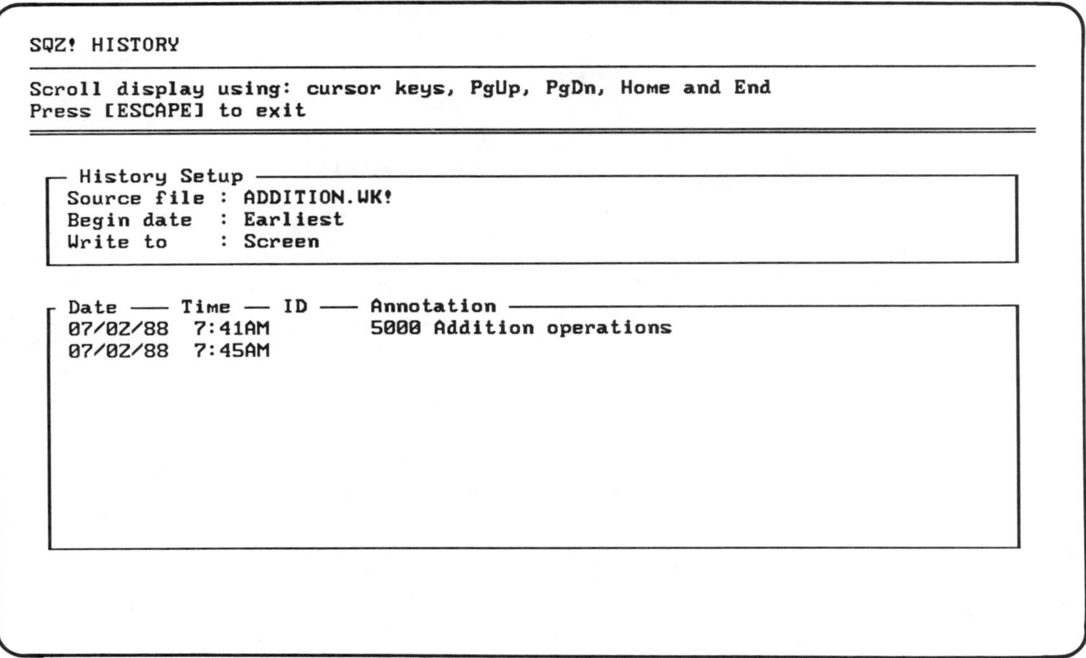

Fig. 23-2. SQZ can display the history of each worksheet including a comment about its contents.

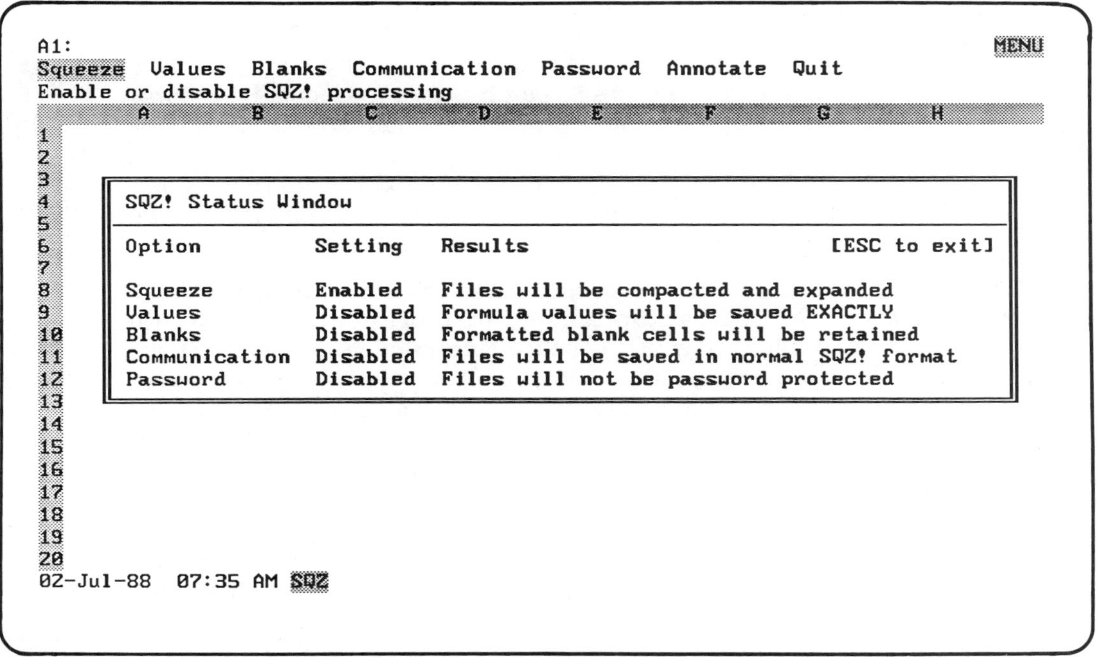

Fig. 23-3. The SQZ main menu makes it easy to set the operating parameters of SQZ.

Table 23-3. **SQZ Plus File Compression.**

File	Compressed Size	Normal Size	Reduction
ADDITION.WK1	3,335	146,727	97.8%
CAR.WK1	17,516	46,506	62.3%
DIVIDE.WK1	3,366	176,719	98.1%
MULTIPLY.WK1	3,368	176,721	98.1%
POWER.WK1	5,426	146,534	96.3%
SUBTRACT.WK1	3,356	146,728	97.7%

cases, the compress was fantastic. I ran all tests with SQZ PLUS not storing values to formulae. That has two drawbacks:

1) Other Programs. Programs that access the files to extract values cannot use the file with the values stripped out even if they are compatible with SQZ PLUS. Generally, you do not store worksheets for use by other programs and when you do you can change this option so this is a minor point.

2) Recalculation. When you first retrieve a file with the values removed, all the formulae evaluate to NA. You must recalculate the worksheet before Lotus will show the values.

SQZ PLUS includes a stand-alone program to convert large numbers of files all at once. This is useful when you first start using SQZ PLUS since Lotus cannot retrieve non-compressed files with SQZ PLUS active. This program accepts DOS paths and wildcards.

SQZ PLUS Tools   This is the stand-alone companion program to SQZ PLUS. Its primary purpose is to compress files in batch mode. It accepts DOS paths and wildcards. It is fast. It took less than 30 seconds to convert all the benchmark programs using an IBM Model 80. SQZ PLUS Tools also has a recovery program similar to Rescue that will try to repair a damaged worksheet file. You will need this since Rescue does not work with SQZ PLUS files. Finally, you use SQZ PLUS Tools to display the History of a file.

Backup   Backup is a separate add-in from SQZ PLUS. It creates files that are fully compatible with the DOS backup and restores programs distributed with DOS 3.3. Figure 23-4 shows the main menu. One interesting aspect of the Backup program is it can create a log. It actually places that log in the current worksheet. One real enhancement over DOS is the ability to analyze the backup specified and report on the number of disks it will need. On short backups, the SQZ PLUS Backup program took much longer than DOS, 20 seconds versus 13 seconds. On longer backups, the times were much closer. Figure 23-4 shows this.

The Backup program can also restore the files it creates, along with backup files created with DOS 3.3. It allows you to be prompted before overwriting files.

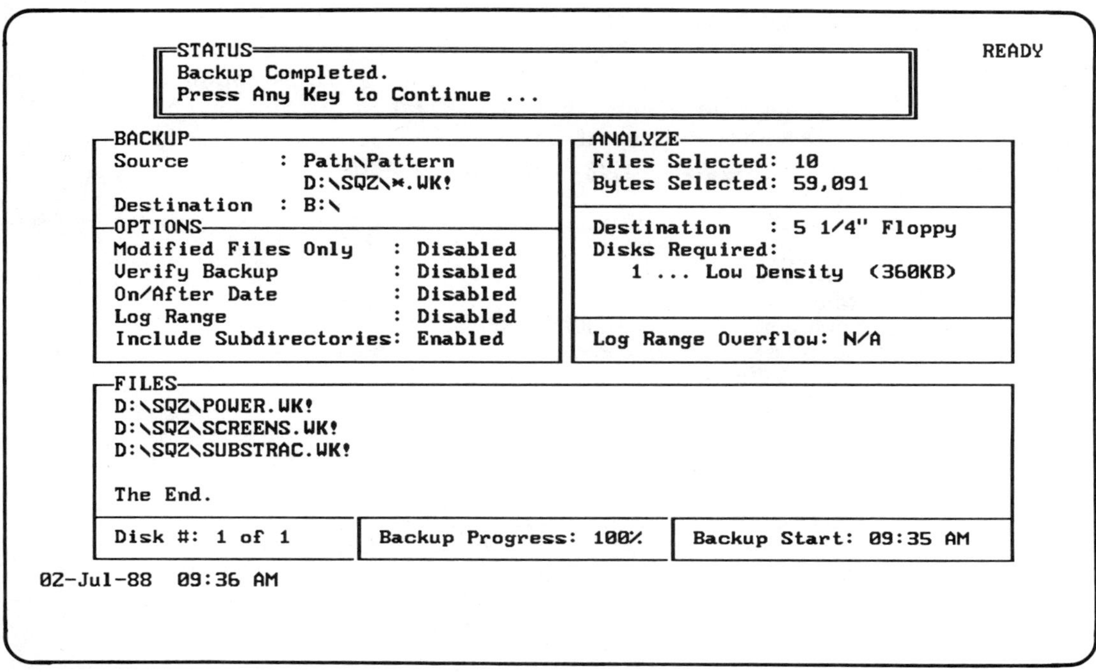

Fig. 23-4. The results of running the SQZ backup program.

Recorder   The Recorder program is another separate add-in. It records your most recent keystrokes invisibly in the background without any input from you. You can use these stored keystrokes to:

- Replay any contiguous combination.
- Convert any contiguous combination into a Lotus macro.

It records all the keystrokes between "milestones". A milestone is two /File Retrieves or one /File Save or /Worksheet Erase Yes.

The Recorder can also automatically save the worksheet at specific intervals specified by you in any increments from zero to thirty minutes. These saves are not to your current file name. Rather they are to a special file name. One option is to have it always to _SAVE1 and the other option is to alternate between _SAVE1 and _SAVE2. Since all worksheets autosave to the same file name, this feature only lets you recover data if you realize your mistake before working on another file. It has the advantage of allowing you to abandon changes to the current worksheet by recalling the same one from disk without saving.

Limitations   The Backup program requires a lot of memory and is slow.

Manual   The manual is very good. It has a number of screen shots so you always know what you are doing and how the screen should look.

Conclusion   SQZ PLUS file compression is worthwhile even if your hard disk has lots of empty space. It makes backups by any method faster and makes it easier and more certain to recover erased files. If you can spare the room, it is one of the few add-ins I would recommend for automatic attachment. The Backup program leaves a lot to be desired, particularly speed. In addition, it is a memory hog. The Recorder is an excellent product for creating simple macros.

Product:	SQZ Plus
Price:	$99.95
Category:	Commercial
Publisher:	Turner Hall Publishing
Address:	10201 Torre Avenue
	Cupertino, California 95014
Phone:	(408) 253-9600
Notes:	The add-in version requires 50K, plus the additional 20K used by the add-in manager.
	The memory resident version requires 40K.
	The add-in backup program requires 84K.
	The add-in keystroke recorder requires 38K.
Memory:	50K/40K

Worksheet Utilities

The *Worksheet Utilities* contains a number of useful features not covered in this book. I included it here only because it offers a file compression option.

The Worksheet Utilities do a poorer job of compressing files than SQZ PLUS. However, they use less memory and offer other features in that same memory.

Installation   The Worksheet Utilities comes with a very non-flexible installation routine. It automatically copies the add-in files to your Lotus subdirectory, supporting files to a \WKUTIL subdirectory off your Lotus subdirectory, and automatically installs the Worksheet Utilities to be automatically loaded.

Operation   The Worksheet Utilities use overlays to conserve memory. Each of the specific functions resides on disk. The program loads these overlays as needed. Rather than being loaded into virgin memory, it loads each utility you use into the memory used by the prior utility. That keeps memory requirements to a paltry 34K.

The file compression works from the FileWorks menu. As shown in Table 23-4 below, FileWorks does a good job of compressing the worksheets but falls far short of SQZ PLUS.

Limitations   The only real limitation of the package is its inflexible installation program.

File	Compressed Size	Normal Size	Reduction
ADDITION.WK1	38,968	146,727	73.4%
CAR.WK1	25,657	46,506	44.8%
DIVIDE.WK1	81,259	176,719	54.0%
MULTIPLY.WK1	81,301	176,721	54.0%
POWER.WK1	27,110	146,534	81.5%
SUBTRACT.WK1	40,216	146,728	72.6%

Manual   The manual is divided into three major parts, getting started, CellWorks, and FileWorks. The two programs have their own indexes and tables of contents. They are further divided by function. It is an unusual arrangement that takes some getting used to. After that, it works ok. The writing is clear and easy to follow, once you find the topic of interest.

Conclusion   This is about the perfect Lotus utility. Funk Software went out of their way to minimize the memory requirements. The result is a program so small you truly can auto-load it. However, a small program is only as good as what it does, and Worksheet Utilities does a lot. The File Editor alone is worth the price of the package. All of the other utilities are useful and easy to use.

Product:	Worksheet Utilities
Price:	$99.95
Category:	Commercial
Publisher:	Funk Software
Address:	222 Third Street
	Cambridge, Massachusetts
	02142
Phone:	(617) 497-6339
Memory:	70K-110K

RONNY'S PICKS

It is important to first decide if you need a file compression program. If you have a hard disk that is only half full, then compressing files will reduce backup times. There is also a tremendous advantage if you must transmit your files over a modem. Even if your hard disk is bulging, file compression programs will only work with data files. If you have mostly programs or games, they will not be much help to you.

Keep in mind that file compression programs effectively increase disk space (which is cheap) at the cost of RAM, which is limited to 640K and expensive. If you are running short of RAM either because you have less than 640K or you use a lot of memory resident software, then you need to be sure you can afford to give up the required RAM.

In addition, your compressed files will be useless if you damage your file compression program, so backups are important. Fortunately, none of the programs are copy protected.

24
Device Drivers to Emulate Expanded Memory

If you build large worksheets and have only 640K, then you occasionally get the dreaded "Memory Full" flashing red error message. You have three defenses against low memory without buying anything:

1) The first defense is to save the worksheet, /Worksheet Erase Yes, and retrieve the worksheet. Lotus is not very efficient in freeing memory when you delete data or convert formulae to values. It does, however, clean all that up when the worksheet is saved. I have seen dramatic improvements, with up to 200K reclaimed.

2) The second defense is to drop your add-ins. The nice thing about add-ins is most of them are so easy to drop through the add-in manager. When you drop an add-in, you reclaim almost all of the memory it was using immediately.

3) Your final defense is to save your worksheet, exit to DOS (/Quit Yes not /System), unload all your memory resident programs (PopDrop or Ramlord will help) and get back into Lotus.

If you do all this and still do not have enough memory, then you need to add expanded memory to your system. At one time memory was cheap and that was no big deal. Now, however, memory is expensive. Luckily, there is an alternative. Emulation programs use your hard disk or extended memory to emulate expanded memory.

WHAT EXPANDED MEMORY IS

Expanded memory is nothing more than a very old technique of bank-switching. Since DOS can address only 640K, part of that memory is used as a window to another set of memory. 64K is allocated for that purpose. That 64K is divided into four 16K "pages". Regardless of how much expanded memory you have, Lotus (or any other program using expanded memory) sees it as a series of 16K pages. The memory is switched in banks of 16K in and out of this 64K window. Anytime Lotus requests information from expanded memory that is not loaded in the 64K page, that memory location is switched into the 64K window while some other 16K page is switched out of memory.

Lotus does not do all this switching. If fact, Lotus does not know it is looking at memory in chunks. The job of managing the memory falls on the memory manager. All Lotus knows is that the memory is available when it requests it.

The time it takes the memory manager to switch banks of memory in and out of the window is the reason applications run slower when accessing expanded memory.

The advantage of this arrangement, with the memory manager acting as gatekeeper, makes the expanded memory specification almost device independent. These programs take advantage of that fact by "tricking" Lotus. Rather than switching data from expanded memory into and out of the 64K window, they swap data between the 64K page and your hard disk. Conventional expanded memory managers usually place this 64K window above conventional memory. Emulators cannot do that, therefore available conventional memory is reduced by 64K plus the size of the emulator's code.

Clearly, emulators will operate much slower. The overhead is the same. However, they are not making fast memory-to-memory swaps. Rather, they are making the much slower memory-to-disk and disk-to-memory swaps.

There are two things you will notice right away while running your spreadsheet under an expanded memory manager. First, as discussed above, it will run slower. Second, your hard disk light flickers on and off constantly especially while the spreadsheet is recalculating. You will want to turn off automatic recalculation.

USING EXTENDED MEMORY

Extended memory was reduced beginning with the IBM AT. While the AT could still only address 640K of conventional memory, it could address 15 Meg of extended memory. However, no programs were introduced to take advantage of extended memory.

There was a good reason. The AT BIOS included on minimal support for extended memory. The BIOS controls extended memory usage through interrupt 15h, the same one used for other little used features like cassette and joystick support. In order to transfer data to extended memory, the computer must be running in protected mode. Currently, DOS cannot run in protected mode, so the BIOS disables all interrupts while working with extended memory.

When the data transfer is complete, the BIOS must switch back to real mode and return control to the calling memory management program. However, the 80286 has no documented way to switch to real mode from protected mode except rebooting. The way IBM solved this problem was to have the BIOS leave a flag to signal to skip over the power-up procedures and then it reboots. It works, however, all this work slows down the emulating program using extended memory.

Using extended memory has two additional problems. First, since the computer is "out to lunch" in protected mode during transfers, background serial communications programs can lose data. The only way to avoid this is to transfer the data in very small blocks, 512-bytes or smaller. A second problem is the lack of memory management in protected mode. The BIOS supports being able to measure total extended memory but not how much is being used by other programs. The program has to do this itself.

LIMSIM

LIMSIM is an expanded memory emulator using only extended memory. Hard disks are not supported.

Installation The easy part of installing LIMSIM is copying LIMSIM.SYS to your root directory and adding a DEVICE=LIMSIM.SYS statement to your CONFIG.SYS file and if you are lucky, that is all you have to do. If you have a special configuration, like an extended memory application LIMSIM cannot detect, then the device line in your CONFIG.SYS file will require complex switches.

Operation LIMSIM allows Lotus and other programs to treat extended memory as though it were expanded memory.

Limitations Does not support a hard disk.

Manual The manual is very complete, down to a list of interrupts. However, it is very technical and not for the faint of heart.

Conclusion LIMSIM does an adequate job of simulating expanded memory.

Product:	LIMSIM
Price:	$65
Category:	Commercial
Publisher:	Larson Computing
Address:	1556 Halford Avenue
	#142
	Santa Clara, California 95051
Phone:	(408) 737-0627
Notes:	Source code is available for an additional $25
Memory:	70K

Above Disk

Above Disk is a expanded memory manager that will use either extended memory or a hard disk.

Installation   Above Disk requires both a device driver statement in your CONFIG.SYS file and loading a memory resident program, typically in your AUTOEXEC.BAT file. Above Disk has an installation program that will install the program and add the necessary command to your CONFIG.SYS file, however, you must modify your AUTOEXEC.BAT file yourself. The manual contains instructions on how to install Above Disk manually if you do not want the installation program to modify your CONFIG.SYS file, a nice touch.

Operation   Above Disk allows Lotus and other programs to treat extended memory and a hard disk as though they were expanded memory.

Limitations   As its default, Above Disk bypasses DOS I/O when accessing disk files. This can be dangerous, for example if you erase the disk file while Above Disk is active it can destroy data. The manual does warn about this problem and Above Disk can be switched to use standard DOS I/O.

Manual   The manual is complete and less technical than the manual for LIMSIM, however, it is still not easy going.

Conclusion   Above Disk does an adequate job of simulating expanded memory.

Product:	Above Disk
Price:	$99.95
Category:	Commercial
Publisher:	Above Software
	(Formerly Teleware West, Incorporated)
Address:	3 Hutton Centre
	Suite 950
	Santa Ana, California 92707
Phone:	(714) 545-1181
Memory:	Depends on the system configuration. On an 80286 machine, it will require between 1K and 78K. On an 80386 machine, it normally requires 14K.

VRAM

VRAM is an expanded memory manager that will use either extended memory or a hard disk.

Installation   There is no installation program. Installing VRAM involves copying VRAM.EXE to either a subdirectory in the PATH or to every subdirectory with a program that uses expanded memory. The process is explained in the manual.

Operation   VRAM requires no statements in either your CONFIG.SYS or

AUTOEXEC.BAT files. Rather, you start your application program with the command:

VRAM 123

That loads VRAM and starts Lotus. When you exit Lotus, you recover the memory VRAM was using.

Limitations   VRAM does not support extended memory directly. Rather, it has you use an extended memory RAM disk program, like VDISK which is included with many versions of DOS, to set a RAM disk. It then treats that RAM disk just as it treats the hard disk. That requires another software package and slightly reduces the memory available to VRAM since a RAM disk needs space for directories and its file allocation table.

Manual   The manual is less technical than the others.

Conclusion   VRAM does an adequate job of simulating expanded memory.

<table>
<tr><td>Product:</td><td>VRAM</td></tr>
<tr><td>Price:</td><td>$49</td></tr>
<tr><td>Category:</td><td>Commercial</td></tr>
<tr><td>Publisher:</td><td>Biologic Corporation</td></tr>
<tr><td>Address:</td><td>11982 Coverstone Hill Circle
Suite 1622
Manassas, Virginia 22110</td></tr>
<tr><td>Phone:</td><td>(703) 368-2949</td></tr>
<tr><td>Memory:</td><td>70K</td></tr>
</table>

RONNY'S PICK

386^{Max} provides expanded memory emulation using extended memory for 80386 computers. Many 386 computers, like the Compaq Deskpro 386, include their own custom expanded memory manager, CEMM.SYS for the Compaq. If you have an 80386 machine, these are the best solutions. If not, then LIMSIM is the best of these programs. However, most any expanded memory emulator will do an adequate job for most applications. Therefore, make your selection based on price and availability.

25
Alternatives To DOS

MULTITASKING AND
ALMOST-MULTITASKING OPERATING SYSTEMS

This is not going to be a detailed analysis of each of these programs. That is simply not possible in the limited space available to discuss them. In fact, most of these programs have entire books written about them. What I hope to accomplish is to give you insight into what each of these programs can and not do. I am going to try to give you enough information so you can decide if the programs are worth your following up on.

Multitasking is when a single user has the computer running more than one task. For example, you start a dBASE accounting program and start the month-end closing procedures. Even on your 80386 rocket, this takes three hours. Under DOS, you would have to sit there and wait on your machine for those three hours. If you were running under a multitasking operating system, you could immediately switch to your word processor to write memos. As you wrote, the machine would continue to run your accounting program—only it would run simultaneously and in the background.

There are basically two types of multitasking operating systems, those that will run on any machines and those that require an 80386. Whether it runs multiple applications by swapping the programs into and out of conventional memory on a non-80386 or it uses the virtual machines of the 80386, all multitasking programs face a major problem. Each application thinks it is running as the sole program. It expects to have full use of the keyboard, screen, ports, hard disk and so on. This is a special problem for the monitor because so many programs have chosen to ignore DOS and write directly to the screen.

None of these operating systems are a different operating system in the true sense of the word different. None of them requires special software. All of them can run "standard" DOS applications. They do differ in how well they run standard DOS programs. That was my main criteria in judging these programs.

EVALUATION CRITERIA

The criteria I used to judge the programs, in order of importance, were:

1) Compatibility. This was far and away the most important criteria. You need complete compatibility with your existing major applications. If you have to swap even one major application, then you are facing having to learn both a new operating system and a new application. I defined major applications as desktop publishing, word processing, databases, spreadsheets and graphics. I was concerned less with minor applications such as disk optimizers and file unerasing. These are generally not difficult to use and you rarely use them enough to become attached to a specific program. While I did some testing with memory resident [TSR] software, that did not enter into my evaluations. It is fairly easy and inexpensive to switch TSR applications. In addition, there are no standard rules for TSR software so it is almost impossible to be compatible with all of them.

2) Speed. You are going to pay a speed penalty. There is no way your computer can run two applications as fast as it can run one. However that penalty does not have to be large. While word processing, your computer spends most of its time waiting on you to press a key. The word processor gets no speed penalty if the computer uses that idle time to run the month-closing in the accounting package. When you run a more processor intensive application, the computer has less idle time to devote to the task running in the background. Of course, the slower the operating system, the less productive you are.

3) Ease of use. This includes three areas. First, how easy is it to get the program up and running? Second, how good is the documentation? And third, how close do the system commands resemble DOS commands? The closer they are, the less there is to learn.

PROGRAMS YOU SHOULD NOT MULTITASK

A few programs take such total control of your machine that you should never run them in a multitasking environment. Disk optimizers are a good example. You do not want your disk optimizer moving cluster 378 to cluster 221 while another program is trying to read cluster 221. Along the same vein, you do not want a program like Disk Technician trying to test cluster 221 at the same time another program is trying to read cluster 221.

Some programs require specific hardware while running. While multitasking programs will let programs share the computer and display, they do not allow the programs to share other peripherals. For example, you could not run two communications programs over one modem. You cannot have two programs printing to one printer. One of them is going to have to wait or use a print buffer.

It is generally easy to find good programs to run in the foreground. The real difficulty is finding good programs to run in the background. A good background task must be a program that runs for a long time without any user intervention and those are not common.

PROGRAMS THAT DO NOT REQUIRE AN 80386

DESQView

DESQView is an impressive multitasking environment that will run, albeit slowly, on a lowly 8088 with 640K.

Installation   DESQView comes with an installation program that will get you up and running if all you want to run are fairly standard applications. Configuring DESQView to run a program for which it does not contain defaults is a complex process.

When you install DESQView, the program scans the hard disk looking for programs it knows about. It automatically configures itself for the programs its finds and understands. They even show up in a menu.

Operation   DESQView is easy to get up and running. You can add the command to start DESQView to your AUTOEXEC.BAT file. You can build a custom DESQView script (very similar to an AUTOEXEC.BAT file) to automatically load programs into specific partitions. You can have a DESQView script that runs each time you start DESQView. You can have others that run each time you open a specific partition.

DESQView offers a great deal of flexibility, especially when run on an XT. In addition to swapping programs between conventional and extended or expanded memory, DESQView will swap them to the hard disk. As a result, DESQView will run on a machine with only 640K of conventional memory.

DESQView traps the Control-Alt-Delete sequence. Rebooting only closes the current window and brings up a DESQView menu. That makes it easier to escape from some lockups without losing the data you have in other partitions. Of course, it does not help when a program locks things up so bad you have to turn the machine off.

Compatibility   DESQView proved to be extremely compatible. I was able to load a number of programs in separate windows without conflicts. It did not have any problems when I loaded memory resident software in a memory. At one point, I even had Windows (another environment) running in one of its windows. DESQView does have minor problems running Microsoft Word in graphics mode in a window.

Speed   DESQView proved to be the fastest of all the non-80386 specific programs. It did not have any significant problems even when running normally slow programs like graphics programs.

DESQView devotes 55 milliseconds to the foreground task and then devotes 33 milliseconds between all the background tasks. As a result, the foreground task always seems to run at about half its usual speed. You can change this ratio if you like. You can also suspend background tasks if you are running a calculation intensive application in the foreground.

Ease of Use   DESQView is very flexible. You must write a PIF file for each application. The PIF file defines such things as how much memory it needs and if it is ok to swap that program out of memory. However, you only have to do this for programs the installation program does not recognize.

Once you have DESQView up and running, it runs fairly painlessly. It has a menu to perform the basic tasks like opening a window, changing window size and so on. This menu is especially nice because it only shows the letters for commands you can actually run at any point in time.

Limitations   If you manage to lock up a program running in one of the DESQView, you have lost all of your work in all of the windows. DESQView is not alone in this respect. This is a problem it shares with Windows and Software Carousel. In addition, it will allow you to close the entire environment even when there are windows that contain data you have not saved yet.

DESQView allows multiple programs to use the printer and other peripherals. However, DESQView makes no attempt to protect these peripherals. If two programs try to print at once, the printer will be printing some mixture of the output of these two programs. DESQView also has problems with the serial ports. It cannot swap a program out of the foreground if that program is using the serial port.

Manual   The contents of the document is excellent. The documentation contains every bit of the information you need to configure and run DESQView. Unfortunately, the documentation gets very technical at times. Users just starting are going to have a very difficult time learning DESQView.

DESQView Companions   DESQView comes without the extra tools many of the other packages include. Quarterdeck Office Systems does sell an additional program called DESQView Companions to overcome that. DESQView Companions includes four programs, a calculator, datebook, telecommunications and notepad. Only the notepad will function outside the DESQView environment. The other programs only work inside DESQView.

The calculator is a straightforward 10-key calculator with an optional tape display on the screen. You can also route the tape display to an ASCII file for use elsewhere. In addition to the standard mathematical operations, the calculator will convert numbers to percentages, take a square root and perform exponential calculations. It also has a single memory register.

The datebook is an on-line personal schedule. It has multiple calendars with dates through 2019. You enter your appointments in half-hour increments. The default times are 8AM to 7PM but you can change this. It will handle repeating appointments. For example, if you enter a doctor's appointment for 4PM on Wednesday, you can have the program repeat that appointment for every Wednesday. You can configure the program to beep for any of the appointments. Finally, the datebook has a flexible print option and it can print to an ASCII file.

The telecommunications program, called Link, is a full-featured communications program with macro script processing. Since it will run completely in the background, you can write scripts to log on and get your e-mail or download large files all while you do something else on the computer.

The notepad program is typical of this type of program. It edits files up to 64K, creates ASCII files and supports the more important word processing functions. The only real drawback to the notepad program is its poor printer support.

There is a separate manual for each DESQView Companions program. These manuals are easy to follow, just like the DESQView manual.

Conclusion   Like most multitasking environments, you will find it fairly difficult to get DESQView up and running. This is especially true if you have a non-standard clone or you are running a non-standard application. Once running properly, DESQView performs very well.

```
Product:      DESQView
Price:        $129.95
Category:     Commercial
Publisher:    Quarterdesk Office Systems
Address:      150 Pico Boulevard
              Santa Monica, California 90405
Phone:        (213) 392-9851
Memory:       170K
```

Double DOS

DoubleDOS is a multitasking program that lets you run two programs at once. Both programs plus DoubleDOS must fit into conventional memory.

Installation   DoubleDOS comes with an installation program that will automatically install the software. If you want DoubleDOS installed in a subdirectory, you must create and log into that subdirectory before running the installation program.

Operation   DoubleDOS is exactly what the name claims, it lets you run two-and only two-programs at once. DoubleDOS does not swap anything to memory or disk so both programs and DoubleDOS must fit into 640K of conventional memory. That effectively limits you to one regular program and one utility or two small programs.

Compatibility   DoubleDOS has a lot of minor compatibility programs. The disk is full of patch files to fix the most popular programs so they will run under DoubleDOS. As a rule, these patches do not change the ability of the program to run as a stand-alone program without DoubleDOS. SoftLogic has many more patches available than would fit on the disk. They invite DoubleDOS users to call them for any patches they need but which were not on the distribution disk.

Speed   DoubleDOS has trouble keeping up with a fast typist. That makes the program seem slower than it really is. Otherwise, the speed is acceptable.

Ease of Use   The numerous patch files make it fairly difficult to get Double-DOS up and running. Once running, using the program is fairly painless. You instantly switch between the two environments using the Alt-Escape key. If either environment begins to run out of memory, you can easily shift free memory from the other environment using a DoubleDOS configuration memory.

Limitations   DoubleDOS is fairly old technology. The review copy SoftLogic sent me in late 1988 has a sticker on the packages saying "NEW!! for 1987." DoubleDOS does not support VGA, extended memory or expanded memory. DoubleDOS has simply let technology pass it by.

Manual   The manual is poorly written and difficult to follow.

Conclusion   DoubleDOS is inexpensive but has little else going for it. Its current version has let technology pass it by to such an extent that the other multitasking programs are far superior.

<table>
<tr><td>Product:</td><td>DoubleDOS</td></tr>
<tr><td>Price:</td><td>$69.95</td></tr>
<tr><td>Category:</td><td>Commercial</td></tr>
<tr><td>Publisher:</td><td>SoftLogic Solutions, Incorporated</td></tr>
<tr><td>Address:</td><td>One Perimeter Road
Manchester, New Hampshire 03103</td></tr>
<tr><td>Phone:</td><td>(603) 627-9900
(800) 272-9900 (orders)</td></tr>
<tr><td>Notes:</td><td>SoftLogic Solutions has released a much improved upgrade to DoubleDOS. It was not released it time to review for this book.</td></tr>
<tr><td>Memory:</td><td>128K</td></tr>
</table>

Windows

Microsoft *Windows* is a graphics-based multitasking environment from the same company that produces DOS itself.

Installation   Windows comes with an installation program that will lead even the most inexperienced user through installing the program. That installation program is extremely flexible in allowing users to select their exact combination of hardware. Depending on your hardware configuration and computer speed, the installation program can take up to an hour. Changing equipment configuration, admittedly something you do not do very often, requires that you run the entire installation program over again.

Compatibility   Windows will run most stand-alone programs without compatibility problems. In fact, more and more programs are being designed with a Windows mode or to run under runtime Windows. For example, *PageView,*

PageMaker and Excel all run using a runtime version of Windows. They will all also run under regular Windows.

Speed   Windows had trouble running some programs in the background. Windows would not run any program that writes directly to the screen in the background. It also had trouble running large programs not written specifically for Windows in the background. Small, well-behaved programs ran fine in the background.

Ease of Use   Windows does more than offer a multitasking environment. It also defines a form of interface between the computer and the user. This interface is different from DOS and can take a long time to learn. However, many applications written especially for Windows use this same interface. As a result, Windows users can often pick up a new Windows-specific program and begin using it immediately without any training or reading at all. Windows-specific programs are available in most major categories, including word processing, graphics, spreadsheets and database. As a result, once a user learns Windows, they can run most types of programs without additional training.

Before you can run a non-Windows-specific application, you must first create a PIF file [Program Information File] for that program. Windows comes with PIF files for many popular programs like Lotus 1-2-3 and dBASE. For less popular programs, you will have to create the file yourself. Microsoft includes a PIF editor to help you with that task. The PIF file gives Windows important information on the program like how much memory it wants and if it writes directly to the screen. The PIF editor makes creating the files as easy as filling in the blanks. However, figuring out what actually goes in the blocks is a difficult and error-prone process. To make matters worse, many errors will cause the system to hang without an error message when you try to run that application.

Other Applications   Windows includes a number of additional programs at no charge. It includes:

- a calculator.
- a calendar.
- a clock.
- a communications program.
- a drawing program.
- a limited database that stores records of graphical representations of index cards.
- a limited word processor.
- a program that allows you to transfer data between different programs running under Windows.
- an Othello game clone.

Limitations   The Windows Clipboard has limited memory. In Windows, you use the Clipboard to transfer text and graphics between programs. To transfer graphics, you load Clipboard and then start the graphics program. When the graph you want to transfer is on the screen, you press Control-Print Screen to send the contents of the screen into the Clipboard. However, Windows does not allocate enough memory to the Clipboard to capture EGA or VGA screens. Clipboard will not do a partial capture so you cannot transfer full page graphics on an EGA or VGA machine. Windows/386 does not have this problem.

Windows is difficult to use without a mouse. Windows does have Alt-keystroke combinations for most of its operations. However, they are often very cumbersome. You really need a mouse to navigate through Windows.

Manual   The manual is a mixed-bag. It does a very good job of explaining how to use Windows. It does a fair job of explaining how to use the Windows applications included with the program. It does a poor job of explaining how to interface Windows with other programs. The manual often leaves you to try a hit-or-miss approach.

Conclusion   Windows is a good multitasking environment if you are running applications written for Windows. If you want to run programs not written specifically for Windows, it is lacking a lot.

Product:	Windows
Price:	$99.95
Category:	Commercial
Publisher:	Microsoft Corporation
Address:	16011 NE 36th Way
	Redmond, Washington 98073
Phone:	(206) 882-8080
Notes:	The price includes all the
	Windows applications
	programs discussed above.
Memory:	512K

PROGRAMS THAT REQUIRE AN 80386

The 80386 programs take advantage of a special feature of the 80386 chip, called virtual mode. Virtual mode allows the 80386 chip to run multiple DOS sessions at once, each in its own memory partition—or so called virtual machine. The chip mimics the 1 Meg memory addressing limit and the register set for the 8086 using a protected-mode mask. The chip can handle interrupts and exceptions in the same fashion as an 8086. Because each virtual machine needs the same logical starting address to mimic an 8086, virtual mode uses the paging feature of the 80386 to map each virtual machine to a different physical address. This lets each virtual machine have the same 640K memory map for its program and data space. This lets 80386-specific programs offer true multitasking by running each program as though it was running on its own 8086 machine.

Part of configuring a virtual machine is providing each virtual machine with a virtual display. With a virtual display, each virtual machine gets its very own display. That means that ill-behaved programs can write directly to screen memory without overwriting other programs. The operating system occasionally copies the contents of the virtual display to the real physical display for the program(s) you are viewing on the screen.

80386 machines have another advantage. You add memory to AT machines by adding a special memory board. Then you have to worry about setting DIP switches to properly allocate conventional, extended and expanded memory. On an 80386 machine, the chip can manage the memory itself. That is what drives the 386^{Max} program. (See Chapter 19 for more details.)

All this combines into one simple fact. 80386-only multitasking programs are far superior to other multitasking programs. In fact, the better non-chip-specific multitasking programs are not as good as the poorer 80386-specific ones.

Concurrent DOS 386

Concurrent DOS 386 is a multitasking and multiuser operating system for the company that developed CP/M. It only runs on 80386 machines.

Installation   Installing Concurrent DOS 386 is painless. You boot off the distribution floppy disk and press F10. The installation program will ask you which drive to use for the software. The installation program automatically creates the subdirectory and copies the files. Most files go to the subdirectory. A few system files go to the root directory. It modifies your AUTOEXEC.BAT file so it prompts you each time you boot to see if you want to run DOS or Concurrent DOS 386. After this, you must run a configuration program to tell Concurrent DOS 386 about your printers, plotters, multiport expansion cards and so on.

The above configures Concurrent DOS 386 to run in conjunction with DOS. That is the way most users will use it. However, Concurrent DOS 386 is a stand-alone operating system in its own right. It can format your hard disk with up to a 512 Meg partition and install itself without DOS. That way, you always get Concurrent DOS 386 when you boot.

In either case, while Concurrent DOS 386 is active you can run either DOS or CP/M 86 applications alone or at the same time. CP/M 86 programs end with a CMD (CoMmanD) extension and are given order preference. That is, it runs a .CMD file instead of a .COM or .EXE file of the same name if you just enter the name. Concurrent DOS 386 can read, write and format both DOS and CP/M 86 disks.

Operation   In addition to running multiple programs on one machine, Concurrent DOS 386 allows multiple users to share the same computer. Of course, each user must have their own "dumb terminal." The host user can run four programs and each remote user can run two. However, the remote users will see very slow operations. Unless they need to share hardware, each remote user would be better off with a fast 8088 clone.

Each Concurrent DOS 386 virtual machine gets its own full window. In the currently active window, Concurrent DOS 386 displays little more than a system prompt. In that respect, it is much like DOS itself. The application on the screen is the foreground application. It can use the keyboard and write to the screen. The other background applications can be running concurrently or just waiting for you to use them. Each partition is independent. You can even load memory resident software in each partition. You switch between different partitions by pressing Alt-number, where the number assigned to the partition you want to switch to.

You can assign a startup file (the CP/M 86 equivalent of an AUTOEXEC. BAT file) to each partition. Concurrent DOS 386 uses these to automatically configure the different partitions. There is only one CP/M 86 version of the CONFIG.SYS file. It uses this file to configure the entire system.

The multitasking capabilities of Concurrent DOS 386 are limited to text-based programs. Concurrent DOS 386 can only run one graphics program and it must stay in the foreground. To switch to another program, you must first exit your graphics program. Of course, the text-based programs continue to run in the background.

While running multiple applications under Concurrent DOS 386, you can dynamically allocate memory where it is needed. Each program takes the memory it needs from a pool of memory and leaves the remaining memory for other programs.

Compatibility   Concurrent DOS 386 has moderately serious compatibility problems. It runs the standard programs, like WordStar and Lotus 1-2-3, without any problems. However, it will not run any Windows programs including those that use runtime Windows. Those programs include PageView, Page-Maker and Excel. In addition, Concurrent DOS 386 will not run some communications programs because it traps serial port interrupts. You cannot use several DOS programs, including FORMAT.COM. You must use the version supplied with Concurrent DOS 386. It does not support some undocumented DOS functions. Some major software packages use these and will not run under Concurrent DOS 386. Microsoft Word 4.0 is the best known example. However, Word 3.1 runs fine under Concurrent DOS 386.

Some programs make calls to COMMAND.COM while running. COMMAND.COM is not part of Concurrent DOS 386. To support these calls, Concurrent DOS 386 includes its own version of COMMAND.COM called CDOS.COM. You have to run CDOS.COM before running any programs that call on COMMAND.COM.

Speed   Programs ran noticeably slower on Concurrent DOS 386 than on the other operating systems. Concurrent DOS 386 uses a straight time slicing approach to give each partition time to run. Each active partition gets 1/60 of a second then Concurrent DOS 386 moves on to the next partition. Each active partition gets 1/60 of a second even if it is idling waiting on keyboard input. As a result, if you load up three active partitions, each one runs at 33% of its normal speed.

The default for each partition is to suspend (stop it from running) that partition when you switch to another partition. Used in the default mode, Concurrent DOS 386 becomes a task switching program. You can issue a SUSPEND=OFF command in any partition you want to run in the background. The startup program can also do this for you.

Ease of Use   The operating system itself is very much a DOS clone. Commands function just like they would under DOS. The few discrepancies are minor and sometimes are things most users will not notice. For example, the COPY command is really a separate program rather than an internal command. Nevertheless, it works the same. A few of the infrequently used commands; like CTTY, EXE2BIN and SHARE; are missing. Most users will not notice.

Concurrent DOS 386 includes a number of new "DOS" commands. There are commands to maintain a password, reboot the system and program the function keys. Concurrent DOS 386 maintains a history of the commands you have entered. You can scroll through prior commands using the up and down arrows.

Other Applications   Concurrent DOS 386 includes several utility programs at no additional charge. They are:

- File Manager. This is a DOS shell program that lets you select most of the commonly used Concurrent DOS 386 commands from a menu. It divides the screen into three parts. One part shows the more important commands. A second part lists files and subdirectories to select from. The third part gives help messages on the command you select.
- Print Manager. This is a print queue. It will queue up to 254 print jobs. It assigns each job a number. Users can delete a file from the print queue using this number. The Print Manager lets you control margins, print format, number of copies and so on.
- DR Edix. This is the Concurrent DOS 386 ASCII editor, in the same vein as Edlin is the DOS editor. While Edlin is a limited function line editor, DR Edix is a full-screen WYSIWYG (what you see is what you get) editor that can edit up to four files at once.
- Cardfile. This is a difficult to use name, address and phone number database program.

Limitations   Concurrent DOS 386 is not as stable as it should be. It sometimes crashes when you load memory resident program or when a remote user tries to run a graphics program. Several times, the crash erased the setup memory in the computer.

Concurrent DOS 386 has no built-in file-locking ability. Rather, it depends on the applications you are running to lock any files that open themselves.

It has problems with programs that write directly to the video memory rather that through DOS. This causes applications to "bleed through" on top of one another. Lotus is one of the worse offenders. Lotus did such a "good job" of overpowering the screen that it proved impossible to leave Lotus running in the background. When Lotus was running in the background, it would completely overwrite the screen so you ended up with a Lotus display on the screen. However, the foreground program still had control of the keyboard. The foreground program was running, you just could not see it.

Manual   The manual is very good. It has a number of screen shots so you know what to expect. There are separate manuals for a couple of sticky topics like reinstallation and 80386-specific commands.

Conclusion   Concurrent DOS 386 is more expensive and slower than the other multitasking programs. It also has much more trouble keeping background tasks from bleeding through onto the screen. However, it offers CP/M 86 compatibility not found in any of the other programs.

<table>
<tr><td>Product:</td><td>Concurrent DOS 386</td></tr>
<tr><td>Price:</td><td>$395.00-Three User System
$495.00-Four User System</td></tr>
<tr><td>Category:</td><td>Commercial</td></tr>
<tr><td>Publisher:</td><td>Digital Research, Inc.</td></tr>
<tr><td>Address:</td><td>70 Garden Court
Monterey, California 93940</td></tr>
<tr><td>Phone:</td><td>(800) 443-4200
(408) 649-3896</td></tr>
<tr><td>Notes:</td><td>The $395 version supports up to eight multitasking programs to run at once. These can be spread among up to three users. A $495 version supports up to 22 multitasking programs running among up to ten users.</td></tr>
<tr><td>Memory:</td><td>512K</td></tr>
</table>

DESQView/386

DESQView running on an 80386 is really the standard DESQView with Quarterdeck's Expanded Memory Manager [QEMM] added, or *DESQView/386* for short. QEMM allows the standard DESQView program to take advantage of the virtual memory mode of the 80386 chip.

In many respects, DESQView/386 is nothing more than DESQView with more memory on a faster machine. QEMM does make setting up DESQView/386 much easier than DESQView. The QEMM automatically takes care of configuring and assigning the memory. You do not have to do that manually. The virtual memory mode of the 80386 makes it less likely that locking up one window will lock up all the applications. However, it does not eliminate the problem.

QEMM manages to store its own code in the areas between 640K and 1 Meg. It also allows you to put DESQView code there as well. That increases the conventional memory that is available for each window. Part of the memory between 640K and 1 Meg is used for the display adapter so the exact memory savings depends on your display mode.

DESQView/386 was the only 80386-specific multitasking program that could run programs designed to run only on an 80386 machine. DESQView/386 successfully ran Paradox 386 and FoxBASE 386 without a hitch. No other multitasking program could do that.

DESQView/386 comes with three manuals in place of the single DESQView manual. One is the DESQView manual, the second is a manual of QEMM and a third is a manual on the combination. The arrangement is confusing. Sometimes the DESQView/386 manual has the information you need. Other times you must switch to the DESQView manual.

Product:	DESQView/386
Price:	$189.90
Category:	Commercial
Publisher:	Quarterdesk Office Systems
Address:	150 Pico Boulevard
	Santa Monica, California 90405
Phone:	(213) 392-9851
Notes:	Price is $129.95 for DESQView
	and $59.95 for QEMM
Memory:	1.5 Meg

Windows/386

Windows/386 is a special version of Windows customized for the 80386 chip. It suffers similar problems as Windows in multitasking non-Windows programs. Many programs either will not run in the background or slow the system to a crawl while running in the background. Unlike Windows, the virtual 80386 mode Windows/386 uses makes it almost impossible to lose all your data by locking up one window. Windows/386 includes a terminate function to help you recover if a window locks up.

Windows has a provision for Dynamic Data Exchange [DDE] between programs. DDE lets programs exchange data automatically without user intervention. However, the only major program currently supporting DDE is Excel so this feature is not yet very useful.

Windows/386 uses time slicing to run each application and each application gets about equal time. However, Windows/386 is smart enough so it does not give any time to applications that are idling or waiting on input. You cannot change the way Windows/386 allocates time to the various applications.

Product:	Windows/386
Price:	$195.00
Category:	Commercial
Publisher:	Microsoft Corporation
Address:	16011 NE 36th Way
	Redmond, Washington 98073
Phone:	(206) 882-8080
Notes:	The price includes all the
	Windows applications
	programs discussed above.
Memory:	2 Meg

RONNY'S PICKS FOR MULTITASKING

To some degree, you can get multitasking without any of these programs. Print buffers store output and feed it to the printer slowly so you can get back to your applications. That is a form of multitasking. Some communications programs will also run in the background, effectively multitasking.

Beyond printing and transmitting large files, most of us do not need multitasking. Even in a corporate office, it is rare for a task to grab a computer and keep it tied up for hours without needing human interaction. Yet that is exactly the type of application it takes to effectively run in the background. If the background program needs constant input, then you spend so much of your time switching that you end up saving nothing over running each task sequentially.

Other programs with multitasking are today's applications. While the multitasking operating systems can force them to run in the background, the operating systems cannot force them to take advantage of the environment. A program designed to run effectively in the background would make it easy on you to quickly queue up any of tasks to run. If those tasks required intervention, it would go ahead and ask its questions during setup. That way, once you were finished queueing tasks, it could run in the background without needing anything from you. Currently, programs do not work that way.

Quite frankly, unless you have applications you start on the computer then walk away for hours while they run unattended, you are probably not going to benefit much from multitasking. Having said that, if you still want a multitasking program, you should get the best one for your needs.

Both DESQView/386 and Windows/386 ran much better and faster than did their 8088/80286 cousins on the same machines. If you have an 80386 machine, you should purchase an 80386-specific program. None of these programs are crash-free. You will spend a significant amount of time as you begin to use either of these programs resolving problems. You cannot avoid that so plan for it. Do not try to get a new environment up and running when on a deadline.

DESQView/386 is faster and less problem prone than Windows/386. DESQView is faster and less problem prone than Concurrent DOS 386. DESQView is also faster and less problem prone than Windows. However, Windows and Windows/386 use an interface that is becoming more popular. In addition, a number of popular programs, like Excel and PageMaker, use the Windows format.

If you want to multitask DOS applications, then DESQView is the best choice. If you run Windows-specific applications, then Windows is a better choice. For multiuser applications, Concurrent DOS 386 is your best choice.

TASK SWITCHING

At first glance, you might tell little difference between multitasking and task switching. Both swap programs around inside the computer. However, there is an important difference. With multitasking, all of the programs are getting attention from the processor. While it may be running only one program at a time, it switches between them rapidly and simulates all of them running at once.

The computer does not do that with *task switching.* Rather, only the program in the foreground runs. The advantage of a task switching program is it has several programs loaded and ready to run. You can switch rapidly between programs at the touch of a key or two. That gives you additional flexibility in using the computer. And giving you that extra flexibility is the purpose of task switching.

In a very real sense, the market is jammed with task-specific task switching programs. Any memory resident program worth its salt will pop up no matter what the computer and its primary application are doing. That is task switching. You are in the middle of running a three hour simulation but need to write a quick memo so you pop up Sidekick and start writing. Task switching programs just give that ability to most any generic program.

Task switching has another advantage. There is a fairly small limit to the number of memory resident programs you can load. They are limited because you have to leave enough conventional memory to load your applications. One way around that limitation is with a memory resident manager like Headroom or RAMLord. Chapter 19 covers these. Another solution are these task switching programs.

Software Carousel

Software Carousel is a task-switching environment. It gives you an easy way to switch between multiple programs.

Installation   Software Carousel comes with an installation program that will automatically install the software. If you want Software Carousel installed in a subdirectory, you must create and log into that subdirectory before running the installation program.

Operation   Software Carousel lets you load up to 10 applications. Each application can get up to 500K each. Since your computer does not have $500*10=5,000K$ of conventional memory, it swaps the programs to disk or to extended or expanded memory. You then select between the different programs using the Alt-Function key combination. If you forget what is where, Alt-Space bar brings up a menu that shows what you have loaded in each partition and how much memory it uses.

In its configuration file, you can define a batch file for it to run the first time it switches to a partition. That is an easy way to configure Software Carousel to load specific software into that partition automatically. It traps the Control-Alt-Delete sequence so you cannot reboot in a partition. That is a plus because a reboot would lose everything in all the partitions.

Compatibility   Software Carousel ran every program I loaded without any problem except Windows applications.

Speed   Because Software Carousel does not multitask programs, the computer is able to devote most of its time to the current task. (Software Carousel takes a little time.) Therefore, programs run at about the same speed under Software Carousel as they do under DOS.

Ease of Use   Software Carousel is extremely easy to use. The only thing you need to know to set it up is how much memory each program needs. Once it is running, you switch between applications using Alt-Function key. Of course, part of the ease of use comes from it doing less than a multitasking program like DESQView.

Limitations   Software Carousel would not allow you to switch out of a Windows application unless you completely exit Windows first. This is especially bothersome when running a program like Excel that uses runtime Windows. The selection of the Alt-Function key hot-keys is a poor choice. Many programs use those so you may have to redefine the Software Carousel hot-keys.

Software Carousel will not multitask. The only program that is executing is the one in the foreground. None of the background programs run until you switch them into the foreground.

Manual   The documentation is brief but it does an adequate job of explaining how to use Software Carousel. Of course, part of this comes from it doing less than a multitasking program like DESQView.

Conclusion   Software Carousel is an inexpensive program that gives users an easy way to switch between tasks. Software Carousel is a solid program that has been around long enough to shake off most of its bugs.

Product:	Software Carousel
Price:	$79.95
Category:	Commercial
Publisher:	Softlogic Solutions, Incorporated
Address:	1 Perimeter Road
	Manchester, New Hampshire 03103
Phone:	(800) 272-9900
	(603) 627-9900
Memory:	32K

Switch-It

Like Software Carousel, *Switch-It* is a task-switching environment. Switch-It lets you easily switch between two DOS programs.

Installation   Switch-It does not have an installation program. The manual adequately explains how to install Switch-It.

Operation   The Switch-It SI command loads Switch-It into memory, sets up two partitions and divides the conventional memory between the two partitions. By default, the second partition gets 128K and the first partition gets the remaining memory. You can change this allocation any way you like using a command-line switch. There is also a command line switch to cause Switch-It to run a batch file called AUTOSW.BAT the first time you switch to the second partition.

Compatibility   Every program I tested would run in a Switch-It partition if it had enough memory.

Speed   Because Switch-It does not multitask programs, the computer is able to devote most of its time to the current task. (Switch-It takes a little time.) Therefore, programs run at about the same speed under Switch-It as they do under DOS.

Ease of Use   Switch-It is very easy to use. Other than have less memory, each partition works just like DOS. As a result, using Switch-It requires very little learning. You can literally have Switch-It up and running in fifteen minutes.

Limitations   Switch-It keeps both programs plus its own code all in conventional memory. That greatly limits the size of programs you can run. It would be impossible to run a spreadsheet in one partition and a large database program in another, 640K is simply not enough memory.

Switch-It is not able to restore the screen properly with some graphics programs that run in EGA or VGA mode. Unless the programs you are running have a command to redraw the screen, you may find the screen unreadable after switching partitions.

Switch-It has no built-in protection to keep both partitions from accessing the same files. While the two partitions are not multitasking, this is still a problem. If programs in both partitions open the same file and write to it, the first program writing to the file will have its file overwritten by the second. This has the potential for other nasty problems.

Switch-It will not multitask. The only program that is executing is the one in the foreground. None of the background programs run until you switch them into the foreground.

Manual   The manual is clear, easy to read and easy to follow.

Conclusion   Switch-It is a fairly inexpensive program that lets you switch between two applications. Only the application in the foreground is running and both applications must fit into 640K.

Product:	Switch-It
Price:	$84.00
Category:	Commercial
Publisher:	Vusoft, Incorporated
Address:	248 Tower Road
	Lincoln, Massachusetts 01773
Phone:	(617) 259-0686
Memory:	36K

RONNY'S PICKS FOR TASK SWITCHING

Headroom (Chapter 19) is a memory resident manager like Extra or RAMLord. Its primary purpose is to swap memory resident software into and out of memory. That lets you load and use more memory resident software than you have room for in conventional memory. However, Headroom also lets you load conventional programs into its partitions. That means it is also a task switching program. It is fairly new and not nearly as solid as Software Carousel. However, it has some very strong points that make it worth a hard look. If you want something solid for switching between a bunch of programs, then Software Carousel is the best choice. Switch-It would be good for keeping small programs in memory almost as memory resident programs. For example, if you have a small ASCII editor, you could load it into the second Switch-It partition and easily go to it to write a quick note. This is, in fact, how the memory resident Boston Documentation for DOS (Chapter 1) stays memory resident.

CommandPlus

CommandPlus is a complete replacement for the DOS COMMAND.COM file.

Installation   Installation is a two step process. First, you must copy the necessary files onto your boot disk. Second, you must add the necessary commands to start CommandPlus. The manual explains both steps but there is no installation program.

For the second step, you have two choices. First, you can load Command-Plus as a shell on top of COMMAND.COM. It still replaces COMMAND.COM, only COMMAND.COM is still in memory. This is the easiest way to get CommandPlus up and running and probably the safest until you are used to it.

The second way to load CommandPlus is using a SHELL= statement in your CONFIG.SYS file. This way, the computer never loads COMMAND.COM. That is fairly easy to do and the manual explains the process; however, there is one problem. Make even one tiny mistake on this line and the computer will not load any command processor. When that happens, you cannot boot the computer. The only way around this is to boot from a floppy diskette. Before modifying the SHELL= line of your CONFIG.SYS file, you should have a boot disk ready just in case. The manual does warn you about this. An even better way is to test your new CONFIG.SYS file on a floppy disk and only transfer it to your hard disk once you know it works.

Operation   Loading CommandPlus in place of COMMAND.COM is not a complete replacement of DOS. To see why, you need to know the steps the computer performs when booting. They are:

1)   The BIOS resets and tests the hardware.
2)   The BIOS loads the DOS bootstrap program into memory and turns control over to it. The bootstrap program is not an intelligent program. All it does is figure out which disk to boot from and reads the operating system from a specific location on that disk.
3)   The bootstrap program loads the two DOS hidden files into memory and turns control over to them. These two files are called IBMBIO.COM and IBMDOS.COM under IBM DOS 4.01. Different versions of DOS by different vendors will have slightly different names. These are the two files transferred by the SYS command. They must be at a specific location on the

disk. If that area is already in use, the SYS command will tell you there is no room for the system on the disk. This can happen even if there is lots of empty space on the disk.

4) DOS processes the CONFIG.SYS file. It sets up room for any BUFFERS = and FILES = statements and loads any device driver.

5) Finally, it loads the command processor specified by the SHELL = statement. If there is no SHELL = statement, it loads COMMAND.COM.

DOS does not load CommandPlus until step 5. As a result, most of DOS gets loaded. That is one reason why almost all programs work fine under CommandPlus, they are still seeing much of DOS. As explained above, you can also load COMMAND.COM normally in the CONFIG.SYS file then load Command-Plus on top of this. Functionally, the two methods produce very similar results. I did most of my reviewing with CommandPlus loaded in the CONFIG.SYS file.

While replacing COMMAND.COM is technically interesting and in this case improves the way DOS works, it is important that the replacement does not cause compatibility problems. After loading CommandPlus, I ran every program I could get my hands on. They all worked. I could not document one single case of incompatibility. Even programs that work very closely with DOS, like disk optimizers and hard disk testing programs, worked identically under CommandPlus.

CommandPlus improves almost all of the DOS commands and functions. While these are too numerous for me to mention them all, I will list the ones I found most useful. They are. . .

Set Alias. With CommandPlus, you can define the equivalent of a keyboard macro for the operating system. For example, the command:

ALIAS D DIR *.DOC /W /P

would configure a new command called ''D'' that was equivalent to the ''DIR * >DOC /W /P'' command. This is an extremely powerful feature. Command-Plus even allows you to use replaceable parameters in the alias.

Command Disabling. CommandPlus uses its alias feature to temporarily disable commands. The commands:

ALIAS FORMAT -
ALIAS DEL -
ALIAS ERASE -

would disable three destructive commands many beginners have a lot of trouble with. You could add any number of these commands to the AUTOEXEC script file to restrict access to any commands. CommandPlus does not limit this command restricting to system commands. You can stop access to any .EXE, .COM or .BAT file this way. This is a great way for experts setting up systems for beginners to control what the beginners can do.

SET Variable Editing. Under DOS, if you want to edit the value of any of your environmental variables, you have to completely enter the new value. For example, to add a subdirectory to your PATH you have to enter the entire

PATH statement. With CommandPlus, you enter the name and press Control-E to exit the value of that variable.

Command Logging. CommandPlus can record what commands the user runs and at what time. It stores this information in a log file.

Subdirectory Storage. CommandPlus can store up to five subdirectory names in a stack. You push a directory into the stack to store it and pop a directory from the stack to use it. Using this, a script file can start in any subdirectory and return to that subdirectory even if it has to move around the disk.

Multiple Command on One Line. With CommandPlus, you can enter multiple commands at once by separating the commands with an ampersand.

Command Storage. CommandPlus stores DOS commands as you use them. You can scroll through old commands using the up and down arrows. CommandPlus has intelligent commands to control this storage area. You can set the number of commands to store, prevent specific commands from entering storage, clear the storage area and turn the recording on and off.

Multiple Arguments. Most CommandPlus commands accept wildcards and multiple arguments. For example, the command . . .

TYPE *.BAT CHAPTER1.CMP *.TXT

would be completely legal under CommandPlus.

You can run most of your DOS batch files under CommandPlus. The exceptions are any batch files that load memory resident software and any that use environmental variables. With one exception, CommandPlus loads another processor to handle batch files. If it is a DOS .BAT file, CommandPlus loads COMMAND.COM to run the batch file. If it is a CommandPlus .S script file, CommandPlus loads a script processor. Either way, memory resident software interferes with CommandPlus's ability to regain control after the processor finishes handling the batch or script file. The single exception is the AUTOEXEC.S script file. CommandPlus processes this file automatically when first loaded without the script processor. As a result, you either load your memory resident software in the AUTOEXEC.S file at boot time or you have to enter the commands manually.

When DOS or CommandPlus loads another program to run, that program gets a full copy of the environment. That copy is called a child and the original is the parent. When the operating system first loads the program, the parent and child environments are identical. If the program makes any changes to the environment, those changes are in the child. When the program terminates, the operating system discards the child environment and the parent regains control. As a result, you lose any changes made to the child. Since CommandPlus loads COMMAND.COM to process batch files, environment variable modifications made by the batch file are reflected only in the child environment. When COMMAND.COM returns control to CommandPlus, you lose those changes.

Note that under DOS, batch files modify the environment directly and you do not lose their changes when the batch file terminates. Since CommandPlus loads a script processor to run its script files, those script files can only modify a child's copy of the environment. Under CommandPlus, the only way to permanently modify the environmental variables is either from the keyboard or in the AUTOEXEC.S special script file.

CommandPlus has script files that are far more powerful than the batch files in DOS. The script programming language looks very much like a small Basic language. It is possible to write extremely powerful script files with CommandPlus.

Some programs give you the option of entering a single command for them to run rather than temporarily exiting to DOS. For example, in Microsoft Word you can enter a command with Escape Library Run. I have got in the habit of entering "COMMAND" as the command for this type of program to run. That loads a second copy of COMMAND.COM and lets me work in DOS until I enter the EXIT command. I tried that with Microsoft Word running under CommandPlus, and it worked. That gave me CommandPlus loaded, then Microsoft Word and then COMMAND.COM loaded on top of all that. The very fact it worked indicates the high degree of compatibility between CommandPlus and COMMAND.COM.

Limitations   A lot of normal DOS internal commands, like DIR, are external commands in CommandPlus. That means you make sure they are always in your PATH. It also means they run noticeably slower than their DOS equivalents.

While CommandPlus improves many DOS commands, it keeps some of the dreadful DOS limits. Like DOS, it limits command lines to 127 characters. Because CommandPlus can enter multiple commands on one line, that is an even more painful limit. Like DOS, CommandPlus limits the type-ahead buffer to 12 characters. That is partially offset since CommandPlus can recall past commands.

You will have to rewrite many of your batch files to run under CommandPlus. Under CommandPlus, you cannot use any batch or script file except the AUTOEXEC script file to load memory resident software. When you run a batch file, CommandPlus shells to COMMAND.COM to run the batch file. That means any SET variables set in the batch file are lost after the batch file terminates. Batch files that call other batch files do not work properly either. Batch files seem to be about the only area where you are going to have to spend any time converting your computer over to CommandPlus.

Manual   The manual needs some work. All the information is there; however, the manual is printed in tiny type that strains your eyes to read. In addition, the manual is moderately difficult to read and understand. I estimate it is only slightly more difficult than the typical DOS manual.

Conclusion   After using CommandPlus for a long time, I do not understand why it is not more popular. This is an excellent program. I do not hesitate at all in recommending it for everyone looking to squeeze a little more power from DOS.

Product:	CommandPlus
Price:	$79.95
Category:	Commercial
Publisher:	ESP Software Systems, Incorporated
Address:	11965 Vinice Boulevard
	Suite 309
	Los Angeles, California 90066
Phone:	(213) 390-7408
Notes:	You can load CommandPlus after booting where it acts as a shell over COMMAND.COM. That way requires 57K. You can also load CommandPlus in your CONFIG.SYS file without loading COMMAND.COM at all. That way, it requires 47K more than COMMAND.COM.
	The exact memory requirements depend of the exact defaults you use, the values listed here are only approximations.
Memory:	57K/47K

## Part Six

Other Programs and Methods

26
Other Programs of Interest

Back Scroll

Back Scroll is a shareware memory resident program that stores a copy of screen information in a buffer of adjustable size. New screens are added to the top of the buffer and once the buffer is full the oldest screens are flushed out as new screens are added.

Installation   Back Scroll consists of two files, the program and a brief documentation file. To install it, you copy it to a directory in the PATH and add the command:

BACKS n

to the AUTOEXEC.BAT file where n is the number of screens to save. Memory requirements are n times 2.5K.

Operation   Once Back Scroll is installed in memory, it works automatically. Text based screens go into the Back Scroll buffer. Once the buffer is full, the earliest screens added to the buffer are flushed out of the buffer. To see the contents of the buffer, you press Control-space. You can scroll around the buffer using the page up and page down keys. You exit the viewing mode by pressing the Return key.

Limitations   The hot-key is not adjustable and there are no provisions for capturing graphic screens or printing text screens once captured.

Manual   The documentation file is very brief but adequately explains how to operate the program.

Conclusion   Back Scroll is useful for viewing directory information and other such things that tend to scroll off the screen before you have time to read them. A setting of two or three for n should be high enough so memory requirements are not very large.

<table>
<tr><td>Product:</td><td>Back Scroll</td></tr>
<tr><td>Type:</td><td>Shareware</td></tr>
<tr><td>Price:</td><td>$20</td></tr>
<tr><td>Category:</td><td>Commercial</td></tr>
<tr><td>Publisher:</td><td>The Kampro Group</td></tr>
<tr><td>Address:</td><td>Post Office Box 90654
Honolulu, Hawaii 96835</td></tr>
<tr><td>Phone:</td><td>Not Available</td></tr>
<tr><td>Notes:</td><td>The size of the buffer is adjustable therefore the memory requirements is variable</td></tr>
<tr><td>Memory:</td><td>2.5K per screen</td></tr>
</table>

Cocoon

Cocoon is a quasi-memory resident program that saves your keystrokes as you work. If there is a power failure or other problem, you can use these recorded keystrokes to recover your work.

Installation   Cocoon does not have an installation program. The manual instructs you to copy all the files to a subdirectory in the PATH.

Operation   I used to work in an office with a manager who liked to do a lot of his own typing. One day he was sitting at the computer typing when the power went out. All of a sudden, I heard a long and loud stream of obsenities coming from his office. It turned out he had been typing for about four hours and had not stopped to save his work even once. He lost all of that four hours of work!

Cocoon was designed to prevent that from happening. More specifically, it was designed for just that type of individual. You can avoid needing Cocoon by saving your work frequently and each time before you enter a dangerous command.

Cocoon requires 12K of memory. However, it is not a memory resident program in the typical sense. Cocoon does not stay in memory all the time. Rather, you start it each time you start an application where you want to log the keystrokes. For example, to start Word and log the keystrokes, you would enter:

LOG WORD

This loads Cocoon and then Cocoon loads Word. When you exit Word, Cocoon closes the log file and unloads itself from memory. You can write batch files to automate this.

Cocoon always stores its log file in the file COCOON.LOG. It always opens this file in the subdirectory you are in when you start Cocoon. If a

COCOON.LOG file already exists, Cocoon renames it to COCOON.BAK. While logging your keystrokes, Cocoon works so fast that you never notice you are using it.

To replay the keystrokes, you first change to the directory containing the COCOON.LOG file you want to replay. Then you enter:

RECOVER

and Cocoon automatically replays the log. There is also a manual playback mode where Cocoon replays one keystroke at a time. In manual mode, you can edit the keystrokes before Cocoon replays them.

If you are a typical computer user, replaying Cocoon to recover data after a long session is going to be more difficult. In order to work, Cocoon must be able to load data files that are identical to the ones you loaded when the keystrokes were logged. However, anytime you save a data file, you write a modified—and therefore different—file back to the disk. To use Cocoon, you must edit the log file and delete all the keystrokes up through the last time you saved the data file. Then you must add in the command(s) to load the data file, since by deleting those earlier commands you removed the load command.

In addition, you must make some recoveries because the user made a mistake. For example, deleting a column in Lotus or exiting without saving. You must delete this mistake from the log file or replaying the log will simply recreate the mistake.

That process is not too difficult if you are working with a single data file. However, it can be difficult or even impossible if you were working with several data files at the same time. For example, as I write this chapter I have four windows open in Microsoft Word. One window has this text you are reading. Another has the summary boxes that appear near the end of each product. The third window has the tables and the last has the figures. I save these at different intervals depending on how much work I have done in each window.

To make these sorts of recoveries easier, Cocoon can convert the log file to an ASCII file. Once the file is an ASCII file, you can edit it with most word processors. Once you finish editing the ASCII file, Cocoon will convert it back to a log file.

Limitations   Cocoon only uses one file name, COCOON.LOG, to log keystrokes. It always stores that in the subdirectory you are in when you start Cocoon. That is dangerous with a program like Word that can start in any subdirectory. First, it makes it difficult to locate the appropriate log file. Second, you can end up overwriting an existing log file. Cocoon cannot log keystrokes going into most memory resident programs. This is a DOS limitation rather than a Cocoon limitation.

Cocoon will not capture selections or actions made with a mouse. Some programs, like Windows and PageMaker, use mice to such an extent that Cocoon is worthless with those programs. You can stop Cocoon from recording keystrokes during a session. Once stopped, you cannot restart Cocoon without exiting your application and reloading Cocoon. That starts a new log file.

Cocoon cannot recover from any action that removes information from the disk. For example it could not recover from the Lotus command /File Erase Worksheet or the Word command Escape Transfer Delete.

Manual   The manual does a good job of explaining how to use Cocoon. Even new users will understand the manual.

Conclusion   I have always used the computer under the operating rule that you stop and save your work everytime you have keyed in more work than you are willing to retype. For me, that generally means I stop and save about every ten minutes. If you frequently save your work, Cocoon has nothing to offer.

```
Product:      Cocoon
Price:        $79.95
Category:     Commercial
Publisher:    FONTEX Technology, Incorporated
Address:      600 South Date Avenue
              Alhambra, California 91803
Phone:        (818) 289-8299
Memory:       12K
```

CutPaste

CutPaste is a memory resident program that lets you modify and capture text screens and paste the captured screen into other applications. It is useful for transferring data between applications as well as capturing screens.

Installation   CutPaste consists of a single memory resident program, a documentation file, and a source code listing. There are no installation instructions. First, you must copy the CutPaste program to a subdirectory in the PATH. To load CutPaste, you place a CutPaste command in your AUTOEXEC. BAT or enter the command from the keyboard.

Operation   Once installed, you activate CutPaste with Alt-F9. At this point, you can move around the screen and edit its contents. The edits are in effect only as long as you are in CutPaste. When you exit, the screen is installed to its original condition. However, any portion of the screen you capture to the buffer is complete with the modifications.

While editing, CutPaste has keystrokes to move the cursor rapidly around the screen. You may enter or modify text at any point on the screen. You can toggle between insert and overwrite mode using the insert and delete keys.

Once any modifications are complete, you capture the screen by moving the cursor to the top left corner on the area to be captured and press the End key. The cursor changes to inverse video. You then move the cursor to the bottom right corner of the capture area. All of the screen in the rectangle between the marked to left corner and current cursor position changes to inverse video. When you reach the bottom right corner, you press the End key. That moves the screen to the storage buffer and exits to DOS. When you are ready to paste the screen, you press Control-F9 while in that application.

Limitations   Graphic screens cannot be captured. Only one screen can be captured at a time and captured screens cannot be saved by CutPaste for future use beyond this session.

Manual   The documentation file is brief but adequately explains how to use CutPaste.

Conclusion   For capturing text screens or transferring data between free-form applications like word processors and text to a spreadsheet, CutPaste is a good program and the price is right.

Product:	CutPaste
Price:	Free
Category:	Public Domain
Publisher:	Gerry Boyd and Larry Weiss
Address:	Post Office Box 83142
	Richardson, Texas 75083
Phone:	N/A
Memory:	6K

EE2 (Environmental Editor)

EE2 is like a word processor only you use it to edit the original copy of your environmental strings rather than editing words.

Installation   EE2 consists of only two files, EE2.EXE and EE2.DOC. EE2.EXE should be copied to a subdirectory in your PATH. The process is not explained in the documentation.

What is the Environment   The DOS environment is a section of RAM [Random Access Memory] that DOS sets aside for specific information. (For your information, this area is called the Master Environment Block.) Three pieces of information are always stored in the environment. They are:

1)   The location of COMMAND.COM.
2)   The PATH, if one has been set.
3)   The PROMPT.

You can see the contents of your environment by entering the command SET followed by a <Return>.

DOS stores each piece of information in the environment as a string. This allows you to enter absolutely anything you want into the environment. The general syntax for placing information into the environment is:

SET variable = value

The only space should be between the SET and the variable name. DOS will actually accept other spaces, for example before and/or after the equal sign. These are treated as part of the variable name or the value and make working with them difficult. The command:

SET TEMP=C:\JUNK

will actually create a variable named "TEMP<Space>" containing the value "<Space>C:\JUNK". You will avoid a lot of problems by avoiding spaces in the SET command, except after SET of course.

The keywords COMSPEC, PATH, and PROMPT have special meaning to DOS. These are the ways you change default values in the environment. The general syntax for these is also:

```
SET COMSPEC = value
SET PATH = value
SET PROMPT = value
```

however, DOS allows you to drop the SET in front of these. WARNING: Changing COMSPEC is dangerous and can cause your computer to lock up. If the command is not just right, you will get the dreaded "Cannot load COMMAND, system halted" error message. You must reboot when you get this message. When experimenting, make sure to save everything first.

In addition to the three entries DOS places into the environment automatically, DOS allows you to store your own information in the environment. This custom information can be accessed by programs and accessed and modified by batch files.

You can remove a variable from memory using the:

```
SET VARIABLE =
```

command. Be sure not to enter any spaces after the equal sign or you will SET the variable equal to spaces. You can check to be sure the variable was removed by entering the SET command by itself.

The default DOS prompt is a C> which tells you almost nothing. The C indicates the default drive. The PROMPT command can be used to change the DOS prompt to a wide range of prompts. The PROMPT command is normally just used in the AUTOEXEC.BAT file. When used by itself, PROMPT resets the prompt to C>.

Any printable character string can be included in the PROMPT command. In fact, one of the first "tricks" most computer users learn is to include their name or company name in the prompt. Special characters can be included in the prompt using the dollar sign and a single letter code. Any non-code character following a dollar sign is ignored. The most popular prompt is:

```
SET PROMPT = $p$g
```

This command adds the current subdirectory to the default disk display.

It is important to remember that any PROMPT you develop is stored in the environmental space, along with the PATH and SET variables. A long PROMPT combined with a long PATH and a SET variable may require you to expand your environmental space. Expanding your environment is explained in my book, *MS-DOS Batch File Programming . . . Including OS/2*.

COMSPEC is short for SET COMmand SPECification. It tells DOS where to find COMMAND.COM when a program overwrites COMMAND.COM. DOS takes up a lot of memory. When your computer is short of memory, either because it has less than 640K or you have a lot of memory resident software, this can be a problem. The lack of memory may prevent some programs from being run or limit the size of others. DOS solves this problem by making part of itself provisionally resident (or transient) in memory. We need this part to enter DOS commands but not to run application programs. If a program needs this space, it can overwrite the transient portion of DOS.

When you exit an application program that has overwritten the transient portion of DOS, DOS is less than complete. If you were to use this version, you would not be able to enter most internal commands. DOS replenishes itself by rereading portions of COMMAND.COM into memory. Usually DOS reloads itself from the drive it booted from. Using:

SET COMSPEC = C:\ COMMAND.COM

you can force DOS to reload itself from some other place. COMSPEC can also be changed using the SHELL command in the CONFIG.SYS file.

Many RAM-disk users copy COMMAND.COM to their RAM disk and then use the SET COMSPEC command to reload COMMAND.COM from the RAM-disk. This is noticeably faster than reloading from disk.

One note, while available in the 2-series of DOS, the SET COMSPEC command does not work reliably in versions of DOS prior to 3.0.

There are four types of commands DOS will accept, internal commands, .EXE program names, .COM program names, and .BAT file names. Every time DOS receives a command, it first checks to see if that command is an internal command, like ERASE. If so, it executes that command. If the command is not an internal command, DOS next checks the current subdirectory for an .EXE file by that name, then a .COM file and finally a .BAT file. If DOS finds a program with the correct name, it executes that program. If DOS does not find a file in the current directory, it searches the PATH for a .COM, .EXE, or .BAT file. If DOS finds a program in the PATH with the correct name, it executes that program. Otherwise, DOS returns the "Bad command or file name" error message.

So the PATH is nothing more than a list of subdirectories for DOS to search when a program is not in the current subdirectory. The syntax is:

PATH = C:\ ;Subdirectory 1;Subdirectory2;. . .;Last Subdirectory

If your PATH is:

PATH = C:\ ;\ SYSLIB;\ DATABASE;\ WORDPROCESSOR

then DOS will only search those subdirectories on the default disk.

If you enter the PATH command with nothing after it, DOS displays the current path. If you enter PATH; then DOS resets the PATH to nothing. This causes DOS to only search the default directory for programs and batch files. If you specify a PATH incorrectly, DOS will not find the error until it needs to search the path. If you enter an invalid directory in the PATH, DOS ignores that entry.

Operation   The problem with the environment is there is no easy way to change it. If you make a mistake entering your PATH command, the only way to correct it is to reenter the entire PATH command. EE2 overcomes this by letting you edit the environment directly.

This is not an easy task. Every time you run a program, it gets a copy of the environment. Any changes it makes are made to the copy, not the original. When the program terminates, its copy of the environment is erased. That is why compilers and other programs set the ERRORLEVEL. They cannot communicate with other programs or batch files through their environment because their copy is erased when they terminate. The single byte ERRORLEVEL is not part of the environment and so it remains intact when a program terminates.

EE2 overcomes this by searching your RAM for the original copy of the environment. It reads that in for you to edit. Any changes are written directly back to this memory location. After booting, the size of the environment is fixed, so EE2 just replaces the existing memory block with the updated one.

Limitations   EE2 will not run under DOS 4.0 and later. It is controlled using the function keys. The assignment is not intuitive, you just have to remember it. However, there is a help screen. Figure 26-1 shows this.

EE2 sometimes appears not to work. EE2 only changes the original copy of the environment. If you are running your system under a menu program that "shells" to DOS to run other programs, then you will be operating under a copy of the environment created before the original was modified by EE2. EE2 only updates the original and not the copy. This is really a limitation of DOS and not EE2.

```
         Graham Systems Environment Edit (EE)
         Copyright June 1, 1987 by Keith P. Graham

    Operation of Keys.
         F1 - Gives this display
         F2 - Updates the Environment and leaves EE.
         F3 - Quits EE without updating the Environment.
         F4 - Clears the Environment completely.
         F5 - Inserts a blank line above the cursor line.
         F6 - Deletes the current line.
         F7 - The 0DH key - allows you to enter the
              carriage return character directly.
         F8 - The 08H key - allows you to enter the
              backspace character without backspacing.
         F9 - Redisplays screen. You may have entered more
              characters than the enviroment can handle.
              This shows the expected results of EE.
         F10- Copyright and Advertising
         ~  - (tilde) joins current line with next line
              when the screen is saved to get lines longer
              then 80 bytes

    Press any key to continue..............
```

Fig. 26-1. The Environment Edit editor has on-line help that explains all the available editing commands.

Manual   The disk file briefly explains the environment and how to use EE2. It could use a better explanation of the environment.

Conclusion   There simply is not an easier way than EE2 to make a temporary change to your PATH or other environmental variables. Experienced users will appreciate this ability. Less experienced users should take care, since some modifications can cause your computer to "lock up" and lose data in the process. EE2 is included on the optional diskette.

Product:	EE2
Price:	$5.00
Category:	Shareware
Publisher:	Keith P. Graham
Address:	238 Germonds Road
	West Nyack, New York
	10994
Phone:	Not Available
Memory:	64K

One-Key DOS

One-Key DOS is a memory resident program that allows you to exit to DOS while running almost any program. For example, you are using WordStar and find that you cannot save a file because the disk is full. You can exit to DOS to format a new disk or erase files. You then return to WordStar to save your file. The program works exactly like the /S option of Lotus 1-2-3 version 2.

Installation   One-Key DOS is copy protected. It installs itself by creating a hidden file called PU.SYS. For hard disk users, you can back up and restore this hidden file using DOS or other backup and restore programs. This is another blessing for hard disk users who are used to having to uninstall programs before backup and install after the backup. For floppy disk users, the installation programs will create an unlimited number of working disks. So these programs can easily work with all your floppy disks.

If you do not read the installation manual and you just copy the program files to your disk, you will get quite a shock. The program will tell you the disk is not bootable and will lock the machine. I did this with my hard disk and I thought the hard disk had failed. The program should use a more meaningful message. I object to copy protected programs and this is no exception. However, the ability to make an unlimited number of working disks makes the copy protection slightly more tolerable.

When you install these programs, they do something that is inexcusable. They add two lines to the top of the AUTOEXEC.BAT file to load the program into memory. These commands are added without the program telling you the AUTOEXEC.BAT file is being modified—although that information is buried in the manual. When an installation program is going to modify an AUTOEXEC. BAT or CONFIG.SYS file, it should always ask permission first.

ASSIGN	BACKUP	BASIC
BASICA	DEBUG	EDLIN
EXE2BIN	FDISK	GRAFTAB
GRAPHICS	KEYBFR	KEYBGR
KEYBIT	KEYBSP	KEYBUK
LINK	MOD	PATH
PRINT	PROMPT	RECOVER
RESTORE	SELECT	SET
TEST		

Table 26-1. **Packages Not Supported by One Key DOS.**

Operation   Using One-Key DOS is easy. Anytime you want to "exit to DOS," you press Alt-F3. You can change this hot-key by adding a / option when loading the program. The program loads a second copy of COMMAND.COM so COMMAND.COM must be present on the default disk. The program changes the prompt to display a short ad, a message telling you to type exit to return, and the current directory. If you change directories while using One-Key DOS, the program will ask if it should pass that change to the original COMMAND. COM. If files were open when One-Key DOS was invoked and your software does not check the directory before writing to the disk, passing a directory change can lose files or even corrupt the entire disk.

Any memory resident programs you load while running One-Key DOS, including the DOS Print and Mode command, are lost when you exit One-Key DOS. One-Key DOS cannot run the DOS programs listed in Table 26-1.

The program will use all the memory available when it is invoked. You can reserve up to 64K for One-Key DOS when starting the program. Additional options at startup allow you to change the hot-key and tell the program to use a graphic screen.

Limitations   The program is copy protected.

Manual   One-Key DOS comes with a two page printed "manual." The sole purpose of this manual is to tell how to install them. You print the program manual using the installation program.

Conclusion   One-Key DOS ran flawlessly. Any problems I had invoking it were caused by the program I was running not playing by all the rules.

Product:	One-Key DOS
Price:	$49.95
Category:	Commercial
Publisher:	Power Up!
Address:	Post Office Box 7600
	San Mateo, California 94019
Phone:	(800) 851-2917
	(800) 851-2917 in California
Notes:	Copy protected
Memory:	44K

Resq

Resq is a public domain program that will search through memory and find word processing text and then recover it to a file called RES.Q. This is useful if you exit your program without saving.

Installation   The documentation does not explain how to install Resq and there is no installation program. All installation requires is copying RESQ. COM to a subdirectory in your PATH.

Operation   What do you do if you exit your word processor without saving your work only to realize that you should have saved it? It turns out that the computer does not clear out memory when you exit your program. Just like your disk, the data stays in memory until it is replaced by something else. Resq will search through memory looking for the text.

Resq is not memory resident. You run it when you need it. First, Resq prompts you for some of the text in your document. You must enter it exactly, including special characters and capitalization. Resq searches for that text. When it finds matching text, it shows you the information and asks if it is a match. If it is, Resq begins writing it to a file called RES.Q. It stops when it hits a Control-Z or you press any key. If it was a false match, it can continue the search.

I first tried Resq after listing text with the Buerg utility LIST.COM and exiting. Resq recovered the text exactly. Next, I tried with WordStar and Microsoft Word. Resq recovered most but not all of the text.

Limitations   Resq always writes to RES.Q so it can overwrite existing text if you happen to have two accidents in a row.

Manual   There is not really much to running Resq. However, the documentation does a good job of telling you how to use the program.

Conclusion   Most modern word processors make it hard to make this mistake. However, it is comforting to have Resq available to recover. While not tested, Resq should work on other text based applications.

Product:	Resq
Price:	Free
Category:	Public Domain
Publisher:	Mike Yarus
Address:	2231 16th Street
	Boulder, Colorado 80302
Phone:	Not Available
Notes:	A copy of Resq is included on the optional diskette set
Memory:	128K

Search

Search is a shareware text searching program. It can also replace one text string with another text string. The optional diskette set has a copy of Search.

Installation   Search does not have an installation program and the manual does not explain how to install Search. All you have to do is copy SEARCH.EXE to a subdirectory in your PATH.

Operation   To search for text, you enter:

SEARCH file var1 [var2] [var3] [var4] [var5] [/P /C /F /R]

where:

- "file" is the file specification to search. These must be ASCII or near ASCII files. Search does not search through multiple subdirectories.
- "var1" is the first text string to match. Search requires at least one string. The next four are optional. If you enter more than one string, the search is an "OR" search where Search returns any line containing at least one of the strings.

- /P sends the output to the printer.
- /F sends the output to a file called SEARCH.LST.
- /R causes Search to replace all occurrences of the text in "var1" with the text in "var2". It does not produce a backup of the text so the user should do that manually first.

If you do not want to deal with command line syntax, Search has a data entry screen you can use instead. To bring up the screen, you enter Search without any parameters and then press F10 at the help screen. Figure 26-2

```
              TEXT SEARCH AND REPLACE PROGRAM Version 6.81

    Select mode of operation               Search mode   Replace mode

    Enter name of file (or wildcard filespec):   C:\BENCHMARK\ASCII\*.ASC
    Enter up to 5 variables to search for:
    Variable 1:      Cogeneration
    Variable 2:      Small Power Producers
    Variable 3:      PURPA
    Variable 4:      buyback rates
    Variable 5:      avoided cost contracts
         Print results? N
         Send results to a file? N
         Ignore case? Y

         Is the above information correct? Y

                    +--------------------------------+
                    | If you find this program of value |
                    | please send $10 to:              |
                    |        Arthur W. Hill, Jr.       |
                    |    936 S. Kensington Ave.        |
                    |      La Grange, IL 60525         |
                    +--------------------------------+


         ESC to End   Arrows(↑ ↓) to Move up or down   Enter Accepts
```

Fig. 26-2. If you prefer to avoid the command line, Search has a data enter screen where you can enter all the information it needs.

```
File----------------->C:\BENCHMAR\ASCII\BERNOULL.ASC
File----------------->C:\BENCHMAR\ASCII\BOTTLING.ASC
File----------------->C:\BENCHMAR\ASCII\BUG.ASC
File----------------->C:\BENCHMAR\ASCII\CERTIFIC.ASC
File----------------->C:\BENCHMAR\ASCII\COMPAQS.ASC
File----------------->C:\BENCHMAR\ASCII\COMPILE1.ASC
 214 compiler.  Figures16 gives the exact time for each
 227 but the first benchmark.  Like the other compilers in this
 969 Neither compiler uses meta commands.  These are instructions
 970 for the compiler to execute at compile time.  A common
1045 compiler purchase)
File----------------->C:\BENCHMAR\ASCII\COMPILER.ASC
  33 protected.  dBASE compilers and runtime modules are a way
 233 In most tests, FoxBASE was faster than the other compilers.
 630 easy as switching compilers.
 718 Quicksilver was the only compiler that had this problem.
1333 Quicksilver demo compiler $75 ($25 applies to full
File----------------->C:\BENCHMAR\ASCII\COMPRESS.ASC
File----------------->C:\BENCHMAR\ASCII\COPYWRIT.ASC
File----------------->C:\BENCHMAR\ASCII\DBASE3.ASC
  26 dBASE III Utilities I reviewed the dBASE compilers and runtime
 103 speed would be using a compiler like Clipper or Quicksilver, or
File----------------->C:\BENCHMAR\ASCII\DHINT1.ASC
  17 dBASE compilers had an INCLUDE statement, I could have used
File----------------->C:\BENCHMAR\ASCII\DISSERT1.ASC
File----------------->C:\BENCHMAR\ASCII\DISSERTA.ASC
File----------------->C:\BENCHMAR\ASCII\DOS1.ASC
 388 basic and compiled using any basic compiler.  If you do not
 389 have a compiler, you can use interactive basic, but it will
File----------------->C:\BENCHMAR\ASCII\FASTBACK.ASC
File----------------->C:\BENCHMAR\ASCII\FIGURES.ASC
File----------------->C:\BENCHMAR\ASCII\FILEFAC.ASC
File----------------->C:\BENCHMAR\ASCII\GOALSEEK.ASC
File----------------->C:\BENCHMAR\ASCII\HAL.ASC
File----------------->C:\BENCHMAR\ASCII\HARD.ASC
 325 files with a .bak extension, and compilers often create
File----------------->C:\BENCHMAR\ASCII\HARD2.ASC
File----------------->C:\BENCHMAR\ASCII\HARDWARE.ASC
File----------------->C:\BENCHMAR\ASCII\LEARNDOS.ASC
File----------------->C:\BENCHMAR\ASCII\LIBRARY.ASC
File----------------->C:\BENCHMAR\ASCII\LOTUS1.ASC
File----------------->C:\BENCHMAR\ASCII\LOTUS2.ASC
File----------------->C:\BENCHMAR\ASCII\LOTUS3.ASC
File----------------->C:\BENCHMAR\ASCII\LOTUS5.ASC
 101 macro commands, like replaceable parameters (%1%9 in DOS
File----------------->C:\BENCHMAR\ASCII\MANNERS.ASC
File----------------->C:\BENCHMAR\ASCII\MATHCAD.ASC
File----------------->C:\BENCHMAR\ASCII\MATRIX3.ASC
File----------------->C:\BENCHMAR\ASCII\MEMORY1.ASC
File----------------->C:\BENCHMAR\ASCII\RESCUE.ASC
File----------------->C:\BENCHMAR\ASCII\SIDEBAR3.ASC
File----------------->C:\BENCHMAR\ASCII\SIDEBAR4.ASC
  22 Quicksilver compiler and linker.
File----------------->C:\BENCHMAR\ASCII\SIDEBAR5.ASC
File----------------->C:\BENCHMAR\ASCII\SIDEBAR6.ASC
File----------------->C:\BENCHMAR\ASCII\SIDEBAR7.ASC
File----------------->C:\BENCHMAR\ASCII\WORDVSWS.ASC
File----------------->C:\BENCHMAR\ASCII\X-LOCK.ASC
******************************************************
(Total lines: searched=  17409  displayed=     18 )
******************************************************
```

Fig. 26-3. Search output.

shows this. As it searches, Search displays the file name, line number and text from any matches it finds. You can redirect that to a printer or a file. Figure 26-3 shows the typical output of Search. When Search finishes, it shows some summary statistics.

Limitations　　The command line mode suffers from the DOS 127-character limit on commands. The menu mode overcomes this and allows much longer variables to search on. Search does not search across subdirectories so it can take a long time to find a file if you do not remember which subdirectory it is in.

Manual　　Search is a fairly simple program to run, especially using the menu. The single screen of information does an adequate job of explaining how to use Search.

Conclusion　　Search is a useful program for finding ASCII information in a file or for replacing one ASCII string with another across multiple files.

```
Product:      Search
Price:        $12
Category:     Shareware
Publisher:    Arthur W. Hill, Jr.
Address:      936 South Kensington Avenue
              La Grange, Illinois 60525
Phone:        Not Available
Notes:        The optional diskette set has a
              copy of Search.
Memory:       128K
```

Time Runner

Time Runner is a utility that will run up to five programs at preselected times. These programs can be .COM, .EXE, or .BAT programs.

Installation　　Time Runner consists of only two files, TIMERUN.EXE and TIMERUN.DOC. TIMERUN.EXE should be copied to a subdirectory in your PATH. The process is not explained in the documentation.

Operation　　Time Runner is very easy to use. At the DOS prompt, you enter the TIMERUN command. Time Runner loads and displays its single screen. Figure 26-4 shows the first screen. First, you select the box to modify. You then enter the date and time to run the program. When you have entered those, you select OK and Time Runner prompts you for the batch file to run. You enter the file name without the extension. You can also enter a .COM or .EXE program file name. You can enter up to five programs to be run at a predetermined time. This information can be saved for repeated use.

Time Runner is an excellent way to run a communications script to log on to a remote database late at night to download information when the rates are lowest. It is also a good way to run your backup program late at night if your backup method does not require you to change diskettes.

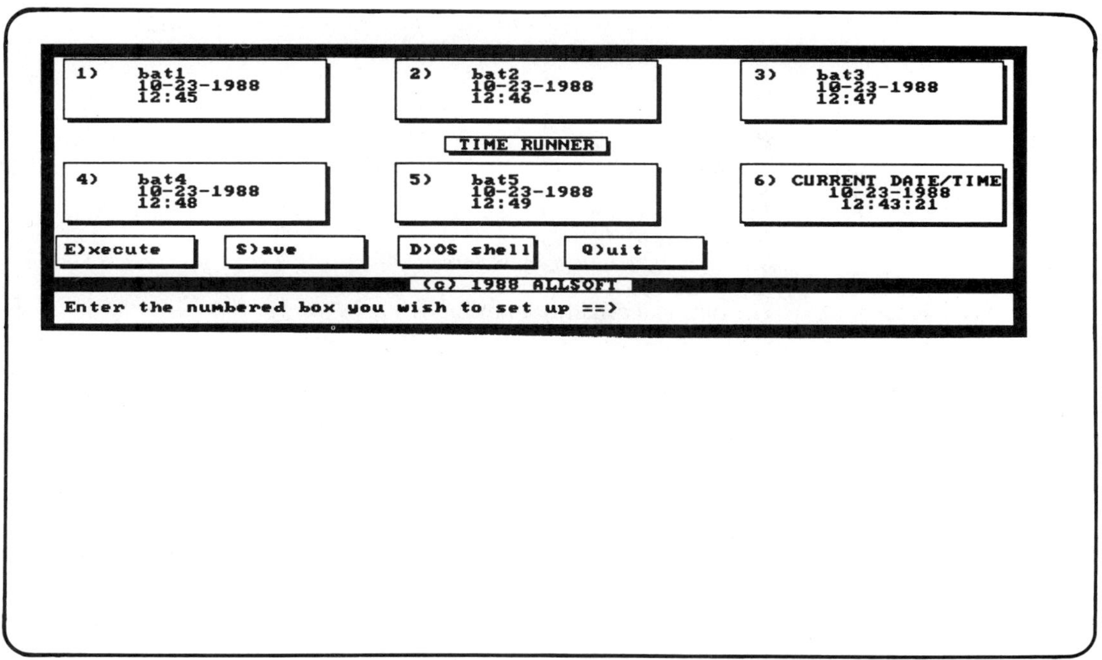

Fig. 26-4. The Time Run screen. Notice that each of five batch files have individual times to run.

Using the above method, you would have to change the date every day you ran Time Runner. You can also start Time Runner with the command:

TIMERUN [1,2,3,4,5 or A]

You place the cells to run inside angle brackets, or A for all, and Time Runner uses the time in those cells but runs them today regardless of the date in the cell. That way, you can easily use Time Runner to perform a repetitive task or tasks every day.

Limitations   The major limitation of Time Runner is not a program limitation, rather, it is a DOS limitation. The only way DOS provides for feeding keystrokes to a program is piping and many programs ignore piped information. If a program requires keystrokes to run and will not accept piped keystrokes and will not use a script file, you cannot run it with Time Runner.

Manual   Time Runner is easy to use and the disk-based documentation adequately explains how to run the program.

Conclusion   Every now and then, I need to run a complex dBASE reporting program. Even compiled with Clipper, it takes about four hours to run. It easily runs at night using Time Runner. In general, any application that can run unattended can be run using Time Runner. That makes Time Runner a very useful program. Time Runner uses 129K so the memory available to the application is reduced by that amount. Time Runner is included on the optional diskette.

<table>
<tr><td>Product:</td><td>Time Runner</td></tr>
<tr><td>Price:</td><td>$5.00</td></tr>
<tr><td>Category:</td><td>Shareware</td></tr>
<tr><td>On Disk:</td><td>Yes</td></tr>
<tr><td>Publisher:</td><td>Allsoft Computer Products
2404 Sugar Maple Court
Monmouth Junction, New Jersey 08852</td></tr>
<tr><td>Phone:</td><td>(201) 422-9254</td></tr>
<tr><td>Notes:</td><td>The optional diskette set includes a copy of this program.</td></tr>
<tr><td>Memory:</td><td>129K</td></tr>
</table>

27
Sharing Data Using Different Disk Drive Sizes

Doing the Floppy Shuffle   When IBM first introduced its personal computer, those computers had 160K single sided drives. Those were quickly replaced with 320K/360K double sided drives. The disks would hold either 320K or 360K depending on the version of DOS used. Later, IBM introduced its next generation of computers and they had 1.2M disk drives. The two drives are supposed to co-exist, but sometimes they have difficulty doing so.

I am unofficially responsible for solving computer related problems in a large office with a mixture of 360K and 1.2M drives. After the 1.2M drives arrived we began having problems. Over the past year, I have investigated these problems and developed procedures for avoiding most of them. The manuals are not much help, so what follows is what I have learned from first-hand experience.

The Systems   The 360K drive spins at 300 RPM's. Data is transferred between the computer and drive at .25 megabits per second [MPS]. The disk is 5.25 inches in diameter and has 40 tracks, numbered from 0 to 39. The disk is coated with iron-oxide.

The 1.2M drive spins at 360 RPM's. It does not slow down when reading from or writing to 360K diskettes. Data is transferred between the computer and drive at .5 MPS and again this does not change when using a 360K diskette. The disk is also 5.25 inches in diameter but it has 80 tracks, numbered from 0 to 79. Packing twice the number of tracks into the same space means the tracks are narrower. That means the heads are designed to write to narrower tracks. The disks are coated with a special cobalt modified iron-oxide so they can handle the additional information. This modified iron-oxide coating requires a higher magnetic field than the 360K disks.

There are four ways to intermix the two disk types, and each is discussed below:

Reading From 1.2M Disk in 360K Drive   Cannot be done at all, period.

Reading From 360K Disk in 1.2M Drive   This is generally not a problem. While it continues to spin at 360 RPM's, the 1.2M drive is able to compensate enough for the 360K drive that most disks can be read. Only very marginal disks or disks created on badly misaligned drives create a problem and these will create the same problems when used on most 360K drives except the one that created them. When a 1.2M drive cannot read a 360K disk, you should look for problems with the 360K drive.

Writing to 1.2M Disk in 360K Drive   Cannot be done at all, period.

Writing to 360K Disk in 1.2M Drive   This is the source of most of the disk interface problems, yet is something you must do to transfer data from most new machines to older machines. Our solution was to finally add a 360K drive to our two most popular AT-class machines. That completely cures the problem and is relatively cheap.

You can format a 360K disk in a 1.2M drive using FORMAT/4 and many 360K drives can read the disks. The problem is that the 1.2M drive creates a much narrower track than does the 360K drive. That makes drive alignment much more critical. A slightly out-of-alignment 360K drive has a much better chance of reading the wide track created on a 360K drive than the narrow one created on a 1.2M drive. The /4 option is best left for using cheap disks in 1.2M drives. So rules one and two are:

1) When intermixing disk types, always format the 360K disk on a 360K drive.
2) Use the FORMAT/4 option only with a cheap disk that is only going to be used in 1.2M drives.

The narrow tracks of the 1.2M drive causes a second, and less obvious problem. When a drive overwrites data on a disk with new data, not only must it store that data to disk, the data must remove all traces of the old data. When a 1.2M drive overwrites data on a 360K disk, it places the new data in a narrow track in the middle of, but not completely overlapping, the existing track. When that data is later read by a 360K drive, it can become confused by reading both new and old data.

That confusion does not have to be major to cause problems. When DOS writes information to disk, it also includes a special checksum, called a Cyclical Redundancy Check or CRC. Writing the same data to disk will always cause DOS to write the same CRC to disk. By including the data and the CRC on the disk, DOS has two representations of the data.

When DOS reads the data from disk, it again computes the CRC and compares the computed CRC to the one read from the disk. If they do not match, DOS knows it has read the data incorrectly. When the two CRC's do not match,

DOS tries several more times. If it cannot read the data where the CRC's match, it responds with the "Abort, Ignore or Retry" error message. All it takes is reading one bit incorrectly to cause the CRC's not to match.

You can avoid this problem by using freshly formatted (on a 360K drive) disks when you must transfer data from a 1.2M drive to a 360K drive. If that is not possible, use a program like WIPEDISK (part of the Norton Utilities) to make sure the disk is blank. So rule three is:

3) Only use freshly formatted disks or disks with no erased files when writing data in a 1.2M drive to be used in a 360K drive.

A Final Word on Floppy Disk Interchange   The only problem you are likely to see is the inability to read information on a 360K drive. Since most computers have a "critical-need" detection circuit, you probably will not even see this error unless the data is critical. When this happens, remember two things:

- Another 360K drive may have better luck reading the disk. Most of the problems result from the narrow tracks used in the 1.2M drives and the ability to read these in 360K drives is very alignment dependent. So try another drive. If you find a drive that will read the data, copy it to a disk formatted in a 360K machine.
- Even if no 360K drive will read the disk, a 1.2M drive probably will. Format a fresh disk in a 360K drive and use the 1.2M drive to transfer the data to the fresh disk.

CpyAT2PC

CpyAT2PC is a commercial program that writes to 360K diskettes in 1.2 Meg drives reliably.

Installation   There is no installation program. The manual instructs you to copy the files to your root directory or a subdirectory in your PATH.

Operation   CpyAT2PC consists of five different programs. They are:

CPYAT2PC.EXE. This is the main program that performs the copying. It does not support subdirectories. You must be logged in to the subdirectories from which the copies will originate. The program supports wildcard copy specifications. If the files you specify to copy are more than will fit on a single diskette, CpyAT2PC will tell you when to swap disks and continue the copy. Each diskette must be preformatted. CpyAT2PC will not, however, copy a single file that is too large to fit on a diskette. In every case, the copies I produced with CpyAT2PC could be read by 360K drives.

4MAT360.EXE. This program prepares the diskette for formatting and then runs the DOS formatting program. It requires that FORMAT.COM be in the current subdirectory when you run the program. 4MAT360 takes about ten seconds to prepare the diskette then FORMAT takes its usual time. 4MAT360 allows you to format 360K disks in your AT, however, if you have access to a PC then you would be better off formatting the diskettes in a 360K drive.

SPLIT.EXE. This program will split a file that is too large to fit on a single diskette into smaller pieces that will file. It took SPLIT one minute and twenty four seconds to split a 394,869 byte file into six files with 65,536 bytes each and one smaller file with the remainder.

COMBINE.EXE. COMBINE reconstructs the individual pieces created by SPLIT into the single large file once you copy the pieces to your target machine.

CKSUM.EXE. This program calculates a checksum on the files specified on the command line. CpyAT2PC also calculates the checksum for the files it copies and writes that to a data file on the target disk. You can use CKSUM to check the integrity of the file after the copy. Since the checksum for a file will not change unless that file is modified, you can also run CKSUM periodically on your programs to see if they have been modified. This would be a weak form of virus detection.

Limitations   CpyAT2PC is very slow copying files. To copy a single 105,472-byte file, it took CpyAT2PC 4 minutes and 53.03 seconds. DOS took 14.28 seconds to copy the same file to a 360K disk in the 1.2 Meg drive and 16.26 seconds to copy the same file to a 360K drive. However, this is not a major limitation. You purchase CpyAT2PC because you need to make reliable 360K copies on your AT, not because you are looking for a fast copy program.

CpyAT2PC is also somewhat cumbersome to use. You must be logged in the subdirectory containing the files to copy. A command like:

```
CPYAT2PC C: \ WORD \ PROJECT \ *.DOC A:
```

would be invalid because CpyAT2PC will not work across subdirectories. In an interesting contrast to that, CpyAT2PC requires DOS 3.x or higher on the source AT machine. It only requires DOS 2.x or higher on the target PC machine.

SPLIT and COMBINE do not deal well with a full target disk. Both continue to work without an error message and do not create the file(s) you are expecting. Since SPLIT.EXE leaves the single large file intact and COMBINE.EXE leaves the smaller pieces intact, this is a minor problem. Neither SPLIT nor COMBINE warn you before overwriting an existing file.

You are licensed to use SPLIT and COMBINE on all of the machines you use. That makes it easier to use CpyAT2PC. You can keep multiple copies of some of the utilities on all your machines legally. You are not licensed to give SPLIT or COMBINE away or sell it so you cannot use them when sharing files with others. It would be especially nice if you were licensed to include COMBINE with any disks you transfer using CpyAT2PC. That would make the utility much more useful.

Manual   The manual does a good job of explaining how to use the main copying program of CpyAT2PC. It does an inadequate job of explaining how to use the other utilities included with CpyAT2PC.

Conclusion   If you need to transfer data between a PC and an AT, you should first try the procedure outlined above. Format the 360K disks and erase files from it on the PC. Use these blank, formatted disks in the 1.2 Meg AT drive.

Most of the time, this will work. If it does not, you have three alternatives; Cpy-AT2PC, install a 360K drive on the AT or install a 1.2 Meg drive on the PC. Cpy-AT2PC is the cheapest solution and is the best solution for low volume transfers. If you need to frequently transfer files, then a hardware solution might be best.

Product:	CpyAT2PC
Price:	$79.00
Category:	Commercial
Publisher:	Microbridge Computer
Address:	655 Skyway
	Suite 113
	San Carlos, California 94070
Phone:	(415) 593-8777
Memory:	20K

Weltec Quad Density Disk Drive

The 360K floppy disk drive in your 8088 machine has one big drawback, it holds only one-fourth the information of a 1.2M drive. That means you must swap four times as many diskettes to back up your hard disk. It also means that some Lotus worksheets will be too large to fit on a floppy diskette. The Weltec quad density disk drive addresses this issue by allowing your standard controller to drive a 1.2 Meg disk drive. This drive also makes it easier for an AT and a PC to share data.

Installation of Hardware   Installing the Weltec quad density disk drive is no more difficult than installing any other half-height disk drive:

1) Unplug computer.
2) Remove cover.
3) Disconnect existing floppy disk drives.
4) Unbolt existing floppy disk drives. Some clones (including my Corona PC–21 require you to remove the bottom "cover" and/or the mother-board.
5) If you have two half-height drives you must disconnect them and replace the B drive with the Weltec unit. If you have a single full height drive, you must replace it with a half-height 360K drive (about $90) and the Weltec unit.
6) Reverse the above procedure to put everything back together. One note, both connections on the Weltec unit are upside-down from a standard 360K drive, no problem since you cannot plug the keyed connectors in wrong.

The above process is not difficult, I was able to complete everything in under an hour—and I had to pull the motherboard. Incredibly, the Weltec drive comes without installation instructions so you must figure all this out for yourself!

Installation of Software   The Weltec drive requires you to install a driver in your CONFIG.SYS file and the enclosed diskette has a readme file that explains the procedure, at least somewhat. The readme file does not explain how to deal with one of several problems you may run into.

The driver installs the Weltec drive as the drive after your last drive, D if you have a single hard disk. The driver must be the first command in the CONFIG.SYS file. If you have a single hard disk, you might have a LASTDRIVE=C command in your CONFIG.SYS file. Since the Weltec drive is now the D drive, this command locks you out of the Weltec drive.

In addition to LASTDRIVE, DOS 3.# allows you to assign a subdirectory a drive letter in your AUTOEXEC.BAT file. This allows older programs, like WordStar 3.#, to work with subdirectories. To use the subdirectory C: \ WORDSTAR \ LETTERS as the D drive, you would have the command

SUBST D: C: \ WORDSTAR \ LETTERS

in your AUTOEXEC.BAT file and a

LASTDRIVE = D

in your CONFIG.SYS file. You now have both the Weltec drive and a subdirectory assigned as the D drive. MS-DOS 3.2 uses the subdirectory and ignores the Weltec drive. Other versions of DOS may do the reverse.

These are not major problems. All you must do is modify you SUBST and LASTDRIVE statements to free the D-drive assignment for the Weltec drive. With no installation manual and only a short readme file, you must figure all this out yourself—or refer to this review.

Operation   The Weltec drive does what it claims, it adds a 1.2M drive to an 8088 machine. 1.2M disks formatted on the Weltec drive, using a special formatting program, can be read by any 1.2M drive. Files copied to the Weltec drive can be read by any 1.2M drive. Disks formatted on any 1.2M drive can be read by the Weltec drive. Unlike most 1.2M drives, the Weltec drive cannot read or write 360K diskettes and therefore cannot be used as the A drive.

While it works, be warned, the Weltec drive is SLOW. Direct comparisons are unfair since AT machines are faster, so 360K times are included. The 8088 machine was a 4.77 MHz Corona PC-21 and the AT machine was a 12 MHz Compaq DeskPro 286. The test times were for copying 35 files totaling about 300K. The times were:

1) It took the AT 2:11 minutes to copy the files to a 360K drive while the PC took 2:36 minutes, 19% longer. It took the AT 1:44 minutes to copy to a 1.2M drive. The PC took 4:43 minutes to copy to the Weltec drive, 172% longer.

2) It took the AT 47 seconds to copy the files from a 360 drive while the PC took 1:16 minutes, 61% longer. It took the AT 36 seconds to copy from a 1.2M drive. The PC took 2:17 minutes to copy from the Weltec drive, 280% longer.

3) It took 53 seconds to format a 360K disk on an AT and 1:13 minutes on a PC, 38% longer. It took 1:54 minutes to format a 1.2M disk on an AT and 2:20 minutes on the Weltec, 23% longer.

Fastback refuses to work with the Weltec. When you install Fastback, it performs a DMA [Direct Memory Access] chip check. A PC, which has only 360K drives, has one DMA chip. An AT, which normally has a 1.2M drive, has two DMA chips. Technical support for Fastback confirmed that it would not work with the Weltec drive. A Weltec official confirmed the problem and added the drive would work with most other backup programs. It does work with PC-DOS BACKUP.COM. Other programs were not checked.

Limitations   The lack of an installation manual gives a good preview of the technical support available from Weltec. When I called, I ask the operator for technical support without indicating I was reviewing the product. The operator indicated that Weltec had no technical support. After identifying myself I was able to get help by asking for the individual I had originally talked to about doing the review. This drive is definitely a do-it-yourself special.

Manual   There is no manual and the "README" file on the software disk is completely inadequate.

Conclusion   The drive is solid and well built. The only problem I had with it was that the screw holes on the bottom were slightly out of place. I wrote a basic program to simulate extended usage. No problems occurred after extended reading and writing.

The Weltec drive is definitely a niche product. First, you have to be very good with both hardware and software to overcome the lack of an installation manual. Second, its inability to read or write 360K diskettes means that you must keep a second disk drive in your system. However, if you must read or write 1.2M diskettes and you want to keep your 8088 system, the Weltec drive can be a cost effective solution.

Product:	Weltec Quad Density Disk Drive
Price:	$149
Category:	Commercial
Publisher:	Weltec Digital
Address:	17875 Sky Park North Suite P Irvin, California 92714
Phone:	(714) 250-1959
Memory:	N/A

Passport

The *Passport* drive from Plus Development is a removable hard disk. The housing stays in the computer permanently but the drive itself can be removed. It is discussed in Chapter 15.

Operation   The Passport drive consists of a couple of components. The first part is a half-length controller card. The second part is the mounting bay. There are two types, a half-height internal unit or an external casing. The external case has room for two drives. The final part is the drive itself. These come in 20 or 40 Meg versions and can be used interchangeably.

The drive itself is a 40-millisecond [ms] drive with a run-length-limited controller with a 1:1 interleave. It has full-track buffers and other speed enhancements to give the drive the performance of a 28 ms drive.

Limitations   The Passport is essentially a sealed Winchester drive. It has a shock rating of 150 g's. While I did not test this, Plus Development claims it will withstand a drop onto a hard surface from one foot away or more. However, rapid decelaration stresses the bearings and other components. It is not likely this drive could take repeated shocks. Plus Development ships each drive with a custom padded carrier to reduce the stress on the drive.

Winchester drives are prone to hard disk head crashes. A head crash is when the heads bump into the surface of the hard drive. At a minimum, this grinds some of the magnetic material off of the hard disk platter. At its worse, it can leave the drive inoperative. Plus Development has designed the Passport with automatic head parking and head locking to minimize this problem.

The only really significant limitation to the Passport drives specifically is the cost. Adding a second 40 Meg cartridge costs $795 or almost $20 per Meg. That is more than most other ways of adding capacity to your system.

Manual   The Passport suffered from too many manuals. An installation manual was included with each component. A much better approach would be to have one single manual. The manuals themselves were not well written and were difficult to follow. However, installation is a one time difficulty. After that, the Passport drives do not require a manual.

Conclusion   The Passport removable hard disk is a pricy but effective way of transporting large amounts of data between different computers.

Product:	Passport Removable Hard Disk
Price:	$1,250 20 Meg Internal
	$1,450 40 Meg Internal
	$100 additional for PS/2
Components:	$659 Adapter and Base
	$759 PS/2 Adapter and Base
	$349 Base
	$595 20 Meg Drive
	$795 40 Meg Drive
	$399 External Chassis
Category:	Hardware
Publisher:	Plus Development Corporation
Address:	1778 McCarthy Boulevard
	Milpitas, California 95035
Phone:	(408) 434-6900
Memory:	Not Applicable

FILE TRANSFER PACKAGES

A file transfer package consists of both hardware and software. The hardware is a cable that goes between the two computers. It will either connect the two serial ports or the two parallel ports. The software is used to control both computers. The computer sending data is called the master computer and the computer receiving the data is called the slave computer.

For these tests, I transferred data between a floppy drive only Datavue Snap 1 + 1 and an IBM Model 70. The Snap computer had two 720K 3.5-inch floppy drives. It is an 8088 machine running at 9.54 MHz. The Model 70 has a 1.44 Meg 3.5-inch drive and a 360K 5.25-inch drive. It is an 80386 machine running at 16 MHz. Both machines have one serial and one parallel port. This configuration would not operate properly in serial mode at 115,200 bits per second [bps] so all tests were performed at 57,600 bps.

Because both computers had a 3.5-inch drive, the file transfer packages were not necessary for data transfer. You normally use these programs to transfer data between a portable computer with 3.5-inch drives and a desktop computer with 5.25-inch drives.

All of the programs support multiple transfer speeds. They all supported 9,600, 19,200, 38,400, 57,600 and 115,200 bps serial transfers. A few support slower speeds. A few programs offer parallel transfers. Their speed is a function of the software.

All of the packages come with a special cable to connecting two computers together. The cable has two connectors on each end, a female 9-pin serial cable (AT) and a female 25-pin serial cable (PC/PS/2.) You can use either connector on each end. A few computers like the old Corona 8088 clones require a male serial connector. None of the cables supported this type of connection. You can, however, purchase a gender-changer at most computer stores for about five dollars if you have one of these computers.

The Brooklyn Bridge (Parallel)

The *Brooklyn Bridge* is a combination program and cable for transferring files between two computers with incompatible drive sizes using the parallel (printer) port.

Installation   The Brooklyn Bridge operates in two modes, menu driven and command-line mode. The menu driven mode is strictly for file transfers while the command-line mode allows one computer to run programs from the drives of the second computer.

Either mode requires you to connect the cable between the two computers. The cable is well made with large thumb screws on each connector.

In menu driven mode, you run a program called F.COM on the master computer and a program called BRIDGEL1.COM on the slave computer. You must copy these programs to a boot disk or a subdirectory on the hard disk. There is no installation program to do this.

The command-line mode requires BRIDGEL1.COM running on the slave computer when the master computer boots and loads its device driver. There is an installation program to copy the device driver and add the necessary lines to the CONFIG.SYS file.

Operation   With serial communication, you must be concerned with transfer speed. That is not the case with parallel communication. The operation speed is defined by the hardware and is not user selectable. On the test configuration, the parallel method was much faster because the IBM Model 70 was incapable of operating at the top speed of 115,200 bps. If it had been, serial and parallel transfers would have taken about the same time.

When you load the slave program, that computer is no longer available for use from the keyboard. You can only access it from the master computer through the menu program. You use the menu program to select which drives and subdirectories will be the source and which will be the target. Either computer can act as a source and target. The menu program shows the source directory on one side and the target subdirectory on the other side. You select files for transferring by tagging them, just as you do with a DOS shell.

For the most part, the command-line mode is functionally equivalent to the menu mode. In fact, you can run the menu program in this mode. The major advantage of the command-line mode is it allows access to all the drives on the slave computer including Bernoulli drives and tape drives. While not reviewed, the command-line mode can be configured so both computers will run as masters and access each other's drives, much like a network.

Limitations   The Brooklyn Bridge parallel version has no significant limitations.

Manual   All of the information is in the manual and the writing is fairly clear. However, you are going to have to look for some on the information.

Conclusion   Even with the problems with its manual, setting up and learning to use the Brooklyn Bridge is fairly easy.

<table>
<tr><td>Product:</td><td>The Brooklyn Bridge (Parallel)</td></tr>
<tr><td>Price:</td><td>$139.95</td></tr>
<tr><td>Category:</td><td>Commercial</td></tr>
<tr><td>Publisher:</td><td>White Crane Systems, Incorporated</td></tr>
<tr><td>Address:</td><td>6400 Atlantic Boulevard
Suite 180
Norcross, Georgia 30071</td></tr>
<tr><td>Phone:</td><td>(800) 344-6783 (Sales)
(404) 446-0660</td></tr>
<tr><td>Notes:</td><td>Since the cable that connects the two computers uses a parallel port, the master computer must have two parallel ports if you plan on printing from the slave computer or from the master computer while the slave is connected.</td></tr>
<tr><td>Memory:</td><td>5K on the Master
70K on the Slave</td></tr>
</table>

The Brooklyn Bridge (Serial)

The *Brooklyn Bridge* is a combination program and cable for transferring files between two computers with incompatible drive sizes using the serial port.

Installation   The Brooklyn Bridge operates in two modes, menu driven and command-line mode. The menu driven mode is strictly for file transfers while the command-line mode allows one computer to run programs from the drives of the second computer.

Either mode requires you to connect the cable between the two computers. The cable is well made with large thumb screws on each connector.

In menu driven mode, you run a program called F.COM on the master computer and a program called BRIDGE.COM on the slave computer. You must copy these programs to a boot disk or a subdirectory on the hard disk. There is no installation program to do this.

The command-line mode requires BRIDGE.COM running on the slave computer when the master computer boots and loads its device driver. There is an installation program to copy the device driver and add the necessary lines to the CONFIG.SYS file. However, the installation program does not allow you to select the speed during installation so you must patch the device driver after it is installed.

Operation   After connecting the cable to both computers and loading the appropriate program on both computers, I started The Brooklyn Bridge menu program. When I tried to configure the program to use the slave computer (the Snap) as the file source, I got the error message that the computer did not respond. I went back and checked all the cables. They were properly installed. I even attached the cable to a modem to make sure it worked. I still could not get the slave computer to respond.

Finally, I saw a brief hint in the manual that suggested trying a slower transfer speed if it would not work at 115,200 bps. Switching the master program was no problem, the speed setting is a menu option. However, switching the slave program proved to be much more difficult. Neither the index nor table of contents told me where to find out how. Finally, I thumbed through the entire manual till I found the instructions. Rather than starting the program with a switch as I had expected, you have to run a program to patch BRIDGE.COM to work at the slower speed. That was easy to do but poorly documented and troublesome if you have to switch speeds a lot.

Once I had both configured at 57,600 bps, everything else worked easily. When you load the slave program, that computer is no longer available for use from the keyboard. You can only access it from the master computer through the menu program. You use the menu program to select which drives and subdirectories will be the source and which will be the target. Either computer can act as a source and target. The menu program shows the source directory on one side and the target subdirectory on the other side. You select files for transferring by tagging them, just as you do with a DOS shell.

For the most part, the command-line mode is functionally equivalent to the menu mode. In fact, you can run the menu program in this mode. The major advantage of the command-line mode is it allows access to all the drives on the slave computer including Bernoulli drives and tape drives. While not reviewed, the command-line mode can be configured so both computers will run as masters and access each other's drives, much like a network.

Limitations   You cannot change the speed on the slave computer "on the fly." Some of the error messages are not very clear. In command-line mode, the two floppy disk drives on the slave machine were automatically configured as the F- and G-drives. (The C-drive was my hard disk and the D- and E-drives were the Passport drives.) My AUTOEXEC.BAT file uses the SUBST command to access two subdirectories as the F- and G-drives. This overwrote the Brooklyn Bridge setting and made the slave computer inaccessible from the DOS command-line until these SUBST's were cleared. The menu program would work normally since it does not use drive letters.

Manual   All of the information is in the manual and the writing is fairly clear. However, you are going to have to look for some of the information. As my problems figuring out how to change speeds illustrates, the manual is very poorly organized.

Conclusion   Even with the problems with its manual, setting up and learning to use the Brooklyn Bridge is fairly easy especially if your computers will operate at 115,200 bps.

<table>
<tr><td>Product:</td><td>The Brooklyn Bridge (Serial)</td></tr>
<tr><td>Price:</td><td>$139.95</td></tr>
<tr><td>Category:</td><td>Commercial</td></tr>
<tr><td>Publisher:</td><td>White Crane Systems, Incorporated</td></tr>
<tr><td>Address:</td><td>6400 Atlantic Boulevard
Suite 180
Norcross, Georgia 30071</td></tr>
<tr><td>Phone:</td><td>(800) 344-6783 (Sales)
(404) 446-0660</td></tr>
<tr><td>Memory:</td><td>5K on the Master
70K on the Slave</td></tr>
</table>

File Shuttle (Parallel or Serial)

File Shuttle is a combination program and connector for transferring files between two computers with incompatible drive sizes using the parallel (printer) port. The connector converts a normal printer cable so it connects to the second computer. The required printer cable is not included.

Installation   File Shuttle does not use any device drivers and is incapable of operating as a device sharing mini-network. Installing the software involved copying one of two programs to either computer. (Computers with a Quadram printer port and all Datavue computers require a special program that is included on the disk. Datavue is a subsidiary of Quadram.) File Shuttle does not include a program to install the program but the process is well explained in the manual.

File Shuttle comes with a connecter that converts a standard printer cable into a file transfer cable. The printer cable is not included so File Shuttle cannot be used directly out of the box. File Shuttle also supports serial transfers. This was not tested as the package does not supply a serial cable with the package.

Operation   Like the other programs, File Shuttle has to run a menu driven program on both computers. With File Shuttle, you run the same program on both. You can easily control the transfer process from either computer. It even has a switch to prevent you from overwriting a file with an older version.

Limitations   File Shuttle comes with a connector to convert a standard printer cable into a file transfer cable. However, some printers have their cable built in where it cannot be removed to use for this purpose. Still other users do not have a printer. Therefore, File Shuttle cannot always be used right out of the box. The company uses this connecter because they claim it saves you from the need to carry a complete cable. However, to be sure you can connect to an unfamiliar computer you are going to have to carry both the connector and a printer cable.

Manual   The manual uses terminology in keeping with the File Shuttle title of the package. Configuring the program is filing a flight plan. Speed setting is called warp drive. Subdirectories are referred to as cargo bays, and so on. If you were going to have to read the manual over and over that might get on your nerves. However, like the other packages a brief reading is all that is required to get you up and running. I found the different terminology refreshing and actually enjoyed reading the manual. This terminology is carried through to the program itself.

The documentation itself is very brief. The manual is only sixteen pages long, far shorter than the other manuals. If you do not have any problems the manual will be adequate. If you do run into problems you will find the manual has inadequate help for finding the problem.

Conclusion   File Shuttle does a good job of transferring data between computers.

Product:	File Shuttle
Price:	$119.95
Category:	Commercial
Publisher:	GetC Software, Incorporated
Address:	Post Office Box 8110-182
	264 H Street
	Blaine, Washington 98230
	In Canada
	1280 Seymour Street
	2nd Floor
	Vancouver, British Columbia
	V6B 3N9
Phone:	(800) 663-8066
Memory:	96K On Both Computers

Lap-Link (Serial)

Lap-Link is a combination program and cable for transferring files between two computers with incompatible drive sizes using the serial port.

Installation Lap-Link runs in two modes, Lap-Link and Lap-Link Plus. Lap-Link mode is strictly for file transferring while Lap-Link Plus, which is not reviewed here, allows the two computers to share printers, drives and other devices. To install Lap-Link, you copy LL.EXE to both computers either on the boot disk or in a subdirectory in the PATH. The manual explains this. There is no installation program. There is an installation program for the Lap-Link Plus mode. Unlike the Brooklyn Bridge, it allows you to set the baud rate during installation.

Operation Operating Lap-Link is simple. You enter the LL command on both computers. Both of the control programs start up and try to connect to the other computer. Once this connection is made, both computers show the same screen. You can control the transfer from either machine. Changes made on one computer are instantly reflected on the other machine. Figure 27-1 shows the control program.

Limitations File transfers were slightly slower with Lap-Link than with the Brooklyn Bridge. This is a significant point if you have a lot of data to transfer. Pressing the first character of a menu option moved the cursor to that menu

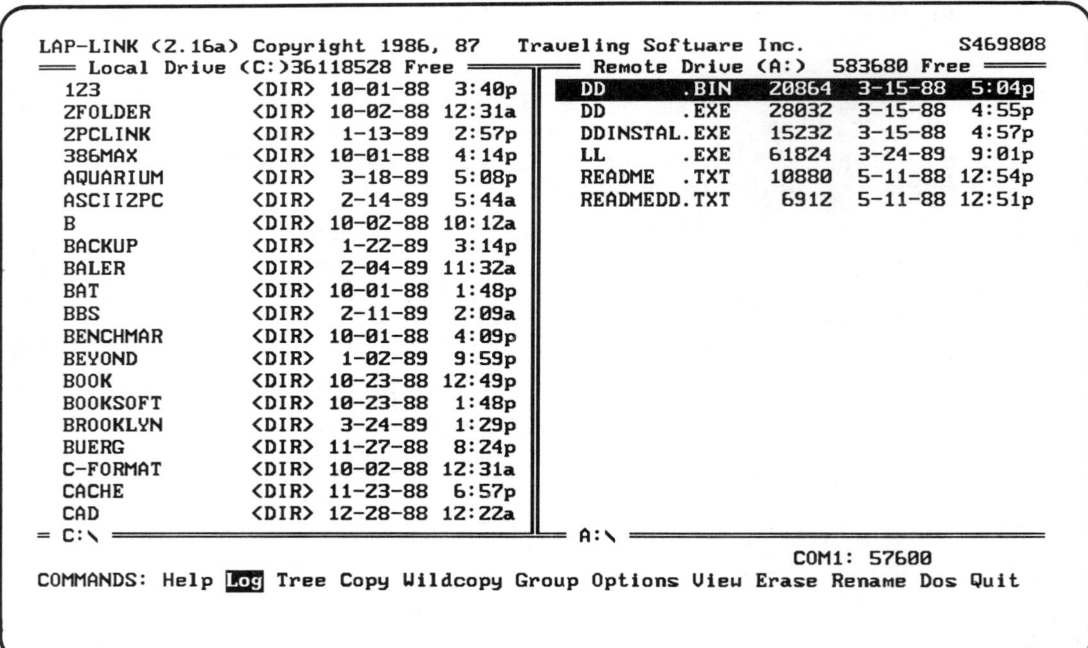

Fig. 27-1. With the Lap-Link control program, you can see a directory of both the master and slave computers on both computers. You can use either computer to control the transfer process.

option. However, unlike most other programs it did not execute the menu option. To do that, you still had to press return.

Manual   The manual is well written and easy to follow. There are a number of typographic special-effects to highlight important information. There is a complete list of error messages and possible causes.

Conclusion   Lap-Link is an easy to set-up, easy to use package. Most users will be able to go from opening the box to transferring files in under an hour.

<table>
<tr><td>Product:</td><td>Lap-Link Plus</td></tr>
<tr><td>Price:</td><td>$139.95</td></tr>
<tr><td>Category:</td><td>Commercial</td></tr>
<tr><td>Publisher:</td><td>Traveling Software, Incorporated</td></tr>
<tr><td>Address:</td><td>18702 North Creek Parkway
Bothell, Washington 98011</td></tr>
<tr><td>Phone:</td><td>(206) 483-8088</td></tr>
<tr><td>Memory:</td><td>192K per machine Lap-Link
32K on master Lap-Link Plus
60K on slave Lap-Link Plus</td></tr>
</table>

RONNY'S PICKS

If you are considering a file transfer program to transfer files between a laptop computer and a single desktop computer, you would be better off installing a 3.5-inch drive in the desktop computer. I checked with several computer dealers and most newer computers will support the drive and installation costs between two and three hundred dollars. If you install the extra drive, you can just switch diskettes and that is much faster.

If you need the file transfer program to use with a number of different computers then parallel mode will be faster if you will be connecting to PS/2 computers. Otherwise, the serial mode will operate at about the same speed.

All of these packages are easy to use. All of them except File Shuttle are ready to run right from the box. File Shuttle requires a printer cable. Otherwise, none of them have a significant advantage. My recommendation is to buy the cheapest one you can find.

Appendices

A

What Shareware Is

THE ORIGIN OF SHAREWARE

Understanding shareware is easier once you know how it began. Shareware was born in two places pretty much at the same time. In Bellevue, Washington a programmer named Jim Button had written a program that would eventually be called PC-File. In Tiburon, California a programmer named Andrew Fluegelman had written a program called PC-Talk.

In 1981, Button had written a database program to print a mailing label program on an Apple computer for his church. Button was an IBM programer so when the original PC came out in November of 1981, he converted his database program to run on the PC. At this point, he called the program Easy File. Button began giving Easy File away. He continually improved Easy File and fixed the bugs that always seem to crop up in programs. He also found it expensive to let all the users know that a new version was available. To recoup these costs, he placed a message in the program asking for $10 if you wanted to be on his mailing list.

In 1982, Button and Fluegelman got together. Button agreed to change the name of his program to PC-File to match Fluegelman's PC-Talk program. He also increased his payment request to $25 to match PC-Talk and shareware was born.

WHAT SHAREWARE IS

There are two basic types of programs, public domain and copyrighted. A public domain program is a program where the author claims no copyright ownership. You can copy and distribute these programs without restriction. A public domain program is really a program that no one owns and no one can own. A copyrighted program is one where the author retains the copyright to the program. A copyright restricts your ability to copy and distribute a copyrighted program by whatever restrictions the author places on you.

There are two types of copyrighted programs, commercial distribution and shareware. (Copyrighted programs that the vendor distributes commercially are the ones you buy at your local computer store or order by mail through a commercial vendor. The copyright holder or his agent authorizes certain individuals or companies to distribute the program. It is illegal for anyone else to copy the program to distribute it.

Copyrighted programs that are shareware distributed are programs where the author allows anyone to copy and distribute the program. Many shareware authors limit the fees the distributor can charge. A few place other significant limitations on how you distribute their program.

Thus, the only difference between commercially and shareware distributed copyrighted programs are the methods of distribution they use. With a commercially distributed program, you buy it and then find out if you like it. Generally, you cannot return the program even if you do not like it. It is a rare commercial vendor that will let you return a program because you did not like it or because it lacked features you needed. Their reasoning is they do not want you to buy the program, copy the program and documentation, return the original for a refund and use the copy.

WHERE YOU CAN OBTAIN SHAREWARE

With a shareware program, there are a number of ways you could obtain the program. You can. . .

- Purchase a disk from a users group or shareware house for $5–$10.
- Download the program from a bulletin board for phone and/or connect charges.
- Get a copy from a friend or coworker.
- Purchase the optional shareware/public domain disk set for this book.

You get to try the program first. If you like it, you pay for it. Otherwise, you erase the program or pass it on to someone else.

WHY THERE IS SHAREWARE

Shareware authors use this unusual distribution method because it is cheap. Distributing software commercially can cost a lot of money. A full page ad in a computer magazine can cost up to $10,000 to run once. and marketing a program requires repeat advertising to be successful. Distributing copies of a program to retail outlets is expensive if you do it yourself. If you pay someone else (a distributor) to do it, then they take a significant portion of your revenue.

Shareware authors avoid these costs. They can upload their programs to commercial bulletin boards for only a few dollars connect fee. Once there, tens of thousands of users have instant access to it. For a few dollars in postage, they can mail copies to the major shareware houses and users groups. They do not, however, avoid any of the costs of writing the program by using shareware distribution. A shareware program will cost the same to write as a comparable commercial program.

Being free to copy and try out a program does not mean you can continue to use the program for free. There are many excellent shareware programs. The authors of these programs have spent the same long hours of hard work developing their programs as have the developers of commercially distributed software. They deserve the same income from their work. That means that if you continue to use a shareware program, you must register it.

DOES IT WORK? YES AND NO

A number of shareware authors make enough money to support themselves. A few make a lot of money. However, most shareware authors estimate that less than 5% of their regular users ever register the program. One author I know personally wrote a shareware program to format text in a special format for a specific bulletin board. He distributed the program to about a dozen people who were posting text on this bulletin. About five people used the program regularly but only one registered the program.

After three years of shareware distribution, an advanced version of the communications program ProComm was shipped as a regular commercial product. After only six months, the commercial program had out-sold the shareware program.

Some shareware authors have tried several tricks to reverse this trend. For example, Wampum (a dBASE-like database) will only run for a certain time after you download it unless you register. At one time, GT Power, a communications program, quits running after a specific number of uses. Currently, GT Power runs progressively slower the more you run it without registering it. Still others distribute limited-function programs. For example, they may limit the size of the files you can work with or will not print. You have to register to get the full version.

However, programs that do not start as and stay fully functional are not true shareware. Some users have suggested names like cripple-ware or demoware.

In addition to cripple-ware, another trend has begun. At one time there was booming activity in public domain software. An author would write a useful, but small program. It was not really large enough to sell so he would upload it to bulletin boards with no requests for money and often no copyright claims. At most, the author would restrict copying to non-commercial applications. Now, programers are tacking on a request for a couple of dollars. Jim Button calls this "what-the-heck-ware."

EVOLUTION OF SHAREWARE

Some authors are leaving the shareware market for the commercial market because many users continue to use a program without registering it. One shareware author told me he received over one hundred requests for technical support during six months yet he only received five registrations in that same period. His program is no longer available as shareware. He sold it to a commercial developer. You can now buy the same program at the local computer store. You pay a lot more for the program while the author gets less because of the chunks taken out by the stores and distributors. If you use a shareware program, it is important that you register it to prevent this from happening to other programs.

CONCLUSION

Developing a program is hard work. It takes a lot of expensive program time and talent along with expensive hardware and software tools. All software of comparable size and function face these same costs. Some authors prefer to give their work to the computing community free and without restriction. These are public domain programs. Other authors allow users to distribute their programs with only minor restrictions but require a payment if, after evaluating the program, you continue to use it. These are shareware programs. The remaining authors place major restrictions on the distribution of their programs and require you to purchase it before you can evaluate it. These are commercial programs. All three sources have good and bad programs and good and bad documentation. One of the things this book will do is point you toward the better products in all three categories.

B

Help File Compilers

Chapter 1 covered help programs. These were programs that read a database and display information from that database on the screen. This is useful, but may not be enough. You may need specific information not available in the database. For example, I use the shareware program LIST.COM for looking at ASCII files and recommend it to anyone I know who buys a computer. If I am setting up a computer for someone, I want the help program to have LIST.COM in the menu. In addition, I want it to give information on how to use LIST.COM. I want the help program to do the same for the other utility tools I add to a system. A help program with a database I can modify lets me do this.

You are not limited to help programs about DOS or even the major software packages. A data entry department could use a pop-up program to display codes for new employees or infrequently used codes for everyone. Foreign users could use a pop-up program to display common English words and their meanings. Students could use a pop-up program to display information in their area of study. A help program that lets you create custom databases will do all this.

Chapter 1 covered the use of these programs with their DOS databases. This appendix will discuss modifying those databases and creating new databases.

DOS Helper

DOS Helper makes it extremely easy to add additional information to the database or to modify existing data.

Installation   Installing DOS Helper proved to be extremely frustrating. I placed the program disk in my B-drive and logged onto that drive to run the installation program. My first problem was DOS Helper expected to use the A-drive even though I logged onto the B-drive. I corrected that with an ASSIGN A=B statement. This ASSIGN A=B is a handy command to remember if you have a PS/2 computer with an external 5.25 inch drive, especially for installations.

After issuing the ASSIGN command, my problems were far from over. Going through the next time, I changed the default directory. DOS Helper expects you to install it in the HELPDOS directory, which I was already using for another program in this chapter. The first time through I changed this to the HELPDOS2. For some unexplained reason, DOS Helper does not work with subdirectories longer than seven characters. DOS allows up to eight with an additional three character extension. When it tried to create this subdirectory, it shortened HELPDOS2 to HELPDOS and quit because it already existed.

I ran the program again and selected the subdirectory HELPER. It modified the program files then tried to create a HELPDOS subdirectory anyway. Once again, it stopped because HELPDOS already existed. At this point, I decided to run DOS Helper from the B-drive. When I logged onto the B-drive and tried to start DOS Helper, it responded that the subdirectory HELPER did not exist. Next, I tried to run the installation program to tell it to use the B-drive. When I told it I wanted to install DOS Helper for a single drive, it responded that running off a single disk required no installation. At this point there was no way to run it off the floppy drive.

Because DOS Helper had to be in my HELPDOS subdirectory, I moved the existing files to a HELPDOS2 subdirectory. Then I deleted the HELPDOS subdirectory so DOS Helper could create it. Once again, I ran the installation program. This time, I made a mistake. I made the mistake of entering the subdirectory as \HELPDOS. The prompt warns you not to do that. When I tried to start DOS Helper, it responded that the directory C:\ \HELPDO did not exist. (Since it only allows seven characters, adding the "\" at the first caused the ending "S" to be dropped.) So I installed DOS Helper once again. This time I got everything right.

There are several other problems with the installation program. To change the hot-key for the memory resident program, you have to enter its ASCII code. The installation program only displays codes for a few combinations of the control, alternate, shift, and function keys. In addition, when it prompts you for the new subdirectory, it does not prompt for something like "Enter the subdirectory for the data files." Rather, it asks you to "Modify F1 (DEFAULT=HELPDOS)". To make matters worse, the default in the prompt is wrong if you have already installed DOS Helper and changed the default. Accepting the default accepts what exists, even though you cannot find out what it is, rather than accepting HELPDOS.

Operation   It stores the information on each topic in a separate data file. For example, it stores the information on the BACKUP command in a file called BACKUP.HLP. Adding a new topic is as easy as adding a new data file. Using the file name to access the file name as the means to access the help data means the keyword cannot be longer than eight characters.

It stores information as straight ASCII data. Figure B-1 shows this. Each line can be no longer than 77 characters and must end with a return. A data file can have at most 250 lines. There are a couple of special dot-commands you can add to your text to format it. These must be entered flush left. They are:

.H.   This highlights the remaining part of the line.
.H2   This highlights the remaining part of the line using the secondary color.
. . .   This causes this line to be treated as a comment and not be displayed.
.##   or .#. This causes ## spaces to be displayed at the beginning of the line. For example, .15 would be replaced with fifteen spaces.

Limitations   Because each topic is a separate file, you end up with a lot of files. Just after installation, I had 112 files. On a floppy disk where the minimum size is 1K this does not represent a major problem. However, with certain types of hard disks and versions of DOS, the minimum file size is 8K. On those systems, these 112 files would require over 900K. (A few of the files are larger than 8K.) In addition, DOS Helper has a very poor installation program.

Manual   The manual does not explain how to create your own help files. All it does is refer you to a DOS Helper help file. That help file adequately explains the process.

```
.h.Command: BACKUP -- Back up disk files -- <E> <2.0>

.h.Typical Usage: BACKUP C:\   A:/S

.h.Syntax:
BACKUP d:[path][filespec]  d:[/S][/M][/A]

.h.Function:
Back up files from a fixed (hard) disk to as many diskettes as needed.

This is the only way to backup a file (or group of files) that is too
large for an individual diskette.

(See other media backup for DOS 3.0 below.)

.h.Detailed Description:

PARAMETERS:

    (FOR DOS 3.00 & up  [d:][path] can be specified before the command to
    indicate where this external command resides (see "TYPES").)

    d:[path][filespec]
```

Fig. B-1. DOS Helper help files are standard ASCII files with only a few special formatting commands.

Conclusion   It is very easy to add your own help to DOS Helper. Its only drawbacks are the user interface and having to store each topic in a separate file.

Product:	DOS Helper
Price:	$35
Category:	Commercial
Publisher:	Aristo Computers, Incorporated
Address:	6700 S.W. 105th Avenue
	Suite 307
	Beaverton, Oregon 97005
Phone:	(800) 537-7417
Notes:	Has both a memory resident
	and stand-alone mode.
Memory:	72K in Memory Resident Mode
	128K in Stand-Alone Mode

Help!!

It is very easy to modify an existing Help!! database or to create a new one. The only difficulty is switching between different databases.

Installation   Installing Help!! is a two step process. First, you copy the files to a subdirectory in your PATH. Next, you run an installation program to tell Help!! where to find its data files. New users (the primary market for this product) could find the manual confusing since it only explains the second step.

Operation   Help!! stores its databases as straight ASCII files with the following restrictions:

1) The lines cannot be longer than 40 characters and must end with a return. It ignores any characters beyond the 40th.
2) Each command explanation must contain at least 128 characters. If the explanation is shorter, you must add spaces to the end to bring it up to at least 128 characters.
3) Each command explanation can have at most 135 lines of text.
4) Each database must contain no more than 500 commands.
5) A database must be reindexed after you modify it.

Help!! databases use a few special characters. They are:

^   Returns text to normal display mode.

^A   You mark each new command by placing this just before each new command. There must not be any spaces between the ^A and the command name, e.g. ^ABACKUP for the BACKUP command. The command name can only be 11 characters long and must end with a return.

^B   In color, Help!! displays the text following this in green. In monochrome, it displays the text as high intensity white.

^E   In color, it displays the text following this command in yellow. In monochrome, it displays this text as high intensity white.

^N   In color, it displays the text following this command as blinking red. In monochrome, it displays this text as blinking high intensity white.

You must index new or modified databases using the included program to do that. Figure B-2 shows the Help!! DOS 4.0 database with a new command added to the top. Figure B-3 shows starting the database indexer. Figure B-4 shows the indexer running. Figure B-5 shows how the new text looks when displayed by Help!!.

Limitations   Help!! includes several different databases of help information, including one on DOS 4.0, however, the program makes it very difficult to switch databases. Only one database is available for use at a time. To switch, you must:

1)   RENAME HELP.DAT to something else.
2)   RENAME the new database to HELP.DAT.
3)   Run an included program to index the new database.

I avoided this by placing several versions of Help!! in different subdirectories under slightly different names (HELP-DOS, HELP-40, and so on) each with a different HELP.DAT file. That is clumsy. The program should handle multiple databases easily if it is going to handle multiple databases.

Manual   As explained above, the manual does a poor job of explaining how to install Help!!. The manual does an adequate job of explaining how to operate Help!! and how to modify the existing databases. It does not explain how to swap databases, I had to figure that one out myself. The missing information does not bode well for beginners.

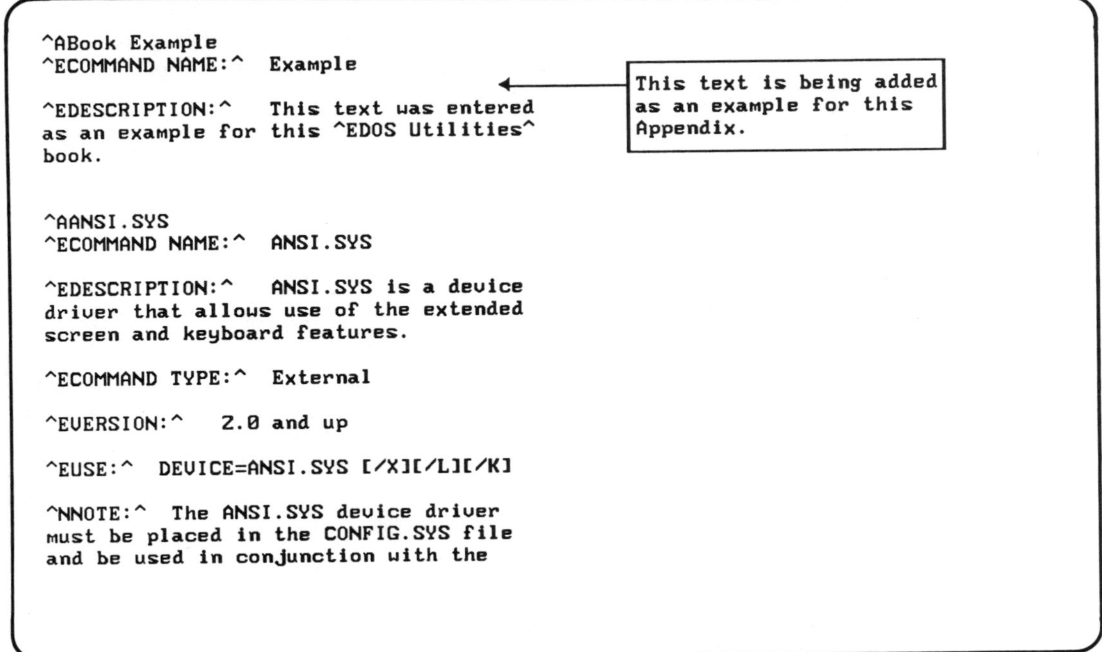

Fig. B-2. Entering new text into the database for display under Help!!. Notice the control codes around the text.

```
                        HELP!! INDEX PROGRAM
----------------------------------------------------------------------

   Enter path and filename of file to be indexed.
   Example C:\HELP\HELP.DAT

   >c:\help!!\help.dat

   Enter full path where Index file should be placed.
   Example   C:\HELP

   >c:\help!!
```

Fig. B-3. To compile a Help!! database, you provide the compiler with the name of the database and the location where you want the resulting file to be placed.

```
      Name          Lines           Commands Indexed:   88
   -------------------------------------------------------------------
   RMDIR            25
   SELECT           75
   SET              30
   SHARE            26
   SHELL            20
   SHIFT            34
   SORT             35
   STACKS           64
   SUBST            53
   SWITCHES         27
   SYS              34
   TIME             39
   TREE             25
   TYPE             25
   VDISK.SYS        60
   VER              15
   VERIFY           24
   VOL              18
   XCOPY            73
   XMAZEMS.SYS      120
   XMAEM.SYS        50

   C:\HELP!!>
```

Fig. B-4. The Help!! compiler reads the database and constructs a special file used by Help!!.

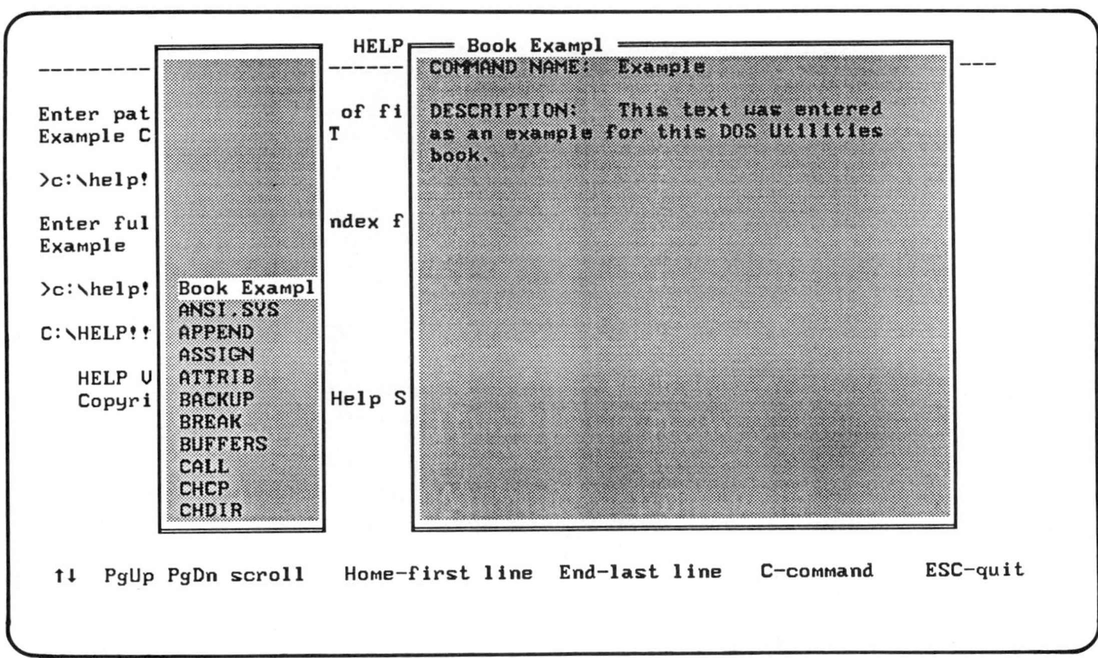

Fig. B-5. The resulting display under Help!!.

Conclusion   It is very easy to create new databases or modify existing ones under Help!!. That, combined with its low cost, makes Help!! an excellent choice for companies or individuals looking to create custom databases for any topic.

Product:	Help!!
Price:	$25
Category:	Shareware
Publisher:	Help Software
Address:	16706 Bradley Court
	Belton, Missouri 64012
Phone:	(816) 331-5809
Memory:	256K Stand-Alone
	67K Memory Resident Mode

Help! Development Kit

Help! Development Kit develops custom databases you use with DOS Help! from Flambeaux Software. You can distribute the first 50 copies for free. After that, you must pay a small fee.

Installation   There is no program to install Help! Development Kit and the brief pamphlet that comes with the program does not tell you how to install it either. All you need to do to run Help! Development Kit from a hard disk is create a subdirectory and copy all the files from the floppy to that subdirectory. You can run Help! Development Kit from the distribution floppy diskette without installation.

Operation   You begin by writing the help file using any editor that can produce straight ASCII code. You have an option, all the text can be in one file or you can include commands to read other files. With a simple database, you would probably produce one file. The option to use multiple files is especially nice for complex databases. No matter how many files you use, it compiles them into a single file for use by the DOS Help! program.

You embed "dot commands" in the text to give major commands to the compiler. A dot command is a line where the first character is a period and a single letter command follows the period. For example:

.A   This defines an alias. When you have a reference in the text called "Formatting" that is a topic the user can read more about, you may want to jump to a page called "The Format Command". You use an alias to define the "Formatting" page to be the "The Format Command" page.

.C   This is a comment line that is ignored by the compiler.

.N   Gives the title of the database. This is shown in DOS Help! when you press F6 to select the database to use.

.P   Signals the start of a new page. You follow the .P by the name of the page. This "page" is not one screen of information. It can extend over multiple screens. The user reads the page using the page up and page down keys. It is, rather, a single topic. A page continues to the next dot command.

Any text surrounded by a set of tildes represents a topic the user can select to read more about. The program displays it in bold on the screen. This text must either be the title of a page or you must map it onto another page by an alias. Figure B-6 shows a portion of Help! Development Kit source code for a database.

Help! Development Kit comes with a neat little utility called Chart Menu to aid in producing fancy screens with your word processor. You pop this 24K utility up while in your word processor. It lets you select extended ASCII characters from a menu and place them in the current document at the cursor position. Chart Menu has a shortcut character selector. Pressing Alt-space bar repeats the last character you selected. Microsoft Word uses Alt-space bar itself and this feature refused to work with Word. Otherwise, Chart Menu worked beautifully.

Once the text is complete, you run it through the compiler. The compiler checks the text for errors and usually reports the line number for any errors. (See below for an exception.) No matter how many files you used in writing the database, the program compiles them into a single database with the extension .H!. The program selects this file automatically if it is the only .H! file

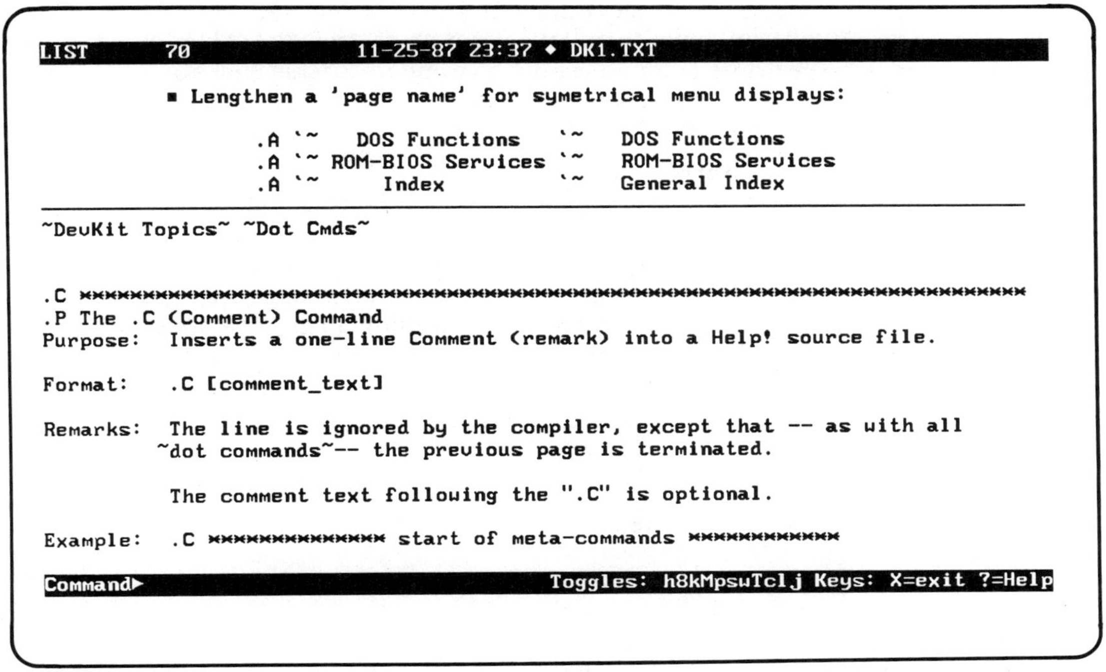

Fig. B-6. Help! Development Kit database source code. Note the use of dot commands to embed compiler commands. Also note the words surrounded by tildes. These will be highlighted in the display and will lead to other topics when the user moves the cursor to these words and presses Return.

available. Otherwise, you can select it from DOS Help! by pressing the F6 key. From there, DOS Help! functions as explained in Chapter 1.

Limitations   Help! Development Kit does not come with a manual per se. Rather, it comes with a brief three page pamphlet that introduces Help! Development Kit. To really learn Help! Development Kit you have to work through the help screens that come with the program. I found this far more difficult than reading a manual. It does have one advantage, however. You can run DOS Help! in memory resident mode and get help as you work.

I created a brief example following the sample in the pamphlet. The compiler compiled it and reported it had no errors. Every time I tried to use it, I received a "Help: Data file format error or other file read error" message and DOS Help! refused to work with the data file. I worked for hours and was never able to resolve the problem. It was especially frustrating because I created several more sample databases that worked without a problem.

Problems are common when writing such things but what I found especially frustrating was the compiler reporting no errors. This would be especially difficult on a large help file. With the compiler reporting no errors and the help program refusing to load the resulting file, you have no indication where the error actually is.

Manual   There really is no manual. You get three pages with the package. Beyond that, you have to read through a custom database included on the disk. You have to use the DOS Help! reader (included) to view this database but the three pages do not tell you how to install the program or get it started. Adding just a few pages to the printed manual would do wonders for this package. I would suggest they start by adding a section on installing the software and a short listing of all the dot commands and other compiler-specific commands available.

Conclusion   If I were Flambeaux Software, I would market Chart Menu as a separate program. I do enough programming where I write fancy screens with high-ordered ASCII that I would be willing to buy Chart Menu alone. It is fairly easy to write databases and they do look good on the screen. Once I got going, I found Help! Development Kit to be very easy to use. I hesitate to give it a broad recommendation because of the poor printed documentation and that one database that would never work properly.

<table>
<tr><td>Product:</td><td>Help! Development Kit
(Hypertext Compiler)</td></tr>
<tr><td>Price:</td><td>$45.00</td></tr>
<tr><td>Category:</td><td>Commercial</td></tr>
<tr><td>Publisher:</td><td>Flambeaux Software</td></tr>
<tr><td>Address:</td><td>1147 East Broadway
Suite 56
Glendale, California 91205</td></tr>
<tr><td>Phone:</td><td>(818) 500-0044</td></tr>
<tr><td>Notes:</td><td>The purchase price includes permission to distribute fifty copies of the reader program with your own databases. More copies can be distributed for an additional fee. Unlimited rights are $200.</td></tr>
<tr><td>Memory:</td><td>64K</td></tr>
</table>

Polaris Rescue

Polaris Rescue is strictly a help construction set. No major databases are available from Polaris, however, the set does come with a sample database. Polaris Rescue offers features not available with other help construction sets but at the cost of ease of use.

Installation   There is no installation program. The manual instructs you to simply copy all the files to a subdirectory on your hard disk or to a working diskette.

Operation   You can use your own word processor to write ASCII files for importation into Polaris Rescue. However, the major editing takes place in the editor included with the program. The main menu of the editors has the following options:

Copy. You use this to copy an entire database to another name.
Delete. You use this to delete an entire database.
Execute. This compiles a database into a format Polaris Rescue can use for display.

Open. This allows you to edit an existing database or create a new one.

Rename. This changes the name of an existing database.

Quit. This exits to DOS. The editor is not memory resident.

You can perform the copying, deleting and renaming just as quickly and easily from DOS.

A Polaris Rescue database consists of a collection of screens. The first menu you see when you select Open from the main menu reflects this. Its options are:

Assign. This makes one of the screens you create the first screen the user sees when he logs on.

Copy. This makes a copy of an existing screen. This is more useful than it sounds at first. I designed a complex border I wanted to use around all my screens. I saved the border by itself and copied it to a new file for each screen I wanted to create.

Delete. This deletes a help screen.

Edit. This lets you edit an existing help screen or build a new one.

Import. This imports an ASCII file created with an external editor. An external editor is probably the best way to create massive amounts of text. The external editor is likely to have features, like a spelling checker, missing in Polaris Rescue.

List. This sends a report on screen names to the printer. The reports list the text on each screen and any errors that exist. You can only send the reports to the printer. If you do not have a printer, it drops you to DOS.

Names. This lets you change the labels for the function keys.

Password. To protect sensitive data, you can apply passwords to a database or any screen in the database.

Rename. This changes the name of a screen in your database.

User. This changes a single line of text the user sees each time he accesses Polaris Rescue.

Quit. This returns to the main menu.

You will spend most of your time using the edit function. This gives you a blank screen to design as a help screen. Figure B-7 shows this with the menu showing. You can only use characters but you can include high order characters on a screen. You move the cursor around and type in your text. This is a menu with the following options:

Abandon. This exits without saving your changes. You are asked to confirm your choice in case you select it accidentally.

Color. This changes the color of the characters you type in. It does not change colors for text already entered. To change them you must retype them. You cannot set colors on ASCII files imported from an external editor.

Erase Screen. This starts you over with a blank screen. You are asked to confirm your choice in case you select it accidentally.

Function Pointers. This is the key to the user moving around the database. You assign function keys to different screen names. When a user presses a function key, the program displays the screen assigned to that function key.

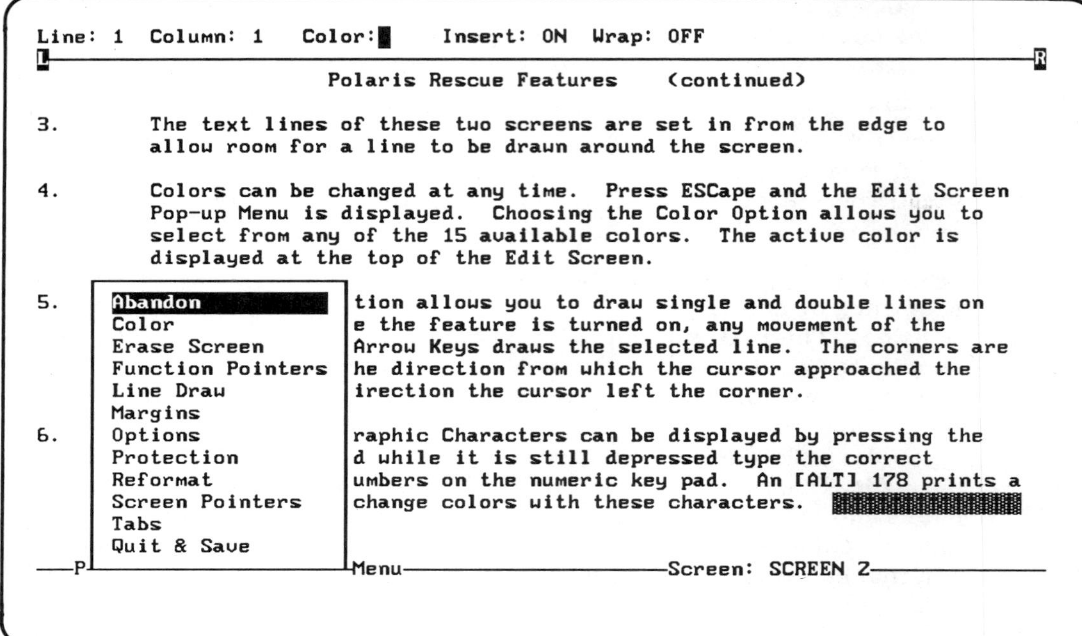

Fig. B-7. The Polaris Rescue editor is used to both create help screens and to link those screens together.

Line Draw. This lets you use the single or double line high-ordered ASCII box drawing characters. Once you select the line type, moving the cursor around draws a line. You go back through this menu again to turn the drawing off. As explained below, this feature has problems.

Margins. This sets the margins that are in place until you press the enter key. Margins can be different for each line on the screen if you like.

Options. You use this to turn word wrap on and off. You also use it to define a screen as normal (displayed until the user selects another screen) or timed (displayed for the period of time you enter).

Protection. Used to assign password protection if you selected that function from the Open menu.

Reformat. This reformats a paragraph.

Screen Pointers. You use this to assign on-screen points to other screens and to remove that assignment. When the user moves the cursor to that screen and presses Return, the programs jumps to the assigned screen.

Tabs. You use this to set the screen tabs for designing the screen.

Quit & Save. This saves the file and returns to the Open menu. You cannot save a screen without exiting.

Once a database is created, you use the Execute option on the main menu to compile the database into a form Polaris Rescue can use. This process goes fairly fast. Since screen connections entered using the editor are checked at that time, it is not likely that an error will slip through to the compiler.

Limitations　　The menu option for box drawing does not get the intersections correct. It always starts off with a corner even when you begin by drawing a straight line. When one line passes over another, it erases the bottom line at the intersection. It replaces the existing line with the character for the top line rather that using the intersection character. You can enter high-order ASCII characters manually using the Alt key and the number pad so you can go back and clean these up.

The editor has other problems in addition to its box drawing problem. You cannot change colors on text already entered on imported text. You cannot save a screen without exiting editing on that screen. That is likely to cause users to go longer than they should without saving a screen.

Using the editor to assign screen connections means the results are usually error free. However, it makes development slower. If a screen is to connect to five other screens, all five of the connecting screens must first exist. You cannot assign the connections before completing the connecting screens. That can be a major limitation when designing a complex database with numerous connections.

Once you compile a database, you display it with the runtime memory resident display program. This program displays the database and allows the user to move around using the combination of function keys and screen attachments built into the database. This part of the program was problem free.

Manual　　The manual was fairly good. Much better than the other help construction sets.

Conclusion　　I found the editor and the Polaris Rescue help construction set in general to be more cumbersome to use than some of the other programs. However, the way its internal editor assigns links makes it very difficult to make mistakes. It also uses a visual point-to-select way of selecting links that is far easier to use than embedding dot commands in text. Inexperienced users may find it to their benefit to use Polaris Rescue for those features.

<table>
<tr><td>Product:</td><td>Polaris Rescue</td></tr>
<tr><td>Price:</td><td>$149
$250 for 10 runtime packs</td></tr>
<tr><td>Category:</td><td>Commercial</td></tr>
<tr><td>Publisher:</td><td>Polaris Software</td></tr>
<tr><td>Address:</td><td>613 West Valley Parkway
Suite 323
Escondido, California 92025</td></tr>
<tr><td>Phone:</td><td>(800) 338-5943</td></tr>
<tr><td>Notes:</td><td>A runtime module is required for each person using a database so the net cost is $25 per user

The RAM resident display program requires 33K and the editor (not memory resident) requires 256K</td></tr>
<tr><td>Memory:</td><td>33K</td></tr>
</table>

About the Author

Ronny Richardson was born in Oak Ridge, Tennessee and raised in Atlanta, Georgia. He has undergraduate degrees in Electronics and Mathematics. He has a graduate degree in Decision Sciences and Business Administration. He is currently a doctoral student in Management at Georgia State University.

He began using computers in 1983. The next year, he won an IBM clone at the Atlanta Comdex. That spurred his interest in learning about computers. Later that year, he began teaching computer classes at a local computer store. In 1986, he began writing articles for *Computer Shopper.* Since then, he has published over 50 articles.

Most of Chapter 17 on computer viruses was written by Curtner Akins. Curtner Akins is currently a software engineering specialist for General Dynamics. He specialized in database applications and user environments. He began his computing career in 1956 writing computer applications for petroleum refineries. He later moved on to writing military applications.

Curtner became interested in personal computers in the late 70's. In 1978 he began running a bulletin board system on a Tandy TRS-80 Model 1. He has remained active in the telecommunications community ever since. Curtner is a founding telecommunications host on the PC-Link network. In the early 80's, Trojan horses first appeared. Curtner responded by testing every program uploaded to his bulletin board so he could guarantee the software on his system was clean. His interest in software viruses and Trojan horses has continued ever since.

MS-DOS UTILITY PROGRAMS
Add-On Software Resources

If you are intrigued with the possibilities of the programs included in *MS-DOS Utility Programs: Add-On Software Resources* (TAB Book No. 3278), you should definitely consider having the disks containing the archived software applications. This software is guaranteed free of manufacturer's defects. (If you have any problems, return the disk within 30 days, and we'll send you a new one.) Not only will you save the time and effort of typing the programs, but also the disk eliminates the possibility of errors that can prevent the programs from functioning. Interested?

Available on disk for the IBM PC at $14.95 for each disk plus $2.50 shipping and handling

5¼	Software order #	3½	Software order #			
	6700		6715	Appendix	03	Fast Screen
				Chapter	01	Help DOS
				Chapter	26	Search
				Chapter	26	Timerunner
	6701		6716	Chapter	01	TUTOR.COM
				Chapter	19	Mark/Release
	6702		6717	Chapter	02	Hard Disk Menu IV
				Chapter	13	Hunter
				Chapter	13	Text File Utilities
	6703		6718	Chapter	02	Magic Menu
				Chapter	03	PC-Menu
	6704		6719	Chapter	03	Point & Shoot Hard Disk Manager
				Chapter	03	Qdisk
	6705		6720	Chapter	03	Qfiler
				Chapter	22	Big Echo
				Chapter	22	Extended Batch Language
	6706		6721	Chapter	02	Automenu
				Chapter	04	Professional Master Key
	6707		6722	Chapter	03	Treeview
				Chapter	05	Baker's Dozen
	6708		6723	Chapter	06	Anadisk
				Chapter	06	HDDiag
				Chapter	06	HDDiag
	6709		6724	Chapter	09	FANSI Console
	6710		6725	Chapter	09	FANSI Console
	6711		6726	Chapter	12	File/Saver
	6712		6727	Chapter	12	Point & Shoot Backup
				Chapter	15	Lockerup
				Chapter	21	Command Editor
				Chapter	21	Con>Format
				Chapter	21	CopyQM
				Chapter	21	DSpace
				Chapter	21	Fastcopy
				Chapter	21	FormanQM
				Chapter	21	Global
				Chapter	21	List
				Chapter	21	Quick Change
				Chapter	21	Resq
	6713		6728	Chapter	12	Norm Patriquin Utilities
	6714		6729	Chapter	21	Tmpspace
				Chapter	21	eXtended Dos
	6730		6731	Archiving disk